An American Genocide

THE LAMAR SERIES IN WESTERN HISTORY

The Lamar Series in Western History includes scholarly books of general public interest that enhance the understanding of human affairs in the American West and contribute to a wider understanding of the West's significance in the political, social, and cultural life of America. Comprising works of the highest quality, the series aims to increase the range and vitality of Western American history, focusing on frontier places and people, Indian and ethnic communities, the urban West and the environment, and the art and illustrated history of the American West.

Recent Titles

Sovereignty for Survival: American Energy Development and Indian Self-Determination, by James Robert Allison III
George I. Sánchez: The Long Fight for Mexican American Integration, by Carlos Kevin Blanton
The Yaquis and the Empire: Violence, Spanish Imperial Power, and Native Resilience in Colonial Mexico, by Raphael Brewster Folsom
Gathering Together: The Shawnee People through Diaspora and Nationhood, 1600–1870, by Sami Lakomäki
An American Genocide: The United States and the California Indian Catastrophe, 1846–1873, by Benjamin Madley
Nature's Noblemen: Transatlantic Masculinities and the Nineteenth-Century American West, by Monica Rico
Rush to Gold: The French and the California Gold Rush, 1848–1854, by Malcolm J. Rohrbough
Home Rule: Households, Manhood, and National Expansion on the Eighteenth-Century Kentucky Frontier, by Honor Sachs
The Cherokee Diaspora: An Indigenous History of Migration, Resettlement, and Identity, by Gregory D. Smithers
Sun Chief: The Autobiography of a Hopi Indian, by Don C. Talayesva, edited by Leo W. Simmons, Second Edition
Before L.A.: Race, Space, and Municipal Power in Los Angeles, 1781–1894, by David Samuel Torres-Rouff
Wanted: The Outlaw Lives of Billy the Kid and Ned Kelly, by Robert M. Utley

An American

Genocide

The United States and the California
Indian Catastrophe, 1846–1873

Benjamin Madley

Yale

UNIVERSITY

PRESS

New Haven & London

First paperback edition 2017. This paperback edition does not contain the appendixes included in the hardcover edition. All appendixes can be found at yalebooks.com/american-genocide-appendix.

This book was made possible in part through the generosity of the UCLA History Department and the Division of Social Sciences and was published with assistance from the income of the Frederick John Kingsbury Memorial Fund.

Yale University Press books may be purchased in quantity for educational, business, or promotional use. For information, please e-mail sales.press@yale.edu (U.S. office) or sales@yaleup.co.uk (U.K. office).

Set in Electra type by Westchester Publishing Services.
Printed in the United States of America.

Library of Congress Control Number: 2015955528
ISBN 978-0-300-18136-4 (hardcover : alk. paper)
ISBN 978-0-300-23069-7 (pbk.)

A catalogue record for this book is available from the British Library.

10 9 8 7 6

For California Indians, past, present, and future

White people want our land, want destroy us. . . . I hear people tell 'bout what Inyan do early days to white man. Nobody ever tell it what white man do to Inyan. That's reason I tell it. That's history. That's truth.

—*Lucy Young (Lassik/Wailaki), 1939, eyewitness to genocide*

CONTENTS

Acknowledgments   xi

List of Abbreviations   xv

Introduction   1

1   California Indians before 1846   16

2   Prelude to Genocide: March 1846–March 1848   42

3   Gold, Immigrants, and Killers from Oregon: March 1848–May 1850   67

4   Turning Point: The Killing Campaigns of December 1849–May 1850   103

5   Legislating Exclusion and Vulnerability: 1846–1853   145

6   Rise of the Killing Machine: Militias and Vigilantes,

April 1850–December 1854   173

7   Perfecting the Killing Machine: December 1854–March 1861   231

8   The Civil War in California and Its Aftermath: March 1861–1871   289

9   Conclusion   336

Notes　361

Bibliography　435

Index　473

ACKNOWLEDGMENTS

At a place called Indian Ferry, not far from where my family's log cabin now stands, whites massacred at least thirty Shasta Indians in the spring of 1852. The victims had not attacked whites. Nor had they stolen from them. Whites killed them near the banks of the Klamath River merely because they were Indians. Few people have heard of this massacre or the many others like it. Yet there were scores of such atrocities. Hundreds of Indian-killing sites stain California from the fog-bound northwestern redwood coast to the searing southeastern deserts. Individuals, private groups, state militiamen, and US Army soldiers carried out these killings, ostensibly to protect non-Indians or to punish Indians for suspected crimes. In fact, the perpetrators often sought to annihilate California's indigenous peoples between 1846 and 1873.

The story of the California Indian catastrophe is almost unrelentingly grim, which helps to explain why relatively little has been written about it, at least compared to other genocides. Until now, no one has written a comprehensive, year-by-year history of the cataclysm. It is, nevertheless, important history, for both California Indians and non-Indians. In researching and writing this book, I received guidance and support from many people and institutions.

Fellow scholars helped shape my ideas, methods, and writing. Gary Clayton Anderson, Ute Frevert, Albert Hurtado, Karl Jacoby, Adam Jones, Paul Kennedy, Howard Lamar, David Rich Lewis, Michael Magliari, Jeffrey Ostler, Russell Thornton, David Wrobel, and Natale Zappia provided crucial insights and direction. My fellow Yale graduate students Adam Arenson, Jens-Uwe Guettel, Gretchen Heefner, Michael Morgan, Aaron O'Connell, Ashley Sousa, Henry Trotter, Owen Williams, and others provided valuable encouragement and advice. Edward Melillo, in particular, devoted his keen editorial eye to every page, and I am grateful for his sage advice. To my dissertation committee I owe unrepayable debts. George Miles helped me to map out a research strategy and provided copies of rare documents. John Demos shaped my writing and encouraged me to address major problems in US history. John Faragher guided me through theoretical and historical problems while suggesting sources and sharing insights into the workings of nineteenth-century California and the western United States. Finally, Ben Kiernan tirelessly read and reread drafts, spent many hours discussing genocide with me, and enthusiastically supported this project at every turn.

People from more than a dozen American Indian nations also informed my research, interpretations, and conclusions. Members of the Big Valley, Blue Lake, Elk Valley, Redding, and Smith River Rancherias, as well as the Round Valley and Yurok reservations, helped me to understand how genocide unfolded in northwestern California. Members of the Klamath Tribes of Oregon, the Modoc Tribe of Oklahoma, and Redding Rancheria provided insights into events in northeastern California. Finally, the Big Pine Paiute Tribe of the Owens Valley, the Bishop Paiute Tribe, as well as members of the Lone Pine Paiute-Shoshone and Fort Independence reservations, guided me in understanding genocide in eastern California. During visits to these communities, members listened carefully to my presentations, pointed out errors and omissions, provided documents and photographs, shared insights, and explained the importance of documenting killings, as well as the reasons that so few oral histories of these events remain. Community members also shared oral histories of massacres and killing campaigns that I used to locate written nineteenth-century sources describing these events. For example, Tom Ball, tribal officer Taylor David, Chief Bill Follis, tribal officer Jack Shadwick, and author Cheewa James spent hours discussing Modoc history with me. Redding Rancheria cultural resources manager James Hayward Sr. provided insights into Achumawi, Wintu, and Yana histories. Joseph Giovannetti provided Tolowa sources. William Bauer Jr. shared insights into Round Valley history and organized my visit there. To all of the American Indian people who guided this project—and whose names are too numerous to list here—I offer my deepest thanks. I am particularly grateful to Loren and Lena Bommelyn of Smith River Rancheria. For years they have acted as teachers, mentors, and friends while generously making important introductions. Finally, Amos Tripp kindly took the time to explain many of the legal issues associated with California Indian history, thus informing my emphasis on legal frameworks.

This manuscript is built upon hundreds of journal entries, manuscripts, government documents, newspapers, books, and other sources buried in libraries, museums, and archives. In California, the staffs of the Autry National Center,

California State Archives, California State Library, Chico State University librar-
ies, Doris Foley Library, Fort Ross Conservancy, Held-Poage Library, Humboldt
State University library, Huntington Library, Los Angeles County Museum of
Natural History, Napa County Historical Society Library, Nevada County Library,
Oroville Pioneer History Museum, San Francisco Public Library, Trinity County
Historical Society History Center, and University of California libraries facili-
tated my research. I am especially grateful for the help and friendship of Susan
Snyder and the Bancroft Library staff. Their warmth, expertise, and camarade-
rie made research a pleasure. Peter Blodgett and the staff at the Huntington Li-
brary also provided extremely valuable help. Beyond California, the list of
institutions that provided materials for this book is even longer: the Beinecke
Library, Biblioteca comunale dell'Archiginnasio, Connecticut State Library,
Dartmouth College libraries, International Museum of Photography and Film,
John Carter Brown Library, Library of Congress, Missouri History Museum Archives, National Anthropological Archives, National Archives and Records Administration, Nevada State Library, New York Public Library, Oregon Historical
Society Library, Sterling Memorial Library, Union League Club of Chicago,
University of Missouri Western Historical Manuscripts Collection, and Univer-
sity of Oregon libraries. Finally, Max Flomen, Timothy Macholz, and Preston
McBride played crucial roles. I relied on their expert research, technological
skills, thoughtful insights, and enthusiastic belief in this project.

Magnanimous grants from the Howard R. Lamar Center for the Study of
Frontiers and Borders at Yale University, the Huntington Library, the Andrew
Mellon Foundation, the Smith Richardson Foundation, the Western History
Association, the Yale Genocide Studies Program, and Yale University made this
monograph possible.

Members of the History Department and Native American Studies Program
at Dartmouth College, where I was an Andrew Mellon Postdoctoral Fellow
from 2010 to 2012, helped me to transform my dissertation into a book. Visiting
scholars such as Christopher Parsons read my work and suggested ideas, while
Robert Bonner, Sergei Kan, Margaret Darrow, Vera Palmer, Melanie Benson
Taylor, and Dale Turner shared insights, input, and friendship. Finally, Colin
Calloway and Bruce Duthu generously read my work and mentored my development as a scholar of the Native American experience.

UCLA's History Department and American Indian Studies Program then
provided an exceptionally supportive environment for editing this manuscript.
Stephen Aron, Paul Kroskrity, William Marotti, David Myers, Peter Nabokov, Angela Riley, Sarah Stein, Craig Yirush, and others read drafts and provided crucial guidance and support.

Cartographer Bill Nelson patiently worked with me over many months to create a dozen detailed maps for this book. His artful cartographic works shed valuable light on the geography of California Indian history past and present.

Meanwhile, my Yale University Press editor, Christopher Rogers, made crucial strategic suggestions, thoughtfully line edited every page twice, met with me repeatedly, and helped to shape my research into the pages you hold in your hands.

Finally, I could not have completed this history without my family. My parents—Jesse Philips and Susan Madley—read and reread chapters, copyedited, commented, suggested sources, and helped me to wrestle with writing about genocide. Alice, Bill, Henry, and Laura Roe, as well as Cory and Lincoln Madley and Brian Peterson, provided emotional, intellectual, and material help. My children—Jacob and Eleanor—gave me both a more profound understanding of life's value and smiles that energized and refreshed my soul. To my wife, Barbara, I can only say thank you, thank you, and thank you. I could not have done this without you.

ABBREVIATIONS

BANC	Bancroft Library, University of California, Berkeley
BLYU	Beinecke Library, Yale University, New Haven, Connecticut
CG	*Congressional Globe*
CSA	California State Archives, Sacramento
CSL	California State Library, Sacramento
DAC	*Daily Alta California* (San Francisco)
DEB	*Daily Evening Bulletin* (San Francisco)
HL	Huntington Library
HT	*Humboldt Times*
IWP	California Adjutant General's Office, *Military Department, Adjutant General, Indian War Papers* F3753
LAS	*Los Angeles Star*
MLRV	*Martial Law in Round Valley, Mendocino Co., California, The Causes Which Led To That Measure, The Evidence, As Brought out by a Court of Investigation ordered by Brig. Gen. G. Wright, Commanding U.S. Forces on the Pacific* (Ukiah City, 1863)
MMR	California, *Majority and Minority Reports of the Special Joint Committee on the Mendocino War* (Sacramento, 1860)
NARA	US National Archives and Records Administration
RG75, M234	US National Archives and Records Administration, "Letters Received by the Office of Indian Affairs, 1824–80"
SDU	*Sacramento Daily Union*
USOIA	US Office of Indian Affairs
WOR	US War Department, *The War of the Rebellion: A Compilation of the Official Records of the Union and Confederate Armies.* 4 series, 130 volumes. Series 1, volume 50, part 1 [WOR 1:50:1]; Series 1, volume 50, part 2 [WOR 1:50:2]; Series 1, volume 52, part 2 [WOR 1:52:2].

INTRODUCTION

As the sun rose on July 7, 1846, four US warships rode at anchor in Monterey Bay. Ashore, the Mexican tricolor cracked over the adobe walls and red-tiled roofs of California's capitol for the last time. At 7:30 A.M., Commodore John Sloat sent Captain William Mervine ashore "to demand the immediate surrender of the place." The Mexican commandant then fled, and some 250 sailors and marines assembled at the whitewashed customs house on the water's edge. As residents, immigrants, seamen, and soldiers looked on, Mervine read Commodore Sloat's proclamation: "I declare to the inhabitants of California, that although I come in arms. . . . I come as their best friend—as henceforth California will be a portion of the United States, and its peaceable inhabitants will enjoy the same rights and privileges as the citizens of any other portion of that nation." As the USS *Savannah*'s sailors and marines hoisted the Stars and Stripes to a chorus of cheers, three ships of the US Pacific Squadron fired a sixty-three-gun salute. The cannons' roar swept over the plaza to the pine-studded hills above the bay before echoing back over the harbor. The first hours of conquest were relatively peaceful, but a new order had come to California. The lives of perhaps 150,000 California Indians now hung in the balance.[1]

The US military officers who took control of California that July under martial law had the opportunity to reinvent the existing Mexican framework within which colonists and California Indians interacted. Instead, these officers reinforced and intensified existing discriminatory Mexican policies toward these Indians. The elected civilian state legislators who followed them then radically transformed the relationship between colonists and California Indians. Together with federal officials, they created a catastrophe.

Yet, the California Indian population cataclysm of 1846–1873 continued a preexisting trajectory. During California's seventy-seven-year-long Russo-Hispanic

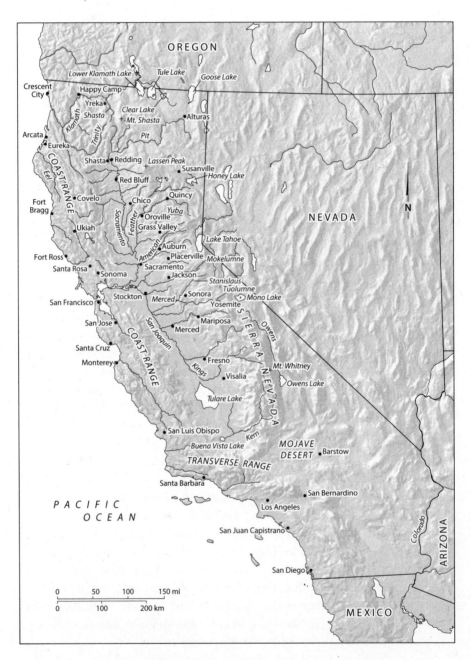

OREGON

Crescent
City

Lower Klamath Lake   Tule Lake   Goose Lake

Happy Camp

Yreka
Shasta   Clear Lake   Alturas
        + Mt. Shasta

Arcata   Pit

Eureka

Shasta Redding   Lassen Peak

Red Bluff   Susanville
            Honey Lake

Fort
Bragg   Covelo   Chico   Quincy
                Yuba
        Ukiah   Oroville
            Grass Valley

Fort Ross   Auburn   Lake Tahoe
        Placerville
    Santa Rosa   Sacramento   Mokelumne
        Sonoma   Jackson
            Stanislaus
                Tuolumne
    Stockton   Merced   Sonora   Mono Lake
        Yosemite

San Francisco

San Jose   Mariposa
        Merced

Santa Cruz

Monterey   Fresno

    Kings   Visalia   Mt. Whitney

            Owens Lake

        Tulare Lake

        San Luis Obispo   Kern

        Buena Vista Lake   MOJAVE
                DESERT   Barstow
        TRANSVERSE RANGE

    Santa Barbara

PACIFIC
OCEAN   San Bernardino

        Los Angeles

    San Juan Capistrano

        San Diego

NEVADA

N

COAST RANGE

Klamath Trinity

Eel

Sacramento Feather

American

San Joaquin

SIERRA NEVADA

Owens

Colorado

ARIZONA

MEXICO

0   50   100   150 mi
0   100   200 km

Nineteenth-century California

Period (1769–1846) its Indians had already suffered a devastating demographic decline. During the era when Spaniards, Russians, and Mexicans colonized the coastal region between San Diego and Fort Ross, California's Indian population fell from perhaps 310,000 to 150,000. Some 62,600 of these deaths occurred at or near California's coastal region missions, and, in 1946, journalist Carey McWilliams initiated a long debate over the nature of these institutions when he compared the Franciscan missionaries, who had held large numbers of California Indians there, to "Nazis operating concentration camps." Today, a wide spectrum of scholarly opinion exists, with the extreme poles represented by mission defenders Father Francis Guest and Father Maynard Geiger, on the one hand, and mission critics Rupert and Jeannette Costo—who called the missions genocidal—on the other. However one judges the missions, Russo-Hispanic colonization caused the deaths of tens of thousands of California Indian people.[2]

Under US rule, California Indians died at an even more astonishing rate. Between 1846 and 1870, California's Native American population plunged from perhaps 150,000 to 30,000. By 1880, census takers recorded just 16,277 California Indians. Diseases, dislocation, and starvation were important causes of these many deaths. However, abduction, de jure and de facto unfree labor, mass death in forced confinement on reservations, homicides, battles, and massacres also took thousands of lives and hindered reproduction. According to historical demographer Sherburne Cook, an often-quoted authority on California Indian demographic decline, a "complete lack of any legal control" helped create the context in which these phenomena were possible. Was the California Indian catastrophe just another western US tragedy in which unscrupulous individuals exploited the opportunities provided in a lawless frontier?[3]

The organized destruction of California's Indian peoples under US rule was not a closely guarded secret. Mid-nineteenth-century California newspapers frequently addressed, and often encouraged, what we would now call genocide, as did some state and federal employees. Historians began using these and other sources to address the topic as early as 1890. That year, historian Hubert Howe Bancroft summed up the California Indian catastrophe under US rule: "The savages were in the way; the miners and settlers were arrogant and impatient; there were no missionaries or others present with even the poor pretense of soul-saving or civilizing. It was one of the last human hunts of civilization, and the basest and most brutal of them all." In 1935, US Indian Affairs commissioner John Collier added, "The world's annals contain few comparable instances of swift depopulation—practically, of racial massacre—at the hands of a conquering race." In 1940, historian John Walton Caughey titled a chapter of his California history "Liquidating the Indians: 'Wars' and Massacres." Three years later, Cook wrote the first major study on the topic. He quantified the violent killing of 4,556 California Indians between 1847 and 1865, concluding that, "since the quickest and easiest way to get rid of [the Northern California Indian] was to kill him off, this procedure was adopted as standard for some years."[4]

In the same year that Cook published his groundbreaking article, Nazi mass murder in Europe catalyzed the development of a new theoretical and legal framework for discussing such events. In 1943, legal scholar Raphaël Lemkin coined a new word for an ancient crime. Defining the concept in 1944, he combined "the Greek word *genos* (tribe, race) and the Latin *cide*," or killing, to describe genocide as any attempt to physically or culturally annihilate an ethnic, national, religious, or political group. The 1948 United Nations Convention on the Prevention and Punishment of the Crime of Genocide (see online Appendix 8) more narrowly defined genocide as "acts committed with intent to destroy, in whole or in part, a national, ethnical, racial or religious group, as such," including:

(a) Killing members of the group;
(b) Causing serious bodily or mental harm to members of the group;
(c) Deliberately inflicting on the group conditions of life calculated to bring about its physical destruction in whole or in part;
(d) Imposing measures intended to prevent births within the group;
(e) Forcibly transferring children of the group to another group.

The Genocide Convention thus provides an internationally recognized and rather restrictive rubric for evaluating possible instances of genocide. First, perpetrators must evince "intent to destroy" a group "as such." Second, perpetrators must commit at least one of the five genocidal acts against "a national, ethnical, racial or religious group, as such." The Genocide Convention criminalizes the five directly genocidal acts defined above and also other acts connected to genocide. The Convention stipulates that "the following acts shall be punishable," including:

(a) Genocide;
(b) Conspiracy to commit genocide;
(c) Direct and public incitement to commit genocide;
(d) Attempt to commit genocide;
(e) Complicity in genocide.

Finally, the Convention specifies that "persons committing genocide or any of the other acts enumerated . . . shall be punished, whether they are constitutionally responsible rulers, public officials or private individuals."[5]

In US criminal law, *intent* is present if an act is intentional, not accidental. The international crime of genocide involves more, comprising "acts committed with intent to destroy" a group "as such." International criminal lawyers call this *specific intent*, meaning destruction must be consciously desired, or purposeful. Yet, *specific intent* does not require a specific *motive*, a term absent from the Genocide Convention. Under the Convention's definition, genocide can be committed even without a motive like racial hatred. The motive behind genocidal acts does not need to be an explicit desire to destroy a group; it may be, but the motive can also be territorial, economic, ideological, political, or military. Moreover, the Convention declares that "genocide, whether committed in time of peace or in time of war, is a crime under international law." If the action is deliberate, and the group's partial or total destruction a desired outcome, the motive behind that intent is irrelevant. Yet, how does a twentieth-century international treaty apply to nineteenth-century events?[6]

The Genocide Convention does not allow for the retroactive prosecution of crimes committed before 1948, but it does provide a powerful analytical tool: a frame for evaluating the past and comparing similar events across time. Lemkin himself asserted that, "genocide has always existed in history," and he wrote two manuscripts addressing instances of genocide in periods ranging from "Antiquity" to "Modern Times." *Genocide* is a twentieth-century word, but it describes an ancient phenomenon and can therefore be used to analyze the past, in much the way that historians routinely use other new terms to understand historical events. Indeed, Lemkin planned chapters titled "Genocide against the American Indians" and "The Indians in North America (in part)," but he died before he could complete either project.[7]

Many scholars have employed genocide as a concept with which to evaluate the past, including events that took place in the nineteenth century, but some scholars have rejected the UN Genocide Convention definition. Some propose expanding, contracting, or modifying the list of protected groups. Others want to enlarge, reduce, or alter the scope of genocidal acts. Still others call for different definitions of *intent*.[8]

Genocide, however, is more than an academic concept. It is a crime defined by an international legal treaty and subsequent case law. On December 9, 1948, the UN General Assembly adopted the UN Genocide Convention and its genocide definition "unanimously and without abstentions." It remains the only authoritative international legal definition. Moreover, unlike at least twenty-two alternative definitions proffered since 1959, it has teeth. Now in its seventh decade, the Genocide Convention has been signed or acceded to by 147 nations and is supported and further defined as a legal instrument by a growing body of international case law. Since 1993, the International Criminal Tribunals for the former Yugoslavia and Rwanda have tried genocide cases using the Genocide Convention. The International Criminal Court at The Hague, established in 2002, and the Extraordinary Chambers in the Courts of Cambodia, which began its first trial in 2009, are also empowered to try suspects using the Genocide Convention. The UN Genocide Convention definition is part of an international legal regime of growing importance and is both the most widely accepted definition and the most judicially effective one. The Genocide Convention provides a powerful, though possibly imperfect, definition for investigating the question of genocide in California. Still, it took decades for scholars to begin using the term in connection with California under US rule. Caughey and Cook, for instance, used terms like *liquidating, military casualties,* and *social homicide,* which fail to capture the full meaning of genocidal events.[9]

Most Americans knew little about the concept of genocide or the Holocaust until the late 1950s. A turning point came in 1961. That year, the media glare illuminating the trial of SS lieutenant colonel Adolf Eichmann—in combination with the release of the Academy Award–winning legal thriller *Judgment at Nuremberg* and the publication of political scientist Raul Hilberg's monumental *The Destruction of the European Jews*—introduced the scope and horrors of the Holocaust to many in the United States. Holocaust-related art, literature, media, and scholarship proliferated during the late 1960s and 1970s. Those turbulent decades also saw continuing civil rights activism, New Left historians' assault on triumphal US history narratives, rising American Indian political activism, emerging Native American studies departments, and a new American Indian history that emphasized the role of violence against indigenous people.[10]

Twenty-five years after the formulation of the new international legal treaty, scholars began reexamining the nineteenth-century conquest and colonization of California under US rule. In 1968, author Theodora Kroeber and anthropologist Robert F. Heizer wrote a brief but pathbreaking description of "the genocide of Californians." In 1977, William Coffer mentioned the "Genocide of the California Indians," and two years later, ethnic studies scholar Jack Norton argued that, according to the Genocide Convention, certain northwestern California Indians suffered genocide under US rule. In 1982, scholar Van H. Garner added that "Federal Indian policy in California . . . was genocidal in practice." Historian James Rawls next made a crucial intervention. He argued that some California whites openly "advocated and carried out a program of genocide that was popularly called 'extermination.'" Following Rawls's important equation of the nineteenth-century word *extermination* with the twentieth-century term *genocide,* anthropologist Russell Thornton went further. In his landmark book addressing genocide in the continental United States as a whole, Thornton argued that "the largest, most blatant, deliberate killings of North American Indians by non-Indians surely occurred in California." Historian Albert Hurtado later described an "atmosphere of impending genocide" in gold rush California, while historian William T. Hagen asserted, "*Genocide* is a term of awful significance, but one which has application to the story of California's Native Americans."[11]

Meanwhile, the field of genocide studies began taking shape. The Holocaust remains "for many, the paradigm case of genocide," but the field's founding publications were emphatically diverse, and some touched on questions of genocide in North America. In 1986, scholars founded the journal *Holocaust and Genocide Studies*, and in the first issue included an article addressing the question of genocide and Native Americans. Historian Frank Chalk and sociologist Kurt Jonassohn included essays on Native Americans in colonial New England and in the nineteenth-century United States in their edited 1990 book addressing *The History and Sociology of Genocide*. They argued that American Indians had suffered genocide, primarily through famine, massacres, and "criminal neglect," and mentioned California's Yuki Indian genocide. That same year, sociologist Helen Fein also touched on the issue of "genocide in North America."[12]

Genocide studies now cross-pollinated with new works on the question of genocide in the Americas, such as American studies scholar David Stannard's *American Holocaust*, and controversial ethnic studies scholar Ward Churchill's *A Little Matter of Genocide*—both of which mentioned genocide in California. During the 1990s, a growing chorus of voices also mentioned genocide in California. By the year 2000, historians Robert Hine and John Faragher had concluded that California was the site of "the clearest case of genocide in the history of the American frontier." Other twenty-first-century scholars agreed that California Indians had indeed suffered genocide.[13]

Still, even though more than twenty scholars have touched on the genocide of California Indians under US rule, little has been written on the topic compared to what has been written on some other genocides. Four scholars—anthropologists Robert Heizer and Allan Almquist, and historians Clifford Trafzer and Joel Hyer—have assembled important edited primary-source volumes highlighting nineteenth-century racism and anti–California Indian violence, some of it genocidal. Others have described the genocides endured by particular California tribes. Only a handful of works, however, analyze the multiple genocides of various California Indian peoples under US rule, and most of these refer to the genocides briefly and incompletely. Only two twenty-first-century monographs have addressed the topic more broadly. Author William

Secrest's *When the Great Spirit Died* provided a general description of anti-Indian racism and violence between 1850 and 1860, but it did not address genocide or the entire 1846 to 1873 period. Historian Brendan Lindsay's *Murder State* then focused on "California's Native American Genocide" as a phenomenon motivated by preexisting racism, facilitated by democracy, and advertised by the press.[14]

Building on previous scholarship, *An American Genocide* is the first year-by-year recounting of genocide in California under US rule between 1846 and 1873. Although newcomers imposed California's political and administrative boundaries on indigenous peoples, these borders form a cohesive unit of analysis with real meaning and repercussions for scholars, California Indians, and non-Indians both past and present. Within and sometimes slightly beyond these boundaries, *An American Genocide* carefully describes the broad societal, judicial, and political support for the genocide as well as how it unfolded. It addresses the causes of the genocide, state and federal government decision-makers' roles, the organization and funding of the killing, and the vigilantes, volunteer state militiamen, and US soldiers who did the killing and how they did it. Further, it details public support for the genocide, the number of California Indians killed, the nature of indigenous resistance, the changes in genocidal patterns over time, and the end of the genocide. These topics call for meticulous analysis and consistent use of an internationally recognized definition such as that of the 1948 Genocide Convention, because the stakes are high for scholars, California Indians, and all US citizens.

If US citizens colonized some regions of California, if not the state as a whole, in conjunction with deliberate attempts to annihilate California Indians, scholars will need to reevaluate current interpretive axioms and address new questions. Scholars could, for example, reexamine the assumption that indirect effects of colonization, like the unwitting spread of diseases, were the only leading causes of death in most or all encounters between whites and California Indians—rather than mass murder or other deliberate acts like forced incarceration under lethal conditions. Exceptionalist interpretations of US history—which suggest that the United States is fundamentally unlike other countries—lose validity when researchers compare the California experience to other genocides and place it within global frameworks. A careful study of genocide in California will also assist scholars in reexamining the larger, hemispheric indigenous population catastrophe and the question of genocide in other regions. Where scholars document a genocide, it will be necessary to evaluate what roles colonial, federal, state, or territorial governments (or private individuals or groups) played, as well as whether or not the event was part of a recurring regional or national pattern. Larger questions follow. What tended to catalyze genocide? Who ordered and carried out the killing? Why do we not know more about these events? Did democracy drive mass murder, and, ultimately, did genocide play a role in making modern Canada, Mexico, the United States, or other Western Hemisphere countries?[15]

Given the political, economic, psychological, and health ramifications of the genocide question, it is urgent for California's approximately 150,000 citizens of California Indian ancestry. Should they press for official government apologies, reparations, and control of land where genocidal events took place? Should tribes marshal evidence of genocide in cases involving tribal sovereignty and federal recognition? How should California Indian communities commemorate victims of mass murder while also emphasizing successful accommodation, resistance, survival, and cultural renewal? The psychological issues related to genocide are also fraught. What happens if a tribal member learns that she or he is a descendant of both perpetrators and victims? How might California Indian people reconcile increased knowledge of genocide—sometimes at the hands of the United States—with their often intense patriotism? Finally, what role might acknowledgment of genocide have on the "intergenerational/historical trauma" prevalent in many California Indian communities and that trauma's connection to present-day physical illnesses, substance abuse, domestic violence, and suicide?[16]

The question of genocide in California under US rule also poses explosive political, economic, educational, and psychological questions for all US citizens. Acknowledgment and reparations are central issues. Should elected government officials tender public apologies, as presidents Ronald Reagan and George H.W. Bush did in the 1980s for the relocation and internment of some 120,000 Japanese Americans—many of them Californians—during World War II? Reparations constitute an important subordinate issue. Should federal officials offer compensation, along the lines of the more than $1.6 billion Congress paid to 82,210 Japanese Americans and their heirs? Might California officials decrease their cut of California Indians' $7 billion in annual gaming revenues (2013) as a way of paying reparations for the state government's past involvement in genocide? Might Californians reevaluate their relationship with California Indian gaming in light of increased awareness of the California genocide? A better understanding of the genocide that took place in California might also affect the federal government's dealings with the scores of California Indian communities currently seeking formal federal recognition. The question of commemoration is closely linked. Will non-Indian citizens support or tolerate the public commemoration of mass murders committed by some of the state's forefathers with the same kinds of monuments, museums, and state-legislated days of remembrance that today commemorate the Armenian genocide and the Holocaust? Will genocides against California Indians be included in public school curricula and public discourse along with these other systematic mass murders? All of these questions have important ramifications, but can be addressed only in limited ways without a comprehensive understanding of relations between California Indians and newcomers during the California Indian catastrophe of 1846 to 1873.[17]

Depending on availability, four kinds of evidence can be used to document a possible crime: perpetrators' assertions and admissions, bystanders' reports, victims' testimonies, and forensic evidence. All four kinds of evidence are important. This book relies primarily on non-Indian perpetrator and bystander accounts because in establishing the case for genocide it is crucial to highlight the voices of killers and witnesses and because there are relatively few written California Indian voices describing the genocide. A host of factors contributed to this dearth of written California Indian accounts. First and foremost, there were not many survivors. Between 1846 and 1873, perhaps 80 percent of all California Indians died, and many massacres left no survivors or only small children. Mass death silenced thousands of California Indian voices, but so did California laws and judges: mid-nineteenth-century California courts usually barred and rarely recorded Indian testimony against whites. Outside the legal system, few nineteenth-century writers recorded California Indians' words either. Moreover, in the face of ongoing discrimination, violence, and intimidation, those who survived often hid their Indian identities—and their traumatic memories—from outsiders. A host of factors further limited the transmission of oral histories within California Indian communities. These included traditional taboos against speaking of the dead, loss of connection to the land where genocidal events took place due to forced removal, systematic government suppression of indigenous languages, the placement of large numbers of California Indian minors in non-Indian homes, and compulsory federal Indian boarding schools' severance of intergenerational oral history conduits. Finally, legal prohibitions against many California Indian religious and cultural gatherings also limited the transmission of oral histories and only abated with the passage of the 1968 Indian Civil Rights Act and the 1978 American Indian Religious Freedom Act. Despite these obstacles, some written California Indian recollections of these events do remain as testaments to both horrific atrocities and heroic defiance.[18]

This book draws on printed California Indian eyewitness testimonials and printed oral histories. Although I interviewed California Indian people and presented elements of my research at thirteen different rancherias and reservations—encountering oral histories describing elements of the genocide—this is not an ethnographic, interview-based oral history project. A history of California's 1846–1873 genocide—told primarily from California Indian perspectives—is important and remains to be written. Nor is this an archaeology-based project. These pages cite very little archaeological evidence.

Written histories draw from imperfect sources, and this book is no exception. The non-Indian perpetrator and bystander reports that form the backbone of this monograph were often written or delivered by biased individuals, sometimes by the very men organizing, inciting, or perpetrating the killing. Some may have deliberately exaggerated, minimized, misconstrued, or concealed genocidal intentions and actions. Moreover, because many sources had little interest in or knowledge of specific California Indian names, tribal groups, or geography, their reports often fail to include important information. This book is the product of the surest available sources and frequently draws on multiple sources to describe a single event.

Genocide is violence, and the study of direct killing is the heart of this book. Disease, starvation, and exposure played major roles in California's Indian population decline between 1846 and 1873, but this project focuses on documenting and analyzing deaths due to direct acts of violence such as shootings, stabbings, hangings, beheadings, and lethal beatings. Ancillary to the direct killings were mass deaths in incarceration—particularly on federal Indian reservations—as well as other genocidal acts described by the UN Genocide Convention. This book does not investigate questions of cultural genocide, the systematic, deliberate destruction of a culture.

To distinguish among genocidal, nongenocidal, and potentially genocidal violence, killings in this book have been divided into four categories. First, *battles*—which are by no means inherently genocidal—constitute the attempted mutual killing of combatant men (and occasionally women). Killings in combat can occur on a small or a mass scale. Second, *massacres* are the intentional killing of five or more disarmed combatants or largely unarmed noncombatants, including women, children, and prisoners, whether in the context of a battle or otherwise. Massacres, when they form part of a pattern targeting a national, ethnic, racial, or religious group, are frequently genocidal. Third, the term *homicides* refers to the killing of four or fewer people, either Indians or non-Indians, including extralegal hangings and small-scale killings, which can also be genocidal when part of a larger killing pattern. Finally, even legal *executions* following a court trial, like homicides, can be genocidal when they consciously contribute to a larger killing pattern, for instance, when they inflict judicially sanctioned violence on all or part of a group rather than on individuals proven to have violated a law.

California Indians did resist conquest. As newcomers took their land, destroyed their traditional food sources, denied them access to what remained, brutalized them, bound them in unfree labor regimes, and murdered them, California Indians sometimes killed livestock or non-Indians. For many whites, Indians defending their homelands against conquest and colonization were intolerable. When California Indians resisted incursions, defended themselves, or took livestock to survive, newcomers often responded with indiscriminate, disproportionate attacks. In classic blame-the-victim style, some claimed that California Indians fully deserved these attacks, and insisted that Indians had brought the attacks upon themselves by daring to resist. This created local cycles of largely one-sided violence in which whites—carrying out what became an unwritten doctrine of collective, mass reprisal—killed large numbers of California Indians. So-called Indian depredations thus became a common justification for indiscriminate killing and great losses of life that cannot be separated from the larger pattern of genocidal killing. According to anthropologists Robert Heizer and Alan Almquist, "For every white man killed, a hundred [California] Indians paid the penalty with their lives." Yet the disproportionate numbers of victims are less important here than the intent to destroy a group.[19]

California Indians also resisted the genocidal attacks routinely camouflaged as "battles" and the genocidal campaigns usually described in written histories as "wars." In so doing, they sometimes did kill attackers. This narrative peels back the heavy nineteenth-century cloak of martial rhetoric to reveal how many of California's so-called battles were in fact massacres in which outgunned California Indians attempted to defend themselves from attack or to save their loved ones and community members from death, lethal incarceration, and often-genocidal servitude. Likewise, this book reveals many of California's so-called Indian wars for what they were: genocide campaigns that California Indians violently resisted.

Perpetrators, bystanders, survivors, and secondary sources indicate that non-Indians killed at least 9,492 to 16,094 California Indians, and probably more, between 1846 and 1873. This more than doubles Cook's calculation of 4,556 California Indians killed between 1847 and 1865. However, due to their large numbers, not all of these reported killings appear in this book. Moreover, these figures do not include those hundreds, and perhaps thousands, whom newcomers worked or starved to death. Likewise, these figures do not include California Indians who died of diseases while incarcerated in US Army forts or on federal Indian reservations. Killings of four or fewer California Indians appear only when part of broader systematic local violence. Otherwise, they are listed in online appendixes 1 and 2. Incidents in which perpetrators killed ten or more California Indians appear in the text and are listed in online appendixes 1 or 3. Likewise, reported killings of non-Indians by Indians—which total fewer than 1,400—appear in online Appendix 4. Tables providing death toll estimates of selected major massacres appear in online Appendix 5. Online Appendix 6 contains information on California state militia campaigns, and online Appendix 7 does the same for US Army operations. Online appendixes can be found at yalebooks.com/american-genocide-appendix.

Recording the numbers of California Indian people killed is not a mere academic exercise. As anyone who has ever lost a loved one knows, the death of a single person is a profound loss. Recording how many California Indians were killed between 1846 and 1873 is, in part, an attempt to understand the magnitude of the rupture and profound pain caused by their loss: each murder severed personal, familial, and tribal links. Each was a tragedy. When multiplied by thousands during a short period, the impact was nothing less than devastating. In the context of genocide, recording deaths also dignifies the slain and gives a voice to the departed.

Genocide is a form of violence in which intention and repetition are defining features. This book shows that, although the pressures of demographics (the migration of hundreds of thousands of immigrants), economics (the largest gold rush in US history), and profound racial hatred all made the genocide possible, it took sustained political will—at both the state and federal levels—to create the laws, policies, and well-funded killing machine that carried it out and ensured its continuation over several decades.

By recounting state and federal policies while supplying evidence of more than 9,400 violent killings, *An American Genocide* constitutes the first comprehensive, year-by-year history of the California Indian genocide under US rule. Chapter 1 sets the stage by describing the precontact California Indian world and narrating California Indian history between 1769 and 1846. Chapter 2 explores pre–gold rush California's anti-Indian violence, economic dependence on Native American labor, and why the gold rush expanded this dependence before ushering in increasingly frequent and lethal violence against California Indians. Chapter 3 explains how the 1848 discovery of gold and the arrival of Oregonians led to rising violence and a regional genocide in the Central Mines. Chapter 4 describes how, in late 1849 and early 1850, regional mass murder campaigns by vigilantes and US Army soldiers opened the door to large-scale statewide killing when the army, press, California Supreme Court, and US Senate effectively condoned them. Lawmakers played a key role in this genocide, and Chapter 5 explores how military, state, and federal legislators made California Indians into easy targets—between 1846 and 1853—by stripping them of legal rights, by making anti-Indian crimes extremely difficult to prosecute, and by refusing to ratify treaties signed by federal agents and California Indian leaders that could have restrained the violence. Bureaucracy also played a central role in this genocide. Chapters 6 and 7 narrate the rise of Indian-killing vigilantes and of paid volunteer state militia expeditions. The chapters explain why state and federal legislators raised up to $1.51 million to fund these campaigns, and describe how these operations facilitated genocide. Chapter 7 also examines the reemergence of the army as a major killing force. Chapter 8 explores California Indian-hunting operations by regular soldiers and vigilantes during and after the US Civil War. Finally, Chapter 9 evaluates the culpability of state and federal officials, explains how the California Indian catastrophe did constitute genocide as defined by the 1948 UN Genocide Convention, and suggests how future studies of possible genocides may be conducted in the United States and beyond.

This book sheds new light on the conquest of California and on US history. At a local level, it provides the first rigorously documented chronological account of the extent, mechanics, and systematic nature of genocide in California. It explains how federal decision makers often appeared to abdicate responsibility to state officials but in fact provided legislative, military, and financial support that made this genocide possible. These pages also narrate how—particularly during the Civil War—the US Army waged genocidal campaigns against California Indians. Major new findings that change our understanding of the catastrophe include the central roles played by state and federal governments, the bureaucratic nature of the killing machine, the major role played by the US Army, the fact that non-Indians killed many more California Indians (at least 9,492–16,094) than had previously been estimated (4,556), and the fact that genocide was inflicted upon more California Indian peoples than existing studies have suggested.

At the national level, the mechanics of California Indian massacres and the model of indirect federal support for local Indian-killing campaigns have important applications to our understanding of other events in Native American and US history. This book contributes to the ongoing American genocide debate—about which relatively little has been written—by providing the first large, detailed regional study of genocide in the United States.[20]

A NOTE ON NAMES AND NAMING

Amid the terror and mass murders of 1846–1873, dislocation and tribal fluidity characterized California Indian life. Forced removal to small, distant reservations shared by multiple tribes was not uncommon. Refugees also fled into new areas, intermarried at increased rates, and sometimes permanently relocated. As a result, it is not always possible to precisely identify California Indians by tribe during these turbulent, poorly documented, and often-chaotic years. Where sources create uncertainty as to tribal identity, I follow the twenty-first-century California Indian practice of using the term *Indian* or *California Indians*. To make this book accessible to nonspecialists, I use the commonly known names for California Indian tribes, rather than the names that they use for themselves in their own languages. That said, I retain idiosyncratic nineteenth-century spellings in order to convey the feeling of the primary sources. I also intentionally quote the offensive epithets deployed to dehumanize California Indians, to reveal the deep and pervasive anti-Indian racism of the period, which was crucial to creating an environment in which the mass murder of thousands of California Indian men, women, and children could take place with broad public support. Naming the heterogeneous non-Indians in this history presents additional challenges.

It is difficult to know what to call the hundreds of thousands of people who flooded into California before, during, and after California's gold rush. Many saw themselves as "settlers," transforming chaos into order, and savagery into civilization. California Indians, of course, saw things differently. To them, the immigrants were invaders who transformed order into chaos, and civilization into savagery. Thus, the term *settler*—with its implications of settling unsettled land, settling a dispute, and creating a legal settlement—is problematic at best. Where possible, I identify these newcomers by profession, place of origin, or other terms. Most US citizens are unused to thinking of "pioneers" and "settlers" as invaders, but in California between 1846 and 1873, they often were.

———— ·⟨∽⟩· ————

CALIFORNIA INDIANS BEFORE 1846

Within a few days, eleven little babies of this mission, one after the other, took their flight to heaven.

—*Fray Junípero Serra*, 1774

We were always trembling with fear of the lash.

—*Lorenzo Asisara (Costanoan)*, 1890

In the centuries before Europeans arrived, California Indians inhabited a world different from the California we know today. Rivers ran undammed to the Pacific, man-made lakes like the Salton Sea and Lake Shasta had yet to be imagined, and vast wetlands bordered many rivers and bays. Other bodies of water were far larger than they are today. Eastern California's now mostly dry Owens Lake covered more than 100 square miles, San Francisco Bay was almost a third larger, and the San Joaquin Valley's now vanished Tulare Lake was the largest body of fresh water west of the Mississippi.[1]

The flora and fauna, in their variety and sheer abundance, would also be unrecognizable to twenty-first-century Californians. Antelope, deer, and elk surged through the vast grasslands of the Central Valley in large herds. Mountain lions and grizzly bears—the latter now extinct in the golden state—searched for food. Forests—far larger than today's and filled with huge, old-growth trees—teemed with animals while oak groves proliferated. Shellfish thronged tidal estuaries. Vast schools of fish navigated rivers and bays. Great flocks of gulls, pelicans, and seagulls wheeled overhead. In the open ocean, fish, whales, seals, and sea otters swam by the thousands along the coast. There were no megacities, freeways, or factory farms. Yet ancient civilizations marked the land.

From a plank house on the redwood coast came the dawn cries of a newborn Wiyot infant. Near the Sacramento River, Wintu people spoke quietly around the morning fire in their subterranean lodge. As the sun climbed, the yells of a Northern Paiute family drove rabbits into a corral of rocks and branches. At noon, the skis of a Washoe man hissed over dazzling snow high above Lake Tahoe, and in the parched Mojave, precious liquid trickled over a young Kawaiisu as she passed into womanhood by "bathing in a wild chrysanthemum solution." On Santa Rosa Island, off the southern coast, a Chumash man and woman bound themselves in marriage by eating from the same dish even as, to the east, conversations rose from the desert as Cahuilla potters fashioned carefully painted and delicately incised earthenware. Up and down California women gathered, as their mothers, grandmothers, and great-grandmothers had before them, to weave baskets bearing intricate designs, each particular to their community.

This rare mission-period California Indian sketch may represent Luiseño Eagle Dancers. The Luiseño scholar Pablo Tac made this drawing while studying in Rome, Italy. Pablo Tac (Luiseño), "Untitled," drawing, ca. 1835. Giuseppe Mezzofanti Archive, folio 105r. Courtesy of Biblioteca comunale dell'Archiginnasio, Bologna, Italy.

As night fell, people gathered to celebrate, pray, and give thanks in the sacred songs and dances of their many traditions.[2]

California on the eve of contact with Europeans was an exuberant clamor of Native American economies, languages, tribes, and individuals. Indigenous people had worshiped, loved, traded, and fought in California for at least 12,000 years—some believe since time immemorial. A number of Southern California Indian peoples, such as the Quechans, farmed—mainly corn, beans, and squash—along the Colorado River. Yet most California Indians depended on carefully managing, harvesting, and processing nature's bounty. Almost everywhere, they modified and maintained their environments in order to maximize hunting and gathering yields. Ethnoecologist M. Kat Anderson has called these practices "tending the wild." California Indians consciously created anthropogenic environments—forests, groves, grasslands, and meadows—fashioned and managed over centuries through techniques that included pruning, tilling, sowing, selective harvesting, and, most important, burning.[3]

Game provided vital components of many precontact California Indian diets and material cultures. Instead of domesticating animals, California Indians frequently modified their environments to increase antelope, bear, bird, deer, elk, rabbit, and other game populations. By selectively and repeatedly burning portions of their land to clear unwanted undergrowth and promote forage for herbivores, California Indians increased the number of herbivores as well as the population of carnivores who ate them, maximizing local game populations and thus their total game supply. These practices bore striking similarities to the ways in which some other Native Americans, elsewhere in North America, shaped and managed their local environments to suit their own needs.[4]

As in other regions of North America, the results of such fire-based indigenous game-management programs deeply impressed early European visitors. These newcomers frequently expressed astonishment at the variety and sheer numbers of game animals in California before colonization. For example, in 1579, the Englishman Sir Francis Drake described how, at one point on the California coast, "infinite was the company of very large and fat Deere, which there we sawe by thousands, as we supposed, in a heard." In 1602, the Spaniard Juan Sebastián Vizcaíno wrote that in the Monterey area, "there is much wild game, such as harts, like young bulls, deer, buffalo, very large bears, rabbits, hares, and many other animals and many game birds, such as geese, partridges, quail, crane, ducks, vultures, and many other kinds of birds." Abundant animal populations formed a cornerstone of life for many indigenous Californians well into the second half of the nineteenth century.[5]

Visitors often commented on the vast numbers of animals thronging California before the gold rush. Emanuel Wyttenbach, "Elk Crossing Carquinez Straits[:] Drawn under the personal direction of William Heath Davis to illustrate his story of the vast herds of these now almost extinct animals so plentiful in California before the discovery of gold by Marshall, January 24, 1848," drawing, 1889, in Davis, *Seventy-Five Years in California*, 31. Courtesy of Yale Collection of Western Americana, Beinecke Rare Book and Manuscript Library, Yale University.

California Indian hunters, usually men, developed a wide repertoire of local techniques and technologies to take game. For example, in the forested Klamath River region near the Oregon border, Karuks used dogs to drive elk into ravines. To the southeast, Atsugewis used deer-head disguises to closely approach, surprise, and take deer. In the mountains around Lake Tahoe, groups of Washoe men on snowshoes hunted deer and mountain sheep. Patwins in the southwestern Sacramento Valley deployed goose-skin-stuffed decoys while duck hunting, and Nisenan people, east of the Sacramento River, constructed net fences into which they drove and entangled rabbits before clubbing them. Farther south, San Joaquin Valley Southern Yokuts set underwater snares to capture geese, ducks, and other waterfowl, and, near what is now San Diego, Luiseños used a "curved throwing stick," or *wakut*, to hunt rabbits.[6]

California Indians prepared and preserved the edible portions of the game that they killed in many ways, often using inedible portions for other purposes.

Mid-nineteenth-century California Indian women often used sticks to place hot rocks into watertight woven baskets in which they cooked acorn mush, soup, meat, and other dishes. Charles Nahl(?), "Indians Cooking, in Front of Their Huts," engraving, undated, in "Scenes among the Indians of California," *Hutchings' California Magazine* (April 1859): 440. Courtesy of Yale Collection of Western Americana, Beinecke Rare Book and Manuscript Library, Yale University.

Cooks frequently roasted meat simply, but some employed more elaborate preparations. The Konkow wrapped game in maple leaves before baking, Miwoks baked or steamed fresh meat, and Lake Miwoks cooked a mixture of pulverized rabbit bones and deer blood between leaves in the coals. California Indian people also preserved meat for future use with salt, sun, smoke, or some combination of the three. Particular tribes also ground dried meat and bone into meal. Beyond nourishment, game animals also provided a variety of materials important to traditional life, including buckskin and pelts for clothing, sinews for bows and bowstrings, feathers for regalia, and bones, horns, and hoofs for fashioning tools and making medicine.[7]

Gathering, generally done by women, added to the richness and variety of California Indian diets. As with game, Californian Indians carefully managed their environments to maximize yields. They also employed multiple technologies to process harvests. Some California Indians constructed substantial earthen ovens to roast soaproot bulbs and cooked other foods by placing hot

Acorns were the foundation of many mid-nineteenth-century California Indian diets. Harvested in the fall, they could be stored and used later in nutritious breads, mush, stews, and other foods. Charles Nahl(?), "An Indian Woman Gathering Acorns," engraving, undated, in "Scenes among the Indians of California," *Hutchings' California Magazine* (April 1859): 439. Courtesy of Yale Collection of Western Americana, Beinecke Rare Book and Manuscript Library, Yale University.

rocks into baskets so tightly woven that they held boiling water. Many California Indian peoples also removed the tannic acid from acorns (generally by grinding them into a powder, then soaking them before cooking), to create that staple of so many indigenous California diets: the acorn meal that could be used to make porridge, bake bread, and thicken soups. Gathering also provided additional important sources of protein and carbohydrates. Some California Indian peoples harvested energy-dense pine nuts from the foothills and mountains. In the meadows and valleys, people often gathered grass seeds, and, according to a Lassik/Wailaki woman, Lucy Young, "Grasshoppers were considered quite a delicacy" with their "sweet, buttery, nutty flavor." A wide variety of berries added nutrients and sweetness to California Indian diets. Some peoples crushed manzanita berries, placed them in a sieve, and poured cool water over them to make a sweet, amber cider. Others brewed and drank fragrant Sierra mint tea. California Indians also saved gathered foods for future use or trade and sometimes stored them in granaries.[8]

California's freshwater ecosystems provided another major source of nutrition in many diets, and California Indians used a wide range of methods to reap this bounty. The Hupa, Chilulua, and Whilkut peoples of northwestern California built weirs, during low water in the fall, to capture river fish. Others, like the Yanas east of the northern Sacramento River, speared fish in streams and pools. Wailakis in the Coast Range deployed nets "made from wild iris fibre," Modocs in the northeast fished from dugout pine shovel-nosed canoes, and the Tubatulabals of south central California built stone and willow-branch fish corrals and held communal fish drives.[9]

To harvest marine species, some California Indians deployed other technologies. Tolowas near the Oregon border harpooned sea lions from oceangoing redwood canoes. Coast Miwoks north of San Francisco set fish traps, and Southern California's Chumash people constructed wooden plank boats—sometimes more than thirty feet long—from which they hunted seals, sea otters, and porpoises. Many California Indian peoples also harvested clams, mussels, and oysters along the coast and in tidal estuaries. They dried, smoked, or sometimes salted fish and seafood, wasting little. For example, the members of some tribes

In this image, California Indians, probably Ohlone
people, cross San Francisco Bay in a reed canoe.
Louis Choris, "Bateau du port de S.ⁿ Francisco" [Boat at
the port of San Francisco], color print, ca. 1815. Courtesy of
The Bancroft Library, University of California, Berkeley.

saved salmon bones and ground them into a nutritious powder that could be added to soups and stews. Preserved fish and seafood provided food in lean times and were also valuable trading commodities.[10]

California's natural bounty, coupled with California Indians' ingenious ability to maximize and use that abundance, supported a population of perhaps 310,000 people before the arrival of Europeans. Thus, through environmental management, hunting, gathering, fishing, farming, and food processing, Indians created a California that may have been the most densely populated region north of Mexico in the years before Christopher Columbus first visited the Western Hemisphere.[11]

These hundreds of thousands of people spoke a dazzling array of languages. Precontact North America was a diverse linguistic landscape. Indigenous peoples between the Rio Grande River and the Arctic Ocean spoke about 300 different languages that can be classified into more than fifty different language families. In contrast, linguists classify Europe's languages into as few as three families. Amid indigenous North America's already varied linguistic landscape, precontact California stands out as one of the most linguistically diverse places on earth. California Indians spoke perhaps 100 separate languages, classified by linguists into at least five different language families, some "as mutually unintelligible as English and Chinese."[12]

Speaking scores of languages, California Indians created dozens of cultural and political units. Anthropologists recognize at least sixty major tribes in California that can, in turn, be divided into many more linguistic and tribal subgroups. For example, anthropologists have classified the Pomo people north of San Francisco Bay into seven different subgroups and the Yana of the Southern Cascades into five subgroups. California's many subgroups can be divided further into about 500 individual bands, given that each village or village constellation tended to act as its own politically and economically autonomous entity. The indigenous peoples of California were thus highly independent but loosely bound to larger tribal groups by shared languages and cultures.[13]

Systems of exchange also connected California Indian peoples to each other and helped to distribute food, raw materials, manufactured goods, and luxuries. Theirs was a mixed economy in which dentalia, or seashell currency, often facilitated transactions within and beyond California. Traded foods included acorns, beans, berries, fish, meat, nuts, roots, salt, seafood, seaweed, and seeds. Traded raw materials included furs, hides, sinew, skins, and obsidian—a volcanic glass used to make knives, arrowheads, and other tools. California Indian people also exchanged manufactured goods. These included arrowheads, baskets, bows, cradle frames, moccasins, nets and snares, redwood canoes, rope, stone mortars

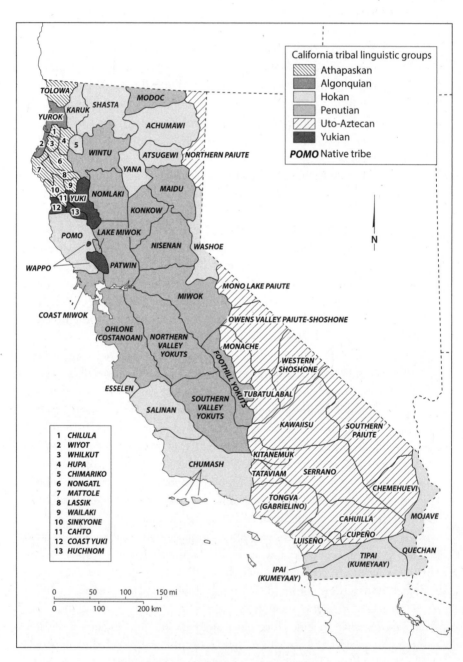

California Indian tribes and language groups

Legend within map:

California tribal linguistic groups
- Athapaskan
- Algonquian
- Hokan
- Penutian
- Uto-Aztecan
- Yukian

POMO Native tribe

Tribe labels on map:

TOLOWA, SHASTA, MODOC, YUROK, KARUK, ACHUMAWI, WINTU, ATSUGEWI, NORTHERN PAIUTE, YANA, NOMLAKI, MAIDU, KONKOW, YUKI, LAKE MIWOK, NISENAN, WASHOE, POMO, PATWIN, WAPPO, COAST MIWOK, MIWOK, MONO LAKE PAIUTE, OHLONE (COSTANOAN), NORTHERN VALLEY YOKUTS, OWENS VALLEY PAIUTE-SHOSHONE, MONACHE, WESTERN SHOSHONE, ESSELEN, FOOTHILL YOKUTS, TUBATULABAL, SALINAN, SOUTHERN VALLEY YOKUTS, KAWAIISU, SOUTHERN PAIUTE, CHUMASH, KITANEMUK, TATAVIAM, SERRANO, CHEMEHUEVI, TONGVA (GABRIELINO), CAHUILLA, MOJAVE, CUPEÑO, LUISEÑO, TIPAI (KUMEYAAY), QUECHAN, IPAI (KUMEYAAY)

Numbered list:

1 CHILULA
2 WIYOT
3 WHILKUT
4 HUPA
5 CHIMARIKO
6 NONGATL
7 MATTOLE
8 LASSIK
9 WAILAKI
10 SINKYONE
11 CAHTO
12 COAST YUKI
13 HUCHNOM

Scale: 0 50 100 150 mi / 0 100 200 km

and pestles, stone vessels, and buckeye fire drills for starting fires. Traded luxuries included tobacco and pipes, decorative woodpecker scalps, ornamental shells, carved nuts, and pigments.[14]

California Indians did have violent conflicts with each other before contact with Europeans, but warfare does not seem to have dominated their lives. As early as 1875, ethnographer Stephen Powers remarked that California Indians "were not a martial race, but rather peaceable." More recently, anthropologists Robert Heizer and Albert Elsasser observed that "except for the Colorado River tribes, who placed a value on warfare, the California Indians were peaceable and unaggressive."[15]

This drawing is one of the earliest known images of California Indians in native regalia at Mission San Jose. Georg Heinrich von Langsdorff, "Ein Tanz der Indianer in der Mission in St. José in Neu-Californien" [A Dance of the Indians in the Mission in San Jose in New California], drawing on paper: ink, wash, and gouache, between 1803 and 1807. Courtesy of The Bancroft Library, University of California, Berkeley.

California before European contact was a thriving, staggeringly diverse place. Peoples speaking scores of different languages organized themselves into hundreds of political entities and connected themselves to each other via dense webs of local and regional cultural exchange while maintaining trading connections with peoples farther away. Their lifeways changed over the course of millennia, but the arrival of Europeans brought rapid, and for many tribes, catastrophic transformations.[16]

In March 1543, Spaniards anchored in the blue waters of San Diego Bay, completing the first European exploration of California's coast. Before leaving, they "took two [Ipai] boys to carry to New Spain to learn to be interpreters." This first European kidnapping of California Indians foreshadowed a dark new chapter in California history. Spaniards, Russians, and Mexicans would impose race-based, two-tiered legal systems, unfree labor regimes, and violence on California's indigenous peoples. These traditions would later cross-pollinate with preexisting Anglo-American practices and policies toward American Indians to create some of the conditions for genocide in California between 1846 and 1873. Newcomers also brought Old World diseases to California, which depopulated and weakened numerous California tribes, thus paving the way for Anglo-American conquest and diminishing the ability of many California Indian communities to resist violence.[17]

In 1769—226 years after its first exploratory visit—Spain sent soldiers and Franciscan missionaries north from Mexico to colonize California. The project sought to preempt possible British, Dutch, and Russian expansion, and create a protective buffer zone for northern Mexico's valuable silver mines, while facilitating what the founder of California's missions, Father Junípero Serra, called the "spiritual conquest" of California. Serra and his fellow Franciscan missionaries viewed California Indians as pagans and *gente sin razón*, or people without reason, to be treated as children. From this infantilizing perspective, these Franciscans—like many other missionaries working in the Americas—aimed to fashion allegedly childlike Indians into Catholic workers by replacing indigenous religions, cultures, and traditions with Hispanic ones. They intended to transform Indians' lives and minds, while purportedly saving Indian souls from the horrors of eternal damnation. It was an ambitious program, deeply compelling for many Franciscans, and one that would come to rely, in part, on force.[18]

Initially, curiosity, food, and gifts drew California Indians to the missions. As time went on, the Spanish inadvertently compelled them to come. Historian Steven Hackel has emphasized that Spaniards introduced "pathogens, plants, and animals that . . . dramatically transformed California's human and natural landscape," destroying traditional California Indian means of subsistence and introducing Old World diseases to which California Indians had little or no biological resistance. The results were hunger, sickness, and death. Thus, many coastal California Indians increasingly came to the missions out of need.[19]

Franciscan missionaries baptized them, often without California Indians understanding what baptism meant to the Franciscans and to Spanish authorities: namely, that baptized Indians put themselves under the Franciscans' physical command, relinquishing the right to control their own lives or leave the mission without permission. In 1773, Serra secured a decree from the viceroy of New Spain and a royal council recognizing that "just as a father of a family has charge of his house and of the education and correction of his children" in California, "the management, control, and education of the baptized Indians pertains exclusively to the missionary fathers." By declaring baptized California Indians the legal wards of the Franciscans, Spanish authorities made them second-class subjects, and established precedents on which Mexican and US authorities would later build. After stripping California mission Indians of substantial rights, Spaniards forced many of them into unfree labor.[20]

By 1823, the Spaniards, and later the Mexicans, would build a network of twenty-one missions, four military presidios, and three civilian pueblos stretching north from San Diego to Sonoma. California Indians constructed most of the buildings, walls, farms, and ranches of this colonial enterprise.

Mission fathers focused on converting indigenous Californians, but both they and their civilian and military counterparts—like others who would follow them under US rule—depended on California Indian workers, often using force to acquire, manage, and retain them. As early as 1780, California governor Felipe de Neve criticized California's missions by writing that "the Indians' fate [was] worse than that of slaves." Many agreed that Franciscans held California mission Indians as unfree laborers. In 1877, the Costanoan Indian Lorenzo Asisara contextualized the 1812 neophyte killing of a Franciscan priest at Mission Santa Cruz by describing early nineteenth-century servitude enforced by violence there. According to Asisara: "The Spanish priests were very cruel with the Indians: they mistreated them a lot, they kept them poorly fed, ill clothed, and they made them work like slaves." Likewise, in 1826, the explorer Harrison Rogers wrote of Mission San Gabriel Indians east of Los Angeles, "They are Kept in great fear, for the least offence they are corrected, they are complete slaves in every sense of the word."[21]

Some scholars, too, have characterized California Indian mission labor as unfree. Cook asserted that "the mission system, in its economics, was built upon forced labor," and historian Robert Archibald maintained, "the result in many cases was slavery in fact although not in intent." Others have defined California's

California missions, forts, and towns, 1769–1823

Legend:
- Mission
- Fort (Presidio)
- Town (Pueblo)
- (1769) Year founded
- IPAI Native tribe

Map labels:
POMO
WAPPO
Fort Ross (1812)
LAKE MIWOK
PATWIN
Sacramento
Russian
San Francisco Solano (1823)
COAST MIWOK
San Rafael (1817)
San Francisco de Asís (1776)
San Francisco (1776)
San José (1797)
Santa Clara (1777)
San José (1777)
Santa Cruz (1791)
Branciforte (1797)
San Juan Bautista (1797)
OHLONE (COSTANOAN)
Monterey (1770)
San Carlos Borroméo (1770)
Soledad (1791)
San Joaquin
NORTHERN VALLEY YOKUTS
Lake Tahoe
Mono Lake
N
Owens Lake
ESSELEN
Salinas
San Antonio (1771)
San Miguel (1797)
SALINAN
Tulare Lake
SOUTHERN VALLEY YOKUTS
San Luis Obispo (1772)
Buena Vista Lake
La Purísima (1787)
CHUMASH
Santa Inés (1804)
Santa Bárbara (1786)
Santa Bárbara (1782)
TATAVIAM
San Fernando (1797)
San Buenaventura (1782)
San Gabriel (1771)
TONGVA (GABRIELINO)
Los Angeles (1781)
CAHUILLA
San Juan Capistrano (1776)
LUISEÑO
San Luis Rey (1798)
CUPEÑO
IPAI
PACIFIC OCEAN
San Diego (1769)
TIPAI

0   50   100   150 mi
0   100   200 km

In the foreground, California Indians march north under the supervision of a mounted overseer carrying a whip or lance. On the left, three other Indians move south under the direction of another overseer on horseback. The water to the right is San Francisco Bay, across which the iconic Golden Gate Bridge now stretches. Louis Choris, "Vue du Presidio s.ⁿ Francisco" [View of the San Francisco Presidio], lithograph, ca. 1815. Courtesy of The Bancroft Library, University of California, Berkeley.

mission labor system as "slavery without the actual sale of the individual," "a communal form of forced labor," "spiritual debt peonage," or "semicaptive labor."[22]

Officially sanctioned corporal punishment underscored California Indians' second-class legal status. Franciscans had mission Indians whipped, shackled, or placed in the stocks for "desertion . . . insolence, tardiness or absence from Mass, carelessness in learning the doctrina, gambling, and bickering between spouses that led to violence, laziness, fornication, adultery, and concubinage." In 1775, Father Serra himself wrote that he wanted some San Carlos Mission Indians to suffer "two or three whippings . . . on different days," explaining that they "may serve . . . for a warning, and may be of spiritual benefit to all." Serra condoned the physical striking of California Indians by missionaries. Indeed, in 1780, he wrote to Governor de Neve, "That spiritual fathers should punish their sons, the Indians, with blows appears to be as old as the conquest of these kingdoms [the Americas]; so general, in fact, that the saints do not seem to be any exception to the rule." Serra geographically and temporally extended what, to him, was a long-established and widespread Catholic missionizing practice in the Western Hemisphere: the deliberate infliction of pain on Native American skin, muscles, and nerves.[23]

Given official sanction and long-standing practice, Franciscan fathers rarely criticized the corporal punishment of California mission Indians. Yet, in 1798, a former Mission San Miguel padre risked his career by reporting to the viceroy of New Spain that "the manner in which the Indians are treated is by far more cruel than anything I have ever read about." He explained, "For any reason, however insignificant it may be, they are severely and cruelly whipped, placed in shackles, or put in the stocks for days on end without receiving even a drop of water." Responding to these accusations, the viceroy ordered California governor Diego de Borica to investigate. De Borica subsequently reported, "Generally, the treatment given the Indians is very harsh. At San Francisco, it even reached the point of cruelty." Despite the governor's strongly worded assessment, in 1805, the viceroy declared the padre's charges "groundless." Corporal punishment thus continued in California's missions.[24]

Floggings, in particular, seared themselves into mission Indians' flesh and memories. Julio César, likely a Luiseño Indian man, recollected of his youth at Southern California's Mission San Luis Rey: "When I was a boy the treatment given to the Indians at the mission was not at all good." He described "flogging for any fault, however slight" and emphasized the caprice with which such whippings could be inflicted: "We were at the mercy of the administrator, who ordered us to be flogged whenever and however he took a notion." The Costanoan Indian man Lorenzo Asisara also vividly recalled floggings. He explained, "The Indians at [Santa Cruz] mission were very severely treated by the padres, often punished by fifty lashes on the bare back" with a whip "made of rawhide." According to Asisara, "any disobedience or infraction" could bring down "the lash without mercy [on] the women the same as the men." Frequent whippings thus ingrained terror into everyday life for many at Mission Santa Cruz: "We were always trembling with fear of the lash." Indeed, throughout California's missions, whippings were an ever-present possibility.[25]

Floggings also informed the mission-era social and legal structures of Hispanic California. Such practices reinforced a racial hierarchy in which California Indians were at the bottom. As Hackel has pointed out, "soldiers and settlers were exempted from corporal punishment, a form of reprimand almost completely restricted to Indians and one that marked them as low and different." Corporal punishment reinforced both the Spaniards' treatment of California Indians as children and the two-tiered legal system on which Mexican and later US citizens built.[26]

Colonists' sexual assaults inflicted further violence and pain on California Indians during the mission period. As early as 1772, Father Luís Jayme of Mission San Diego reported hearing that local Indians, probably Ipai or Tipai people, "leave their huts and the crops which they gather . . . and go to the woods and experience hunger. They do this so that the soldiers will not rape their women as they have already done so many times in the past." Jayme also received multiple eyewitness reports of gang rapes and concluded of Spanish soldiers: "Very many of them deserve to be hanged on account of the continuous outrages which they are committing in seizing and raping the women. There is not a single mission where all the gentiles have not been scandalized." The following year, Serra himself wrote: "The soldiers, clever as they are at lassoing cows and mules, would catch an Indian woman with their lassos to become prey for their unbridled lust. At times some Indian men would try to defend their wives, only to be shot down with bullets."[27]

Sexual violence against California Indians was apparently routine at some times and in some places under Spanish rule. One Indian woman accused soldiers of raping her daily in her cell at Monterey Presidio. San Diego commandant José Francisco Ortega wrote simply that soldiers "go by night to nearby villages for the purpose of raping Indian women." Serra also received a report of soldiers sexually assaulting Indian children, probably Tongvas, at Mission San Gabriel. The Chumash man Kitsepawit, or Fernando Librado, described the routine rape of females at Mission San Buenaventura, as recounted by Woqoch, or Old Lucas, who had been the Indian sacristan there: "They took all the best-looking Indian girls . . . and they put them in the nunnery [*monjerío*]; the priest had an appointed hour to go there. When he got to the nunnery, all were in bed in the big dormitory. The priest would pass by the bed of the superior [*maestra*] and tap her on the shoulder, and she would commence singing. All of the girls would join in, which . . . had the effect of drowning out any other sounds." Then, "While the singing was going on, the priest would have time to select the girl he wanted [and] carry out his desires." According to Woqoch, "In this way the priest had sex with all of them, from the superior all the way down the line. . . . The priest's will was law."[28]

Some sexual assaults were lethal, and at least one high-profile reported rape went unpunished. In 1773, Pedro Fages charged a trio of soldiers with raping three California Indian girls, one of whom subsequently died. Yet Governor Fages himself may have been guilty of raping a California Indian child. In 1785, his wife formally declared having caught him "physically on top of . . . a very young Yuma [Quechan] Indian girl." The girl was eleven years old. Authorities then temporarily imprisoned Fages's wife and deemed Fages innocent of rape.[29]

When Spanish authorities did punish colonists for sexually assaulting California Indians, the sentences were less severe than for similar crimes committed against non-Indians. In 1789, after one colonist raped an Indian woman, the authorities incarcerated him for only twenty days. In 1805, another colonist received a six-month sentence for raping an Indian girl, and, in 1818, a third received six months of hard labor for raping a married Indian women. Predictably, such sentences did little to protect California Indians from sexual assault, and reinforced the violent, two-tiered colonial legal system under which California Indians suffered.[30]

Unsurprisingly, thousands of California mission Indians resisted by fleeing; perhaps 4,000 left in 1817 alone. Their motives varied, as the interrogations of a dozen California Indians captured after fleeing Mission San Francisco in 1797 make clear. Tiburcio had suffered five whippings for crying when his wife and child died. Magin had endured incarceration in the stocks while sick. Tarazon had visited home and stayed. Claudio had been "beaten . . . with a stick and forced to work when ill." José Manuel had been bludgeoned. Liberato "ran away to escape dying of hunger as his mother, two brothers, and three nephews had done." Otolon had been "flogged for not caring for his wife after she had sinned with the vaquero." Milan had been worked "with no food for his family and was flogged because he went after clams. Patabo had lost his family and had no one to take care of him." Orencio's niece had starved to death. Toribio had been "always hungry," and Magno had "received no ration because, occupied in tending his sick son, he could not work." Thousands of others, up and down the mission system, had their own reasons for running away. In doing so, they established an enduring tradition of resisting unfree labor regimes under Spanish, Mexican, and later US rule.[31]

Franciscan fathers and their advocates, usually Spanish and later Mexican soldiers, frequently used force to recapture escapees. That force sometimes turned lethal. For example, in 1782, Governor de Neve wrote of Esselen Indians who had escaped from San Carlos Mission: "The repeated patrols that have been sent out to importune them to come back have resulted in deaths among the non-Christian natives." In 1829, the Mexican soldier Joaquín Piña recorded how his unit attacked escaped mission Indians, killing perhaps thirty or more Indian people, including male and female prisoners.[32]

Corporal punishment at the missions often followed recapture, particularly after a California Indian fled repeatedly. Father Estevan Tápis frankly explained that if a Santa Barbara Mission Indian ran away more than once, "he is chastised with the lash or with the stocks. If this is not sufficient . . . he is made to feel the shackles, which he must wear three days while at work." Visitors to California

This sketch depicts the way that Rumsen or Costanoan men would defend themselves from a Spanish dragoon. Tomás de Suria, "Modo de pelear de los Yndios de Californias" [Mode of combat of the Indians of the Californias], pencil drawing, 1791. Original in Museo Naval, Madrid, Spain. Photograph courtesy of Iris Engstrand.

also remarked on the corporal punishment of repeat escapees. In 1786, French navigator Jean François de La Pérouse visited Monterey and explained the Spanish thinking behind such punishments: "The moment an Indian is baptized, the effect is the same as if he had pronounced a vow for life." Violating this implied vow triggered an institutionalized response that could end in corporal punishment: "If he escapes to reside with his relations in the independent villages, he is summoned three times to return; if he refuses, the missionaries apply to the governor, who sends soldiers to seize him in the midst of his family and conduct him to the mission, where he is condemned to receive a certain number of lashes with the whip." Despite the threat of corporal punishments, thousands of California Indians fled and refused to return voluntarily. The Chumash woman María Solares of Santa Inés later recollected that her grandmother had been an *"esclava de la misión,"* or mission slave, who "had run away many, many times, and had been recaptured and whipped till her buttocks crawled with maggots." Such was the tenacity of one California Indian woman's desire for freedom.[33]

Punishments for recaptured escapees were sometimes lethal. One early nineteenth-century Russian American Company hunter described Spaniards torturing recaptured Indians at what seems to have been Mission San Fernando, northwest of Los Angeles:

> They were all bound with rawhide ropes and some were bleeding from wounds and some children were tied to their mothers. The next day we saw some terrible things. Some of the run-away men were tied on sticks and beaten with straps. One chief was taken out to the open field and a young calf which had just died was skinned and the chief was sewed into the skin while it was yet warm. He was kept tied to a stake all day, but he died soon and they kept his corpse tied up.

In 1831, British Navy captain Frederick Beechy summarized Spanish and Mexican responses to California Indian mission escapees, observing, "The services of the Indian, for life, belong to the mission, and if any neophyte should repent of his apostacy from the religion of his ancestors and desert, an armed force is sent in pursuit of him, and drags him back to punishment." Such treatment reinforced both Spaniards' and Mexicans' dehumanization of California Indians and the two-tiered Hispanic legal system on which US citizens later built. Meanwhile, some California Indians organized mass resistance.[34]

Like Native Americans in other parts of the Hispanic Americas, California Indians repeatedly attacked or rose up against the missions' oppression and conquest of indigenous lands. As early as 1775, some 600 Ipai and/or Tipai warriors stormed Mission San Diego, burning buildings and killing three people. The following year, Indians fired flaming arrows into the reed roofs of Mission San Luis Obispo, burning down buildings. Further incendiary attacks on San Luis Obispo eventually led to the universal adoption, from Sonoma to San Diego, of the California missions' iconic red-tile roofs. The Franciscans thereby incorporated the need to protect themselves from California Indian resistance into the missions' very architecture. Indeed, the Franciscans had reason to worry. In 1781, Mojaves and Quechans in southeastern California permanently destroyed the colonial outpost of Purísima Concepción, across the Colorado River from present-day Yuma, Arizona, as well as San Pedro y San Pablo de Bicuner ten miles upstream.[35]

California Indians repeatedly resisted or rose up against colonialism in the nineteenth century. From 1820 to 1823, a former San Rafael Mission Indian man named Pomponio, likely a Coast Miwok, led other escapees in raiding missions around the San Francisco Bay area. Authorities eventually captured this "most rebellious Indian," whom they executed by firing squad and buried on February 6, 1824. Just weeks later, Chumash people launched the largest uprising of the mission period. It soon involved missions Santa Inés, La Purísima, and Santa Barbara. The Chumash burned buildings, killed non-Indians, and held La Purísima for almost a month as many fled to the interior, some permanently. Four years later, large numbers of Indians escaped missions San Jose, San Juan Bautista, and Santa Cruz. A Yokuts man named Estanislao, born at Mission San Jose, led the uprising that now bears his name. "About six feet in height, of skin more pale than bronze, of slender figure, with a head of heavy hair and a heavy beard on his face," Estanislao held off multiple Mexican military expeditions before suffering defeat in 1829. By repeatedly burning buildings, killing Spaniards, Mexicans, and their allies, and escaping in large numbers, California Indians established a tradition of resistance to colonialism and helped to pave the way for their own emancipation.[36]

Mexico won independence from Spain in 1821 and immediately made Indians citizens, thus setting the stage for the gradual legal emancipation of California mission Indians. In 1826, California governor José María de Echeandía allowed potentially self-sustaining and married or adult mission Indians to request emancipation "provided they had been Christians from childhood, or for fifteen years." Mission Indians promptly began petitioning for their "freedom," but officials did not always grant such requests. In 1833, California governor José Figueroa issued "Provisional Preparations for the Emancipation of Mission Indians," and the Mexican Congress secularized the missions. Figueroa continued the official legal secularization process the following year, which liberated many mission Indians. Kitsepawit (Fernando Librado) later explained that at Mission San Buenaventura, "When all the Mission Indians heard the cry of freedom, they said, 'Now they no longer keep us here by force'." That December, Captain Pablo de la Portilla reported from San Luis Rey Mission, "These Indians will do absolutely no work nor obey my orders." Instead, "All with one voice would shout, 'We are free! We do not want to obey! We do not want to work!'" The protracted process of California mission secularization then continued well into the 1840s.[37]

California's missions had taken a terrible human toll. When the Franciscans concentrated California Indians, and held unmarried females in locked, crowded, and poorly ventilated buildings, they facilitated the transmission of pathogens, including those borne by Europeans and Mexicans to which California Indians had little or no immunity. The results were devastating. According to Hackel, "Across the California missions one in three infants did not live to see a first birthday. Four in ten Indian children who survived their first year perished before their fifth [and] between 10 and 20 percent of adults died each year."[38]

Spanish and Mexican officials knew of this trend and its relentless death toll because Franciscans carefully recorded baptisms and mortalities. For example, in 1774, Serra reported that "within a few days, eleven little babies of this mission, one after the other, took their flight to heaven. . . . A number of adults went also: some we baptized just before dying; others had been baptized before." Despite high mortality rates, authorities maintained and expanded the mission system for decades, thus facilitating and tolerating the mass death of tens of thousands of incarcerated California Indian civilians. By 1833, Franciscans had baptized 81,586 California Indians and buried some 62,600. Hardest hit were the indigenous peoples of the coastal zone between the San Diego area and the region north of San Francisco Bay. In 1769, perhaps 72,000 California Indians lived in this area. By 1830, their numbers had plunged. In total, if 310,000 Indians populated California in 1769, an estimated 245,000 California Indians were alive in 1830. Whether or not this constituted genocide is a hotly contested topic and deserves a separate, detailed study of its own.[39]

On a much smaller scale, Russians also colonized and coerced California Indians beginning in 1812 at Fort Ross Colony on the wave-lashed coast north of San Francisco. In 1958, a Kashaya Pomo man, James Herman, described the Russians' arrival, based on oral traditions: "Unexpectedly, they detected something white sailing on the water. It later proved to be a boat, but they didn't know what it was—the Indians hadn't seen anything like that before. Then it came closer and closer, and unexpectedly it landed, and it proved to be a boat. They turned out to be the undersea people—we Indians named those people that." Thus began Russian colonization in Northern California.[40]

There, and at nearby ranches, Russian agents sometimes forced Pomo and Miwok Indians to labor for them beginning in the 1830s. According to scholar Richard Steven Street, "Sweeping into interior villages, they rounded up entire rancherías at gunpoint and took hostages—women and children—to ensure that the men would labor diligently." Such practices replicated the established Russian system of taking hostages to compel first indigenous Siberians and later Native Alaskans to hunt for them. Yet Russians also seized and held California Indians as captive laborers. In 1833, Russian American governor Ferdinand Wrangel visited Fort Ross and reported that for some harvests "they forcibly collect as many Indians as possible, sometimes up to 150 persons, who for 1½ months are occupied without rest in Company field work." Moreover, "The Factory found itself forced to seek them in the tundras, attack by surprise, tie their hands, and drive them to the settlement like cattle to work: such a party of 75 men, wives, and children was brought to the settlement during my presence." The following year, California's Mexican governor, José Figueroa, visited another Russian ranch

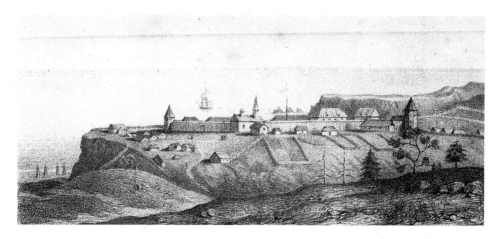

From 1812 to 1841, Fort Ross was the southernmost outpost of Russia's North
American empire. This Northern California colony was also a site to which
Russians brought Pomo and Miwok people to work as unfree laborers. Duhaut-Cilly,
"Vue de l'etablissement russe de la Bodega, à la Côte de la Nouvelle Albion,
en 1828 [View of the Russian establishment of the Bodega, on the coast of New Albion,
in 1828]," lithograph by Landais and Martenelle in A. Duhaut-Cilly, *Voyage Autour
du Monde, Principalement A la Californie et aux Iles Sandwich, Pendant les
Années 1826, 1827, 1828, et 1829 . : .* (Paris, 1835), frontispiece. Courtesy of
Fort Ross Conservancy Photo Archives, Fort Ross, California.

and recorded how Russians "were using, for labor . . . some Indians from the
villages whom they brought usually by force." Although Russian colonialists—
who formally withdrew from California in 1841—did employ forced labor, it
affected too few California Indians to approach the mass death of Spanish and
Mexican colonialism in California. Still, it did reinforce the dehumanizing
and violent policies toward California Indian people on which others later seem
to have built.[41]

Even as Mexican authorities emancipated mission Indians, many indigenous
Californians found themselves bound into new forms of unfree labor under
Mexican rule. Mexico outlawed slavery throughout its possessions in 1829,
but abolishing unfree California Indian labor proved difficult to enforce given
that many colonists depended on various forms of Indian servitude. Anglo-
Americans, Europeans, and Mexicans in California demanded laborers to work
their fields, manage their cattle, and staff their homes and businesses. Yet Mexican California suffered from a persistent non-Indian labor shortage. In the
search for labor, colonists turned to California's large Indian population. As

Hurtado has noted, "In the 1840s Indians were practically the sole source of agricultural labor and whites used every possible means to obtain their services. Slavery, debt peonage, and wage labor all had a place in Mexican and Anglo California." Many Californians operated their vast ranchos almost entirely with Indian labor, much of it coerced. According to Native American studies scholar Edward Castillo, by 1840 there were perhaps a dozen large "feudal establishments, each with 20 to several hundred Indians, in all perhaps as many as 4,000." Contemporary sources sometimes described these workers as slaves. For example, in 1844, rancher Pierson B. Reading—who had spent thirteen years in Mississippi and Louisiana—wrote that "the Indians of California make as obedient and humble slaves as the negroes in the south, for a mere trifle you can secure their services for life." Some Californians obtained such laborers, in part, by force. Two years later, at "'Hopitse-wah,' or 'Sacred Town',," a Pomo Indian village on the west shore of Clear Lake, the chief Hallowney told US Navy lieutenant Joseph Warren Revere, "as if he were spitting some fiery substance from his mouth [that] 'the Californians . . . hunt us down and steal our children from us to enslave them.'"[42]

Mexican Californians inherited the missions' deeply ingrained racial hierarchy, which placed Indians at the bottom and depended on them for labor. Rancheros ensnared some of these Indians in what scholars have defined as "debt peonage," "seigneurialism," or a "paternalism . . . similar to that which bound black slaves to white masters." Thus, multiple forms of California Indian servitude—as well as the profound racism that made the coercion of California Indians ideologically acceptable—existed on the eve of the Mexican-American War. These conditions set local precedents onto which US citizens and administrations then grafted their own racist traditions and unfree labor systems, even as they undid Mexican rule.[43]

In addition to systems of servitude, the United States would inherit a recently depopulated California. The 1830s and early 1840s had brought mass destruction to California Indians as sweeping epidemics killed more than 60,000 California Indian people. In 1833, malaria—with its debilitating fevers, headaches, and death—swept through the Sacramento and San Joaquin river valleys, spread by whining mosquitoes. Many thousands of California Indians inhabited these food-rich regions, and the impact was awful. According to former trapper J.J. Warner, "late in the summer of 1833, we found the valleys depopulated." He explained:

From the head of the Sacramento, to the great bend and slough of the San Joaquin, we did not see more than six or eight live Indians; while large numbers of their skulls and dead bodies were to be seen under almost every shade tree, near water, where the uninhabited and deserted villages had been converted into graveyards; and, on the San Joaquin river, in the immediate neighborhood of the larger class of villages, which, the preceding year, were the abodes of a large number of those Indians, we found not only many graves, but the vestiges of a funeral pyre.

Perhaps 20,000 to 50,000 Central Valley Indians died in 1833 alone.[44]

As for many indigenous peoples, from the Arctic to Patagonia, such "virgin soil epidemics" devastated populations and left survivors in shattered worlds. Luiseño Indian scholar Pablo Tac of Mission San Luis Rey may have been describing the 1833 epidemic when he later wrote: "In Quechla not long ago there were 5,000 souls, with all their neighboring lands. Through a sickness that came to California 2,000 souls died, and 3,000 were left." What Tac did not emphasize—perhaps because he was writing in Rome as he studied for the priesthood—was that the loss of 40 percent of his people was a result of contact with non-Indians and that the epidemic likely smashed his world by depriving him of friends, relatives, and much of his community's social fabric. Tac's experience was hardly unique.[45]

Other, smaller disease outbreaks followed the 1833 epidemic as California became more tightly knit into the transpacific trade networks that brought increasing numbers of disease-bearing ships from distant ports. As in other parts of the Americas, smallpox proved both highly contagious and extremely lethal to Native Americans. In 1837, smallpox arrived at Fort Ross—likely from Russian Alaska—spread east and killed as many as 10,000 California Indians, including many Pomo, Wappo, and Nomlaki people, in what is known as the Miramontes Epidemic. In 1844, smallpox arrived again, this time from what is now Mexico on a ship crewed by Native Hawaiians. The disfiguring disease—which causes painful, oozing sores—killed at least eighty-five Indians at Monterey. It then spread east to the Miwok people of what is now Amador County, killing an unknown total number of California Indians. In sum, according to Cook, if the "acute epidemics" of the 1830s killed roughly 60,000 California Indians "another 40,000 . . . perished, throughout the occupied portion of the state, as the result of endemic disease, armed conflict, and destruction of food supply" by 1845.[46]

Violence also took many California Indian lives under Mexican rule, albeit on a much smaller scale than did disease. In the 1820s, 1830s, and early 1840s, Mexicans killed hundreds of California Indians in battles and massacres. For example, in 1826 Lieutenant Juan Ibarra's men killed at least thirty-eight

Indians—likely Quechans or Yumas—near Santa Ysabel in Southern California before sending their severed ears to Ibarra's commander. In 1833, Father Jesús Mercado's forces slew twenty-one Southern Pomos, and the following year General Mariano Vallejo's men killed 200 Satiyomi Wappos in two separate battles. On several occasions, Mexicans also massacred Northern California Indians. In about 1837, José Maria Amador's forces slew 200 Sierra Miwok Indian prisoners of war in two mass executions, and in 1841 or 1842 Captain Salvador Vallejo led fifty or sixty men in an expedition to Clear Lake. Attacking the local Indians— likely Pomos—in their village, Vallejo's men "shot or cut down . . . about 150 men, women and children." In 1843, some 270 men under Salvador Vallejo left Sonoma to attack Indians suspected of plotting against colonists. Near Cape Mendocino, Vallejo's force launched an amphibious night assault on Moth Island, where they killed 170 Indian people. Massacres—although relatively unusual under Mexican rule—may have set local precedents for much larger-scale and more widespread violence against California Indians under US rule. Such atrocities may also have been driven by genocidal impulses. Indeed, the Pomo chief Hallowney explained to Revere in 1846 that Californios "are always ready to wage a war of extermination against us." Thus, Mexican-era massacres and the thinking behind them may have helped to pave the way for genocide in California between 1846 and 1873.[47]

In sum, the period between the secularization of the missions in the 1830s and 1846 was harrowing and catastrophic for many California Indian peoples. In combination with the mass death of the mission period, devastating epidemics and violence dramatically diminished California Indian populations in the 1830s and early 1840s, destabilized many of their social structures, wreaked havoc on multiple indigenous economies, and critically weakened many California Indian peoples' ability to resist the invasion and violence that began in 1846. At the same time, the dehumanization, the race-based two-tiered legal system, the unfree labor regimes, and the violence of the Russo-Hispanic colonial period set precedents for US citizens and others who later moved toward genocide.[48]

Still, perhaps 150,000 California Indian people survived the unfree labor, epidemics, and violence of Russo-Hispanic colonization. Spanish, Russian, and Mexican colonialism environmentally and demographically transformed much of the coastal region between Fort Ross and San Diego, while diseases depopulated much of the Central Valley. Yet some areas of California remained relatively unchanged. In 1846, immense flocks of pigeons still darkened the skies, huge herds of deer and elk continued to roam many plains and foothills, and vast runs of spawning salmon still turned California's rivers and streams silver with life. In much of the state, oaks continued to provide rich acorn harvests, pines still bore shiny nuts, grasses produced seeds, and other plants continued to yield traditional foods. California still provided a livelihood for tens of thousands of Indian people on the eve of conquest by the United States.[49]

Smoke curled into the blue skies from underground Pomo dance houses north of San Francisco Bay. Modoc paddles dipped quietly into Tule Lake to propel canoes near the Oregon border. Pine nuts clicked softly into woven Owens Valley Paiute-Shoshone baskets near the Nevada line. Pacific waves pounded against the redwood coast as Yuroks gathered shellfish. Southern Yokuts in the San Joaquin Valley continued to construct tule mat houses, and throughout much of California the steady thudding of stone pestles crushing acorns into meal sounded from villages and sun-dappled acorn groves. Conversations resonated on Mojave Desert footpaths, singing echoed against the sheer glacier-polished walls of Yosemite Valley, and flute players from north to south wove delicate melodies. Prayers rose amid towering redwoods and children's laughter accompanied celebrations and gatherings up and down the land of California.[50]

PRELUDE TO GENOCIDE:
MARCH 1846–MARCH 1848

It was a perfect butchery.

—Kit Carson, ca. 1856–1857

My son, remember, that from this hour there is blood between us and the pale-faces.

—Miwok(?) chief to his son, Chechee, 1847

Army captain John C. Frémont was blatantly disregarding orders. In the spring of 1846, he was not supposed to be in California. In fact, on February 12, 1845, a colonel had ordered him to survey the streams flowing east from the Rockies. Yet the ambitious topographical engineer—who in 1856 became the first Republican presidential candidate—made other plans. Instead of surveying rivers, the young Virginian marched his men 900 miles west to California, where Mexico's rule was tenuous. Captain Frémont's decision was likely a calculated attempt to be in the right place at the right time. Journalist John O'Sullivan had just coined the phrase "manifest destiny," the Texas storm clouds of the Mexican-American War were gathering, Anglo-Americans in California were chafing under Mexican rule, and Frémont knew—from a personal meeting with US president James K. Polk—that the new leader had "a fixed determination to acquire California."[1]

Frémont had led troops into California before, during his 1843–1844 expedition, and he now apparently reasoned that he could seize fame and power by playing a leading role in its imminent acquisition. Thus, after he reached the headwaters of the Arkansas River on September 2, 1845, he abandoned his Rocky Mountain assignment and—guided by Kit Carson—marched his men across mountains and deserts to California. Once there, he provoked Mexican authorities by raising the Stars and Stripes outside Monterey before retreating to explore the northern part of the state. According to one Frémont biographer, "He was killing time." Soon he was killing people.[2]

On March 30, 1846, Frémont and his men arrived at Danish immigrant Peter Lassen's ranch amid the high grasses of California's upper Sacramento River Valley, some ninety miles northwest of what would become Sacramento. Kit Carson recalled, "During our stay at Lawson's [Lassen's], some Americans that were settled in the neighborhood came in stating that there were about 1000 Indians in the vicinity making preparations to attack the settlements, [and] requested assistance of Fremont to drive them back." Frémont soon responded.[3]

Moving north up the Sacramento, Frémont's group presented a formidable sight: sixty buckskin-clad white men, each armed with a "Hawkens rifle, two pistols, a butcher knife" and other weapons, advanced with nine Delaware (Lenape) Indians and two California Indians. Joining these seventy-one Frémont expedition members were five volunteers from a nearby trading post. "Late in the afternoon," on or about April 5, 1846, they came to a halt.[4]

Close to Reading's Ranch, near the present-day city of Redding, Frémont spotted his objective. Expedition member Thomas S. Martin recollected, "At the foot of the low hills where the Sac. riv. comes out of the mtns. on the left hand side of [the] river going up we found the indians . . . on a tongue of land between the bends of the river." The people gathered there on the Sacramento that afternoon were probably Wintus, California Indians whose territory sprawled across hundreds of square miles of grasslands, oak-studded foothills, and conifer-clad mountains in and around the upper Sacramento River Valley and upper Trinity River drainages. Theirs was a land of plenty. From the plains and woodlands they harvested berries, pine nuts, clover, roots, seeds, and that foundation of so many California Indian diets: the acorn. Wintus also hunted bears, deer, and rabbits while burning grasslands in order to gather grasshoppers in woven conical baskets. Twice a year, the Sacramento and its tributaries ran silver with spawning Chinook salmon, which Wintus speared, clubbed, or netted before preserving for future use. These varied foods supported perhaps 5,300 Wintu people before contact with non-Indians.[5]

Led by hereditary chiefs, Wintus lived in politically independent villages in which residents gathered for communal hunting, fishing, feasting, and ceremonial dancing. Although sometimes at odds with neighboring California Indian peoples, they traded with them and with each other, often facilitating transactions with seashell currency. To Shasta Indians they sold deer hides and decorative woodpecker scalps in return for dentalia and obsidian. With the Achumawi they exchanged salmon flour for salt and also traded for salt with the Yana Indians.

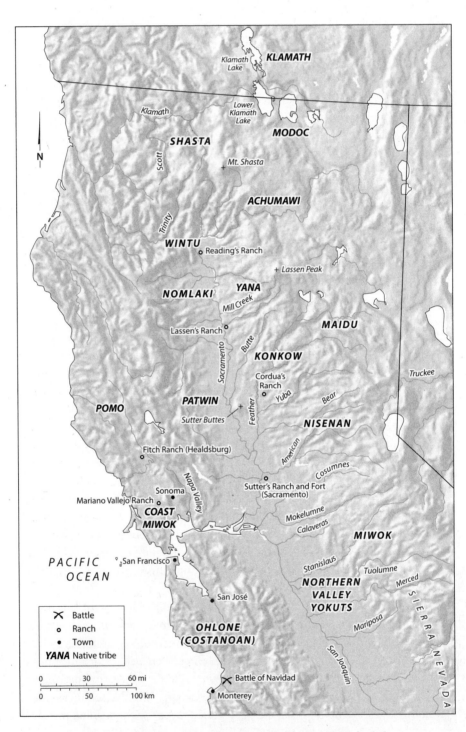

KLAMATH

Klamath
Lake

Klamath

Lower
Klamath
Lake

MODOC

SHASTA

Scott

Mt. Shasta

ACHUMAWI

Trinity

WINTU

Reading's Ranch

Lassen Peak

NOMLAKI

YANA

Mill Creek

Lassen's Ranch

Sacramento

Butte

MAIDU

KONKOW

Cordua's
Ranch

Yuba

Bear

PATWIN

Feather

Sutter Buttes

NISENAN

POMO

American

Cosumnes

Fitch Ranch (Healdsburg)

Sutter's Ranch and Fort
(Sacramento)

Napa Valley

Truckee

Sonoma

Mariano Vallejo Ranch

COAST
MIWOK

Mokelumne

Calaveras

MIWOK

PACIFIC
OCEAN

San Francisco

Stanislaus

Tuolumne

Merced

San José

NORTHERN
VALLEY
YOKUTS

Mariposa

⚔ Battle
○ Ranch
● Town
YANA Native tribe

OHLONE
(COSTANOAN)

San Joaquin

S
I
E
R
R
A

N
E
V
A
D
A

| 0 | | 30 | | 60 mi |
| 0 | | 50 | | 100 km |

Battle of Navidad

Monterey

Frémont's movements and events of March 1846–March 1848

In this image, a mounted man gazes across the upper Sacramento River, surveilling what is likely a Wintu village or fishing camp. Henry B. Brown, "On the Sacramento near Shasta Head of Great Sacramento Plain April 1852," pencil with gouache, 1852. Courtesy of Huntington Library, San Marino, California.

They also carried on considerable traffic—within and beyond Wintu territory—in dried salmon, freshwater clams, and dentalia in return for bows, acorns, and manzanita berries. Trade brought prosperity and connected Wintu people to a wider California Indian world. Contact with newcomers from beyond California would prove far less advantageous.[6]

After sighting the Wintus gathered on the banks of the Sacramento, the members of Frémont's expedition recalled no tribal name, but did remember a great many Indians. The laconic Kit Carson recollected, "Found them to be in great force, as was stated [by those who had requested Frémont's help]." Expedition member Thomas E. Breckenridge later estimated 150 men and about 250 women and children. Martin, however, recalled: "4000 to 5000 . . . having a war dance prepa[ra]tory to attacking the settlers." These widely divergent estimates—in conjunction with additional estimates to which we shall turn shortly—suggest that as many as 1,000 or more Wintus were there that day.[7]

Seeing seventy-six heavily armed men approaching, and being surrounded by the snowmelt-swollen Sacramento on three sides, the Wintus reacted quickly. There were many women and children in camp and to retreat across the river would be difficult, if not disastrous. The Wintu men thus hastily prepared to

With a snowcapped Mount Shasta towering in the distance, these presumably Wintu
people enjoy a summer day on the shores of what is probably the upper Sacramento
River near modern-day Redding, California. Henry B. Brown, "Summer Lodges.
California Indians near Shasta 1852," pencil with gouache, 1852. Courtesy of
Huntington Library, San Marino, California.

defend themselves and their families. William Isaac Tustin, an eyewitness, remembered, "When we arrived . . . on the Sacramento River the Indians quickly
formed themselves into [a] line of battle." Their caution proved warranted. Having effectively surrounded them, Frémont eschewed diplomacy and instead
launched a well-planned, preemptive assault of a kind that would later become
common in California.[8]

According to Breckenridge, "the or[d]er was given to ask no quarter and to
give none." The massacre began with long-range small-arms fire. Tustin described how "as soon as we got within rifle shot, they began to fall fast." Using
their Hawken rifles, which had a range of some 200 yards, Frémont's men could
kill from well beyond the reach of Wintu bows and arrows. Overwhelmingly
superior range meant that, as in the many California battles and massacres
that would follow, "arrows thrown against us were harmless on account of the
distance." Still, the attackers' rifle barrel grooves probably soon clogged with
burned powder after several shots and Frémont's men charged in an example of
what would become the second phase of many California massacres. Martin
recalled a well-executed military assault: "Our advance guard of 36 first came

in sight of them & immediately charged & poured a volley into them killing 24, they then rushed in with their sabers." Soon, "The res[t] of the party coming up they charged in among them." Once engaged in close-quarter killing, the attackers began using their sabers and perhaps their pistols and butcher knives, the third phase in a progression of massacre tactics that would later become common. Breckenridge bitterly criticized the assault, but blamed the "five volunteers from the trading post," presumably to spare his fellow soldiers' honor: "The settlers charged into the village taking the warriors by surprise and then commenced a scene of slaughter which is unequealled in the West. The bucks, squaws and paposes were shot down like sheep and those men never stopped as long as they could find one alive."[9]

With their defenses breached, if they had any defenses at all, Wintu survivors fled west into the hills, or east into the Sacramento River. Frémont's men turned both escape routes into death traps, thus initiating the fourth and final phase of this and many subsequent California Indian massacres: executionary killing. Tustin recalled: "They took flight and run, some made for the river, but the majority took the plains towards the foothills." Attackers pursued them: "Kit Carson and the Delaware Indians who were with Fremont followed those who took the plains, and being mounted they literally tomahawked their way through the flying Indians." Meanwhile, "the rest of the party stationed themselves on the bank of the river, and kept up a continual fire on the Indians who had gone into the river and were swimming across." It was "a slaughter."[10]

During the next twenty-seven years, massacres like this became all too common in California. Encirclement, surprise attack, an initial barrage of long-range small-arms fire, close-range attack, and executionary noncombatant killing would become a kind of unwritten tactical doctrine in California Indian-hunting campaigns. The Sacramento River Massacre was the prelude to hundreds of similar massacres and ultimately an American genocide.

Frémont's men killed a great number of people that April day in 1846. Breckenridge, who claimed not to have participated, wrote: "Some escaped but as near as I could learn from those that were engaged in the butchery, I can't call it any thing else, there was from 120 to 150 Indians killed that day." Martin, who did participate, estimated that "in less than 3 hours we had killed over 175 of them," but that "most of the inds. escaped to the neighboring mts." Tustin, a man with no professional interest in downplaying the number killed and whose unpublished eyewitness account has never before been cited in connection with this massacre, reported a far greater death toll: "The Indians killed was somewhere between six and seven hundred by actual count." He specified, "I am speaking of those killed on land, as we could not count those killed in the river, but I have no doubt there was fully two or three hundred more." If Tustin was correct, Frémont's force killed as many as 1,000 California Indian men, women, and children in what may have been one of the largest but least-known massacres in US history.[11]

Highlighting the one-sided nature of the attack, no extant primary source documented any member of Frémont's force being killed or even injured in what was apparently an assault on largely unarmed Wintu civilians gathered to catch and process salmon. On March 5, Frémont recorded that "salmon was now abundant in the Sacramento," and Tustin recalled that, after the massacre, "We camped there all night and ate up all their salmon." If the Wintus were assembled for a war dance, why did women and children outnumber men, as Breckenridge asserted? Any war dance should have contained enough armed warriors to inflict at least one casualty, particularly during close-quarters fighting. The Sacramento River Massacre thus presaged the many later attacks that targeted California Indian civilians for slaughter, based on hearsay.[12]

The massacre also foreshadowed what would become a common rationalization for such atrocities: the notion of pedagogic killing. In 1894, Breckenridge remained stunned by the extent and cruelty of the massacre. "I think that I hate an Indian as badly as any body and have as good reason to hate them, but I don't think that I could have assisted in that solaughter[.] It takes two to fight or quarrel but in that case there was but one side fighting and the other side trying to escape." Still, although he criticized "that solaughter," Breckenridge articulated an idea that would become increasingly prevalent in California: the notion that killing indigenous Californians would teach survivors not to challenge whites. As Breckenridge saw it, "The Indians had received a wholesome lesson from our party," and, as a result, Sacramento Valley Indians "did not desire any farther evidence of our fighting qualities" and left Frémont's party unmolested. Carson agreed: "(it) would be long before they ever again would feel like attacking the settlements." He concluded, "It was a perfect butchery."[13]

Killing as they went, Frémont's expedition now moved north, after a brief return to Lassen's Ranch, to head up the Sacramento and into southern Oregon. Martin remembered, "About the 10th of May, I think, we started with about 57 men for Oregon. We followed up the Sac. river killing plenty of game, and an occasional indian. Of the latter we made it a rule to spare none of the bucks." Breckenridge explained that Frémont's men "had orders while in camp or on the move to shoot Indians on sight," and concluded, "While on the [m]arch the crack of a rifle and the dying yell of a native was not an unusual occurrence."[14]

Unsurprisingly, Indians retaliated. On May 9, US Marine Corps lieutenant Archibald H. Gillespie caught up with Frémont in southern Oregon, north of

John C. Frémont was responsible for the killing of
perhaps hundreds of California Indians, but went on to
an illustrious career. He later represented California as
one of its first US senators, became the first Republican
presidential candidate, and served as a general during
the US Civil War. George Peter Alexander Healy, "Portrait
of John C. Fremont," oil on canvas, undated. Courtesy
of the Union League Club of Chicago, ULI895R.4.

Klamath Lake, to deliver urgent dispatches and letters, one of which instructed
Frémont to return to California. That night, as Frémont was falling asleep under
the branches of a cedar, "fifteen or twenty [Klamaths] attacked," killing two or
three of Frémont's men and wounding perhaps one. Frémont now "determined
to square accounts with these people." Two days later, his Delaware scouts took
two Klamath scalps with his help, but Frémont wanted more. Like many later
immigrants to California, Frémont and Carson seemed to think that in matters of revenge any American Indians would do. On May 12, Carson assaulted
a village on the southern shores of Klamath Lake and killed at least fourteen

Klamath people without suffering a single casualty. Marching south, Frémont's men continued killing and scalping Native Americans. It was a portentous prelude to US rule in California, which began three months later when military officers took possession of the northern portion of the state.[15]

The 1846 Sacramento River Massacre foreshadowed the new regime's propensities for preemptive mass violence against California Indians as well as the specific tactics and justifications that they would use. It was a "genocidal massacre"—which sociologist Leo Kuper defined not as genocide itself but as "the annihilation of a section of a group—men, women and children, as for example in the wiping out of whole villages." Still, it did not signal the immediate commencement of genocide throughout California. Before the gold rush, during the first twenty months of US rule (between July 1846 and March 1848), US sailors and soldiers, along with other US citizens, Mexicans, and Europeans, established other patterns of violent and destructive behavior, supported by local officials and federal authorities. For instance, mountain men, ranchers, farmers, soldiers, and sailors attacked California Indians and abducted them. They also crippled some tribes' traditional economies. Nevertheless, although California's non-Indian society was fundamentally racist toward California Indians and routinely exploited them, there were relatively few killings of California Indians during this period.[16]

Three factors explain why. First, with some exceptions, California Indians posed little threat to whites or their property. Second, because California's 10,000–14,000 Anglo-Americans, Spanish-speaking Californios, and Europeans were collectively outnumbered by as much as fifteen to one, this small, thinly spread, and heterogeneous population was relatively cautious in its dealings with the perhaps 150,000 Indians inhabiting California during these early years. Third, and most important, colonizers needed California Indians—who constituted the overwhelming majority of laborers in California's cattle, grape, and grain economy—too much to annihilate them. Yet Frémont's Sacramento River Massacre did foreshadow a new approach to California Indians. Indeed, these twenty months of 1846–1848 were a transitional period between the Hispanic tradition of assimilating and exploiting indigenous peoples and the Anglo-American pattern of killing or removing them. California Indians, for their part, participated sometimes voluntarily and sometimes unwillingly in these varied relationships, but during this period few Indians launched concerted efforts to drive non-Indians away, in part because so many colonized areas had been heavily depopulated during the Russo-Hispanic era.[17]

California Indians played important roles in colonists' pastures, fields, houses, bedrooms, and barracks. Yet the dehumanization inherent in many of these relationships and in the low-intensity anti-Indian violence that flared between July 1846 and March 1848 foreshadowed the genocide to come.

PASTURES, FIELDS, AND HOUSES

Three days after Frémont began his drive north toward Klamath Lake, the United States declared war on Mexico. On May 9, 1846, he received orders to return south from Oregon. Slowly riding south through Northern California and still unaware of the war, Frémont waited for his moment. His was an unhurried march, traversing a world where Anglo-Americans, Californios, and Europeans depended on the California Indians who were enmeshed in the colonial economy but were generally hostile toward those who were not. Some supported the Sacramento River Massacre. Breckenridge recalled, "The fight that we had had with the Indians in the Sacramento Valley . . . had been noised about and recruits were plenty." Nevertheless, many farmers and ranchers, and particularly the wealthy and powerful major estate owners, relied on California Indian labor. Thus, although some admired the massacre, their economic dependence on California Indians limited violence to attacks primarily on so-called wild Indians, those outside the colonial economic matrix. Simultaneously, the non-Indian population's small size, compared to the California Indian population, constrained the number and scope of these attacks.[18]

The California Indians who worked in colonists' pastures, fields, and houses included free and bound laborers. Some Indians worked voluntarily to earn trade goods or food. Bound labor, however, was common in Mexican California. Many California Indians worked for Anglo-Americans, Europeans, and Californios who had appropriated their land. These Indians had to do this if they wanted to remain in their ancestral homes, with their tribe, and near their sacred places. In addition, colonists' livestock depleted traditional California Indian food sources, particularly grasses, seeds, acorns, and the game that fed on them. Ranchers and farmers often denied Indians access to what remained, unless they became laborers. Thus, if they wanted to stay, and eat, many California Indians exchanged work for food rather than face the dangers inherent in hunting, fishing, and gathering on neighboring tribes' land.

In this way, large estate owners often developed semifeudal relationships with California Indians. Such Indians provided labor, and sometimes military service, in return for food, the right to remain on their land, and some combination of shelter, clothing, trade goods, and protection. Although they sometimes paid Indian laborers, ranchers often coerced them into work with the threat of violence. For example, Nisenan man William Joseph recalled that on the

Sacramento River Valley estate of Swiss emigrant Johann Sutter, Indians who did not work suffered flogging "with a big whip made of cowhide." Pre–gold rush eyewitnesses described Indian workers on California's ranches as "legally reduced to servitude," "the bond-men of the country," or "little better than serfs [who] performed all the drudgery and labour." The forty-niner William M. Case concluded, "a genuine European feudal system was in force."[19]

Other California Indians labored completely against their will. Captured by armed kidnappers who sold them, they worked as slaves. In 1845, one US citizen wrote that "the natives . . . in California . . . are in a state of absolute vassalage, even more degrading, and more oppressive that that of our slaves in the south." The gregarious, handsome, and hard-drinking Johann Sutter built a small empire, in part, by employing substantial numbers of unfree Indian laborers. His Swiss employee, Heinrich Lienhard, recalled that Sutter "had many mountain Indians [who] were furnished by the various chiefs [and who] had to slave two weeks for a plain muslin shirt, or the material for a pair of cotton trousers." Although nominally paid, they were unfree: "I had to lock the Indian men and women together in a large room to prevent them from returning to their homes in the mountains at night [and] the inmates were forced to sleep on the bare floor." Sutter also bought and sold Indians. Irishman John Chamberlain recalled: "While I was living at the Sacramento [in the 1840s], it was customary for Sutter to buy and sell Indian boys and girls." Sutter himself recalled that it was "common in those days to seize Indian women and children and sell them, this the Californians (Mexicans) did as well as Indians." Unfree Indians filled roles integral to California's colonial ranching and farming economy. Thus, colonists chose not to dispense with them as long as there were few non-Indians in California.[20]

Riding south into the broad, rolling upper Sacramento Valley in May 1846, Frémont crossed the northern frontier of California's already vast pastoral industry. Geared toward the export of cattle hides and tallow—mainly to New England—these operations formed California's economic backbone. That year, Thomas J. Farnham wrote that "there is now believed to be in the country about 1,000,000 black cattle, 500,000 horses, 420,000 sheep, 3000 mules, 3000 goats, and 2000 swine." Journalist Edwin Bryant ventured that in 1847, some 150,000 hides would be shipped, and in 1848 he estimated that "the value of the hides and tallow derived from the annual *matanzas* [killings] may be estimated at $372,000." To wrangle and process the bovine multitudes ranging over their vast domains—which routinely exceeded 10,000 acres and contained thousands of animals—ranchers turned to California Indians, who served as cowboys, broncobusters, butchers, skinners, tanners, and tallow renderers. This Indian labor was indispensable to pre–gold rush California cattle ranchers.[21]

Many of these ranchers also cultivated grain, and they employed California Indians in this endeavor as well. On March 25, 1846, Frémont visited German immigrant Theodore Cordua's ranch on the Yuba River, which was "stocked with about 3,000 head of cattle, and cultivated principally in wheat." He reported: "The labor on this and other farms in the [Yuba] valley is performed by Indians." In an August 30, 1846, journal entry, Bryant wrote of "Indian servants" on the Johnson ranch, north of Sutter's Fort, who apparently helped to farm wheat, barley, and corn. Two days later, Bryant visited Scotsman John Sinclair, east of Sutter's Fort, where he found Sinclair threshing wheat with Indians. Nearby, Sutter supervised several hundred to 1,000 California Indians, depending on the season, to manage thousands of cattle and to raise and harvest crops on his 48,000-acre land grant.[22]

By 1847, grain was a small but thriving economic sector. On July 10, the San Francisco *Californian* reported, "There was never better crops of wheat raised in any country, than there is this season in California, and there is much more cultivated than ever before." Three days later, a correspondent for San Francisco's *California Star* asked, "What will the farmer of the New England States think when I inform him that one *farmer* in this valley cuts two thousand acres of wheat this year, which if carefully harvested will yield over forty thousand bushels of the best wheat on the globe?" What indeed? Naturally, in New England, "Our little ten acre farmer would say, that it was decidedly a large 'crap,'" on the grounds that no one farmer, even with the help of his immediate family, could possibly cut by hand 40,000 bushels—320,000 gallons—of wheat in a single harvest season. How was this possible without mechanization? "Most of this enormous crop is cut with the sickle by the wild Indian." In addition, a select number used more efficient scythes with an attached frame for catching the cut wheat: "some half a dozen of the *tame* Indians have this season been taught the use of the cradle, and use it as well as the white men of the East." California Indian labor was crucial to the region's grain boom. Without it, farmers could not harvest their vast crop yields.[23]

California Indians also played vital roles in non-Indian homes. On September 21, 1846, Bryant stayed in the residence of Virgin Islander William A. Leidesdorff, where, he wrote, "The servants waiting upon the table were an Indian *muchachito* and *muchachita*." In October, Bryant visited the home of a Mr. Murphy in San Rafael where coffee was "prepared by the Indian muchachos and muchachas," and, in December, he reported an English family "with two or three

Indians servants" at San Miguel mission. In addition to working in pastures, fields, and homes, California Indians also worked as guides, loggers, ferrymen, and sailors.[24]

California's vast estates were particularly dependent on California Indian labor. The ranching and farming operations of a handful of men dominated the economy from Healdsburg, in the west, to Sacramento in the east, and from the Upper Sacramento in the north to Southern California. Every one of them depended on California Indian workers. Salvador Vallejo, the Californio owner of a 30,000-acre Napa Valley estate, summarized large landowners' dependence on Indian laborers: "They tilled our soil, pastured our cattle, sheared our sheep, cut our lumber, built our houses, paddled our boats, made tiles for our houses, ground our grain, killed our cattle, and dressed their hides for market, + made our unburnt bricks; while the indian women made excellent servants, took good care of our children, made every one of our meals." In addition to this vital work, California Indian women and girls also played important roles in the personal lives of some Anglo-American, Californio, and European men.[25]

BEDROOMS

Although some non-Indian families migrated to California between 1821 and 1848, most newcomers were single men, many of whom presumably desired women for some combination of companionship, love, sex, labor, or political or economic connections. Arriving in California, they found just a few thousand Anglo-American, Californio, European, and Native Hawaiian women. By contrast, tens of thousands of Indian women inhabited California and many were working for non-Indians. As a result, immigrant men often married or cohabited with California Indian women in the established tradition of white fur trappers and traders working in the North American borderlands. It is difficult to estimate how many liaisons existed between such men and California Indian women in pre–gold rush California. As historian Albert Hurtado has observed, "American society scorned 'squaws,' 'squaw men,' and their 'half-breed' children." As a result, white men married to California Indian women rarely recorded such liaisons and often maintained them only temporarily. This helps to explain historical demographer Sherburne Cook's conclusion that "there are few reliable, concrete data on this subject."[26]

Fortunately, some observers did report relationships between white men and California Indian women. Sutter's Fort was one locus of interracial cohabitation and intermarriage. According to Sutter's employee Lienhard, fellow employee Michael C. Nye had an "Indian squaw" with whom he had two children, and

Indian females, like this young woman who may have
been from what is now Stanislaus County, sometimes
cohabited with non-Indian men and sometimes suffered
sexual manipulation, coercion, rape, and sexual slavery
at colonizers' hands. Unknown artist, "Indienne
Californienne du Sud 16 ans [a]u prix d'une livre de
poudre de chasse et une bouteille de brandy"
[Sixteen-year-old Southern California Indian female
at the price of a pound of gunpower and a bottle of
brandy], print on paper: engraving, hand colored,
185?. Courtesy of The Bancroft Library,
University of California, Berkeley.

"two of the squaws claimed [fellow employee John] Yates as their husband."
Yates, in turn, recalled that German employee Nicholaus Allgeier had an
"adopted wife (a California native)," and that another employee, John Chamberlain, "had been married nineteen times to native women." How consensual
these relationships were remains unclear. Lienhard charged that Sutter, "a typical
Don Juan with women," kept a "harem" that included "Indian girls" as young

as "ten or twelve." Given the unequal power dynamics between Anglo-American, Californio, and European men, on the one hand, and California Indian women and girls, on the other, sexual manipulation, coercion, rape, and sexual slavery were likely common in pre–gold rush California.[27]

Beyond Sutter's estate there are other examples of intermarriage from the early years of US rule. Forty-niner William Case recollected that most of the traders who had gone to California before the gold rush "had married native Indian women." In the summer of 1849, William J. Shaw met "an American" in Sacramento, "from the mountains, with a squaw for wife" and "a number of children." That same year German immigrant John A. Bauer encountered a hunter named Green with an Indian spouse. Lienhard reported on Clements's "Indian squaw and several children" on the Sacramento, "Cordua's Indian wife" on the Yuba, and Perry McCoon's Indian "mistress," Mary, on the Co-sumnes River. Marriages and liaisons between non-Indian men and California Indian women were not confined entirely to the interior. William Redmond Ryan described his San Francisco business partner's wife as "a beautiful half-caste Indian girl, who had an infant at the breast," and wrote that in 1849 men could be seen "perambulating the streets" of San Francisco in the company of "Indian squaws."[28]

Despite the degrading, racist terms with which they frequently objectified and insulted California Indian women, some newcomers candidly described their physical attraction to such women and even risked their lives to ap-proach them. New York journalist E. Gould Buffum arrived in California in March 1847 and recorded an episode in which he and his companion Higgins encountered two "mountain beauties." The two quickly became "flying beau-ties" but the smitten men followed, even when the "two female attractions" re-treated into a village filled with armed California Indian men. The women were evidently extremely compelling, but they were frightened—perhaps with good reason—by the attentions of Buffum and Higgins. Such pursuits also likely sparked resentments among California Indian men, thus leading to con-flict and violence.[29]

Encounters between non-Indian men and California Indian females spanned the gamut from marriage to temporary companionship to rape and sexual en-slavement. However, in at least some instances—we are unlikely ever to know how many—California Indian women were integral to male colonists' personal lives. Just as economic factors created a demand for California Indian labor, demographic conditions drove accommodation, cooperation, and other forms of contact in the pre–gold rush era. Indeed, Frémont himself employed dozens of California Indians in the US Army.

BARRACKS

As Frémont bivouacked north of Sutter's Fort in the summer heat of 1846, rumors suggesting that Mexican governor José Castro intended to expel all foreigners began circulating among Anglo-Americans and Europeans in Northern California. The swirling rumors, combined with the presence of Frémont and his soldiers, inspired some men to action. On the morning of June 14, Anglo-Americans entered Sonoma, an adobe mission village north of San Francisco Bay, seized the local barracks, and imprisoned several leading Mexicans—including General Mariano Vallejo and his brother Captain Salvador Vallejo—before declaring their political independence and raising a flag emblazoned with a star, a grizzly bear, and the words, "CALIFORNIA REPUBLIC."[30]

This was precisely the kind of opportunity for which Frémont had come to California. Indeed, the Bear Flag revolutionaries probably expected him to join them. Thus, when they brought the Sonoma prisoners to his camp on the Sacramento on June 16, Frémont was ready, but cautious. Still unaware that Mexico and the United States were at war, Frémont sent the prisoners to be interned in Fort Sutter, and waited. Receiving word, on June 20, that Governor Castro planned to attack the Bear Flaggers at Sonoma, Frémont finally felt he had a legitimate casus belli. With ninety mounted men, he rode into Sonoma on June 23, and several days later spiked the San Francisco Presidio's six guns without encountering resistance. On July 5, he officially took command of the Bear Flaggers and combined them with his own unit, renaming the resulting 250 men the "California Battalion." On July 11, Frémont requisitioned Sutter's Fort—with its fifteen-foot-high "whitewashed . . . crenulated walls, fortified gateway, and bastioned angles"—by raising the Stars and Stripes. The ambitious topographical engineer planned to conquer California, but had fewer than 300 men for the campaign.[31]

Just before appropriating Sutter's Fort, Frémont had attacked another community of unsuspecting Sacramento Valley Indians (probably Patwins) under the Sutter Buttes, near modern-day Meridian, and had killed "several Indians." Still he needed more troops, and US military officers now recruited California Indians. Fort Sutter's new commander, Captain Edward M. Kern, first enrolled thirty of Sutter's 100 to 200 battle-hardened California Indian troops to garrison the fort as paid infantrymen. Dressed in red-trimmed green and blue surplus imperial Russian uniforms and armed with muskets, bows, and arrows, these Miwok and probably Nisenan soldiers were more than mere colonial exotica. Drilled and deployed in combat for more than seven years to subdue neighboring California Indians, they were "expert in the use of firearms," according to

California Indian soldiers, like the men standing at attention here, served in the
US Army during the campaign to wrest control of California from Mexico.
Joseph Warren Revere, "Sutter's Fort—New Helvetia," lithograph,
undated, in Revere, *Tour of Duty in California*, 72. Courtesy of
The Bancroft Library, University of California, Berkeley.

navy lieutenant J.S. Missroon. These qualities made them particularly attractive to Frémont, many of whose Bear Flaggers were unseasoned volunteers.[32]

Sutter's California Indian soldiers proved themselves useful. US Navy lieutenant Joseph Revere, grandson of Paul Revere, visited Fort Sutter soon after the
proclamation of the Bear Flag Republic and reported: "These Indians indeed
were important auxiliaries to the Revolutionists, during the short period of strife
between the parties contending for the sovereignty of California." Soon, twenty
more enrolled as US soldiers. On September 2, 1846, Frémont became military
commandant of California and the following day Bryant described Sutter's Fort
as "manned by about fifty well-disciplined Indians, and ten or twelve white men,
all under the pay of the United States." They were not the only California Indians to serve under the Stars and Stripes during California's conquest.[33]

Others served in a variety of capacities. Lieutenant Revere assumed command of the Sonoma military post, where "ten Indian horse boys" were serving.
Indian guides led Revere's patrols and when he received rumors of "one thousand
Wallawalla Indians" invading the Sacramento Valley from Oregon, he raised
"a force of one hundred and fifty white men . . . and nearly three hundred Indians,

all well armed." California Indians also worked with Anglo-Americans around Monterey. In October 1846, the Yale-trained Navy chaplain turned Monterey mayor Walter Colton wrote: "Our Indian scouts, who came in yesterday, reported the discovery of a large band of Californians in the cover of the hills within the vicinity of Monterey."[34]

California Indians also served under Frémont in the final phase of California's conquest, between October 1846 and January 1847. Still undermanned, Frémont left Fort Sutter garrisoned with fifty Indians while recruiting others to help secure the tenuous hold of the United States over Southern California. On November 17, and 18, 1846, thirty Indians joined Bryant and others on their way to join Frémont's forces at Monterey. "Walla-Wallas from Oregon" also joined these "native Californian" volunteers to form Company H of Frémont's California Battalion.[35]

The men of Company H made important contributions to Frémont's campaign to conquer Southern California. They scouted for the battalion, served as night pickets, and fought aggressively, as demonstrated by their forceful response to a Californio surprise attack at the Battle of Natividad, northeast of present-day Salinas, on November 16. After campaigning some 300 miles south to Santa Barbara and then another 100 miles southeast to Campo de Cahuenga, on the edge of Los Angeles, Company H and the California Battalion halted. On January 13, 1847, the Mexican General Andrés Pico sat down with Frémont in Tomás Feliz's adobe house and capitulated, signing the Treaty of Cahuenga Pass. The Mexican-American War in California was over. Two weeks later, officers discharged thirty members of Company H. As in the state's fields, pastures, homes, and bedrooms, California Indians had played a role in the region's conquest by the United States that is now largely forgotten.[36]

DEHUMANIZATION AND RISING VIOLENCE
(JULY 1846–DECEMBER 1847)

Even after the Sacramento River Massacre of April 1846, demographics and economics favored a continuation of the Mexican status quo. Yet dehumanization, punctuated by anti-Indian violence, characterized the first twenty months of US rule. Continuing unfree labor regimes, US military campaigns, slave raiding, and other forms of dehumanization further eroded the moral restraints of Anglo-Americans, Californios, and Europeans against killing California Indians, while simultaneously stoking aggression and the desire for revenge among their victims. This period thus helped to lay the foundations for the mass killing that followed.

Dehumanization took many forms during these twenty months, but unfree California Indian labor was particularly corrosive to colonists' views of California Indians. Unfree Indian labor reaffirmed and perpetuated existing Mexican racial hierarchies, which excluded most California Indians from colonial society. Local Mexican racial hierarchies then cross-pollinated with the deeply entrenched anti-Indian racism that many US citizens carried to California. The net result was the steady erosion of cultural barriers to anti-Indian violence and, ultimately, the fraying of many immigrants' moral fiber, at least with regard to Indians. Indeed, the degradation associated with some forms of unfree California Indian labor confronted immigrants with an economic system and society in which some colonists treated Indians as animals. These encounters had a powerful psychic effect, fueling racism and emotionally hardening colonists, soldiers, and sailors to cruelty toward California Indians.

Sutter's vast semifeudal ranch, with its partly clothed or naked Miwok and Maidu Indian laborers and its "harem" of Indian women and girls, exemplified this process. Situated along the overland route into California, Sutter's domain was a Sacramento Valley portal through which many overland immigrants passed on their trek from the eastern United States in the late 1840s and early 1850s. Sutter, who built and maintained his fiefdom with Indian labor, extended his hospitality to many immigrants. What these newcomers saw during their visits with the gregarious, hard-drinking Swiss colonist often had a profound effect on them and several immigrants recorded witnessing scenes of institutionalized dehumanization at his ranch.[37]

Sutter's method of feeding his California Indian laborers shocked pre–gold rush visitors. In 1845, James Clyman wrote that Sutter "keeps from 600 or 800 Indians in a state of complete slavery, and . . . I had the mortification of seeing them dine[:] 10 or 15 troughs, 3 or 4 feet long were brought out of the cook room, and seated in the broiling sun, all the laborers great and small, ran to the troughs like so many pigs, and fed themselves, with their hands, as long as the troughs contained even a moisture." The following year, as Bryant described it: "The laboring or field Indians about the fort are fed upon the offal of slaughtered animals, and upon the bran sifted from the ground wheat." This was "placed in wooden troughs standing in the court, around which the several messes seat themselves and scoop out with their hands this poor fodder." It was hardly the "good soup," roasted and fried meat dishes with onions, "bread, cheese, butter and melons" that Sutter served Bryant in separate courses on china with silver utensils that evening. The contrast could not have been more pronounced.[38]

By feeding California Indians like hogs, Sutter, who routinely presented himself as a European gentleman, suggested that they were animals. Bryant, a perceptive journalist who trumpeted his friendly interactions with American Indians, seems to have interpreted it this way. Yet, as a newcomer trying to fit into California's colonial society and understand its peculiar institutions, he struggled to rationalize an obviously odious practice: "Bad as it is, they eat it with an apparent high relish; and no doubt it is more palatable and more healthy than the acorn, mush, or *atóle*, which constitutes the principal food of these Indians in their wild state." By feeding Indians like pigs, Sutter ostracized, humiliated, and dehumanized them. These effects were perhaps by-products of efficiency: It was expedient to feed Indian workers cheaply, as with useful animals. Yet Bryant's struggle with what he saw suggests that men with morals could be confused, and potentially corrupted, by the pervasive dehumanization of Indians in pre–gold rush California.[39]

In part as a result of the degrading ways in which many treated California Indians under early US rule, some came to see them as subhuman. In September 1847, the *Californian* rhetorically asked, "What is lower in the scale of humanity than a California Indian?" The author then offhandedly, and without any evidence, declared some Indians he met on "the Sui Sun Ranch, the property of General Vallejo" to be "cannibals." It was a surprisingly simple rhetorical step to move from dehumanizing to demonizing. Demonization—playing on long-standing Anglo-American fears of American Indians—would justify and encourage anti-Indian violence. It was a crucial precursor to establishing a collective mindset in which genocide would become possible.[40]

US soldiers and sailors began sporadic operations against Northern California Indians even as Northern California Indian soldiers were helping them to conquer Southern California. On August 8, 1846, less than a month after the Stars and Stripes began flying over San Francisco, forces at San Juan set off in pursuit of Indians who had driven off more than 200 horses from San Jose. Twenty mounted soldiers and sailors caught up to the rustlers and killed three or four of them. The *Californian* then proclaimed, "We shall urge the organization of interior defences sufficient to protect the property of citizens from the depredations of the wild indians."[41]

California's first US military governor set an aggressive tone for martial law policies toward California Indians. On August 17, 1846, Commodore Robert Stockton proclaimed that the California battalion would remain "constantly on duty to prevent and punish any aggressions by the Indians." Five days later, the *Californian* reported that mounted infantrymen had just returned from another sortie against Indians. The paper concluded by invoking a doctrine of collective, that is, indiscriminate, reprisal against California Indian villages that would come to be widely accepted and that all but guaranteed the killing of large numbers of noncombatants: "The only effectual means of stopping [Indian] inroads upon the property of the country, will be to attack them in their villages." Some military officers were more circumspect in identifying Indian targets. On September 6, Lieutenant William T. Sherman advised San Jose mayor John Burton to "tell the people of your District that if they catch indians in the act of stealing, or of attempting to steal their horses, they should shoot them" or "collect together, pursue and kill them, or at least show them that a pursuit was made." However, military pursuits also resulted in attacks on California Indian communities and consequent casualties. The *Californian* reported that forty men under navy purser James H. Watmough, reached San Jose on September 14, after a two-week campaign against Indians, during which Watmough "recaptured over 100 horses, and killed and wounded several Indians, in the various skirmishes at the Indian camps." In 1847, violence against California Indians was not yet genocidal. But whites were discussing the doctrine of indiscriminate, collective reprisal, which would become central to the genocide yet to come, and military officers were conducting lethal reprisals for stock raiding.[42]

Early in the new year, Frémont finally seized the prize that had apparently lured him to California. On January 16, 1847, Commodore Stockton turned the military governorship over to him. However, in late February, orders arrived from Washington, DC, substantiating General Stephen Kearney's supreme authority. On March 1, Kearney became governor, and in June he and Frémont headed east to Washington, where Frémont would face twenty-three charges of "mutiny" for not quickly surrendering the governorship to Kearney. Meanwhile, the dry season brought renewed military assaults on California Indian villages.[43]

On February 28, 1847, sixteen Mill Creek men petitioned US Army captain Edward M. Kern for assistance against local Indians so that they would not "be forced to abandon our farms and leave our property [or] perhaps [face] something worse." Captain Kern quickly marched up the valley with twenty men to "chastis[e]" the Indians. On March 23, he and Sutter led fifty men into the upper Sacramento Valley where they killed twenty Indians in a violent, one-sided campaign in which "Kern lost none" of his men.[44]

The army also organized punitive operations in Southern California. Indian stock raiding was a serious problem for California ranchers at this time and on April 10, 1847, Colonel R.B. Mason ordered every ranch to provide one or two mounted men, with spare horses, to unite with US troops at Los Angeles "for the purpose of repelling and destroying the Indians who are now committing such extensive depredations."[45]

California Indian slave raiding—a Mexican period carryover—also continued under US rule. Methods were often murderous. As early as August 24, 1846,

Bryant wrote of meeting an Indian "Chief" near the Truckee River and the Sierra Nevada crest. According to Bryant, "If I understood it," the chief explained that "whites, had slaughtered his men, taken his women and children into captivity, and driven him out of his country." Bryant concluded: "I have but little doubt, that these Indians are the remnant of some tribe that has been wantonly destroyed in some of the bloody Indian slaughters which have occurred in California."[46]

California Indian slave raiding often involved killing the adults and taking young women and children into captivity. Frequently it entailed the genocidal acts of "killing members of the group" and "forcibly transferring children of the group to another group." By intentionally separating California Indian men and women from their home communities and tribal members of the opposite sex, those who imposed the institution of California Indian servitude also hindered reproduction, which—according to the UN Genocide Convention—constituted "imposing measures intended to prevent births within the group." As such raids increased, when they were conducted with intent to destroy the group in whole or in part, systems of California Indian servitude came to play an important role in the genocide of California's Indians.

California Indians developed a diverse variety of architectural styles for their houses and communal gathering places. The Maidu people depicted here constructed subterranean lodges that remained cool during the heat of summer and warm in the depths of winter. Henry B. Brown, "Chino [Konkow Maidu] Village near Monroeville, California," pencil and gray wash, May 1852. Courtesy of the John Carter Brown Library at Brown University.

Patterns of murderous slave raiding were readily discernible in 1847. Early that year seven Rancheria Tulea Indians told Napa magistrate E.J. Babe that after some of their community escaped bondage, their captors attacked the village "killing five and wounding many more." On May 18, Sutter, now a US federal Indian agent, reported that slave raiders "with little or no cause would shoot them, steal away their women and children, and even go so far as to attack whole villages, killing, without distinction of age or sex, hundreds of defenseless Indians." In late June or early July, several Spanish-speaking men "started from Sonoma or vicinity, and proceeded" to a point "sixty miles above [Sutter's Fort] to a tribe of friendly Indians" near present-day Chico. The Konkow Maidu received the visitors with "the most friendly feelings, offering acorn bread, and other food." However, "The Spaniards, after having partaken of their hospitality, commenced making prisoners of men, women and children, and in securing them, [shot ten to thirteen who tried] to escape." The raiders next tied at least thirty people together, "principally women and children," and drove them to "the settlements." The killing continued: "Young children who were unable to proceed, were murdered on the road. In one instance an infant was taken from its mother, and killed in her presence."[47]

Such treatment was not anomalous. As Konkow Maidu man John A. Clark recollected, some white men "had absolutely no regard for Indian life, and . . . would wantonly murder an Indian with no more compunction than if they were killing a coyote." Some officials, moreover, did not consider such behavior worth punishing. Sutter reported that Antonio Armijo, Robert Smith, and John Eggar were the perpetrators of the murderous slave raid north of Sutter's Fort and that the army had arrested them. Yet, at their trial, judges acquitted all three. California's military government never again tried to stop the kidnapping of Indians. Judicial impunity for California Indian kidnapping would continue for decades, virtually uninterrupted, thus indirectly encouraging both lethal kidnapping and related killing.[48]

Military decision makers focused on punishing California Indians for crimes against whites. In September 1847, after Indians stole stock near San Jose and a white man was found killed, Lieutenant Sherman ordered New York Volunteers captain Henry Naglee to capture the thieves and bring them to Monterey for trial. Captain Naglee's men then burned an Indian village to the ground in the Sierra Nevada Mountains near the Tuolumne River and captured two Indians, probably Miwoks. An expedition member recounted to Ryan what happened next. The chiefs proclaimed their innocence, but Naglee replied that "he did not believe them; that they were all the same colour, and, therefore, all thieves and murderers alike; and he should insist upon the culprits being given up.

Again the chiefs remonstrated and protested against the injustice that had been done them; it was in vain." Naglee "pointed to a small space that had been recently cleared, and a firing-party took up its position there." The older chief bid a final farewell to his son, Chechee: "The two took leave of each other with great emotion; and the old man, after embracing his son, said to him—'My son, remember, that from this hour there is blood between us and the pale-faces.'" Following this injunction to avenge, "The two chiefs then folded their arms, and deliberately stalked to the place of execution—of murder, rather." The firing squad shot both chiefs and left them "stretched on the ground stone dead."[49]

Given that soldiers and sailors were attacking and killing California Indians but failing to punish civilians who kidnapped and killed California Indians, it is unsurprising that those who harbored anti-Indian sentiments became increasingly bold. Nevertheless, in comparison to what came after, the August 1846 to December 1847 period was one of relatively little recorded violence. The events of these months helped to spread the hostile and permissive attitudes, as well as the increasingly lax official protection of California Indians, that policy-makers institutionalized over the coming years and that eventually created an atmosphere conducive to genocide.

In January 1848, a Sonoma correspondent of the *California Star* proposed that a California Indian apprentice system be established for this "inferior order of our race" and that Indians be prohibited from passing through colonized parts of California without passes. The correspondent concluded that unless authorities adopted such a plan, California Indians would become thieves, and that "a continual war will necessarily be waged, for depredations committed, till all are exterminated." It was an important moment in California history, portending a fundamental shift in California Indian policy away from coexistence, however exploitative, and toward genocide. That same month Captain Charles Weber led a punitive raid into the mountains of what is now San Joaquin County, attacking a presumably Miwok village and killing "most of the bucks."[50]

On the eve of the gold rush, some whites were beginning to speak of "getting rid" of California Indians altogether. On February 26, 1848, the same Sonoma newspaper correspondent who had suggested making California Indians into apprentices now proposed total elimination. Again marshaling the myth of sub-humanity, the correspondent called California Indians "the nearest link of the sort, to the quadrupeds of any [Indians] on the continent of North America." As such, he claimed, "They are a burden and pest to the country, and gladly would I behold the exit of every one of these miserable creatures from our midst." As to how California Indians would "exit," his prior reference to "a continual war . . . till all are exterminated" had provided a strong hint. Two and a half weeks later, San Francisco's other major newspaper—the *Californian*—printed a similarly ominous statement, proclaiming: "We desire only a white population in California, even the Indians amongst us, as far as we have seen, are more of a nuisance than a benefit to the country; we would like to get rid of them." The California Gold Rush thus began in an atmosphere of rising hostility toward California Indians and an escalating Anglo-American interest in their forced relocation or physical extermination.[51]

Between July 1846, when the United States raised its flag in California, and March 1848, when the gold rush began, war and a change in government convulsed California. US armed forces launched several murderous local campaigns against California Indians during this period, but the old Hispanic system of marrying and employing California Indians (often without the freedom to quit) remained largely intact, as did the colonial economy and the power of prewar Anglo-American, Californio, and European elites. In fact, in their new possession, US military administrators perpetuated the prewar economic system and its dependence on California Indian labor. Between July 1846 and March 1848, despite outbursts of mass murder and the rise of an ominous rhetoric of elimination, relations between California Indians and colonists remained largely unchanged. However, when thousands of gold seekers began arriving from beyond California, that relationship began sliding toward catastrophe.

GOLD, IMMIGRANTS, AND KILLERS FROM OREGON: MARCH 1848–MAY 1850

The late emigrants across the mountains, and some Oregon trappers and mountaineers, had commenced a war of extermination upon them, shooting them down like wolves, men, women, and children, wherever they could find them.

—Johann Sutter, 1849

White men who were washing gold further up the [American] river killed my uncle and another Indian, scalped them, and took their heads.

—Konnock (Nisenan), n.d.

Sutter tried to keep James Marshall's January 24 gold strike on his land a secret, but journalists soon broke the news. On March 15, 1848, the *Californian* announced, "Gold has been found in considerable quantities" near Sutter's Mill on the South Fork of the American River. Still, many Californians remained skeptical. Then, in early May, an exultant Samuel Brannan strutted through the village of San Francisco's sandy lanes "holding up a bottle of [gold] dust in one hand, and swinging his hat with the other," bellowing, "Gold! Gold! Gold from the American River!" The California Gold Rush began in earnest and soon triggered mass migration to the goldfields.[1]

As news of the gold found by James Marshall and his Nisenan employees spread, the Central Mines drew people with almost irresistible force, emptying California's towns, farms, and ranches. By June 10, "Every seaport as far south as San Diego, and every interior town; and nearly every rancho from the base of the mountains in which the gold has been found, to the Mission of San Luis [Obispo], south, has become suddenly drained of human beings." They initially converged on the gold-rich watersheds of the American, Feather, Stan-islaus, and Yuba Rivers. There, amid the Sierra Nevada's western slopes, geologi-cal forces had deposited the glinting mineral millions of years earlier. Internal migration to these watersheds concentrated thousands of California Indians and non-Indians together into relatively small areas in what became known as the Central Mines. The arrival of at least 80,000 immigrants from beyond Califor-nia then intensified the crowding even as prospecting increased in the Northern Mines and the Southern Mines. The three gold-mining regions would ultimately stretch from the Klamath River near the Oregon border to Central California's Mariposa Creek and become the setting for new relationships, new conflicts, and, ultimately, the first local genocide against California Indians under US rule. This local genocide—an attempt to annihilate the people of a relatively limited geographic zone—began in the Central Mines but soon spread to the Northern and Southern Mines. These mass killings were the first of many such local campaigns that would stretch across decades and target dozens of tribes to cumulatively constitute the wider California genocide that ended only in 1873.[2]

Miwok and Nisenan Indian people were the primary inhabitants of what became the Central Mines. Traditional Miwok territory covers a vast region stretching roughly from what is now Walnut Creek, in the eastern San Francisco Bay Area, to the high peaks of the Sierra Nevadas and from just north of the Cosumnes River south to modern-day Mariposa. To the north, Nisenan territory covered the majority of the Central Mines and spread north from what is now Sacramento to the jagged Sutter Buttes and east to the Sierra Crest. Although they spoke different languages, Miwok and Nisenan people had much in com-mon: they both wove beautiful baskets, lived in politically autonomous villages, practiced tattooing, gathered and hunted to create similar cuisines, and often built substantial structures. Like most California Indian peoples, neither pos-sessed a centralized social hierarchy or military command able to mobilize armies, and neither was particularly warlike. In fact, Miwoks and Nisenans in the gold-laden Sierra foothills generally allowed newly arrived "forty-eighters" to prospect relatively unimpeded in their homelands. Gold-rich watersheds flowed through their territories, and thus both the Nisenan and Miwok peoples felt the full effects of the gold rush. However, because the Nisenans lived along the American River—where the gold rush began—they seem to have borne the brunt of the early violence, which began to escalate in the second half of 1848.[3]

Several thousand California Indians, including many Miwok and Nisenan people, became gold miners in 1848, many entering the colonial economy for the first time. Some came as ranchers' employees, serfs, or slaves. After mili-tary governor Richard B. Mason toured the Central Mines with Lieutenant

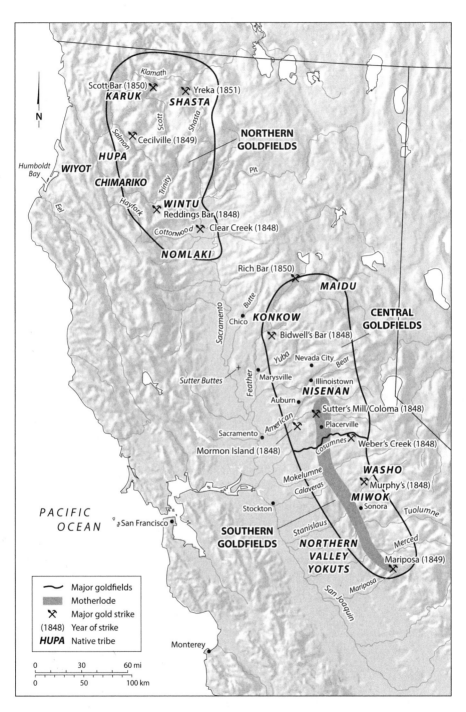

Klamath

Scott Bar (1850) ✗
KARUK   ✗ Yreka (1851)
          SHASTA

N

✗ Cecilville (1849)

NORTHERN
GOLDFIELDS

HUPA

Humboldt
Bay
WIYOT

CHIMARIKO

Pit

WINTU
Reddings Bar (1848)
Cottonwood ✗ Clear Creek (1848)

NOMLAKI

Rich Bar (1850) ✗
          MAIDU

Butte

CENTRAL
GOLDFIELDS

Chico
KONKOW
          ✗ Bidwell's Bar (1848)

Sacramento

Yuba Nevada City
Marysville   Bear
Sutter Buttes   Illinoistown
          NISENAN
Auburn
          Sutter's Mill/Coloma (1848)
Sacramento ✗   • Placerville
          American ✗
Mormon Island (1848)   Weber's Creek (1848)

Cosumnes

WASHO

Mokelumne   ✗ Murphy's (1848)
Calaveras   *MIWOK*
          • Sonora
Stockton   Tuolumne

PACIFIC
OCEAN
🪸 San Francisco •

SOUTHERN
GOLDFIELDS   Stanislaus
          *NORTHERN
          VALLEY
          YOKUTS*   Merced
          Mariposa (1849)

San Joaquin   Mariposa

Major goldfields
Motherlode
✗   Major gold strike
(1848) Year of strike
HUPA Native tribe

0   30   60 mi
0   50   100 km

Monterey •

California's Northern, Central, and Southern Mines

William T. Sherman in July, he reported that the rancher Sinclair employed some fifty Indians from his ranch as miners on the North Fork of the American River. In August, Monterey mayor Walter Colton wrote that a group of men mining on the Feather River, "employed about thirty wild Indians, who are attached to the rancho owned by one of the party." Edward McIlhany recollected that the rancher John Bidwell employed forty Konkow Maidu men from a village near his house at his Feather River mine. Sutter himself recalled taking some 100 California Indian laborers from his vast ranch to the mines.[4]

Surging gold rush labor demand also spurred further slave raiding, which ensnared more Indians in California's systems of servitude and brought them to the mines. In 1850, the *Sacramento Transcript* explained that "when the first operations were commenced in the diggings, the Indians were employed . . . to perform the heavy labors of mining" and "to get together a sufficient number, a few whites would go to the places frequented by them, and drive away as many as they chose." Bidwell provided a vivid example, recalling that in 1848, three men "went across the Sacramento valley and brought in some 30 or 40 Indians to help them dig gold. They compelled them to come." Moreover, "If the Indians did not bring a sufficient amount of gold to suit them, they were whipped." Bidwell concluded: "The Indians would often try to escape but were always brought back by these men, and treated like slaves." Still, many California Indians voluntarily joined the rush of 1848.[5]

Some Indians mined as employees, as partners in mining companies, or as independent entrepreneurs. On August 14, the *Californian* reported: "Indians engaged at the mines, and from the fact that no capital is required, they are working in companies on equal share or alone with their basket." Former gold rush–era Indian trader William Robinson Grimshaw recollected: "Few persons now living have any idea of the enormous quantity of gold taken out in the summer of 1848 before the advent of white strangers." He explained that California Indian miners made this possible. They "worked with great energy to acquire the heretofore unheard of luxuries supplied by the traders." That same month, according to Governor Mason, "Large quantities of goods were daily sent forward to the mines, as the Indians, heretofore so poor and degraded, have suddenly become consumers of the luxuries of life." Yet, if some California Indians mined to acquire luxuries, many others did so to survive.[6]

As thousands of gold seekers poured into California Indians' homelands—in what amounted to an uninvited and sudden mass invasion—many indigenous Californians found their traditional food supplies rapidly declining. The Nisenans and Miwoks, for example, depended on gathering a variety of foods including wild onions and sweet potatoes, freshwater clams and mussels, seeds, nuts, berries, grasshoppers, and, most important, acorns. They also caught salmon, sturgeon, and other fish while hunting bears, birds, deer, elk, and small animals. The surge of gold seekers wrought havoc on traditional California Indian economies in and around the mines, and threatened local Indians' very ability to feed themselves. Newcomers shot or drove off game and grazed cattle, horses, pigs, and other stock on the meadows that had supported game animals. Domesticated animals also ate the grasses, nuts, seeds, and tubers crucial to the diets of California Indians living in and around the sand and gravel areas, known as placers, where prospectors were panning and digging for gold.

California Indians were thus motivated to mine, in part, by the pressing need to buy food to compensate for declining hunting and gathering yields. As German forty-niner Friedrich Gerstäcker observed, "The gold discovery has altered their mode of life materially; they have learned to want more necessities, while the means of subsistence diminishes in the mean time." California Indians in the mining regions purchased wheat flour to replace acorn meal as well as beef, mutton, and pork to replace fish and game, and European-style clothing to replace animal skins and traditional woven garments.[7]

Throughout 1848, observers noted increasing numbers of California Indian miners. On August 17, Mason reported some 2,000 Indians working in the placers. Charles M. Weber and William Daylor alone reportedly employed 1,000 Indians, probably Nisenan people, near Coloma, where Marshall and his Nisenan employees had first struck gold. By Christmas Day, James Clayman reported, "not less than 2000 white men and more than double that number of Indians washing gold." If more than 4,000 California Indians were mining gold by the end of 1848, their numbers likely increased in 1849, as gold strikes proliferated within and beyond the Central Mines. Indeed, one miner wrote that early that year, "thousands of . . . Indians were [reportedly] employed by the whites in gold gathering." The gold rush also drew many California Indians into other work and contact with non-Indians, amid a booming colonial economy that rapidly expanded to support the mining operations and those who toiled in the mines.[8]

Internal California migration to the goldfields in 1848 left an acute labor shortage in its wake. Towns, farms, and ranches emptied, causing severe economic disruption. After May 1, relatively few San Franciscans remained in town, and by June, the former US consul Thomas O. Larkin reported that three-fourths of San Francisco houses had been deserted, while at Monterey, "Every blacksmith, carpenter and lawyer is leaving; brick yards, saw mills, and ranchos, are left perfectly alone." The results were social upheaval and economic stagnation in some sectors. In August, Colton wrote that "the gold mines have upset all social and domestic arrangements in Monterey; the master has become his own servant,

Published in 1848, this is probably the earliest extant
image of California Indians mining gold. Henry I.
Simpson(?), "Untitled [California Indian Gold Miners,
August 1848]," drawing, undated, in Simpson, *Emigrants'
Guide to the Gold Mines*, 9. Courtesy of The Bancroft
Library, University of California, Berkeley.

and the servant his own lord." That same month, Sherman explained that "no
less a personage than the Governor himself has had to cook his own breakfast."
Tens of thousands of immigrants arrived in the second half of 1848 and in 1849,
and most headed to the mines in search of gold. Given colonial California's
long-standing dependence on California Indian labor, many Anglo-Americans,
Californios, and Europeans saw employing more Indians as the obvious solution
to their intensifying labor demands.[9]

California Indians not only worked in the mines but also helped to fill the labor vacuum created by mass internal migration to the placers. On ranches some continued working as skilled laborers. For example, in June 1848, hundreds of California Indians still worked for Sutter in occupations as varied as blacksmithing, tin work, carpentry, and weaving. Other California Indians continued nurturing colonists' crops and wrangling ranchers' huge cattle herds. Meanwhile, as California towns grew into cities built on the wealth created by gold mining, California Indians worked as cooks and domestics in these expanding urban centers. By 1849, Indians and other nonwhite servants were common in both Monterey and San Francisco. Indeed, the domestic roles played by California Indian women were often central in newcomers' lives, as some partnered, either informally or in wedlock, with Anglo-American, Californio, and European men.[10]

The first half of 1848 was relatively peaceful, even as sporadic killings, lethal slave raiding, and destructive slavery proliferated. Although Nisenan and Maidu peoples were experiencing an invasion of their sovereign territory in the placers, they did not violently impede the thousands of gold seekers who surged into the homelands. Nor did California Indian peoples at first offer substantial violent resistance to the newcomers' quest for riches within their lands. Instead, many Indian people aided in or joined that quest, either voluntarily, out of need, or in response to coercion. In sum, the vanguard of gold seekers who mined during the first half of 1848 had few reasons to attack California Indians.

In fact, during the first two years of the gold rush many of California's colonists became increasingly dependent on California Indian workers. In the context of an enduring non-Indian labor shortage and a rising demand for labor, increasing numbers of indigenous men, women, and children played indispensable roles in the colonial economy, even as gold mining rapidly overtook agriculture as California's economic mainstay. During the first two years of the gold boom, therefore, the number of California Indians connected to the colonial economy increased within and beyond the placers. At the same time, a murderous countercurrent began sweeping the mines with the arrival of large numbers of gold seekers, who had no preexisting relationships with California Indians.

KILLERS FROM OREGON

In the second half of 1848, tens of thousands of people from beyond California began arriving in search of wealth. These newcomers rarely had connections to California's Hispanic economy and society, in which indigenous peoples played important roles and in which mestizos were among the economic and

political elites. Some of these new prospectors saw California Indians as dangerous obstacles to wealth, rather than as potential employees or mates. Among these
newcomers, white men from Oregon played a leading and decisive role in increasing violence against California Indians. Their propensity for systematically
and indiscriminately murdering substantial numbers of indigenous civilians
ultimately created a local genocide in the Central Mines. This local genocide,
in turn, helped to pave the way for even more widespread and larger-scale killings by triggering escalating cycles of asymmetric violence and by normalizing
the killing of California Indians.[11]

By September, a relatively small but steady stream of forty-eighters began arriving from beyond California. That month, San Francisco's *Californian* exulted,
"Our town is completely crowded with new comers, thirty-five having arrived in
one vessel, thirty in another and nineteen in another, while every vessel that
comes brings more or less. Verily, gold is a powerful magnet." By mid-November,
the forty-eighters were pouring into California. San Francisco harbor, once a
remote and rarely visited port, became a jungle of masts and rigging into which
"upward of six hundred vessels had entered." The ships often sat rocking idly on
the blue bay, abandoned by sailors eager to trade their meager maritime wages for
the risky but potentially huge remuneration of the mines. Others made similar
calculations. They left homes, families, and jobs around the world for the chance
to strike it rich. In all, 10,000 to 13,000 wealth seekers arrived in 1848, roughly
doubling California's non-Indian population.[12]

Living just north of California, thousands of white Oregonians were among
the first people beyond California to gravitate toward its gold that year. On
July 31, the schooner *Honolulu* brought news of the gold rush to the Columbia
River, and the following month confirmations arrived by land and sea, triggering
an exodus. Oregonians often traveled hundreds of miles south in wagon trains
or in smaller groups to join the rush. By late October, 400 had arrived, and by late
November, perhaps 2,000 had made the trip. Oregon men made up the domi-
nant non-Indian mining group in some regions. For example, on December 2, the
California Star & Californian reported, "On the 'Middle-Fork,' . . . the 'diggers'
are mostly of the Oregon emigration." As Oregonian forty-eighter Peter H.
Burnett—who later became California's first civilian US governor—recollected:
"I think that at least two thirds of the population of Oregon, capable of bearing
arms, left for California in the Summer and fall of 1848. The white population
of Oregon . . . must have then amounted to from eight to ten thousand persons."
Their arrival would prove disastrous for California's indigenous peoples.[13]

Some Oregonians arrived full of murderous hostility toward American Indians. On November 29, 1847, Cayuse Indians had attacked an Oregon Trail mission

operated by Dr. Marcus Whitman and his wife Narcissa, near present-day Walla Walla, Washington. For many whites, the incident corroborated their stereotype of unpredictable American Indian violence. Yet the Cayuse of the Columbia Basin had four intense grievances against the Whitmans and other whites that animated the assault. First, Cayuse men—coming from a culture renowned for its equestrian skills—had served as US soldiers in Frémont's California Battalion during the Mexican-American War, but felt that they had not been adequately paid. Second, some local Cayuse people were profoundly insulted by what they considered to be the Whitmans' lack of respect and unfair trading practices. Third, some saw the Whitmans as aiding a dangerously increasing number of immigrants. Fourth, and most importantly and immediately, a substantial number of Cayuse people held Dr. Whitman personally responsible for unleashing a devastating measles epidemic that brought fevers, rashes, and ultimately death to perhaps half of the local Cayuse community. Whitman's ineffective treatment of stricken Cayuse people (often with cayenne pepper) only reinforced Cayuse suspicions that the doctor was intentionally poisoning them. In an early twentieth-century interview, Nez Perce man Yellow Bull and his Cayuse wife, whose father Tamáhŭs slew Whitman, explained:

> An employé at the mission . . . told the Indians that Doctor Whitman was putting poison in their medicine and killing them. One of the Indians made himself sick in order to test the Doctor, saying that if the Doctor's medicine killed him they would know that he was the cause of the death of the others. He took the medicine and died. Then the head-men met in council and made an agreement that the Doctor should be killed because two hundred of the people had died after taking his medicine.

Some sixty warriors now sought to defend their community and redress their grievances with tomahawks, guns, and other weapons. In total, fourteen people died, including Marcus, Narcissa, and their children. The Cayuse took fifty-three others prisoner. The Cayuse War had begun.[14]

By January 1848—the same month in which Marshall and his Nisenan employees found the gold that would trigger the California Gold Rush—fifty volunteer Oregon militiamen were marching east toward the Cayuse. This single company of riflemen soon grew into seven companies, a regiment totaling 537 men, many of whom would cover hundreds of miles searching for perpetrators of the Whitman Massacre. Although seeking the Cayuse, these volunteers killed various other American Indian people on multiple occasions. Indeed, the Oregon militiamen fought several pitched battles. They also saw the site of the killings they had come to avenge. Two companies of volunteers visited the

Whitman mission's charred wreckage, where they encountered the remains of the victims, disinterred and mangled by wolves. The grim scene likely hardened and infuriated the militiamen, but they failed to capture any perpetrators and most mustered out of service in July. The men responsible for the Whitman killings had eluded the expedition. As a result, many Anglo-American Oregonians remained deeply frustrated, their appetite for vengeance unsated as the California Gold Rush began pulling them south.[15]

The Whitman Massacre and the Cayuse War inspired some Oregonians to kill California Indians out of revenge or frustration. An article in San Francisco's *Daily Alta California* explained how, following the Whitman killings, "A protracted war with several of the most warlike and powerful tribes of Indians inhabiting Oregon" broke out. However, "It was for naught that company after company of volunteers proceeded against these well mounted and equipped warriors, and the attempt to visit vengeance upon the savage foe pitiably failed." The article emphasized that some Oregonians' "insatiable thirst for revenge" then generated new conflicts. As the Oregonians migrated south toward California's mines, they "had difficulties with Indians all along the route [presumably a variety of Oregon and Northern California Indian peoples]. Disdaining to treat otherwise with the most friendly in pretension than through the muzzles of their rifles, it is well known their trail was marked with Indian blood." Cayuse War veteran John E. Ross—who would participate in some California Indian killing campaigns and organize others—recollected blandly that during their 1848 journey he and thirty-six other Oregonians had repeatedly fought American Indians.[16]

Violent Oregonian forty-eighters continued killing Indians once in Northern California, fundamentally worsening relations between Indians and non-Indians there. Others also sometimes massacred California Indians. For example, around April 1848, a group of men ruthlessly killed eight Indian horse thieves. However, the Oregonians introduced more systematic and sustained killing, routinely targeting noncombatants. In 1849, an Oregonian named Grover explained, "Fresh from the Cayuse war, and exasperated by the atrocities of the Indians, [Oregonians] no sooner reached the head waters of the Sacramento Valley, than they avenged every theft of the California Indians by the rifle." Numerous primary sources recount 1848 Oregonian attacks on California Indians. Alfred A. Green recalled: "At Mokolumne [in October 1848], some Oregon people came in, and as they had had some trouble with the [Miwok] Indians, they regarded all Indians as their enemies. . . . About a week after, some Indians came there, and no sooner had they got there, than these Oregon men rushed at them, firing at the same time, exclaiming, 'Out of here, you black Devils!,' and commenced shooting them down." Nearby, Oregonians later conducted another "fierce onslaught on the Indians."[17]

The Oregonian attacks continued. On November 18, 1848, the *California Star & Californian* attributed to Indians, presumably Nisenan people, the disappearance of two miners, "between the [Y]uba and American rivers," but the report ultimately blamed Oregon men: "The Indian perpetrators of the above deed are of a numerous tribe highly incensed against the whites, particularly against the emigrants late from Oregon, having received injuries from the latter not long since, it is said." William Grimshaw concluded, "The first to commit outrages upon them were emigrants from Oregon: who, with the massacre of the Whitman family by the Indians of that territory fresh in their minds, fully carried out the proposition that the Indians had no rights whatever as human beings." Oregonians' profoundly racist 1848 assaults marked the beginning of what in 1849 would become a murderous drive to eliminate California Indians from the Central Mines.[18]

Oregonian attacks on California Indians catalyzed violent conflict while simultaneously corroding other whites' resistance to Indian killing by normalizing such behavior. "The ire of the savage was stirred," according to the *Daily Alta California*. "Here may be dated the commencement of disturbances between our people in the Placer, and the Indian tribes of the North." Green recalled simply that "war was introduced by" Oregonians. Indeed, Oregon men helped initiate an intensifying, but largely one-sided, cycle of violence that would soon turn genocidal and ultimately spread to become a major catastrophe in Native American and US history. In 1848, there were still too few non-Indians to either remove or annihilate California Indians in the Central Mines, but that would soon change.[19]

On December 5, 1848, President James K. Polk publicly confirmed that California's gold rush was based on solid, conclusive evidence. "The accounts of the abundance of gold in that territory," he pronounced, "are of such an extraordinary character as would scarcely command belief were they not corroborated by the authentic reports of officers in the public service, who have visited the mineral district and derived the facts which they detail from personal observation." Polk's widely republished message convinced tens of thousands of skeptics and helped to transform the stream of forty-eighters into a torrent of forty-niners.[20]

FRIGHTENED, HEAVILY ARMED IMMIGRANTS, 1849

On January 1, 1849, California contained approximately 25,000 non-Indians. By the end of June, that number had surged to 30,000 or more. By late December, at least 94,000 were in California. The non-Indian population had more than tripled in a year. Recollecting his July arrival in San Francisco, Dr. William M'Collum estimated at least 100 ships in port. Arriving five months later, French aristocrat Ernest de Massey marveled, "Around us ride three hundred ships or more which have arrived or are just arriving, from all over the world."[21]

Many of these tens of thousands arrived bearing exaggerated preconceptions, shaped and amplified by unscrupulous eastern writers, of Native Americans as hostile and dangerous. The supposed Indian peril constituted a consistent theme in books about the Trans-Mississippi West. Journalists thus calibrated the lens through which newcomers viewed Indians well in advance of actual contact. For example, writing in 1846, a *New York Herald* reporter warned of "the daring and predatory habits of the roving bands of Indians" of California, and in 1849 a St. Louis journalist insisted, "Many of the overland companies bound thither have been attacked by Indians."[22]

Yet, the overland routes were not nearly as full of dangerous Indians as many forty-niners imagined. Between 1840 and 1860, Indians killed 362 whites on all the overland trails, or about eighteen per year. This was a significant toll, but overland emigrants were twenty times more likely to die from diseases than from Indian attack. On these trails, "emigrants killed by Indians during the antebellum era represent a mere 4 percent of the estimated 10,000 or more emigrant deaths." Still, mid-nineteenth-century authors and journalists convinced thousands of emigrants to fear Indian attacks. More important, few emigrants distinguished between Indians they encountered on the long overland trail and those in California itself. The specter of being shot or scalped by Indians consequently remained vivid in the minds of many forty-niners and animated their behavior before, during, and significantly, after their migration to California.[23]

Fear of Indians led many forty-niners to heavily arm themselves, a practice subsidized by the US War Department policy—authorized by Congress—of selling handguns, rifles, and ammunition at cost to California emigrants. At Fort Kearney, Nebraska Territory, one observer described, "Wagons . . . rolling along towards the Pacific, guarded by walking arsenals." One gold seeker bore a long rifle, two revolvers, and a Bowie knife. Others brought even more firepower. A Charlestown, Virginia (now West Virginia), group issued every man a rifle, a double-barreled shotgun, and a brace of pistols. These men were so afraid of being attacked by Indians that they even hauled a cannon across the United States. In total, emigrants headed to California between 1848 and 1852 spent more than $6 million on knives and pistols alone.[24]

Forty-niners arriving by sea also came well armed. The forty-person Camargo Company embarked from Philadelphia on February 1, armed with guns, revolvers,

In 1848, the village of San Francisco hosted relatively few vessels.
J.C. Ward, "San Francisco in November, 1848," lithograph, undated, in Taylor,
Eldorado, frontispiece. Courtesy of Yale Collection of Western Americana,
Beinecke Rare Book and Manuscript Library, Yale University.

In 1849, San Francisco grew rapidly and the port became literally filled with ships
abandoned by crews eager to seek their fortunes in California's gold-rich hills.
William Shew, "Untitled [Panorama of the Waterfront]," photograph, undated.
Courtesy of The Bancroft Library, University of California, Berkeley.

This 1846 book cover exemplified the popular theme of Indians as hostile and
dangerous, which calibrated the way that many immigrants viewed California
Indians even before they arrived in California. ORR SC(?), "Untitled," lithograph(?),
1846, in Farnham, *Life, Travels and Adventures,* cover image. Courtesy of
Milstein Division of United States History, Local History & Genealogy,
The New York Public Library, Astor, Lenox and Tilden Foundations.

and knives. Dr. William M'Collum left New York four days later: "We had revolving pistols, and Bowie-knives, dirks, and other offensive weapons, as if we were
so many sons of Mars." Leaving San Francisco for the mines on October 19,
German prospector Friedrich Gerstäcker listed a pistol, a rifle, a large cudgel,

rifle guns, a double-barreled gun, and a cutlass among the weapons carried by his party of six. Ananias Pond—who owned both a revolver and a rifle—summed the situation up in December: "This Country is certainly better supplied with arms + ammunition than any I ever had a knowledge of."[25]

Fears of Indian attack also inspired some overland forty-niners to organize their well-armed groups along paramilitary lines, by electing captains, drilling in preparation for anticipated assaults, and posting sentries around their bivouacs en route. Irishman Francis Cassin recalled that his Ohio expedition armed and drilled before departing, to prepare for potential conflict with Indians. Michael Kane left Pittsburgh, Pennsylvania, in March with some 250 others and later explained, "as we thought we might encounter the Indians, it was considered advisable to have a large body of men. We equipped ourselves with arms, ammunitions, and provisions . . . and organized in military form, with regular officers." Some New Englanders also followed this paramilitary pattern. The forty-seven men of the Sagamore and California Mining and Trading Company left Lynn, Massachusetts, in March 1849, "armed, equipped and uniformed after the manner of military companies." The overland journey thus primed many gold seekers for martial conflict with Indians and provided them with rudimentary paramilitary training.[26]

Most overland forty-niners experienced no violent encounters with Indians during their trek. In his December 3, 1849, report to the president, US interior secretary Thomas Ewing explained that the American Indian peoples "who have their hunting grounds in the great prairie, through which our emigrants to California pass, have, during the present year, been more than usually pacific." Secretary Ewing emphasized: "They have suffered our people to pass through their country with little interruption, though they traveled in great numbers, and consumed, on their route, much grass and game." Still many overland migrants kept their weapons once in California. For example, the Glaswegian William Downie described twenty to thirty men arriving at the placers near Marysville in the summer of 1849 with pistols, knives, rifles, and shotguns.[27]

Other forty-niners concluded that weapons were of little use in California, suggesting by association that its Indians were relatively unthreatening. On July 14, 1849, Sacramento's *Placer Times* recommended to miners: "Take no gun with you, you will not require it for safety." Miners echoed this sentiment because, particularly in the first two years of the gold rush, California Indians rarely attacked miners without provocation. In a November 21, 1849, letter from Weaverville, in the Northern Mines, a Mr. Taylor suggested bringing only "a small rifle, if . . . any at all—no pistols, and but little powder and lead." Writing of his early gold rush experiences, M'Collum suggested that "California

Many prospectors arrived in California heavily
armed. Note this miner's rifle, holstered pistol, and
the knife handle protruding from his boot.
Charles Nahl, "Miner Prospecting," lithograph,
1852. Courtesy of The Bancroft Library,
University of California, Berkeley.

Adventurers . . . take no guns or pistols, dirks or bowie knives; they are almost
as useless there as they would be at a Quaker meeting." For that matter, Edward
McIlhany of the Charlestown expedition recalled that once in Sacramento the
members of his company sold their cannon, after having dragged it across the
continent, for a single dollar. Still, most forty-niners did not give up their weapons.
They remained heavily armed and often deeply afraid of Indians and each other.[28]

SYSTEMATIC KILLING IN THE CENTRAL MINES, 1849

In 1849, Oregonians' attacks on California Indians increased in both frequency
and lethality, particularly in the Nisenan and northern Miwok lands east of
Sacramento where the Central Mines were booming. W.T. Sayward, who mined

near Placerville in 1849, explained: "Oregon people had been used to shooting Indians, and they did shoot them freely." Forty-niner John Letts described one Oregonian who was hunting Indians there based on vague suspicions and racist assumptions: "The first man I met after my arrival in the interior was an Oregonian on horseback, armed with a revolving rifle in search of Indians. He had had a horse stolen, and presumed it was taken by an Indian; he swore he 'would shoot the first red-skin he met,' and I had no reason to doubt his word; still the chances were ninety-nine out of the hundred, that the horse was stolen by a white man." Indeed, newcomers often murdered California Indians, even massacred them, based on hearsay or the fixed hypothesis that any missing animals must have been taken by Indians. Some Oregonians apparently needed no pretext and aimed to kill every Indian they encountered. Forty-niner James L. Tyson recollected that the killing was systematic and unrelentingly merciless in the foothills near Sacramento: "The Oregonians . . . were severe on all Indians, whenever they met a naked or wild one, unhesitatingly shooting him down."[29]

New Englander J.A. Perry provided a chilling example of some Oregonians' penchant for killing California Indians without provocation. According to Perry, "Two men from Oregon were walking along one day when an Indian came in sight, and as he passed within reach of their rifles, one drew a piece of money from his pocket to send into the air, while his partner guessed which side it would fall; the only difference it would make, was to see which should shoot the Indian, and he was shot dead on the spot." Perry added, "This is not the case with every man from Oregon but it is a fair specimen of two thirds of what I saw among them." He concluded that Oregonians' unprovoked and indiscriminate homicides turned some California Indians against newcomers: "The Oregon men . . . would shoot an Indian as soon as they saw one, and this had a tendency to strengthen their hatred toward the whites." Such unprovoked attacks on California Indians tended to initiate escalating spirals of violence in which Indians found themselves the victims of mass killings and massacres if they sought to punish the individuals who had attacked them. Unfortunately, Oregonians were not the only newcomers interested in killing California Indians simply for being Indians.[30]

Some non-Oregonian forty-niners—arriving by both land and sea—also displayed tendencies toward unprovoked Indian killing. As he and his fellow overland immigrants reached the eastern edge of California's Sierras in 1849, Ananias Pond wrote that "two of them appear rather anxious to Shoot, Diggers [Indians]." Lienhard recalled that in 1849, while sheepherding with California Indians from Sutter's Fort, some heavily armed men who had arrived on the steamer *California* stopped in his camp. "Glancing at the Indians" and motivated perhaps by fear, hatred, or a craving for blood sport, "they said they would like to try their guns on them." Lienhard theorized, "What flashed through their minds was something like this: 'See that black devil. Look at his wild eye. Why not blow his brains out[?]'" Lienhard dissuaded the would-be murderers, but in many other instances, there was no white man to advocate for California Indians in the face of such racist bloodlust.[31]

During 1849, more than 65,000 emigrants—often heavily armed, experienced with paramilitary organizations, and full of fear and hatred toward Indians—arrived in California. They entered an increasingly violent borderland in which colonists often dehumanized California Indians. Others, notably Oregon men, gratuitously killed them. Such killings generating Indian reprisals that fed a pre-existing fear of Indians, creating an escalating cycle of violence that led to more frequent, lethal sorties against California Indians.[32]

The Nisenan foothills near Sutter's Mill, where California's gold rush began, became the epicenter of the 1849 killing of Indians. Eliminating California Indian mining competition and acquiring Indian wealth were central motives behind much of this violence. In January, the *Daily Alta California's* Sacramento correspondent reported fighting between there and what is now Placerville—a region where southern Nisenan territory abuts northern Miwok lands. Indians retreated, and whites torched their villages. The correspondent also reported that an Oregonian took a horse from an Indian who was visiting his camp and that when "the Indian . . . rode off, making use of expressions which were not agreeable to the Oregonian . . . he took up his rifle and shot" the Indian. Later, when other Indians visited the camp, the Oregonians "*presumed* they had come to take revenge" and "whipped" the surprised visitors.[33]

More killings followed, often motivated by whites' desire to avenge an alleged Indian crime or misdemeanor in the mines. According to the *Sacramento Transcript*, in late February 1849, "a company of about sixty, horse and foot, left Sutter's Fort to chastise the Indians" for the alleged killings of "about thirty" whites, "principally Oregonians . . . on various occasions," crimes that remain undocumented elsewhere. The posse "took the direction of Sutter's Mill or Culloma, and the [Nisenan] Indians fled before them." However, the Nisenans could not outrun the mounted company, which overtook them and killed "several." Anglo-Americans soon blamed "further depredations" on local Nisenans and several weeks later "another company of about twenty whites left the region of Culloma, and followed the Indians to their encampment," where they took 200 to 300 prisoners before driving them to Sutter's Mill. There, "A sort of trial was then given them, after which thirty of their number where shot" and the rest released. This was the largest extrajudicial mass execution yet in California under US

Tom Lewis (Nisenan) wears a robe of gopher
tails or squirrel pelts, a flicker quill headband, a
stick with woodpecker scalps or quail scalps,
and an abalone gorget. Lewis was a leader of
the Auburn Indian community. Alexander W.
Chase, "Portrait of Captain Tom [Lewis], from
Auburn, California, in Partial Native Dress,"
photograph, ca. 1874. Courtesy of National
Anthropological Archives, Smithsonian
Institution, NAA INV 01527500.

rule. It portended a slide toward even more indiscriminate homicides and massacres.[34]

"About the end of March," Mexican miner Antonio Coronel followed an
expedition led by Californio rancher Sisto Berreyesa against a Nisenan "Indian
village on the American River because two Americans had turned up dead,

and the Indians were blamed." Berreyesa carefully orchestrated a massacre. According to Coronel, "At first light they surrounded the village and opened fire. What followed was a scene of utter horror. Out came old men, women, children—everyone . . . running in every direction, even throwing themselves in the river. They were all rounded up and shot down." Soon thereafter, at Mr. Hicks's ranch near the Cosumnes River, Coronel "saw several Indians fleeing in different directions, and the men who had passed us earlier hunting them down and killing the ones they caught" in the kind of executionary killing that increasingly characterized the final phase of attacks on California Indian communities. There were no sanctuaries. The Indians sought refuge in Hicks's house, but the killers "entered and dragged the Indians out to murder them." The next month, similar events took place as the killing escalated into a local genocide.[35]

Heading east across the broad Sacramento River Valley in early April 1849, prospector Theodore T. Johnson met Sutter, who described exterminatory violence against local Nisenan people and the accompanying rhetoric of annihilation. According to Johnson's summary of Sutter's report, "The late emigrants across the mountains, and some Oregon trappers and mountaineers, had commenced a war of extermination upon them, shooting them down like wolves, men, women, and children, wherever they could find them." Lienhard, who worked with California Indians in the region at the time, recalled that many non-Indian miners advocated a doctrine of indiscriminate and annihilationist collective reprisal against California Indians, even when it was not clear who had committed a particular theft. According to him, "Whenever anything was stolen the so-called Christian miners would invariably say, 'Kill every d—Indian you can find!' "[36]

During and after homicides in the mines, killers sometimes severed and collected the body parts of California Indians. In one instance, Konnock, a Nisenan man, told Lienhard that "some white men who were washing gold further up the [American] river killed my uncle and another Indian, scalped them, and took their heads." Modern white society tends to view scalping in US history as a predominantly American Indian activity. Yet whites also scalped many Indians in a tradition that stretched back to colonial times, and that policymakers sometimes codified as official, state-sanctioned scalp bounties. In California between 1846 and 1873, scalping was an almost exclusively non-Indian practice, inflicted on California Indians. Scalping served as a way to inventory killing, collect macabre trophies, and express a profound disdain for victims. Collecting the severed heads of California Indians served similar purposes. The prospector Johnson soon came into personal contact with the killing, sadism, and scalping of what Sutter described as a "war of extermination against the aborigines."[37]

Jane Lewis (Nisenan) was a member of the
Auburn Indian community. Alexander W.
Chase, "Portrait of Captain Tom's Wife [Jane
Lewis] in Partial Native Dress, Wearing
10-Yard Necklace of 1160 Clam Shell Money
Beads, and Deerskin Girdle and Headdress
with Abalone Pendants," photograph, ca. 1874.
Courtesy of National Anthropological
Archives, Smithsonian Institution,
NAA INV 01527600.

On April 12, Johnson entered the epicenter of a local genocide: Coloma, at
Sutter's Mill. Oregonian miners—bent on raping Nisenan women—had killed
several Nisenan men who had attempted to protect these women. Nisenans then
killed five Oregonians at Murderer's Bar on the American River's Middle Fork,
presumably in keeping with the Nisenan tradition of sometimes avenging murder

with the retaliatory killing of the perpetrator or perpetrators. Soon thereafter, Nisenan people reportedly killed two more men, upstream.[38]

In response, James Delavan recollected, "A war of extermination was therefore declared, and carried on by well armed and well mounted parties, determined on revenge." Sutter also used the same expression, "war of extermination," a nineteenth-century phrase for what we would today call genocide. Some local miners threw down their picks, shovels, and pans to prepare rifles, load revolvers, and sharpen knives.[39]

The day after Johnson arrived in Coloma, "A war party of ten or twelve men, including the two Greenwoods, went out, well mounted, to attack a neighboring *rancheria* of Indians, and revenge the murder of two Oregon men by some of the latter. . . . As they galloped away . . . Old Greenwood . . . shouted, 'Be sure, boys, you bring me a squaw!'" whereupon one of Johnson's party "jocosely added, 'Bring *me* a scalp!'" The joker soon got his wish. On April 14, the vigilantes returned and "young Greenwood, as he passed our tent," flung "an Indian scalp, the long, black, bristly hair clotted with blood," at Johnson and his companions. Johnson "ascertained that they had killed four, made several prisoners, burnt the *rancheria*, and carried off some gold dust."[40]

Soon thereafter, whites captured "one of the warriors of the tribe" and "his life was spared on the condition that he should guide the whites to their *rancheria*." On April 16, another "war party was made up of about twenty mountaineers, mostly Oregon men." According to William M. Case, an Oregon forty-niner in Coloma at the time, "The Oregonians concluded . . . that the only way to put an end to the murders was to . . . wipe out the tribe." This "was accordingly done."[41]

No one in Coloma seems to have been willing to stand in the way of the well-armed Oregonians. Storekeeper Norman Bestor reported, "Many of these men are so violent that they denounce every one who advances any reason why a wholesale slaughter should not be made." The vigilantes were, according to Johnson's eyewitness account, "Well mounted, and equipped. . . . Each man carried besides his inseparable rifle, a long Spanish knife . . . and many were also provided with a brace of pistols or bowie knife, worn in the red Mexican sash around the waist. Old Greenwood shouted, 'mind the scalps and squaws for me, and be sure to bring 'em all in, boys,' and away they went, at a thundering *lope*." One E.G.B. reported that at about twilight they encountered a village on Weber's Creek. According to Case, "The Oregonians rode among the Indians. They had been friendly and were not afraid of them. Our men saw at once that these were the Indians they were looking for, and decided then and there to kill every one of them if they could. Each Oregonian had about thirteen shots a piece. I do not suppose the battle lasted more than one minute." After some sixty seconds as many as thirty Nisenan people lay dead and the Oregonians took forty to sixty survivors prisoner.[42]

Johnson encountered these captives being marched through a deep and narrow ravine near Weber's Creek. They included, "Warriors and boys, squaws with *papooses* tied on boards and slung at the back, all were prisoners. Clustered together like sheep driven to the slaughter, they hastened through the gorge with uncertain steps, the perspiration rolling off their faces now pale with fright." Their palpable terror and the possibility that they might all be slaughtered apparently bothered Johnson. Like others who would later witness violence and cruelty toward California Indians, he tried to rationalize their treatment by portraying them as less than human: "Many of them were quite naked, and the men and boys especially, looked more like ourang-outangs than human beings."[43]

Johnson then vividly described the vigilantes:

> Every man's rifle lay across the pommel of his saddle, and dangling at both sides hung several reeking scalps. Among them was a dashing young mountaineer [and Oregonian] named John [E.] Ross, who had two scalps for his share, and sticking in his sash was the red-sheathed bowie knife, which I had sold him a few days previous for an ounce of gold dust. Used previously to sever the rinds of pork, or shovel in rice and frijoles, it had now been "wool gathering" or collecting wigs for old Greenwood's fancy stores.

Posse members explained that "the night before" they had attacked and killed "some twenty to thirty" at a *rancheria* on Weber's Creek." The riders also reported: "Their chief fought until shot the third time, rising each time to his knees and discharging his arrows, Ross finally killing him, cutting off his head and scalping him." Like many California Indians, this Nisenan leader fought tenaciously and sacrificed his life to protect his community. "Their *rancheria* was then searched and burned."[44]

The posse drove the prisoners to Coloma. There "the mountaineers and miners had a grand revel and jollification to celebrate their achievement" and "most of the prisoners were released." However, the posse kept some seven warriors for questioning about their possible participation in the killing of Oregonians. Ross recollected that when James Marshall stood up for the seven, one ruffian nearly shot Marshall, and the man who helped initiate California's gold boom "was given five minutes to leave the place." On April 19, understanding that they were to be murdered in another extrajudicial mass execution, the seven ran for their lives. A "massacre" then commenced. Accounts vary, but it seems that one man, at most two, escaped alive. Killers gunned down the rest. Johnson concluded, "This is what they call fighting the Indians!"[45]

Such "fighting" continued. According to Case, a few days later someone murdered an Oregonian named Dougherty some eleven miles from Coloma, and fifteen men set out to exact revenge "in accordance with an agreement made by the Oregonians that all Indians would be killed on sight until all were destroyed, or else sufficiently subdued to stop any further molestation." The squad first killed "three Indians . . . mining." Later that day they found eleven more California Indians mining. Aware of the Oregonians' reputation, the Indian miners fled into the log cabin of an Englishman named Goff. Hoping to protect them, Goff initially defied the Oregonians' summons. The Oregonians then began removing the chinking from between the logs and threatened to shoot through the gaps. Goff surrendered the eleven Indians, "who were then immediately hanged." Following this atrocity, the Oregonians tracked surviving members of the tribe to "the tules of a swamp of a marshy lake" where they were hiding. Attacking on horseback, the Oregonians killed "all the men, and one woman." Ross added that others "were shot" in the yard of an Englishman named Daly as far away as the Cosumnes River and estimated that, in all, "some sixty Indians were killed in retaliation" for Dougherty's murder. Case concluded that "seventy-six of the tribe . . . fell, the Oregonians having lost by secret murder thirty-three." This Nisenan death toll may have been an underestimate. According to Delavan, the killing stopped only "after more than a hundred had been sacrificed to appease the manes of the slaughtered Oregonians."[46]

Nisenan survivors of the Oregonians' campaign now fled for the "the snowy mountains, about fifty miles" away. Benevolent whites found them "almost starving" in this food-poor alpine environment. There the devastation continued, ironically facilitated by well-meaning merchants. According to Case, "beef and flour were sent to the women by the California traders. . . . Such a diet they had not been accustomed to, however, and as a result of overeating of food they were not used to, took some disease, and the whole tribe—numbering altogether one hundred and fifty-two Indians—died," including the wife and child of a white man named Smith.[47]

In contrast to this attempt to rescue victims, the killing of California Indians was, in part, motivated by racial hatred, fear, and greed. Recalling his 1849 encounters with Indians in the Southern Mines, M'Collum wrote, "They need watching about as much as the wolves." M'Collum's sentiment seems to have animated many Oregonian killers, who saw California Indians as a dangerous, less-than-human threat in need of elimination. Of course, Indian miners also presented lucrative targets for the impatient, lazy, greedy, and bloody-minded. Most forty-eighters and forty-niners came to California to obtain wealth as rapidly as possible. In pursuing that aim, some of them murdered California Indian miners. In the short term, valuable booty—including Indian slaves and, more important, gold dust and gold nuggets—could be obtained by attacking California Indian miners. There was a cold calculus to killing Indian miners rather than non-Indian miners. Those who murdered Indians miners were very rarely punished, so it was less dangerous than killing and stealing gold from non-Indian miners. Equally important, the killing of Indians also frequently facilitated the theft of their valuable mining claims, whereas there was little tolerance for anyone jumping the claims of white men. As William Grimshaw recalled, "Instances were by no means rare where an Indian[,] working a piece of ground and hesitating about giving it up at the command of some white ruffian[,] being ruthlessly shot down and his body tossed aside." In the longer term, killing California Indian miners facilitated a larger economic end: it eliminated competition and helped to level the economic playing field between established colonists like Weber and Daylor, who employed Indian miners, and newcomers like the Oregonians, who did not. Ideological agendas also motivated mass murder.[48]

In an era when slavery debates permeated national politics, many forty-niners subscribed to Free Labor ideology, and some attempted to justify the killing or driving off of California Indian miners as the righteous elimination of unfree labor from California's placers and eventually from the state as a whole. It may seem contradictory to combat unfree labor by exterminating unfree workers, but liberating unfree workers was not the aim of such violence. Case insisted that although the murder of Nisenan people around Coloma "was rough and terrible," it helped to replace "the old California system . . . of inequality—of proprietors and peons" with "the system of free labor." As Hurtado has explained, many whites "regarded the use of Indians in the diggings as something akin to slavery, which was abhorrent not because Indians were abused but because command over Indian labor was unfair competition with free white men." California Indians thus sometimes paid with their lives for being employed or enslaved in the mines. Oregonians played a central role in the killing and expulsion of many California Indians. Case described "conflicts between the Oregonians and the California ranchers and importers of a semi-slave labor," and concluded, "Oregonians in California during the mining days became the backbone of American government, and from this sprang the splendid free state." In a free state increasingly defined in part as one free of Indians, genocide could occupy the moral high ground in some men's minds.[49]

White miners, motivated by a combination of short- and long-term economic goals, attacked California Indian miners working for William Daylor in Nisenan territory on the American River in late April 1849. As Daylor wrote, "About the 26th, a party of armed white men came to their camp, or where they were at work, and killed an Indian while working with a crow-bar, and on his knees; they then shot another through the arm [and] thigh [before] his brains were beat out with rocks and stones." Other whites forced off the murderers, and the surviving Indians fled. The attackers had driven away Daylor's Indian mining force. In so doing, they had hamstrung a local competitor, and probably stolen some or all of the valuable gold that these Indians had toiled to gather. Still, merely running them off and taking their gold did not satisfy the attackers. Their aims were more comprehensive. They pursued the fleeing Indians, and about ten miles from Daylor's house overtook and surrounded a group of them. Separating fourteen unarmed men from the women and children, they massacred the men and took the women and children into captivity. The following day, the gang proceeded to Daylor's Ranch on the Cosumnes River, where they murdered one Indian and wounded another.[50]

The total number killed in these incidents remains uncertain. Daylor reported seeing eighteen dead Indians and described how the perpetrators proudly told him that they had "killed 27 before coming to the house." According to the *Placer Times*, the body count was at least twenty, whereas "the Indians report twenty-three missing of their Indian men in all." The death toll may have been as high as eighty-three. As Daylor noted, "Twenty-two men, and thirty-four women and children are yet missing from the rancheria."[51]

This *"Terrible slaughter of Indians"* was part of a wider local genocide against California Indians in the Central Mines. On May 1, the *Daily Alta California* made this clear: "Whites are becoming impressed with the belief that it will be absolutely necessary to exterminate the savages before they can labor much longer in the mines with security." Three days later, Yale graduate Chester Lyman wrote in his diary, while at Suisun in the San Francisco Bay Area, of another asymmetric death toll: "Bad news from above, collisions between the whites (chiefly Oregonians) & indians, 30 or 40 indians killed, 5 or 6 whites . . . whites doubtless the aggressors. Will probably result in a general indian war." Whether this was news of a battle or a massacre, Lyman did not say. Yet the killing of substantial numbers of California Indians was clearly an increasingly common event and Oregonians were often to blame. Even so, California Indians were not the only group targeted for violence in the mines.[52]

Attacks on California Indians were the most lethal element of a loosely organized but growing xenophobic campaign to forcibly expel all nonwhites from

California's gold-mining regions. As early as May 1, 1849, the *Daily Alta California* reported, "The feeling is very general among the Americans and Californians that foreigners should not be allowed to dig for gold," and it soon became clear that "foreigners" did not mean white immigrants from the United States. On June 30, the *Placer Times* reported hostilities against Spanish speakers. Three weeks later, the newspaper announced that "the Peruvians and Chileans have been pretty thoroughly routed in every section of the Middle and North Forks [of the American River], and the disposition to expel them seems to be extending throughout the whole mining community." Chinese miners would also come under attack, particularly in the 1850s, as whites forcibly drove them out of many placers and surrounding communities. Yet, if whites violently expelled Hispanic and Chinese miners, they routinely murdered and massacred California Indian miners, whom many attackers considered little better than animals.[53]

Attacks on California Indians continued through 1849. Recalling Indians in the Southern Mines that summer, M'Collum wrote: "The Oregonians, especially, hunt them as they would wild beasts." According to him, their craving to avenge past events in Oregon sometimes trumped even their lust for gold: "An Oregonian will leave a rich placer to wreak his vengeance on one of a race that he has learned to regard as his foe, by the outrages they have committed upon the whites in Oregon." Briton William Shaw went on one such expedition, led "by two Englishmen, hunters from Oregon," east of Stockton during the 1849 rainy season. Responding to an Indian attack, the dozen men, "mostly Yankee backwoodsmen," tracked the Indians to a village of about fifty people, probably Miwok or Northern Valley Yokuts.[54]

The massacre that followed typified a pattern that became increasingly common during the coming years. After silently encircling the village, the attackers fired their long-range rifles to devastating effect: the "first volley killed five instantly, and wounded six more severely." Next they charged in to use short-range pistols and bowie knives for close-quarter killing. Finally, they pursued and slew those who fled and murdered some of the wounded as well as an old woman. After killing at least nine people, and probably more, Shaw and his companions sat "down to supper" and ate their victims' food: "roots, venison, acorn-bread, boiled horse-chesnuts, and a dish of vermin." Other attacks followed in December.[55]

In Placer County, one annihilation squad organized along lines that soon became widespread. During a "howling storm," on December 15, whites found Nisenans raiding an unattended store near present-day Colfax. The following day, after mules went missing in the snow, whites organized the twenty-one-man

Some have criticized Edward S. Curtis's
twentieth-century photographs of American
Indians for hiding the modern and presenting
Indians as unchanging. These are valid critiques.
Still, his images provide both stunning portraits
and windows on traditional material culture.
Curtis's portraits adorn some contemporary
California Indian homes as well as some official
California rancheria and reservation gathering
places. Edward S. Curtis, "A Miwok Head-man,"
photograph, 1924, in Curtis, *North American
Indian,* 14: plate 493. Courtesy of Yale Collection
of Western Americana, Beinecke Rare Book and
Manuscript Library, Yale University.

"California Blades," and voted to destroy local Indian villages, wrecking several
and killing two men before the Indians retreated across Bear River. The "Blades"
continued to destroy villages the next month.[56]

New York forty-niner John W. Connor described his participation in an
assault in December 1849 near the town of Volcano, southeast of Placerville.

Local Miwok Indians had allegedly provoked whites by stealing stock and killing a miner in early December. In response, "we organized a party of about twenty persons, all these were in the camp, and started for the Indian camp to punish the rascals and recover our animals if possible. . . . About three miles from the camp," the miners "came upon a hundred of them" and attacked. The skirmish ended quickly, the assailants' triumph a product of surprise and the military asymmetry created by their weapons' superior range and killing power. The "rifles and shotguns scattered them in all directions. They had nothing but bows and arrows." Several miles further on, the posse burned a "rancheria, and destroyed all the dried locusts they had laid up for food and the nuts they had stored away to make bread by."[57]

Destroying California Indians' food supplies—particularly in winter when they would be extremely difficult to replace—became an increasingly common tactic. It also became progressively more lethal, as California Indians' traditional food supplies dwindled under the mounting pressure of tens of thousands of immigrants, these newcomers' hunting, and the spread of their livestock. The attack was also typically one-sided. Connor reported no vigilante casualties, but recalled: "We killed several of the men, seven I think." Yet this engagement was unusual in that it ended with a degree of rapprochement. After the attackers took women and children as prisoners, "The Chief of the tribe" sued for peace. "So we gave up the women and children to this old man, and had no further trouble after that." Whites repeated similar attacks elsewhere but negotiations became less and less common as genocidal violence spread.[58]

At about the same time, miners also attacked Indians near what is now Chico. Following the killing of several miners by unknown people, near the confluence of Rock Creek and the Sacramento River, twenty-seven men attacked what was either a Nomlaki Wintun, Northern Maidu, or Yahi Yana village east of the Sacramento. The massacre was typical in its pedagogic aims: one participant recollected that the planned "summary punishment" was intended to "teach them a lesson." It was also typical in its California massacre tactics: the killing squad attacked just after dawn and effectively surrounded the village by pinning it "on an elbow of land, formed by the bend of a creek, that was so swollen and swift as to leave them very poor chances of retreat." The villagers soon began fleeing, but received no quarter, "rushing back amongst the wigwams, and many plunging into the stream, followed by women holding little children in their arms, who were soon swallowed up in its curling eddies." Exterminatory killing followed, after all resistance had ceased: "We fired a few more shots into their bark tenements, and, from the howls that followed, I should say with fatal results; but deeming that our measure of retribution was amply filled, we ceased firing, and retired in a cool deliberate manner, after counting twenty-three bodies on the ground." People murdered in their homes remained uncounted as did the drowned women and children. Just two attackers were wounded, both mortally.[59]

Exterminatory killing now spread north, beyond the Central Mines, as gold seekers initiated repeated attacks against Wintu people that month. On December 27, miner Augustin Hale recorded the massacre of some twenty Wintu north of Cottonwood Creek on the valley's west side. On January 2, 1850, he wrote: "17 [Wintu or Yana] killed on east side Sacramento." On January 31, "27 men cross[ed] Clear Creek to fight the Indians," and Hale reported, "Many [Wintu] killed." The next month he described the killing of more Wintu and twice reported "several Indian Ranches" in flames.[60]

In early 1850, the future of the California Indians remained an open question. As new goldfields opened, Indian killings increased. Many miners wanted to eliminate Indian mining competition, acquire Indian miners' gold, and, perhaps most important, seize Indian lands. Simultaneously, miners destroyed Indian communities' traditional means of subsistence and denied them access to what remained. Indian attacks and thefts—motivated by hunger and the desire to repulse invaders and slave raiders—became a pretext for assaults that eliminated Indian mining competition, provided looting and kidnapping opportunities, and opened new areas to white miners. The process was, as historian Philip J. Deloria has written of other "Indian Wars," one of "defensive conquest," that is, conquest that whites described—somewhat disingenuously—as a reaction to Indian aggression, theft, or threat.[61]

Such processes continued and increasingly led to what perpetrators sometimes described as annihilation campaigns. In January 1850, one group campaigned high in the Sierras, east of Sonora, in reaction to a murder and the theft of six mules. William Perkins's posse first launched a surprise attack on "more than a hundred well built huts" after which "we set fire to . . . the whole amount of worldly goods possessed by the tribe." Indiscriminate, disproportionate, and fueled by the intent to destroy the group, the attack was typical of hundreds that would follow. Perkins observed, "We invade a land that is not our own; we arrogate a right through pretense of superior intelligence and the wants of civilization, and if the aborigines dispute our truths, we destroy them!" The next day, Perkins's group incinerated two more hamlets. Destroying Indian villages and their food stores would become a crucial tactic for creating "conditions of life intended to destroy the group."[62]

Like destroying whole villages, summary extrajudicial executions of California Indians became increasingly common in the 1850s. Indiscriminate murders often initiated new cycles of violence that led to wider killing. H.D. La Motte arrived at Humboldt Bay in March 1850. In an unpublished memoir, he recollected that soon after arriving, two Eel River Indians boarded a wrecked schooner—after whites had largely stripped it—to salvage "some light sails and ropes." This infuriated local "Oregon and Sonoma" men who set out after the salvagers. Near "where Eureka now is . . . a man by the name of Stansberry" found two Wiyot Indians and proclaimed, "'I judge these fellows know too much about this'" before drawing his pistol and murdering them. According to La Motte, these were "the first Indians shot on Humboldt Bay." Following the double homicide, other Indians killed "two white men, perfectly horrible fellows, but they had to pay the penalty for the wrong done by the Oregon men. These Oregon men would kill Indians wherever they saw them."[63]

To the east, miners continued massacring Wintu people in and near the Northern Mines. In March 1850, a miner executed a sixteen- or seventeen-year-old Wintu boy with "a bullet [to] his brain." The miner later recollected that, at the time, when Wintu stole property, "About twenty or thirty miners, all armed with rifles, revolvers and bowie knives, would start out on a road into the Indian country, discover a rancheria, take it by surprise, rush upon it, and shoot, stab and kill every buck, squaw and pappoose." One newspaper later reported: "In 1850 we saw the scalps of Diggers hanging to tent-poles in the Shasta and Trinity country. The Oregon men who first settled that part of the State thought it sport to kill a Digger on sight, as they would a coyote."[64]

Genocidal campaigns against the Nisenan people also seem to have continued that month. In a March 10 journal entry, Dr. Israel Lord recorded groups of men on the Yuba River setting out to attack Indians and concluded, "These 'Diggers' are bound to be exterminated." Washington, DC, policymakers now began to comprehend the demographic catastrophe unfolding under US rule in California. In his March 22 "Report on California," special agent and presidential envoy T. Butler King reported to US secretary of state John Clayton that "the whole race seems to be rapidly disappearing," but concluded that, despite this, California Indians "ought to be chastised for the murders" they had "already committed." Some whites clearly agreed.[65]

Northwestern California's Trinity River placers now began to draw more gold seekers to the Northern Mines. As in the Central and Southern Mines, prospectors created frictions with the local Indians. Yuroks resisted invasion and the miners responded with massacres and village burnings. Frenchman Ernest de Massey reported that around March or April, "several miners were robbed and wounded [in Yurok territory] and [as a result] an expedition . . . from [Trinidad Bay], destroyed five huts, killed several natives, and captured one young woman." That spring, prospector Thomas Gihon witnessed an attack on a Yurok village north of Trinidad Bay in response to a theft. Gihon "protested strongly against this cowardly and wanton murder . . . but . . . there were several killed." Later that day the prospectors encountered "a young Indian girl in the greatest distress, sobbing and waving her hands. We had doubtless killed her father, or some one dear to her. As she passed by, she looked back at us with such agonized reproach that it lessened the courage of those bravoes perceptibly."[66]

The Nisenan people in the Central Mines also suffered further attacks. In late March or early April, some dozen vigilantes attacked a group of Nisenan, "whom they accused of stealing animals, and killed four or five men and one squaw." Nisenan sought to defend themselves, and the subsequent fighting "lasted two days." The vigilantes killed seventeen more Nisenan men and one woman, and themselves suffered two men wounded, "it is believed fatally." A week later, the *Sacramento Transcript* reported that vigilantes were searching for suspected cattle rustlers near "Rough & Ready Diggings," southwest of Nevada City: "The last news was a rumor that the thieves had been found, and that twenty-five of the Indians had been killed." Possibly reporting the same massacre, Myron Angel wrote that the "California Blades" of Illinoistown and others had killed and scalped "some twenty or more Indians" that month and by May, "At nearly all of the wayside houses on the road from Illinoistown were scalps on exhibition." The Nisenan did not practice scalping, and the display of the skin and hair from loved ones' heads must have been truly horrifying. Vigilantes were now launching more frequent sorties, and killing more Indians in each attack. A correspondent from "North Fork of North Fork, Yuba" reported that, after alleged Indian thefts, vigilantes "burnt one or two of their rancherias." Nisenan now retaliated in defense of their land and communities. Thus "commenced the war in earnest." If a war, it was grossly asymmetrical: "At the least calculation, seven whites have been killed, and seventy or eighty red skins."[67]

Whites launched further attacks on the Nisenan people in early May 1850. A robbery on the North Fork of the American River became the pretext for the killing of seven Nisenan people. Nisenan then killed one miner and wounded another. In response, on May 4, twenty to forty-five men, "started from Auburn and Kelly's bar." They found a Nisenan community of about 100 people "in a valley, near Illinoistown. . . . They were armed with bows and arrows, and had one gun." The mob did not negotiate. Instead, "The whites immediately fired upon them, whereupon they ran, scattering in all directions." The attackers offered no quarter. Consequently, "Small parties" of Nisenan mounted a desperate holding action, firing from concealed positions. Overwhelming vigilante firepower nevertheless made it impossible for these valiant Nisenan to hold their positions once whites had determined their location. Like hundreds of California Indians during the decades to come, some of these Nisenan likely made the ultimate sacrifice in giving friends, family, and fellow community members time to escape death.[68]

What happened that day in a valley near Illinoistown was typical of the massacres that were becoming increasingly common. Two whites suffered wounds, but neither one died. And although "the loss of the Indians could not be ascertained" precisely, "twenty-five dead bodies were found, and it is supposed they concealed and carried off others of their dead. Among their dead were found a woman and a child." The vigilantes "returned to Auburn, having with them several scalps, which were exhibited in that place." Still, some locals wanted to hunt down and kill survivors. "A meeting was held at Auburn" on May 6, "to raise a company of volunteers, for the purpose of scouring the country and making war upon the Indians wherever found, so long as they maintain a hostile position." How they planned to determine which Nisenan were "hostile" the article did not say, but like other California vigilantes they probably considered most, if not all, mountain Indians hostile and therefore, legitimate targets.[69]

For Nisenan people, many white attacks must have seemed completely random, and thus all the more terrifying. Army captain Hannibal Day explained, "On the night of [May] 6th . . . ten white men . . . attacked a small band of natives, killing two . . . under the impression that the Indians had stolen their cattle; but behold, the next day, their cattle *were found*." Whether or not they understood the whites' motives, Nisenan avengers killed two uninvolved whites. Day concluded: "The result is most deplorable; and let me say entirely attributable to the wreckless, if not cowardly and certainly unjustifiable killing of two Indians, on a mere surmise that they (or some other natives) had stolen their cattle for subsistence." Unfortunately, the cycle of violence that routinely escalated to the point of massacring entire California Indian villages often began with such reckless, cowardly, and unjustifiable murders.[70]

Responding to violence on and near Deer Creek, seventy-five whites organized a posse and attacked local Nisenan. The resulting assault left eleven whites dead. The correspondent did not indicate how many Nisenan people died but mentioned the execution of a prisoner. Twenty-four soldiers under Captain Day took the field, killing three chiefs and presumably some of their people. "One hundred miners from Deer Creek also poured in, and in a couple of days they killed and run off all the Indians." The loss of Nisenan life was devastating. By mid-May, "some four or five hundred Indians" were mourning near Deer Creek. In keeping with tradition, they commemorated the loss of their loved ones and community members by shaving their heads and covering them with ash.[71]

Due to spotty primary source coverage, we will never know the exact number of California Indians murdered by whites in and around the mines in 1849 and early 1850. It is plausible that hundreds, if not thousands, suffered violent deaths. What was clear to contemporary observers was the exterminatory nature of such killings, both in their intent and impact. On March 11, 1850, a report in the *Daily Alta California* summarized the genocidal killing of the previous year: "Early last spring . . . difficulties disturbed the tranquility of the miners on the American river, and the grounds of complaint against the Indians were sufficiently strong to arouse the whole mining populations to arms and unite them in the work of extermination." The author understood that this was the result of a cycle of violence initiated and then dramatically escalated by white men: "The Indians committed several brutal murders, but they sought savage redress for outrages committed by the whites. The desperadoes of our people who went among the Indians to communicate with them through the muzzles of their rifles brought down the deadly vengeance of the various tribes around them, and the consequence was the shedding of much innocent blood. The Indians were mercilessly hunted down and order finally restored by the expulsion of the Indians from the grounds occupied by the miners." The article's grim conclusion was that only the merciless hunting and violent expulsion of California Indians from the American River placers brought order. By implication, newcomers, more of whom were arriving by the day, might soon impose this merciless order elsewhere, with disastrous consequences for California's original inhabitants.[72]

Gold rush emigrants—and Oregonians in particular—initiated demographic, military, economic, and ideological revolutions in relations between California Indians and non-Indians, each of which removed barriers to anti-Indian violence or escalated existing conflict. The 80,000 or more emigrants who arrived in 1848 and 1849 revolutionized California demographics. Before the gold rush, California Indians had outnumbered non-Indians by perhaps ten to one. This numeric imbalance helped to mitigate anti-Indian violence by imposing a degree of caution on non-Indians. Yet by the end of 1849, there were fewer than two California Indians for every non-Indian. Their numeric advantage fast slipping away, California's indigenous peoples also confronted a military revolution in which whites became not only much more numerous but also suddenly very well-armed, which exacerbated the preexisting military asymmetry.

Argonauts and other immigrants also revolutionized many California Indian economies. Newcomers, through their hunting and pastoral animal grazing, crippled many Indians' traditional means of subsistence but also drove Indians away from the gold mines on which they had become increasingly dependent in the face of declining traditional economies. This was a process of radical

Charles Nahl's engraving of California Indians leaving—perhaps driven by the
miners behind them—as others arrive, may be a play on the European art
trope of Adam and Eve being driven from the Garden of Eden. It may thus
suggest that California Indians themselves are somehow to blame for their
expulsion from their homelands. Charles Nahl, "A Road Scene in
California," wood engraving, probably not before 1854. Courtesy of
The Bancroft Library, University of California, Berkeley.

economic destabilization for many California Indian people, which threatened
their basic food security. The process would soon spread and intensify as many
more immigrants arrived in California.

Forty-eighters and forty-niners also helped to transform how the majority of
non-Indians in California thought about California Indians. Gold rush immigrants were typically ignorant of the Californio tradition of tolerating Indians,
always limited but based on the cultural acceptance of mestizo hybridity and
economic dependence on indigenous labor. Many were better versed in the
Anglo-American tradition of eliminating Indians from colonized areas. Moreover, some—particularly Oregonians—were committed Indian killers who did
not discriminate between tribes, and shot all Indians on sight. Their murderous
violence, coupled with the general rise of Indian killing in the Central Mines
in late 1848 and 1849, further eroded cultural and moral barriers to such behavior in California. In keeping with general Anglo-American and emerging local
traditions, many Anglo-Americans sought to drive away or destroy California
Indians and as their numbers grew, their approach prevailed.

Miners and immigrants generally arrived heavily armed, afraid of and often opposed to all Indians—regardless of their tribe—and intent on the rapid acquisition of wealth. This vanguard of newcomers provided both the initial means (a large, heavily armed male population) and multiple motives for mass murder. Chief among the factors animating their atrocities were fear, hatred, greed, and the impulse to teach Indians to fear whites by physically destroying them. Some newcomers were quick to use their overwhelming firepower in 1848 and 1849. However, their violence against California Indians, although horrific, remained relatively limited because it was not yet openly condoned or sponsored by the state. When state and federal officials became involved, between December 1849 and May 1850, they catalyzed a far more widespread genocide. Indian killing had begun in earnest, and it soon spread like a bloodstain across California.

4

TURNING POINT: THE KILLING CAMPAIGNS OF DECEMBER 1849–MAY 1850

Their position being entirely surrounded, they were attacked under most embarrassing circumstances; but as they could not escape, the island soon became a perfect slaughter pen.

—US Army brevet captain Nathaniel Lyon, 1850

His mother told him to climb high up in the tree, so he did and from there he said he could see the solders running about the camp and shooting the men and women and stabing the boys and girls. [H]e said mother was not yet dead and was telling him to keep qui[e]t. [T]wo of the solders heard her talking and ran up to her and stabed her and child.

—Pomo survivor, n.d., paraphrased by William Ralganal Benson, 1832

Perhaps Shuk leaned too far when he threw his lasso. Maybe the young Pomo Indian's horse, borrowed from his white employers without permission, reared when the rope shot over its head. Or, perhaps his mount slipped chasing that ox. Whatever the reason, the horse fell and Shuk landed on the sodden ground. Horse and ox then vanished into the rain-streaked night. Thus began, in December 1849, a cascading series of events that plunged the region's Indian peoples into mortal danger and changed California forever.

By December 1849, the Eastern Pomo and Clear Lake Wappo Indians working for Charles Stone and Andrew Kelsey on Big Valley Ranch, ninety miles north of San Francisco, were starving. William Ralganal Benson, an Eastern Pomo man born in 1862 near Lakeport—just north of Big Valley—spoke with five Indian men who had lived on Big Valley Ranch at the time: Shuk, Xasis, Ba-Tus,

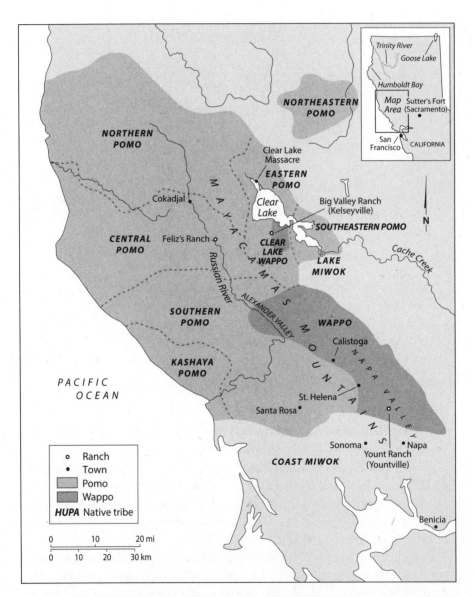

The killing campaigns of December 1849–May 1850

This photograph shows a Pomo man paddling a tule canoe on Clear Lake in what is now Lake County, California. Edward S. Curtis, "In the Tule Swamp—Upper Lake Pomo," photograph, 1924. Courtesy of Library of Congress, Prints & Photographs Division, Edward S. Curtis Collection, LC-USZ62-98670.

Kra-nas, and Ma-Laxa-Qe-Tu. Benson was in a unique position to do so. In early adolescence, he became "the hereditary chief of both the Xolo-napo and the Xabe-napo divisions of" the Eastern Pomo people. Many years later, in 1932, Benson published a detailed account of their story.[1]

According to Benson, "the Indians who was starving hired a man by the name of Shuk [later known as Chief Augustine] and another man by the name of Xasis. to kill a beef for them." While trying to lasso an ox, "Shuks horse fell to the ground. the horse and the ox [then] go away." Returning to the Indian people who had hired them, Shuk and his partner Xasis called an all-night council in Xasis's home. The gathering was deadly serious. When livestock went missing, some California ranchers were quick to blame nearby Indians. The loss of one horse could trigger indiscriminate retaliatory killings and even mass violence against entire indigenous communities. Thus, the men who met in Xasis's house that night had reason to be afraid as they considered how to respond to the loss of their employers' horse.[2]

The Eastern Pomo and Clear Lake Wappo people who labored for Stone and Kelsey at Big Valley Ranch were longtime residents of the Clear Lake region. Eastern Pomo peoples traditionally lived in intimate connection with Clear Lake. They resided near that nineteen-mile-long body of water in villages largely organized along kinship lines and led by a *ká•xa•lik^h*, or chief. They built circular or elliptical houses—sometimes dozens of feet long and large enough to accommodate multiple families—of tule reeds collected from along the lakeshore. They navigated its waves in tule canoes, traversed its islands and shores wearing woven tule leggings with laced tule moccasins, and nestled their sleepy infants in beds of shredded tules. Their annual cycles likewise centered on the lake. In February, March, and April they speared pike and trapped suckers, hitch, and chay from streams flowing into Clear Lake. In May and June, they snared blackfish and carp in the lake itself. In June and July, they harvested Clear Lake's freshwater clams. Eastern Pomo people then transitioned to gathering bulbs, berries, clover, pinole seeds, roots, and acorns. In fall and winter they hunted waterfowl. Clamshell beads of standardized value served as currency and Eastern Pomos traded extensively with other California Indians, presumably including their neighbors, the Clear Lake Wappos. Less is known about the Clear Lake Wappo people, but although their language was different, they likely shared the Eastern Pomo focus on the lake.[3]

Both Eastern Pomo and Clear Lake Wappo people were part of larger Pomo and Wappo groups. Traditional Pomo territory can be divided into seven distinct language regions stretching across an area more than twice the size of Rhode Island. These lands ranged from the hills northeast of Clear Lake to the redwood coast and from the lower Russian River region to north of what is now Fort Bragg. Wappo territory was smaller. It included a five-square-mile area adjoining southern Clear Lake, parts of what are now the Napa and Alexander valleys, and adjoining regions. Wappo people spoke five geographically specific dialects and lived in villages led by male or female chiefs elected, appointed, or chosen by other Wappos. By periodically traveling to the Pacific or buying foods with clamshell beads or magnesite cylinders, they created a varied cuisine. Their fare included abalone, clams, crabs, eels, and salmon, as well as duck, goose, quail, venison, and rabbit. Acorns, clover, roots, and dried seaweed added to their menus, and honey, sweet pitch, and salt provided additional seasonings. As neighbors, Pomo and Wappo people seem to have shared musical instruments and pastimes. Both peoples played the cocoon rattle, double-boned whistle, flute, plank drum, and rattle. Both also enjoyed similar games including dice, the grass game, guessing games, a stick-and-ball game called shinny, and contests of strength. Some Pomos and Wappos also shared less pleasant experiences.[4]

Stone and Kelsey routinely seared terror and pain into the minds and bodies of the Eastern Pomo and Clear Lake Wappo people living on Big Valley Ranch. They also sometimes killed them. Shuk's loss of the pair's horse threatened to unleash additional, possibly lethal violence. So the men meeting in Xasis's house carefully considered three possible responses to the lost horse: appeasing Stone and Kelsey, admitting the loss of the horse, or killing the two men.

That they considered killing Stone and Kelsey may at first seem extreme, but the Indian people on Big Valley Ranch harbored six profound grievances against the two ranchers. These included de facto slavery, institutionalized starvation, torture, rape, abandonment at gold mines, and the threat of imminent forced removal. Examining each grievance provides insight into the range of crimes perpetrated by ranchers against California Indian laborers during the late 1840s, 1850s, and 1860s, the demographic carnage these acts inflicted, and the reasons that California Indian laborers sometimes violently resisted their oppressors.

Charles Stone and Andrew Kelsey were reportedly the first Anglo-American colonists in the Clear Lake region. There were three Kelsey brothers, all of whom seem to have joined the Bear Flag Party that hoisted the Bear Flag at Sonoma in 1846, and all three were among the region's Anglo-American vanguard. In the fall of 1847, Stone, Andrew Kelsey, his brother Benjamin Kelsey, and a man named Shirland bought perhaps 15,000 cattle and 2,500 horses from the Mexican landholder Salvador Vallejo along with "the right to use the lands where the animals were pastured." They began grazing these and other animals on Vallejo's vast Clear Lake ranch. However, according to nineteenth-century historian L.L. Palmer, it remains unknown "whether Stone and Kelsey ever purchased any right to the land or not, or indeed any right of any kind, as the place was very far removed from civilization then, and they were not likely to be molested." Stone, Shirland, and the two Kelseys also took possession of the Eastern Pomo and Clear Lake Wappo people living on the ranch. They did this in accordance with the Mexican custom by which California ranchers transferred control of indigenous people with the land, much as some European landowners transferred serfs with estates. Thus, along with many newcomers who acquired Mexicans' California ranches in the 1840s, 1850s, and early 1860s, the trio assumed control of an existing unfree labor system. Charles Stone and Andrew Kelsey, who remained at the ranch as managers, became overseers.[5]

Stone and Kelsey treated the Pomo and Wappo people on Big Valley Ranch as slaves. According to Palmer, Indians performed all of the work, and it was "slave labor of the worst kind," the only pay consisting of "very short rations and a few bandana handkerchiefs." From the five Indian men he interviewed, Benson

This photograph shows William Ralganal Benson,
a master basket maker, toward the end of his life,
with what was probably one of his own works.
Benson was "hereditary chief of both the Xolo-
napo and the Xabe-napo divisions of" the Eastern
Pomo people, according to legal scholar Max
Radin. See Radin, "Introduction," in Benson,
"Stone and Kelsey 'Massacre,'" 266. Roger
Sturtevant, "William [Ralganal] Benson
[Eastern Pomo] holding a fine Pomo feathered
basket," photograph, ca. 1931. Courtesy of
Phoebe A. Hearst Museum of Anthropology and
the Regents of the University of California,
Catalogue No. 15-18497.

learned how Stone and Kelsey imprisoned Eastern Pomo and Clear Lake Wappo people on the ranch:

> These two white men had the indians to build a high fence around their villages. and the head riders were to see that no indian went out side of this fence after dark. if any one was caught out side of this fence after dark was taken to stones and kelseys house and there was tied both hands and feet and placed in a room and kept there all night. the next day was taken to a tree and was tied down. then the strongs man was chosen to whippe the prisoner.

Shuk, who would have been about eighteen years old in 1849, later became the Hoolanapo Pomo chief Augustine, the leader of an Eastern Pomo clan that Stone and Kelsey seem to have held at Big Valley Ranch. In 1881, Palmer described Augustine as "a very intelligent man" who "bears a good name among the white citizens for probity and veracity." In an interview with Palmer, Augustine recalled that Kelsey "took Indians down to the lower valleys and sold them like cattle or other stock." Indeed, Stone and Kelsey practiced chattel slavery, but with a lethal twist. To them, their Indian slaves were disposable.[6]

Unlike antebellum slave owners in the Southern United States, who in the 1850s often paid hundreds of dollars for an African American slave, and sometimes more than $1,500, Californians typically spent between $35 and $200 to acquire de facto ownership of an Indian. Supply and demand, in combination with rising tobacco and cotton prices, dictated this radical price difference. By the 1840s, the South's supply of African American slaves came almost exclusively from biological reproduction. The federal government's 1808 ban on the transatlantic slave trade to the United States limited new supply to births and a very small illegal international slave trade. Supply grew more slowly than demand and, in combination with rising demand for cotton and tobacco, pushed African American slave prices dramatically upward in the 1840s and 1850s. By contrast, the supply of potential de facto California Indian slaves remained relatively elastic (there were still tens of thousands of California Indians) and acquisition costs were low. Anglo-Californians, Californios, and Europeans could purchase California Indians from ranchers who already held them as unfree laborers, or from slave raiders. Alternatively, they could become slave raiders themselves, kidnapping California Indians and paying nothing to acquire de facto slaves. This factor was crucial in determining the relatively low cost of de facto California Indian slaves. At the same time, demand—undercut by a rapidly growing immigrant labor supply—rarely pushed prices to the levels of those for African American chattel slaves.[7]

The relatively low cost of acquiring de facto California Indian slaves—combined with profound racism—sometimes led to their treatment as disposable laborers. Some Californians treated Indians as disposable laborers based on a profound disregard for their value as human beings and how cheaply they could be replaced. This twisted moral and economic calculus helps to explain the brutal logic behind Stone and Kelsey's abysmal treatment of Indian workers, including their institutionalized starvation.[8]

Thomas Knight, who settled in the nearby Napa Valley in 1845, explained that at Big Valley Ranch, Indian workers received so little food that they occasionally took and ate a bullock, despite the threat of corporal punishment. The Indians on Big Valley Ranch had difficulty augmenting insufficient rations with game because Stone and Kelsey held the Indians' hunting weapons in "the loft of the house," for fear that the workers might use these weapons against them. Benson explained that the people "were starving" because "stone or kelsey would not let them go out hunting or fishing." He also reported that, one year, "about 20 old people died during the winter from starvation." According to Benson, starvation was the primary reason some Big Valley Ranch Indians wanted to kill Stone and Kelsey—but hardly the only motive.[9]

Stone and Kelsey also tortured their workers and sometimes killed them in the process. Chief Augustine (Shuk) recollected, "Stone and Kelsey used to tie up the Indians and whip them if they found them out hunting on the ranch anywhere, and made a habit of abusing them generally." Knight recalled that if a worker broke a rule, Stone and Kelsey would hang the worker "up by his thumbs, so that his toes just touched the floor . . . and keep him there two or three days, sometimes with nothing to eat." After interviewing Pomo people between 1903 and 1906, anthropologist S.A. Barrett concluded that torture was routine: "Any offence of a worker was punished by whipping, a trivial offense drawing sometimes as many as fifty lashes." Benson described torments, "such as whipping and tieing their hand togather with rope. the rope then thrown over a limb of a tree and then drawn up untill the indians toes barly touchs the ground and let them hang there for hours. this was common punishment." Stone and Kelsey also brutalized Indians for entertainment. According to Palmer, "It is stated by white men that it was no uncommon thing for them to shoot an Indian just for the fun of seeing him jump, and that they lashed them as a sort of a recreation when friends from the outside world chanced to pay them a visit." Torture sometimes led to death. Benson wrote: "From severe whipping 4 died."[10]

Stone and Kelsey also routinely raped Indian women and girls, and countered resistance to their sexual assaults with torture and threats of violence. George C. Yount of Napa Valley recalled that Stone and Kelsey had sought

This portrait shows a young Pomo woman wearing strands of clamshell beads, which Pomo people used as currency. The dark colored bead on one strand is probably a magnesite cylinder, a highly valued object. Edward S. Curtis, "Pomo Girl," photograph, 1924, in Curtis, *North American Indian*, 14 supplement: plate 482. Courtesy of Rauner Library at Dartmouth College.

"freedom for their unbridled lusts among the youthful females." According to Benson, "When a father or mother of young girl. was asked to bring the girl to his house. by stone or kelsey. if this order was not obeyed. he or her would be whipped or hung by the hands . . . such punishment occurred two or three times a week. and many of the old men and women died from fear and starvation." The terrible repercussions of resistance may explain why Augustine initially endured it when, "by all it is stated that they took Augustine's wife and forced her to live with one of them as his concubine, and compelled her to cease all relations with her legal spouse." These sexual assaults perpetrated by Stone and

Kelsey were likely another major consideration for the men in Xasis's house as they considered their options.[11]

Stone and Kelsey also murdered Indians outright. Benson reported that Stone shot a young man "to deth" for taking wheat to his "sick and starveing" mother. Local whites added that Stone and Kelsey repeatedly slew their workers. Knight recollected, "Sometimes they would kill an Indian outright on the spot for some small offence. In driving them in to their place they would shoot any of the old or infirm ones by the wayside." Yount recalled simply: "They murdered the indians without limits or mercy."[12]

Like his brother Andrew, Benjamin Kelsey—a part owner of the ranch— treated Indians as disposable laborers. Like many California ranchers, Benjamin Kelsey redeployed Indian ranch hands as miners during the gold rush. In the spring of 1849, he went to Clear Lake. There he obtained between 50 and 100 Eastern Pomo and possibly Clear Lake Wappo men from Charles Stone and his brother Andrew and took them east to the goldfields. On arriving, Benjamin Kelsey began selling off supplies to other miners and eventually had no supplies left with which to feed the men he had brought from Clear Lake. From interviews with Pomo people, Barrett concluded that these men "were forced to do the hardest kind of work and were kept on very meager rations. Informants freely used the term 'starved' to describe the plight of these workers." Augustine recalled simply that Kelsey "did not feed the Indians." Conditions deteriorated further when malaria broke out. Benjamin Kelsey fell ill and abandoned the 50 to 100 men he had brought to the mines. Augustine explained, "Two . . . died there" and the rest "got dissatisfied and wanted to go home. . . . On the road they all died from exposure and starvation, except three men, who eventually got home." According to other sources, Benjamin Kelsey's willful neglect, combined with disease and exposure, killed as many as ninety-nine Indian men. Surviving Big Valley Ranch Indians were thus profoundly concerned when, in a new turn of events, Stone and Kelsey began preparing to move the community's women, children, and elders east over the mountains to the Sacramento Valley.[13]

This menace of imminent forced removal was likely another major factor under discussion in Xasis's house that night. Augustine recollected that Stone and Kelsey "tried to get the Indians to go to the Sacramento River, near Sutters Fort, and make a big rancheria there. They would thus get rid of all except the young men." Benjamin Kelsey's disastrous mining expedition—and the many men who had died as a result—preyed on their minds. Anxieties rose as Stone and Kelsey ordered the people to braid ropes with which to bind their friends, relatives, and neighbors for the impending march.[14]

This Pomo mother holds her child in a cradleboard in front of their lakefront tule reed shelter. Edward S. Curtis, "Pomo Mother and Child," photograph, 1924, in Curtis, *North American Indian*, 14: plate facing page 90. Courtesy of Yale Collection of Western Americana, Beinecke Rare Book and Manuscript Library, Yale University.

For several years, Charles Stone and Andrew Kelsey had ruled over them with fear, sadism, and murderous force. Hard men, Stone and Kelsey were likely to exact terrible vengeance for their lost horse. Barrett concluded that Shuk "knew from past experience that the punishment that would come to him [for losing the horse] would be most severe; in fact, he feared he might be killed. He therefore advocated that the Indians should rise up against Stone and Kelsey and free themselves once and for all from their tyranny." Based on their own experiences, the other men gathered in Xasis's house also predicted that Stone and Kelsey would respond violently. Indeed, the two had murdered Indians for lesser offenses. The assembly thus carefully considered multiple solutions, including paying Stone and Kelsey "16000 beads or 100 dollars" or simply telling Stone or Kelsey "that the horse was stolen," but "no one agreed." Finally, as dawn broke, five men—including Shuk and Xasis—chose a more dangerous path.[15]

Cruelty, starvation, sexual abuse, and the desire to avenge lost Indian lives motivated Shuk, Xasis, Ba-Tus, Kra-nas, and Ma-Laxa-Qe-Tu to kill Stone and Kelsey at what is now Kelseyville, near the western shores of Clear Lake. Augustine (Shuk), "said by all to have been the originator" of the plan, explained: "Finally the Indians made up their minds to kill Stone and Kelsey, for, from day to day they got worse and worse in their treatment of them, and the Indians thought that they might as well die one way as another, so they decided to take the final and fatal step."[16]

Shuk, Xasis, and the other organizers could not envision the scope of retaliatory mass murder that killing Stone and Kelsey would provoke. In just five months, between December 1849 and May 1850, vigilantes and US Army soldiers would kill as many as 1,000 Indians, or more, across four Northern California counties. This response, as well as its sheer scale and geographic scope, were beyond the experience of Shuk, Xasis, Ba-Tus, Kra-nas, and Ma-Laxa-Qe-Tu. Nor could they imagine how these massacres would become the turning point that led to the increasingly widespread genocide of California Indians after May 1850.[17]

KILLING STONE AND KELSEY, DECEMBER 1849

Though conceived in desperation, careful preparation preceded the killing. Before attacking, the five leaders made a decisive tactical move. Shuk and Xasis had the Pomo children who served Stone and Kelsey "carrie out allthe guns. bows and arrows. knives and every thing like weapons . . . so the two white men was helpless in defense."[18]

Shuk, Xasis, Ba-Tus, Kra-nas, and Ma-Laxa-Qe-Tu then rendezvoused with eleven other men outside Stone and Kelsey's adobe house, where "indian herders" received boiled wheat for breakfast early each morning. Emerging to kindle the breakfast fire, Stone walked into the trap. Yet Shuk hesitated. Kra-nas then

said to the men. I thought you men came to kill this man; give me these arrows and bow. He jerk the bow and the arrows away from Shuk and drew it and as he did.Stone rose quickly and turned to Qka-Nas [Kra-nas] and said what are you trying to do . . . and as Stone said it. the indian cut loose. the arrow struck the victim.pith of the stomach. the victim mediately pull the arrow out and ran for the house. fighting his way. he broke one mans arm with the pot he had. and succeeded in getting in the house and locked the door after him.

Kelsey then emerged and tried to placate the sixteen men: "he said to them. no matar kelsey [don't kill Kelsey]. kelsey bueno hombre para vosotros [Kelsey good man for you]." There would be no forgiveness.[19]

According to Barrett, "Kanas [Kra-nas], a Lileek [Clear Lake Wappo], replied, 'Yes, you are such a good man that you have killed many of us.'" Kra-nas then "shot Kelsey with an arrow." Benson continued: "the indians charged and two of the indians caught kelsey and the fight began . . . kelsey was stabbed twice [but] managed to brake loose. he ran for the creek and the indians after him . . . Xa-sis . . . was in pursuit [and] shot kelsey in the back." Still Kelsey ran. He pulled out the arrow and swam across the creek, but to no avail. On the far shore two Indian men, "Big Jim and Joe," caught and held him by the arms. "Big Jim [then] said to his wife. this is a man who killed our son. take this spear.now you have the chance to take revenge. Big Jim's wife [Da-Pi-Tauo] took the spear and stabed the white man in the hart." Meanwhile, "Xasis and Qra-Nas was trailing [Stone's] blood up stairs and for a hour almost." Eventually they found his "lifeless body [in the loft] and threw it out the window." Stone and Kelsey were dead—but the Pomo and Wappo people on Big Valley Ranch were far from safe.[20]

Kra-nas and Xasis understood that they had taken what Augustine later called, "the final and fatal step." Immediately after the killings, they "called all the people to come and take what wheat and corn they could." They also slaughtered stock for meat to help feed hungry people and to prepare them for a long concealment. Kra-nas and Xasis anticipated that whites would probably retaliate and thus told the Big Valley Ranch Indians to "go to-a hiding place." Everyone then dispersed. Augustine explained, "The Indians then all went to Scotts Valley and Upper Lake, or wherever else they pleased, as they all now felt that they had their liberty once more and were free men." They awaited the whites, likely believing that they could retreat to the safety of the mountains cradling Clear Lake, or to the islands within it.[21]

THE 1ST DRAGOONS' CAMPAIGN, DECEMBER 1849

Word of the two killings soon reached the adobe houses and dirt streets of Sonoma, some seventy miles south of Big Valley. The US 1st Dragoons—a battle-hardened, elite mounted infantry unit—were stationed in the sleepy village. They responded almost immediately. Founded in 1832 to police the frontier and fight American Indians, by 1850, the 1st Dragoons had served on the Oregon Trail and in the Mexican-American War. Their ranks had included some of the army's brightest and most ambitious men: Daniel Boone's son Nathan,

Stephen Kearny (fourth military governor of California), Richard Mason (fifth military governor of California), and Jefferson Davis (later secretary of war). Predecessors of the 1st Cavalry Regiment, the 1st Dragoons were mobile, heavily armed, and well-versed in irregular warfare. This was the kind of operation for which Congress had created them.[22]

On Christmas Day, 1849, First Lieutenant John W. Davidson learned that Indians had killed Stone and Kelsey. The following morning, the West Point–trained Virginian, accompanied by a Lieutenant Wilson, saddled up to lead twenty-two 1st Dragoons north from Sonoma through the oak-studded hills, dense brush, and shoulder-high grasses on the way to Clear Lake. With Kit Carson's brother Moses as their guide, they covered the seventy miles in just three days. However, their rush did not prevent them from making two significant stops en route.[23]

As was becoming increasingly common among Northern Californians on so-called punitive expeditions against Indians, Lieutenant Davidson chose not to differentiate between the guilty and the innocent. The killing of a non-Indian by an Indian was increasingly a pretext for the mass murder of any California Indians in the vicinity, regardless of their age, gender, identity, location, or tribal affiliation.

Moving northeast from Sonoma, the twenty-five riders traversed the mountains into Napa Valley and Central Wappo territory, an area inhabited by people related to the Clear Lake Wappos who lived some thirty miles north. Central Wappo people called the valley *Talahalusi*, meaning "Beautiful Land." Today, thousands of acres of grapevines—which yield some of the most sought-after wines in the world—score the basin in orderly parallel rows. But for thousands of years, grasses and trees dominated this Central Wappo homeland. Here Wappo people harvested acorns, seeds, and other foods while fishing, hunting, and trading for additional items.[24]

Near the top of the lush valley, the twenty-five riders halted at "a very large Indian village . . . about three miles south of Calistoga." This was probably the Central Wappo village of Mayacama. In 1902, a white man named Nash, who lived near this village at the time, told Barrett what happened next: "When these soldiers reached this village, they entered without incident and, as the Indians were standing around and all unsuspecting, the soldiers suddenly opened fire and killed about thirty-five of the Indians." Nash observed, "The people of this village had had apparently nothing whatever to do with the deaths of Stone and Kelsey, but nevertheless they had to pay the penalty." Little evidence of the massacre remained. Nash concluded, "As soon as the soldiers left the village, the Indians brought together a large quantity of wood and built a huge pyre for the cremation of their dead," in keeping with traditional Wappo funerary rites. The soldiers then rode on, to a point just north of Calistoga, and stopped at the Cyrus family ranch.[25]

Elizabeth Cyrus Wright based her 1928 account of what transpired on pre-existing notes of things told to her by her parents and older cousins, some of whom, including her parents, were adults living in the upper Napa Valley in 1849. According to Wright, after Stone and Kelsey died, "Some of Kelsey's friends came to Upper Napa Valley and wanted the settlers to band themselves together and drive back the Indians." Local farmers and ranchers found the proposal contrary to their interests and sensibilities, for in 1849 upper Napa Valley's colonial economy depended on California Indian labor. Thus, they "replied that [driving back the Indians] was unnecessary as the Indians, if well treated, were friendly, and an advantage rather than otherwise, as they were not only willing but glad to work if they were left free, well treated, and properly paid for their labor." The vigilantes then departed and "thus the matter stood for some time."[26]

"Then came a small detachment of soldiers under a snappy young officer from Benicia saying that he had been sent to exterminate the Indians." Wright explained, "The people were gone from the two lower villages on a hunt, so he [the officer] came on up to the one of the Cyrus place. Enoch Cyrus [Wright's grandfather] tried to argue him out of it but was sharply commanded to 'shut up and go away or he would be shot.'" Cyrus apparently complied. "The Indians," however, "not knowing their danger, and never having seen men in uniform before, were clustered in a group watching these strangers when the officer gave the order 'Fire.' His men fired point blank at the harmless natives killing some and wounding others." Wright concluded, "Evidently feeling that he had made a sufficient show of his authority, the young officer retired with his men and the frightened, grief stricken Indians carried their dead away to the thick timber where they held a great 'cry' that night," in keeping with the Wappo mourning tradition of ritual wailing. Lieutenant Davidson made no mention of these events in his official report.[27]

Leaving Napa Valley, Davidson's cavalcade rode into Big Valley Ranch on December 28. There they encountered one of the surviving Kelsey brothers with fifteen armed men. Less pleasant discoveries were also in store. Davidson found Stone's body "in a vat, covered with hides, and shockingly mangled. The house was robbed of everything it contained, and the rancherias abandoned." Soon thereafter, Davidson captured twelve "Isla" Indians, probably Pomos, "who live upon the lake." Davidson, apparently wanting to question them, initially kept the prisoners alive. However, when the detainees reportedly tried to escape, "They were promptly fired into by the dragoons and citizen sentinels, and three

This woodcut provides a rare glimpse into the interior of what is probably a traditional Wappo house in Napa Valley. Whitney Jocelyn-Annin SC(?), "Interior of Indian Huts, California," woodcut, before 1855, in Bartlett, *Personal Narrative*, 2: plate between pages 30 and 31. Courtesy of Yale Collection of Western Americana, Beinecke Rare Book and Manuscript Library, Yale University.

of their number fell, who died the next day." Davidson then continued searching for those who had killed Stone and Kelsey, proceeding to the shores of Clear Lake.[28]

Seeing Indians gathered on an island "about 300 yards from shore," Davidson assumed that they were harboring those who had slain Stone and Kelsey. He repeatedly asked the islanders to surrender the killers, but according to him they only replied: "'It was good if we could catch them.'" Davidson interpreted this ambiguous reply as both a taunt and a collective admission of guilt. Then he made a major interpretive leap—without citing specific evidence—to report: "There is no doubt but all the Indian tribes upon the lake are more or less concerned in this atrocious murder." Yet, in 1849, four different California Indian groups lived around Clear Lake and they spoke at least three separate languages. Consequently, Davidson's conclusion now seems irrational. However, it was not inconsistent with the notion of collective Indian guilt then popular in California.[29]

Many mid-nineteenth-century whites came to think of California Indians as one nearly indivisible corporate body where criminal law and punishment were concerned, and Davidson was no exception. He supported his claim with no evidence but echoed the increasingly common Anglo-American notion that when one or more California Indians committed a crime, all Indians in the vicinity should be severely punished. This collective-guilt argument became a routinely cited pseudo-juridical rationale for both the indiscriminate killing of California Indians (including men, women, children, and elders) and the theft or destruction of their property.

Davidson would have liked to attack the Indian people he saw on the island that day. In his report, he explained that his unit's tired horses, lack of tools, and inability to find timber with which to build rafts, prevented such an immediate assault. Instead, he and Lieutenant Wilson proposed bringing sixty soldiers to Clear Lake with "two or three boats, capable of carrying ten men each," to "surprise them in their rancherias, and cut them to pieces." The intended targets: "All the Indian tribes upon the lake."[30]

How could a West Point–trained officer of an elite military unit plan such a large, expensive, logistically difficult military operation to kill untold numbers of mostly unarmed Indian civilians from multiple tribes, for the killing of two white men? Large-scale army operations against California Indians were unusual at this time. But US Army general Persifor F. Smith's written acceptance of Davidson and Wilson's audacious plan sheds light on the Anglo-American attitudes toward Indians and Indian violence in California that made the operation acceptable to General Smith and thus to the US government.

Philadelphia-born and Princeton-educated, Brevet Major General Persifor F. Smith was a lawyer and a decorated veteran of the Seminole and Mexican-American Wars. He accepted Davidson and Wilson's plan. On January 12, 1850, General Smith wrote, "As soon as troops can move in the spring . . . the Indians . . . who committed the murder on Clear Lake must be chastised." Smith believed in collective punishment. On February 26, he ordered Brevet Brigadier General Bennett Riley to execute a modified version of Davidson and Wilson's plan by targeting neither the individual killers nor all Clear Lake tribes, but rather "the exact tribe that is guilty." The notion of a "guilty tribe" would soon be pervasive.[31]

In his orders to Riley, Smith explained how and why the operation should be carried out. He began, "The time will soon be here in which the state of the roads and waters will permit the movement of troops, and must immediately be taken advantage of to chastise the Indians near Clear Lake." Smith then enlarged the troop strength proposed by Davidson and Wilson, calling for "at least one hundred men." Further, the expedition should include not two but "three boats or skiffs capable of containing [not ten, but] fifteen men each." Smith thus increased Davidson's proposed amphibious strike force from twenty or thirty soldiers to forty-five. The general also narrowed the expedition's aims and detailed its scope. Its commander was to "ascertain positively the exact tribe that is guilty, which, in regard to the murders at Clear Lake, is not difficult, as there are witnesses at hand [presumably Davidson]; to attack at once wherever he finds them, and to pursue them as long as he is able, without proposing or attempting any parley or communication with them; to inflict such a blow on them as will intimidate them and others and prevent like offences." Smith concluded by attempting to explain the logic undergirding his draconian orders: "The future tranquility of the borders and security from Indian aggressions requires that the first attempt to punish Indian murders should be effectual and thorough. Lenity now would be the extreme of cruelty to both parties." General Riley could not immediately execute Smith's orders. Winter rains made the roads to Clear Lake temporarily impassable for a military expedition.[32]

THE VIGILANTE CAMPAIGNS, FEBRUARY–MARCH 1850

Meanwhile, violence flared in the hills south of Clear Lake. Perhaps frustrated by the army's inaction, ad hoc groups picked up where Davidson's 1st Dragoons had left off. Rumors of Davidson's Calistoga region massacres and the planned severity of General Smith's Clear Lake operation likely did little to restrain them.

Throughout 1849, a dangerous pattern was emerging in Northern California. When Anglo-Americans suspected Indians of stealing from or killing whites, they formed ad hoc vigilante parties, often killing any Indians they encountered. These campaigns never extended beyond small geographic areas, did not aim to annihilate an entire tribe, rarely included more than a few men, and never lasted more than a week. The vigilante operations of February–March 1850 broke this mold and set new precedents. Roused by the slaying of Stone and Kelsey and perhaps inspired by Davidson's killing of Wappo people, Napa and Sonoma men organized groups to exterminate or drive away local Coast Miwok Indians, some of whom inhabited the Sonoma River Valley but were unrelated to any Clear Lake Indians. These Napa and Sonoma vigilantes also targeted Pomo and Wappo people. Violence soon engulfed Napa Valley, Sonoma Valley, and the Santa Rosa region.[33]

Curtis created this rare early twentieth-century portait of a Wappo man in 1924. Edward S. Curtis, "Wappo," photograph, 1924, in Curtis, *North American Indian*, 14 supplement: plate 490. Courtesy of Rauner Library at Dartmouth College.

On March 2, 1850, a correspondent from Sonoma reported: "Ever since the murder of Andrew Kelsey . . . a party of men have caused much excitement among the peaceful inhabitants of this place and Nappa." The correspondent explained, "On the 31st [of January] a meeting was got up in Nappa for the purpose of driving all the Indians from the country." Soon thereafter, "A party of twenty-four armed horsemen . . . proceeded to Mr. Yount's rancho [now Yountville in Napa Valley], set fire to the rancherie [probably the Southern Wappo village of Caymus] and chased near one hundred Indians to the mountains." Yount himself recalled these horsemen "killing a few Indians" in the area. The vigilantes now rode further up Napa Valley.[34]

Approximately eight miles upriver, or north of what is now St. Helena, the riders came to a halt at Henry Fowler's Rancho Carne Humana, or "Human

Flesh Ranch." According to court documents, "Several Indians in the Napa Valley were shot on the twenty-seventh day of February, their lodges burned, and a considerable quantity of wheat, barley, and other property destroyed . . . at and about the ranch of Henry Fowler and William Hargrave." A Sonoma correspondent reported, "fifteen innocent Indians," presumably Central Wappo people, shot down "at Fowler's ranch." This may have been an underestimate. Yount recollected, "On reaching Fowlers Ranch, on which was a large Rancheria they executed their bloody work & perpetrated a multitude of murders, & left the Ranch covered with the slain, men, women & children—Thus they passed the day in murder & butchery."[35]

The vigilantes next moved, by night, west to Santa Rosa and then back to Sonoma. Yount concluded, "How many victims fell in this murderous forey has never been & never will be known." The Sonoma correspondent reported that at Santa Rosa, in Southern Pomo territory, the vigilantes "chased the Indians from thence" and that at "Jesse Beasley's ranch in Sonoma," within Coast Miwok territory, they "killed two of his household, Indian servants." On March 1, "the party that is said to have killed the Indians, passed through this town [Sonoma], and threatened to hunt and kill every Indian, male and female, found in the country." Meanwhile, others opposed the posse, and "a courier was dispatched from here [Sonoma], and two from Nappa to the Governor, for instructions how to proceed."[36]

Observers provided additional details of the expanding violence. On March 4, one J.W.B. reported from Napa Valley that "During the past week most outrageous acts of lawlessness and cruelty have been perpetrated in Napa by an armed body of Americans, who publicly organized themselves in the village of Sonoma for the avowed purpose of exterminating the Indians in this valley and burning the ranches and lodges where the innocent and laboring people live." J.W.B. added that, in upper Napa Valley, "Bandits commenced their work by murdering a large body of Indians and burning their houses and provisions. Ten of the dead bodies of those murdered people were found about six miles above Harbins' Mills." C.A. Menefee later described how:

> In 1850 a party of Americans came over from Sonoma to avenge upon the Indians in general the murder of Kelsey in Lake county, in which the Indians of Napa had no hand. This party were on their way to Soscol to attack the Indians there, but were turned back by another party of white men at Napa, who prevented them from crossing the ferry. They then returned to Calistoga, and murdered in cold blood eleven innocent Indians, young and old, as they

came out of their "sweat house," and then burned their "wickeyups," together with their bodies.

To the south, "forty to fifty [men] headed by Samuel Kelsey and a Mormon named Smith" burned more rancherias and chased Indians away, three of whom drowned in Napa Creek while trying to escape.[37]

Napa, Santa Rosa, and Sonoma had no local newspapers at this time. Consequently, limited information exists on the number of Miwok, Pomo, and Wappo people killed in February and March 1850. However, extant sources suggest that vigilantes killed a substantial number. On June 1, 1851, Justice of the Peace Peter Campbell reported to the US Commissioner of Indian Affairs, "The brother of the murdered man [i.e., Samuel or Benjamin Kelsey] collected a strong force and . . . commenced an indiscriminate Slaughter of the Indians who reside on farms working for Americans and in one night slew Twenty." Campbell concluded, "They were [only] prevented by the citizens from utterly annihilating them." Knight, too, recalled indiscriminate murders: "The two [surviving] Kelseys also killed a good many . . . many of those they massacred being old or infirm and had never made any trouble." As late as September 13, 1850, the *Daily Alta California* reported, "Since [Andew Kelsey's] death frequent and daring have been the acts of retaliation and revenge visited indiscriminately of sex or age upon either *Indian manzos*, or *Indian bravos*, in the vicinity of Sonoma." Because of the limited number of sources and their often incomplete descriptions, we are unlikely to ever know the total number murdered or exactly how long this killing spree lasted.[38]

Despite these widespread attacks on Indian men, women, and children, General Persifor F. Smith, "head of the Pacific Military Division," was reluctant to intervene. According to J.W.B., "Despatches were speedily sent to General Smith at Benicia for military aid," but Smith "thought the civil arm ought first to be proven powerless for the arrest of the desperadoes, before the military could be called upon." Smith's reluctance probably stemmed from his own views of Indians: he had recently ordered a military operation to attack an entire Indian tribe based on the suspicion that one or more of them might have been connected to a crime. He may also have been motivated by respect for California's new political status.[39]

California had not yet been admitted as the thirty-first state, but it was newly self-governing. On November 13, 1849, California voters had ratified a constitution and elected representatives. On December 15, the legislature met for the first time. Five days later, "the State government of California was established."

Tennessee lawyer and "Oregonian" Peter H. Burnett became the first civilian US governor of California. That same day, Brevet Brigadier General Riley resigned as military governor. California thus became self-governing. However, from December 20, 1849, to September 9, 1850—when Congress admitted California to statehood—California was neither a territory nor a state. The transition to self-government and statehood created an ad hoc rule of law that effectively granted impunity to those who killed Indians. Self-government for California would have catastrophic results for California Indians. Federal officials and army officers largely abdicated responsibility for protecting California Indians to local and state officials, who demonstrated a consistent lack of interest and initiative in taking on this responsibility.[40]

Smith may have earnestly interpreted vigilante violence against California Indians as a matter for the new civil authorities, based on the principle of states' rights. Given national politics in 1850, he may have been reluctant to order federal troops to arrest the citizens of a nascent state. On the other hand, he may also have wished the vigilantes success. According to Yount, "On being interrogated," the vigilantes "averred that they came commissioned by Gen. Smith to destroy & drive off into the mountains all the Indians in Napa Valley." Whatever motivated Smith's decisions, not all Napa Valley colonists were content to wait for him to act while vigilantes massacred and drove away local Indians.[41]

Ranchers motivated by moral conviction and economic interests came to the aid of Indians under attack. J.W.B. reported great excitement at Napa. Indians were part of the economy and social fabric of the Napa and Sonoma valleys and had been for decades. They were also human beings, and some non-Indians, including J.W.B., considered the vigilantes' actions "cruel." Thus, local ranchers and law enforcement officials took preventive action.[42]

Yount recollected that after the vigilantes left Sonoma "with numerous recruits," they "burned one Rancheria" but "soon after . . . were routed by a band of bold Rancheros, hastily armed & mounted to give them battle, & some fled, others were made prisoners & all were routed." On March 19, the Sonoma correspondent celebrated this dispersal of the "band of lynchers" by Napa residents and the arrest of some of them by the mayor of Benicia. Those arrested included Benjamin Kelsey, Samuel Kelsey, Captain Smith, James Lewis, Julian Graham, James Prigmore, John Kelly, and W. Anderson. A Benicia magistrate examined these suspects and held them on the US Navy frigate *Savannah* before a San Francisco court released them "on bail to appear for trial." However, California courts tried none of these eight men and, until now, no one has explained why.[43]

The trial of the eight was, in fact, the first case brought before California's new Supreme Court. Charged with "various felonious acts," the octet's legal defense team included Charles D. Semple and John B. Weller, who later became governor of California. California's Supreme Court provided two reasons for releasing the eight on bail. First, California's district courts were not yet fully organized, the laws regulating them had yet to be promulgated, and it was not yet clear when they would begin operation, making it difficult for the accused to first be tried by a lower court before being tried by the state Supreme Court. Second, the court asserted that there was no jail or prison in which the accused could be securely held. Apparently the fifty-gun USS *Savannah*, manned by some 480 navy sailors and marines, was insecure. Yet, the octet never had to escape their guards, leap over the side, or swim to freedom. Upon release, all eight men jumped bail and authorities never rearrested them, even though several remained prominent citizens.[44]

California superintendent of Indian Affairs Thomas J. Henley later explained, "The excitement ran high during the confinement of the parties, and the responsibility of conducting the prosecution was very great, and even dangerous to personal safety." We may never know exactly why authorities failed to try the eight suspects, but we do know that the arrests halted the killing campaign and that the two Kelsey brothers soon moved north to California's then remote Humboldt Bay and Trinity River regions, likely to distance themselves from the law.[45]

For the Indian survivors—who included Coast Miwok, Pomo, and Wappo men, women, and children—continued existence was a challenge. Driven from their villages, employment, food stores, houses, sacred places, and bountiful ancestral valleys by indiscriminate attacks, they sought refuge in remote mountain areas. Amid these peaks, there were fewer murderous newcomers but also far less food, particularly in the lean months of winter and early spring. The recent loss of expert hunters and gatherers—who were also loved ones and family members—presumably added to their difficulties, making subsistence challenging if not impossible. Many likely cut their hair in mourning and struggled to survive. On March 19, the *Daily Alta California* reported that "Hundreds of the Indians are in the mountains in a starving condition, afraid to return to the Ranchos." For these refugees, the sense of danger remained acute, and the prospects of returning safely to their homes in the Napa and Sonoma valleys and Santa Rosa region was still uncertain.[46]

On March 11, the *Daily Alta California* railed against the vigilantes: "The victims upon whom the sins of criminals of their own color have been visited, were, as is usually the case, innocent of offence, and by their uniform, quiet demeanor have thoroughly established a name throughout the portion of California inhabited by them, for tractability and usefulness. They were the Indian

Benjamin Kelsey's willful neglect combined with disease and exposure to kill as many as ninety-nine Indian men in 1849. Following the murder of his brother Andrew in 1850, Benjamin Kelsey seems to have joined a vigilante group that killed an unknown number of Indians. Released on bail in California's first Supreme Court case, he never stood trial. Carlton E. Watkins, "Ben Kelsey," photograph, before 1889. Courtesy of Humboldt Room, Humboldt State University Library, Arcata, California.

employees of the several settlers in Sonoma and Nappa Vallies, and for many years they have maintained a relationship of perfect amity with the whites." The editorial continued: "We can readily imagine why the chivalrous 'hounds' of the red woods have concentrated and commenced indiscriminate slaughter of the Indians," and opined, "The cause of the recent aggressions in Sonoma valley on the part of the whites is said to be the murder of white men by the Indians last fall, and for which, it would appear the slaughter of whole tribes has not sufficiently atoned." The editor opened with a lament: "We had hoped to hear no more of Indian butcheries in California," and culminated with a plea: "We hope and trust the U.S. troops in California will prevent further violence." As we shall see, the opposite occurred. Two days later, even as he again condemned the killers, the editor predicted, "The work of blood is not yet ended."[47]

Vigilante violence was, in part, a response to the killings of Stone and Kelsey. But why did their deaths cause such widespread violence so far from the site of that double murder? Four factors may also have motivated vigilantes to chase away and kill local Indians. First, some probably failed to distinguish between California Indian tribes or may have believed that their victims were from the group that killed Stone and Kelsey. Second, some probably believed—as did General Smith—in the efficacy of pedagogic violence: the idea that extreme violence against one tribe would "teach" others to respect whites. Third, some may have sought to physically eliminate what they perceived to be the unfair economic and social advantages then enjoyed by ranchers and farmers who employed Indians. And fourth, some who simply wished that local Indians would go away may have decided that killing and chasing off Indians were the most effective means of attaining this end. All four factors would animate later vigilante, state militia, and US Army killing campaigns against other California Indians. However, the next campaign, launched by the US Army in May, was primarily motivated by conflicting desires to "teach" and to destroy.

TO BLOODY ISLAND, MAY 1–15, 1850

By early May, the boats were ready and the roads were dry. Despite citizens' pleas for conciliation, troops in Benicia were preparing to execute Davidson's plan to "cut" Clear Lake Indians "to pieces." The expedition included company C of the 1st Dragoons, detachment M of the 3rd Artillery, and detachments A, E, and G of the 2nd Infantry. The *Daily Alta California* reported on May 28 that, according to US Army captain John B. Frisbie, "on the 1st of the month an expedition was fitted out . . . (75 [men] in all) with orders to proceed against the Clear Lake Indians, and *exterminate* if possible the tribe."[48]

As the expedition marched north, pulling a mountain howitzer or two and portaging at least two boats, it does not seem to have encountered Indians. When the troops reached the southern shore of Clear Lake, they found the lakeside deserted. Benson explained, "Every Indian around the lake knew the soldiers were coming up the lake." The time had come to retreat to the perceived safety of the mountains around Clear Lake or to the islands within it.[49]

Connecticut-born and West Point–educated, expedition commander and Brevet Captain Nathaniel Lyon reported on the approach. Following special department orders number 44, Lyon left Benicia on May 5. After a seven-day march, his men, horses, wagons, boats, and artillery reached Clear Lake on May 11. The infantry then moved by water up the lake as the dragoons, led by Davidson, with help from West Pointer George Stoneman, rode north along the western shore. Local Indians, meanwhile, retreated to an island at the north end of Clear Lake. Lyon then "took position on the afternoon of the 14th, the Indians still gathering rapidly on the [mile-long] island." That same day, Davidson's dragoons and Lieutenant Haynes's artillery "attacked a rancho . . . killing four and securing an Indian chief." By May 15, Lyon had positioned troops in a crescent on the northern rim of the lake, to the north, east, and west of the island. A cordon of regular soldiers thus closed off escape to all three nearby shores.[50]

The Pomo were trapped, and the moment was ripe for negotiation. However, General Smith had specifically instructed Lyon to negotiate neither for custody of those who had killed Stone and Kelsey nor for a general surrender. Smith made this plain in his May 25 report to US Army Headquarters: "My instructions, conveyed through General Riley, were, to waste no time in parley, to ascertain with certainty the offenders, and to strike them promptly and heavily." Smith evidently relied on Davidson's report of January 6, 1850, to conclude, "There was no difficulty in determining the guilty, for they boasted of the deed and defied punishment, secure of a retreat on their islands in a lake surrounded by mountains impassable for any carriage." In neither his orders to Riley nor in his report to army headquarters did Smith address the high probability that such orders would lead to large numbers of civilian casualties.[51]

Like Davidson, the Napa and Sonoma vigilantes, and many others who would follow in their footsteps, General Smith rejected the US legal system where Indians were concerned. Like the vigilantes, Smith seems to have believed that a special, extralegal process applied to Indian crimes against non-Indians. He presumed Indian guilt, circumvented courts, and ordered an operation that amounted to summary capital punishment of the many—including women, children, and elders—for the crimes of a few. Smith's primary concern was not justice, as defined by law. His goal was "to chastise the Indians near Clear Lake," that is, to inspire fear by killing large numbers, regardless of whether or not the victims were guilty of committing, aiding, or abetting the killing of Stone and Kelsey.[52]

Brevet Captain Lyon zealously carried out General Smith's order not to negotiate. Augustine explained that, prior to the assault, Lyon's soldiers first "killed their two Indian guides, one being shot and the other hung," thus presumably denying his force any translators and the possibility of negotiation. Having taken this extraordinary final step, Lyon was ready. Early on the morning of May 15, Lyon's infantrymen loaded themselves, their weapons, and ammunition into boats and crossed the water. Meanwhile Davidson, Stoneman, and their dragoons patrolled the shore.[53]

Unaware of Lyon's orders, Pomo leaders apparently attempted to negotiate. According to Benson, when "the white warriors" landed "the indians said they would met them in peace.so when the whites landed the indians went to welcom them.but the white man was determined to kill them. Ge-Wi-Lih said he threw up his hands and said no harm me good man but the white man fired and shoot him in the arm and another shoot came and hit a man staning along side of him and was killed.so they had to run and fight back." Perhaps trying to buy time for friends and relatives to hide or escape—as California Indians so often did in the face of such attacks—a small group of Pomo men mounted a courageous, but brief, resistance.[54]

Lyon reported that "the landing on the island was effected, under a strong opposition from the Indians." Based on information from Lyon's fellow expedition officers, Smith reported that the Pomos "received them manfully with showers of arrows." Chief Augustine presented a distinctly different, Pomo perspective: "Five Indians went out to give them battle; one with a sling and the other four with bows and arrows." Benson concurred: "Four or five of them gave a little battle." Though valiant, five men armed with a sling and bows could not hold off dozens of heavily armed attackers.[55]

Lyon—who provided the only eyewitness account of the assault—specified only that "the Indians . . . perceiving us once upon their island, took flight directly, plunging into the water." According to what Smith heard from other officers present that day, "only those could escape who could reach the water and conceal themselves." The US troops then pressed the attack.[56]

Thirteen days later, in an article titled "Horrible Slaughter of Indians," the *Daily Alta California* described the assault, using information provided by army captain John B. Frisbie:

They . . . poured in a destructive fire indiscriminately upon men, women and children. "They fell," says our informant, "as grass before the sweep of the scythe." Little or no resistance was encountered, and the work of butchery was of short duration. The shrieks of the slaughtered victims died away, the roar of muskets . . . ceased; and stretched lifeless upon the sod of their native valley were the bleeding bodies of these Indians—[n]or sex, nor age was spared; it was the order of *extermination* fearfully obeyed.[57]

Frisbie's fellow officers almost immediately disputed his vivid report. On May 30, Lieutenant Davidson wrote to the *Daily Alta California* claiming, "No order of extermination was given, and consequently no such order obeyed." The next day, General Smith himself wrote to the *San Francisco Herald* denying that "'an order of extermination without sparing sex or age' was ever given or carried out." On June 1, the *Daily Alta California* reported that Frisbie's "account has caused a great commotion in camp, and excited a great deal of indignation." As a result, Frisbie recanted: "In an accidental interview with General Persifor F. Smith, yesterday, [Frisbie] pronounce[d] . . . our account *false*, in the very strongest possible language, and with a very decided evidence of anger, and also . . . question[ed], indirectly, our motives for its publication." A cover-up was in the making.[58]

Benson provided a Pomo perspective that revealed the Davidson, Smith, and Frisbie denials as pure deception. According to him:

> Many women and children were killed on around this island. one old lady a (indian) told about what she saw while hiding under abank,in under aover hanging tuleys [bulrushes]. she said she saw two white man coming with their guns up in the air and on their guns hung a little girl. They brought it to the creek and threw it in the water. and alittle while later, two more men came in the same manner. this time they had alittle boy on the end of their guns and also threw it in the water. alittle ways from she, said layed awoman shoot through the shoulder. she held her little baby in her arms. two white men came running torge the women and baby, they stabed the women and the baby and, and threw both of them over the bank in to the water. she said she heard the woman say, O my baby; she said when they [the survivors] gathered the dead, they found all the little ones were killed by being stabed, and many of the women were also killed [by] stabing. . . . They called it the siland creek. (Ba-Don-Bi-Da-Meh).[59]

On June 27, 1850, the *Daily Alta California* lamented: "We quite dispair of getting access to a copy of the original report of Captain Lyon, commander of the expedition, to General Smith." The army did not distribute Lyon's May 22 expedition report to the press, and for good reason. In it he stated that his troops "rapidly cleared the island." Survivors then began "plunging into the water, among the heavy growth of tula which surrounds the island." To maximize casualties, in compliance with General Smith's orders, Lyon "saw no alternative but to pursue them into the tula, and accordingly orders were given that the ammunition be slung around the necks of the men, [to keep the gunpowder dry] and they proceed into the tula and pursue and destroy as far as possible." Palmer later wrote that, according to locals, "the soldiers killed women and children indiscriminately, following them into the water and shooting them and clubbing them with their guns and oars."[60]

Those who swam away from the island to the shores of Clear Lake had little chance of reaching dry land alive. According to George Gibbs, who met with local Pomo people in 1851, "On their trying to escape to the shore, [they were] attacked by the dragoons, who met them waist-deep in the tulé." Davidson, Stoneman, and their dragoons apparently cut these survivors down. By nearly encircling the island, Lyon had sought to prevent escape. He never offered the surrounded Pomo people quarter, and in compliance with Smith's orders, he took no prisoners. His intention seems to have been to annihilate every Pomo on the island, much as Captain Frisbie had originally reported.[61]

Counting corpses is unpleasant work, and in this case water, tule, and cremation made it extremely difficult, if not impossible, for Lyon's men to obtain an accurate body count. The soldiers murdered many people in the water or threw them into it after killing or mortally wounding them. Some bodies presumably drifted away on the lake or disappeared beneath its surface. The dense tule cloaking the shores of both the island and Clear Lake also probably obscured corpses. For anyone returning to the island and the surrounding shoreline in subsequent weeks or months, human remains would have been difficult to find given that Pomo survivors cremated the dead, in keeping with their traditional funerary customs, less than a week after Lyon's force departed. One survivor explained to Benson: "It took them four or five days to gather up the dead. and the dead were all burnt on the east side of the creek."[62]

Even as surviving Pomo women were likely singing mourning songs for their slain loved ones, Lyon officially reported "most gratifying results." He explained, "The number killed I confidently report at not less than sixty, and doubt little that it extended to a hundred and upwards. The Indians were supposed to be in number about 400." Three years later, a Sonoma correspondent reported: "The slain were numbered by hundreds, nobody knew how many." In 1862, Lyon's biographer Ashbel Woodward claimed, "Nearly a hundred of the enemy perished." In 1873, Menefee estimated, "About two hundred . . . slain." However, in

1881, Palmer reported that Chief Augustine had emphasized to him that "there were only *sixteen* of them killed there that day." Did Palmer misunderstand Augustine? Perhaps "there" referred to a specific location; maybe "them" referred to a specific group of victims—Big Valley Ranch refugees, Eastern Pomos, Northern Pomos, Southeastern Pomos, Clear Lake Wappos, warriors, or some other subset of those on the island that day. It is highly improbable that only sixteen died, given Lyon's report and other accounts. According to ethnographer C. Hart Merriam's early twentieth-century interviews: "The Indians tell me that Lyon's men killed 120 men, women and children." Another twentieth-century writer, Virginia Hanrahan, estimated "one hundred per cent . . . Indian Casualties" out of "more than five hundred indians." She concluded: "Out of this entire group of natives only Chief Prieta and fourteen men survived because they were away on a trip at the time." Did US soldiers kill 500 people that day? The toll may have been even higher.[63]

In July 1850, two months after this genocidal massacre, Major Edwin Allen Sherman arrived in the Clear Lake area to help locate Stone and Kelsey's missing stock. In his early twentieth-century recollections, Sherman contended, "Captain Lyon was rather too modest in his report." According to Sherman, "There were not less than four hundred warriors killed and drowned at Clear Lake and as many more of squaws and children who plunged into the lake and drowned, through fear, committing suicide. So in all, about eight hundred Indians found a watery grave in Clear Lake." If Sherman's estimate is correct, the May 15, 1850, attack may rank among the most lethal of all Native American massacres in the history of the United States and its colonial antecedents. According to Sherman's figures, it would have exceeded the 260–300 Hunkpapas and Miniconjous murdered at Wounded Knee in 1890, surpassed the 400–700 Pequots massacred at Mystic, Connecticut, in 1637, and rivaled the 600–800 Puebloan people killed at Acoma, New Mexico, in 1599.[64]

In contrast, Lyon reported, "Their fire upon us was not effective, and no injury to the command occurred." Not a single soldier was killed or wounded. The isle in the northwest portion of Clear Lake became known as "Bloody Island." Today, two stone and steel historical markers bear mute testimony to the many people murdered in the Bloody Island Massacre.[65]

What did the Bloody Island Massacre accomplish? Soldiers killed between 60 and 800 Pomo men, women, and children. For survivors, life became exceedingly difficult. Lyon seems to have intended this suffering; his men burned the village to the ground "together with a large amount of stores collected in it." However, the massacre may not have had much to do with the killing of Stone and Kelsey, except in the minds of some soldiers. According to Barrett's informants, "Almost none of those directly concerned with the deaths of Stone and Kelsey" were among the victims. Many of the Pomo people gathered on the isle were simply there to fish.[66]

Following the massacre, Lyon continued to "chastise" Indians, per Smith's orders. In a cryptic 1851 journal entry, Gibbs recorded that, following the massacre, "Three Indians had been implicated in the Clear Lake murder [of Stone and Kelsey], and were accordingly chastised by Captain Lyons on his return from Clear Lake." Benson partially decoded Gibbs's enigmatic phrase, using Pomo oral history. After the massacre, expedition members encountered several Pomo near the lake: "This old lady also told about the whites hung a man on Emerson siland this indian was met by the soldiers while marching from scotts valley to upper lake. the indian was hung and alarge fire built under the hanging indian. and another indian was caught near Emerson hill. this one was tied to atree and burnt to death." Lyon now continued his "search" for those who had killed Stone and Kelsey. As Benson explained, "The next morning the soldiers started for mendocino county. and there killed many indians."[67]

TO THE "PERFECT SLAUGHTER PEN"
AND BEYOND, MAY 15–25(?), 1850

In his official report, Lyon explained why he marched his force northwest: "Being satisfied that the Indian tribes on Russian river had participated in the murders of Stone and Kelsey, and were now harboring one or two tribes known to be the most guilty, I now proceeded to the headwaters of that river." Lyon may have been tracking Shuk, among others. Reaching the upper Russian River in Northern Pomo territory, Lyon sought "a tribe whose chief is called Chapo; but finding the rancheria deserted," he followed the river downstream for twenty-two miles.[68]

Early on the morning of May 19, on an island formed by a Russian River slough, Lyon found "the Yohaiyaks," or Yokaya, a Central Pomo group at Cokadjal. Located "about four miles and a half south-southeast of Ukiah," Cokadjal was, according to Barrett, "the largest of the Yokaia villages and the largest village in the southern part of Ukiah valley." Lyon deemed Cokadjal yet another criminal population. He believed that "Preesta [Prieta?] and his tribe, the most active participants in the [Stone and Kelsey] murders," were there during those early morning hours.[69]

When Lyon's men attacked, the Yokaya of Cokadjal seem to have been surprised. A large military expedition had suddenly appeared on the edge of their village and Benson gathered that "The indians wanted to surrender, but the solders did not give them time, the solders went in the camp and shoot them down as tho if they were dogs." General Smith had, of course, instructed Lyon not to negotiate.[70]

Once under attack, Yokaya people fought desperately to protect themselves and their families, their resolve possibly strengthened by knowledge of what had happened four days earlier on Bloody Island. Whatever their motives, they defended themselves "with great resolution and vigor," according to Lyon. Smith reported—based on information from officers who participated in the attack— that the Yokaya conducted "a spirited defense." If Shuk was there, he had no interest in describing Cokadjal as an army victory against an equal or superior foe. As Chief Augustine, he offered a more qualified assessment: "The Indians fought well considering their arms." Still, the army's overwhelming firepower, which presumably included at least one howitzer, rapidly transformed Cokadjal into another killing field.[71]

According to Barrett, "The superior arms of the soldiers gave them such an advantage that they soon had the village at their mercy and killed many of the Indians." Lyon himself was not proud of the assault. He explained, "Their position being entirely surrounded, they were attacked under most embarrassing circumstances; but as they could not escape, the island soon became a perfect slaughter pen." According to Benson, the soldiers "killed mostly women and children." Benson also retold accounts he heard from survivors:

> One old man said that he was a boy at the time he said the soldiers shoot his mother, she fell to the ground with her baby in her arms, he said his mother told him to climb high up in the tree, so he did and from there he said he could see the solders running about the camp and shooting the men and women and stabing the boys and girls. he said mother was not yet dead and was telling him to keep quit. two of the solders heard her talking and ran up to her and stabed her and child.[72]

As at Bloody Island, Lyon's troops were relentless in their search for victims.

Some Yokaya people did manage to escape the carnage. According to Benson, "Som of them escaped by going down a little creek leading to the river. and som of them hed in the brush. and those who hed in the brush most of them were killed. and those who hed in the water was over looked." In 1982, Salome Alcantara of Yokayo Rancheria explained how her grandmother—presumably a child in 1850—escaped, first by crawling under a thick growth of wild grapevines as the soldiers searched for survivors, then holding onto her aunt's neck and swimming downriver to hide under more "grapevines on the bank." Others were less fortunate. "Salome's great grandmother on her mother's side was shot."[73]

The Yokaya Pomo men who defended Cokadjal
from Lyon's assault may or may not have had time
to don armor like this, but they did fight back until
Lyon's men, with their superior firepower,
overwhelmed them. J.W. Hudson, "Yokeya Warrior
with armor," photograph, before 1903. Courtesy of
the National Anthropological Archives,
Smithsonian Institution, OPPS NEG T11797.

As at Bloody Island, the number of people killed at Cokadjal proved difficult
for Lyon's troops to determine. There were "many trees, both dead and alive, in
a horizontal position, interwoven with a heavy growth of vines," as well as watery
surroundings, into which bodies may have disappeared. Pomo sources reported
between 75 and more than 100 killed. Lyon reported: "Their number killed I
confidently report at not less than seventy-five, and have little doubt it extended
to nearly double that number." It was another one-sided atrocity: just two of
Lyon's men were wounded.[74]

After Cokadjal, Lyon divided his force in two to pursue yet more Indians supposedly connected with the Stone and Kelsey killings: "A body of Indians
supposed to have been concerned in the outrages at Kelley's [Kelsey's] rancho,
and who it was believed were harboring one of the tribes known to have been
concerned with the Kelley murder, lay about ten miles below; and in order that
action might promptly be taken against them . . . I detached Lieutenant Davidson with his (dragoon) company [with Stoneman], to proceed hastily to . . .
Fernando Feliz, upon whose land these Indians lived." Lyon did not report
another massacre, but specified: "On arriving at Fernando Feliz's rancho [David-
son] found the Indians had fled through fear" and "The intelligence that the
hostile tribe was harbored by them proved unfounded." Yet, Davidson's men did
kill Indians on and possibly also just north of the ranch. In 1980, Alice Elliot of
the Hopland Band of Pomo Indians explained that most of the Central Pomos
of Shanel, a village on Feliz's Ranch, "ran up and hid on Duncan's Peak" after
"a Spanish man . . . told them that soldiers were going to kill them." Still, "Soldiers
killed few who stayed and burned village."[75]

Lyon's report may also have omitted an additional massacre, carried out by
Davidson's detached force, just north of Feliz's 15,000-acre ranch. Leaving San
Francisco on May 6, 1850, Herman Altschule and several fellow prospectors
headed north and traveled up the Russian River. Several hours' ride north of
Feliz's Ranch, Altschule came upon a strange sight. From a hilltop he saw "blaz-
ing fires, and marching down the valley towards us were two files of dragoons
and infantry. A fight had indeed occurred, and the rancheria of the Indians was
in flames." Altschule then "met the army, composed of forty dragoons and sixty
infantry, under the command of Lieutenant Davidson." According to Altschule,
"The story of the fight—or more properly slaughter—was briefly given as follows:
The Indians had taken refuge in a few acres of timber and brush in a bend on the
river, and shouted defiance. The dragoons then fired the brush woods through
and through, when the infantry entered and picked off every Indian that could
be found. Then the rancheria was set on fire, and the soldiers boasted that the
tribe was exterminated."[76]

Altschule and his companions "were not allowed to visit the battlefield." The
soldiers kept the grisly evidence off-limits while survivors cremated the bodies,
in keeping with Pomo tradition. Like many of history's mass murderers, these
soldiers seem to have understood that bystanders are more willing to accept
extermination as an abstract concept than as large numbers of visible corpses.
They may also have wished to cover up the killing of friendly Indians, and
Altschule now rode back to Feliz's Ranch with them. Still, they could not silence

grieving Central Pomo people there: "At nightfall the weird wail of mourning went up from the wigwams along the river" and "it was late when the wailing ceased."[77]

Despite the "wail of mourning," not all of Altschule's companions sympathized with the victims. In keeping with the spreading philosophy of pedagogic violence against California Indians, one of Altschule's companions approved of the massacre: "The Indians, he said, had been taught a wholesome lesson which would have a lasting effect, and we could now go ahead with safety."[78]

Two days later, Altschule and his companions did visit "the battlefield," a short ride from their camp on the ranch. They "found that the entire rancheria had been burned to the ground. The charred corpses of several Indians lay among the smoking ruins. Evidences of a conflict were visible in the brush by the river brink." There was little else to see. Altschule concluded his recollection with a haunting image: "All the Indians had not been killed however, for we discovered one lonely survivor feeding with sticks his evening fire in the timber, and left him to his labor and his mourning."[79]

Still, the expeditions' commanding officers were unconvinced that they had yet done enough to "teach" the Pomo people. Years later an elderly man told Benson that after Cokadjal, "he and another boy about the same age was taken [captive] by the soldurs." The boys were repeatedly impaled and when their feet began bleeding, a soldier took a handful of salt and "rubed it in the cuts on the bottom of their feet" and "in the wounds on their seats and backs wher they jabed them with the solders big knife." According to Benson's informant, "The tears were rolling down his cheeks" and as he and the other boy "roled and twested for about two hours . . . all the solders came and stood around them laughing." Then "two or three days later the chif solder [Lyon?] told them" that they were free to go. The officer apparently wanted other Pomos to know that soldiers would not only kill but also torture children in retaliation for the killing of whites. Thus, he gave the two boys bread and meat upon releasing them. After binding their feet, the two finally reached their village. Benson's informant told him that once he reached home, "He said to himself. hear Iam not to see my mother and sister but to see thir blood scattered over the ground like water and thir bodys for coyotes to devour. he said he sat down under a tree and cryed all day."[80]

Meanwhile, having reunited with Davidson, "Captain Lyons and his men continued their march southward, but news of what had happened preceded them and few of the Indians remained in their villages." Lyon and Davidson then parted ways again. Lyon marched his men northeast, following General Smith's orders, on a new expedition against Indians—presumably Modocs and

Northern Paiutes—in "the Goose lake country" of northeasternmost California. Once there, infantry and dragoons under his command shot at least fifteen Indian people. Davidson rode south to Benicia, via Sonoma. Although most Pomos fled, "Nevertheless, [Pomo?] informants say, the soldiers killed many more Indians as they journeyed on toward Sonoma."[81]

MEDIA, COURTS, CONGRESS, AND THE ARMY RESPOND

San Francisco newspapers quickly disseminated news of the Napa and Sonoma vigilante killings, but Lyon's campaign found an even broader audience. California newspapers covered the operation, reports from Lyon and Smith reached US Army Headquarters in July, and in December the US Senate published these reports, as well as military correspondence associated with the operation. Although spectacularly bloody and the source of numerous newspaper articles, the vigilante and army campaigns attracted surprisingly little criticism. Instead, they were the subject of temporizing, silent condoning, and open adulation.[82]

California Supreme Court justices effectively condoned the vigilantes' killings. During the early years of the gold rush California was a violent place, and the criminal justice system was weak. In these years, as Bancroft observed, "Grand juries were extremely negligent in bringing evil-doers to trial, frequently ignoring assaults with intent to kill, and manslaughter." As a result, "Men of criminal reputation often went free for years, committing numerous crimes against life without being punished." Was this why California courts never tried Anderson, Graham, Kelly, Lewis, Prigmore, Smith, and the two Kelseys? No. Their crimes extended far beyond "assaults with intent to kill" or "manslaughter." Their own neighbors and a local mayor arrested them for repeated multiple homicides. Their release on bail, given the gravity of the charges, indicated how lightly California Supreme Court justices took Indian killing. It is almost impossible to imagine the justices releasing, on bail, eight men accused of killing dozens of white civilians—including women and children—in 1850. More important, the court's failure to prosecute the accused amounted to a grant of judicial impunity for large-scale California Indian killing by vigilantes. This message, conveyed by newspaper reportage, was not likely lost on Californians. California newspapers, US senators, and the US Army granted similar impunity to Brevet Major General Smith, Brevet Captain Lyon, and First Lieutenant Davidson for the subsequent Bloody Island and Cokadjal massacres.[83]

Northern California newspaper reportage on Lyon's campaign ranged from condemnation to guarded support, but over time even the most assertive critics retreated. The public thus came to know about the massacres, but came to understand—through both perpetrator impunity and a shoddy cover-up—that killing California Indians was not a crime that would be punished or even thoroughly condemned.

The *Daily Alta California* quickly moved from condemnation to cowed reticence. As early as May 27, the paper reported on Lyon's campaign: "Captain C.C. Catlett . . . stated . . . that a Lieutenant of Dragoons [Davidson] had just returned to Benicia, bringing reports of two engagements between the Indians and our troops. It appears that a company of infantry, and another of dragoons, had left Sonoma and overtaken and fought the Indians at Clear Lake [Bloody Island], and again on Russian River [Cokadjal]. Two of the troops were badly wounded, and from 180 to 300 Indians killed." The next day, the paper published its account of the Bloody Island Massacre and *"extermination,"* as told by Frisbie. Later, the denials issued by Davidson and Smith, as well as Frisbie's retraction, apparently pressured the *Daily Alta California* into retreat. On June 8, the paper printed what amounted to a retraction of its own: "We are just as anxious as any one else to hold Captain John B. Frisbie responsible as he has been the means of causing us to do injustice to General Smith and the officers of the expedition." Other newspapers, such as the *Stockton Times*, joined in downplaying the "rumored massacre of the Clear Lake Indians." Like the *Daily Alta California*, the *Stockton Times* cited the *San Francisco Herald's* defensive May 31 article, which had claimed, "The statement that women and children were massacred, is wholly unfounded," and even argued in purported contradiction: "Some of the squaws were drowned in attempting to swim away, and it is said that some of the children were put to death by their own mothers."[84]

While the *Daily Alta California* and *Stockton Times* backpedaled, San Francisco's *Watchman*—a Christian periodical—temporized. In a June article titled "Indian Difficulties," the paper wrung its hands over Lyon's expedition: "Under the most plainly justifiable circumstances, such fearful destruction of human life as that which recently occurred in the case of the Clear Lake and Russian River Indians, cannot be thought of without a shudder of horror. If a deserved retribution, surely it cannot but be regarded as a most deplorable retribution." The paper admitted, "The order to *exterminate* the tribe appears to have been given to the expedition," but the author refused to openly criticize Lyon, his men, or their superiors. The writer came closest to open condemnation only when arguing: "We cannot for one moment entertain the thought that [all] Indians of California . . . *must be* at once and entirely *exterminated*." Immediate and total physical annihilation was now a topic of public discussion, in part as a result of the exterminatory campaign ordered by General Smith.[85]

As we have seen, the *San Francisco Herald* defended Lyon. On May 31, 1850, the paper also inaccurately described the "rumored massacre of the Clear Lake Indians" as a battle in which "many of the soldiers were seriously wounded." The *Herald* argued that Lyon had righteously followed orders to "punish and dislodge the Indians" and that whatever civilian deaths took place during the attack were deserved. The *Herald's* story then became the definitive national interpretation reprinted in the New Orleans *Daily Picayune*, the *New York Herald*, and the Washington, DC, *Daily National Intelligencer*, with the endorsement that other accounts had "entirely misrepresented" the Clear Lake violence. In July, the *New York Herald*—the most widely read US newspaper in 1850 with a circulation of some 90,000—also reprinted an article reporting "from 160 to 300 Indians" killed "at Clear Lake and again on Russian River." The *New York Herald's* death toll estimates, printed side by side with the *San Francisco Herald's* laudatory interpretation, communicated a deeper message to the nation: massacring American Indians was acceptable, so long as perpetrators provided excuses.[86]

Celebrating the massacre of American Indians as a justifiable military necessity, and as battles rather than atrocities, was hardly new in the United States or in its colonial antecedents. In 1637, colonial church and government leaders celebrated the Mystic Massacre of Pequot Indians, rationalizing it as both necessary and laudable. Massachusetts Colony governor John Winthrop wrote in his journal, "There was a day of thanksgiving kept in all the churches for the victory obtained against the Pequods." William Bradford, Plymouth Colony governor at the time, wrote that while "it was a fearfull sight to see them thus frying in yᵉ fyer, and yᵉ streams of blood quenching yᵉ same, and horrible was yᵉ stinck & sente ther of; but yᵉ victory seemed a sweete sacrifice, and they gave the prays therof to God, who had wrought so wonderfuly for them." Such praise for the massacre of Indians, often supported by justifications and camouflaged with martial rhetoric, continued in California and beyond. Following the 1890 massacre of 260–300 Hunkpapa and Miniconjou people by members of the 7th Cavalry at Wounded Knee, the US government awarded twenty of these cavalrymen the country's highest military award: the Congressional Medal of Honor.[87]

Whether newspapers censured or celebrated Lyon's campaign, they circulated information on both the operation and the massacre tactics used while publicizing the fact that none of the officers involved were censured or punished. In conjunction, this reportage can only have helped erode cultural barriers to further violence against California Indians, both among those in California and those who would soon move there from elsewhere in the United States. If army officers could massacre Indians with impunity, could vigilante groups and individuals not do the same?

US senators seem to have been even less divided and more adulatory than California journalists. According to Lyon's twentieth-century biographer, "Lyon's official report of the expedition was heard in the US Senate, where both its explicit detail and the officer's meritorious service to his country against an obviously dangerous and subversive Indian 'menace' were met with warm approbation."[88]

Army officers, too, rallied around Lyon and his operation. According to General Smith, Lyon's fellow expedition officers "all unite in awarding to [Brevet] Captain Lyon the highest praise for his untiring energy, his zeal and skill, and attribute his success to the rapidity and secrecy of his marches, and skilful disposition on the ground." Smith's report of May 25, 1850, to US Army Headquarters enthused: "I cannot let the mail go off without communicating . . . my highest praise of [Brevet] Captain Lyon's conduct, and that of the officers and men under him." To underline why he awarded Lyon his "highest praise," Smith concluded: "The officers here think that two hundred Indians, at least, were killed in the two affairs." Smith assumed that fellow generals at army headquarters would agree that killing hundreds of Indians, in retaliation for the murder of two whites, deserved "the highest praise." His assumption proved accurate.[89]

The army did not court-martial General Smith. Nor was he censured. In October 1851, headquarters selected Smith to command the Department of Texas and to prosecute the army's expanding operations against the Comanches and other American Indian peoples there. In Texas he told his officers: "All predatory Indians, no matter where discovered, will be pursued, attacked, and put to death. It is not advisable to take prisoners." In 1856, headquarters awarded him command "of the Department of the West," comprising the region west of the Mississippi River and east of the Rocky Mountains, excluding the departments of Texas and New Mexico. On December 30, 1856, Smith received promotion to the rank of full brigadier general.[90]

Lieutenant Davidson, who co-planned the Clear Lake campaign and led its dragoons, likewise rose steadily through the ranks. On January 20, 1855, Davidson received promotion to captain, in 1861 he became a major, in 1865 a Civil War brevet major general, and in 1879 a full colonel in the regular, postwar US Army. He is buried in Arlington National Cemetery.[91]

Second Lieutenant George Stoneman followed an even more meteoric professional trajectory. Like Davidson, Stoneman obtained promotion to the rank of captain in 1855. In 1862, he became a Civil War major general of volunteers and in 1870, he assumed command of the Department of Arizona. He retired as a full major general. Stoneman then settled in Southern California, and in 1882 voters elected him governor of California by a landslide.[92]

As field commander of the Clear Lake campaign, however, Nathaniel Lyon enjoyed the most direct and immediate rewards for his participation. On July 9, 1850, army headquarters received his campaign report, detailing the Bloody Island and Cokadjal massacres. Eleven months later, he received the rank of captain. In July 1852, President Millard Fillmore and Secretary of War Charles Magill Conrad signed the promotion, "By and with the advice and consent of the Senate." According to Lyon's twentieth-century biographer, the promotion came "primarily as a result of his decisive actions with the Indians in northern California." Lyon was a brigadier general of volunteers when he was killed at the Civil War Battle of Wilson's Creek, Missouri, in 1861.[93]

Even in death, Lyon's name continued to be associated with the slaughter of American Indian civilians. Beginning at dawn on November 19, 1864, Colorado and New Mexico volunteers surrounded and methodically massacred at least 150 mostly unarmed and peaceful Cheyenne and Arapaho men, women, and children, at a place called Sand Creek, Colorado. The assembled Cheyenne and Arapaho people believed themselves safe. They were cooperating with the local soldiers garrisoned at nearby Fort Lyon.[94]

The vigilante and US Army campaigns that followed the slaying of Stone and Kelsey dwarfed the relatively isolated murders and massacres that had characterized the killing of Indians during the first three years of US rule in California, from 1846 to 1849. An important new factor was at work. The period between late December 1849 and the end of May 1850 might have comprised just another, albeit larger, series of killing operations, but for the policy- and opinion makers in the California media, the state Supreme Court, US Army Headquarters, and the US Senate, who effectively condoned the campaigns. By failing to prosecute or condemn the perpetrators, newspaper editors, judges, generals, and US senators effectively approved the large-scale killing of California Indians. Thus began a new, much more violent era in California history: an era of protracted genocidal campaigns that targeted large numbers of Indian civilians in so-called punitive assaults.

The killing campaigns of December 1849 to May 1850 marked three major changes in relations between Anglo-Americans and California Indians. First, the two vigilante operations that rampaged through Napa and Sonoma counties were the first large, organized, widespread campaigns against the still-prevalent Mexican practice of employing California Indians as agricultural laborers. The

This hagiographic depiction of Lyon's charge at the 1861
Civil War Battle of Wilson's Creek may have resembled,
in some ways, his infamous 1850 attack on Bloody Island.
Here he leaps over a fallen Confederate soldier on the cover
of a "Journal of Civilization." Unknown artist, "General
Lyon at the Battle of Springfield [Wilson's Creek],"
Harper's Weekly Journal of Civilization, August 31, 1861, 1.
Courtesy of General Collection, Beinecke Rare Book
and Manuscript Library, Yale University.

vigilantes sought to destroy California's old agricultural system—which was
built upon California Indian workers—and seriously eroded that institution in
the Sonoma and Napa valleys as well as in the Santa Rosa region. Second, and
more important, by releasing eight of these vigilantes on bail and then failing

to prosecute them, California's new Supreme Court undid law enforcement efforts and initiated a policy of granting effective impunity to those who killed California Indians, further weakening accommodation and cooperation while removing legal restraints to mass killing.

Third, and most important, the army's May 1850 Clear Lake operation was the first extended, large-scale military campaign against California Indians aimed at inflicting mass deaths, and arguably extermination, a goal reported by multiple sources. Both the US Army and the US Senate tacitly approved this campaign, ex post facto, thus demonstrating the support of many federal policymakers for large-scale, indiscriminate killing in response to isolated California Indian crimes. In combination with widespread media coverage, federal leaders' acquiescence in these army massacres helped to unleash later large-scale vigilante and state militia killing campaigns by further eroding cultural and legal barriers to the killing of California Indians. This helped to normalize mass murder. Federal leaders' acceptance of these massacres also established a pattern of indirect congressional and federal agency support for the killing of California Indians, which would become more direct—in the form of massive material and financial support—in the coming years.[95]

The mass killings of the last month of 1849 and the first five months of 1850 ignited an inferno of anti-California Indian violence that would last until 1873, and beyond. These six months, culminating in Lyon's massacre campaign, mark a turning point in California history. On May 29, 1850, the *Daily Alta California* editor warned, based on recent events, that if relations between whites and California Indians degenerated into an "open collision—here will then be *safety* only in a war of *extermination*, waged with relentless fury far and near." It was the first time that a California newspaper had suggested the possible necessity of a widespread genocide. The editor then argued that this "war of *extermination*" was unavoidable, but in keeping with past killing campaigns: "Such is the destiny of that miserable race, and . . . we are but fulfilling our own by the enactment of scenes on the Pacific similar to those which have stained with blood our Indian history on the shores of the Atlantic, from the first dawnings of civilization." It was a grim view apparently shared by many. Acting on this growing consensus, legislators in California and Washington, DC, added fuel to the flames.[96]

5

LEGISLATING EXCLUSION AND VULNERABILITY:
1846–1853

Either a brilliant destiny awaits California, or one the most sordid and degraded. . . .
Much will depend upon her early legislation.

— *Governor Peter H. Burnett, 1849*

They were totally deprived of land rights. They were outlawed and all treated as wild
animals . . . murdered . . . enslaved and worked to death . . . driven back to totally
barren vastness . . . and they died of starvation. Their life was outlawed and their
whole existence was condemned . . . and they died.

— *US Indian Affairs commissioner John Collier, 1935*

Soon after the Stars and Stripes began cracking in the Pacific breeze over the
seaside village of Monterey, the US Army and Navy officers governing California faced a choice. They could continue Mexico's policies toward California
Indians or chart a new course. Like other recent arrivals, these officers quickly
realized that California's cattle, grain, and grape economy depended on Indian
laborers, many of whom toiled as unfree workers, despite Mexico's having
banned slavery in 1829. To avoid disrupting this economy, which might have
risked pushing thousands of Californios into revolt, the officers administrating
California sought to maintain existing labor relations. This was a choice driven
by economic and political calculus as well as notions of American Indian racial
inferiority, which allowed the denial of civil rights to California Indians. Yet
because slavery in US territories was a vexed question that increasingly polar-
ized the nation, the officers sought to maintain existing systems of Indian servitude without overtly legalizing slavery.[1]

Thus began a protracted process by which military and civilian lawmakers, law enforcement officials, and judges stripped California Indians of legal power and rights, excluded them from colonial society, deprived them of their land, denied them protection, legalized their exploitation as both de jure and de facto unfree laborers, and ultimately all but erased legal and cultural barriers to their abuse and murder. The result was an ever-narrowing space in which California Indians could peacefully coexist with whites and an ever-widening scope for exploiting and killing California Indians under the laws of California and the United States. Legal exclusion was a crucial enabler of mass violence, and the process began just months after the United States invaded California.

MARTIAL LAW, 1846–1849

On September 15, 1846, the commandant of the Northern Department of California, navy captain John B. Montgomery, issued the United States' first official California Indian policy. In a public decree, he began by acknowledging the existence of unfree Indian labor in California: "Persons have been and still are impressing and holding to service, Indians against their will, without any legal contract, and without due regard to their rights as freemen." He then called for the continuation of existing labor relationships between Indians and non-Indians under new rules: "All [p]ersons so holding or detaining Indians, shall release them, and permit them to return to their own homes, unless they can make a legal contract with them, which shall be acknowledged before the nearest Justice of the Peace." Montgomery continued, "The Indian population must not be looked upon in the light of slaves, but it is deemed necessary that the Indians within the settlements, shall have employment with the right of choosing their own master or employer."[2]

Under Montgomery's proclamation, California Indians could select an employer, but were then legally required to continue working for the "master or employer" until the master, employer, or a justice released them. Montgomery thus legalized indenture without term limitation and institutionalized the holding and working of Indians indefinitely. To ensure a dependable Indian labor supply—then California's economic backbone—Montgomery made escape difficult and participation mandatory. His proclamation defined unemployed Indians "within the settlements" as vagrants: "All Indians must be required to obtain employment and not permitted to wander about in an idle and dissolute manner, if found so doing, they will be liable to arrest and punishment, by labor on the public works, at the discretion of the Magistrate." Montgomery enlisted both the armed forces and civil bureaucracy to enforce this state-sponsored unfree Indian labor system: "All officers, civil or military, under my command, are required to execute this order, and take notice of every violation thereof." Montgomery made Indians either captive laborers or outlaws, thereby criminalizing Indian freedom.[3]

Four months later, Monterey officials announced a municipal version of Montgomery's edict. On January 11, 1847, magistrate Walter Colton and the town council stipulated: "That no person whatever shall . . . hire or take into his service any Indian without a certificate from the former employer of that Indian stating that the said employer has no claims on the services of that Indian for wages advanced." Possibly borrowing from the contemporaneous Southern slave pass system or Mexican California's 1836 Indian pass program, Monterey's government apparently formulated their certificate system to diminish conflicts between non-Indians over control of Indian workers and to limit Indians' freedom of employment. By claiming that an Indian owed them labor "for wages advanced," unscrupulous employers could retain physical control over them indefinitely. The ordinance thus allowed non-Indians to force Indians into the legal position and lived reality of debt peonage. This was hardly new in California. Still, without the all-important certificate, an Indian could not legally be employed elsewhere. To encourage compliance, Colton and the council stipulated fines of $5 to $20 for employers who violated the ordinance.[4]

San Francisco magistrate Washington A. Bartlett then announced that his town would also enforce Indian labor laws. On February 20 and March 6, Bartlett republished Montgomery's proclamation in the *California Star*, San Francisco's new paper. The proclamation placed San Francisco Indians under tighter control, but failed to stop de facto Indian chattel slavery. That August, a journalist reported on thirty-four Indians there, "mostly employed as servants and porters," noting, "Some of the Indians are considered by persons having them as their property, and I am told, though I have never known of such a case, there have been instances of the sale and transfer of them from one person to another."[5]

In November 1847, California's military rulers tightened control over California Indians within and beyond the colonial labor system. With probably not more than 1,500 soldiers to cover 155,779 square miles, they sought to supplement their limited troop strength by engaging civilians in the control of Indians. To this end, California's secretary of state under martial law, West Point–trained lieutenant Henry W. Halleck, instituted a statewide Indian pass system that inaugurated a new California Indian policy. Halleck, who later became President Abraham Lincoln's Civil War general in chief, began publicizing the system, both in English and Spanish, in September 1847. He put it into effect on November 1.

Unlike prior regional and municipal proclamations issued under martial law, Halleck's pass system sought to control California Indian laborers and to help colonists and authorities differentiate between Indians employed by non-Indians and Indians not enmeshed in the colonial economy whom he automatically defined as either runaway laborers or "thieves and marauders." The pass system criminalized all Indians not employed by non-Indians as well as any Indians employed by non-Indians who left their employers without written permission: "Any Indian found beyond the limits of the town or rancho in which he may be employed, without such certificate or pass, will be liable to arrest as a horse thief." Without the all-important pass, Indians could be arrested, tried, and punished as stock rustlers, then the bane of California ranchers.[6]

By officially requiring "any Indian" to obtain a pass from an employer, Halleck legalized and intensified Hispano-American systems of California Indian servitude, making all Indians within the colonial economic matrix legally bound laborers who could not freely change employers without becoming criminals. Halleck's pass system also placed new controls on Indians' movement: "Wild Indians, and other Indians not employed as above, wishing to visit settlements or towns for the purpose of trade, must have a passport from the Sub-Indian Agent of their district." To enforce these new restrictions on Indian employment and movement, Halleck proclaimed: "All Indian Agents, and civil Magistrates will use their best endeavors to have it carried into effect, and to bring to trial and punishment all persons who may act in violation of its provisions." Like the contemporaneous slave pass system in the antebellum South and the 1836 California Indian pass program from which he may have borrowed, Halleck's ambitious new policy sought to control Indians and their movements while making it easier to identify, capture, and punish those who were not part of the system or who were in violation of its draconian rules.[7]

Halleck's pass system legally segregated California Indians and the results were fourfold. The passes dehumanized California Indians, profoundly weakened the military's proclamations banning Indian slavery, severely limited Indians' freedom of movement, and made it easier for non-Indians to distinguish which Indians they could kidnap or kill without offending municipal and federal authorities. Ultimately, Halleck's pass system made captive laborers of Indians working for non-Indians, while potentially criminalizing those tens of thousands who were still free. Nevertheless, this legal perpetuation and intensification of Hispanic policies toward California Indians would not necessarily define California Indians' future under civilian US rule.

Less than two years after Halleck's pass system became law, California's military governor began preparing to hand government over to civilians elected by

California's rapidly growing non-Indian population. On June 3, 1849, Governor and Brevet Brigadier General Bennett Riley issued a proclamation "Recommending the formation of a State Constitution, or a plan of a Territorial Government," calling a special election so that US citizens in California, and Baja Californians who had come to help the United States in its war with Mexico, could elect regional delegates for a constitutional convention. This provided another opportunity for the radical reinvention of California Indian policies. Three months later, delegates to California's Constitutional Convention began arriving in Monterey, and their discussions soon turned to the legal status of Indians in the future state of California.[8]

THE CONSTITUTIONAL CONVENTION, 1849

On the morning of September 1, 1849, delegates began passing between the tall white columns framing the entrance to Colton Hall, an imposing two-story sandstone schoolhouse still standing in Monterey. Juxtaposing a red-tile roof with neoclassical columns, candelabras, and New England–style fittings, the 4,200-square-foot building elegantly merged Hispanic and Anglo-American architectural traditions. Over the coming weeks, however, Colton Hall would become a battleground between the Hispanic tradition of assimilating and exploiting Indians and the Anglo-American tradition of excluding them. The outcome of these contentious debates would prove crucial to determining the future of California's Indian policies.[9]

Climbing Colton Hall's stairs, the forty-eight delegates reached the second floor and entered a spacious room with fireplaces at either end. They seated themselves at four long wooden tables, and on September 4 elected Dr. Robert Semple of Sonoma as their convention president. The imposing Kentuckian, six feet eight inches tall, then ascended the speaker's platform, over which hung two US flags and a portrait of George Washington. The flags and the painting implied that this would be an Anglo-American-style constitution, and that delegates would continue the US tradition of excluding Indians by writing anti-Indian laws into the document. Yet, multiple factors mitigated against such an outcome. The delegates were mostly young—their average age was under thirty-seven—and hence potentially open-minded. They were also heterogeneous: a dozen were foreign born and thus not necessarily inculcated with Anglo-American beliefs and practices regarding Indians. Finally, some employed Indians, were married to them, or had Indian blood in their own veins— particularly the six Californio delegates—and these men were likely to protect their own political rights, those of their heirs, and perhaps those of their

Within these walls, California's 1849 constitutional convention delegates vigorously
debated whether or not to enfranchise some or all California Indians. The outcome
shaped California's history in the years to come. Unknown artist, "Capitol at
Monterey—1849 [Colton Hall]," in *Pioneer* (December 1899): 145. Courtesy
of The Bancroft Library, University of California, Berkeley.

employees. However, on September 8, when delegates first touched on Indian
enfranchisement, Semple insisted: "Particular classes must necessarily be deprived of the right of suffrage." It was a portentous beginning.[10]

Once again, the future of tens of thousands of California Indians hung in the
balance. Convention delegates could either continue the military's policies or
chart a new course by granting California Indians political rights and freedoms.
Some pro-Indian delegates wanted to do just that. Others believed Indians had
to be granted rights in order for California's new constitution to be accepted by
Congress. Still others held deeply anti-Indian views, saw Indians as a threat to
democracy, and sought to push some or all Indians out of California's political
and social system. The stage was set for contentious deliberations.

On the morning of September 12, the first of three debates over California
Indian voting rights began in earnest. Delegates considered suffrage for nonwhites and soon divided into two camps. The first to speak out against was lawyer
and magazine editor Charles T. Botts, representing the Monterey district. Botts
articulated the racism of his faction, stating that he "would be perfectly willing
to . . . exclude the African and Indian races." Delegates next explored the suf-

frage question as it bore on compliance with the Treaty of Guadalupe Hidalgo. The 1848 treaty, which ended the Mexican-American War, ceded present-day California, Nevada, and Utah to the United States as well as parts of what are now Arizona, Colorado, New Mexico, and Wyoming. It stipulated that all Mexican citizens in California—including Indians, who were technically Mexican citizens—would be eligible to become US citizens. Such people were to be "incorporated into the Union of the United States and be admitted, at the proper time (to be judged of by the Congress of the United States) to the enjoyment of all the rights of citizens of the United States." The treaty thus specified that Congress could choose when to admit such Mexicans to full citizenship, but some delegates considered quick compliance crucial. For if California's new constitution did not comply with a treaty recently ratified by the Senate, Congress might reject the new constitution and with it California's bid for statehood. Because taking the wrong course might jeopardize statehood, delegates questioned each other about Indian citizenship under Mexican law, to determine how to comply with the treaty.[11]

The delegates quickly agreed that Indians were Mexican citizens, per the 1824 Mexican Constitution. However, Yale-educated Stephen Foster of Los Angeles pointed out that "very few of the Indian race were admitted to the right of suffrage" in Mexico as "they are restricted by some property qualification, or by occupation or mode of livelihood." Indeed, the 1836 Mexican Constitution limited the franchise to people with an income of at least 1,000 pesos and the 1842 *Bases Organicas* (Mexico's new constitution) required each voter to have an income of at least 200 pesos. Presumably referring to these laws, Foster introduced the idea that California's constitution could comply with the Treaty of Guadalupe Hidalgo while only granting some form of restricted franchise to Indians, not based on the treaty but on Mexican voting laws.[12]

Other delegates objected to enfranchising any Indians. Sacramento delegate Lansford W. Hastings began by raising the specter of whites manipulating large numbers of California Indian voters: "There are gentlemen who are very popular among the wild Indians, who could march hundreds of them to the polls." Hastings also objected to enfranchising Indians who were not enmeshed in the colonial economy, using that issue as a means to disenfranchise those who were: "An Indian in the mountains is just as much entitled to vote as anybody, if Indians are entitled to vote." Convention chairman Kimball Dimmick, representing San Jose, generally agreed, stating that "he would be very unwilling to see the Indians of this country brought to the polls to vote in our elections." Nevertheless, Dimmick suggested that "where there was here and there a good Indian, capable of understanding our system of government, he had no objection to making such provision as would entitle him to vote." William Gwin, a former Mississippi congressman who would soon become one of California's first two US senators, then insisted: "The pure uncivilized Indians should not be permitted to vote." Representing San Francisco, Gwin also echoed Hastings's concern that a few whites might control and direct many Indian votes. Like Hastings, the politically savvy Gwin invoked the menace of potentially corrupted democracy to rally support for excluding Indians from a democratic process.[13]

Building on the momentum of opposition to Indian enfranchisement while seeking to comply with the Treaty of Guadalupe Hidalgo, some delegates began to consider making Indians nonvoting California citizens. Botts pointed out that thousands of US citizens could not vote. Gwin supported Botts's argument and Dimmick added: "We are not necessarily compelled to make Indians citizens, entitled to the elective franchise, when many of our own citizens in the United States are not entitled to such privilege." The converse, that both should be granted voting rights, remained unmentioned.[14]

Amid this crucial discussion of California Indians' political place in the future state, the delegates broke for dinner, spilling out into Monterey's dusty streets. Passing through the adobe village, many probably headed to the only restaurant in town. At the Fonda de la Union, a smoky cantina run by a Mexican and his Indian cook, delegates dined on beef, cucumbers, corn, red pepper, potatoes, "and two or three cups of execrable coffee." Their bellies full and their minds likely intoxicated by drink, the delegates returned from the moonless streets to the lights of Colton Hall to reconvene at eight o'clock.[15]

Reinitiating the debate, the Kentuckian M.M. McCarver asserted that the Treaty of Guadalupe Hidalgo did not give Indian citizens the right to vote. The Marylander Jacob D. Hoppe then insisted: "The whole Indian race should be excluded from the elective franchise" and the Ohioan Oliver M. Wozencraft agreed. McCarver later added that he was against enfranchising even taxpaying Indians because "the privilege would be greatly abused." Like Hastings and Gwin, McCarver claimed that Indian voters would be manipulated and democracy perverted. It does not seem to have entered McCarver's mind that barring Indians from voting was perhaps not in keeping with his own democratic ideals.[16]

As the evening grew late, two young men advocated Indian enfranchisement. Louis Dent, a twenty-seven-year-old Monterey delegate from Missouri, reminded listeners that California Indians "were the original proprietors of the soil" and that "from them we derived it, and from them we derived many of the blessings which we now enjoy." He added, "They have already been deprived of their original independence," before asking, "Why should we pursue them, and drag them down to the level of slaves?" Dent concluded: "Indians should enjoy the right of suffrage." Just twenty-six, New Yorker Henry A. Tefft, a San Luis Obispo delegate, then cited precedents for Indian enfranchisement by pointing out that other states, including Wisconsin, had enfranchised Indians. He begged delegates to carefully consider the matter: Tefft "hoped this question would be considered calmly and dispassionately in all its bearings, and that gentlemen would not, by acting hastily, exclude all Indians, absolutely and entirely, from the right of suffrage." Tefft pointed out that many Californians were of mixed heritage, and also appealed to delegates' sense of justice ("Has not injustice enough already been visited upon the Indian race?"), their identification with the civilizing mission ("Shall we deprive them of the advantages of civilization? Shall we prohibit them from becoming civilized?"), their humanity ("Surely the prejudice against color does not extend so far!"), and, finally to delegates' sense of humility as relative newcomers to California ("This native population was better entitled to the right of suffrage than [I am], or a thousand others who came here but yesterday").[17]

After additional squabbling, the forty-one delegates present voted on whether or not to grant suffrage to all adult men except "citizen[s] of Mexico, Indians, Africans, and descendants of Africans." There were twenty "ayes" and twenty "noes." The delegates were deadlocked. To break the tie, Chairman Dimmick cast his "vote in the affirmative" and the convention adopted the amendment by a single vote. Indian suffrage advocates had been dealt a serious defeat, albeit by the slimmest of margins. Had all forty-eight delegates been present, the vote might have swung in favor of enfranchisement and California history might have unfolded quite differently. By a single vote, the delegates prohibited most Indians from voting, which largely excluded them from electing legislators and shaping California Indian policy. This single vote excluded most Indians from the political process. Had it gone differently, enfranchised Indians might have been in a position to stop their mass murder. Still, having come so close to victory, Indian enfranchisement advocates fought on, in an attempt to secure voting rights for at least some Indians.[18]

Seventeen days later, on the evening of September 29, the second California Indian enfranchisement debate began as Halleck suggested that not enfranchising Indians might conflict with the Treaty of Guadalupe Hidalgo. The Californio Pablo de la Guerra of Santa Barbara now eloquently addressed the assembly "through an interpreter." He highlighted California Indians' humanity, intelligence, economic utility, and social malleability while emphasizing the "very great importance" of suffrage and warning against excluding "all Indians." Finally, de la Guerra recommended "that those [Indians] who were holders of property and had heretofore exercised all the rights and privileges of freemen, might still be permitted to continue in the exercise of those rights." De la Guerra's arguments seem to have changed at least one man's position.[19]

Chairman Dimmick now proposed enfranchising taxpaying Indians. Halleck, keen on treaty compliance, quickly transformed Dimmick's idea into an amendment that Dent, Tefft, and twenty-seven-year-old Irish immigrant William E. Shannon of Sacramento supported. Opponents of Indian enfranchisement counterattacked. Hoppe of San Jose bluntly asked if anyone "was willing to place himself on a level with the Indian or the negro?" He then recycled and embellished the threat of Indian vote manipulation: "There was not a *rancho* where you would not find fifty or a hundred buck Indians, and the owner could run these *freemen* up to the polls, and carry any measure he might desire." McCarver opposed allowing propertied Indians to vote and Winfield Sherwood of Sacramento claimed that if Indian landowners were enfranchised, his fellow delegate "Captain Sutter . . . could, by simply granting a small portion of land to each Indian, control a vote of ten thousand." As historian Albert Hurtado observed, "Sherwood's claim bordered on hysteria." Nevertheless, "No one bothered to point out that creating ten thousand Indian freeholders by making donations of land would be a ruinously expensive way to cadge votes." De la Guerra countered, however, that "all the Indians in the entire Territory who owned land and were entitled to vote, under the laws of Mexico, were not more than two hundred."[20]

Delegates now voted on the question of enfranchising propertied Indians and, once again, the decision came down to one man. With five delegates absent and many of those present eager to leave—seventeen had voted to adjourn earlier that evening—opponents of Indian enfranchisement won by a single vote. The delegates largely split between Californios and long-term residents, on the yea side, and new arrivals in opposition. California history might have followed a different course had several of the absent delegates attended that night or had so many of the present delegates not been itching to leave Colton Hall. Indeed, the lives of tens of thousands of California Indians hung in the balance.[21]

Although J. Ross Browne's official record of the debate does not make this clear, the Indian suffrage battle almost blew the convention apart, nearly aborting the constitution and with it California's bid for statehood. Writing to his wife two days after the September 29 debate, Browne explained: "The question of the right of suffrage of Indians which occasioned so much trouble on Saturday, and which it was feared would end in the withdrawal of the Spanish delegation, and the consequent breaking up of the whole Convention, has just been decided to the satisfaction of all parties. My fears therefore on that subject

Manuel Dominguez owned a substantial Southern
California ranch and served in various official
capacities under Mexican rule. Bayard Taylor called him
the 1849 California Constitutional Convention's "Indian
member." Taylor, *Eldorado*, 1:107. Maria de los Reyes
Dominguez de Francis(?), "Don Manuel Dominguez,"
painting, undated. Courtesy of the Seaver Center for
Western History Research, Los Angeles County
Museum of Natural History.

are at an end. There is now no doubt but the Constitution will be adopted."
Browne's prediction proved only partly prescient. Some delegates—particularly
Californios—remained determined to include some form of Indian enfranchise-
ment in the constitution. As the convention observer Bayard Taylor recalled in
1850, "Many of the most wealthy and respectable families in California have
Indian blood in their veins, and even a member of the Convention, Manuel
Dominguez [representing Los Angeles], would be excluded from voting" under
the existing clause as he was the convention's "Indian member."[22]

Determined to obtain enfranchisement for at least some Indians, on October 3, de la Guerra proposed allowing "the Legislature," to admit "such Indians to the elective franchise as they may in future deem capable thereof." On October 4, after a brief discussion, Thomas Vermeule—who had voted against enfranchising propertied Indians four days earlier—effectively crippled de la Guerra's amendment. Vermeule proposed allowing state legislators to enfranchise only particular Indian individuals and then only if two-thirds of the legislature voted in favor. For those opposed to Indian enfranchisement, Vermeule's amendment was hardly a compromise given the cumbersome nature of individually approving each California Indian's right to vote and the difficulty of getting two-thirds of both houses of a future legislature to agree on something as obviously contentious as Indian enfranchisement. On the other side of the debate, Indian enfranchisement proponents may have sensed that, after two defeats, this was all they could hope to salvage. At least, it would keep open the possibility of voting for powerful Californians of Indian ancestry. Whatever their motives, both camps united to adopt Vermeule's amendment unanimously.[23]

When delegates gathered for the last time in Colton Hall, on the morning of October 13, 1849, to sign California's new constitution, "The windows and doors were open, and a delightful breeze came in from the bay, whose blue waters sparkled in the distance." The view "was bright and inspiring." Yet the constitution left the legal future of California's Indians uncertain. Article II specified that "nothing . . . shall be construed to prevent the Legislature, by a two-thirds concurrent vote, from admitting to the right of suffrage, Indians or the descendants of Indians, in such special cases as such a proportion of the legislative body may deem just and proper." The constitution did not ban all Indian voting outright, but it made the possibility remote at best, while overturning Mexican laws that had enfranchised some California Indians. As the *Daily Alta California* later asked, "To what does this magnanimity amount, except the sublimity of ridicule?"[24]

Realizing the contentious nature of Indian-related issues, the conventioneers made no other mention of Indians or their rights in the constitution. With the exception of enfranchisement, they avoided provisions on Indian citizenship and rights. Instead, they deferred these questions to a future legislature, in which ten of them would soon serve. By denying Indians the vote (at least until a California legislature came into being), California's 1849 constitution all but eliminated Indian political influence along with the possibility that elected state officials would either advocate for Indians' rights or spend state money on their needs. Excluding Indians from California's political process soon bore bitter fruit.[25]

NEW LAWS, NEW SYSTEMS OF SERVITUDE,
MARCH AND APRIL 1850

On November 13, 1849, California voters (Indians now excluded) approved the new constitution and elected representatives. On December 20, California established a civilian government and became self-governing. On September 9, 1850, Congress admitted California to the Union as the nation's thirty-first state. The transition to civilian rule, coupled with the new constitution's vague position on Indians, provided the new state legislators with yet another opportunity to refashion California Indian policies.[26]

State legislators largely decided the legal position of California Indians under state law during their first session in early 1850 at the new capital in San Jose. On December 21, 1849, California's first civilian governor under US rule, Peter H. Burnett, presciently predicted: "Either a brilliant destiny awaits California, or one the most sordid and degraded. She will be marked by strong and decided characteristics. Much will depend upon her early legislation." In the realm of Indian policy, few existing laws bound California's first elected state legislators. The constitution had made enfranchising Indians extremely difficult, but beyond that, the sixteen senators and thirty-six assemblymen had a free hand with regard to Indians. In 1850, it was not too late to remake California's Indian policies.[27]

State senator John Bidwell of Chico submitted a bill that would have done just that. On March 16, 1850, state senators heard "An Act in relation to the protection, punishment, and government of the Indians" in the new, two-story adobe legislative building. Bidwell's bill had eight major points. First, it divided California counties into Indian law-enforcement zones, each policed by a "Justice of the Peace for Indians" to be elected by voters, who would include adult "male Indians of the district." Second, it defined Indian crimes and penalties for each while allowing the "Justice of the Peace for Indians" to punish non-Indians who abused Indians. However, it prohibited the conviction of non-Indians on the basis of Indian testimony alone. Third, the "Justice of the Peace for Indians" could approve adoptions of Indian children by non-Indians with the in-person consent of Indian parents. Fourth, the "Justice of the Peace for Indians" would have to approve any labor contracts between Indians and non-Indians. Fifth, Indians would be paid "two good suits of clothes" when their contract expired. Sixth, the bill imposed fines on those who forced Indians to work in the mines. Seventh, it guaranteed Indian freedom of movement. Eighth, it provided Indians with limited land rights and protected their access to food-gathering places. By proposing this bill, Bidwell, himself a major employer of Indians, likely hoped to forestall violence between California Indians and non-Indians while human-izing Indian policies. Unfortunately, it was far too progressive for most California legislators in 1850.[28]

One week after Bidwell introduced his bill, the legislature voted to limit en-franchisement to "white male" citizens, thereby barring even a limited number of Indians from voting. Bidwell's bill clearly granted more rights and protections to Indians than most California legislators would tolerate. In addition to out-lawing Indian voting, these men had elected John C. Frémont, the well-known killer of Indians, and William M. Gwin, an outspoken opponent of Indian enfran-chisement, to represent California in the US Senate just three months earlier. In keeping with their anti-Indian stance, the state senators let Bidwell's bill wither on the vine. Meanwhile, Assemblyman Elam Brown of the San Jose district began a high-speed legislative end-run around it.[29]

On April 13, Assemblyman Brown, who as a Constitutional Convention del-egate had voted against enfranchising propertied Indians, introduced what he euphemistically called "a Bill for the Government and Protection of Indians." The bill moved rapidly through both the Assembly and Senate. On April 21, the last day of the legislative session, Governor Burnett signed the infamous, ironi-cally titled "Act for the Government and Protection of Indians." The govern-ment of California had, in just nine days and with almost no deliberation, both banned Indian voting—which under both Mexican law and the 1849 constitu-tion had at least been a possibility—and passed an act that made Indians vul-nerable to violence and exploitation. First, the act made Indians criminals until proven innocent, counter to all of the stated ideals of the young American nation. Second, the act established a new de jure system of California Indian servitude. Finally, it legalized the corporal punishment of Indians.[30]

According to legal scholar David J. Langum, California "Indians within the settled areas were definitely protected by the [Mexican] legal system, and there are many cases in which they were victims of a crime for which a non-Indian was prosecuted. Alternatively, they would be tried as ordinary defendants." Brown's 1850 act swept this old legal standard aside, beginning a new, more draconian era in California Indian history. His act severely limited Indians' legal rights and placed them in acute danger of physical abuse, murder, and—quite explicitly—unfree labor.[31]

The act legalized de jure custodianship of Indian minors and two types of Indian convict leasing. Children could, with the consent of "friends," an extremely vague legal category, or "parents," be held and worked without pay until age fifteen, for females, or eighteen, for males. "Any white person" could also visit a jail and pay the "fine and costs" for any "Indian . . . convicted of an offence . . .

punishable by fine." Because few Indians had access to sufficient money, California jails became low-cost labor suppliers. Under this convict-leasing clause, which resembled debt peonage, employers paid fines on behalf of Indian convicts, who then worked to repay their employers. A closely related Indian convict-leasing clause allowed for almost any free Indian to be legally detained and worked without pay by empowering whites to arrest Indian adults "found loitering and strolling about, or frequenting public places where liquors are sold, begging, or leading an immoral or profligate course of life." When a court received a "complaint" along these broad lines, the act required court officers to capture and lease "such vagrant within twenty-four hours to the best bidder." Winning bidders could then legally hold and work Indian convicts for up to four months without compensation. This second form of convict-leasing legislation created what historian John Walton Caughey called "the Sunday slave mart." According to historian Richard Steven Street, "Over the next thirteen years, thousands of natives were arrested and sold." The state itself facilitated such arrests and sold California Indians into state-sponsored servitude.[32]

The act also legalized the corporal punishment of California Indians. It stated that "an Indian convicted of stealing . . . any valuable thing, shall be subject to receive any number of lashes not exceeding twenty-five or shall be subject to a fine not exceeding two hundred dollars, at the discretion of the Court or Jury." Such floggings exposed California Indians to a form of legalized torture from which the law exempted whites, thus reinforcing the preexisting Hispanic social and legal structures in which California Indians were at the bottom.[33]

The 1850 act provided Indians with limited legal remedies, in relation to its rules, while overtly denying Indians full protection from whites under state law. The act allowed Indians to complain to a justice of the peace and to take whites to court. It also stipulated that "forcibly convey[ing] any Indian from his home, or compel[ling] him to work" was punishable by a fine of at least $50. However, the act simultaneously proclaimed that "in no case shall a white man be convicted of any offence upon the testimony of an Indian, or Indians." Further, it stipulated that Indian testimony against a white man could be rejected by "the Court or Jury after hearing the complaint of an Indian." Given that few whites were willing to testify against another white on behalf of an Indian and that the 1850 act made Indians nearly voiceless and defenseless in court, for the next twenty-three years the system almost completely precluded Native Americans from using state courts as an effective system of redress in cases against whites.[34]

State legislators even more severely restricted Indian participation in criminal and civil court cases unrelated to the 1850 act. On April 16, they barred Indians with "one half of Indian blood" or more from giving "evidence in favor of, or against, any white person" in criminal cases. Four days later, they denied Indians the right to serve as jurors. Further limiting Indians' access to the courts, on February 19, 1851, they specified that only "white male" citizens could become attorneys. On April 29, 1851, lawmakers banned Indians with "one fourth or more of Indian blood"—along with the mentally incompetent—from serving as witnesses in civil cases involving whites. In combination, these race-based laws largely shut Indians out of participation in and protection by the state legal system.[35]

In succeeding years, state lawmakers tinkered with the judicial exclusion of Indians from California courts, but left the system essentially intact. In 1854, they made the witness box accessible to more Indians in civil cases by allowing those with less than "one-half . . . Indian blood" to testify. Still, they barred people with Indian ancestry of one half or more from testifying. The next year, they made it easier for Indians to be witnesses in cases related to the 1850 act, stipulating that: "Complaints may be made before a Justice of the Peace, by white men or Indians, and in all cases arising under this Act, Indians shall be competent witnesses, their credibility being left with the jury." Still, the amendment left juries (from which Indians had been barred since 1850) free to summarily reject Indian testimony. Few juries determined California Indians credible witnesses in either criminal or civil cases. Moreover, until 1873, any person of half Indian ancestry, or more, could be barred from providing admissible testimony in criminal cases. At the same time, California law banned anyone of half Indian ancestry, or more, from serving as a witness in civil cases involving whites. California courts accepted all Native Americans as full witnesses only in 1873 and as attorneys only in 1878.[36]

By denying most Indians the right to testify, serve as jurors, or work as attorneys—on an explicitly racial basis—against whites in California courts, state legislators placed them in the same legal category as felons and mental incompetents, which communicated to California's white population that they could commit crimes against Indians with little or no fear of punishment by state courts. Indeed, according to historian Clare McKanna, nineteenth-century California prosecutors "rarely charged white defendants who killed Indians." Moreover, between 1850 and 1873 California state judges found whites guilty of very few crimes against California Indians and sentenced only a handful of whites for such crimes. During these twenty-three years, California courts hanged numerous Indians, but there are very few records of California courts executing a white man for the murder of an Indian. As General George Crook later recollected of 1850s California, "It was of no unfrequent occurrence for an Indian to be shot down in cold blood, or a squaw raped by some brute. Such a things as a white man being punished for outraging an Indian was unheard of. It was the fable of the wolf and lamb every time."[37]

The 1850 act and additional race-based laws catalyzed mass abduction and a boom in involuntary California Indian servitude. Wages for white agricultural laborers in California during the 1850s were frequently more than four times the average of those for farm laborers in New York or Pennsylvania. As a result, California farmers and ranchers sought cheaper labor. State laws, meanwhile, made it easy to legally ensnare California Indians in systems of servitude. As Bancroft explained, "It was easy to charge any one with vagabondage, especially by enlisting the potent aid of liquor, and obtain his condemnation to forced labor. The impressments generally occurred toward harvest time; and this over, the poor wretches were cast adrift to starve, their own harvest season was by this time lost to them." Indeed, according to one superintendent of Indian Affairs, eighteen enslaved Clear Lake Indians (probably Pomo and/or Wappo) starved to death after being abandoned following the 1852 harvest at Rancho San Pablo near San Francisco Bay. Indeed, California's systems of Indian servitude — directly linked to murderous kidnapping raids and massacres, the forcible removal of children from their tribes, and frequently lethal working conditions — would become a major component of California's genocide.[38]

To the south, law enforcement officials arrested and sold Indians weekly with devastating results. Lawyer Horace Bell recalled: "Los Angeles had its slave mart . . . only the slave at Los Angeles was sold fifty-two times a year as long as he lived, which did not generally exceed one, two, or three years. . . . They would be sold for a week, and bought up by the vineyard men and others at prices ranging from one to three dollars, one-third of which was to be paid to the peon at the end of the week, which debt, due for well performed labor, would invariably be paid in 'auguardiente' [fiery water]," thus catalyzing rearrest by the marshal and another week "as slaves." Bell concluded, "thousands of honest, useful people were absolutely destroyed in this way." Indeed, between 1850 and 1870, Los Angeles's Indian population fell from 3,693 to 219, presumably in part due to the state's selling of California Indians into a lethal form of servitude.[39]

In 1852, some federal officials began protesting California's new unfree Indian labor policies. In September, California's first Indian Affairs superintendent, Edward F. Beale, wrote to the US Commissioner of Indian Affairs in Washington, DC, to protest the "new mode of oppression of the Indians, of catching them like cattle and making them work, and turning them out to starve and die when the work-season is over." Two months later, Beale implored the commissioner to act, explaining how, "Hunted . . . like wild beasts, *lassoed*, and torn from homes [they are] forced into slavery," while insisting, "I have seen it; and seeing all this, I cannot help them." Beale concluded: "It is a crying sin that our government, so wealthy and powerful, should shut its eyes to the miserable fate of these rightful owners of the soil." Still, Beale's protests—like the scores of letters and reports that would flow from the pens of others in the years to come— failed to compel Washington to stop California's violent systems of Indian servitude.[40]

The violent kidnapping continued, supported by state laws. In late 1852, Contra Costa County district attorney R.N. Woods wrote that four Napa County men "are in the habit of kidnapping Indians in the mountains near Clear lake, and in their capture several have been murdered in cold blood." Such men kidnapped substantial numbers: "There have been Indians to the number of one hundred and thirty-six thus captured and brought into this county, and held here in servitude adverse to their will." Woods concluded, "The statutes of this State afford no adequate protection against cruel treatment of Indians." In fact, California courts handed down very few guilty verdicts in such cases.[41]

By effectively denying California Indians legal protection from kidnappers and slave raiders, while granting human traffickers legal cover in the form of de jure minor custodianship and prisoner-leasing laws, California legislators created a legal environment in which violent kidnapping and unfree Indian labor flourished. By April 1856, California Indian Affairs superintendent Thomas Henley reported to the US Commissioner of Indian Affairs: "Hundreds of Indians have been stolen and carried into the settlements and sold; in some instances entire tribes were taken en masse." Henley emphasized the murderous nature of these raids: "In many of the cases . . . fathers and mothers have been brutally killed when they offered resistance to the taking away of their children." Henley was not alone in issuing such reports. Three months later, Indian agent E.A. Stevenson reported from Mendocino County on a "system of slavery" in which whites "seem to have adopted the principle that they (the Indians) belong to them as much as an African slave does to his master." As we shall see, the California Indian unfree labor trade—facilitated by state laws and federal unwillingness to protect California Indians—played a central role in the overall genocide of California's indigenous peoples. Further legislation enacted in 1860 would only intensify the problem.[42]

Now largely excluded from access to the state court system and protection under state laws, California Indians became the victims of a wide variety of crimes at the hands of non-Indians. These included abduction, assault, kidnapping, rape, theft, murder, and massacres. The results included dispossessions and thousands of deaths. By excluding Indians from the community of citizenship, legislators, law enforcement officials, and judges also severely eroded non-Indians' moral boundaries in dealing with Indians, particularly for those non-Indians who equated citizenship with humanity. Mass dispossession facilitated by the federal government also dramatically increased California Indians' vulnerability.

DISPOSSESSION, REJECTED TREATIES, AND INCREASED VULNERABILITY

The day after Congress admitted California to the Union, John C. Frémont entered the US Senate and proposed ten bills aimed at unilaterally transferring vast tracts of California Indian land to non-Indians and to the new state government. The two largest of Frémont's land bills dealt with millions of acres. The first was "a bill to grant to the State of California one million six hundred thousand acres of land for the purposes of internal improvement, in addition to the half million of acres granted for such purposes to each new State by a general law." These 2.1 million acres represented roughly 2 percent of California's territory. This bill died in committee, but Frémont's second land bill was even more extensive. It aimed to dispossess California Indians by "providing for the extinction of their territorial claims in the gold mine districts." The bill covered millions of acres in existing "gold mine districts" and presumably any future "gold mine districts." It opened the door to an assault on all California Indian landownership.[43]

Frémont's interest in transferring legal title from California Indians to the new state built on his understanding that, under Spanish law, the seizure of Indian lands amounted to illegal invasion by force. He sought to extinguish California Indian title altogether. The day after he introduced his ten land bills, Frémont told fellow senators: "The Spanish law clearly and absolutely secured to Indians fixed rights of property in the lands they occupy, beyond what is admitted by this Government in its relations with its own domestic tribes." Consequently, "Some particular provision will be necessary to divest them of these rights." Many senators agreed. On September 16, they passed Frémont's bill "extinguishing [Indian] territorial claims in the gold mine district."[44]

Other members of Congress argued that California Indians had no legal title to their lands. California senator William M. Gwin—who had opposed California Indian enfranchisement during the constitutional convention—asserted that "With regard to the title which Indians may have to tracts of land in California, they are disputed." Gwin insisted, "They are not recognized as having any titles there by the Mexican law. That is the impression of the [non-Indian] population of California." Perhaps as a result, when Frémont's bill reached the House, congressmen removed his language related to "extinguishing territorial claims." On September 28, they voted simply "to authorize the appointment of Indian Agents in California" but failed to define their work or authorize appropriations.[45]

Nevertheless, in late 1850 the majority of US congressmen and senators still felt that the federal government should make treaties with California Indians and set aside land for their exclusive use. This was in keeping with the prevalent US policy of negotiating treaties with Indian leaders that transferred Indian land to the federal government in exchange for other pieces of land, peace, annuities, and other benefits. Accordingly, on September 30, Congress authorized the appropriation of $25,000 for negotiating "treaties with the various Indian tribes of the State of California," but did not mention land. On October 15, US Indian Affairs commissioner Ardavan S. Loughery appointed Virginian Redick McKee, Colonel George W. Barbour of Kentucky, and Dr. Oliver M. Wozencraft (who had voted against Indian enfranchisement in the California Constitutional Convention) to negotiate these treaties. The public initially supported treaty making. Indeed, in December, San Francisco's leading newspaper emphasized: "We must have treaties with our Indian tribes," the next month adding: "The Indians have a right to a portion of the soil, a better right than we have to the whole of it." However, many Californians soon turned against the establishment of California Indian reservations.[46]

From the outset, treaty makers and pundits framed the treaties—and removal to reservations—as the only alternative to extermination and genocide. Before setting out to negotiate treaties, Special Commissioners Barbour, McKee, and Wozencraft wrote a letter, published in the *Daily Alta California*, on January 14, 1851, "To the People of California, residing in the vicinity of the Indian Troubles," in which they argued: "As there is now *no farther west*, to which they *can* be removed, the General Government and the people of California appear to have left but one alternative in relation to these remnants of once numerous and powerful tribes, viz: *extermination* or *domestication*." The *Daily Alta California* agreed. On May 31, 1851, its editors predicted that the alternative to treaties would be, "a war . . . of extermination, long, tedious, cruel and costly." The article then reiterated that without treaties, "subduing and keeping them quiet . . . could be done [only] by a war of extermination." By February 1852, a letter to the *Daily Alta California* warned, in support of treaties, "You have but one choice—KILL, MURDER, EXTERMINATE, OR DOMESTICATE AND IMPROVE THEM." Reservations presented a clear alternative to genocide.[47]

The three treaty commissioners did not have an explicit congressional mandate to include land in the treaties that they negotiated, but they did and the Office of Indian Affairs supported their work. After receiving their first treaty,

US Indian Affairs commissioner Luke Lea replied, "The department . . . is highly gratified with the results you have thus far achieved; especially with your energy and dispatch in procuring a location for several tribes of Indians and promptly removing them to it." Land thus became a crucial component of these treaties, as was typical of treaties between the US and American Indian tribes in the mid-nineteenth century.[48]

Between March 19, 1851, and January 7, 1852, McKee, Barbour, and Wozencraft signed eighteen treaties with no fewer than 119 California tribes, in which Indian leaders agreed to surrender almost all of their land in return for promises of protection, clothing, blankets, tools, food, education, and nineteen federal reservations. Heavily armed regular troops and, in some cases, state militiamen and artillery, enhanced the commissioners' negotiating power. White violence was also a major consideration in some Indian leaders' decision-making. In one instance, Wozencraft reported that "the Indians complained very much, and only consented to go [to the reservation] that they might have a home in which they would be protected from the white man." The nineteen reservations totaled 7,488,000 acres (11,700 square miles) or approximately 7.5 percent of California's 155,779 total square miles. Still, many Californians resisted allowing Indians to retain even this land. In March 1852, the *Los Angeles Star* opined: "To place upon our most fertile soil the most degraded race of aborigines upon the North American continent, to invest them with the rights of sovereignty and to teach them that they are to be treated as powerful and independent nations, is planting the seeds of future disaster and ruin." Other California newspapers joined in attacking the treaties that year.[49]

Following this turn of public opinion, on January 30, 1852, California governor John Bigler insisted, in a message to the state legislature: "A decided expression should be transmitted to the Senate of the United States, and a rejection of the treaties, by which these reservations are secured, earnestly urged." Several legislators followed Bigler's advice. In February, these men, whom the *Daily Alta California* described as "seekers for political popularity," formed committees to attack the treaties. Their reports bristled with arguments against creating Indian reservations in California.[50]

On February 11, 1852, the California Senate's Majority Report on the issue marshaled legal, economic, and humanitarian arguments to assault the treaties. The authors began by claiming that there was no legal precedent for creating California Indian reservations in either the Mexican Republic or the United States. They also argued that removing Indians who were enmeshed in the colonial economy would create an economic disaster by denying the state "the labor, without which, it will be long before California can feed herself."

Federal treaty commissioner Oliver Wozencraft (seated center) met with these four Maidu leaders in July 1851. Unknown artist, "Maidu Indians and Treaty Commissioners," ambrotype, 1851. Courtesy of George Eastman House, International Museum of Photography and Film.

The authors also raised the specter of misery and mass death: "The Indians, moreover, would be happier, safer, and longer preserved from that destruction which seems to be inevitable" if not relocated. Yet, the authors simultaneously advocated the forcible expulsion—and thus, by their own definition—the destruction of those Indians already legally defined as outlaws: "As to the wild Indians now located within this State . . . remove all Indian tribes beyond the limits of the State in which they are found with all practicable dispatch." Removal, the authors insisted, aligned with long-standing US Indian policies and therefore constituted "an undoubted right." The Majority Report concluded by calling for three resolutions. The first described federal Indian policy in California as "wholly and radically wrong." The second called for "removing the wild Indians beyond" California, and the third suggested "that our Senators in Congress be instructed to oppose the confirmation of any and all treaties with Indians of the State of California, granting to Indians an exclusive right to occupy any of the public lands in the State."[51]

Two days later, state senator J.J. Warner issued a courageous one-man Minority Report. Warner advocated plans to "civilize, refine and enlighten" California Indians and championed the idea of allowing California's senators in Washington, DC, to consider the treaties without state legislators' interference. However, the rising din of anti-treaty demagoguery, in both houses of the California legislature, drowned out Warner's lone voice.[52]

Issued three days later, the state Assembly report on the treaties was even more inflammatory than the Senate's Majority Report. Its five authors asserted that if ratified, the treaties would impose hardships on "not less than twenty thousand American citizens," who would be forced to evacuate reservations "to make room for . . . a few tribes of ignorant barbarians." The report also invoked the potent threat of increased taxes: "The taxable property which would be swept from the State would be immense, which would bring on a corresponding increase of taxation upon other portions of the state." Finally, the authors made the dire prediction that placing Indians on reservations near whites would lead to "frequent depredations upon the white settlements [that] would cause certain retaliation, which would [in turn] result in their complete extermination." Echoing the Senate Majority Report, the Assembly report also called for the treaties' rejection by California's congressional delegation. Finally, the Assembly report attacked both the character and actions of the treaty negotiators, baying for "a rigid inquiry into the official conduct of the several Indian Agents, in California, as . . . high-handed and unprecedented frauds have been perpetrated by them, against the General Government, and the citizens of California." On March 22, the Assembly overwhelmingly endorsed the resolution against the reservations by a vote of thirty-five to six. Where did all of this rage come from?[53]

Greed and racism animated California legislators' intense hostility to the treaties. Many of their constituents wanted unfettered access to California Indian lands, all of which they considered valuable or possibly valuable, and most legislators advocated for their constituents' demands for entitlement. Immigrants came to California largely for the new state's economic potential and few wanted to share that potential with Indians. Accordingly, the California Senate's Majority Report fretted: "They have undertaken to assign to the Indian tribes, a considerable portion of the richest of our mineral lands [and] an extensive surface of the most valuable grazing land of the earth." The Assembly report then speculated: "The aggregate value of those reservations is not less than one hundred millions of dollars." The current and potential future value of the 11,700 square miles set aside for reservations became a central point in rhetorical attacks on the treaties. California representative Joseph McCorkle complained to his fellow congressmen that the reservations "comprise, in some cases, the most valuable agricultural and mineral lands in the state." Soon thereafter, Governor Bigler wrote to treaty negotiator McKee opposing any Northern California reservations and boasting that the state's congressional delegation would ensure their rejection by the US Senate. Tragically, Bigler's haughty forecast proved prescient. As Chauncey Shafter Goodrich has noted, "In Washington, at that moment, California's Senators held the balance of power in the nice adjustment between Whigs and Democrats [and] the natural result followed."[54]

President Millard Fillmore submitted the eighteen treaties, along with a letter of support from California Indian Affairs superintendent Edward F. Beale, to the US Senate on June 1, 1852. On July 8, 1852, US senators, meeting in a secret session, unanimously repudiated all eighteen treaties. The Senate then placed the eighteen treaties and associated documents under an "injunction of secrecy." These documents were on file and presumably accessible in the US Department of the Interior, but the Senate did not lift its injunction until January 18, 1905, fifty-three years later.[55]

The eighteen treaties comprised evidence related to a deceitful crime of vast proportions and documented a massive betrayal. California Indians had surrendered vast tracts of land for reservations, varied forms of remuneration, and protection. By failing to ratify the treaties, the Senate took back the reservation lands promised to California Indians and canceled federal treaty negotiators' promises to provide animals, clothing, cloth, blankets, tools, food, education, and physical protection.[56]

The Senate's rejection of the eighteen treaties placed California Indians in grave danger. US Navy lieutenant George Falconer Emmons connected the absence of treaties to the mass murder of California Indians. In a report written on May 20, 1852, Emmons warned: "What justice most demands for these Indians is, that they should have immediate protection from lawless whites . . . while we are discussing the propriety of Indian agencies and treaties, they are falling by tens, fifties, and hundreds, before the western rifle." Emmons warned that California Indians "are rapidly diminishing in numbers, that they cannot keep up their tribal organization many years longer, and if not removed, or reinforced by bands lying east of them, that very few will be found alive in 1870."[57]

On November 22, 1852, California Indian Affairs superintendent Beale painted a desperate picture of the unfolding California Indian catastrophe for US Indian Affairs commissioner Luke Lea and requested $500,000 to help them survive. According to Beale, "The wretched remnant which escapes starvation on the one hand, and the relentless whites on the other, only do so to rot and die of a loathsome disease, the penalty of Indian association with frontier civilization."

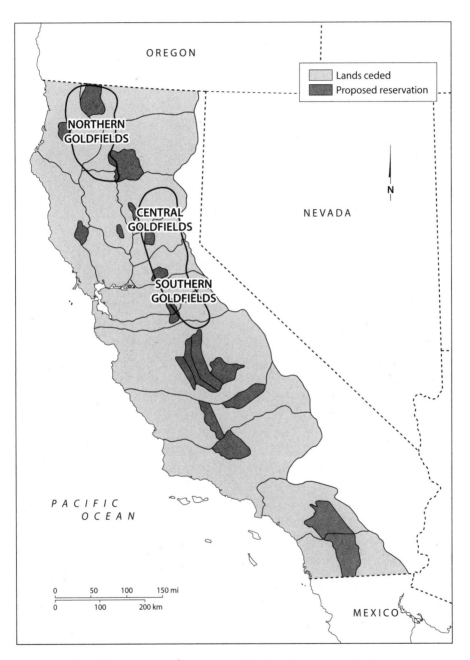

Lands ceded and reservations proposed by the eighteen unratified treaties,
1851–1852, based on map in Rawls, *Indians of California*, 143

Beale asserted, "I have seen it; and seeing all this, I cannot help them. I know that they starve; I know that they perish by hundreds; I know that they are fading away with a startling and shocking rapidity, but I cannot help them." Beale emphasized, "They are not dangerous," before applying moral persuasion: "It is a crying sin that our government, so wealthy and so powerful, should shut its eyes to the miserable fate of these rightful owners of the soil." Beale concluded by noting that it would be far cheaper to feed and protect Indians than to wage war against them. Federal officials, at the highest levels, were also deeply concerned about the effect of the treaties' rejection.[58]

In his annual report on December 4, 1852, US interior secretary Alexander H.H. Stuart explained: "In consequence of the rejection of all the treaties . . . our relations with [California Indians] are of a very unsettled and precarious character." He then warned Fillmore, "If measures are not speedily adopted to declare by law what is to be the extent of the rights of the Indians, and to protect them from aggression, collisions and bloodshed will ensue."[59]

President Fillmore listened. Two days later, in his annual message to Congress he devoted three paragraphs to the issue. He began by explaining, "In California and Oregon there has been no recognition by the Government of the exclusive right of the Indians to any part of the country. They are therefore mere tenants at sufferance, and liable to be driven from place to place, at the pleasure of the whites." Fillmore blamed the Senate: "The treaties which have been rejected proposed to remedy this evil [but] no substitute for it has been adopted by Congress." Fillmore then added, "If it be the desire of Congress to remove them from the country altogether, or to assign to them particular districts more remote from the settlements of the whites, it will be proper to set apart by law the territory which they are to occupy, and to provide the means necessary for removing them to it." The president concluded with an emphatic call to action: "Justice alike to our own citizens and to the Indians requires the prompt action of Congress on this subject."[60]

Congress acted on Fillmore's call two days before he left the White House. On March 3, 1853, Congress authorized "five military reservations not exceeding 25,000 acres each" and "appropriated $250,000 to defray the expenses of maintaining the Indians in California and removing them to the reservations," but conferred no legal recognition or land titles on California Indians. The results were fivefold. First, California Indians were to be allocated not more than one-sixtieth of the acreage promised by the treaties, and they received nothing for relinquishing their claims to the entire remainder of California. Second, no reservations were patented and jurisdiction over them was left uncertain. Third, because jurisdiction remained uncertain, confusion and conflict prevailed between and among state and federal authorities. Fourth, California Indians did not explicitly become wards of the US government. Fifth, Pacific Department commander major general John Wool's 1857 interpretation of the California reservations' legal status denied these reservations full army protection: "Until these reservations are . . . perfected the United States troops . . . have no right to . . . exclude the Whites from entering and occupying the reserves, or even prevent their taking from them Indians, squaws and children. In all such cases, until the jurisdiction of the State is ceded to the United States the civil authority should be invoked to correct the evil."[61]

Supreme Court chief justice John Marshall had ruled in 1831 that Indian tribes constitute "domestic dependent nations" and that "their relation to the United States resembles that of a ward to his guardian." Yet, in California, the US Senate denied Indians both permanent reservations and full protection by the US Army. The Senate thus denied California Indians their lands and made them particularly vulnerable to kidnapping, slavery, assault, and murder at the hands of California citizens, including state militia forces, while often denying federal troops the mandate to intercede.[62]

Between 1846 and 1853, US military officers, California state legislators, and federal lawmakers expelled California Indians from mainstream colonial California society and relegated them to a shadowy legal and social status between man and beast. This was not preordained. In each phase of legislation, anti-Indian views prevailed over more sympathetic voices, each time pushing Indians farther beyond the bounds of citizenship and community. Through a succession of laws, legislators slowly denied California Indians membership in the body politic until they became landless noncitizens, with few legal rights and almost no legal control over their own bodies. Indians became, for many Anglo-Americans, nonhumans. This legal exclusion of California Indians from California society was a crucial enabler of mass murder.[63]

Legislation made the California Indian catastrophe possible. Military, state, and federal policymakers first stripped California Indians of legal power and rights, excluded them from society, denied them protection, and all but erased legal and cultural barriers to their abuse and murder. The result was even more widespread exploitation and violence. In 1935, US Indian Affairs commissioner John Collier explained the "swift depopulation" of California Indians after 1850: "They were totally deprived of land rights. They were outlawed and all treated as wild animals, shot on sight." He emphasized, "They were actually murdered . . . enslaved and worked to death . . . driven back to totally barren vastness . . . and they died of starvation. Their life was outlawed and their whole existence was condemned . . . and they died."[64]

State and federal legislation against California Indians created the legal framework within which non-Indians carried out a variety of genocidal actions, as defined by the 1948 UN Genocide Convention. By effectively denying California Indians protection in the courts, legislators granted non-Indians what amounted to legal impunity for many anti-Indian crimes. This legal system all but guaranteed that authorities in California rarely arrested, and even less frequently punished, non-Indians for "killing members of the group." The legal system likewise nearly guaranteed that authorities almost never punished non-Indians for the rapes and beatings that constituted "causing serious bodily or mental harm to members of the group." Furthermore, the legal system made it extremely difficult for authorities to punish non-Indians for destroying California Indian villages or their food stores or for driving California Indians into inhospitable mountain areas, each of which amounted to "deliberately inflicting on the group conditions of life calculated to bring about its physical destruction in whole or in part." By legalizing multiple forms of unfree California Indian labor, legislators also laid the legal groundwork for a system that routinely separated California Indians during their peak reproductive years, which amounted to "imposing measures intended to prevent births within the group." Kidnappers and their clients also used these laws to "forcibly transfer children of the group to another group." The US Senate's rejection of treaties, meanwhile, denied California reservation Indians the status of federal wards, thereby denying them full federal protection from attacks.

The legal exclusion of California Indians from the rest of society not only deprived them of their land and of political and legal rights. It also represented a broad, anti-Indian consensus among voting non-Indians, while creating a legal framework in which non-Indians could treat Indians as outsiders at best and nonhumans at worst. This exclusion facilitated violence by eliminating Indians' rights and legal recourse while eroding legal and moral barriers to kidnapping, enslaving, starving, raping, murdering, and massacring California Indians. Over the coming decades, vigilantes and militias took full advantage of the state of California's anti-Indian legal system to kill thousands of California Indians. The establishment of a state militia system would play a central role in this genocide.

6

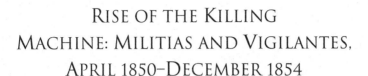

RISE OF THE KILLING MACHINE: MILITIAS AND VIGILANTES, APRIL 1850–DECEMBER 1854

A war of extermination will continue to be waged between the races, until the Indian race becomes extinct.

—*Governor Peter H. Burnett, 1851*

If we lose this war, all will be lost—the world.

—*Antonio Garra (Cupeño), 1851*

By April 1850, state legislators had set the stage for legally sanctioned genocidal crimes against Indians, but it was not clear that establishing a California militia system would create a state-sponsored killing machine. During the past year, soldiers and vigilantes had slain hundreds of Indians in northern counties, but the Clear Lake and Cokadjal massacres were yet to come. Militias, moreover, were integral to the United States and its colonial antecedents. In 1607, Virginia established the first colonial militia, and other colonies followed suit. Militiamen served in the French and Indian War, the War for Independence, the War of 1812, and the Mexican-American War. In fact, with its small antebellum peacetime army, the United States depended on militias to provide troops for every major national conflict up to and including the Civil War.[1]

There was, however, another militia tradition. In 1610, Jamestown militiamen massacred the Indian men, women, and children of "Paspahas towne." In 1637, Connecticut and Massachusetts militiamen slaughtered as many as 700 Pequots at Mystic, Connecticut. In 1675, New England militiamen attacked Narragansetts in Rhode Island, inflicting perhaps 1,000 casualties. Militia massacres of Indians continued during the early years of the republic. In 1782, Pennsylvania militiamen murdered at least ninety Delaware Indians, including not less than fifty-four women and children, at Gnadenhütten, Ohio. Thirty-one years later, Tennessee militiamen slaughtered at least sixty Hillabee Creeks in Alabama, and, in 1832, Illinois militiamen joined regular soldiers, at Bad Axe, Wisconsin, to massacre "at least 260" Sauk and Fox Indians. Colonial and state militias could be devastating instruments of atrocity. Yet California's leaders funded and controlled their militiamen. Thus, policymakers would determine the militias' role amid rising violence against California Indians. Militiamen could be deployed to protect or to destroy.[2]

California's rarely studied 1850 militia acts—signed into law on April 10 by Governor Peter Burnett—called for two militias, one compulsory and one voluntary. The "Act concerning the organization of the Militia" called for a permanent militia of "all free, white, able-bodied male citizens" ages eighteen to forty-five. Planners imagined that this standing militia would be a reserve force to be mobilized in major military crises. Yet underfunding and disorganization made California's compulsory militia "essentially a paper army."[3]

In contrast, the "Act concerning Volunteer or Independent Companies" gave rise to over 303 militia units in which more than 35,000 Californians served between 1851 and 1866. This act allowed citizens to organize a volunteer company by following procedures that included advertising an enlistment location, electing officers, and reporting the unit's name and members. California's adjutant general administered the process, but only the governor could commission volunteer militia officers or call their units into service. Once the company had been organized and uniformed, its commander could petition the governor for weapons and supplies, as long as he sent along a bond certified by his county judge. The governor could then order California's quartermaster general to provide arms and supplies. The "Volunteer" militia act, in turn, created two distinctly different kinds of volunteer militia units.[4]

Social volunteer militias served primarily as fraternal social and athletic clubs. San Francisco's First California Guards, with its elite social roster, was the oldest, the most prestigious, and the model to which many other social militias aspired. Its calendar of events included evenings of dining, dancing, and drinking; drill and target practice outings followed by picnics, formal dinners, theater outings, and drinking; dress parades followed by elegant meals and drinking; balls followed by dining and yet more drinking. The First California Guards enjoyed a "commodious" clubhouse "elegantly furnished" with "a fine drill room," "billiard saloons," and a "reading room." Not all militia headquarters were so luxurious. Yet social militias offered an alluring mixture of prestige, networking opportunities, sartorial splendor, fraternity, recreation, and interactions with scarce white women.[5]

Hundreds of social volunteer militias sprang up in California between 1850 and 1866. Many were urban. Seventy-one emerged in San Francisco alone, and while they wore uniforms, owned weapons, marched, and shot at targets, their primary raison d'être was social. They rarely went far from home, except to visit other social militias for new rounds of target practice, marching, balls, dining, and drinking.[6]

Rangers constituted the second kind of volunteer militia unit. They were in many ways the inverse of the social militias. Inspired by the rugged Bear Flaggers (Frémont's largely volunteer California Battalion) and the vigilantes who had already begun killing Indians in 1849 and early 1850, the ranger militias' raison d'être was fighting, not fraternizing. Where social militias were largely urban, permanent, self-funding, and sedentary, ranger militias were generally rural, temporary, state-funded, and mobile. Most important, social militiamen shot targets whereas rangers shot people, mainly California Indian people.

Between 1850 and 1861, some 3,456 militiamen enrolled in twenty-four volunteer militia expeditions and killed more than 1,342 California Indians. However, their impact was greater than these numbers suggest. Indirectly, ranger militias encouraged many more killings by vigilantes. Ranger militia operations provided a widely publicized state endorsement of Indian killing, communicating an unofficial grant of legal impunity for Indian killing, and eroding cultural and moral barriers to the homicide and mass murder of Indians. Simultaneously, the money, arms, and material showered on ranger militias inspired vigilantes to mount their own Indian-hunting operations in hopes of becoming similarly well-supplied and well-funded ranger militia companies. By funding, arming, and supplying militias—and, moreover, allowing them to kill Indians—state and federal officials increased the frequency, size, lethality, and geographic scope of Indian-hunting operations. These twenty-four expeditions set an example that a far greater number of vigilantes followed, with devastating effect.

The number of California Indians killed by US Army soldiers, California militiamen, and vigilantes from 1850 through 1854 will likely never be known. Published and archival sources indicate that the numbers exceed at least 2,776. Yet, these findings are flawed because the people who were most likely to know how many died—the survivors—left scant written evidence. Ethnohistory, in the context of genocide, is difficult because genocidal acts and state policies silenced so many indigenous witnesses. Few survived massacres to tell their stories. Those who did were often children, frequently raised as the legal wards or apprentices of non-Indians and sometimes by the very people who had murdered their families. Forced relocation to federal Indian reservations also severed

The widespread California Indian funerary tradition of cremation made counting
Indians killed by diseases or by whites difficult. C. Nahl del [Charles Nahl], "Burning
Their Dead," wood engraving, 1854(?), in "The California Indians," *Hutchings'
California Scenes* (Placerville, 1854), n.p. Courtesy of Huntington Library,
San Marino, California.

many survivors' links to the places where genocidal events took place. Removal
to federal Indian boarding schools then took many California Indians away from
their homes and the relatives and other community members who could share
oral histories of genocide. When these children returned home, sometimes after
years away, they often had difficulty communicating with members of their communities because of federal educational policies designed to strip Indian youth
of their traditional languages and cultures. Policies against traditional California Indian cultural and religious gatherings further limited the transmission
of oral histories. For these reasons, any accounting of the number of California
Indians killed between 1846 and 1873 is almost certainly underestimated.

Individually, the many murders and massacres of this period may not initially
seem to comprise genocide because non-Indians often framed killings as either
individual acts of vigilante justice or justified acts of war. Yet, this was not the
justice of the Wild West. Punitive anti-California Indian violence was altogether
different. Vigilantes and militiamen did not routinely massacre the villages of
whites who stole horses or cattle. In fact, that never happened in California.
Moreover, it is difficult to imagine white men responding to a white crime this
way. Yet, almost any excuse could trigger the mass killing of California Indians,
which suggests that their routinized massacre, in response to simple theft, was

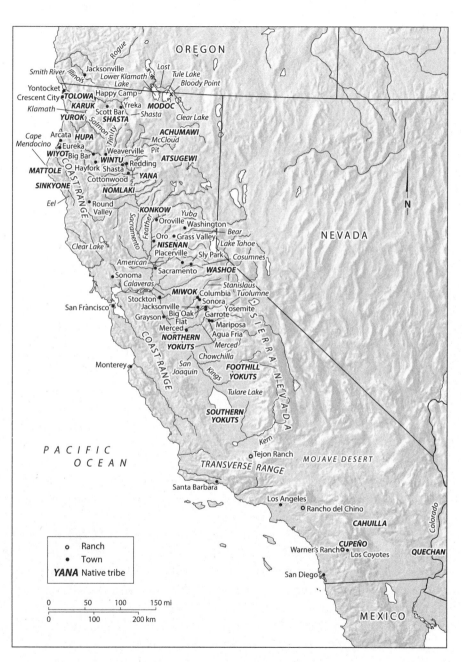

OREGON

Rogue

Smith River • Jacksonville
Yontocket • Lower Klamath
Crescent City • **TOLOWA** Lake
Illinois Happy Camp
Klamath **KARUK** Scott Bar • Yreka **MODOC**
YUROK **SHASTA** — Shasta
Salmon
Trinity
Cape Arcata **HUPA**
Mendocino • Eureka
WIYOT Big Bar • Weaverville Pit
MATTOLE Hayfork Shasta
SINKYONE Cottonwood
Eel
NOMLAKI
Clear Lake • Round
Valley
Sacramento
KONKOW
Yuba
• Oroville Washington
Oro • Grass Valley Bear
NISENAN Lake Tahoe
Feather Placerville
Sly Park
American
Sonoma Sacramento **WASHOE**
Calaveras
MIWOK *Stanislaus*
Stockton Columbia *Tuolumne*
San Francisco • Jacksonville Sonora
Grayson Big Oak Yosemite
Flat Garrote
Merced • Mariposa
NORTHERN Agua Fria
YOKUTS *Merced*
Chowchilla
Monterey • San *Kings*
Joaquin **FOOTHILL**
YOKUTS
Tulare Lake

Lost
Tule Lake
Bloody Point

Clear Lake

ACHUMAWI
McCloud

ATSUGEWI
WINTU Redding
YANA

SOUTHERN
YOKUTS

Tule Lake

NEVADA

N

SIERRA NEVADA

Kern
• Tejon Ranch MOJAVE DESERT
TRANSVERSE RANGE

PACIFIC
OCEAN

Santa Barbara

Los Angeles
○ Rancho del Chino

Colorado

CAHUILLA

CUPEÑO
Warner's Ranch ○ •
Los Coyotes

San Diego ○

QUECHAN

○ Ranch
• Town
YANA Native tribe

0	50	100	150 mi
0	100	200 km	

MEXICO

Events of April 1850–December 1854

part of a larger project of annihilating them, in order to take possession of their lands and natural resources. California Indians did violently resist invasion, theft, and exploitation. Yet this was no regular war. Many whites articulated genocidal intent, that is "intent to destroy, in whole or in part," either mentioning particular California tribes or all California Indians. To realize this intent—and it is important to note that the UN Genocide Convention did not address motive—whites routinely carried out acts defined as genocidal, most conspicuously by killing thousands of California Indians, often by surrounding and massacring whole villages. As in some other genocides, war provided the context and the smokescreen for intentional mass murder. Thus, many have used California Indian resistance to camouflage the genocide with martial rhetoric. Comparing casualties—and noncombatants in particular—reveals that although California Indians resisted, they also suffered genocide. Indeed, whites suffered very few losses even as they destroyed California Indian peoples "in whole or in part." Taken together, the many genocidal acts perpetrated against California Indians indicate a broad-based, state-supported project aimed at their physical annihilation.[7]

GENERAL GREEN'S TEST

A standing California militia general soon tested the new system in the Central Mines. On May 16, 1850, militia major general Thomas J. Green reported to Governor Burnett that he had assumed command of a volunteer company that would set out from Oro, "three miles above the mouth of Bear River," to attack Nisenan people in response to a Deer Creek "engagement" that left fifteen Nisenan and eight whites dead. Amid the evergreen-studded hills and meadows of the Nisenan homeland, Green tested the volunteer militia act, perhaps hoping to lead the nascent state's first ranger militia expedition. For Nisenan, who had already lost untold numbers of people during the localized genocide of 1848 to 1849, the impact would be devastating.[8]

On May 25, Green penned a field report to Burnett that California newspapers widely republished, thus alerting thousands to the existence and tactics of a new form of hunting California Indians. Green described two preemptive attacks launched with little or no pretext. On May 17, eleven men "encountered a large number of [Nisenan], killing five and bringing in six prisoners." Three days later, Green located "between two and three hundred [Nisenan] upon an elevated conical hill." The Nisenan did not attack. Nor did Green negotiate. Instead, his pincer attack crushed them in a vise, perhaps massacring them. Green described only "a smart skirmish" before his men "pursued them for several miles in the hills and ravines, killing and wounding a number, and took eight prisoners." He concluded, "Their chiefs report eleven of their men killed, besides wounded." In contrast, Green suffered only four wounded, one "accidentally." The assault was typically asymmetrical, but that afternoon, Green offered terms. Likely persuaded by the threat of further attacks, on May 25, chiefs Weima, Buckler, and Poollel signed a treaty that promised peace in return for Nisenan disarmament in colonized areas and the surrender of Nisenan who attacked or robbed whites. Never ratified by the US Senate, the treaty provided the Nisenan with scant protection.[9]

Indeed, Green's expedition heralded the rise of anti-Indian militia operations and signaled the potential for expanded genocidal campaigns. The *Placer Times* predicted: "The repeated [Indian] outrages in every direction will induce a more general militia organization throughout this part of the State." The *Daily Alta California* then anticipated that unless "the flame of excitement . . . subdued, the whole [Deer Creek] district will revolt, and declare, perhaps, a war of extermination against the Indians." Militias could expand the range and duration of killing campaigns. Perhaps with this in mind, on May 29, the *Daily Alta California* warned that if relations between whites and California Indians degenerated to the point of an "open collision—there will then be *safety* only in a war of *extermination*, waged with relentless fury far and near." This "war of extermination" was what the 1948 Genocide Convention defined as genocide: "Killing members of the group" with "intent to destroy [them] in whole or in part." California's leading newspaper thus described a statewide genocide as potentially necessary and justifiable.[10]

The next day, the Clear Lake operations became public knowledge. Vigilantes could now claim powerful precedents. State-sanctioned killing operations were becoming part of California's political landscape, approved by generals and now the governor. On June 3, Burnett assured General Green—after reading his reports: "Your course in reference to this expedition is entirely satisfactory and is fully approved." Governor Burnett never enrolled Green's volunteers as militiamen, but the operation set a deadly precedent.[11]

Widely reported and endorsed by the governor, Green's campaign likely inspired others to murder and massacre California Indians. On May 23, without any provocation, whites murdered at least five Nisenan people. On June 6, a Texan murdered "Lutario, the chief of the tribes of the Tuolumue and Mercedes Rivers," leading to a skirmish in which five to eleven Indians and "four Americans" died. Meanwhile, after Yuroks avenged the massacre they had suffered earlier that year by wounding two whites, vigilantes slew at least five Yuroks and destroyed their village on the redwood coast. Yurok oral history also recorded an assault on Mä'äts in which vigilantes massacred every villager save a single child.[12]

Still, Green's campaign did not inspire every white man to become a ruthless killer. Some maintained their moral compass. Following a Miwok raid near Big Oak Flat, miners "followed the Indians . . . found their Settlement, and killed Old Men, Squaws, and Children." Yet, one L. Armstrong protested this genocidal massacre, refused to participate, and helped women and boys to escape. He was not alone. According to one observer, "it was with difficulty that a few humane persons present interfered to prevent the cruel treatment of some aged and sick females left behind." As elsewhere, some whites protected Indians, particularly women, children, and elders. But when whites suspected an Indian of stealing from or attacking a non-Indian, the doctrine of massive, disproportionate, and indiscriminate retaliation was increasingly the rule. The many resulting massacres—perpetrated in the name of pedagogic violence—constituted an expanding genocide that the state increasingly legalized and financially incentivized.[13]

THE 1850 GILA EXPEDITION AND VIGILANTE KILLINGS

As early as 1849, some of the Quechan, or Yuma, people living along the Colorado River were profiting handsomely from the gold rush without pan or pick. Some Quechans, long familiar with crossing the river running through their homeland, found that gold seekers heading west would pay generously for passage across its waters. In January 1850, however, a company of whites began competing for this lucrative ferry traffic—worth perhaps $20,000 per month—later destroying a Quechan boat and murdering an Irishman employed by the Quechans. When a Quechan leader offered to share the ferry traffic with the white ferrymen, they beat him with a club. In the violence that followed, they killed and scalped four Quechans. This was their last mistake. Quechans had violently ejected Spanish colonists from the region in 1781, and they now drove out the white ferrymen, reportedly killing eleven of them in late April. This massacre catalyzed the transformation of California Indian policy. For the first time, a governor called out militiamen, and the resulting Gila Expedition became the first California ranger militia operation materially supported by the state.[14]

On June 1, 1850, Governor Burnett ordered standing militia major general Joshua Bean to recruit volunteers from Los Angeles and San Diego to "punish the Indians, bring them to terms, and protect the emigrants." Three days later Burnett authorized Bean to raise 120 men. Bean, in turn, placed militia quartermaster general J.C. Morehead in command. By August 25, Morehead was marching east and soon had 125 volunteers, a number that eventually swelled to 142. Having traversed rugged mountains and arid desert, he met Quechan chiefs at the Colorado, where he demanded hostages and money that Quechans had supposedly taken. A battle or massacre then ensued. The volunteers suffered a single wound while killing perhaps a dozen Quechans. On September 4, Burnett ordered Bean to disband his unit, and they mustered out on November 20. Once again the aim of pedagogic violence animated the killing. Moorhead wrote to Burnett, "The [Quechans] were taught to know that they could not trifle with the American Government with impunity."[15]

The Gila Expedition communicated important lessons to would-be volunteer militiamen and their suppliers. The ninety-one-day operation set a precedent for extended campaigns as well as the expectation that the army might provide arms. By loaning Moorehead twenty-five carbines, twenty-five pistols, and twenty-five sabers, army major Edward H. Fitzgerald indicated to future ranger militia expeditions that they too might receive federal arms. Just as important, the Gila Expedition—in combination with the Clear Lake Operations, the 1850 acts, and Green's campaign—publicly reemphasized state sanction for Indian killing, encouraging more vigilante attacks that summer.[16]

When whites suspected Indians of crimes or wished to avenge violence, they increasingly attacked whole communities, in keeping with the unwritten but more and more popular doctrine of disproportionate, collective reprisal in the name of pedagogic violence. Some killings took relatively few lives. In June, whites slew at least four Indians in a mountain village near Redding following the theft of two horses. In July, prospectors murdered five Karuk or Shasta Indians after an attempted theft. Others killed greater numbers of Indians. That month, following a skirmish between whites and Nisenan people above American Bar, "Maine and Massachusetts men . . . took fearful vengeance, and the deadly rifles of the Kentuckians and Missourians told with terrible effect." Meanwhile, Ernest de Massey reported that, after Indians supposedly stole from them, Canadians burned a village and massacred at least fourteen Tsnungwe in the Northern Mines. He concluded: "This is typical of the tales we hear around here." Joseph Warren Revere recalled that after Indians took stock near Cape Mendocino, he and a group of slave raiders attacked a Mattole or Wiyot village so violently that "as 'order reigned in Warsaw,' so did it in the little 'rancheria' when resistance ceased." Finally, on August 13, a correspondent reported the burning of three Hupa villages and the massacre of "some fifty or sixty Indians." Employing pedagogic rhetoric, he concluded: "The effect has been decidedly good, their thieving and other annoying propensities having sensibly decreased."[17]

California Indians resisted invasion because, among other things, it so often led to genocidal acts. Backed by the state and broad-based support for the physical annihilation of California Indians, the invaders routinely destroyed California Indians' means of subsistence and imposed measures that denied them access to what remained, which may be considered, "Deliberately inflicting on the group conditions of life calculated to bring about its physical destruction in whole or in part." The invaders also enslaved California Indians, often separating tribal members during peak reproductive years and kidnapping children, which may be considered, "Imposing measures intended to prevent births within the group" and "Forcibly transferring children of the group to another group." All too often, the invaders were also guilty of "killing members of the group." Thus, it is unsurprising that California Indians resisted invasion.

However, firepower disparities and the relatively consistent white intent to kill all adult males, and sometimes entire villages, led to massacres. On August 10, Augustine Hale recorded meeting miners returning from the headwaters of the Trinity and Shasta Rivers after "many fights with the [Shasta and Wintu] Indians." They reported suffering one wound and one death, but had "many trophies taken from the Indians," likely meaning scalps. They boasted of killing nine Indians in one skirmish. Soon thereafter, a battle broke out at the confluence of the Klamath and Salmon rivers, where fifty whites attacked hundreds of Karuks. Firing across the Salmon River, Karuk archers stood their ground for hours but suffered twenty-four killed while inflicting only a few wounds. The Karuks then proposed peace, and the whites "consented to 'bury the tomahawk.'" Unlike many massacres, this battle apparently ended without the slaughter of noncombatants and concluded with negotiations rather than indiscriminate killing or enslavement. Such encounters were a rarity, but accommodation remained possible in 1850. Nevertheless, Indian killers had little to fear from state authorities that year.[18]

As Indian killing spread and became increasingly common, California law enforcement officers took little action to protect Indians. This is unsurprising. State legislators had banned Indians from serving as jurors or testifying against whites in criminal cases. California's Supreme Court had released the octet arrested following the Napa and Sonoma massacres of early 1850, and leaders like Governor Burnett supported Indian-hunting ranger militias. Thus, prosecutors may have felt they faced an impossible battle in prosecuting and punishing white homicides of California Indians. Indeed, it seems that in 1850 authorities arrested and convicted only one white person for killing a California Indian, despite many known homicides and massacres. That summer, authorities convicted a white man for killing an Indian near Grayson. Had he killed a white man, the murderer would almost certainly have been hanged by authorities or by a mob. The murder of an Indian was different. According to the *Stockton Journal*, "The Sheriff . . . set him at work to wash his clothes, and after hanging the first half dozen up to dry he made his escape," which the Sheriff "permitted." In the absence of meaningful law enforcement or legal consequences, vigilantes continued murdering and massacring California Indians that fall.[19]

THE FIRST EL DORADO EXPEDITION, 1850

A third ranger militia expedition now reinforced state support for Indian killing. On October 23, El Dorado County sheriff William Rogers petitioned Governor Burnett to call out 200 militiamen "to punish the Indians engaged in the late attacks in the vicinity of Ringgold, and along the emigrant trail." Two days later Burnett issued the order. Rogers's four militia companies then killed at least nineteen Nisenan people and "severely wounded" large numbers while suffering just two men killed and two wounded. For the Nisenan, who had by now endured repeated massacres, the impact must have been devastating. The operation—which grew to involve 352 militiamen—would also have ominous implications for many other California Indians.[20]

The First El Dorado Expedition—which one miner later called "a war of extermination"—encouraged future Indian-hunting ranger militia operations, in part, because it was so lucrative. Before being reduced to 100 men, it cost roughly "$3,500 per day" and Rogers disbanded his remaining 100 men only on November 28. Thus, long before the legislature approved a single cent to pay these militiamen or their suppliers, it became clear that hunting Indians could be financially advantageous. For enlisted militiamen, operations provided food, the promise of pay, and potential loot, including gold mined by Indians. Officers earned higher salaries and could develop cozy remunerative relationships with expedition suppliers. Businesspeople, in turn, anticipated windfall profits from supplying ranger militias in remote locations where prices could be inflated even beyond already high gold-rush rates. As a result, the lure of lucre created powerful temptations to fabricate or exaggerate in order to justify anti-Indian ranger militia expeditions that routinely targeted noncombatants. The Genocide Convention does not mention motive. Thus, while greed often helped to drive such operations, what made them genocidal were the participants' expressions of intent to destroy and the genocidal crimes that they committed.[21]

The anticipation of state financial support for the First El Dorado Expedition was likely one motivation for its organization and operation. The *Placer Times* concluded that the "ridiculous attempt to get up an Indian war in El Dorado

County had its origin in a desire on the part of a few provision dealers to supply the troops with their 'grub.'" The *Daily Alta California* agreed: "This farce . . . was got up by speculators." Others were even more critical. In 1877, forty-niner Alfred Barstow recollected that El Dorado County Indians "were always peaceable. I never knew them to commit a depredation or to steal." Thus, the operation "was a great slaughter of Indians for the benefit of the contractors and county officers." The expedition was indeed bloody and expensive. Yet, like the many ranger militia campaigns that followed, its popularity stemmed, in part, from its potential to line the pockets of militiamen and their suppliers.[22]

The First El Dorado Expedition likely encouraged vigilantes that fall. In November, a mob massacred "perhaps fifteen or twenty" Indians following the killing of a white man in Eel River Valley. To the east, in Trinity County, "Americans surrounded [a] rancheria at night, and destroyed the whole tribe, excepting a few children." And, on December 14, a miner told J. Goldsborough Bruff that after finding "one of the[ir] oxen dead, and full of arrows.—They attacked the [Yahi Yana] Indians, killing several of them, and burnt the village." During 1850, whites killed at least 716 Indians and destroyed many villages, even though the *Daily Alta California* concluded, "Generally we have found the Indian here peaceable and disposed to live on friendly terms with us."[23]

Meanwhile, the promise of wealth drew tens of thousands to California in 1850. By May 14, US mints had received at least $15,425,452 in California gold. The riches mined that year remain staggering. According to economist John Kenneth Galbraith, "In but one year, 1850 . . . California produced as much gold as the whole world had in an average year of the preceding decade." Seeking this wealth, the immigrants of 1850 intensified pressures on California Indians' traditional food supplies. In 1850, the *Daily Alta California* explained that immigrants had "broken up or occupied" California's fisheries while driving off and destroying the state's game. Immigrants had thus driven California Indians "to the brink of starvation." The editorial concluded that immigrants bore responsibility for Indian thefts and attacks but could stop these acts by peaceful means. The next month the paper warned, "If we drive the poor Indian from his old hunting grounds, and break up his fisheries, and cut down his acorn orchards, and burn up his grass seeds, and drive him from his old haunts which the god of nature has given him, it is to the mountains and starvation that we drive him."[24]

California Indians' search for food often triggered annihilationist white violence, particularly when Indians took horses, which some California Indian communities had been eating since the 1840s. In January 1851, William Graham explained that when he and eight others found a village containing horse-meat near the Middle Fork of the Cosumnes, they massacred ten Miwok or Nisenan people and badly wounded fourteen others. Graham then led another attack, killing six Nisenan and wounding "a great many" near the South Fork of the American. The next month, Redick McKee explained to the US Commissioner of Indian Affairs that "The Whites have driven most of the Southern Tribes up into mountains—from where, as opportunities serve, they sally out into the vallies to steal, + drive off Cattle, + mules, as an only alternative for starvation. Then comes up the cry of Indian depredations, Invasion, murders + the absolute necessity for Exterminating the whole race!" Many attempted to justify such total annihilation with the pervasive notion that Indians were fated to vanish.[25]

THE MYTH OF INEVITABLE EXTINCTION

The myth of inevitable extinction conveniently displaced agency from human beings to amorphous forces such as Providence, fate, and nature. This falsely but convincingly absolved both individuals and white society of moral responsibility for the destruction of American Indians in general and California Indians in particular. As early as 1830, President Andrew Jackson told the US Congress, in his annual message, that although "humanity has often wept over the fate of the aborigines of this country . . . its progress has never for a moment been arrested, and one by one have many powerful tribes disappeared from the earth." Jackson apparently saw such extinctions as inevitable, adding that while "tread[ing] on the graves of extinct nations excite[s] melancholy reflections . . . true philanthropy reconciles the mind to these vicissitudes as it does to the extinction of one generation to make room for another." Eight years later, the nation's preeminent newspaper editor Horace Greeley flatly predicted, in "The Doom of the Indian," that "Indians are to be annihilated—it is their fate." By divorcing American Indian demographic cataclysms from human agency and individual or government responsibility, both Jackson and Greeley conveniently elided the human agency driving the violence of conquest and colonialism. Instead, they suggested that mass American Indian death was the product of powers beyond human control. The myth of inevitable extinction thus hid the agency of conquerors and colonizers in the destruction of Indian peoples while suggesting that if they did kill Indians, they were only a small part of a much larger, inevitable process.[26]

By the 1840s, pundits began applying the myth of inevitable extinction to California Indians. In 1844, traveler Thomas J. Farnham wrote that California

Indians "must fade away," and by 1848 the myth was taking root in what would become the Golden State. That year, a *California Star* correspondent asked readers to "let the destined doom (an early extinction) of the red man hasten towards its close, without enlisting . . . fruitless sympathies and efforts to avert his fate." Journalists continued propagating the myth. On December 15, 1850, the *Daily Alta California* joined the chorus of doom, describing California Indians' destruction as unavoidable, suggesting that they would evaporate "like a dissipating mist before the morning sun, from the presence of the Saxon." The inevitability of extinction as an intention now hung in the air.[27]

A PROPHECY OF EXTERMINATION, THE MARIPOSA BATTALION, AND MONEY FOR MILITIAMEN

On January 7, 1851—just weeks before special commissioners Barbour, McKee, and Wozencraft began their California treaty-making campaign— Governor Burnett transformed passive acquiescence into active acceleration by inaugurating a new, state-sponsored phase in the destruction of California Indians. During his "Annual Message to the Legislature," delivered two days before he resigned, Burnett prophesied that "a war of extermination will continue to be waged between the races, until the Indian race becomes extinct." Dismissing nascent federal treaty making while ignoring his own past support of Indian-hunting ranger militia expeditions, Burnett declared annihilation inevitable and unstoppable: "The inevitable destiny of the race is beyond the power or wisdom of man to avert." By invoking the inevitable extinction myth, on one hand, while supporting Indian killing, on the other, Burnett leveraged his authority as California's first civilian US governor to endorse further ranger militia operations against California Indians. In this way, he pushed his successor, lieutenant governor and fellow Democrat John McDougal, as well as state legislators, to institutionalize the state-sponsored hunting and killing of California Indians.[28]

Burnett's portentous prophecy directly challenged federal treaty commissioners Barbour, McKee, and Wozencraft as well as Washington's entire California treaty-making strategy. By preemptively dismissing treaties before their negotiation, Burnett initiated a struggle between advocates of domestication (i.e., treaties and reservations) and proponents of extermination. The dichotomy became increasingly clear. On January 13, Barbour, McKee, and Wozencraft wrote—in a letter published in major California newspapers—that "the General Government and the people of California appear to have left but one alternative in relation to these remnants of once numerous and powerful tribes, viz: *extermination*

In 1851, Governor Peter Burnett prophesied "That a
war of extermination will continue to be waged between
the races, until the Indian race becomes extinct"
(Peter H. Burnett, "Governor's Message," in California,
California Legislature, 1851, 15). Unknown artist,
"Untitled [Peter Hardeman Burnett (1807–1895), first
governor of California]," albumen print on ambrotype
plate, ca. 1860(?). Courtesy of The Bancroft Library,
University of California, Berkeley.

or *domestication.*" More immediately, Burnett's speech also likely referred to
the Southern Mines and the question of whether or not to transform vigilantes
there into ranger militiamen. Given his prior policies, Burnett almost certainly
meant to endorse what would become the largest and most expensive California
Indian-hunting militia operation yet.[29]

In December 1850, Southern Mines violence intensified, prompting calls for
a new militia campaign and even for genocide. On December 23, C.D. Gibbes
of Washington, California, "hoped that the Governor will order out the militia,
and let us drive them back to the mountains, or kill them all." On New Year's

Day 1851, the *Daily Alta California* described an Indian-related panic in the Southern Mines, and, on January 2, Adam Johnston asked Governor Burnett for "aid from the State Government" to protect "persons and property." Some locals were unwilling to await gubernatorial help. The following day, vigilantes killed nine Indian people at "Pleasant Valley . . . in El Dorado county." More killings soon followed.[30]

After Indians captured and killed or mortally wounded three whites, sixty-five miners took to the field. They assaulted a village some twenty-five miles from Columbia at dawn, massacring twenty Miwoks without incurring a single fatality. To the south, Mariposa County sheriff James Burney reported to Burnett that on January 6, he had raised seventy-four additional men from around Agua Fria and marched into the mountains. The vigilantes' ranks swelled. On January 7, Robert Dowling "from the north fork of the Calaveras" reported that after Indians took animals, miners began to "work a terrible vengeance upon the Indian tribes." Participants included "200 old Mexican campaigners from the Calaveras, and about an equal number from the neighbourhood of Moquelumne Hill." In addition, "100 of . . . the [French] Garde Mobile filed out and tendered their services." Dowling estimated some 400 men in the field. It was by far the largest California vigilante expedition yet, and in late January, vigilantes massacred thirty Indian people near James Savage's store.[31]

Meanwhile, at two in the morning on January 8, Sheriff Burney's force located a village when they heard Indians singing, likely during an intertribal religious ceremony attended by "Kee-chees . . . Chow-chil-la[s and] several of the Chuc-chan-ces." The exhausted celebrants eventually went to sleep but at dawn found themselves under assault. Fighting desperately, they wounded at least six attackers, including two mortally, but could not prevent a massacre. Forty to sixty Indian people, or more, soon lay dead. Burney now burned some 100 houses, several tons of dried meat, and bows and arrows before stealing four horses and six mules. By routinely destroying Indians' houses, provisions, and means of subsistence, such attacks, although meant to "teach" Indians not to steal, forced them to raid white settlements in order to eat and survive. Some of the destruction was not necessarily against the interests of would-be volunteer militiamen. Indian raids could be used to justify new operations. Indeed, some may have intentionally stoked a cycle of violence to provide justifications for mass murder, which, in turn, facilitated the ultimate goal of physically eliminating California Indians. Understanding the militia system, Burney concluded his report to Burnett by requesting authorization, commissions, weapons, provisions, and pay for his men.[32]

Following the First El Dorado Expedition precedent, Mariposa County men began lobbying the governor for another militia campaign, and, on January 13, Burney requested gubernatorial authorization and material while reporting the attack in which his vigilantes had massacred at least forty Indians. Governor John McDougal, who took office on January 9, responded by reinforcing Burnett's policy of approving campaigns against California Indians. On January 13, McDougal ordered Burney to call out 100 men "to punish the Indians." Remuneration would "depend upon . . . the State or General government" but "one or the other . . . will, I make no doubt, provide for their pay." The treaty commissioners would soon be negotiating in the Southern Mines, but McDougal nevertheless launched a militia campaign there.[33]

Five days later, Governor McDougal began politicking to institutionalize Burnett's Indian policies, making an argument that helps to explain why state legislators funded California's volunteer militia operations. On January 18, McDougal wrote to the California Senate president requesting pay for volunteers. Understanding that state senators might resist assuming the burden of such a substantial expense, McDougal made a two-part argument to convince them that Washington would ultimately pay. First, he insisted that because the federal government had failed to "protect our citizens against the hostile incursions of Indian tribes," the state had been forced to mount militia operations. Second, McDougal added that because the US Constitution bound the federal government "to protect each state against foreign invasion and domestic violence," Washington would "no doubt" ultimately pay. Blaming federal inaction would become a common justification for launching California militia expeditions. In combination with the notion of a federal obligation to protect the states from Indians, it was essential to the argument that the federal government would eventually pay for them. This oft-repeated two-part argument, in turn, helps explain state legislators' willingness to fund such expeditions. In essence, they believed that Washington would ultimately pay. That same day, McDougal wrote to the state legislature requesting an act to pay veteran and future volunteer rangers.[34]

Vigilante-led killings, meanwhile, continued in the Southern Mines near Agua Fria. According to Dr. Lafayette Bunnell, after a January 11 skirmish "high up on the Fresno," vigilantes retreated with one man killed. Then they pursued "the Indians to near the North Fork of the San Joaquin river, where they had encamped on a round rugged mountain." Among "the Tribes represented were the Chow-chilla, Chook-chan-cie, Noot-chu, Ho-nah-chee, Pot-to-en-cie, Po-ho-no-chee, Kah-we-ah and Yosemite. The number of fighting men or warriors was estimated at about 500, while that of the whites did not exceed 100." After reconnoitering the rough terrain, the vigilantes—led by John Bowling, John Kuykendall, and James Savage—waited. Then, "before daylight," thirty-six of them "dashed in and with brands from the camp fires, set the wigwams burning, and at the same time madly attacked the now alarmed camp." Another genocidal massacre ensued: "No prisoners were taken; twenty-three were killed; the number of wounded were never known." In contrast, just one attacker "was really wounded" and none killed. Governor McDougal now moved to transform these vigilantes into state militiamen. On January 25, he gave militia colonel J. Neely Johnson substantial autonomy in commanding the impending operation. Meanwhile, leading 210 men from Agua Fria, Burney and Savage "had a skirmish, the [Miwoks or Yokuts] Indians retreating" before killing ten and wounding forty. Soon thereafter, many of these vigilantes joined the Mariposa Battalion, California's newest volunteer militia force. James Savage would lead this troop of 211 men—which soon grew to 560—with Bowling and Kuykendall as his lieutenants. Ultimately, the Mariposa Battalion took the lives of at least seventy-three California Indian people.[35]

State legislators now put the power of the purse behind anti-Indian ranger militia campaigns. They endorsed the Mariposa Battalion and provided substantial financial support to the three officially mustered 1850 militia expeditions. On February 15, 1851, legislators voted to borrow $500,000 for past and future anti-Indian operations necessitated by "the absence of adequate provision being made by the General Government." On March 7—confident that Congress would reimburse them for "debt legitimately due by the General Government"—they established a generous daily pay scale for volunteer ranger militiamen:

Majors: $15
Captains: $12
Quartermasters, Commissaries, Surgeons, and Adjutants: $12
Lieutenants: $10
Sergeants: $7
Corporals: $6
Privates: $5

These wages were relatively high. In contrast, laborers and prospectors in the Central and Southern Mines of 1851—where most militia operations were taking place—typically garnered $3 to $8 per day, although some lucky miners earned more. By offering $5 to $15 per day, legislators offered a financially attractive alternative to mining that helped to recruit militiamen.[36]

Retroactive pay for First El Dorado Exhibition and Gila Expedition militia-men and outfitters underscored the state's commitment to anti-Indian ranger militia operations. The act of March 7 allocated $100,000 to the First El Dorado Expedition, and the state ultimately spent $101,861.65 on the campaign. Several privates earned $150, a captain $450, and a major $750, all for less than a month of service at a time when men in the Central and Southern Mines typically earned roughly $72 to $192 per month. In total, the 352 men earned $76,619.86, on average $217.67 each. Outfitters were likewise well paid. They received $1,185 for animals and $24,056.79 for supplies. The Gila Expedition's longer duration made it even more expensive. The act of March 7 allocated $125,000 for it, and the state ultimately disbursed $113,482.25. The 144 volunteers earned $90,450.49, or about $628 each, the value of more than thirty-nine ounces of gold. Meanwhile, the state paid outfitters $5,571.00 for animals and $17,460.76 for supplies. By spending $215,343.90 on the first two paid ranger militia operations, California legislators broadcast lucrative support for Indian hunting and helped to institutionalize both vigilante and volunteer ranger militia operations against California Indians.[37]

For miners accustomed to toiling in ice-cold streams under a broiling sun for uncertain rewards, the promise of pay was attractive, particularly when it exceeded what they could earn mining. Generous militia wages established important precedents. They ensured that when governors called for militiamen, many volunteered. More important, high wages incentivized men to initiate expeditions in hopes of receiving gubernatorial authorization and substantial officers' pay from legislators, ex post facto. Raising a militia company to hunt Indians would be financially risky until the governor and legislators signed off, but the new legislation reduced that risk.

Generous payments to suppliers likewise encouraged prospective outfitters to take similar risks in return for potentially high profits. Ranger militia operations promised windfall earnings for suppliers willing to gamble that the governor would approve an expedition and that legislators would pay. The promise of generous remuneration to outfitters resulted in well-armed and well-supplied ranger militia operations that killed increasing numbers of California Indians. These militia expeditions, in turn, encouraged even more killing by vigilantes. The generous pay allocated to the First El Dorado and Gila expeditions also boded well for Mariposa Expedition volunteers and suppliers.

Why were state legislators willing to spend so much money to fund anti-Indian ranger militia operations? One reason was that they fully expected Congress to reimburse California. The expeditions thus garnered broad support among California voters (a category from which Indians were excluded) because they promised to use federal funds to enrich participants and suppliers, eliminate a perceived threat, and unlock access to California's gold. According to the *Sacramento Transcript*, "Savages . . . infest a great part of the richest mines. . . . Thus we are cut off perhaps from thousands of square miles of the richest mines in the country." Indeed, the desire to eliminate Indian miners as competitors and to possess Indian land and the gold it contained motivated some Indian killers. As in some other wars against American Indians, the desire to take Indian land helped to drive killing campaigns aimed at physically destroying Native Americans. But the lure of plunder and high wages probably motivated the majority of men who volunteered for ranger militia expeditions.[38]

As legislators institutionalized Burnett's Indian policies, killings and village burnings continued in the Southern Mines, even as treaty negotiations proceeded. In January, after Miwoks wounded five miners near Sonora, "hunters" took "twenty Indian scalps." That same month, a Texan near [Big?] Oak Flat killed at least three Sierra Miwoks "with a double-barreled rifle," and soon thereafter twenty Big Oak Flat men attacked Sierra Miwoks "on the North Fork of the Tuolumne," killing and wounding many while losing two men. The next day, a steamer carried 150 US Army soldiers to Stockton *"en route* for the scenes of the Indian difficulties." By February 11, an Agua Fria correspondent warned of what we would call genocide: "I would not be astonished . . . if a general massacre was to take place of all the tame Indians and all wild ones that could be found in the mines, whether hostile or not. There is great excitement amongst the men." Meanwhile, an expedition from "Gerote" destroyed a rancheria and, after the killing of one prospector and the wounding of another "between the middle and south forks of the Stanislaus," Columbia men "killed one woman and a number of [Sierra Miwok or Washo] men," before burning their village.[39]

C.D. Gibbes of Washington then prophesied a statewide anti-Indian war. In a public letter of February 15, he asserted that "a general Indian war from one end of the State to the other has been planned for months." Gibbes's pro-war advocacy and implicit preemptive treaty rejection provide a window into the thinking of war supporters. Gibbes argued that the success of California's mining-based economy depended on subduing its indigenous peoples. Invoking paternalism, naked self-interest, and historical precedent, he concluded, "It is no use to talk about the poor Indians; it has to be done, and has been ever the case since America was first settled, and the sooner done the better for them, and us, too."[40]

Powerful men now threatened genocide. As treaty negotiations proceeded, Mariposa Battalion commander and militia colonel J. Neely Johnson (who later became governor of California) warned the treaty commissioners that failure on their part would lead to the annihilation war that Governor Burnett had predicted. On or before February 17, 1851, Johnson "promised" commissioners Barbour, McKee, and Wozencraft that if negotiations "were unsuccessful he would then *make war upon the* [Indians], *which must of necessity be one of extermination to many of the tribes.*" Johnson's—and presumably Governor McDougal's—calculus was clear: without treaties California Indians would be annihilated by militiamen.[41]

Some Mariposa County miners were uninterested in waiting for the outcome of treaty negotiations. On March 7, Indian agent Adam Johnston reported from Mariposa to the US Indian Affairs commissioner that "many of the whites in the region have lost either property or friends by the Indians and openly declare they will shoot down any and all Indians they meet with, whether a Treaty be made or not." Two days later, a frustrated James Savage of the Mariposa Battalion reported to Governor McDougal, "Eight [white] men killed and six wounded" in the Mariposa region between February 15 and March 3. He then begged McDougal to let him attack, arguing that "all . . . might have been saved, had it not been for the fact that my command was restrained from acting, lest we might thwart the mission of the Indian Commissioners, and incur the displeasure of the General Government."[42]

Some California leaders apparently agreed, troubling even General Persifor Smith, who had ordered the 1850 Clear Lake Campaign. On March 13, General Smith pointed out to the US Army adjutant general that the army and federal government could increase the number of troops under his command in California. Smith—aware of white resolve to attack California Indians—also predicted: "Whatever may be the result of the efforts of the commissioners in making treaties with the Indians, I have now no hope that peace will be maintained, for certain persons have determined that there shall be a war, and there is not sufficient military force and no judicial authority to restrain them." Smith's prediction proved prescient.[43]

Two days later, Governor McDougal insisted to the Senate and Assembly that a war was raging and that, despite ongoing treaty negotiations, "offensive measures [are] the only alternative left." Legislators concurred. The next day, they authorized McDougal to muster 500 additional militiamen to "punish into subjection" so-called hostile tribes. Anticipating further campaigns and a substantial Mariposa Battalion bill, on March 17, legislators reduced daily militia pay rates to:

Majors: $10
Captains: $8
Quartermasters, Commissaries, Surveyors, and Adjutants: $8

Lieutenants: $6
Sergeants: $5
Corporals: $5
Privates: $4

Legislators wished to minimize costs to the state, until Congress reimbursed them. Still the pay remained generous enough to attract plenty of recruits.[44]

That same day, a *Daily Alta California* editorial on the Mariposa Battalion insisted, "We must now chastise these mountain thieves and murderers into submission, or annihilate them." The *Stockton Times* disagreed, supported treaties, and argued: "The Indians have been shamefully maltreated and imposed upon." Meanwhile, Mariposa Battalion firepower took Indian lives. Robert Eccleston's journal entry of March 16 noted, "Capt. Kierkendall has had a fight with some Indians & taken 10 sca[l]ps & one or two prisoners."[45]

Three days later, the battalion attacked Chief Tenaya's Ahwahanees, thus becoming the first whites to visit the soaring, glacier-polished granite walls and verdant meadows of Yosemite Valley. Although the presence of treaty commissioners and regular soldiers likely modulated the battalion's Yosemite campaign, the invaders marked their way with blood and ashes. In no fewer than seven separate incidents, they killed at least twenty-four to thirty Ahwahanees and perhaps many more. By systematically torching villages and food stores, the battalion also made survival difficult for retreating Ahwahanee survivors. Their settlements and supplies destroyed and Chief Tenaya in captivity, Ahwahanees eventually signed a treaty, and on July 1, the last of the 518 Mariposa Battalion men mustered out. These volunteers would be well paid. The Ahwahanees would face death and starvation at Fresno Reservation, the treaty they signed never ratified by the US Senate.[46]

The mechanics of militia campaigns sponsored and paid for by the government were now in place. Even as the Mariposa Battalion scythed through the Southern Mines, the lure of lucre and violent solutions to Indian-related concerns stirred others to action further south. In late January, a large group of Indians—possibly Yokuts—reportedly attacked Tejon Rancho, north of Los Angeles. Whites then killed forty or more of them. Following a report that Indians "massacred" thirteen immigrants "at the Four Creeks," whites demanded a fifth ranger militia operation. On March 1, McDougal called up volunteers "to punish and repel the aggressing Indians." The resulting Utah Expedition rangers roamed Southern California until July 14, 1851, murdering at least two Indian prisoners before being discharged and given valuable "drafts of indebtedness."[47]

THE SECOND EL DORADO AND MONTEREY
EXPEDITIONS, 1851

The pull of mammon now enticed Sheriff Rogers to organize a Second El Dorado Expedition. On February 22, he wrote to militia general A.M. Winn reporting miners driven from claims and "several dead bodies found cut to pieces by the Indians." On these pretexts, Rogers raised 107 men, and, on May 13, Governor McDougal authorized him to enroll militiamen. Two days later, the *Daily Alta California* explained, "We do not believe that there is any necessity whatever for raising the volunteers or commencing warfare with the Indians." Rather, "The whole movement looks like a mere pecuniary speculation." However, because most California legislators expected Congress to reimburse the state for anti-Indian militia operations, no one stopped this sixth militia campaign. It soon became the largest yet, swelling to 633 militiamen.[48]

The Second El Dorado Expedition killed Nisenan people and burned their villages even as it sometimes forced Nisenan leaders to sign treaties. On May 21, militiamen slew one, lost two men killed, and two days later burned "ranches." On May 25, they killed perhaps twelve or fifteen Nisenan on the American River's South Fork, while suffering two killed and two wounded. Still, federal treaty making restrained the killing machine. After May 24, Rogers's rangers forced a large group of Nisenan under Chief Santiago and five other chiefs to surrender before turning them over to Wozencraft for negotiations. Rogers then launched a final attack on "the enemy and one of the troops was killed." He failed to report Nisenan casualties, but near Sly Park, militiamen slew eight Nisenan, and lost one ranger killed. By the time the last militiaman mustered out on July 24, the expedition had killed perhaps twenty-four or more Nisenan, at the same time more deeply institutionalizing California Indian hunting. In twelve months, California had supported six well-publicized Indian-hunting ranger militia expeditions that had killed at least 143 California Indians. Still, treaty making remained a priority in 1851, which limited the lethality of militia operations.[49]

One 1851 militia expedition demonstrated that treaties could be signed with little or no bloodshed. Organized by Governor McDougal to punish both white and Indian stock rustlers near Monterey, the twenty-two Monterey Expedition volunteers operated for one month, ranged as far south as Southern Valley Yokuts territory in the lower San Joaquin Valley, and negotiated "a sort of treaty of friendship" with "*Attache*" Indians apparently without killing any Indian people. The state had established a legal code and a militia system conducive to Indian killing, but the Monterey Expedition demonstrated that treaties could be signed without killing, particularly in the context of federal treaty-making policies. Such

This image of a Nisenan or Maidu man with arrows
may be the earliest existing photograph of a California
Indian person. In 1954, Frank A. Robertson found it
in "a lot of trash from the attic of an old house in
Los Angeles" and donated it to the Southwest
Museum. M.R.H., "Rare Maidu Portrait," in *Masterkey*
(September–October, 1954): 195. Unknown artist,
"Untitled," daguerreotype, 1850s(?). Courtesy of the
Braun Research Library Collection, Autry National
Center, Los Angeles, 1346.G.1.

nonviolent operations might have led to a dramatically different history in California. Unfortunately, this seventh state militia operation proved a rarity.[50]

VIOLENCE EXPANDS IN AND AROUND THE NORTHERN MINES

In the spring of 1851, new gold strikes and reports of high earnings in the Northern Mines catalyzed a rush to the lands of northwestern California Indians.[51]

As prospectors poured into the homelands of the Hupa, Karuk, Shasta, Tolowa, Wintu, Yurok, and others, they carried genocidal tendencies and tactics with them. Killings in and around the Northern Mines then spread in the context of state policies that gave Indian killers little to fear and much to gain. Following the theft of stock by unidentified rustlers near "Mosquito Cañon," a posse massacred five Indians. After Indians killed three explorers near Happy Camp, other Indian-killers attacked a "[Karuk] village and put a majority of them to death." On March 25, a distraught white man from Ranch de Luise warned General D.F. Douglas that "the Kirks have raised a band of 25 men, and are hunting the Indians in this neighborhood; they this morning 'run' the Rancherie from Williams & Atherton's . . . they are (the Kirks) watching to kill any of them that they can find." In April, bloodless robberies in the upper Sacramento Valley led to the genocidal massacre, near Cottonwood, of "about thirty" Nomlaki, Wintu, or Yana people. Soon thereafter, whites seeking to punish rustlers massacred forty Indians in "the Coast Range." Then, after pursuing white stock rustlers who had pretended to be Indians, four men from Big Bar "reached the Sacramento valley . . . with fourteen Indian scalps tied on a string."[52]

Attackers sometimes articulated genocidal intent as killings proliferated. On April 22, John Marshall wrote from "Marshall's Ranch" that because three whites and two Indians had died in a skirmish, "We are going out to kill the whole tribe." Indian resistance would increasingly be met by annihilation, with the smoke of conflict, however small, camouflaging genocide. In May, eighty Scott Bar miners avenged a white man's death by killing four Shastas on the Klamath, including a woman and two children, burning every village they found. Such attacks inspired reprisals that, in turn, intensified white violence. In June, thirty whites responded to the killing of a white man on Churn Creek by massacring fourteen or fifteen Wintu people. Soon thereafter, one G.R.S. described how, on June 29, he and some twenty whites and fifty-five Indian auxiliaries—who participated for unexplained reasons—attacked a village about thirty miles west of Sears and Swift's upper Sacramento Valley ranch. This "slaughter" of completely unarmed people involved "killing of all of the men who did not escape" and perhaps some women and children too.[53]

Shasta City "authorities" now institutionalized Indian killing by offering "five dollars for every Indian head brought to them." Swiss Argonaut Carl Meyer recollected that "Human monsters of Americans made a regular business of getting these. A friend of mine who was in Shasta City at that time assured me that in one week he saw several mules laden with eight to twelve Indian heads turn into the precinct headquarters." While uncommon, local head and scalp bounties offered new financial incentives to indiscriminately murder California Indians, mutilate their bodies, inventory their deaths, and ultimately carry out genocide.[54]

By early July 1851, California's leading newspaper had become resigned to a brutal colonial killing campaign, hinting that massacres would eventually clear California of Indians. Reviewing the past few years, the *Daily Alta California* observed: "Bloodshed has followed on the track of civilization and settlement." Looking to the future, the paper echoed Burnett's January speech: "From this time forward we must be prepared to hear of encounters with Indians in the settlement of the soil comprising their homes. We will hear of massacres and strife and bloodshed, which no local nor borrowed power will have the means to prevent." Tolerated by state officials, unchecked by federal authorities, and predicted by the press, Indian-hunting operations increased in frequency and lethality.[55]

Shasta City, with its local head bounty, may have become a center for men who abandoned gold mining for head hunting. Whether or not body part bounties motivated the killings, Shasta City became the base from which vigilantes repeatedly set out to massacre nearby Wintu Indians. On the morning of July 6, some 800 presumably Wintu people gathered about twenty miles from Shasta City on the west side of the Sacramento. They were not at war with whites. So when sixteen men under a captain B.F. Harvey arrived, the Wintu may have welcomed them. Yet, at nine o'clock the visitors opened fire. As Wintus fled, "some sixty or seventy were killed, and a large number mortally wounded." So surprised were the Wintu that they did not inflict a single wound on the attackers. Harvey's killing squad soon set out again. Returning on July 14, he reported assaulting another village, "killing some fifty Indians, and wounding many more." Again, Harvey reported no casualties on his side. The next day another posse returned to Shasta City. Responding to the murder of an employee sixteen miles from town, supposedly by an Indian, James Macklay had organized fifteen men and attacked another Wintu village "killing some twenty . . . and wounding as many more." As in Harvey's operations, Macklay's men apparently suffered no casualties. Both killing squads took only a handful of prisoners, presumably to sell into slavery. And, each may have collected lucrative head bounties. Both the frequency and lethality of vigilante attacks were on the rise.[56]

This escalation led to California Indian counterattacks, but they were often both qualitatively and quantitatively different from newcomers' attacks on California Indians. The motives driving Indian violence against non-Indians included protecting their homelands from invasion and theft; obtaining nourishment as immigrant mining, hunting, ranching, logging, and industry destroyed traditional foods; and preserving themselves and their communities from assault, abduction, unfree labor, rape, murder, massacre, and, ultimately, obliteration. Indian counterattacks were also quantitatively less lethal, rarely killing more than a handful of whites. Nevertheless, violent California Indian resistance deeply concerned California state policymakers, who now moved to intensify whites' killing power.

BUILDING A STATE ARSENAL WITH FEDERAL SUPPORT

Superior weapons and ample ammunition were essential to the martial asymmetry that allowed whites to kill many California Indians while themselves suffering relatively few casualties. Immigrants arrived well armed, but in 1851 some California leaders, who wanted more weapons and ammunition for militiamen, began building a state militia arsenal. By March it contained "one hundred and twenty stand of arms." By April, it held 400 muskets and 90,000 cartridges.[57]

In the meantime, Governor McDougal sought direct federal support for California ranger militia operations. On March 1, 1851, he wrote an audacious letter to US president Millard Fillmore requesting that Washington equip, provision, and pay volunteer California militiamen, at the same time leaving California's governor in sole control of launching and commanding all militia operations. McDougal added, "You will remember that we occupy an extraordinary situation," perhaps hinting at the tens of millions of dollars in gold that California contributed annually to the national economy.[58]

On April 30, Secretary of War Charles Conrad responded on President Fillmore's behalf. He pointedly suggested that whites had initiated much of the conflict with California Indians and that McDougal had exaggerated Indian belligerency and numbers. Conrad then wrote that Fillmore questioned the inevitability of "perpetual war" between whites and California Indians and suggested seeking a peaceful solution. Conrad also refused McDougal's requests both for funds and authorization to call out militiamen, noting that the president could not legally authorize either. Conrad then asked, "Is there not some reason to fear" that in California "the love of adventure with some and the high pay with others, would operate as inducements to perpetual collisions with the Indians?" Having noted that adventurism and greed motivated some ranger militia volunteers and thus catalyzed anti-Indian expeditions, Conrad answered his own question: "The plan recommended by your Excellency has already produced these results in California. The President deems it his duty to make these suggestions, not doubting that your Excellency will do all in your power, to prevent abuses as injurious to the State as they are revolting to humanity." This insightful rebuke stung, but neither Conrad nor Fillmore acted to prevent such abuses. In fact, Conrad supported them. While appearing to abdicate authority to the state of California, federal authorities were actually complicit in this genocide.[59]

Conrad now provided weapons, ammunition, and accoutrements to McDougal. The 1808 federal militia act required the US government to distribute "arms and military equipments" to "each state and territory . . . in proportion to the number of the effective militia." However, because California had no standing militia, California senator William Gwin and Governor McDougal had no documents proving the existence of a substantial "effective militia." Instead, they applied directly to Conrad for weapons and ammunition. Gwin and McDougal both lied, telling Conrad that California's standing militia was 100,000 men strong. Despite the absence of any supporting documents, Conrad accepted their estimate, perhaps fearing that if he did not do so he might violate the 1808 militia act. California then received 200 muskets, 198 rifles, 100 Colt pistols, 10,000 percussion caps, and hundreds of belts, gun slings, cartridge boxes, and other accoutrements from one "Capt. Schaeffer, U.S.A." On June 27 and August 7, California's quartermaster general distributed most of these weapons to ranger and social militias, giving 100 rifles, 75 Colt pistols, ammunition, and accoutrements to the governor, presumably for future distribution. War Secretary Conrad thus helped to arm and supply future California militia Indian-hunting operations, increasing their firepower and lethality while lending an indirect stamp of federal approval to unprovoked attacks on California Indians that he himself foresaw.[60]

Over the coming years, the army provided more weapons, accoutrements, and ammunition to California's quartermaster general who, in turn, distributed them to militias that used them to carry out genocidal campaigns against California Indians. Since most immigrants were already well armed and the quartermaster general gave many of these items to social militias, most ranger militia expeditions were not heavily dependent on these items. Still, army supplies helped ranger militias while making the War Department accessory to California's increasingly systematic Indian-killing militia campaigns. Most profoundly, army donations to the state armory communicated a powerful message: indirect army, and thus federal, sanction of California militias' Indian-hunting operations.

THE TRINITY, KLAMATH, AND CLEAR LAKE EXPEDITION, 1851

One volunteer ranger militia that received weapons following Conrad's arms transfers—six Colt pistols and other items—was militia general James Estill's Trinity, Klamath, and Clear Lake Expedition. Following the Monterey Expedition, Estill's was the second militia operation to focus on compelling California Indians to sign treaties but without killing them. Mustered in on August 12, 1851, its 122 men accompanied Commissioner McKee's treaty-making expedition as auxiliaries to US Dragoons. In the field for fifty days, this eighth California militia operation helped provide the force that convinced many Indian leaders to sign federal treaties. Yet, as before, US senators refused to ratify these treaties.[61]

Even in 1851, some suggested that the treaties were merely an expeditious temporary alternative to extermination. In September, the *Daily Alta California*—the state's leading newspaper—argued that "To exterminate them would be impossible at present; pacificatory measures [treaties] were consequently adopted." Given such attitudes, it is hardly surprising that treaty making proceeded in parallel with mass murder and the wholesale destruction of California Indian property in many parts of the state.[62]

THE MODOC KILLING CAMPAIGN, 1851

Tensions had long been rising in Modoc territory, in northeastern California and south central Oregon, as immigrants traveling through ravaged the game and grasses that the Modocs depended on and clashed with Modoc people. Modocs called themselves *Maklaks*, or "People," and before contact, they inhabited a Connecticut-sized region. On their lake-studded plateau between the high Cascades and the parched Great Basin they built semi-subterranean houses, fished from dugout pine canoes, hunted waterfowl and game, and gathered seeds, fruits, berries, nuts, and tubers. As one observer wrote in 1873, "Their country was rich in everything necessary to sustain aboriginal life." Their hills, grasslands, lakes, and lava beds constituted a fragile, semiarid ecosystem. It had supported the Modocs since perhaps 5,000 B.C.E. or, as some believe, "since time immemorial." Men—traditionally wearing aprons or fur robes, as weather and status dictated—fished, hunted, worked wood, and wove nets. Women—often wearing fiber skirts, buckskin thongs, or robes—wove baskets, tanned hides, and made clothing. Traditional Modoc diversions included footraces, ball and dice games, and archery competitions. The early nineteenth-century introduction of horses and guns revolutionized their world, making the Modocs an equestrian people while intensifying trade and hostilities with neighboring tribes. Growing migration prompted by the discovery of gold to the west, in 1851, brought far more dramatic changes.[63]

In April or May 1851, Modocs allegedly "stole forty mules and horses" at or near Yreka. Veteran Indian hunter John Ross then led twenty men and "surprised them in Butte Valley," killing fifteen Modocs and taking seven scalps. That fall, after whites traced forty-six head of stock—which may or may not have been stolen by the Modoc—to a village "to the east side of Tule Lake," or perhaps on Lost River, some twenty men, including the Quaker turned Indian hunter Ben Wright, launched a dawn attack there. According to William Fanning, "The Indians came rushing out of their wickiups in confusion, and fought desperately for a while, having nothing but bows and arrows and protecting themselves with shields made of tule rushes, old tin pans, etc." In response, "We fired as fast as we could load our rifles" and after the Modoc fled, "found some sixteen dead Indians." Fanning's group continued patrolling and several weeks later killed "a number of Indians" in "a running fight" before attacking another village at dawn "near the mouth of Lost river." There the vigilantes captured about thirty Modocs while chasing others "who plunged into the icy water at our approach, and hid in the grass like so many ducks. We spent the entire day in hunting them, and killed fifteen or twenty." The vigilantes later killed a prisoner and in November marched south to the Modoc stronghold in the lava beds southeast of Tule Lake, where they "killed several" others. When Smith and Wright's campaign ended, at least thirty-seven Modocs, and perhaps many more, were dead. In contrast, participant W.T. Kershaw later testified that only two of Wright's men were wounded. The Modoc would eventually endure seven such campaigns at white hands that, in total, took perhaps as many as 1,106 Modoc lives, reducing them from 1,000 or 2,000 people to some 250, a decline of roughly 75–88 percent.[64]

THE GARRA UPRISING AND CALIFORNIA
LEGISLATORS' ACQUIESCENCE

Indian killing also took place under Southern California skies that fall. In November, the *Los Angeles Star* reported an affray some months earlier "in which five or six Indians were killed," as well as the recent massacre of up to eight Indians outside a Los Angeles cantina. As a result of such incidents and the multiple effects of an increasingly invasive colonialism, Southern California Indians now rose up against white domination. Across the desert to the east, Indians launched a coordinated attack on November 11, 1851, four miles west of the Colorado River, where five sheepherders and twelve Indians died in the assault. What became known as Antonio Garra's Uprising had begun.[65]

Paramount Cupeño chief Antonio Garra sought to unify Southern California tribes to expel all white Americans. He understood the risks, but felt the uprising represented Southern California Indians' best last chance: "If we lose this war, all will be lost—the world. If we gain this war, then it is forever; never will it stop; this war is for a whole life." Garra's son and others struck early on November 21, killing four whites near Warner's Rancho while suffering two casualties. Three days later, San Diego area men met with militia General Bean, organized a volunteer ranger militia company, and elected US Army major Edward H. Fitzgerald as captain, forming the ninety-two men of Fitzgerald's Volunteers. Army major Samuel P. Heintzelman promised San Diego County sheriff Agoston Haraszthy fifty muskets and ammunition. The volunteers then reported these activities to McDougal and requested enrollment as militiamen. Organizing a volunteer ranger militia unit was now a smooth, routinized process.[66]

Fitzgerald's Volunteers reached Warner's Ranch on December 1, and burned the village of Kupa. Other volunteers soon joined, including George B. Fitzgerald's Los Angeles Expedition, which mustered in on December 1 and comprised at least forty-four men. By mid-December Thomas Whaley reported "volunteers and regulars . . . coming to our aid from all parts of the state." Meanwhile, the Cahuilla chief Juan Antonio captured Garra and turned him over to whites. Fitzgerald Volunteers captured four others—Bill Marshall, Sonoran Juan Verdugo, and the Cupeños José Noca and Santos—whom they then tried in a San Diego court martial in which the sheriff acted as judge and an army major as defense counsel. On December 12, they hanged Marshall and Verdugo, gave Santos twenty-five lashes, and released Noca. The rule of law thus triumphed over naked genocide in these cases. Still, army operations catalyzed additional violence. On December 20, as Heintzelman and his regulars moved into their territory, Cahuilla chief Chapuli attacked them at Los Coyotes, losing as many as eight men. Three days later, the army began the court martial of four more Indian prisoners, and executed them on Christmas morning.[67]

On Christmas Eve, General Bean convened a third court martial to try Antonio Garra's son and ten other prisoners. Conducted by militiamen at Rancho del Chino, it executed Garra's son and one José Luis while inflicting fifty lashes on a third Indian deemed too young to execute. The court acquitted two others and turned the remaining six over to a magistrate due to insufficient evidence. The rule of law again averted a mass killing on these rare occasions of relative restraint. Still, on January 10, following convictions for theft and murder by a fourth court martial, a blindfolded Antonio Garra "kneeled at the head of his grave" to receive the fatal bullet. Two days later, McDougal ordered the militiamen disbanded. California ultimately spent $23,000 on Edward H. Fitzgerald's ninety-three-man operation as well as additional money on George B. Fitzgerald's forty-four

Los Angeles Expedition volunteers. The campaign had killed perhaps seventeen California Indians, but stopped short of murdering all Indian combatants, probably due to US Army involvement, which in this case mitigated genocidal violence.[68]

Elected by largely anti-Indian constituencies, California legislators were far less interested in curbing genocide. In a speech to California legislators on January 30, 1852, Commissioner Wozencraft warned, "He who would pursue the exterminating policy . . . shows a want of mental capacity and humane feeling." Yet his exhortation failed to move policymakers to action. Soon thereafter, vigilantes went on a rampage of punitive village burnings and massacres. On February 17, the *Sacramento Union* reported that forty-two Churn Creek men had ravaged Achumawi communities on Pit River for two weeks, killing "about thirty Buck Indians," burning and destroying twenty-five villages, and capturing seventeen prisoners. On February 19, the *Marysville Herald* described how, after "Thomas Kearns, was killed by the Indians" in upper Feather River country, whites massacred "some six or eight" Konkow or Maidu people. The next day, following Indian thefts near "Reading's," and the killing of a white man, vigilantes surrounded and massacred thirty Wintu villagers "without losing any of their own number." They then ordered survivors to "kill every Indian belonging to the Rancheria, where" the white man had been killed. On February 22, some of these Wintus "returned with the scalps of two Indians." Reading also apparently sent out "his Indians" who soon returned with two severed heads and two prisoners who they then hanged with the two heads dangling beside them. Genocidal expeditions were now commonplace. As the *Sacramento Daily Union* observed, immigrants needed "but little . . . provocation to commence a war of extermination."[69]

It did not help that John Bigler, another Democrat and California's third elected US governor, had assumed office on January 8. He would continue indirect gubernatorial acquiescence to genocide. In April, Indian agent Redick McKee reported to Governor Bigler that after the killing and robbing of two white men on Eel River, whites "commenced an indiscriminate attack upon the poor, defenceless, and wholly unsuspecting" Wiyot on and around Humboldt Bay "and the mouth of Elk river, killing several; then proceeding out to Eel river [murdering] fifteen or twenty naked and defenceless natives." These "rash, cruel, and blood-thirsty proceedings," McKee added, ended only after "some three or four other Indians who *were suspected* of being concerned in the murder, (*if committed by Indians at all,*) were overtaken on Eel river, and summarily shot."[70]

Governor Bigler responded by defending immigrants as blameless participants in an unstoppable conquest. He insisted: "The career of civilization, under the auspices of the American people, has heretofore been interrupted by no dangers, and daunted by no perils. Its progress has been an ovation, steady, august and resistless." Bigler then attacked McKee, asserting: "An investigation of the circumstances . . . will fully acquit the American citizens residing in the northern counties of the charge of 'murdering naked and defenceless Indians in cold blood.'" California Indians could expect no sympathy from the new governor. Still, McKee replied that "the Indians of this country are not disposed to war with the whites; they are afraid of our long rifles, and seldom attack or steal from parties traveling, unless driven to desperation by hunger, or the supposed necessity of killing a pale face, to make good the death of one of their own people." The new governor was unmoved.[71]

Nevertheless, McKee kept Californians informed of genocidal attacks. In a letter to the *Daily Alta California*, he reported that after Karuks or Shastas threatened miners upriver from Happy Camp, miners "went down to Happy Camp, raised a crowd, came up the Klamath River, collecting miners on their way up, and on the morning of [March] 12th surrounded two lodges at the Indian ferry, and shot all the men, several squaws, and destroyed the rancho. The same scene was enacted at Indian Flat, two miles above—but one escaping, and he wounded." McKee concluded that in these two genocidal massacres "some thirty or forty Indians were killed, and two whites wounded." In another public letter, McKee asserted, "All accounts agree in stating that the attack was wholly unlooked for by the Indians, who from the date of the treaty at Scott's Valley in November, had been perfectly quiet and inoffensive." Still, "A war of extermination had been declared by the whites against the Indians, and many aborigines have been killed."[72]

To Governor Bigler and some other California legislators, annihilation campaigns were an acceptable phenomenon because anti-Indian sentiment and even the massacre of Indians was tolerable or even popular among their political constituents. McKee reported the Klamath River massacres to Bigler, but the governor made no policy changes. Still, at least one state legislator did excoriate state-sponsored killing. While debating a new militia bill, Frank Soule "facetiously suggested an amendment providing that the soldiers in future Indian wars shall receive as pay $10 for each scalp they bring in." Soule, the only Whig elected to the state senate in 1851, sarcastically noted, "had this rule been adopted before some of the brave warriors who had gained titles and epaulettes would find their pockets in the end rather flat." A macabre joke about the state-funded murder and mutilation of Indians, Soule's statement condemned state legislators' acceptance of widespread mass violence against California Indians. However, Soule's critique went largely unheeded. Other state legislators actively organized lethal new militia expeditions.[73]

INTENSIFYING GENOCIDE IN THE NORTHERN MINES AND CONTINUED SUPPORT FOR MILITIA OPERATIONS

On April 6, 1852, five state senators from Klamath, Shasta, Siskiyou, and Trinity counties claimed that Indians had killed some 130 whites in their districts and stolen or destroyed $240,000 in property. They blamed Indians for all conflict and called on Governor Bigler to deploy regulars north or muster militiamen, warning that if he did neither, their constituents "must either unite and exterminate the Indians in their neighborhood, or withdraw from it." The *Shasta Courier* countered that Indians had probably killed twenty or thirty (not 130) whites, but Bigler had already acted. The day after Commissioner McKee wrote begging Pacific Department commander and brigadier general Ethan A. Hitchcock to send regulars north to protect Indians, Bigler asked Hitchcock for help against them, warning that if the army failed to intervene, Bigler would muster volunteers.[74]

While these letters were being exchanged, vigilantes continued killing. On April 13, the *Sacramento Daily Union* reported forty Indians killed in the Trinity River region. Three days later, Hitchcock wrote to Bigler promising to establish "a post on the Klamath or its vicinity." For at least 140 Nor-rel-muk Wintu people, the promise came too late.[75]

On April 18, 1852, J.A. Luckett reported the disappearance of a Mr. Anderson and his cattle near Weaverville. Finding Anderson's dogs shot with arrows, whites blamed local Nor-rel-muk Wintu Indians. A mob assembled, and Luckett outlined a genocidal sortie, "We will . . . overtake them, and kill all we find." That same day 123 people at Weaverville petitioned Governor Bigler for permission to raise "at least two companies of Riflemen."[76]

Without awaiting a reply, County Sheriff Dixon organized a killing squad at Weaverville: "Every man [was] required to swear that no living thing bearing Indian blood should escape them, when found with those who committed the murder." On the afternoon of April 22, scouts located a Nor-rel-muk Wintu village in a small valley on the South Fork of Trinity River, near Hayfork. Setting out at midnight, Dixon's men surrounded it and attacked at dawn. According to an April 25 letter from Weaverville, "Each rifle marked its victim with unerring

precision—the pistol and the knife completed the work of destruction and revenge, and in a few brief moments all was over." According to non-Indian sources,
Dixon's mob massacred 140 to 200 or more Nor-rel-muk men, women, and
children during that bloodstained dawn. Nor-rel-muk matriarch Grace Mc-
Kibbin later "placed the number of those killed at three hundred, as told to her
by her [father's] uncle [Bob Brown or *tawin t*ᵸ*ewis*] who survived the attack as a
small boy" by "crawling uphill through a gulch." In contrast, Dixon's death
dealers suffered a single wound. They returned to Weaverville in gory triumph
with "Indian scalps posed on standard poles [that] fitly portrayed the nature as
well as the issue of the battle." According to Augustus W. Knapp, "When they
entered Weaverville with one hundred and forty-seven or one hundred and
forty-nine scalps hanging to their girdles, you can well imagine the wild excitement and joy at the extermination of this tribe. Indian scalps were nailed to
many door posts in that town for quite a while." This atrocity, in which Dixon's
posse murdered almost every single villager, was clearly animated by the intent
to destroy the group.[77]

After this widely reported genocidal massacre, state legislators further institutionalized Indian killing. On May 3, 1852—less than fifteen months after raising $500,000 for ranger militia expeditions against Indians—legislators passed a
new $600,000 bond *"for the payment of the expenses of the Mariposa, Second El
Dorado, Utah, Los Angeles, Clear Lake, Klamath, and Trinity, and Monterey
Expeditions against the Indians."* The act specified the expectation that Washington, DC, would reimburse California, but that meanwhile the state would
pay 7 percent annual interest to bondholders. Such generous interest encouraged both banks and individuals to buy "war bonds," thus drawing both institu-
tional investors and others into collusion with legislators to support past and
future state Indian-hunting operations. The bond issue lured many Californians
into financially supporting the killing machine.[78]

Twenty-three days later, in response to requests from Commissioner McKee
and Governor Bigler, the army established Fort Reading, where Redding now
stands in the upper Sacramento Valley. Apparently mollified by the recent massacre, the new fort, or both, Bigler decided not to call out the militia at Weaverville.
However, the fort and its small staff of regulars did not stop regional violence.[79]

Large-scale killings continued in the spring and early summer of 1852 from
the Northern to the Southern Mines. Englishman William Jackson Barry recollected that, thirty-five miles from Yreka, en route to the Salmon River, he and
a group of prospectors engaged "about seventy Indians, with eight mules loaded
with swags, evidently stolen property." The prospectors "fired as fast as [they]

These bonds came in multiple denominations and displayed a stylized Indian man at
the center as well as President George Washington on the right margin. This bond
no longer has its payment coupons, which would have been attached to the bottom of
the bond, presumably because the bondholder redeemed them for a tidy profit.
California, "Bond of the State of California, for War Indebtedness in Conformity
with an Act Authorizing the Treasurer of the State to issue Bonds for the payment of
the expenses of certain Expeditions against the Indians," 1854. Courtesy of The
Bancroft Library, University of California, Berkeley.

could . . . wiped-out forty of the savages, and captured the mules." That May,
whites accused Indians on the Klamath of stealing and threatening to kill. They
then massacred "some thirty Indians." Whites also reportedly massacred "some
seventy Indians . . . on the Trinity for similar offences." At about the same time,
in response to theft and violence near Shasta City, miners gathered in Shasta to
push away "or exterminat[e]" Wintus. In June, a Pit River sortie killed ten to fifteen Achumawi and on June 29 John Bidwell—a politician who had once
championed California Indians' rights—led forces in an engagement that killed
at least eleven Indians, possibly Maidus or Yahi Yanas, at the head of Chico
Creek. A massacre also stained Independence Day that year when a Lieutenant
Moore attacked and massacred six people in a village that had been accused of
involvement with the killing of two miners. Even on federal reservations California Indians were not safe. On July 13, Commissioner Wozencraft reported to
Governor Bigler that "a party of men are charged with having made an attack

on some Indians living within a reservation [on Kings River] and have killed some several of them." Four days later, following the killing of a white man, the *Shasta Courier* reported the massacre of fourteen Shasta Indians in Scott Valley before describing the July 20 vigilante hanging of an Indian man they called "Scarface" at "the head of Shasta Valley."[80]

To the west, the Tolowa suffered their first major massacre at about this time. For eight centuries or more, the Tolowa inhabited the redwood coast and inland meadows and watersheds of northwestern California and southwestern Oregon. Before whites arrived, they employed a complex legal system to resolve disputes, used seashell currency to facilitate exchange, paddled seagoing redwood dugout canoes to hunt pelagic sea mammals, and constructed permanent rectangular redwood plank houses in politically independent villages united by a shared language. From the Pacific, Tolowa took crustaceans, seals, sea lions, and stranded whales. From the Smith River and various creeks they fished salmon, smelt, and trout. On the land they hunted elk, deer, and other game while collecting berries, seeds, tubers, and that California Indian staple, the acorn. These varied and abundant food sources supported 2,400 to 5,000 Tolowa in some twenty-three different settlements. Like many other California Indians, the Tolowa made densely woven baskets, lived in close-knit communities, and enjoyed saunas, games of chance, and storytelling. With the arrival of whites, the near extinction of the Tolowa began.[81]

In 1880, former US Indian Affairs commissioner George Manypenny, who had served from March 1853 to March 1857, wrote that "at an early day a party [sailed] up the coast from San Francisco on a gold hunting expedition" and landed "near the southern boundary of Oregon," in other words in Tolowa territory. Some thirty Indians "at the request of the 'Americans' proceeded to help unload the vessel." Unaware of some whites' annihilationist enmity, "The Indians labored faithfully." As the unloading proceeded, the prospectors placed two cannons on a large rock "near the landing and close to the vessel." Then, "When the work was completed, the Indians were requested to come on the rock to receive pay for their labor. As they passed up in Indian file . . . the guns were brought to bear upon them, and all but two were killed." Manypenny thus reported the murder of twenty-eight Indians.[82]

California Indians' experience of such massacres is challenging to piece together. In many cases few survived to tell the story. Those who did were often children, raised by non-Indians or constrained by traditional taboos against speaking of the dead. Many survivors were probably afraid to tell their stories, and relatively few non-Indians recorded them. Moreover, as mentioned earlier, government policies such as forced removal, boarding schools, and bans on traditional gatherings, mitigated against the transmission of oral histories between generations. Written eyewitness California Indian accounts of massacres nevertheless do exist.

Sinkyone woman Sally Bell—now honored by a redwood stand named after her at Sinkyone State Park—provided a rare California Indian eyewitness account of the coastal Needle Rock Massacre, which took place in the 1850s. Like many California massacres, the killers' surprise attack apparently targeted every person in the village. Bell remembered:

> My grandfather and all of my family—my mother, my father, and we—were around the house and not hurting anyone. Soon, about ten o'clock in the morning, some white men came. They killed my grandfather and my mother and my father. I saw them do it. I was a big girl at the time. Then they killed my baby sister and cut her heart out and threw it in the brush where I ran and hid. My little sister was a baby, just crawling around. I didn't know what to do. I was so scared that I guess I just hid there a long time with my little sister's heart in my hands. I felt so bad and I was so scared that I just couldn't do anything else.

Despite profound anguish and terror, Bell collected herself and fled:

> Then I ran into the woods and hid there for a long time. I lived there a long time with a few other people who had got away. We lived on berries and roots and didn't dare build a fire because the white men might come back after us. So we ate anything we could. We didn't have clothes after awhile, and we had to sleep under logs and in hollow trees because we didn't have anything to cover ourselves with, and it was cold then—in the spring. After a long time, maybe two, three months, I don't know just how long, but some time in the summer, my brother found me and took to me to some white folks who kept me until I was grown and married.

Bell's recollection suggests the perseverance against incredible odds necessary for an Indian to survive in California during the 1850s.[83]

Even when Indian-hunting expeditions did not result in mass killing, vigilantes made survival difficult by destroying Indian houses and food stores. For example, on July 21 a "Middle Yuba" correspondent reported that after "a white man was killed, and another [went] missing," miners blamed Indians, and "a party of about sixty men started out in search of the perpetrators." The vigilantes did not find them, but after hanging "an Indian boy" at Little Grass Valley they "burnt two of the Indian ranches, with all their food, &c."[84]

Sally Bell (Sinkyone) provided a rare California Indian
account of surviving a massacre. A redwood grove at
Sinkyone Wilderness State Park is now named in her
honor. Unknown artist, "Sally Bell, Needle Rock
Crossroads. August 1923," photograph, 1923. Courtesy of
The Bancroft Library, University of California, Berkeley.

NEW FEDERAL POLICIES AGAINST CALIFORNIA INDIANS

That same month, US senators exposed California Indians to more attacks
when, on July 8, they repudiated all eighteen California Indian treaties. This
comprehensive treaty rejection had deadly consequences. With federal Indian
policy having voided the diplomatic agreements, militia and vigilante campaigns became increasingly annihilationist. Simultaneously, betrayed and em-
bittered California Indians became more likely to attack whites. In accordance
with treaty provisions, many had relocated to provisional reservations. Once
senators rejected the treaties and nullified the reservations, immigrants began

encroaching on them. Responding to these intrusions and disillusioned by the Senate's rejection of the treaties that their leaders had signed in good faith, many California Indians returned to their ancestral lands, hunting grounds, and mining claims, only to find that they had been appropriated. Newcomers and the threat of violence now drove them to less hospitable locations—typically in the mountains—where survival was more difficult due to less available food and a colder climate. Even in the mountains they faced attack. And now that California Indians were no longer explicit federal wards, the army rarely protected them. In 1944, California attorney general Robert W. Kenny vividly described the impact of the Senate's failure to ratify the treaties: "The results of the rejection of the treaties left the Indians of California exposed, helpless and largely unprotected to ruthless evictions, unprovoked aggression, bitter persecution, conscienceless exploitation, dispossessed and despoiled of their property without recourse, to become homeless wanderers in the lands of their fathers." Kenny concluded, "In the bitter struggle for existence thousands perished . . . as the result of unprovoked war, massacre, disease and famine."[85]

It was worse than that. Elected California leaders continued spewing the rhetoric of inevitable extermination and genocide. On August 11, 1852, California senator John B. Weller—a Democrat who became California's governor in 1858—predicted to his fellow US senators that California Indians "will be exterminated before the onward march of the white man," explaining: "It has been the policy of the Government to drive [Indians] to the West; but the white man is now in the West." Therefore, "The Indian is placed in between the upper and nether millstones, and he must be crushed!" Warming to his topic Weller proclaimed: "The fate of the Indian is irrevocably sealed. He must soon be crushed by the encroaching tide of emigration. The hand of destiny has marked him, and soon he must fade away. The reflection to every humane heart is a melancholy one, but it is unavoidable. In the providence of God they must soon disappear before the onward march of our countrymen." Weller even emphasized that whites should assist Providence in what was nothing less than a declaration of his support for genocide: "Humanity may forbid, but the *interest* of the white man demands their extinction."[86]

Congressmen made life increasingly difficult for California Indians on August 30, 1852, by slashing the Senate's appropriation for California Indians by 17 percent. California senator Gwin explained the impact during a conference between senators and congressmen to discuss the issue: "We have taken their acorns, grass-hoppers, fisheries, and hunting-grounds from them." Thus, "The Indian must perish from cold and hunger, if this Government does not interpose to save him. From his hunting-ground we export an annual average value of $60,000,000 in gold, and the revenue paid to the Treasury, from one port in California, exceeds $3,000,000 annually, and yet the miserable pittance of $120,000, to feed and protect these original inhabitants of the country, is refused and cut down $20,000, by the grossly unjust policy adopted by the other House." Summing up Gwin warned, "If this is to be the policy of this Government towards these people, it will form a dark page in our history, if it does not bring the vengeance of Heaven upon us as a nation." The cut weakened the Indian Affairs Office in California, and, as a result, large numbers of California Indians struggled on reservations without sufficient food, clothing, medical care, or shelter. Reservation Indians were also largely unprotected from attack. As early as October 1852, Pacific Department commander and general Ethan A. Hitchcock endorsed the plan of stationing federal troops on reservations as "perhaps, the only one calculated to prevent the extermination of the Indians."[87]

THE SISKIYOU VOLUNTEER RANGERS EXPEDITION, 1852

In the summer of 1852, an inferno of Indian killing raged through Modoc country. Siskiyou County sheriff Charles McDermitt reported that on August 6, "forty packers arrived" in Yreka and urged him to send "assistance and protection [to] some three or four families" at Tule Lake in danger of being killed by Indians. McDermitt wasted no time. On August 7, he led twelve men east through high grasses and lava boulders to Tule Lake. He arrived too late. The emigrants "were all murdered by the Indians." On August 30, McDermitt lost three men to a Modoc attack.[88]

Ben Wright, later described in the *New York Times* as "a genuine Indian-killer," organized twenty-one volunteers who rode east from Yreka on August 29 to reinforce McDermitt. According to an 1884 history, this was "an expedition to annihilate utterly and without remorse" the Modocs who had attacked McDermitt. En route, Wright's men shot down two Modoc women gathering roots. An eyewitness reported that "one was an old woman of seventy, quite dead, and the other a young mother, who was only wounded [but] weeping bitterly." Wright then "plunged a knife twelve inches in length into her breast, with the cool remark that he would put her out of her misery." Arriving at Tule Lake on August 31 to find circled wagons besieged by Modocs, Wright attacked. According to him, Modoc people, including women and children, "Broke for the [shoreline] Tulies" and "we followed them about an hour and a half firing whenever we could get a sight of the Red Devils, about sixty shots were fired by our company and ten or twelve Indians killed," plus "a number of women and children" who "must have been drowned." Death toll estimates for this encounter range from

Ben Wright was a Quaker turned Indian killer
who led attacks against the Modocs. He
committed multiple genocidal atrocities.
Unknown artist, "Captain Ben Wright,"
photograph, undated. Courtesy of the Oregon
Historical Society, Portland, Oregon, OrHi 1711.

fifteen to sixty-four, probably because some Modoc bodies slipped below Tule
Lake's surface or were lost on its bulrush-choked shores. Moreover, white (and
perhaps some Indian) accounts tended to count only California Indian men
killed in attacks. No matter how many Modocs died, the killing was one-sided.
W.T. Kershaw later testified, "Our company sustained no loss whatever." That
evening, Wright's men killed and scalped a prisoner. Wright's volunteers soon
found new motives for additional atrocities.[89]

After the massacre, Wright's men reportedly discovered eighteen immigrant
bodies near Bloody Point, according to John Ross—now an Oregon territorial
militia officer—who with twenty-two Oregon volunteers, had joined Wright's

operation that September after reportedly finding fourteen other immigrant corpses at Lost River. Decades later, one source suggested that the Modocs killed as many as seventy-five whites in 1852. Although this estimate—made in the aftermath of the 1872–1873 Modoc War—smacks of exaggeration, in 1873 the Modoc chief Old Schonchin did recollect that the Modocs "made legitimate war . . . the whites had imposed upon them in the beginning, and they undertook to kill them off." The Modocs were, after all, a people resisting invasion and massacres.[90]

Having discovered the immigrant bodies on September 2, Wright requested supplies and additional volunteers. Five days later, fifty-five Yrekans petitioned Governor Bigler for help and authority to enroll a state militia company, enclosing with the petition Wright's report and the proceedings of a public meeting. Genocidal rhetoric now began to suffuse anti-Modoc operations. That same day, Yrekan H.S. Lewis wrote to Bigler asking him to assign authority "to enlist men here and procure the necessary supplies for a company to go against these Indians and subdue or exterminate them."[91]

General Hitchcock, meanwhile, changed the army's objectives. No longer deploying dragoons as peacekeepers, on September 15, he reported to Bigler, "Major Fitzgerald has about Eighty mounted men with him and I cannot doubt he will be successful in punishing the Indians." Wright's reported discovery of "the bodies of three men, one woman, and two children . . . butchered by the Indians" east of Yreka probably informed Hitchock's new position. When the dragoons entered Modoc territory, Fitzgerald's company gave Wright a boat, and by scouting the shores of Tule Lake forced Modocs to retreat to an island. Meanwhile, Fitzgerald's dragoons "burned fourteen Indian rancherias" and "somebody killed an Indian." Additional violence probably accompanied the dragoon's systematic burning of villages, but by early November, Fitzgerald's cavalcade was in Yreka en route to "winter quarters at Scott's Valley." Wright, in the meantime, relieved McDermitt and continued "hunting Indians" until November 24, with a command that grew to thirty-six men. Yet, following his Bloody Point Massacre, Wright found the Modocs elusive.[92]

This consummate Indian killer now became creative in his quest for Modoc blood, capturing a Modoc woman and releasing her with an invitation to attend a diplomatic meeting. As a result, "On the north bank of Lost River, a few hundred yards from the Natural Bridge," Modocs "attended, and, as agreed upon by both parties, no weapons were brought." Yet Wright's intentions were hardly peaceful. Early on November 8, Wright's men armed themselves, surrounded the Modoc peace delegates, and opened fire. Whites estimated thirty-one to fifty or more massacred that morning. Modocs and a white eyewitness married to a Modoc, who were likely more intimately familiar with Modoc casualties, estimated forty-three to ninety Modocs murdered in the trap.[93]

Wright's men paraded into Yreka sometime before November 29, with "Indian scalps dangling from their rifles, hats, and the heads of their horses. Scores of scalps were thus flaunted to show to the admiring crowd [and] cheers and shouts rent the air as they slowly rode through the dense throng." Then "the enthusiastic crowd lifted them from their horses and bore them in triumph to . . . the saloons, and a grand scene of revelry commenced." Faith in Indian killing moved one Yreka correspondent to praise pedagogic violence: "They have, by their bravery, taught the redskins that they cannot rob and murder the white man with impunity." It apparently did not occur to the writer that immigrants were trespassers destroying Modocs' means of subsistence or that Wright and McDermitt's campaign had shattered Modoc families and communities. Nor did he understand that the Modocs would continue to resist white attacks for decades to come.[94]

The Siskiyou Volunteer Rangers Expedition, as the Wright/McDermitt campaign came to be called, was the most lethal militia Indian-hunting operation yet. California's Senate Committee on Indian Affairs later asserted that Wright's "Mounted Rangers" had killed "in all, seventy-three of the enemy." The death toll was likely much higher, possibly 158 or more, according to other sources. In 1873 the Modoc chief Old Sc[h]onch[in] estimated that Wright's 1852 "Summer campaign" killed half of all Modoc warriors and "nearly 200" Modocs in all. By contrast, Wright lost only two or three men killed and three wounded. As historian Erwin Thompson observed, the violence of 1852 marked a turning point: "The prevailing attitude among [local] whites that all Indians should be exterminated was greatly reinforced."[95]

California legislators resoundingly endorsed Wright's campaign while Oregon's Indian Affairs superintendent did so indirectly. Despite evidence of premeditated massacre, on April 16, 1853, California legislators passed an act appropriating $23,000 to reimburse the "Volunteer Rangers under Captain B. Wright and Charles McDermitt." State legislators thus directly sanctioned these rangers' killings retroactively. The following year, Oregon's Indian Affairs superintendent rewarded Wright with the position of "special sub-Indian agent" in southwestern Oregon.[96]

The Modoc campaign represented three new trends in California ranger militia operations: it was small, inexpensive, and focused on killing as many Indians as possible. With just sixty-one men, it was a bantamweight compared to some previous militia expeditions in which hundreds had served. Whereas prior campaigns had cost at least $96,184, Wright's operation—on which the state would ultimately spend $14,987—was a relative bargain. Finally, whereas some previous expeditions had sought to use violence to force California Indians into treaties, Wright employed diplomacy only as a ruse with which to lure Modocs into a death trap. Killing was Wright's aim, and state legislators—who had rallied to sunder treaties—emphatically endorsed this emphasis. By streamlining the killing machine, the state entered an era of smaller, cheaper, and more lethal ranger militia operations.[97]

CONTINUED KILLINGS AND NEW FORMS OF STATE SUPPORT

As slayings multiplied, some journalists continued to invoke the notion of pedagogic killing. An October 1852 *Sacramento Daily Union* article on Indian hunting reported that "Owing to some depredations recently committed on Clear Creek by [Wintu?] Indians, Capt. Larabee organized a small party and gave them chase. The party returned a few days since, bringing with them a number of squaws and children. During their absence on the scout they killed fifteen Indians." The *Union* coldly concluded, "It is probable that this wholesome and impromptu chastisement will effectually check the serious depredations which had lately become alarmingly frequent on Clear and Cottonwood Creeks."[98]

As in previous years, the mass immigration of newcomers to California during 1852 had added fuel to the inferno of violence consuming California Indian communities. That fall, census agents reported 264,435 people, including some 33,000 Indians and 231,000 non-Indians, in the state. Although the census count was almost certainly an underestimate—Governor McDougal, for one, contended that California's 1852 population was 308,507—it indicated the magnitude of the immigrant tidal wave rushing ever deeper into California Indian lands, intensifying pressures on traditional Indian food supplies and increasing demand for unfree Indian labor. Pushed out of fertile valleys and bottomlands, many California Indians retreated even farther into the mountains where food was scarce and conditions were more difficult. To feed themselves and their families, more and more began raiding valleys to take food and stock from whites. These raids, in turn, inspired new vigilante campaigns in 1853 that further deprived Indians of food.[99]

Indeed, starvation was apparently claiming the lives of thousands of California Indians. On March 3, Arkansas senator William Sebastian told the US Senate, "The Superintendent has received information of a character beyond all dispute, that fifteen thousand [California Indians] have perished from absolute starvation during the last season." This was, in large part, due to the Senate's rejection of treaties and state-supported violence that forced California Indians into food-poor areas, and, even in those areas, to continue moving frequently to avoid attacks. In sum, these policies may be considered as "deliberately inflicting on the group conditions of life calculated to bring about its physical destruction in whole or in part." Yet, the state and federal governments maintained their California Indian policies, and when starving California Indians tried to feed themselves and their families by raiding, whites responded with massively disproportionate attacks that routinely targeted entire communities.[100]

However, California's looming Indian "War Debt" halted paid volunteer militia expeditions in 1853. Elected state officials still supported Indian hunting, but by December 15, 1852, the "War Debt" amounted to $771,190.05, or most of the $1.1 million raised in 1851 and 1852. Many legislators thus resisted additional militia-related spending, and in 1853 the State Senate deadlocked over whether or not to fund Wright's "Siskiyou Volunteers." The lieutenant governor broke the tie, but, knowing that they needed to retain funds to service the "War Debt," legislators opposed funding additional operations without receiving federal money.[101]

In 1853, vigilante operations continued, unchecked by federal treaties, unimpeded by regulars, and unconstrained by California's government. In January, vigilantes killed at least twenty-two Indians and burned or destroyed several villages. On January 29, thirty or forty men set out toward a Dry Creek Miwok village "to complete their work of driving the Indians off, or exterminating them." Miwok marksmanship drove them back, but the *Sacramento Daily Union* later explained that "the war of extermination" against the Dry Creek Miwok had only been "suspended."[102]

Whites attacked Mariposa County Indians that same month. After the theft of a "large fine horse," a posse tracked it to a presumably Yokuts village "near the Chowchilla" River. Following discussions, a white man shot the village chief dead, and Indians then killed the white man with arrows. The posse fled, but others returned and "burned the village, with all their traps, &c." A third group of twenty-five then tracked the retreating Indians. Launching a dawn attack, the vigilantes left "some ten or twelve dead on the ground," while sustaining a single "flesh wound." Hunger had probably motivated the theft that provoked these attacks. As a correspondent explained, "These Indians think the government of the United States has not acted in good faith with them, in not carrying out the stipulations of the treaty, and they complain that the Americans have cut off their supply of fish, destroyed their acorn trees, and have killed or driven away the deer from their hunting grounds, and that they are in a state bordering on actual starvation." In February and March 1853, hungry California Indians continued stealing stock, and whites responded by killing, hanging, and, on March 1, massacring thirteen of them, including three women.[103]

Theft frequently triggered massacres. In the spring of 1853, fifteen whites tracked stolen horses to an Achumawi village near "Squaw Valley mountain." Had the rustler been white, vigilantes would likely have tracked and lynched him. The response to an Indian theft was entirely different, often serving as the catalyst for genocidal massacre. Having surrounded the village at night, they could have captured its horses and inhabitants. Instead, as the sun rose, they murdered "every occupant of that little camp" including "some half dozen bucks and the usual complement of squaws and children." To the west, "a party of Indians," probably Wintu people, took "sundry blankets, flour, bacon, etc." from some miners and went to Hayfork. There, "Trinity River boys" caught them asleep and killed seven or eight of them. By March 5, G.C. Lusk of Trinity announced: "The Indians have committed so many depredations in the North of late, that the people are enraged against them, and are ready to knife them—shoot them—or inoculate them with small-pox—all of which have been done." Indeed, whites often killed without any provocation. In March, prospectors murdered two Indians who peacefully visited their camp near the Trinity and then killed another the next day before one of them "straddled [his companion] and scalped him alive."[104]

Economic ambition was one motive for attacking Indians. As a Shasta correspondent opined, "The Indians, the pests of the northern country, have thus far prevented the full development of our wealth." Fear of Indian attack was another motive. According to the *Daily Alta California*, "Throughout Colusa, Shasta, and in portions of Trinity and Siskyou, they are waging a most active and ruthless warfare against all whites." In this atmosphere, it took little to galvanize annihilationist Indian hunters. On March 26, the *Shasta Courier* proclaimed: "They must be whipped—if needs be, exterminated," or, more specifically, "hunted through the mountains and shot down without mercy." The newspaper's logic was simple, "What are the lives of a hundred of these savages to the life of a single American citizen?" After all, "Their total annihilation is certain, and it is now but a question of time—whether that event shall not be hastened by a war of extermination waged by the whites."[105]

Although they rarely killed California Indians in 1853, the 631 US Army regulars stationed in California did little to restrain Indian killers that year. A few miles from Fort Reading, the *Shasta Courier* reported that, on March 11, Indian hunters Henry Lutman and John Breckenridge pursued a party of Coast Range Indians suspected of stealing horses, "killing eight" of the Indians. Local California Indian people were so fearful of annihilationist attacks that some tried to preempt mass murder by themselves killing Indians who stole from whites. In April, for example, the *Shasta Courier* explained that Cow Creek Chief Numtarimon, likely Wintu, executed one of his own tribe for stealing "property from one of the Ranch men near Cow Creek." The chief was likely motivated by fear: "Numtarimon sees the speedy and utter annihilation of his tribe, unless they will live on terms of friendship with the whites." Moreover, the *Shasta Courier* asserted, "Numtarimon is what we call 'much good Indians'— that is, an Indian who refrains from stealing through fear." The chief was desperately trying to protect his people from "utter annihilation" amid a firestorm of mass murder. Soon thereafter, vigilantes started up the South Fork of nearby Cottonwood Creek, attacked a village, and massacred "some ten or fifteen" Wintu people.[106]

It was a terrifying time to be a California Indian: vigilante operations were often unpredictable, indiscriminate, and genocidal. In Crescent City that spring, someone saw a Tolowa man with a pistol. When a mob discovered that the weapon had once belonged to a white man, they stormed the nearby Tolowa village at Battery Point, "killing the one who had the pistol and eight others," and incinerated the rancheria. Meanwhile, in late April a man named Tomlinson who had lost two dozen oxen demanded "a scalp for every ox stolen." He and a dozen others went "to the head of Clay Bank Creek, 75 miles in the mountains" to "a rancheria . . . containing a population of some three or four hundred Indians, three of whom they succeeded in killing" before burning "the whole." On May 6, miners surprised and massacred thirty Nisenan people. Further south, the *Columbia Gazette* warned that Indians might soon face "extermination or expulsion."[107]

That summer, vigilante campaigns declined as traditional foods became more readily available with the season. Still, killings continued around Yreka. On July 20, vigilantes left town in pursuit of "stock stolen by the Indians" and "overhauled the thieves in a large and beautiful valley watered either by the M'Cloud's or Pitt's river, about 120 miles distant from Yreka." The ten vigilantes turned the peaceful meadows into killing fields. "The whites attacked them just at daylight, each man picking an Indian with his rifle, and then pitching into them promiscuously with their revolvers." When the slaughter ended, "20 or 25 were killed, only five of the band having escaped." Several weeks later, on August 7, the *Yreka Mountain Herald* reported "five or six Indians"—probably Shastas—killed in Scott Valley. Soon after, whites encountered "thirty armed

Indians" near Yreka and killed five. Finally, the Modoc man Jeff Riddle later wrote that "about the year 1853" vigilantes led by Jim Crosby (almost certainly Cosby) massacred eleven Modocs near the eastern shore of Tule Lake as well as "several" Hot Creek Modoc men, women, and children before returning to Yreka with "quite a few scalps to show their friends."[108]

For the Modocs, the patterns of exterminatory attacks were now clear. According to Riddle, "After the Modoc Indians had been killed by Crosby's men," a Modoc leader announced at a council that "God put our fathers and mothers here. We have lived here in peace [but] we cannot get along with the white people. They come along and kill my people for nothing. Not only my men, but they kill our wives and children." He added, "They will hunt us like we hunt the deer and antelope."[109]

In August 1853, events in Oregon once again intensified white violence against California Indians. The Rogue River War—between southern Oregon Indians and newcomers—terrified many whites in far Northern California. They feared the war would spread south. Some responded by marching north to join the conflict. Others called for extermination. In short order, the Rogue River War fever inspired a new surge of annihilationist violence that soon swept through Northern California.

On August 7, the *Yreka Mountain Herald* called for the state-sponsored total annihilation of all Northern California Indians: "Now that general Indian hostilities have commenced, we hope that the Government will render such aid as will enable the citizens of the North to carry on a war of extermination until the last red skin of these tribes has been killed. Then, and not until then, is our lives and property safe." The editorial continued: "Extermination is no longer even a question of time—the time has already arrived, the work has been commenced, and let the first white man who says treaty or peace be regarded as a traitor and coward." Imagining a vast alliance of California and Oregon Indians, the *Herald* saw enemies everywhere: "The Rogue River, Cow Creek, Grave Creek, Applegate Creek, Umpqua, Shasta, and Klamath Indians, and probably the Pitt River's, and also the Indians about the Klamath and other Lakes have united and declared an open and general war against the whites." This was fantasy. Still, local whites did think it important to crush Oregon's Rogue River Indians, presumably to stop the war from spreading south. On August 8, 1853, "twenty or thirty volunteers and fifteen soldiers left Yreka" for the Rogue Valley. Three days later, the Marysville *Daily Evening Herald* announced that "the citizens of Yreka have recently killed twenty-five out of a band of thirty thieving Indians," referring either to the Rogue River War or operations against Modocs east of Yreka. Later that month the *Yreka Mountain Herald* roared, "Let extermination be our motto!"[110]

Whites in the Crescent City area expressed similar sentiments and also sent volunteers north from the redwood coast. On August 14, a Crescent City correspondent worried that "the Rogue River, Klamaths . . . and Shastas are combined" against all whites. And Benjamin Franklin Dowell of Jacksonville, Oregon, recalled that, in August or early September of 1853, "a company . . . organized at Crescent City . . . marched . . . through Jacksonville and Rogue River valley to the council ground on Rogue River near Table Rock waving a flag on which was inscribed in flaming colors *Extermination*." Genocide was hardly a hidden agenda, and many rallied around it.[111]

The conflict that California volunteers encountered in Oregon likely only reinforced the belief of many in the necessity of annihilation. The Rogue River War soon became, according to the *Daily Alta California*, "A War of Extermination" in which "Citizens are arming in all directions to march against the Indians and scatter them or exterminate them wherever they can be found." The *Daily Alta California* later asserted: "The people are highly exasperated, and have determined to show no mercy in their warfare." Some Northern California whites adopted similar policies. Genocidal violence against the Achumawi, Atsugewi, Shasta, Tolowa, and Yurok increased as whites launched preemptive strikes and massacres. According to the *Daily Alta California*, both the *Shasta Courier* and the *Yreka Mountain Herald* demanded "a war of extermination [and] 'death to all opposition, white men or Indians.'"[112]

That fall vigilantes and soldiers killed scores of Indian people in northwestern California. By September 3, a party from Arcata had reportedly killed fifteen or twenty "Redwood Indians." About that time, whites also massacred some seventy Tolowas at Howonquet, near the mouth of the Smith River, before incinerating the town. And, sometime before October 24, soldiers killed eight to fifteen Indians, almost certainly Tolowa refugees fleeing white violence, near "Illinois creek" in the Siskiyou Mountains. Worse was to come. On October 16, a correspondent wrote from Scott Bar, "All this northern Cal. has been in a perfect fever of excitement about the [Rogue River] Indian war." Such fears soon catalyzed a massacre of staggering scale.[113]

In the late fall of 1853, large numbers of Tolowa proceeded to Yontocket, the largest Tolowa town, near Yontocket Slough, south of Smith River. There, Tolowa rendezvoused with Yuroks from the south, and Chetcoe, Winchuck, and other Oregon Indians from the north. These spiritual pilgrims came to pray on the sacred ground of Yontocket—the center of their universe—and to celebrate the World Renewal Dance, the *Nee-dash*, or "Feather Dance" at the place where the world was born. The Tolowa were not at war. Nevertheless, as celebrants prayed, danced, and socialized, whites led by J.M. Peters encircled them.[114]

Peters recalled that, when it became known that survivors of the Battery Point massacre were at Yontocket, he formed a thirty-three-man company, "well armed and resolved upon the extermination of all the Indians concerned in the killing of" California Jack and his companions. Peters's men encircled Yontocket and, as "the first rays of morning began to streak the Eastern horizon," opened fire. "Immediately the Indians came creeping out of their huts, armed with bows and arrows. But these primitive weapons were no match to the improved arms of the whites. . . . On all sides as the savages attempted to escape they were shot down and the crack of rifles and Indian yells, intermingled with the screams of the women and children, made the scene one of wild confusion." Peters's men burned Yontocket to the ground and "scarcely an Indian was left alive." He reported no women or children intentionally killed, but called the attack—in which he lost no men—"a saturnalia of blood."[115]

In 1923, thirty-four-year-old Tolowa Sam Lopez, his wife, and his father-in-law concisely described that nightmare dawn: "A large number of Indians were caught during a ceremonial dance and ruthlessly slaughtered." In 1963, eighty-seven-year-old Tolowa Eddie Richards summarized "stories told to him by his relatives" and an eyewitness:

> The white people got all around them. . . . Every time someone go out, never come back in. . . . They set fire to the house, the Indians' house. You could see them just cutting heads off. They stick them things into them; pretty soon they pick them up and throw them right into the fire. Some of 'em tried to get away, run down the slough. Soon as they get down there, if they don't get 'em right away, they get 'em from the other side when they come up. Shoot 'em right there, waiting for them.

Richards quoted a survivor reporting "hundreds and hundreds" of Indians at Yontocket, and related that after the massacre, "the water was just red with blood, with people floating around all over." Also in 1963, ninety-three-year-old Tolowa Amelia Brown explained that, based on what she had been told, "The white people were all around, they just watched. Then they set fire to the place. Women try to get away, they grab 'em, throw 'em in fire. Take pot shots at 'em when they try to run. Just two men got away." Three years later, Sam Lopez added that the vigilantes "killed so many Indians they could not bury them all, so they took the bodies and tied rocks around their necks and took them in the slough . . . and buried them that way." In 1979, Tolowa dance maker and tribal historian Loren Bommelyn related a harrowing view of the massacre's conclusion: "Over 450 of our people were murdered or lay dying on the ground. Then the whitemen built a huge fire and threw in our sacred ceremonial dresses, and regalia, and our feathers, and the flames grew higher." Then "they threw in the babies. Many of them were still alive." Finally, the attackers "burn[ed] the village to the ground."[116]

So many victims were incinerated, submerged, or floated away that the attackers could not obtain a complete body count. White sources estimated as many as 150 massacred that morning. Still, this may have been an underestimate. Tolowa sources—recorded first in oral histories and later written down in the twentieth century—insist that whites massacred as many as 600 people at Yontocket. Even if we halve the latter estimate, Yontocket may rank among the most lethal of all massacres in US history. Yet, it remains unknown except to a few scholars, locals, and, of course, the Tolowa.[117]

To the south, whites launched massacres that were less connected to fears swirling around the Rogue River War. When "Tiger Indians [probably Yahi Yana] stole cattle from Clark's ranch" in Butte County, vigilantes led by Manoah Pence caught and hanged their chief before massacring twenty-five people. That fall, after the killing of ten Chinese, Pence led the massacre of forty to sixty more Indians near the Feather River's West Branch. In stark contrast, that December soldiers killed three Indians at "Four Creeks," wounding six others and taking a dozen prisoners. The attack was bloody, but it highlighted a crucial difference between the army and vigilantes. Between 1851 and 1854, the army tended to kill small proportions of those California Indians whom they attacked and to take higher quantities of prisoners. Civilians, vigilantes, and militiamen tended to be more genocidal: shooting, beheading, burning, enslaving, and scalping most of those Indians they attacked.[118]

California's premier purveyor of racial loathing, the *Yreka Mountain Herald*, provided a window into the intensity of Indian hating and its connection to the Rogue River War. The day after Christmas 1853, the paper called the native peoples of Port Orford, Oregon, "enemies of the human family." Moving from the demonization of one Indian nation to an imagined need to annihilate all Native Americans, the paper proclaimed, "We can never rest in security until the red skins are treated like the other wild beast of the forest," that is, presumably exterminated.[119]

Encouraged by the press and unchecked by authorities, vigilantes continued to put these sentiments into practice in 1854, both near the Oregon border and further south. On New Year's Day 1854, Sacramento's *Pictorial Union* summarized the nature of vigilante campaigns: "Exasperated men arm themselves, meet at some rallying point, seek the trail of the savage foe, and follow it to his secret fastnesses, where an assault is made, which terminates in a general massacre." Newspapers published announcements of multiple massacres that month.[120]

In the meantime, California officials were arming Indian hunters. Although the state's voluminous "War Debt" made them reluctant to dole out militia funding, it cost the state very little to distribute the arms and ammunition provided by the US army. Thus, the state supported Indian hunting even when it had little money. Some California whites apparently understood this. Klamath state assemblymen Stephen G. Whipple and W.D. Aylett, as well as one A.J. Butler, asked for ten rifles, twenty muskets, and 1,000 cartridges for use against "hostile Indians." Governor Bigler agreed and on January 31 California quartermaster general William C. Kibbe sent the requested arms and ammunition to the Klamath County judge. As we shall see, these weapons and bullets probably found their way into the hands of annihilationist militias, some of whom organized later that year to hunt Tolowa people.[121]

By early 1854, the sources of conflict on both sides were settling into discernible patterns. As the *Daily Alta California* observed on February 1, "In the north the difficulties have again commenced. The Indians complain that some of their tribes have been shot down without provocation and that the treaties are not observed. The whites complain that the Indians are constantly stealing stock." Army captain Henry M. Judah led "a force of more than fifty" regulars and volunteers against Indians of the Klamath for killing four white men who had tried to kidnap Indian women, steal Indian ponies, and had killed seven Indians. The Yreka *Mountain Herald* proclaimed, "We hope our citizens will render him such aid as will secure the speedy subjugation, if not extermination, of these thieving tribes" and the operation ended only after Judah fired a howitzer on a group of Indians, probably Shastas, seeking refuge in a cave.[122]

To the south, the Upper Sacramento Basin was another site of continuing violence. On "McCloud's river, about twenty miles east of Pittsburgh," a town now submerged under Lake Shasta, Wintu or Achumawi Indians killed two whites and twelve or thirteen Chinese on February 3. Three days later, whites from Pittsburgh, Stillwater, Oak Run, and Clover Creek met at Pittsburgh and requested assistance from nearby Fort Reading, in the form of "supplies and men for an expedition against the Cloud River Indians." Colonel Wright, with "about 15 effective men—scarcely enough to protect the government property," refused. In keeping with established patterns, locals took matters into their own hands, killing nine Indians later that month.[123]

THE SHASTA EXPEDITION, VIGILANTE KILLINGS,
AND NEW LEGISLATION

On February 20, Pittsburgh, California, men organized 1854's first state militia Indian hunting operation and elected D.C. Johnson as captain. The thirty-five officially enrolled Shasta Expedition militiamen now marched into the McCloud River Valley. After scouts located an Indian camp—probably Wintu—they attacked the twenty-six people there, killing twenty-one or twenty-two and severely wounding three others. Only one or two escaped unharmed. From "friendly Indians" Johnson's men now learned of "an encampment of others who had a hand in the massacre of the 13 [white and Chinese] men." On March 3, the Shasta Expedition assaulted this village and killed seven more people. The company now disbanded, but reformed at Stillwater about mid-March after Indians reportedly stole some stock.[124]

Gathering at "Dribbelbis' Ferry," the group crossed the Pit River. Four days later, "midway between the Sacramento and [Mc]Cloud," they found an Indian target:

> Just at sunset, ten of the party discovered their fires about four miles distant. . . .
> At two o'clock next morning, sixteen of the company started for the ranch, and just at the dawn of day had the pleasure of taking a peep into their temporary encampment—halting a few minutes for light sufficient to draw a *hair sight*, we, by twos and threes completely surrounded them, and then the *charge*, and crack! crack! bang! bang! "Yopitoo! yopitoo!" echoed and re-echoed along that bloody gulch, till none were left to tell the tale save one squaw and a small boy, taken prisoners, and one "buck" that escaped, and he left many a purple drop in his trail, being shot through and through with a rifle bullet.

In total, they killed fourteen or seventeen that morning and sixteen or seventeen during this second sortie. The attackers then told prisoners to send a chief to make a local treaty, warning that "they would all be destroyed, if they did not desist from their thieveries and murderings." Finally, on April 13, the group's adjutant wrote to Bigler describing the operation and requesting compensation. Eventually, the state—now hard-pressed for militia expedition funding—dispensed $4,068.64 for the sixteen-day operation, paying thirty-five men. The Shasta Expedition demonstrated a new level of efficiency in state-sponsored Indian killing. The least expensive state militia operation yet had killed at least fifty-eight California Indians.[125]

Even if militia payments were now lower, vigilantes feared no repercussions from state or federal authorities and they continued killing Indians. Around

March 4, "about twenty persons organized themselves under the direction of Mr. W. Williams—whose bronzed visage, iron-grey locks and trusty rifle have long made him a terror to the Indians—and proceeded to the mountains near the source of Thomes' Creek [Dry Creek]." Three days later, "the party returned, having succeeded in burning five rancheries and killing and bringing in some twenty-three [Yahi Yana] Indians." On March 8, after the theft of "a large number of cattle and horses," vigilantes went back into the mountains and "found a number of them hid in caves," probably because their villages had recently been torched by Williams's men. Here, the vigilantes massacred as many as twenty-three Yahi Yana people, including three women. "They took twenty men and children prisoners, and brought them to the settlements." The report concluded: "A wounded squaw was left under a tree, where she would be found by her friends." Yet, after attacks in which so many of her countrymen had been killed or taken away, few were likely left to rescue her. Indeed, by 1854, the mere survival of many California Indian communities was in serious question.[126]

The March 1854 Battle of Yreka Pass, near the southern edge of Oregon's Rogue River War, if accurately reported, was an anomaly and the last of its kind. According to army colonel W. Willer, "On the 25th, with a command of 72, officers and men" he "pursued the savages into . . . the pass, near the Oregon line." Although extremely unusual, given Shastas' reluctance to fight large set-piece battles, Willer wrote that "about 500 . . . made a most bold and vigorous attack, but were repulsed after a well conducted fight, with the loss of sixty or seventy, and driven into the mountains." Willer reported himself and three other soldiers wounded as well as "five privates killed." Never again would regulars and Northern California Indians engage in such a large battle. The demographic toll of white attacks would make it impossible for any Northern California tribe or tribes ever again to field such a large force.[127]

As sustained but sporadic killing continued, state legislators further weakened Indians' ability to feed and defend themselves by denying them access to arms and ammunition. The March 24, 1854, "Act to Prevent the Sale of Fire-arms and Ammunition to Indians" made the sale or transfer to Indians of arms and ammunition punishable by a fine of $25 to $500 and/or a jail sentence of from one to six months. In effect until 1913, the act severely threatened California Indians' physical and food security. As legal scholar Chauncey S. Goodrich has pointed out, "The prohibition . . . was double edged to the Indian to whom hunting was both an occupation and a necessity, and to whom game, after the whites had scattered it by the use of firearms, was now beyond easy reach of bow and arrow." By making it more difficult for Indians to hunt, the act limited their direct access to food, in the form of game, as well as their indirect access to food purchased with money earned from the sale of buckskin, furs, and meat. As a result, the act forced some California Indians to take from non-Indians in order to survive, which fueled new genocidal attacks on Indian communities.[128]

The act also had more ominous implications. It bolstered whites' major tactical advantage: firearms. By blocking California Indian access to guns and ammunition, the act gave whites a monopoly and diminished Indians' ability to protect themselves and their families. With the superior range of muskets and rifles, miners, ranchers, and farmers could kill California Indians from beyond the effective range of bows and arrows, thus ensuring one-sided fights, and often slaughters. This 1854 legislation helped to make murders, massacres, and slave raids less dangerous for perpetrators by perpetuating if not exacerbating the existing military asymmetry between California Indians and non-Indians. Unsurprisingly, killings and massacres continued.[129]

By the spring of 1854, Indian killing was so common that it sometimes required no provocation, and guns allowed small numbers of whites to repeatedly massacre large numbers of Indians, with few or no white casualties. In 1854, the Yuki had yet to experience sustained contact with whites. They inhabited a "400 to 900 square mile" area, but most lived in Round Valley, which supported 6,000 to 20,000 Yuki people. The valley was so important to them that they called themselves "Ukomno'm," or "valley people." Amid meadows of grasses and clover, they lived in conical bark-and-hide dwellings. Along the Eel River and its branches, they built community halls thirty to forty feet in diameter, near water for cooling swims following dances, ceremonies, gaming, and gatherings. Able to shelter in their houses and halls, most wore minimal clothing and rarely donned footwear. As with some other California Indians, tattooing was common, and elaborate dances anchored traditional life. Both Yuki men and women donned dance regalia—which included feather headdresses, feathered capes, and special skirts—before dancing to the music of rattles, bone whistles, log drums, and human voices. Their complex valley culture flourished within a protective oval ring of mountains, creating a refuge the Yuki defended when at war, and from which they traded when at peace. Economic cornucopia and martial stronghold, Round Valley nurtured them for centuries. The land provided birds, small game, deer, acorns, and other foods. The rivers and streams yielded salmon, trout, and steelhead. Beginning in 1854, however, this bountiful sanctuary became a place of horror, in part because Yuki people did not have firearms. For them, Round Valley became a death trap.[130]

On May 15, six Missourian explorers entered Round Valley, some 150 miles north of San Francisco, in Mendocino County. According to Frank Asbill, son of one of the six, "the tall, waving, wild oats began to wiggle in a thousand dif-

Yuki ceremonial dance regalia included
elaborate feather capes and headdresses like those
displayed here. Philip M. Jones, "Yuki Indian
Head," photograph, 1900. Courtesy of the
Phoebe A. Hearst Museum of Anthropology and
the Regents of the University of California,
Catalogue No. 15-689.

ferent directions all at the same time." Pierce Asbill, the group's leader, called
out, "We've come a long way from Missouri to locate this place . . . an' be
damned if wigglin' grass 'ull keep us away! Git a-hold of yer weapons—we'uns
are goin' in!" Reaching a creek bed, the six horsemen reportedly encountered
thousands of Yuki people. "A war hoop went up from the Missourians [who] just
lay over the horse[s'] neck[s] and shot. . . . They just rode them down. . . . When
the shootin' was over, thirty-two dead and dying [Yuki] lay scattered." By day's
end perhaps forty Yuki lay dead.[131]

Meanwhile, Governor Bigler began preparing for new Indian-hunting militia
campaigns by working to obtain federal reimbursement for California's staggering "War Debt." His campaign seems to have been motivated by both a desire

to lower California's debt and an understanding that it would be difficult to raise money for future militia campaigns without obtaining reimbursement for monies already spent. Thus, on June 30, Bigler appointed State Comptroller Winslow S. Pierce to procure and organize the documents related to the militia expeditions of 1850, 1851, and 1852. Pierce was to document Indian "depredations," the army's "inability to respond," and militia expedition costs. It took months to organize the documents but on December 7, 1853, California Senator Gwin introduced "A BILL to refund to the State of California the expenses incurred in suppressing Indian aggressions in that State." Five days later, United States senators sent the bill to the Senate Committee on Military Affairs for review.[132]

On January 30, Governor Bigler ordered Comptroller Pierce to Washington, DC—where he remained for months—to help California's congressional delegation pressure Congress into assuming the state's "War Debt." With assistance from California's anti-Indian senators Gwin and John B. Weller, Pierce helped convince Congress to add a financial rider to the 1854 army appropriations bill. According to this August 5 bill, then Secretary of War Jefferson Davis was to "ascertain the amount of expenses incurred and now actually paid, by the State of California, in the suppression of Indian hostilities . . . prior to" January 1, 1854, and pay not more than $924,259.65 into California's treasury. This money would be used to retroactively help pay the costs of killing at least 200 California Indian people. The promise of Congress to potentially pay all of California's towering "War Debt" had a huge impact. It dramatically diminished elected state officials' fear of not being reimbursed by Washington for past militia operations and, more important, it fed hopes of federal support for future militia campaigns against California Indians. The result was a further institutionalization of California's killing machine.[133]

7

PERFECTING THE KILLING MACHINE: DECEMBER 1854–MARCH 1861

A relentless course of punishment for the most trivial offences is adopted, which is putting into operation without a declaration of war, the policy of extermination.

—*San Francisco* Daily Evening Bulletin, *1856*

I saw the white men chop off women's heads with axes, and build up a big fire into which they threw the bodies of infants. . . . About a hundred and sixty were killed.

—*Chief of the Fall River Band (Achumawi), 1923*

The World Renewal ceremony began late in the evening and continued until just before dawn. Illuminated by the dancing flames of a central fire, the line of celebrants moved together in ancient rhythms, the women's clamshell necklaces clicking against their shell dresses. Between the girls and women, male dancers, dressed as birds, deer, or hunters, supported the females in their heavy ceremonial regalia. From behind the line of dancers, singers raised their voices to fill the hall with the songs of the *Nee-dash*, or Feather Dance. It was a time of joy and thanksgiving. Between songs, the singers offered prayers of thanks for both the creation and the renewal of the world. Casting long shadows against the walls, the dancers moved for hours in the redwood dance house.[1]

Finally, the exhausted celebrants stopped. A singer offered a closing prayer of thanks and the World Renewal celebrants walked away under a full moon. Nearby, they passed through small round doorways into snug redwood plank houses with gently sloping peaked roofs. Outside, Lake Earl lapped softly at the shore. Inside, the Tolowa and their Indian guests bedded down and slept near kith and kin. Vigilantes had attacked World Renewal celebrants at nearby Yontocket a year earlier, but now, in the final days of 1854, the Tolowa had reason to feel safe. There had been no violence between whites and Tolowa for months, and whites had recently made peace overtures. The Tolowa thus likely assumed that they and their guests could carry out the sacred annual rites of the *Nee-dash* and sleep without fear at the Tolowa village of Etchulet, four miles north of Crescent City. The celebrants were unaware that Crescent City men had established their own branch of California's killing machine, with the support of both state legislators and the governor.[2]

Organized and enrolled in the spring of 1854, Crescent City's Coast Rangers and Klamath Mounted Rangers had been well armed by Governor Bigler for the purpose of Indian killing. In January 1854, California's state quartermaster general, William Kibbe, had sent the Klamath County judge twenty muskets, ten rifles, and 1,000 cartridges to arm Indian fighters. In July, Kibbe ordered the distribution of fifty rifles and twenty muskets to the Klamath Mounted Rangers. By November, the Coast Rangers had thirty-five rifles and appendages, 3,000 percussion caps, 2,000 rifle ball cartridges, and four swords. These two well-armed militia units now prepared to use the weapons, accoutrements, and ammunition provided by the state of California and the US Army to do one thing and one thing only: kill Indians.[3]

In the predawn hours of December 31, 1854, as many as 116 militiamen, accompanied by an unknown number of Smith River Valley whites, quietly surrounded Etchulet and took up concealed positions in the brush. At daybreak, as men, women, and children emerged from their houses to begin the day, the militiamen and vigilantes opened fire. They shot them down as fast as they could reload. Unable to see their attackers and possessing only three guns, the Indians could not defend themselves. Amid the carnage, a few evaded the crossfire and plunged into Lake Earl. There too they became targets, and those who swam across the lake encountered a second group of well-armed killers laying in wait. This was a slaughter of men, women, children, and elders—everyone in sight. When the shooting stopped, perhaps "hundreds" were dead; not more than five seem to have survived. The attackers apparently suffered only a single casualty.[4]

Some white and Tolowa sources suggest that Etchulet was the largest single massacre yet perpetrated by California militiamen, and that it introduced a new, more lethal era in the history of California's state-sponsored Indian killing machine. It also announced a new genocidal campaign. Two days later, the *Crescent City Herald* proclaimed, "The die is cast and a war of extermination commenced against the Indians."[5]

Still, some Tolowa sought to use diplomacy to save their people from annihilation. Just days after the December 31 Etchulet massacre, Tolowa leaders

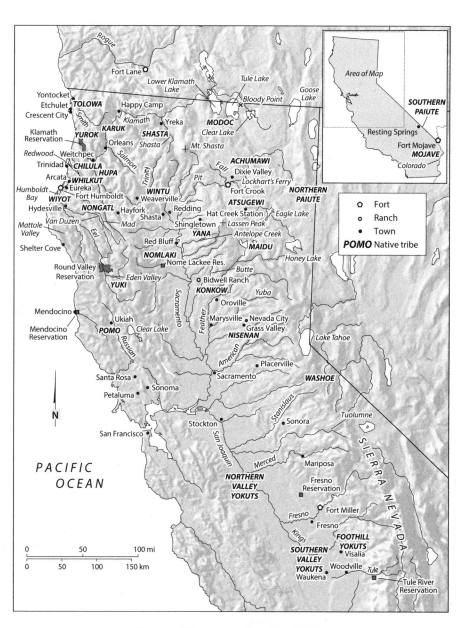

Fort Lane

Rogue

Yontocket
Etchulet **TOLOWA**
Crescent City

Smith

Happy Camp

Lower Klamath
Lake

Tule Lake

Bloody Point

Goose
Lake

Klamath
Reservation
YUROK

Klamath

KARUK

Yreka

MODOC

Clear Lake

SHASTA

Orleans   *Shasta*

+ Mt. Shasta

Redwood Weitchpec
Trinidad **CHILULA**
HUPA
Arcata **WHILKUT**

Salmon

Trinity

Fall

ACHUMAWI
• Dixie Valley

Pit

Lockhart's Ferry
Fort Crook

**NORTHERN
PAIUTE**

Humboldt
Bay
WIYOT

Eureka
Fort Humboldt
• Weaverville

Hydesville •
NONGATL

Van Duzen

Hayfork
• Shasta

WINTU

Redding •

ATSUGEWI

Hat Creek Station • Eagle Lake

Mattole
Valley

Mad

Shingletown
+ Lassen Peak
YANA

Antelope Creek

Shelter Cove •

Red Bluff •

Eel

NOMLAKI
• Nome Lackee Res.

MAIDU

Honey Lake

Round Valley
Reservation

Eden Valley

Butte

• Bidwell Ranch
KONKOW

YUKI

Sacramento

• Oroville

Yuba

Mendocino ■

• Ukiah
POMO

Clear Lake

Feather

Marysville • Nevada City
• Grass Valley
NISENAN

Mendocino
Reservation

Russian

Lake Tahoe

Santa Rosa •

American

• Placerville

• Sonoma

Sacramento •

WASHOE

Petaluma •

N

Stockton •

Stanislaus

• Sonora

Tuolumne

San Francisco •

S I E R R A   N E V A D A

**PACIFIC
OCEAN**

San Joaquin

Merced

• Mariposa

**NORTHERN
VALLEY
YOKUTS**

Fresno
Reservation
■

Fresno

• Fort Miller

Kings

• Fresno

**FOOTHILL
YOKUTS**
• Visalia

**SOUTHERN
VALLEY
YOKUTS**

Woodville

Tule

Waukena •

Tule River
Reservation ■

| 0 | 50 | 100 mi |
| 0 | 50 | 100 | 150 km |

Area of Map

**SOUTHERN
PAIUTE**

Resting Springs •

Fort Mojave
MOJAVE

Colorado

⬠ Fort
◯ Ranch
● Town
POMO Native tribe

Events of December 1854–March 1861

"CHY-LUS, COSE-TOOTTI, [and] YUT-SAY" negotiated with whites, signing a local treaty with two Smith River men in which they surrendered all of their firearms. The *"Great Chief"* explained "that he wanted to live in peace, that he always told his Indians not to steal from the Whites . . . and that the conditions of this treaty were all very good." Yet, on January 17, the *Crescent City Herald* reported that another committee seeking to make other Tolowa people sign a similar treaty had murdered three of them. Other whites apparently employed betrayal in their quest to annihilate the Tolowa. According to local historian Doris Chase: "In January, 1855, some of the whites told some of the Indians they would furnish them with meat for a feast if they would invite Indians from another village. The Indians invited their neighbors and had a big feast. Then, in the very early morning, the whites came and killed all the Indians they could find." Chase's narrative suggests another preplanned massacre.[6]

The Klamath Mounted Rangers were less creative. After Etchulet, they killed "several" Tolowa on the Smith River, and a correspondent reported that between Trinidad and Crescent City "whites are shooting [Yurok and Tolowa people] whenever an opportunity offers." The Coast and Klamath Mounted Rangers officially took the field for only four weeks, but by January 25, 1855, they may have killed hundreds of Tolowa and Yurok people. The *Yreka Herald* agreed with the *Crescent City Herald* that this was a "war of extermination," what we would today call genocide. A new era of increasingly lethal state-sponsored Indian killing had begun as the US government, state legislators, militiamen, and vigilantes perfected the killing machine.[7]

THE "RED CAP WAR" AND THE KLAMATH AND HUMBOLDT EXPEDITION

Known as the "Red Cap War" or "Klamath War," this tangle of vigilante and militia operations targeted Karuk, Hupa, and Yurok people between the Pacific and the confluence of the Salmon and Klamath Rivers even as the army became involved. Like many so-called wars in California, a relatively small Indian act triggered massively disproportionate genocidal killing in the form of a state-sponsored annihilation campaign. On or about December 10, 1854, a white man attempted to rape a Karuk woman and mortally wounded an accompanying male Karuk. In retaliation, Karuks killed an ox that they thought belonged to the killer. Learning that the murderer had sold this ox to another man, Karuks offered to pay the current owner for the ox but he refused. Likely assuming that whites might now launch the kind of genocidal reprisals that typified white responses to lost stock, "The Indians became frightened."[8]

It was only an ox, and the Karuks had offered compensation, but some white men now articulated genocidal intent, underscoring how lost stock was sometimes a pretext for mass murder. On January 5, Stephen Smith wrote from Big Bend, "We have organized ourselves up this river in order to exterminate the treacherous tribe that we now exist amongst." The following day, miners at Orleans, on the Klamath, resolved to disarm local Karuks, warning that "noncompliance would be visited with death" after January 9. Others advocated more ominous aims. On January 16, militia captain Frank Buzelle—who had raised a volunteer company—wrote from Orleans to warn that "it was in contemplation to make a general attack on the tribes, wheresoever they might be found. No exception was to be made." All were "marked down for slaughter." Buzelle offered to help prevent killing and reestablish peace, but his warning came too late.[9]

How many villages the vigilantes assaulted remains unclear, but on January 16 a slaughter ensued. Many villages apparently complied with the disarmament decree. However, some Karuks and Yuroks refused, and a party attacked the "Red Caps [Yuroks] to destroy the ranches." Red Caps resisted, killing three attackers and wounding "four or five others." The vigilantes now retreated, after burning "the Indian Ranches" and killing "a number" of warriors. Now well-versed in camouflaging genocidal operations with the rhetoric of a just war, whites used Yurok resistance to these unprovoked attacks to launch a wider, state-sponsored killing campaign.[10]

While admitting that whites had caused the conflict, the *Humboldt Times* proclaimed, "A peace *must be conquered.*" Others agreed. Between January 11 and 23, Humboldt and Siskiyou counties raised five volunteer militia companies totaling 234 men. Coastal Yuroks, with no connection to the conflict, soon came under attack. Militiamen killed two or three near Redwood Creek, five near the creek's mouth, "and others at the Lagoon." Meanwhile, US Army captain Henry Judah rushed to stop the conflict.[11]

Many local whites were bent on genocide. Buzelle, an unusual militia captain who defended California Indians, reported reaching the mouth of the Salmon River on January 24, "Just in time to save a general massacre" of the Karuks. The *Humboldt Times* described miners "determined to commence an indiscriminate massacre of all the Indians" in the Klamath watershed, and the *Sacramento Daily Union* added that "people look upon it there as a war of extermination, and are killing all grown up males." The killing spread like a pool of blood. As Captain F.M. Woodward's militiamen approached "the Cappell and Morro ranches" on February 4, "Red Caps" fired, probably to repel the rangers. Woodward then shot one of his Indian guides as a traitor, and one of the captain's

Yurok people, like this man, paddled dugout redwood canoes as a traditional form of transportation and to fish on the Klamath and Trinity Rivers in northwestern California. Edward S. Curtis, "Yurok Canoe on Trinity River," photograph, 1923. Courtesy of Library of Congress, Prints & Photographs Division, Edward S. Curtis Collection, LC-USZ62-118588.

men shot an Indian. The following day, his militiamen massacred "twenty warriors" and captured "eighteen squaws" at Morro, also killing "six warriors" and capturing "five squaws" at Cappell. Like many California militia massacres, these were one-sided atrocities: the militiamen suffered a single wound. And, like many attacks, this one had little to do with the original casus belli.[12]

This was no war, but rather a thinly veiled annihilation campaign. By mid-February, Judge Fletcher of Klamath County reported that Indians had retreated to the mountains, where "whites are hunting them down like deer." He added that just eight white men but seventy to eighty Indians had been killed. Meanwhile, some sought a final solution. On the Klamath, Captain Judah encountered opposition from men advocating "the total extermination of all the Indians in this section." Genocidal intent persisted even as the campaign wound down. On February 4, Buzelle's militiamen mustered out. Still, some advocated "exterminating all the Indians." Indian hunting thus continued. Almost a month later, the *Crescent City Herald* reported that the Klamath Rifles of Weitchpec "killed a large number [of Indians] and compelled the main body to sue for peace." On March 22, Judah reported that the Woodward brothers (C. and M.) took their militiamen to an Indian village "called the Indians from their homes, shook hands with them, and immediately afterwards, each white man picking his man, numbers of the Indians were shot."[13]

Demonstrating the army's power to stop genocidal killing campaigns, Captain Judah ended this so-called war. On March 23, he dismissed two of the remaining militia companies. At the same time, he used diplomacy and his thirty regulars to pressure Indians into surrender. On April 7, Judah held a peace conference with tribal leaders, but continued capturing and killing Red Caps. Sometime before May 26, vigilantes "at the mouth of Salmon" murdered two Karuk(?) people. The last two militia companies now mustered out, and on June 1 the campaign ended, after killing a minimum of forty-five Indian people. Surviving Red Caps—who had simply tried to defend themselves and their families—lost their freedom, consigned to California's new Klamath Indian Reservation, which, as we shall see, imposed hunger on its inmates and exposed them to physical attacks.[14]

Since 1850, California militia expeditions had been supported, in part, by state funding. As a Nome Lackee Indian Reservation correspondent argued in an open letter of February 10, 1855, "If the nine hundred thousand dollars expended . . . to exterminate them, had been appropriated in teaching them the arts of civilized life and habits of industry, how much better it would have been, and how many persons would now have their consciences clear of guilt, and their skirts clear of blood." The three major supports for militia expeditions had included, up to this point, laws, state funding, and state-supplied weapons and material that, in turn, came primarily from the US Army. To these three foundations, the US Congress now added a fourth pillar that strengthened California's killing machine while enlarging the federal government's supporting role.[15]

FEDERAL LAND BOUNTIES, THE 1855 STATE MILITIA ACT, AND UNFREE INDIAN LABOR

On March 3, 1855, Congress dramatically expanded the 1850 and 1852 Bounty Land laws that offered federal acreage to military veterans. Under the 1855 act, Congress promised 160 acres to any regular, militiaman, or volunteer who had participated in a battle or served for at least fourteen days, as long as the United States eventually paid for the operation. At a time when War Secretary Jefferson

Davis refused to release any of the funds appropriated by Congress to pay down California's 1850–1853 "War Debt," this act helped to maintain interest in volunteering for militia expeditions by linking participation to potential pay and plunder as well as possible bounty land warrants, which could be converted into land or sold. The 1855 Bounty Land Act thus provided powerful new federal incentives that further rewarded participation in volunteer California militia Indian-killing campaigns.[16]

The following month, state legislators began working to help California militia veterans obtain such bounty land warrants. On April 16, the Assembly asked the governor to provide the US Department of the Interior with muster rolls of all the volunteers who had served against California Indians so that such men could obtain bounty land warrants "more expeditiously." By rewarding those who campaigned against Indians with 160 acres of federal land—itself taken from California Indians without treaties—the federal government remunerated men who participated in the killing machine at little cost to itself and thus incentivized militia campaigns against California Indians.[17]

That same month, California legislators bolstered the state militia system with a bill of their own. The measure increased the salary of the militia's adjutant and quartermaster general to $3,000 per year, provided for state militia units to be armed in parity with comparable army units, exempted volunteer militiamen from jury duty, mandated regular drill exercises, and required all white men ages eighteen to forty-five not enrolled in a militia unit to pay an annual $0.25 tax to fund the militias. The tax raised just $664.33 between July 1, 1855, and June 30, 1856, but in his December 1855 annual report, Adjutant and Quartermaster General Kibbe praised the bill for creating new militia companies, swelling the ranks of existing ones, and improving drill, discipline, and efficiency. Kibbe was also brutally clear about the militia's genocidal purpose: "There are but two alternatives before us, viz: either to wage a war of extermination, or abandon a large and productive territory."[18]

General Kibbe, Governor Bigler, and War Secretary Davis also professionalized California militia units in 1855 by providing them with military manuals. Kibbe assembled *The Volunteer: Containing Exercises and Movements of Light Infantry, Riflemen and Cavalry, Compiled from the Most Approved Works and Dedicated to the Volunteers of California*. This 268-page primer covered topics ranging from artillery to bayonets, training, and tactics. Targeting volunteer militiamen, Kibbe sought to provide "thorough and practical Elementary Instruction . . . to remedy one of the greatest defects of the Militia System." On September 10, Governor Bigler officially approved and adopted Kibbe's "System of Military Tactics" as "the Tactics of the State of California." That

As California's quartermaster and adjutant general
from 1852 through 1863, William C. Kibbe
oversaw the state militia and played a major role
in the genocide of California Indians. He
facilitated the state-recognition and arming of
volunteer companies, authored a militia manual,
and directly organized and oversaw some
campaigns. In all, his militiamen killed well
over 1,000 California Indian people during his
tenure. Thomas B. Sherriff, "W.C. Kibbe,"
photograph (carte de visite), 186-?. Courtesy
of the California History Room,
California State Library, Sacramento.

Christmas Eve, Davis sent the California militia "ninety two copies of the system of Tactics recently adopted for Light Infantry and Riflemen." Kibbe, Bigler, and Davis thus sought to professionalize California militiamen and, ultimately, make them a more lethal killing force.[19]

Meanwhile, demand for unfree California Indian labor, in combination with acquiescent officials and permissive state laws, drove a murderous slave-raiding surge. The *Grass Valley Telegraph* reported that near Clear Lake "during the last season," Mexican kidnappers first murdered the adults before capturing and selling "three or four hundred of the [Pomo?] tribe." The genocidal crimes of "killing members of the group" and "forcibly transferring children of the group to another group" were typically indivisible from such raids. Indeed, an April *Daily Alta California* article explained that kidnappers frequently killed Indian parents who tried to protect their children. California's anti-Indian laws and passively consenting officials supported this murderous trade. As the *Daily Alta California* concluded, "It is not only hard to get testimony necessary to convict, but some of the officials are said to exhibit a willingness to see the unholy practice continued."[20]

The US Army also refused to intervene, thus emboldening kidnappers and slave raiders. In 1855, War Secretary Davis pointedly refused California superintendent of Indian Affairs Thomas Henley's request for US soldiers to arrest California slave raiders, responding that this was "the appropriate duty of the civil officers [and if] necessary, the *posse comitatus*." Given state officials' reluctance to capture and prosecute kidnappers and slave raiders, their crimes continued. On August 9, Robert White wrote from Mendocino to inform Henley that "Ind. reports . . . say the Spaniards stole twenty or twenty five young women" and on August 20 he wrote from Mattole Valley that an Indian reported "a lot of Squaws and children and men" recently stolen. Davis's refusal to deploy United States troops already in California amounted to a tacit grant of federal legal impunity to those involved in California's de jure and de facto systems of Indian servitude. The results were a continuation of murderous kidnappings as well as the widespread forced separation of California Indian children from their communities, both of which constituted genocide.[21]

California now had a legal, political, and social system that allowed lethal slave raids against California Indian communities and that overtly supported ranger militia expeditions and their massacres. It took little to inspire Eureka and Yreka papers to call for mass murder. When packers "lost ten mules" in May or early June of 1855, the *Yreka Mountain Herald* roared that Indians "should be pitched into and exterminated this time." Later, after someone killed a white man near Eureka, the *Humboldt Times* wrote of Eureka vigilantes, "We have every confidence that they will make a good report of themselves by the number of scalps they bring in."[22]

Suspicion alone was the pretext for some massacres. P.A. Chalfant recalled participating in the May 1855 "Cow Creek Massacre," launched because some suspected that a Yana village there was harboring an Achumawi leader who supposedly planned to burn the nearby mill. Attacking the "six or eight . . . pine-bark wickiups" just before dawn, some twenty-five attackers unleashed a withering fire and after sunrise, persuaded "three or four squaws and about as many little ones" to surrender. "The arm of a papoose was dangling by its side, broken by an unwitting rifle shot. The blood poured from a deep wound in the shoulder of its mother. The others were unhurt." The men received no mercy. The attackers torched the houses and as men emerged "dazed, half suffocated . . . the crack of three or four rifles is heard, the Indian convulsively draws himself together, and goes down, right at the edge of the fire!" Chalfant counted thirteen Indian men shot dead and concluded that the atrocity amounted to "Butchering Indians on Suspicion." It is difficult to imagine vigilantes committing a similar massacre against whites in California and even harder to imagine such an atrocity being motivated by rumor alone. Yet vigilantes and ranger militiamen increasingly targeted whole California Indian villages and tribes for destruction in the 1850s, killing and enslaving Indians indiscriminately with no legal restraints.[23]

Attempted crimes often led to similar atrocities. In late June or early July, after Indians reportedly "attempted violence upon a lady" in Humboldt County, whites killed "three warriors" on the Wiyot River. According to the *Humboldt Times*, "Since that time, rumor has it that fifteen [have] been killed" in the same area. The doctrine of mass, indiscriminate retaliation was central to the destruction of untold numbers of California Indians, and continued state-sponsored militia expeditions—which routinely followed this doctrine—were crucial to maintaining the legal and political environment in which this doctrine was practiced throughout the state.[24]

THE SISKIYOU EXPEDITION, OR "HUMBUG WAR," 1855

Several weeks later, the murder of an Indian initiated a cycle of violence that triggered a genocidal ranger militia campaign against Shasta Indians on the upper Klamath. On July 26, a miner named Peters shot one of three Shastas and they, in turn, killed him. Shastas then slew eleven whites "between Little Humbug and Horse creeks" along the Klamath. The response to this unusually large killing of whites was predictable: the killing machine went into operation with devastating effect. Albert G. Walling and J.P. Munro-Fraser later explained, "Excitement knew no bounds; every man constituted himself an exterminator of Indians." Locals mustered five militia companies in late July, and killed "a great many" Indians "without the least reference to their possible guilt or innocence." By July 31, Horsley & Barrow's Express predicted, "Every buck Indian that can be seen in the mountains, will be shot." Walling and Munro-Fraser believed militiamen made no such distinctions: "Many miserable captives were deliberately shot, hanged or knocked into abandoned prospect holes to die. Over twenty-five natives, mostly those who had always been friendly, were thus disposed of. Even infancy and old age were not safe from these 'avengers.'"[25]

On August 2, a sixth militia company mustered in and, based on reports that the Shastas who were suspected of shooting Peters had fled north, five companies (about 200 militiamen) marched to "the reservation at Fort Lane," in southern Oregon. There they threatened to attack if the army garrison did not surrender the suspects. When the army refused, the militiamen retreated to California, again demonstrating the army's ability to stop mass murder if they so chose. The Siskiyou Expedition ended on Halloween. Involving 237 men over more than three months, the operation eventually cost Californians more than $14,000. Ultimately, Siskiyou whites did get their men or, more likely, two scapegoats. Yreka authorities later tried, acquitted, and released two Indians suspected of killing a miner. However, this judgment did not protect the acquitted men. After the two left the jail, vigilantes "took them a little south of town, where they were summarily shot and tumbled into an old mining shaft."[26]

Whites' desire to rid California of its indigenous peoples was increasingly clear to some Indian leaders. At an October 1 diplomatic meeting between whites and Nisenan people near Nevada City, Nisenan Chief Weimah summarized California Indians' frustration with government policies and their determination to resist. Although a white man recorded and thus mediated his speech, Weimah's meaning remained clear: "American man come—Indian here first. . . . But you want send Indian away—Indian no go." Weimah concluded by emphasizing his moral outrage, "White man no keep promise—no good—white man no good." Not far to the north, vigilantes massacred some twenty-five Indians, probably Yana, later that month.[27]

PREDICTING TOTAL ANNIHILATION

By the fall of 1855, the possibility that many, or all, surviving California Indians might soon be physically exterminated was apparent to multiple journalists. On

October 20, the *Daily Alta California* asserted that in upper Northern California, whites were "determin[ed] to 'exterminate' the Indians," later adding that "throughout the North . . . many Indians may be killed, and even the whole race 'exterminated.'" The *Marysville Herald* then predicted "a thorough and merciless war of extermination" in Northern California. The *Sonora Herald* emphasized that the "work of extermination" against North American Indians was nearing "termination." According to the *Herald*, whites should complete this "work" and "destroy the implacable enemies of our race." The *Herald* concluded: "The border wars now in progress are but the beginning of the final end of the red man." Joining the chorus of doom, the *Sacramento Daily Union* stated that "a war of extermination is bound to be waged against the tribes of Indians who inhabit that portion of the continent lying westward of the Sierra Nevada." The editorial did acknowledge an Indian perspective: "The unerring rifle has cleared the forests of game, and mining operations, or other branches of industry have driven the fish from the streams. It is not astonishing that they should be driven to thieving, and even murder, to provide themselves with the means of livelihood." Nevertheless, "nothing save complete extermination will mollify that insatiable spirit of revenge which actuates the greater number of those who have volunteered to inflict chastisement." Two weeks later, the *Nevada Journal* attempted to justify California Indians' "final extermination" with a familiar argument: "The inevitable fate of the Indian is to vanish like mist before the all-powerful blaze of civilization." The fact that five different papers were discussing, and sometimes trying to justify, California Indians' annihilation likely normalized and justified the process as inevitable in some readers' minds. Regardless, the extermination of California Indians was now a widespread public media topic, which made the ultimate outcome of continued killing clearer than it had ever been before.[28]

Whites continued to hunt California Indians. According to an early twentieth-century interview with the chief of the Fall River Band of Achumawi, "About 1855 the Warm Springs band went to Yreka and stole a number of horses and mules" after which "white men tracked them to their camp and killed a good many." The Achumawi leader added that soon thereafter an Achumawi band "drove off a bunch of horses from Shasta valley" and "were followed and overtaken near Danaville [where] fifty to sixty men, women, and children were killed." As the US Army's Pacific Department commander, General John Wool, reported to War Secretary Davis that November, "In the northern part of California, many whites are for exterminating the Indians." California Indians resisted "with the desperation of despair" but whites routinely attacked when Indians thought that they were safe. "On Christmas night," 1855, vigilantes surrounded and attacked a house filled with Indians who had come "to spend the night in frolic and fun" with Bidwell's Ranch Indians, near present-day Chico. The revelers resisted, but whites gunned them down, killing five people.[29]

If 1855 was violent—with at the very least 433 California Indian deaths reported—1856 was only somewhat less so. During January and February, when food was particularly scarce due to winter weather and to white strategies that involved destroying food and shelter, hungry Indians raided for sustenance. Vigilantes retaliated ferociously, capturing and then executing five Wintu "on Trinity River, near Robinson's." They also shot and killed six Yana people near Shingletown, and some thirty others nearby, including "men, women and children!" In April, vigilante killings reached a fever pitch. Sometimes vigilantes killed Indians for entertainment—for example, when "men on the borders of Mendocino county" attacked "'Tatoe Indians,' and wantonly killed eleven of them . . . 'just to see them jump.'" In other instances, vigilantes responded to Indian resistance with similar massacres. Whites slew five Nongatl or Whilkut after they attacked an Eel River Valley mill.[30]

Suspicion also continued to catalyze killing. On April 15, vigilantes massacred twenty to thirty Yana on Cow Creek, to prevent a possible Yana attack on a nearby mill. Days later, whites killed thirteen Indian men at Clover Creek, and on April 20, they slaughtered seven Karuks near Happy Camp. In late April, more than fifty vigilantes repeatedly attacked Karuks, killing a minimum of ten people. Finally, after a white man and three "friendly indians" were killed "eighty miles [north of] Petaluma" while trying to capture an Indian boy, Parker Valley men began "arming and preparing for a war of extermination against the [Yuki?] tribe."[31]

THE 1856 MILITIA ACT, KLAMATH EXPEDITION, AND TULARE EXPEDITION

Amid these vigilante massacres, state legislators passed yet another militia bill, on April 25, reinforcing the killing machine, reiterating their commitment to it, and thus encouraging new ranger militia expeditions while adding fuel to California's inferno of anti-Indian vigilante violence. The new act doubled California's militia tax to $0.50 per nonserving white adult male and required volunteer militia officers to contribute $5 to the state military fund in return for their commissions. Most important, it provided for the state-funded distribution of General Kibbe's militia manual on training and tactics to all commissioned and noncommissioned militia officers. Soon thereafter, the state launched three new militia campaigns against Indians.[32]

On May 3, 1856, California governor J. Neely Johnson's local representative enrolled thirty militiamen in Klamath County. Thus began the brief Klamath Expedition. Local Tolowa people largely eluded the operation, but state documents recorded five Indians killed between May 5 and May 31. Meanwhile, a far more lethal expedition had unfolded hundreds of miles to the southeast in the hills to the east of the San Joaquin Valley.[33]

On April 22, presumably hungry Yokuts Indians risked their lives to drive off 500 cattle in Tulare County. Whites recovered the stock, but the county sheriff called out Captain Foster De Master's standing militia company of some sixty mounted riflemen. They proceeded to attack a Yokuts community on the Tule River's north fork. The Yokuts resisted, and after a two-hour battle De Master retreated with an injured man, leaving six Yokuts dead and eight or ten wounded. Other "men on White or Quartz river [also] killed five or six Indians." It is almost impossible to conceive of militiamen or vigilantes responding to white cattle rustling in this way much as it is difficult to imagine the governor supporting such violence. Still, Governor Johnson provided De Master's riflemen with officers' commissions and probably sixty rifles, accoutrements, and 2,000 percussion caps from the state militia arsenal, a cache largely supplied by the US Army. By May 6, some fourteen Indians had been killed but no whites had died.[34]

Militiamen now received a report that some 700 Yokuts had gathered in the mountains east of Woodville. Leading eighty men, a Captain Poindexter attacked them on May 7. They were reportedly "in such a position that it would have been impossible to dislodge them with treble the force which Capt. Poindexter had." Three hours of fighting later, Poindexter retreated. Having been assaulted without provocation, the Yokuts now pursued him "nearly to Woodville, burning all the houses they came across and destroying all kinds of property. Several of the whites were injured, but none were killed" while the Yokuts' losses "must have been considerable." Enraged local whites now planned to attack the Fresno Indian Reservation, but twenty US regulars stopped them, again demonstrating that the army could halt mass murder when its officers chose to do so.[35]

As the genocide intensified in 1856, the US Army increasingly protected California Indians with one hand while killing them with the other. Tulare Mounted Riflemen surgeon Dr. S.G. George met with Governor Johnson to request assistance, and Johnson—who in 1851 had threatened to "make war upon the [Indians], which must of necessity be one of extermination"— agreed. Johnson gave George permission to take eighty guns, 5,000 rounds of ammunition, and commissions to raise two more ranger militia companies to support De Master's men. To augment this lethal force—which eventually grew to 132 militiamen—US Army general Wool ordered Captain Stewart, of Fort Miller, to bring his regulars to the aid of the militiamen. Thus, federal troops joined the Tulare Expedition. On May 13, a Lieutenant Livingston led twenty-six regulars—accompanied by twenty of De Master's militiamen—to charge a fortified Yokuts village. The combined army and militia force killed as many as forty people before survivors fled. In keeping with well-established tactics, attackers burned the rancheria and almost everything in it. According to militia brigadier general Edward F. Beale—who had served a few years earlier as California's first federal superintendent of Indian Affairs—"the whites [were determined] to prosecute the war to extermination against the Indians."[36]

General Beale now brought the Tulare Expedition to a close. Beginning at "midnight on the 5th of June," he sent runners to invite a dozen chiefs, representing tribes "living between Tule River, and the County line on the waters of Kings River" to a peace conference. Having sustained perhaps 100 casualties, all twelve arrived to find Beale accompanied by seventy regular soldiers. Beale threatened "summary and severe chastisement" if they did not sign his prepared treaties. "Very anxious" chiefs did so on June 10. That same day, Beale reported dispatching runners to initiate negotiations with a thirteenth, Tule River tribe. By July 1, the one-sided Tulare Expedition was over. According to Beale, only one white man "had been killed, and a very few wounded." The campaign had ended, but the killing had not. After reported thefts that August, King's River region whites murdered five or six people at a nearby Yokuts village.[37]

Vigilante violence also flared elsewhere in California that summer. A Smith River Valley farmer named Ward Bradford recalled that "in July, 1856, five or six roughs [were] killing all the [Tolowa] bucks they could find. They had already surrounded two small villages and killed twenty or thirty of the inhabitants." Then they threatened a Tolowa community of "about one hundred persons." Bradford tried to help save them from being massacred by leading them to Crescent City's lighthouse island, where he hoped they would be safe. In August, a North Cow Creek rancher reported that, following Yana(?) stock rustling, "parties have been or are out of course, on another 'digger hunt.'" The rancher predicted: "A few years and the like depredations and excursions will not be heard of. Neither will the Indians." That same month, after receiving "reports of outrages by Indians on Redwood Creek," twenty men left Arcata and assaulted a Whilkut village along Pine Creek, killing seven warriors. At the same time, another ranger militia campaign was already unfolding.[38]

THE MODOC EXPEDITION, 1856

In the fall of 1855, some Siskiyou County whites advocated the total annihilation of California Indians. As one Yrekan reported, "The citizens of Siskiyou . . . are determined to leave not a vestage of the savage race alive." Winter weather delayed a new "war of extermination," but not for long. On June 12, 1856, state senator and militia general John D. Cosby reported on "isolated parties of miners and herdsmen . . . murdered and robbed," possibly by Modocs, Klamaths, Shastas, or others. That day he dispatched "thirty mounted men to ascertain the position and strength of the enemy, and for the immediate protection of the threatened country." Cosby thus used the rhetoric of protecting the vulnerable to initiate a campaign that would last for months, deploy more than 230 militiamen, and kill scores of Achumawi, Atsugewi, and Modoc people.[39]

On June 17, Governor Johnson wrote to General Wool of Cosby's expedition and warned that unless Wool sent additional regular troops, he would enlist militiamen. Wool apparently responded that he had no troops to spare. Thus, between July 17 and 23, Cosby raised and mustered in three companies of mounted volunteers totaling 204 men—with Johnson's authority—and rode east for "Modoc country." Modocs protected their homes and families as best they could. On July 29 or 30, militiamen attacked a village, burned it to the ground, and killed two Modocs while one militiaman was mortally wounded. Several days later, Lieutenant H.H. Warman attacked warriors near Tule Lake and Bloody Point. After Warman died and two of his men sustained wounds, the militiamen retired, leaving the Modocs "master of the field." Such was the valor and skill of Modoc resistance. Yet, with eight Modocs dead, it was a victory won at great cost. The tribe—worn down by four previous killing campaigns—could ill afford such losses. That same day, Cosby's militiamen took the lives of three more Modocs.[40]

Not yet aware of these killings, on August 4, Governor Johnson ordered Cosby "to take such measures and employ all the power you may possess, as the Major General commanding the 6th Division Cal. militia under the laws of this State, which may be absolutely necessary for the protection from Indian hostilities of the persons and property of the people within your command." The state militia's supreme commander thus granted Cosby carte blanche to do as he saw fit. Cosby took his men on a killing spree.[41]

Before contact, the Achumawi inhabited a region about the size of Connecticut, ranging from the snowfields and geothermal vents of Mount Shasta and Lassen Peak in the west to the alpine summits of the Warner Range in the east and from the waters of Goose Lake in the north to beyond Eagle Lake in the

In this photograph, an Achumawi woman, wearing a rabbit-fur cloak and an
intricately decorated woven hat, displays one basket while beginning work on
another. Edward S. Curtis, "Achomawi Basket-maker," photograph, 1923.
Courtesy of Library of Congress, Prints & Photographs Division,
Edward S. Curtis Collection, LC-USZ62-98674.

south. In their forests, meadows, mountains, and lava beds, the Achumawi lived
in summer teepees covered with tule or, in winter, cedar bark lodges. The lower
altitudes of the Pit River watershed cradled the Achumawi heartland, but their
diverse ecosystems yielded a rich variety of foods. Wearing shoes of woven tule
and clothing sometimes fashioned of cedar bark or plant fibers, they gathered
acorns, berries, clover, insects, roots, and seeds, maximizing yields through fire-
based land management. From their politically autonomous villages, Achumawi people also hunted badgers, bears, beavers, deer, elk, waterfowl, and other
game. They carried or stored these foods in the tightly woven and intricately
patterned baskets for which the Achumawi are renowned to this day. A variety
of fish and freshwater clams provided additional protein in their diet and helped
to support perhaps 3,000 or more Achumawi people before contact. However,
successive killings and massacres took hundreds of Achumawi lives, reducing
their number to perhaps 1,000 people by 1910.[42]

On August 6, Cosby's force rode south into Achumawi territory. On August 7, a militiaman murdered a lone Indian with a revolver. That same day, Cosby's men surrounded, surprised, and stormed a village, killing all nine men there and possibly a woman, without any militia casualties. The militiamen now seized human spoils: "Two of the men took a fancy to a couple of very good looking squaws, which they now have in camp. Gen. Cosby also took a boy, which he has with him." In all, they captured some thirty women and children, human beings presumably swallowed up by California's genocidal traffic in unfree Indian labor. Cosby then returned north to Tule Lake where his men killed at least two or three Modocs before a correspondent in the militia camp ominously suggested that remaining Modoc warriors "need a good cleaning out of the worst kind."[43]

Cosby's militiamen now rode to Goose Lake, Russian Springs, and Klamath Lake. For Indian people, Cosby's attacks likely came as bolts from the blue. One day, between August 21 and September 4, Cosby's force surprised a community at "Great Klamath Lake," possibly in Oregon, "who were so completely surprised that the squaws and papooses were playing and laughing together, and the bucks sitting around and enjoying the sport." As in so many similar situations, the militiamen could have forced these peaceful villagers to surrender. Instead, they charged, killing four Indian men. They likewise stormed another village, where they killed another Indian man. At Clear Lake they massacred eight or ten Modocs, who never had "an opportunity to fire a shot or an arrow." The following day they attacked another camp, killing "two men and one squaw." Ruthless and relentless, some of Cosby's rangers continued to hunt Achumawi people.[44]

During twenty days on Pit River, a detachment of Cosby's force stormed several villages and killed at least five men, but had a plan to utterly annihilate the Achumawi. Their commander explained: "In the winter . . . the Indians are compelled to take up quarters in the valley; then one company of men could kill the whole tribe." Meanwhile, US Army captain Judah arrived to punish Achumawis for allegedly attacking a wagon train. Surprising the suspected band near Lockhart's Ferry, Judah's regulars killed at least six Achumawi men in early September from beyond the range of their arrows.[45]

To the north, Cosby's militiamen continued hunting Modocs with a lethal new asset: eight boats. Once sanctuaries, the Modocs' lake islands and marshes became killing fields. On or just before October 3, using three boats on Tule Lake, Cosby's men massacred twenty-six Modocs "in the tule [and] but four made their escape." Cosby's officers next located a Modoc community on a Lower Klamath Lake peninsula. Attacking at dawn on October 9, they slew "several" Modocs on land. Militiamen waiting in boats then sank three escaping Modoc canoes while the land-based attackers "destroy[ed] their ranches, *muk-a-muk, ic ters, etc.*" and captured "several children." Cosby's militiamen counted five Indians killed, but the bodies of others likely disappeared in the lake. Meanwhile, on Pit River, another Cosby unit killed five Achumawis before Modoc Expedition members began mustering out.[46]

Celebrating the work of his 237 ranger militiamen, Cosby officially reported having killed some 185 Indian people. His Modoc Expedition may thus have been the most lethal California militia expedition to date, although the 1854–1855 Coast and Klamath Mounted Ranger Expedition may have killed hundreds at Etchulet and beyond. Momentous events taking place that August and September in Washington, DC, now lay the groundwork for more California militia campaigns.[47]

THE 1856 CONGRESSIONAL FUNDING BILL

By July 1856, California senator John B. Weller's patience with War Secretary Davis was at an end. Weller's constituents had waited almost two years for the money appropriated by Congress for California's 1850–1853 militia expeditions. Still, Davis refused to release any of the funds. It was to Congress that Weller again turned for help, and he found a legislative ally in Louisiana senator Judah P. Benjamin. Benjamin was a connected southern politician who later served as the Confederacy's attorney general, war secretary, and finally as its secretary of state.[48]

On July 21, Senator Benjamin introduced a bill to pay California's "War Debt." Some senators objected to paying California's creditors, rather than sending the money to the state treasury, but no senator offered any recorded objection to the lethal Indian-hunting militia campaigns that the money would retroactively fund. The United States Senate passed Benjamin's bill and, after a similar debate, the House did so as well. The bill directed Davis "to pay to the holders of the war bonds of California the amount of money appropriated by" the August 1854 act of Congress: "to wit" $924,259.65. Congress then appropriated money for both principal and interest up to January 1, 1854, "amounting in all to $840,648[.]65." By November 15, 1856, the US government had given California $814,456.84 for distribution to bond holders as reimbursement for their financial support of genocidal killing. This enormous cash transfer provided crucial funding for California's killing machine and made the genocide an increasingly state and federal project.[49]

The congressional act had a profound impact in California, reaffirming Washington's support for the state's anti-Indian militia killing campaigns while

The same year that a photographer made this image, US senator Judah P. Benjamin of Louisiana sponsored a senate bill that ultimately gave California more than $800,000 to pay for militia campaigns. This money provided crucial funding to California's killing machine and made the genocide there an increasingly state and federal project. Unknown artist, "Judah Philip Benjamin," photograph, 1856. Courtesy of Library of Congress, Prints & Photographs Division, LC-USZC4-12291.

dramatically confirming that the federal government would help to pay for them. The US Congress fed the killing machine with money provided by taxpayers from across the country and, in so doing, the nation's elected representatives in Congress sanctioned the machine's operation. Congress thus catalyzed a new series of militia expeditions. As the *Sacramento Daily Union* later observed,

"The necessity for Indian wars has apparently arisen since Congress assumed and paid the war bonds issued for Indian war expenses."[50]

Unsurprisingly, vigilante killings continued in California. On September 30, a group of men took the shooting of several cattle near Hempfield's Ranch, in Humboldt County, as an opportunity to kill three to fifteen Chilula or Whilkut Indians in their village at daybreak. The next month, after a white man received a mortal wound in an Indian village, gunmen massacred seven Wiyot people "near Grizzly Bluff." Nineteenth-century historian Theodore H. Hittell concluded: "In 1856 there were a number of small expeditions by whites against [Nongatl, Sinkyone, Wiyot, and other] Indians in the Eel river and Humboldt bay regions, in each of which, though little or no provocation had been given, from six to ten Indians were killed . . . when volunteers went on the hunt they made it a point to avoid ridicule on their return and were sure to bring back scalps."[51]

Much as they had done in 1855, observers again commented on extermination wars in 1856. A front-page editorial in the San Francisco *Daily Evening Bulletin* framed the issue in terms of race and land: "If [Indians] refuse to move upon the demand of the settlers, a relentless course of punishment for the most trivial offences is adopted, which is putting into operation without a declaration of war, the policy of extermination." From Yreka, George Metlar added that "in seven out of ten cases of violence and outrage, the white man has been the aggressor" and that "at this moment the work of blood is going outward." Metlar warned: "In a little time the race of the red men will have become extinct— their career will be closed forever." Despite such dire warnings, neither state nor federal officials stopped sanctioning and funding the killing. Instead, they incentivized it.[52]

Round Valley, in northern Mendocino County, saw the beginnings of intensive vigilante killings targeting local Yuki Indians in 1856. Hungry Yuki were eating stock, and ranchers' responded with genocidal ferocity. As several California legislators later wrote of Indian killing in and around Round Valley, "From the imperious and pressing demands of hunger, [the Yuki] kills the stock of the settler as a means of subsistence, and in consequence thereof, a war is waged against the Indian." Benjamin Arthur later testified that in 1856, "the Indians were killing stock, and the whites were killing Indians." John Burgess added, "For every beef that has been killed by them ten or fifteen Indians have been killed." Farmer John Lawson explained, "I lost twenty hogs; I found the meat in the rancheria. We went after the Indians; we shot three; the balance, five in number, were tried at the reservation, found guilty, and hanged. . . . It is the common practice when the Indians kill stock to pursue them and kill them."

Arthur estimated that during the winter of 1856–1857 alone, whites "killed about seventy-five Indians." Yet, the total number slain was far higher. In 1860, rancher Dryden Lacock testified that in 1856: "The first expedition by the whites against the Indians was made, and have continued ever since; these expeditions were formed by gathering together a few white men whenever the Indians committed depredations on their stock; there were so many of these expeditions that I cannot recollect the number . . . we would kill, on an average, fifty or sixty Indians on a trip . . . frequently . . . two or three times a week." According to another record of this deposition, Lacock testified: "We could kill, on an average, 15 or 20 Indians on a trip." Either way, if his memory is credible, Lacock seems to have participated in the *killing of thousands of Indians* between 1856 and 1860.[53]

THE 1857 MILITIA FUNDING BILL

By agreeing to help pay California's 1850–1853 "War Debt," Congress turned the state's genocide campaign into a federally supported program. Congress effectively told California legislators that they could expect additional federal money for past and future California Indian-killing expeditions. Indeed, on January 7, 1857, Governor Johnson announced to state legislators, "The balance of War Debt"—then totaling $218,020.19—"will probably be paid by the General Government." In response, California legislators introduced a series of small militia-related bills to fund past operations.[54]

Federal financial support also helped to concoct and catalyze new ranger militia expeditions. In March, the *Daily Alta California* explained that the federal payment of California's "war debts" has *"no doubt, tended to encourage certain classes of whites to create new causes of strife with the Indians,* or at least to repel their aggressions in a way that would enable them to establish new claims upon the public authorities for their services. Thus, we have had an Indian war in progress on our northern borders, with some intermission for two or three years." Even if most killers did not receive pay, such federal funding reinforced the notion of Indian killing as an acceptable, US government–sponsored project. The very day that this editorial appeared, some intoxicated Wintus on Hay Fork Creek drove a white woman from her tent. Vigilantes reportedly took this as a reason to massacre fifteen Wintu people.[55]

The following month, federal financial support for past operations inspired the passage of a major new state militia bill. The April 25 bill appropriated up to $410,000 for the so-called War Fund. Of this fund, legislators earmarked up to $210,000 for 1850–1856 campaigns and "depredations." This included up to $14,000 for the 1855 Siskiyou Expedition, $10,000 for an 1852 Klamath Expedition

(Siskiyou Volunteer Rangers Expedition?), $110,000 for the 1855 Klamath and Humboldt Expedition and "property destroyed in the Indian war," and $10,000 for the 1856 Tulare Expedition. The bill also appropriated $5,000 for an 1850 Sutter County "expedition against the Indians," $1,000 for the 1855 San Bernardino Expedition, $20,000 for the 1850 and 1851 Nevada County expeditions and "property destroyed by the Indians" there during those years. It also allocated $20,000 for 1852–1855 Los Angeles County "expeditions, wars and depredations," and, finally, $20,000 "for the expeditions, wars and depredations in Yuba County, since" January 1, 1850, perhaps including Green's 1850 expedition. These were all reimbursements for past events but left at least $200,000 for future operations. Unsurprisingly, the major anti-Indian expedition of early 1857 continued previous patterns of state support for genocidal militia campaigns.[56]

MOUNTED VOLUNTEERS OF SISKIYOU COUNTY EXPEDITION, 1857

Senseless white violence triggered the campaign. The chief of the Fall River Band of Achumawi later recollected that Harry Lockhart and "Buckskin Pants" lost their horses and sent their "two young Indians," presumably Achumawi, to search for them. When the youths failed to find the steeds, Lockhart "shot them both." Responding to this double murder, in early 1857, Achumawi attacked Lockhart's Ferry on Pit River, killing Harry Lockhart and four other men, burning the settlement, and suffering five men killed. In response, the US Army planned a spring campaign, but eighteen impatient Yrekans led by Samuel Lockhart—Harry Lockhart's brother—launched their own expedition. Deep snow and storms forced them back to Yreka, but not before they left a poisonous calling card on Pit River. According to the *Shasta Republican*, Samuel Lockhart reportedly "mixed a considerable quantity of strychnine with flour, and placed it where it would be found and consumed by the starving Indians." This was not the first time that Samuel Lockhart had poisoned Achumawi people: "He also stated, with apparent gusto, his poisoning achievements during the last summer while living with his brother in Pitt River Valley. According to his own story a number of the Indians of that section of the country were treacherously poisoned by him." The article concluded, "We have lost our wonder at the untimely fate of the settlers of Pitt River Valley."[57]

Samuel Lockhart may not have been the first or only person to poison Achumawi people and he was certainly not the first colonist to poison American Indians. He noted that others left poisoned sugar "on the roadside for [Achumawi] Indians" in 1856. Still others likely preceded these poisoners. In 1897, an unidentified man explained that "in early days," he and a partner baked 200 loaves of bread at Shasta, kneading eighteen bottles of strychnine into the dough. Then they rode "sixteen miles east of where Redding now stands" to the outskirts of an Achumawi village. There they intentionally dropped the loaves from their pack animals—being sure to make it look like an accident. According to the man, a Sacramento *Union* reporter later "counted ninety-three bodies" in one place, but "that figure didn't represent the complete returns." Poisoning American Indians was not a new mass murder tactic. As early as 1623, English colonists reportedly poisoned "some tooe hundred" Powhatans at a diplomatic conference on the Potomac River. Rancher H.L. Hall also reportedly used poison to kill California Indians in the Round Valley region. In 1860, William Scott testified that "Hall said he had . . . put strychnine in their baskets of soup, or what they had to eat." Still, those killing California Indians generally preferred bullets to poison, and Samuel Lockhart was no exception.[58]

On February 9, 1857, militia brigadier general David D. Colton enrolled a volunteer company to attack the Achumawi on Pit River, and on March 16, Samuel Lockhart and thirteen others joined the dozen Mounted Volunteers of Siskiyou County. Between about April 1 and April 18, they attacked the Achumawi three times, killing some twenty people including at least "two or three women and one child." The chief of the Fall River Band of Achumawi—then "a little boy"—survived a massacre that may have been part of this campaign. He re-called: "At dawn one day a party from Yreka, headed by Lockhart's brother, at-tacked the camp and killed ten or twelve women and children" near "Dixie Valley." He survived because "His grandmother dragged him out at the first sound of shooting and crept under the edge of the bluff, where she hid in a cave, concealing the entrance with stones. Others saved themselves in the same way." Still, the militiamen continued to hunt for Achumawi, and in late April they found them. Camouflaging the atrocity as "another battle," they presumably massacred thirty-nine people, reporting that "the whole number of Indians killed [in the expedition] is fifty-nine." The militiamen then gave thirteen Achumawi children—deliberately taken from their communities—"to [Yreka] families" thus "forcibly transferring children of the group to another group" in another act of genocide. The company mustered out on May 2 and the state later paid them more than $5,000 for their services.[59]

Still, Samuel Lockhart continued relentlessly hunting Achumawi people. The chief of the Fall River Band of Achumawi described how Lockhart "established him-self on the north side of Pit river at the mouth of Fall river." From this base he would set his "huge dogs" to tearing Indian people "to pieces" while shooting every Indian he found alone. Thus, "It was said that he alone killed at least twenty Indians."[60]

Population dynamics help to explain why California Indians in relatively remote areas, like the Achumawi, were now subject to killing campaigns. Between 1853 and 1857, 228,059 passengers disembarked at the Port of San Francisco and 139,002 departed. California's population thus seems to have increased by at least 89,957 people in fewer than five years, to say nothing of those immigrants who arrived via other ports and overland routes. As these tens of thousands rushed into previously uncolonized areas, they seized land and imposed new pressures on California Indians who were already resisting invasion, thus creating new conflicts. Yet it was the killing machine—which effectively granted whites legal impunity and often arms, ammunition, and money for killing Indians— that made genocidal campaigns so common. The army's renewed willingness to launch its own murderous operations only strengthened the killing machine.[61]

THE 1857 PIT RIVER ARMY CAMPAIGN AND VIGILANTE KILLINGS

In late May, the army launched its first major California Indian-hunting expedition since 1850. Some considered the Achumawi less than threatening. In June, a Mr. Jenner reported that even if a single man met twenty or twenty-five Achumawi, they would run away if he showed a gun. Nevertheless, Lieutenant George Crook's regulars picked up where the Mounted Volunteers of Siskiyou County had left off, with murderous effect. Crook—a West Point graduate who later became a famous "Indian fighter"—gunned down the first victim in late May. In June, he and his men killed six to eight Achumawis, while Crook received an arrow to the thigh that he carried for the rest of his life. Still, Crook and his men were only beginning to spill blood.[62]

July of 1857 was a catastrophic month for the Achumawi people. On July 2, Crook's soldiers massacred thirty-five of them, wounding thirty-five others. On July 4, they slew another, and on July 7 massacred twenty-one more. Crook's men later killed two others. He then used martial rhetoric to camouflage a July 25 massacre, describing how his troops "had a glorious fight, leaving twenty-three dead on the ground that we knew of, and nine wounded; besides there must have been a great many more killed and wounded that they could not tell any thing about." For killing at least eighty-nine Achumawi people without losing a single soldier, the *Shasta Republican* hailed Crook as "one of the best Indian fighters attached to the service in the State." In a subsequent foray against the Atsugewi, Crook killed two "and took two prisoners." His rampage finally ended in early September, wrapping up a genocidal US Army campaign that underscored the increasing importance of the federal government as both a funder and a direct perpetrator of genocide in California.[63]

To the south and east, vigilantes also launched killing campaigns that summer and fall. Following the murder of a white man "near Antelope Mills," fifteen vigilantes attacked a Yahi Yana village in Mill Creek Canyon on June 15. But this time their intended victims had rifles. The Yahi returned fire, counterattacked, and pushed the vigilantes down-canyon. Yet it was a costly victory. One attacker reported just two whites injured but "at least 50 Indians . . . killed and wounded." Several months later, in Honey Lake Valley, whites used the loss of five cattle as a pretext for destruction and indiscriminate murder. Vigilantes first destroyed two Achumawi rancherias on October 9 before others murdered three Washoe Indians in Honey Lake Valley. On October 17, whites slew at least seven Washoe people, while suffering just one wound.[64]

Forensic evidence of past mass murder also seems to have surfaced in 1857. That spring, the *Sacramento Daily Union* reported that "the skeletons of forty Digger Indians were sluiced out . . . on Trinity river, by a company of miners." The evidence of past and ongoing genocide was difficult to ignore.[65]

REMOVALS AND RESERVATIONS

Although California Indians often resisted, civilians and officials carried out large removal operations in the late 1850s to concentrate California Indians on federal reservations. In May 1857, authorities took 300 Indians "to the Nome Lackee Reservation" and that fall took 169 Konkow and/or Maidu Indians there. Eventually, authorities held thousands of Indians on California reservations. The federal government–sanctioned forced removal of American Indians was a national program that began in the east and steadily spread across the country with cataclysmic results. It repeatedly led to mass death. More than 4,000 Choctaws died during and immediately after their deportation to Oklahoma in 1832 and 1833. Approximately 700 Creeks died while being marched there in 1836, and at least 3,500 others perished during their first year in Oklahoma. As many as 8,000 Cherokees "may have died as a more or less direct result of the Trail of Tears," before, during, and after 1838. Despite substantial evidence pointing to the lethality of forced removals and incarceration on reservations, such policies proliferated.[66]

The removal process itself was sometimes lethal in California. For example, on or about October 8, 1856, ten whites tried to force a large group of unidentified Indians near the Mendocino Reservation to relocate there. The Indians reportedly responded with "a volley of arrows," and the whites massacred fifty-five people before taking a roughly equal number of women and children to Mendocino Reservation. Survivors vividly recalled the violence of such forced removals. In 1937, Yoi'-mut, a Choo'nut woman, recollected how, while her family was living near Waukena, "ranchers came on horseback to take them with all of the other Lake [Yokuts] Indians to the Fresno river reservation." They "beat the Indians with whips and hit them with their swords and ran their horses over them when they would not go." When they ran, "some Indians were shot" and "my mother said she saw 12 Indians killed." During the subsequent forced march to the reservation, "The Indians only had a few things to eat [and] about 10 Indians died on the way." As Nomlaki man Andrew Freeman later explained, "When they took the Indians to Covelo [Round Valley Reservation] they drove them like stock [and] shot the old people who couldn't make the trip. They would shoot children who were getting tired. Finally they got the Indians to Covelo. They killed all who tried to get away and wouldn't return to Covelo." Limited documentation makes it difficult to know exactly how many California Indian people died during forced removals, but the numbers were substantial. For the Yana alone, researcher Theodora Kroeber concluded, "Forced migrations account for some hundreds of . . . deaths."[67]

Once they arrived at reservations, California Indians often encountered institutionalized malnutrition and lethal starvation. According to Yoi'-mut, "When they got to Fresno river there was nothing to eat there. The soldiers there killed some cows and gave them [rotten] acorns." To the north, at Mendocino Reservation, at least ten Indians starved to death in the spring of 1857, according to historian Frank Baumgardner. The following year, colonist J.L. Clapp reported that at Tule River Reservation "two-thirds of the time the Indians have been starved and forced to steal. Only those who worked on the buildings were fed. The rest were left to shift for themselves, and no attention was paid to them." Institutionalized starvation—yet another component of genocide—then continued to stalk Mendocino Reservation. In April 1858, Matteo, "Chief of the Kineamares," explained to Superintendent Henley that his "people were starving." In August, Mendocino reservation subagent Henry L. Ford testified that during the previous winter and spring "Indians were very short of provisions on the reservation . . . and suffered from hunger." He also heard rumors that Mendocino Reservation inmates died of starvation, and reservation employee John P. Simpson testified having heard "that two or three Indians had died during that time of starvation." Later, US Army major Gabriel J. Rains reported that starving Indians were fleeing Mendocino Reservation in 1858 or 1859. One source

Rations at Mendocino Reservation were often inadequate, which caused starvation conditions and death. Unknown artist, "The Headquarters of the Mendocino Reservation. Distribution of Rations to the Indians," drawing(?), 1858(?), *Hutchings' California Magazine* (October 1858), cover. Courtesy of Yale Collection of Western Americana, Beinecke Rare Book and Manuscript Library, Yale University.

was more emphatic about death by starvation there. Konkow leader Tome-ya-nem recollected that after volunteers had forcibly removed his people to Mendocino Reservation, "The times became very hard, for often we were very hungry, and did not know where to get enough to eat, and the Con-cows began to die very fast." Other reservations were little better. In about 1860, Tome-ya-nem and his people relocated to Round Valley Reservation where "there was even less to eat."[68]

If some California reservation inmates died of institutionalized starvation, malnutrition weakened the immune systems of others, making them more susceptible to lethal diseases. The federal officials who created and maintained these conditions for years would now be considered guilty of genocide for, according to the UN Genocide Convention, "deliberately inflicting on the group conditions of life calculated to bring about its physical destruction in whole or in part." Starvation and malnutrition also predictably decreased fecundity while increasing miscarriages and stillbirths. Thus, along with suppressing demographic rebound, institutionalized starvation and malnutrition may be considered "imposing measures intended to prevent births within the group."

Observers were well aware that California reservations imposed institutionalized neglect, and some writers emphasized the lethal results. In 1858, Indian Office special agent Goddard Bailey reported that at California reservations, "Indians are insufficiently fed and scantily clothed." In 1859, US Army brevet major Edward Johnson reported eight to ten Indians dying each day at Round Valley Reservation due to syphilis and inadequate rations. The total number that died on California reservations from institutionalized neglect is difficult to know. Still, journalist J. Ross Browne—writing based on what he had learned during his investigation for the Office of Indian Affairs—concluded of Henley's 1855–1859 tenure as California superintendent of Indian Affairs that at California reservations, "A very large amount of money was annually expended in feeding white men and starving Indians. . . . Every year numbers of [Indians] perished from neglect and disease, and some from absolute starvation." Despite such reports, federal officials failed to increase California reservation funding. Instead, they made conditions worse. In 1859, congressmen cut appropriations for California Indians by almost 70 percent, from $162,000 to $50,000 per year.[69]

Even as many Indians suffered and died from a federally imposed program of hunger, California Indians confined to reservations suffered lethal exploitation and attacks. Pacific Department Commander Wool's 1857 interpretation of California reservations' legal status denied the reservations full army protection: "Until these reservations are . . . perfected the United States troops . . . have no right to . . . exclude the Whites from entering and occupying the reserves, or even prevent their taking from them Indians, squaws and children. In all such cases, until the jurisdiction of the State is ceded to the United States the civil authority should be invoked to correct the evil." By design, federal troops thus provided limited protection to Indians on California reservations. The results were lethal. For example, locals worked hundreds of Round Valley Reservation Indians to death, treating them as slaves who were no more than disposable laborers. According to one Round Valley resident, "About three hundred died on the reservation [during the winter of 1856–1857], from the effects of packing them through the mountains in the snow and mud. . . . They were worked naked, with the exception of deer skin around their shoulders—some few had pantaloons and coats on; they usually packed fifty pounds, if able." Because federal reservations were so dangerous, California Indians sometimes rose up against those who held them there or sought to escape.[70]

In 1857, the conditions at the Klamath Reservation were intolerable. Tolowa today recall this place as the "Klamath Concentration Camp," and an 1856 army report explained: "The Indians . . . say that lies have been told them; that they have been told . . . that if they came here they would be protected [and] given fisheries[,] helped to build new houses, and that they would be fed . . . but that no such thing has been done, that no preparations have been made, and that they . . . will not . . . come down here to freeze and starve." The report added that authorities routinely failed to protect detainees, who "are continually exposed to the brutal assault of drunken and lawless white men; their squaws are forced, and, if resented, the Indians are beaten and shot." In response to these conditions, many Tolowa fled. In at least one later instance, reservation personnel shot at escapees, hitting one or more and in the summer of 1857 redeported many others back to the reservation. Desperate inmates now organized an uprising. On November 17, "an old squaw came to the station and told the Agent that the *Yon-tak-et Mow-e ma* was very sick and wanted to see him." The agent and a Mr. Goodspeed then walked into a trap. Once they "entered the house of the supposed sick man . . . *Requa Mike* . . . presented a yager [rifle] to the breast of the Agent and fired," just missing him. A fight commenced, fifteen minutes later US soldiers arrived, and ten to twenty Indians soon lay dead.[71]

For Indians incarcerated at the Klamath Reservation in 1858, the situation remained dangerous and lethal. In July, the *Humboldt Times*—hardly a pro-Indian newspaper—warned, "Government must take some steps to provide for these [reservation] Indians or they will be exterminated," and in October concluded that "no attempt has ever been made by the officers in charge . . . to look after, or care for any" of the Indians relocated to Klamath Reservation. Here too federal officials may have been guilty of committing genocidal crimes, as defined by the UN Genocide Convention, including "deliberately inflicting on the group conditions of life calculated to bring about its physical destruction in whole or in part" and "imposing measures intended to prevent births within the group."[72]

VIGILANTE CAMPAIGNS, 1858

The rate of killing increased steadily during the first half of 1858. In the first three months, whites killed at least twenty-nine Indians. Then, after the murders of three Washoe and four Achumawi people, a Honey Lake Valley posse launched an unprovoked massacre, slaughtering as many as fifty Modoc or Northern Paiute people at Goose Lake on May 6 without suffering a single fatality. Vigilantes also massacred Yana people that spring, murdering fifteen on Battle Creek following the escape of "George Lane's squaw" and "his Indian boy" in April. On May 3, a correspondent reported "a rumor" that following thefts near Lassen Peak, men set out to exterminate a Yana group "and killed nearly every one, men, women and children, to the number of forty or fifty." Another writer later reported the complete extermination of a Yana village that spring.[73]

Organized killings continued that summer. On June 19, following the slaying of a white man, in "upper Mattole Valley," the *Humboldt Times* reported that whites "in the Valley have been waging a general war against the Indians [killing] some fifteen or twenty [Mattole or Sinkyone] Indians." After the June 23 shooting of William E. Ross on the Trinity Trail, the *Humboldt Times* helped whip whites into a murderous froth, proclaiming, "If they murder a white man without cause, kill ten Indians for it." Vigilantes listened. According to Major Rains, they "fired into every 'Indian Ranch' they could find, killing indiscriminately all ages and sexes." On July 15, vigilantes killed "quite a number of Indians" at Grouse Creek according to the *Humboldt Times*. This bland language, as well as reports of just ten or fifteen Indians and one white man killed, may have camouflaged a major massacre. According to a 1969 history, "After Ross was killed, parties were formed to hunt Indians on upper Grouse Creek, a rancheria was attacked and [Wintu?] Indians numbering 107 men, 83 women, and 67 children were killed by a party of 27 men." This massacre may have taken the lives of 257 people. Five days later, one F.E.W. reported the killing of "fifteen Indians and squaws" as well as one attacker. On August 2, the posse struck again, killing "some Indians" while suffering one man dead and two wounded. Vigilantes also marked their paths with blood elsewhere that summer. In early July, the *Trinity Journal* reported a dozen presumably Nongatl or Whilkut people slain on Mad River and predicted, "Extermination will be their fate." Finally, on July 31, the *Shasta Courier* reported that in the upper Sacramento River Valley and its tributaries "some twenty or thirty [Indians] have been killed."[74]

By September, Mattole Valley killings were coming to a close. On September 4, colonists met to draw up treaty terms, and on September 29 Special Treasury Agent J. Ross Browne reported: "A treaty of peace is here made with the Mattole Indians, some forty or fifty of whom it will be remembered were killed by the whites during the past summer for alleged murders of white[s]." However, while the Mattoles' diplomatic efforts did stop the killing in their valley, organized men targeted nearby Indians: "A war of extermination has been declared against the Cascurise Creek, Bear River, Eel river and other neighboring Indians. Some twenty or thirty armed men are said to have been busily occupied during several months past in killing [Nongatl and Sinkiyone] Indians South and East of the Mattole."[75]

THE SECOND KLAMATH AND HUMBOLDT EXPEDITION, OR "WINTOON WAR," 1858–1859

That August, political pressure for a major ranger militia operation was building. Humboldt, Siskiyou, and Trinity County citizens and politicians began petitioning California's new governor, John B. Weller, for a ranger militia operation, arms, and ammunition. On September 5, Weller agreed but then "deemed it unnecessary" after the army agreed to dispatch regulars to the area. As promised, forty-eight US Army soldiers arrived at Humboldt Bay on September 19.[76]

Some felt that no real local Indian threat existed. On September 30, a "Klamath river country" informant explained that "there has been no hostile disposition manifested by the Indians towards the whites in general, and that the only depredations that have been committed have been provoked by a parcel of abandoned [white] characters, who live in the vicinity of the villages, and who are in the constant habit of committing the grossest outrages upon the squaws." Thus, "in a few instances these outrages have been avenged by the Indians, by shooting their aggressors or killing their stock. These acts of retribution are called Indian outrages, and are made the pretext for fresh outrages upon the poor red skins." The source concluded that despite "years, of making weekly trips . . . through the heart of the country in which the hostilities are reported," he had "seen no disposition manifested to molest the whites who behave themselves as white men should."[77]

Others vehemently disagreed. During a public meeting in Arcata, extremists called for "a war of extermination, total extermination, of every man, woman and child in whose veins coursed the blood of the Indian race." From Weaverville, Isaac Cox joined the genocidal chorus: "Let the Indians be exterminated;— that is their destiny, alas!—but let it be done at one stroke, the better for them." Still others petitioned Governor Weller, requesting "a military post [and] the removal of the Hoopa Valley Indians." Meanwhile, the *Humboldt Times* again called for forced removal to reservations, threatening that "a war of extermination will be waged against all who are caught off of it."[78]

Weller—who would later authorize California's most lethal Indian-hunting ranger militia expeditions—heeded his constituents' calls. On September 28, he ordered the enlistment of militiamen. Consequently, on October 6, militia general S.H. Dosh advertised for eighty volunteers to serve against Indians between Weaverville and Arcata. Meanwhile, thirty-five regular US Army soldiers left Fort Humboldt "to operate against" Indians "about half way between [Arcata] and the South Fork of Trinity." But the call for volunteer militiamen had already gone out. On October 14, eighty volunteers enlisted under militia captain I.G. Messic, while militia quartermaster and adjutant general Kibbe retained command of a force that eventually swelled to ninety-two ranger militiamen. Kibbe's expedition was both a forced removal operation and a killing campaign. For every four Indians that they captured, his rangers killed at least one.[79]

In October and November, Messic's militiamen slew a minimum of eight Whilkut people while taking at least twenty-nine prisoners. Some local journalists explicitly called for a genocidal campaign. The *Humboldt Times* announced: "We hope that Capt. Messic will succeed in totally breaking up or exterminating the skulking bands of savages in that section." In December, Kibbe expanded his operation, dividing his force into three groups. They captured large numbers of Indians, but their tactics and treatment of prisoners were often lethal. In attacking Indian communities along the Van Duzen and Mad Rivers his militiamen killed at least three people and wounded an unspecified number of others, including "two so badly that they may almost be called 'good Indians'." Militiamen also shot a prisoner, and a woman and three children "died in the guardhouse." By New Year's Day 1859, the *Shasta Courier* reported forty or fifty Indians killed and 225 taken prisoner.[80]

Late January saw a surge in killings. Messic's men massacred twenty Nongatl men "in the Redwoods," sustaining two wounds before capturing thirteen women and children. At about the same time, militiamen killed one Nongatl or Whilkut "on Redwood Creek," before Indians injured a militiamen. On the morning of January 28, Messic's men assaulted a village of log houses and killed fifteen Wiyot "waarriors." Messic now retreated with thirteen prisoners and two wounded militiamen. That same day "Lieut. Winslett came upon a band of [Nongatl or Whilkut] Indians on Redwood" and killed "several" while suffering a man wounded. In a later, conflicting report, Kibbe wrote that on January 21, 22, and 23, detachments under Messic, Winslett, and "private McNeil" assaulted thirty redwood houses, killed thirty-five to forty men, and took fifteen women and children prisoners, while five militiamen suffered wounds.[81]

By late March this long, deadly winter campaign was winding down. On March 26, the *Humboldt Times* reported 300 prisoners taken and nearly 100 Indians killed. On April 4, the expedition's last militiamen mustered out, and on April 7, Kibbe summarized the operation, reporting 75 to 100 Indians killed, "a large number wounded," and 350 prisoners taken. Kibbe likely underestimated the number of Indian deaths during this operation, as a tally of other sources suggests that as many as 125 Indian people were killed in this campaign. Kibbe presumably underestimated because the death toll was entirely one-sided: Indians did not kill a single one of his militiamen. Kibbe insisted that "in no case have their women and children been killed or separated" but admitted, "The plan of moving upon and attacking their ranchos by night was the only one which promised much success, and . . . was . . . pursued until every river, creek, and gulch, in this large section of country, was scouted over and cleared of Indians." His surprise night assaults on villages almost certainly led to indiscriminate killing. Thus, Kibbe's claim that no woman or child was ever killed during more than five months of campaigning strains credulity. Nevertheless, on April 16, California legislators, knowing that they were financially backed by Congress, voted to pay for this genocidal campaign after the fact. Meanwhile, authorities deported 300 prisoners—primarily aboard the bark *Fanny Major*—to suffer the starvation conditions of the federal government's Mendocino Reservation.[82]

ROUND VALLEY KILLINGS, NOVEMBER 1858–APRIL 1859

While Kibbe's campaign raged in the northwest, vigilantes and federal officials killed even greater numbers in and around the Round Valley Reservation. In November or early December 1858—after cattle, horses, and hogs went missing in Round Valley—whites killed nine Indians. The next day, Indian agent Simon Storms "ordered the Indians to produce among them those who had been engaged in the stealing. Twenty-one were given up." Storms planned to hang "some of the worst," but when the prisoners allegedly ran, "fourteen of them were killed." On December 31, after Indians stole six or seven horses from nearby Eden Valley and killed them for food—amid the starvation conditions caused by white hunting, stock grazing, and exclusion from traditional hunting and gathering areas—ranchers "went to the *rancheria* of the robbers" and massacred fourteen or fifteen Yuki people. On New Year's Day, Round Valley whites massacred another "forty Indians, for stealing stock and killing their hogs." The following day, they slew at least twelve other Indians in the valley.[83]

These five massacres were part of a loosely organized regional campaign. By January 13, 1859, the *Sacramento Daily Union* published reports "that more than one hundred Indians have been killed by whites within three or four months" in the Eden Valley region. J. Ross Browne later wrote: "At [Round Valley], during the winter of 1858–'59, more than a hundred and fifty peaceable Indians, including women and children, were cruelly slaughtered by the whites who had settled there under official authority." He explained, "Armed parties went into the rancherias in open day, when no evil was apprehended, and shot the Indians down—weak, harmless, and defenseless as they were—without distinction of age or sex; shot down women with sucking babes at their breasts; killed or crippled the naked children that were running about." On January 20, the *Daily Alta California* reported "the slaughter of *one hundred and seventy Indians*, in the locality of Round Valley, since November last."[84]

As in some other instances in the 1850s, the army temporarily stopped this rampant slaughter. In January, the Sixth Infantry deployed seventeen dragoons to Round Valley. Yet, these soldiers soon learned that neither state nor federal authorities supported their peacekeeping mission. In February, commanding officer lieutenant Edward Dillon arrested a white man for beating a reservation Indian with a club. The news spread, and twenty-five angry whites soon surrounded Dillon's house, threatening violence if the accused was not released by the following morning. Dillon stood his ground for two days. Then, inexplicably, his prisoner escaped. The incident seemed over, but Superintendent Henley complained to Washington that the dragoons were overstepping their authority by protecting California Indians. Army command in San Francisco then ordered Dillon to avoid confronting or incarcerating whites. Despite deploying seventeen soldiers, US Army commanders ordered Dillon to stop protecting Round Valley Indians from a now profoundly lethal killing machine, thus underscoring federal culpability in the expanding Round Valley region genocide. The results were disastrous.[85]

On April 2, Dillon reported from Round Valley that "the party that went to Eden Valley to hunt [Yuki] Indians . . . have been for nearly two weeks hunting Indians and . . . it is currently reported here, that *two hundred* and *forty* Indians were killed." By mid-April, an informant who had just arrived from Round Valley reported that "in the vicinity of Round Valley . . . within the past three weeks, from three to four hundred bucks, squaws and children, have been killed by the whites." In total, these reports suggest the killing, primarily by vigilantes, of at least 550 and perhaps as many as 910 Indian people in the Round Valley region between November 1858 and mid-April 1859.[86]

Vigilantes killed more Indians elsewhere in early 1859. On January 23, after an attempted stock theft on Battle Creek, vigilantes massacred "not less than ten" Yana people without suffering a single casualty. Ten days later, three men attacked a Pomo village "near the head of the Russian River Valley, and killed fourteen of them, on the supposition that the Indians had been stealing their cattle." Indian resistance to such attacks, which was often nothing more than

self-defense against a relentless killing machine, soon triggered even more vigilante and army massacres in the Mad River Basin.[87]

MAD RIVER, MAY–SEPTEMBER 1859

On May 10, James C. Ellison took an arrow to the groin while attacking and
killing two or three Nongatl people near Yager Creek. Five days later, thirty
regular soldiers left Fort Humboldt for Yager Creek. The army generally sought
to capture California Indians and forcibly remove them to often deadly federal
reservations. Local whites frequently favored another objective: immediate extermination or enslavement. On the third day of the army's march, a man
named Lindley explained to Lieutenant A.B. Hardcastle that Indians "will not
run from us as fast as they will from volunteers because they know we will take
prisoners." As the *Daily Evening Bulletin* had observed in 1856, "the officers of
the U.S. Government, and the settlers and frontiersmen" pursued opposing objectives: "the one, the policy of protection; the other, that of extermination."
Indeed, on May 20, Hardcastle met six vigilantes who were hunting Indians.
The following day, after reporting the killing of a Mr. Ellison at Iroquois Ranch
and the loss of fifty head of stock on the north fork of Yager Creek, the *Trinity
Journal* warned that a "war of extermination will ensue," and proclaimed that
"nothing but extirpation will subdue the ferocious devils."[88]

As if heeding this call, on May 24, vigilantes organized at Hydesville—
southwest of Eureka—to hunt "the Indians who murdered Ellison, and who
have been killing stock in the Bald Hill and Yager Creek country." Two days later,
at least twenty men set out for a six-week-long killing operation. On North Yager
Creek, they encountered Nongatl or Whilkut people harvesting clover and
murdered two while "severely wounding" a third. The following week, they
"stormed several ranches and killed quite a number of Indians." Soon, the vigilante and army operations came into conflict, underscoring their opposing
objectives.[89]

On May 31, Hardcastle captured seven Indian men in an attempt to initiate
the negotiation of their rancheria's surrender. However, six of them "ran away"
because—according to one recaptured—"they were afraid of being taken to San
Francisco," presumably to be enslaved. According to Hardcastle, they may have
suffered a worse fate. The next day, "the volunteers found some Indians just
about where I had met my party and I should not be at all surprised if they had
come on the same Rancheria, whilst they were waiting for me to return—the
volunteers killed those [five] bucks and two squaws." Two days later, Hardcastle's

commander told him that he thought "a white man" had shot even the expedition's vanished Indian translator, Tamarisk. On June 5, Hardcastle reported that volunteers had killed five Nongatl "in redwoods near Yager" and two Nongatl women and a man "on Van Dusen's." Regular soldiers did kill during this operation, despite proclaiming their desire to quell the violence. After Indians killed a deserter and wounded another, soldiers massacred seven Nongatl "on Van Duzen Fork." Nevertheless, although regulars were less violent than the volunteers that spring, soldiers killed and did little to stop vigilante massacres. It remained a desperate time for many California Indians.[90]

By the summer of 1859, most of the California Indians who had been living ten years earlier were now dead. The following year, federal census takers counted only 17,798 Indians in California. This was almost certainly an undercount. The ethnographer C. Hart Merriam later estimated 35,000 California Indians alive in 1860, down from some 100,000 in 1849. Perhaps 65,000 people had died in a decade, not counting intervening births. For individual California Indian tribes, this population catastrophe had major impacts. It devastated families, creating widows, widowers, and orphans. As leaders died, it also played havoc with political systems, by denying California Indian communities experienced leadership when they needed it most. Economies also suffered. The fallen left traps untended, acorns ungathered, nets abandoned, and bows unstrung. Decreased food intake, in turn, weakened survivors, making it more difficult for them to escape, resist, and survive. On June 26, 1859, the *Daily Alta California* blamed mass murder for this disastrous population decline: "More than three-fourths of the red men living in 1849, in the State north of latitude 36°—that is, in all those districts where white men are numerous—have been killed off." Resigned to genocide, California's leading newspaper announced: "That the extermination will continue, no reasonable man can doubt." Indeed, killing campaigns proliferated and, increasingly, the US Army participated while the US Congress continued to support the killing machine.[91]

THE MOJAVE WAR, 1859

Far to the southeast, a war erupted in Mojave territory along the Colorado River, involving white civilians, Mojave Indians, and the US Army. As early as February 1859, a correspondent reported troops "at the Barracks . . . practicing" in preparation for Indian fighting near "the southern boundary." Meanwhile, some Mojaves wanted to actively resist immigrants and the colonization of Mojave lands. Chooksa Homar, a Mojave who was about fifteen years old in 1859, later paraphrased their arguments: "If we let the whites come and live here, they will

This photograph of a young Mojave woman named Mosa is one of Edward S. Curtis's most famous portraits. Edward S. Curtis, "Mosa—Mohave," photograph, 1903. Courtesy of Library of Congress, Prints & Photographs Division, Edward S. Curtis Collection, LC-USZC4-8920.

take your wives. They will put you to work. They will take your children and carry them away and sell them. They will do that until there are not Mojave here. That is why [we] want to stop them from coming, want them to stay in their own homes." The army soon had its casus belli. On March 12, Mojaves attacked and killed thirteen out of seventeen whites on the west side of the Colorado River. Following this unusually large killing by California Indians, on April 17(?), Samuel A. Bishop wrote of "the attack made on him when he was about to cross the Colorado." He continued: "I then gave orders to the men to kill and scalp every one that could be seen. It was a warm time for about three hours, my men killing at least two Indians for every three shots fired, and taking some of their hair." Despite April 22 negotiations that seemed to end this particular conflict, that summer the Mojave suffered the impact of army firepower.[92]

On August 5, US Army regulars under Major Lewis Armistead engaged Mojave Indians fifteen miles "below" Fort Mojave in a one-sided slaughter. Soldiers counted twenty-three Mojave bodies but estimated killing fifty or sixty while just three of their own soldiers were "slightly wounded." By late August, a correspondent at the fort reported nearby Indian villages "destroyed" and the region's Mojave people driven downriver. In addition to this killing by federal troops, civilian vigilantes unleashed a new campaign far to the northwest in Tehama County.[93]

THE BRECKENRIDGE EXPEDITION, 1859

On May 9, forty-eight Antelope and Deer Creek men petitioned Governor Weller for help in dealing with Yana Indians' "frequent depredations." Three days later, 240 Red Bluff residents petitioned Weller for "relief," claiming that, on May 11, Indians had set fire to Colonel E.A. Stevenson's house, killing two women, four children, and probably one man. Three more local petitions followed. For these communities, killing Yana people was routine. In March, the veteran Indian killer Harmon Good had led a night massacre of fourteen near Mill Creek. In April, locals raised money to establish a scalp bounty fund, and vigilantes massacred fourteen more, mostly children and women. It was thus unsurprising when, on May 21, vigilantes hanged "the Indian boy of Col. Stevenson," on suspicion of setting Stevenson's house ablaze.[94]

The army now acted, as did vigilantes. Ordered to arrest Indian "marauders," Captain Franklin F. Flint's sixty federal infantrymen searched the rugged hills and canyons between Battle and Mill Creeks but found no Indians. In late May, frustrated local whites thus raised money for an extended Indian-hunting vigilante operation. The veteran Indian killer John Breckenridge led some ten men into the hills, and on May 25, the *Red Bluff Beacon* called for, "*total extermination.*" In the second week of June, local whites "resolved to petition the Governor again for authority to raise a volunteer force [that the state would then fund] to drive the Indians from their fastness, or exterminate the tribe." Ultimately, local whites raised $3,000 to pay the vigilantes under "Breckenridge, to chastise the Indians on the head-waters of Deer, Mill, and Antelope Creeks."[95]

Before departing, the posse received state recognition and US Army leadership. Militia general Kibbe sent a "Captain Burns of the army to take command," and the party departed on June 15. Burns soon left, but the ten vigilantes moved south. There they located a Konkow Maidu camp. After killing and scalping one man, the posse massacred "about forty" people while suffering only a single wound, according to participant Robert Anderson. The *Red Bluff Beacon* reported a smaller death toll, announcing that during the last week of July the posse had killed *"Fifteen Indians and one white man"* in two incidents near "the headwaters of Butte and Deer Creeks."[96]

The Breckenridge expedition now swung north into Yahi Yana territory and massacred perhaps a dozen people, including two prisoners, "on the head waters of Deer Creek," before taking women and children to a reservation. Newspapers and correspondents provided additional accounts of the expedition's massacres, and "citizens of the 'Forks of Butte'" accused the posse of "shooting down like a dog a poor old blind Indian, and his squaw . . . and making an indiscriminate slaughter on defenseless women and children" there. Finally, following an August 31 interview with Breckenridge, the *Red Bluff Beacon* summarized the expedition: "They killed twenty-nine Indians, wounded about twenty more, a great portion of them severely [and] took thirteen women and children to the [Nome Lackee] Reservation." However, if Anderson's recollections are accurate, the Breckenridge posse killed well over forty-two Indians, both Konkow Maidu and Yahi Yana. Either way, a militia campaign now absorbed most of the posse into a larger and more lethal state-sponsored ranger militia operation supported by and augmented with US Army soldiers.[97]

THE PIT RIVER MILITIA EXPEDITION, 1859

In the summer of 1859, the surviving Achumawi, Atsugewi, Maidu, and Yana people east of the Sacramento River were living under increasing pressure and intensifying fear. All three of these peoples had suffered repeated lethal attacks. To avoid slave raiders, soldiers, militiamen, and vigilantes, many of them had retreated ever higher, up valleys and canyons and into the rugged mountains where food was relatively scarce. Yet, with the coming of summer, food supplies increased and the need to raid whites for food diminished. The Achumawi, Atsugewi, Maidu, and Yana peoples thus likely thought themselves in relatively less danger that summer as the days warmed. They did not know that they would soon be the targets of a major state militia operation.

On Independence Day, 1859, Governor Weller ordered militia general Kibbe north, to determine whether or not ranger militiamen should be mustered to fight Tehama County Indians. Kibbe responded by reporting a far bigger problem: a pan-Indian force of 175 to 250 well-armed warriors united against whites in a region extending from Butte Creek to Little Cow Creek and covering much of Butte, Tehama, and Shasta counties. Kibbe's claims were uncorroborated but provided the pretext for a major Indian-hunting operation. On August 2, Governor Weller ordered him to enroll up to eighty militiamen. Weller did warn Kibbe that "there must be no indiscriminate slaughter of the Indians" and that "women and children must be spared." Yet this was purely lip service to protect Weller against future criticism. He clearly commanded Kibbe to punish at a time when punishing California Indians routinely meant massacring them. Two weeks later, the general organized a ranger militia company and at Red Bluff, ninety-two volunteers—including Anderson and his group—enlisted for a three-month-long killing campaign.[98]

General Kibbe's plan was bold. The operational area—ranging from Butte Creek to the headwaters of the Pit River—encompassed a huge swath of mountainous geography, extending from northern Maidu territory, through Yana lands, and north and east into Achumawi and Astugewi country. To cover this region with ninety-two men, Kibbe divided them into three detachments. Each pierced the campaign zone at a different point, and they all moved south to north, in three subcampaigns. By August 31, the Indian agent Vincent Geiger reported: "An Indian war, under the auspices of the State government, is now being waged against the Indians east of the Sacramento river." Kibbe's rangers were marching north.[99]

Soon after Kibbe's campaign began, vigilantes and US soldiers took to the field in the Hat Creek and Pit River regions, the northernmost portion of Kibbe's campaign zone. Local events triggered these operations, but their temporal and geographic overlap with Kibbe's expedition suggests that the vigilantes and soldiers involved may have taken his presence as carte blanche to launch their own local Indian-killing campaigns. In mid-August, whites found John Callahan and his cook dead at Hat Creek Station. Pit River colonist George Lount reported that because they had been "shot with guns," the Achumawi, who "have no guns," could not have committed the killings. Nevertheless, Fort Crook regulars deployed to the Hat Creek region, killing one or two Achumawi or Atsugewi. Two more white men's corpses now appeared, and John Longley organized the nineteen Pit River Rangers. He collected $600 from local whites as well as guns from Fort Crook's commander in another case of local army support for California's wider genocide. Soldiers also participated directly. On August 27, the *Shasta Herald* reported that Fort Crook soldiers had killed thirteen Indians. The *Shasta Courier* next described another engagement that left five of Kibbe's militiamen and twenty-one more unidentified Indians dead.[100]

"Fired with a spirit of deep revenge," according to Kibbe, the Pit River Rangers entered Pit River Valley. On September 2, 1859, these vigilantes halted near Fort Crook at the ranch of Joseph Rolf, who had a contract to cut wild grass and sell it to the government. "He lived with an Indian woman," and an Achumawi village was near his house. George Lount described the genocidal massacre that ensued. The twenty-two vigilantes surrounded the village at night and began firing at daylight. According to Lount, "The massacre was almost entirely of squaws and papooses—the greater part of the Indians having fled directly after the attack. The camp was taken completely by surprise, as the Indians knew that they were innocent of any depredations, and were confident in the kind feelings of the whites towards them." Lount continued, "The attacking party rushed upon them—blowing out their brains, and splitting open their skulls with tomahawks. Little children in baskets, and even babes, had their heads smashed to pieces or cut open. Mothers and infants shared the common fate. The screams and cries of the victims were frightful to hear, but no supplications could avail to avert the work of devilish butchery." The Pit River Rangers shot others "as they ran. Where whole families had been butchered, was indicated by heaps of bodies composed of the mother and her little ones. The children, scarcely able to run, toddled towards the squaws for protection, crying with fright, but were overtaken, slaughtered like wild animals, and thrown into piles."[101]

The rangers were relentless. The Achumawi were helpless. According to Lount: "From under the haycocks where some of them had taken refuge, they were dragged out and slain. One woman got into a pond hole, where she hid herself under the grass, with her head above water, and concealed her papoose on the bank in a basket. She was discovered and her head blown to pieces—the muzzle of the gun being placed against her skull, and the child was drowned in the pond." Lount continued, "The ground was covered with blood, and the brushwood ranches, of which there fifty or sixty, were filled with the dead bodies. Old decrepit squaws, young girls and infants, none were spared. Guns, knives, and hatchets were used, but the favorite method appears to have been staving in the head with tomahawks. The blush of dawn shown upon this fearful spectacle, and still the massacre went on." In some cases, the killers even knew their victims.[102]

Some of the women and children "had lived with the very men who now struck them down. . . . One of the butchers named Lee, had been attended while sick—almost to death—by the Indian women, who had shown him all the simple kindnesses." These women "looked around in their terror, some of them recognizing the man whose life they had saved, cried out 'Lee! Lee!' raising their hands towards him with gestures of supplication—but in vain. Lee was among the most infuriate of the party and afterwards boasted of the number of skulls he had split open, and exhibited his tomahawk, hacked and broken in the dreadful work." Eventually, "When the slaughter was over, the shambles were examined and more than sixty squaws and children, and ten Indian men were found dead." Then, "after the last squaw and child had been killed the brushwood ranches or huts were set on fire and the bodies burnt." Finally, "the Indians crept down at night and carried away a few of the remnants of the bodies, and continued to do so until they became so offensive and decomposed that they could not be removed." Other white sources reported as many as ninety Achumawi people massacred that morning, the majority of whom were women and children. Still, because perpetrators incinerated many bodies while survivors removed others, these were likely underestimates.[103]

The chief of the Fall River Band of Achumawi band chief later provided an eyewitness account of that nightmare sunrise:

> In the summer, a band of white men from Red Bluff attacked the Fall River Achomawi in camp at Beaver creek and slaughtered the entire number except thirty or forty men, who escaped. [I] was then a young man, and with an Indian companion, both of [us,] being in the employ of a white man who was cutting hay for the Government, [we] stood on a hill overlooking the scene. [I] saw the white men chop off women's heads with axes, and build up a big fire into which they threw the bodies of infants.

He estimated that "About a hundred and sixty were killed. . . . When the slaughter was ended, [we] started for the house . . . thinking that the men had gone. To [our] surprise [we] came upon the settlers laying beside a haystack, and saw them leap up and level their guns." Their employer then saved the future chief and his companion. He "went up to the leader of the settlers and put a pistol to his head" while several armed men covered the other killers. The future chief's relief was short-lived. He soon learned that his "mother, sister, and grandparents had been killed."[104]

Following a rest at Rolf's Ranch, the rangers—who by all accounts suffered only a few injuries during the massacre—"killed several of the Fort Crooks [Achumawi] tribe" who were "perfectly peaceable and well disposed to the whites." Several days later, they "killed a number" near Fall River. In September, Shingletown men en route to join the Pit River Rangers killed six or seven Indians. Finally, in early October, the veteran Indian killer Captain Weatherly returned to Honey Lake Valley "from the Indian hunt, he having been with the company of Shasta volunteers." According to a man named Belden, the Honey Lake expressman, "It is stated that this company had taken some twelve prisoners, and killed twenty-three."[105]

Meanwhile, Kibbe's militiamen arrived at Rolf's Ranch, where lethal violence continued. According to Henry Landt, Achumawi men came in to negotiate with Kibbe—lured by Kibbe's display of two captured infants—and Kibbe promised to protect these diplomats and treat them kindly. Yet when they tried to leave, Kibbe's men shot down two of them and captured the chief. Unsurprisingly, the chief "very readily came to terms."[106]

Kibbe's militiamen captured hundreds of Indians, but also perpetrated one-sided genocidal killings. On October 5, a detachment at Eagle Lake encountered six Atsugewi and killed every one of them. Indeed, Kibbe spoke of both capturing and exterminating. In early October, he boasted that "in six weeks" he would "have all the Indians in the mountains, east of [Red Bluff] on the Reservation or exterminated." Some saw his campaign as exclusively genocidal. On October 15, the *Shasta Herald* reported: "KIBBE still continues to wage a war of extermination against the hostile Indians, in the eastern portion of Shasta and Tehama counties," explaining that "small detachments . . . can move more rapidly from one point to another—penetrating to the Indian's hiding places—visiting on them swift and certain destruction." The newspaper concluded with a thinly veiled call for total extermination: "A chastisement must be inflicted on them that will forever put an end to their atrocities." News of Kibbe's tactics spread and Kibbe responded by claiming that "not more than two squaws and one child have died from wounds received from his troops within the past year."[107]

Public criticism now intensified. On October 18, the *Sacramento Daily Union* chided: "It has not been much of a war . . . the truth being that nobody has been hurt [except Indians] 'being skinned.'" Pundits understood that this was no normal war. A week later, the *Union* asserted that Kibbe's hunt of "inoffensive people" was merely a boondoggle supporting his "wholly unnecessary office," the "rotten" reservation system, "certain politicians, the demand created for supplies and the employment of men who would otherwise be idle." Assessing California's anti-Indian campaigns to date, the *Union* concluded that "the Indian wars in this State . . . have all one and the same origin, are prosecuted from one and the same motive, and have each a secret history that shrinks from exposure." The *Plumas Argus* then suggested that readers consider "killing" Kibbe's influence. Still, Governor Weller declined to recall General Kibbe or end his expedition.[108]

By November 1, a Pit River correspondent wrote that Kibbe's men had killed eighty warriors. By December 7, the *Red Bluff Beacon* reported that 200 Indians had been killed in the northern half of Kibbe's campaign zone. Yet his strategy transcended killing and capturing. By keeping Indian communities running, denying them the opportunity to hunt, fish, or gather food "sufficient for winter," he forced the survivors of his campaign to die by the gun, surrender, or face death by starvation. For Indians who had suffered multiple massacres and had little faith in whites or the reservation system, it must have been an agonizing choice. Many chose not to surrender. According to local historian May Hazel Southern, "It was said 50 starved to death in the mountains that winter."[109]

Kibbe's tactics remained predictable to the end. He explained, "The plan of moving upon, and attacking, the rancherias of the Indians at night, I had learned by experience, was the best and only one calculated to be attended with happy results." Kibbe aimed to clear the land for white possession by killing and capturing its California Indian owners: "From time to time small parties of Indians were captured, until the southern portion of the country operated in [Maidu lands] contained not a warrior to offer resistance. The intermediate section was next visited [Yana territory], and the Indians occupying it, after several severe skirmishes, compelled to flee for safety to the country occupied by the" Achumawi and Atsugewi. Kibbe concluded his operation in the Pit River and Hat Creek region. Here he assaulted an "Indian stronghold with forty men, completely routing those who defended it, killing several of their number and taking others prisoners; those who escaped were pursued. A number of engagements subsequently occurred with them, in which a great number were killed or captured." He then reported a mass surrender of "four hundred and fifty," followed by many "skirmishes."[110]

The Pit River Expedition was both a forced removal operation and an extermination campaign. On December 15, Kibbe brought some 450 prisoners to San Francisco, en route to the Mendocino Reservation and its life-threatening conditions. The following day, a *New York Times* correspondent wrote of white Californians' attitudes toward the campaign: "They wanted the Indians exterminated, and to all intents and purposes they have been." Summing up his expedition, Kibbe reported about 200 killed (not counting army or Pit River Ranger operations), and 1,200 captured. Despite his admission of launching surprise assaults on sleeping villages, Kibbe improbably claimed: "No children were killed, and but one woman, during the whole campaign." He also reported: "Not a single [white] life was lost, and the wounded all recovered." Kibbe's Pit River Expedition amounted to a ruthless operation intended to capture or exterminate the northern Maidu, Yana, Achumawi, and Atsugewi. It partially succeeded in achieving both goals.[111]

THE MENDOCINO EXPEDITION, 1859–1860

Just weeks after Kibbe launched the Pit River Expedition, a smaller, but even more lethal militia company mustered into service in Round Valley. The Mendocino Expedition would kill more California Indians than any other militia operation, but like many others, it grew directly from ongoing vigilante Indian killing. Whites in the Round Valley region had killed at least 550 Indians between November 1858 and April 1859. On May 1, 1859, US Army major Edward Johnson, commanding the military district including Round Valley, explained: "The whites have waged a relentless war of extermination against the Yukas [Yuki]. . . . They have ruthlessly massacred men, women, and children . . . some six hundred have been killed within the last year." He continued, "I have endeavored to put a stop to the aggressions of the whites against the Indians, but without effect." Denied the freedom to confront or arrest whites by commanding generals after the Dillon incident, soldiers had little capacity to protect Indians in and around Round Valley. Up the chain of US Army command, generals rarely acted to protect California Indians. More often, the generals refused to protect them or supported killing them.[112]

Meanwhile, the powerful local ranch owner and former California state Supreme Court chief justice Serranus C. Hastings gave Governor Weller a petition drawn up by Round Valley colonists. It requested militia support against local Yuki Indians. Weller responded by commissioning a US Army investigation. On May 1, Major Johnson reported to Weller that "the Yukas have not been, for the last two years, nor are they now, at open war with the whites; But the whites have waged a relentless war of extermination against the Yukas." Apparently dissatisfied with this report, Weller commissioned Captain Flint to conduct a second inquiry. Flint contradicted Johnson and recommended organizing volunteers to fight, rather than protect, the Yuki.[113]

As Weller pondered his options, stockman Walter S. Jarboe organized "the Eel River Rangers." Jarboe engaged men to hunt Indians, promising them payment from the state, or if Sacramento failed to pay, from the operation's extremely wealthy mastermind, Judge Hastings, who owned an Eden Valley ranch and may have wanted to eliminate the Yuki in order to protect his stock. On July 11, 1859, sixteen men elected Jarboe captain. On August 10, his "Rangers" massacred sixteen Yuki near Round Valley. Johnson reported that by August 21, Jarboe's men had slain at least sixty-four Yuki, concluding: "I believe it to be the Settled determination of many of the inhabitants to exterminate the Indians." That same day, Johnson alerted Weller that Jarboe and his men had recently murdered dozens of men, women, and children. Rather than condemn Jarboe, on September 6, the governor authorized Jarboe "to muster into the service of the State twenty men to act against the Indians in Mendocino county."[114]

Newspapers now reported nine massacres by Jarboe's rangers and vigilantes. In late September, the Eel River Rangers slaughtered twenty-five presumably Yuki males. On October 12, they massacred twenty Yuki or Wailaki north of Round Valley. On November 18, they killed seven Indians in the "Eel River country." On December 9, Jarboe's rangers surprised and slew at least thirty Indians on or near South Eel River, wounding thirty others. Meanwhile, after

Indians stole five horses from Agent Storms's Round Valley ranch, Captain Lacock's "Rangers . . . overtook them in the night and [killed] seventeen." On December 13, Jarboe's rangers massacred some thirty more Indian men near Round Valley. Six days later, "settlers" massacred thirty-two Yuki in Long Valley. Finally, in late December, Jarboe's company massacred thirty Indian people in Round Valley before slaughtering "some sixty South Eel River Indians" on New Year's Eve.[115]

During the Mendocino Expedition, federal Indian Affairs officials and US Army generals failed to challenge California's Yuki policy or order their subordinates to protect Indians, even as Indian Affairs officers and soldiers issued warnings and objections. On September 4, California Indian Affairs superintendent James Y. McDuffie warned US Indian Affairs commissioner Alfred B. Greenwood that "in round valley and its vicinity. . . . The killing of Indians is a daily occurrence." He added, "If some means be not speedily devised, by which the unauthorized expeditions that are constantly out in search of them can be restrained, they will soon be exterminated." On October 18, after visiting Round Valley, Agent Browne reported to Greenwood that Jarboe "has been engaged for some months past in a cruel and relentless pursuit of the Indians in this vicinity, slaughtering miscellaneously all with whom he comes in contact, without regard to age or sex." Four days later, Johnson warned his commanding general that Jarboe's men were "slaughtering indiscriminately all the Indians they meet; men, women and children." Johnson also wrote to the army department adjutant to protest Governor Weller's unwillingness to stop this state militia killing campaign: "Can not the Executive of this state be induced to stay the hands of this Jarboe and his assassins?" Aware of the slaughter, neither Indian Affairs leaders nor army generals intervened. Without new directives from their superiors, local Indian agents and soldiers had little power to deter this horrific killing or punish whites who murdered Indians.[116]

On January 24, 1860, outgoing governor Weller disbanded the "Eel River Rangers." Jarboe then reported to the new governor, John Downey that "from [September 20] to the 24th of January, I fought them 23 times, killed 283 Warriors, the number of wounded was not known, took 292 prisoners, sent them to

---

This drawing accompanied an article by J. Ross Browne in which he described the mass murder of Yuki people at Round Valley. J. Ross Browne, "Protecting the Settlers," drawing, 1861(?), *Harper's New Monthly Magazine* (August 1861), 313. Courtesy of Yale Collection of American Literature, Beinecke Rare Book and Manuscript Library, Yale University.

the Reservation." Jarboe then billed California $11,143.00. Jarboe's claim that he killed only "Warriors" was dubious. He and his militiamen were notorious for murdering women and children, and there is no reason to dismiss the reports of Browne and Johnson stating that Jarboe targeted every Indian, regardless of age or gender. Jarboe's report was likely designed to conceal his slaughter of civilians. However, he boasted, according to H.H. Buckles, that "his company had killed more Indians than any other expedition that ever had been before ordered out in this state." If accurate, his claim of "283 Warriors" killed did make his the most lethal of all officially reported California militia campaigns. Yet, his unit almost certainly killed many others who were not warriors. The *Daily Alta California* reported that in fifteen engagements over seventy days, Jarboe's rangers killed more than 400 Indians, took 600 prisoners, and suffered only three militiamen wounded and one killed.[117]

In commissioning and supporting Jarboe's Eel River Rangers over more than four and a half months of sustained killing, Governor Weller had likely known that Jarboe was waging a campaign of extermination. Indeed, Weller voiced this concern twice. In two different letters, he admonished Jarboe first not to wage "indiscriminate warfare against a whole tribe," and then "not to suffer a war of extermination against a whole tribe." Yet Weller commissioned Jarboe knowing, through Johnson, of his bloody record, and still kept him on. As historian Gary Garrett astutely observed, "Notwithstanding Governor Weller's hypocritical puling about deploring the death of Indian women and children, he was more aware of Jarboe's activities than almost anyone in the state." Like his August 1859 order commanding Kibbe that "there must be no indiscriminate slaughter of the Indians" and that "women and children must be spared" during the Pit River Expedition, Weller's September and October 1859 letters to Jarboe appear to have been political insurance against future criticism. Indeed, Jarboe candidly explained his aims. In an official December 3, 1859, report to Weller, he wrote: "However cruel it may be . . . nothing short of extermination will suffice to rid the Country of them [the Yuki]." It took Weller more than a month to disband the Eel River Rangers, and he did so only as he was leaving office. Even then, Weller thanked "the volunteers for the manner in which the campaign was conducted," an operation that had killed perhaps as many as 400 or more Indian people.[118]

SOUL-SEARCHING AND THE HUMBOLDT BAY MASSACRES, FEBRUARY 1860–APRIL 1861

Exactly how many California Indians were killed by whites in 1859 will never be known, but the *Daily Alta California* observed that "during 1859 there were three Indian wars in this State—one in the valley of the Mojave; one in the valley of Pit river; and one in the valley of Eel river" and estimated that "the three cost the red man not less than several thousand lives, exclusive of those slain in casual encounters in other parts of the State." By early 1860, writers from the northern border south to Los Angeles were analyzing the past year's meaning for California Indians and state policies. On January 20, the *Sacramento Daily Union* warned that if Indians did not receive protection, they would "be gradually killed off by volunteer expeditions." The same day, a Sacramento correspondent cautioned: "The antipathy of race . . . will in a very short time, unless regulated and mitigated by legislation, cause the speedy extermination of the Indian population of this State." In February, the *Yreka Northern Journal* warned that "The red men of California are fast passing away, and if left to roam at will around and in the settlements, but a few more years will suffice to exterminate the race." Finally, in March, the *Los Angeles Star* observed, "The war of extermination continues upon the poor aborigine."[119]

This discussion overlapped with a public debate over whether or not to pay for the Pit River and Mendocino expeditions. Some praised these killings. On January 18, a Sacramento correspondent wrote of Kibbe's Pit River rangers: "Numberless scalps attest to their prowess." Others affirmed an outright genocide. One observer opined of Jarboe's Eel River Rangers that "nothing short of a war of extermination would seem to be practical, however cruel this may appear, in order to rid the county of such intolerable and dangerous pests in human form."[120]

Still others critiqued the two expeditions as financially profligate and morally outrageous. On January 15, a Pit River correspondent scathingly noted that Kibbe "styles his [Pit River] expedition a *war!!*" and admonished legislators not to pay for "such a 'war.'" The *Petaluma Argus* then disparaged Jarboe's campaign as "an outrage upon the Indians, and a swindle against the Government," and on February 2, the *Sacramento Daily Union* criticized Weller for commissioning Jarboe to raise a ranger militia company when regular army troops were already there. Three weeks later, the *Union* warned that the state must stop funding such expeditions or empty the treasury, and the next day, the *Daily Evening Bulletin* castigated Jarboe's actions as a "deliberate, cowardly, brutal massacre of defenseless men, women, and children."[121]

State legislators also debated the two 1859 ranger militia expeditions, which had killed at least 483 California Indians. Assemblymen considered investigating Kibbe's Pit River Expedition because of the size of the slaughter, but voted against doing so. However, on February 13, 1860, they discussed Northern California "Indian hostilities, real and alleged" until late in the evening, eventually voting, thirty-nine to eighteen, to investigate Jarboe's expedition by sending law-makers to Mendocino County. For the first time, the killing machine came under legislative threat.[122]

Events in Humboldt County then shook the killing machine to its core. In mid-December, 1859, Hydesville area whites raised and provisioned perhaps a dozen men to protect stock and "hunt Indians," despite the army's preparations for a local pacification expedition of its own. After two white men disappeared near Mattole Valley, vigilantes massacred fifteen Mattole people and captured two others. Mattole and Wiyot Indians could not have known it, but such killers were just getting warmed up.[123]

On February 6, 1860, with the fishing season over and many white men unemployed, Hydesville residents organized a vigilante group that they called the Humboldt Cavalry and elected Seaman Wright captain. By mid-month, they had at least forty-six members and rode to the Eel River's south fork where they killed forty unidentified Indians. They then applied for enlistment as state militiamen. Governor Downey rejected the request because a company of regular soldiers was already operating in the area. However, another factor also likely influenced his decision. As Fort Humboldt's commander, Major Gabriel J. Rains, observed, the state legislature was then reviewing "the reports of a Committee adverse to payments to murderers of women and children in Jarboe's case and others analogous to what already had been perpetrated in this region." Following Weller's rejection of their request, an enraged Humboldt Cavalry faction "resolved to kill every peaceable Indian man, woman and child in this part of the country."[124]

Indians at Tuluwat on Duluwat Island, just across from Eureka in Humboldt Bay, were apparently unaware of this declaration. That day, large numbers of Wiyot, Eel, and Mad River Indians had gathered there to dance and celebrate life in their annual World Renewal ceremonies. They were not at war. Yet, early on February 26, a vigilante party slipped across the bay and at about 4:00 A.M. began murdering them. Eyewitnesses penned searing accounts of the carnage. On February 29, journalist Bret Harte wrote: "Neither age or sex had been spared. Little children and old women were mercilessly stabbed and their skulls crushed with axes. When the bodies were landed at [Arcata], a more shocking and revolting spectacle never was exhibited to the eyes of a Christian and civilized people. Old women, wrinkled and decrepit lay weltering in blood, their brains dashed out and dabbled with their long gray hair. Infants scarce a span long, with their faces cloven with hatchets and their bodies ghastly with wounds." Another eyewitness provided additional detail:

The writer was upon the ground with feet treading in human blood, horrified with the awful and sickening sights which met the eye wherever it turned. Here was a mother fatally wounded hugging the mutilated carcass of her dying infant to her bosom; there, a poor child of two years old, with its ear and scalp tore from the side of its little head. Here, a father frantic with grief over the bloody corpses of his four little children and wife; there, a brother and sister bitterly weeping, and trying to soothe with cold water, the pallid face of a dying relative. Here, an aged female still living and sitting up, though covered with ghastly wounds, and dying in her own blood; there, a living infant by its dead mother, desirous of drawing some nourishment from a source that had ceased to flow.

The eyewitness continued, "The wounded, dead and dying were found all around, and in every lodge the skulls and frames of women and children cleft with axes and hatchets, and stabbed with knives, and the brains of an infant oozing from it broken head to the ground." Reports of the death toll at Tuluwat soon began circulating in California newspapers and beyond, with estimates ranging from forty to sixty-two people killed, the vast majority women and children.[125]

That same morning, vigilantes also stormed nearby South Beach and Eel River communities. According to Wiyot man Dandy Bill, at South Beach a killing squad slew at least thirty-six Wiyots, including eleven women, fourteen children, and four elders. Others estimated as many as fifty-seven massacred there, again mostly women and children. In total, the *Humboldt Times* reported at least 150 killed in the three massacres, but J.A. Lord thought that "not less than two hundred Indians—men, women and children—were killed on this Sabbath morning." Eureka resident Robert Gunther, who owned land on Duluwat Island and heard many screams across the dark water between the island and his home in Eureka, recalled, "It was said that about 250 Indians were killed that night." Even the *Humboldt Times* excoriated the three attacks as an "indiscriminate slaughter of helpless children and defenseless squaws."[126]

Determined to destroy Humboldt Bay area Wiyot communities, the killing squads selected new targets. On the morning of February 29, they stormed a village at or near Eagle Prairie, on Eel River, and massacred as many as thirty-five Wiyots. The following night, they assaulted a nearby village, slaying an unknown number. In less than a week, killing squads had murdered as many as 285 or more Indians in five different massacres. On March 17, the *Humboldt Times* used the massacres to reiterate its opinion that there were "two—and only two— alternatives for ridding our county of Indians; either remove them to some reservation or kill them." Meanwhile, Bret Harte fled Arcata—his unflinching description of the Tuluwat atrocities dangerously unpopular among certain local readers—while the massacre perpetrators went unpunished.[127]

For some pundits, the justifications for such carnage were starting to wear thin. San Francisco journalists censured the massacres and used them to attack both the Mendocino Expedition in particular and California's Indian-killing program in general. The *Daily Evening Bulletin* quoted a Eureka correspondent who reported that "the murderers were creatures calling themselves volunteers from Captain Wright's Company." The state's leading newspaper went further. A February 29 *Daily Alta California* editorial titled "OUR INDIAN MASSACRE POLICY" pointed out that where "this policy of exterminating the Indians" was concerned, "the Legislature is disposed to come to the assistance of the exterminators." The article then attacked "Jarboe and his hired exterminators." A *San Francisco Herald* writer now censured this and other state-sponsored militia killing campaigns with the biting wit of satirist Jonathan Swift's *Modest Proposal*: "We . . . propose to the Legislature to create the office of Indian Butcher, with a princely salary, and confer it upon the man who has killed [the] most Indians in a given time, provided it be satisfactorily shown that the Indians were unarmed at the time, and the greater portion of them squaws and papooses." Still, the overwhelming majority of California legislators continued to support genocidal campaigns, reflecting a broad political consensus among enfranchised Californians.[128]

After weeks of debating whether or not to pay for the Pit River Expedition, the state Assembly passed "the Kibbe War Appropriation Bill" by a vote of more than two to one and the state Senate passed it by five to one. Although unstated in the legislative records, it seems clear that lawmakers' support for this bill was, in part, due to past congressional funding for state militia campaigns and the expectation of future support. Once again, federal financial support proved crucial to state militia campaigns against California Indians.[129]

However, some state legislators did resist funding such expeditions. Two state senators announced that "it was the last scheme of this character they would ever support," explaining, "The system inaugurated in this State [is] a pernicious one, and should be abolished." Most explicitly, in the *Majority and Minority Reports of the Special Joint Committee on the Mendocino War*, four senators proclaimed: "We are unwilling to attempt to dignify, by the term 'war,' a slaughter of beings, who at least possess the human form, and who make no resistance, and make no attacks." These senators then asked, "Shall the Indians be exterminated, or shall they be protected?" Such scathing critiques revealed profound, if numerically limited, legislative opposition to the killing machine, and the report's damning testimony underscored the genocidal nature of Jarboe's campaign. It is thus possible that someone conspired to withhold the report from the legislature. As the *Sacramento Daily Union* observed, "For some cause it [was] delayed in the hands of the printer until the bill ha[d] passed." Assemblymen and senators thus appropriated $9,347.39 to pay for Jarboe's Mendocino Expedition before they received the report. Still, given its scale, geographic scope, and state-supported nature, the wider genocide in California could not be hidden.[130]

On May 26, 1860, the debate over systematic California Indian killing reached the US Senate. After California senator Milton Latham called recent "outrages . . . greatly exaggerated," Massachusetts senator Henry Wilson referred to the Humboldt Bay Massacres and had the Senate secretary read aloud accounts of Jarboe's massacres, the Rolf's Ranch Massacre, and the murder of a wounded Indian by California superintendent of Indian Affairs Thomas Henley. Senator Wilson then unleashed his oratorical talent: "I am informed by officers of the Army that it is a fact which they personally know to be true, that Indians are hunted down in some portions of the State of California; that the old bucks . . . are killed, and the children . . . in certain cases sold as slaves." He continued, "Sir, the abuses that have been perpetrated upon the Indians in California are shocking to humanity, and this Government owes it to itself to right their wrongs." Latham then claimed that steps had been taken. Yet Kentucky senator John Crittenden pressed the attack, asking, "Can the gentlemen tell us of any of these murderers who have been prosecuted and punished? Have they been hung, as Jarboe ought to have been twenty times over[?]" Crittenden concluded, "If you suffer them to be murdered, the blood falls directly upon you; your garments are stained with it; and you are responsible for it."[131]

During this exchange, neither Wilson nor Crittenden acknowledged that Congress had lavished more than $800,000 on past California militia expeditions. Their censure nevertheless indicated that they—and perhaps other federal legislators—would oppose additional funding for California militia operations and might also oppose US Army Indian-killing operations in California. Nevertheless, California senator William Gwin now defiantly declared, "I look upon it as a mere question of time when these Indians of California are to be exterminated." Despite Gwin's expectation that the killing machine would continue until all California Indians were dead, the political situation was changing, and the federal tide seemed to be turning against further financing of California's killing machine.[132]

Increased scrutiny, strident public critiques, the shrinking state war fund, and the possibility that the federal government might not pay for additional state militia campaigns against California Indians combined to weaken the killing machine. Indeed, Governor Downey authorized no ranger militia expeditions in 1860.

Vigilante killings did continue that year, but at a reduced rate. In February, a Van Duzen River rancher slew six Nongatl people because his Nongatl servant, who was related to the victims, visited them too often. This rancher also "boasted of having killed *sixty infants* with his own hatchet." That same month, vigilantes massacred perhaps seventeen Yahi Yanas on Mill Creek. In March, Wright's Humboldt Cavalry "fired into a canoe, laden with old squaws and children," killing several on South Eel River before capturing "a couple of 'bucks'" and "a couple of NICE young squaws." They tied the men to a tree and shot them. The women they "reserved for future disposition." Summarizing Wright's ninety-day vigilante campaign, Major Rains reported that they "killed all of three men." Women and children were a different matter. Wright's operation was an attempt to annihilate Indians north, south, and east of Hydesville.[133]

Spring, summer, and fall brought fewer killings. In April, vigilantes murdered and scalped six Sinkyone people at Shelter Cove. On June 2, whites attacked a Mad River rancheria, massacring ten Whilkut men and two women. On July 20, "Eight or ten [Miwok] Indians and three Americans were shot" in a "quarrel" in the Tuolumne region. Around December 2, a white gunman killed seven Indians near South Eel River. Finally, after Nongatl reportedly stole and killed cattle "on Van Dusen Fork," vigilantes followed, and "some half dozen" Nongatl were "effectually cured of stealing beef."[134]

Regular army soldiers may also have massacred Mojaves and Southern Paiutes that year. From April to July, Major James Henry Carlton led two companies of dragoons into the Mojave Desert, following the killing of three whites there. Non-Indian sources reported that Carlton killed at least three Mojaves, gibbeting their bodies and displaying their severed heads. However, "At the Vegas an Indian [reported] that the soldiers had killed about forty [presumably Southern Paiute] Indians, including women and children, at the Resting Springs." Still, whites killed far fewer Indians in 1860 than in previous years, in large part because the state decreased support for ranger militia Indian-hunting operations.[135]

EXPANDING UNFREE CALIFORNIA INDIAN
LABOR LAWS, 1860

That spring, however, California legislators expanded de jure Indian servitude. First, they expanded the 1850 act by sanctioning the "indenture" of "any Indian or Indians, whether children or grown persons," including "prisoners of war" and vagrants as "apprentices." Legislators thus blended two traditionally separate forms of unfree labor: indentured servitude and apprenticeship. Second, lawmakers gave judges the power to "bind" and apprentice Indian minors without the consent of the minor's parents or guardians. Third, they allowed white employers to retain Indians indentured as minors beyond the age of eighteen: girls and boys under fourteen could be indentured until they turned twenty-one and twenty-five, respectively. Fourth, teenagers indentured between the ages of fourteen and twenty could now be held until their twenty-fifth birthday, if female, or their thirtieth birthday, if male. Finally, Indians over age twenty could be indentured for a decade. The 1860 law thus dramatically lowered legal barriers to acquiring involuntary Indian servants and substantially expanded de jure servitude terms.[136]

The issue of California Indian servitude reached the United States Senate floor the following month, as senators from Massachusetts and Kentucky attacked its immorality and lethality. Yet the federal government—now struggling to keep the Union together in the months leading up to the Southern secessions—took no action. This was unsurprising, insofar as slavery was the issue driving the North and South apart. Still, federal inaction had terrible consequences, as we shall see. Many kidnappings involved the murder of parents, the separation of men and women during peak reproductive years, and the forcible removal of California Indian children from their communities, which constituted the genocidal crimes—as defined by the UN Genocide Convention—of "Killing members of the group," "Imposing measures intended to prevent births within the group," and "Forcibly transferring children of the group to another group."[137]

Despite the new legislation that expanded unfree California Indian labor, by early 1861, the killing machine was under threat from both recent legislative attacks and the state executive. In his January 7 annual message, Governor Downey explained that by not calling out state militia units in 1860, he had avoided both "a very onerous tax upon the treasury" and the "indiscriminate slaughter of defenseless women and children." It was an unprecedented and direct public gubernatorial attack on the monetary cost and profound immorality of California's state-sponsored Indian-hunting militia expeditions in particular and the rampant killing of California Indians in general. Indeed, it suggested the possibility of a new direction in California's Indian policy.[138]

Still, killings in the Eel River basin and surrounding areas continued during the early months of 1861. In January, vigilantes massacred eighteen Yuki near Round Valley and thirteen Nongatl near "Inqua Ranch, Middle Yager." Regular soldiers meanwhile slew "several" Indians on the Eel River's South Fork. In February and March, vigilantes killed seven Mattole people in "Upper Mattole," thirty-nine Sinkyone "on main Eel river," and at least nine others in various locations. Some approved of these killings. On February 22, a Ukiah correspondent reported that Mendocino, South Eel River, Mattole, and North Eel River Indians were again killing stock and insisted: "A war of extermination is the only means that suggests itself as a remedy."[139]

The will to destroy remained strong, with a substantial base of non-Indian support, but the killing machine, and the California Indian-hunting militia expeditions that formed the heart of the apparatus, appeared to be in decline. Journalists, legislators, and even Governor Downey were publicly criticizing the killing of Indians, and a growing number of state legislators, including the governor, appeared not to support militia expeditions as funding dried up. Still, the well-oiled machinery of extermination stood by, idle but ready to be put back into full, murderous operation against California's surviving indigenous peoples. In March and April of 1861, developments in Washington, DC, and Fort Sumter, South Carolina, unleashed a new phase of state-sponsored California Indian killing.

The Civil War in California and Its Aftermath: March 1861–1871

A mean "Digger" only becomes a "good Indian" when he is dangling at the end of a rope, or has an ounce of lead in him.

—*Correspondent from Orleans, 1864*

White people want our land, want destroy us.

—*Lucy Young (Lassik/Wailaki), 1939*

On December 20, 1860, South Carolina became the first state to secede from the Union. The following morning, US senators ascended Capitol Hill to once again discuss the country's uncertain future. Still, some business proceeded as usual. That day, California senator Milton Latham introduced a bill to pay "expenses incurred in the suppression of Indian hostilities" in California. By March 2, both houses of Congress had passed the bill. Even as southern states seceded and the country careened toward civil war, Congress once again emphatically endorsed and generously financed California's killing machine.[1]

The new act appropriated up to $400,000 to pay the expenses of the nine California militia campaigns that had killed at least 766 California Indians from 1854 through 1859. The euphemistically titled "Act for the payment of expenses incurred in the suppression of Indian hostilities in the State of California" rejuvenated state militia Indian-hunting operations even as outrage against such campaigns became public at local, state, and federal levels. Genocide in California was becoming a national issue, and the US government would soon become even more directly involved.[2]

LOVELL'S ARMY CAMPAIGN, 1861

Soon after Congress passed the March 1861 funding act—which communicated emphatic federal support for California Indian hunting—a change of command at Fort Humboldt helped reorient the army's local Indian policy. From his base on a bluff overlooking Humboldt Bay, West Point graduate Major Gabriel J. Rains had emphasized protecting and negotiating with Indians. He told Lieutenant J.W. Cleary that "the hostility of these Indians is questionable" and that "something may be done with a pacific understanding" while ordering Lieutenant R.W. McLearry to emphasize taking prisoners, promising food, and using diplomacy. But his superiors reassigned Rains to Washington Territory. Captain Charles S. Lovell assumed command and soon waged the most lethal US Army expedition in California since Crook's 1857 Pit River Campaign.[3]

Pacific Department commander and brevet brigadier general Albert Sidney Johnston, another West Pointer, played a decisive role in implementing a new round of genocidal killing led by the US Army. He ordered Lovell to launch an Indian-hunting campaign and, on March 25, asked Governor Downey to enroll thirty volunteers for three months to serve as guides at the army's expense. On March 26, Lovell's regulars headed into the interior: Lieutenant Joseph B. Collins left Fort Humboldt with forty-five men for Yager Creek and the South Fork of Eel River under "orders to chastise hostile Indians wherever found on his route." On April 14, Collins's men massacred "between 15 or 20" Nongatl Indians. The next morning, US troops killed five more and wounded three, suffering one soldier injured. Meanwhile, Downey authorized the enrollment of guides. Johnston and Downey thus integrated volunteers' local knowledge with professional soldiers' training and discipline to lethal effect.[4]

On February 25, the *Daily Alta California* reported the "formation of a Southern Confederacy" and Jefferson Davis's election as its president. On April 9, General Johnston resigned his commission to head east where he would become a Confederate general. Still, the fragmentation of the United States did not stop California Indian-killing operations and the volunteer guide company mustered in on April 17.[5]

Captain Lovell now hurled a three-pronged attack into the heartlands of northwestern California Indian peoples. Captain Edmund Underwood commanded this lethal trident's northern point near the headwaters of Redwood Creek and Mad River, into Whilkut, Nongatl, and Lassik territory. On May 14, volunteer guide corporal Green Wilkinson led thirteen soldiers and volunteers to massacre at least six Whilkut people on Boulder Creek, leaving "twenty or

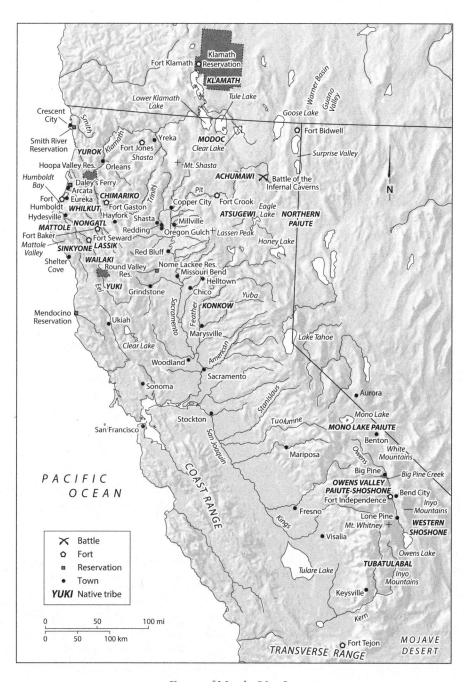

Crescent City

Smith River Reservation

YUROK

Humboldt Bay

Hoopa Valley Res.

Daley's Ferry

Fort Humboldt
Eureka
Arcata

CHIMARIKO

WHILKUT

Hydesville
Hayfork

Fort Baker

MATTOLE

NONGATL

Fort Seward

SINKYONE

LASSIK

Mattole Valley

Shelter Cove

WAILAKI

Round Valley Res.

YUKI

Ukiah

Mendocino Reservation

Clear Lake

Woodland

Sonoma

San Francisco

PACIFIC OCEAN

Smith

Klamath

Yreka

Fort Jones

Shasta

Orleans

Trinity

CHIMARIKO

Fort Gaston

Shasta

Redding

Oregon Gulch

Red Bluff

Nome Lackee Res.

Missouri Bend

Helltown

Grindstone

Chico

Eel

Sacramento

Feather

KONKOW

Marysville

American

Sacramento

Stockton

San Joaquin

COAST RANGE

Klamath Reservation

Fort Klamath

KLAMATH

Lower Klamath Lake

Tule Lake

Goose Lake

Warner Basin

Guano Valley

Fort Bidwell

MODOC

Clear Lake

+ *Mt. Shasta*

Pit

Copper City

Fort Crook

ACHUMAWI

Battle of the Infernal Caverns

Surprise Valley

Millville

+ *Lassen Peak*

ATSUGEWI

Eagle Lake

Honey Lake

NORTHERN PAIUTE

N

Yuba

Lake Tahoe

Aurora

Mono Lake

MONO LAKE PAIUTE

Stanislaus

Tuolumne

Benton

White Mountains

Mariposa

Big Pine

Big Pine Creek

OWENS VALLEY PAIUTE-SHOSHONE

Fort Independence

Owens

Bend City

Inyo Mountains

Fresno

Lone Pine

Mt. Whitney +

WESTERN SHOSHONE

Kings

Visalia

Owens Lake

TUBATULABAL

Inyo Mountains

Tulare Lake

Keysville

Kern

Fort Tejon

MOJAVE DESERT

TRANSVERSE RANGE

✗ Battle
⬠ Fort
◼ Reservation
• Town
YUKI Native tribe

| 0 | 50 | 100 mi |
| 0 | 50 | 100 km |

Events of March 1861–1871

more wounded." Underwood's men killed five to eight more Indians by June 1, while just one of his men was wounded. Then, on June 21, local whites—including Wilkinson—"sent eight [Mad River Indians] to their happy hunting grounds."[6]

Lieutenant Joseph B. Collins's soldiers and guides—the trident's central spearhead—waged a particularly lethal campaign in the Larabee Creek region. For Sinkyone and Nongatl people, who had yet to experience genocidal massacres by regular army soldiers, such attacks likely came as a surprise, given that regular soldiers had previously focused on capturing, rather than killing, them. This element of surprise, in combination with army professionalism and integrated local guides, led to substantial death tolls. By May 9, Collins reported having killed fifteen Indians since April 19. In the next nine days, his men killed eight more. Collins then reported killing ten on May 23, four on May 26, and twenty-five on May 30, while wounding ten others that day. Collins's killers were relentless. On June 2, they massacred at least twenty. On June 8, they slew at least four. Eight days later, they killed four more, and on June 17, they massacred "6 Indians, only 1 escaped." Meanwhile, just two of Collins's men sustained wounds and, although he attacked villages that presumably contained substantial numbers of noncombatants, Collins improbably claimed that his men "killed and wounded" only "males, competent to bear arms." Yet he did not say that they were in fact armed.[7]

The *San Francisco Herald* minced no words in describing Collins's subcampaign: "The troops are not engaged in 'fighting' the Indians, but in slaughtering them. They have Indian battues [hunts], not battles, on Larabee Creek. We are not told that the Indians were punished for any offences they had committed, but were shot down as they were 'going out a hunting.'" It was a clearly genocidal US military operation: "The purpose of the troops is to exterminate." On June 22, the *Humboldt Times* summarized Collins's campaign to date: "The troops have followed the Indians night and day," killed 117, and suffered just three men wounded.[8]

Lieutenant James P. Martin, with sixty men, led the trident's southern point into the Eel River's South Fork region, where ranchers had recently massacred fifteen Indians. Martin's volunteer guides and regular soldiers proved lethal to local Sinkyone people. On May 28, Martin's men slew eight on the South Fork "about one mile above its mouth." On June 4, they massacred sixteen, including "three squaws." On June 14, they killed seven more and, on June 16, they took the lives of at least nine others in three separate incidents. Responsibility for these unprovoked murders weighed heavily on Martin's conscience. He lamented, "I do not know positively what depredations, if any, have been committed by the Indians killed by this command," but his orders encouraged indiscriminate killing: "My instructions are to consider all who run on approaching them as hostile and to fire upon them. In every case where any have been killed they ran at the first sight of the men." Martin's men even killed some who could not run. According to historian William F. Strobridge, "Apparently unreported by Martin was the act of a volunteer who . . . tied an Indian child to a tree, and shot him or her."[9]

By the time Captain Lovell mustered out the thirty guides on July 16, his US Army command had killed more than 190 California Indians. Still, they were not finished. Five days later, Martin's men attacked a South Fork Eel River village and massacred a dozen Sinkyone Indians, including two women. In November, US Indian Affairs commissioner William P. Dole issued a scathing critique of the army's Humboldt and Mendocino County operations: "This so-called 'Indian war' appears to be a war in which the whites alone are engaged. The Indians are hunted like wild and dangerous beasts of prey; the parents are 'murdered,' and the children 'kidnapped.'" Still, despite evidence of what we would today call genocide, Washington decision makers made few plans to protect California Indians. Instead, they supported genocidal actions by paying the killers' salaries after the fact.[10]

THE 1861 SLAVE-RAIDING BOOM

Meanwhile, California's 1860 legislation unleashed an 1861 slave-raiding boom. In January, a correspondent described "WHOLESALE KIDNAPPING," noting that the Tehama County judge was indenturing "all of the 'most valuable'" Nome Lackee Reservation Indians to individuals for terms of ten to twenty years. In February, the *Humboldt Times* observed: "This law works beautifully. . . . V.E. Geiger, formerly Indian Agent, had some eighty apprenticed to him. . . . We hear of many others who are having them bound in numbers to suit." Indeed, the Colusa County court indentured dozens of Indians in 1861, and the Humboldt County court indentured seventy-seven others that year, the youngest a two-year-old indentured for twenty-three years. State-sponsored legislation thus supported the genocidal crimes of "Forcibly transferring children of the group to another group" and, by compulsorily separating members of the group, "Imposing measures intended to prevent births within the group."[11]

Kidnapping raids also routinely involved the genocidal crime of systematic killing. Raiders regularly murdered parents. A *Boston Transcript* correspondent visited northwestern California and described "Indians . . . being hunted *for their children*." At one house in the mountains, the correspondent saw six naked

In this image, a white man—possibly a judge—exhorts one California Indian man to
whip another as the Stars and Stripes flies in the background. The 1850 *Statutes of
California* stated that "An Indian convicted of stealing . . . any valuable thing, shall
be subject to receive any number of lashes not exceeding twenty-five or shall be
subject to a fine." The law specified that "the Justice may appoint a white man,
or an Indian at his discretion, to execute the sentence in his presence." California,
Statutes of California, 1850, 409. A. Gandon, "Untitled," drawing, ca. 1859(?), in
Gerstäcker, *Scènes de la Vie Californienne*, plate between pages 246 and 247.
Courtesy of Yale Collection of Western Americana, Beinecke Rare Book and
Manuscript Library, Yale University.

Indian children. Their captor "pointed to one boy and said, with the greatest
coolness imaginable, that he 'had killed his daddy yesterday, and thought he was
not quite big enough to kill, so he brought him in.'" That same month, the
Marysville Appeal railed against slavers "killing the Indians in the mountains,
or running them off, and kidnapping their children . . . to sell, at retail or
wholesale."[12]

In at least one instance, Northern California district superintendent of Indian
Affairs George Hanson did prosecute slavers but found the court stunningly un-
supportive. In October, he captured three men, near Marysville, holding nine

Indian children, ages three to ten. However, the court discharged one of the three kidnappers "upon the testimony of the other two, who stated that 'he was not interested in the matter of taking the children.'" Once released, the man testified on behalf of the other two that "'it was an act of charity on the part of the two to hunt up the children and then provide homes for them, because their parents had been killed, and the children would have perished with hunger.'" Hanson's "counsel inquired 'how he knew their parents had been killed?' 'because,' said he, 'I killed some of them myself.'" Authorities then released the suspects on bail, placing the children in "good homes." By New Year's Eve, a despondent Hanson reported that "kidnapping Indians has become quite a business of profit, and I have no doubt is at the foundation of the so-called Indian wars." Thus, the cogs of the state-sponsored killing machine meshed with the gears of California's genocidal systems of servitude to create a powerful machine of extermination.[13]

VIGILANTE KILLINGS, 1861

During and after Lovell's army campaign—which underscored continuing federal support of California Indian killing—deadly vigilante squads continued operating, sometimes with organized local support. For example, in early May, "citizens" near Shasta raised money to pay for Indian scalps, and the *Shasta Herald* warned that "the extinction of the tribes who have been to settlers such a cause of dread and loss, will be the result." Accordingly, "the Diggers can only be saved from forcible extermination by the intervention of Uncle Sam." Yet, federal government help was not forthcoming even as many immigrants demonstrated their determination to physically annihilate California Indians, including women and children. Instead, the federal government ultimately bankrolled many genocidal campaigns.[14]

On June 18, whites and Sinkyone people clashed at Shelter Cove on the southern Humboldt coast, which resulted in the deaths of perhaps four Sinkyone and one William Oliver. John Biaggi Jr. later recollected that, in response, a posse of fifteen men went to Shelter Cove. As Sinkyone villagers slept, Oliver's friend Hamilton "led the charge with the cry 'Kill them all,' and most of them were either driven into the surf with whips and drowned or were shot. The children were put into some sort of a stockade for the night, but during the night" a posse member "cut the throats of most of the children." Another posse killed three more Indians in late July and early August. Meanwhile, Trinity County vigilantes killed and wounded twenty or thirty Chimarikos(?) at Ketcupomene that summer, suffering just one man injured. Soon thereafter, a Hayfork gang killed five Wintu people. Although at first glance seemingly unconnected, these and other Northern California massacres were, of course, part of the broader genocidal program allowed and supported by state and federal policymakers and their treasuries.[15]

Round Valley Reservation was also a locus of genocidal Indian killing that summer. Some of the carnage targeted the reservation's Indians. On July 16, Northern California Indian Affairs Superintendent Hanson reported Round Valley Reservation Indians "being hunted down like wild beasts and killed." Still, federal officials did not stop the killing. Earlier, in February, the *Mendocino Herald* had proclaimed that nearby mountain Wailakis "must gradually become extinct, else forever be a pest and trouble to the white man." In October, some Long and Round Valley colonists decided to accelerate that process, apparently with the support of the reservation superintendent.[16]

As in many other genocidal California massacres, killers used missing stock as a pretext for mass murder, and, in this instance, recruited Round Valley Reservation Indians to join them. Sometime after October 10, 1861, Charles Baume led as many as thirteen whites and eighty Achumawi, Atsugewi, Konkow, and Yuki reservation Indians against Wailaki people living to the north. Some or all of these Indian auxiliaries participated at the behest of Round Valley Reservation supervisor James Short. Konkow chief Tome-ya-nem resisted joining this expedition "to kill the Wylackies," later explaining that "they had done no harm either to me or mine." But Short "asked me to go." Given that Short controlled rations on a reservation that had very little food, as well as other aspects of life at Round Valley, this may not have been much of a choice. Moreover, given that Round Valley Reservation agents sometimes killed reservation Indians, the threat of lethal force may have compounded the coercive pressures that compelled Tome-ya-nem and other reservation Indians to participate.[17]

Full of remorse, Tome-ya-nem recalled that Baume's force found the Wailaki at Horse Canyon. "The trees were full of meat hanging in the sun to dry," but "I told my braves to be sure and not kill . . . the women and the little children." Baume's men initially spared women and children until a white man "commanded to kill them all and they were killed." Still, some of the Indian auxiliaries subverted these orders. Tome-ya-nem explained, "We hid a great many little *koh-las* [children] among the rocks, and perhaps they did not die. I remember one, White Chief, a beautiful brown little girl with eyes as bright and as large as two stars; she was running away and trying to escape . . . her foot tripped and she fell the tomahawk cleft her little head in two." By such means, "very soon the water in the creek became red . . . tomahawks crushed through the brain of the old and the young alike." Eventually, "dead Wylackis were strewn over the ground like the dead leaves in the fall, and for many days the sky was black with the ravens fattening on the dead." Of the 400 or more people surprised that morning, nineteenth-century sources reported at least 100 and perhaps as many as 240 massacred. As the *Red Bluff Beacon* explained, it was "an indiscriminate slaughter of men, women and children." Just two to five attackers died, but more Wailaki blood soon pooled in Horse Canyon.[18]

A few days later, according to the *Red Bluff Beacon*, "another party discovered" Wailaki survivors "burying their dead, and killed about forty more." The newspaper concluded, "The settlers are determined to exterminate them, root and branch, if possible." California newspapers reported these genocidal massacres, but none of the men involved faced legal charges or even substantial censure in California's press. Few whites were willing to stand up against the killing machine, in part because most state and federal officials either openly tolerated or supported the destruction of California's Indian peoples.[19]

RESERVATIONS AND STARVATION, 1861

When not subject to violent attacks, California reservation Indians faced continued institutionalized starvation as rations declined. In July, Northern California Indian Affairs Superintendent Hanson frankly reported, "As hitherto conducted, the indians have looked upon the reservations rather as a hell than as a home." The following month, Browne suggested in *Harper's* that starvation conditions prevailed on California reservations. With his signature sarcasm, he quipped that detainees liked the Mendocino Reservation "so well that they left it very soon, and went back to their old places of resort, preferring a chance of life to the certainty of starvation." Browne added that internees "were very soon starved out at the Fresno [Reservation], and wandered away to find a subsistence wherever they could. Many of them perished of hunger on the plains of the San Joaquin." Of California reservations as a whole, he concluded, "In the brief period of six years [California reservation Indians] have been very nearly destroyed by the generosity of Government." Such destructive federal Indian reservation policies thus seem to have constituted the genocidal crimes of "Deliberately inflicting on the group conditions of life calculated to bring about its physical destruction in whole or in part" and "Imposing measures intended to prevent births within the group." To Browne, reservations were clearly another component in California's machinery of genocide: "What neglect, starvation, and disease have not done, has been achieved by the co-operation of the white settlers in the great work of extermination."[20]

Official reports corroborated starvation conditions on California reservations. In July, Hanson reported that, at Nome Lackee Reservation, "The Indians, who formerly numbered from two to three thousand, being left destitute of food and clothing, have mostly scattered." On New Year's Eve, Hanson reported on the relationship between starvation at the Klamath Reservation and violent mass murder, predicting that internees "will either perish from lack of food or return to their old haunts, and renew a war (perhaps to their own extermination) by the recommencement of depredations on the settlers' stock, which they *must do from necessity or die*." Some California Indians thus fled starvation conditions on federal reservations only to be killed when they tried to feed themselves and their families off the reservation. Reservations and killing campaigns thus worked together to facilitate the genocide of California Indian peoples.[21]

HUMBOLDT HOME GUARDS MILITIA EXPEDITION, 1861

Likely to obtain food and retaliate against slave raiders, Indians south of Humboldt Bay continued to attack colonists. Attendees at a July 24 Eureka meeting thus resolved—despite the killing of over 190 Indians during Lovell's recent army campaign—to request another army expedition or, failing that, a state militia unit. They sent Stephen G. Whipple to present their grievances to the governor. Three days later, unidentified Indians killed George Cooper and an Indian boy near Hydesville. That day, Captain Lovell dispatched a dozen US Army soldiers "to the scene." Governor Downey then ordered out a state militia company for three months, secure in the knowledge that Congress had approved payment for previous campaigns. Downey had returned to business as usual, and the *Daily Alta California* predicted that Jarboe's genocidal ranger militia campaign would now be repeated. On September 9, the Humboldt Home Guards state militia unit mustered in, elected G.W. Werk as captain, and in October swelled to seventy-five men as they began killing Indians.[22]

Two San Francisco newspapers now openly condoned genocide. The *Daily Alta California* asserted that "since the existence and persistence of one race implies the annihilation of the other, we are content that the red men should be that 'other.'" The *Daily Evening Bulletin* announced: "While we believe the manner in which the Indians are being exterminated is perfectly horrible, we are disposed to make every possible allowance for our own people." The *Bulletin* then predicted that Indians between Clear Lake and Oregon, "on both sides of the Coast Range . . . will all be killed within a short time unless Government assumes the task of saving their lives." Moreover, "If Government fails to act in putting into operation its humane policy of reclaiming the savages, its inactivity must be regarded as constructive license to the horrible butchery." When federal policymakers failed to act, many presumably agreed that the genocide was indeed proceeding with federal "license." The US government abetted the genocide both by failing to stop the massacres and by consistently funding California's Indian-hunting militia operations after the fact.[23]

As the army stood by, the Humboldt Home Guards scoured the hills and valleys for targets. By November 9, Werk reported having killed thirty-four Indians. In two subsequent massacres, his militiamen slew an additional thirty-five Whilkut people. On December 18, Werk filed his final report, enumerating fifteen engagements, the killing of seventy-seven men "and a few women" as well as the wounding of "nearly" as many. On his side, Werk reported two killed and eight wounded. Tellingly, he mentioned no prisoners. Thus ended California's last ranger militia Indian-hunting operation before the US Army transformed the killing machine. Three months later, army colonel Francis J. Lippitt frankly characterized Werk's genocidal expedition as "a mere series of Indian hunts, whose only object was to slaughter." In the meantime, violence on the Atlantic seaboard of the United States began a cascading series of events that would remake California's killing machine.[24]

TRANSFORMING THE KILLING MACHINE

At 4:27 A.M. on April 12, 1861, mortar shells exploded in the darkness over the Stars and Stripes at Fort Sumter in Charleston Harbor, South Carolina. The American Civil War had begun. Several months later and thousands of miles away, these events precipitated the departure of most regular army soldiers from California, leaving a military vacuum in their wake. On July 24, Secretary of War Simon Cameron telegraphed Governor Downey, urgently requesting that he enroll an infantry regiment and five cavalry companies to serve for three years. On August 12, Downey called for volunteers. Two days later, Secretary Cameron requested four more infantry regiments as well as another cavalry regiment.[25]

Cameron issued similar calls to the governors of other states, and like their brethren across the Union, many Californian men responded enthusiastically. During 1861, they volunteered to join the US Army and formed the First and Second California Cavalry and the First, Second, Third, Fourth, and Fifth California Infantry. Often referred to as "California Volunteers," these men chose to join the US Army as wartime soldiers—armed, uniformed, fed, supplied, and paid by the federal government—for terms of three years. By war's end, 15,725 would enlist, dwarfing all previous military mobilizations in California history.

The continuing flood of immigrants arriving in California helped to make such recruitment possible. By 1860, the state's population had grown to more than 362,000, an increase of at least 53,000 people over eight years. This enabled the army to deploy thousands of California Volunteers north and east, beyond the Golden State, to patrol areas vacated by regulars while also keeping thousands of others in California.[26]

The California Volunteers who remained in the state revolutionized the killing machine. Before 1861, bureaucracy had mediated, limited, and delayed federal funding for state militia operations against California Indians. Under this system there was also the possibility that the US government would not fund some or all of each expedition. With the creation of the US Army's California Volunteers, federal authorities could now directly pay and supply California men to conduct anti-Indian operations. As US troops, the California Volunteers replaced relatively small, short-term state militia campaigns with larger, longer army campaigns. Often commanded by veteran regular officers, the California Volunteers sometimes received support from soldiers in neighboring Nevada. No longer limited in size or duration by state legislators' concerns about congressional reimbursement or participants' worries that they might not get paid, the army took over from militias, fielding the most sustained campaigns yet seen in California. Not surprisingly, vigilante operations flourished alongside these campaigns. Still, the federal government and its army now took the lead in directly manning and funding the killing machine. The genocide was now primarily a federal project.

The US Army's California Volunteers quickly grew into a substantial military force within California. By December 10, 1861, the army's Pacific Division commander general George Wright reported three artillery companies, one ordnance company, one cavalry regiment, and thirty-seven infantry companies in Northern California as well as five companies of cavalry and an infantry regiment in Southern California. These 5,900 men were a much larger armed force than had ever existed in antebellum California, and Wright soon began deploying them against California Indians with devastating effect.[27]

THE CALIFORNIA VOLUNTEERS' FIRST CAMPAIGN, 1862

On January 9, 1862, California Volunteers colonel Francis J. Lippitt—who had come to California in 1847 and had served as a California constitutional delegate—assumed command of Fort Humboldt and reinstated Major Rains's diplomatic approach to Indian relations. In one set of orders, Lippitt commanded an officer "not to make war upon the Indians, nor to punish them for any murders or depredations hitherto committed, but to bring them in and place them permanently on some reservation where they can be protected . . . without bloodshed whenever it is possible." Lippitt also prohibited, on penalty of death, "killing or wounding an Indian, unless in self-defense, in action, or by orders of a superior officer." Nor did Lippitt approve of vigilantes. Three days after taking command, he reported "many whites . . . constantly killing Indians, often making up parties for that purpose, and as they generally find them in their rancherias, they kill as many of the women and children, perhaps, as bucks."[28]

Many local immigrants did consider themselves at war with northwestern California Indians and planned to win by killing, rather than negotiating. On January 21, Humboldt County resident James Beith insisted, "We are in the midst of a terrible Indian war," and warned, "God help the Indians *now*." On February 9, after Indians drove off cattle near Big Bend, on Mad River, vigilantes massacred five Whilkuts. Political pressure for another official anti-Indian campaign intensified, and at an April 2 Arcata meeting, whites resolved to demand that local Indians be removed to "some distant Reservation." They sent copies to the new governor, Leland Stanford, as well as General Wright and Colonel Lippitt. Meanwhile, state senator Walter Van Dyke urged Wright to deploy additional US Army troops to Humboldt County, emphasizing "that the war should be vigorously prosecuted." Killings continued. On April 7, Wright agreed to send two new companies "to act vigorously." That same day, Captain D.B. Akey's California Cavalry company shot two Whilkut men on sight. These murders marked the first steps in California Volunteers' journey toward becoming the driving force in California's killing machine between 1862 and 1866.[29]

That same day, US Army general Wright ordered Colonel Lippitt—who had been capturing dozens of Indians with relatively few killings—to radically alter his tactics. Wright ominously commanded Lippitt "to make a clean sweep," and declared his determination to settle "Indian difficulties in the Humboldt District . . . for the last time." Although "women and children" were to be spared, Wright ordered the execution of prisoners, *"Every Indian you may capture, and who has been engaged in hostilities present or past, shall be hung on the spot."* Under these draconian directives—which clearly broke traditional laws of war— Lippitt issued "General Orders No.4" on April 9, 1862: "Every Indian captured in this district during the present war who has been engaged in hostilities against whites, present or absent, will be hanged on the spot, women and children in all cases being spared." Lippitt did not explain how his troops were to determine who was innocent. Thus, his order seems to have been read as a general command to kill all adult Indian men. He issued even more explicitly murderous orders to his troops on Mad River. They were to kill all male adults: "No quarter will be given, except to the women and children." As a result, between early April and June 7, Lippitt's soldiers killed or mortally wounded at least thirty-eight Mattole, Yurok, and other Indian people while taking 147 prisoners, with reports suggesting that most prisoners were women, children, and teenagers. Wright's "clean sweep" policy—and orders to kill all adult males—involved repeated, systematic killings. At the same time, the destruction of villages and their contents made survival for those who escaped extremely difficult.[30]

Some continued to express genocidal intent. On June 7, California Volunteers lieutenant colonel James M. Olney ordered Captain Charles D. Douglas to help in "exterminating the band of Indians engaged in the murders and depredations at Daley's Ferry." Lieutenant Charles Hubbard then concluded of Mattole Valley colonists: "Cold-blooded Indian killing [is] considered honorable, [even the] murdering [of] squaws and children. . . . Human life is of no value in this valley."[31]

Wright's operation captured substantial numbers, but his officers' official reports likely concealed the full extent of the killing. On June 21, the *Humboldt Times* reported that Captain Thomas Ketchum's company alone had "killed forty Indian warriors, and taken 272 prisoners." Soon thereafter one anonymous volunteer reported that "our troops [presumably another company] thus far have killed some 70 or 80 but have very rarely succeeded in taking any of them prisoners." These unofficial reports suggest that the campaign killed at least 120 Indian people before imposing the lethal conditions that killed others in confinement. By July 12, Lippitt was holding 365 people prisoner at Fort Humboldt, where an unspecified number died, "probably owing to the close confinement."[32]

Despite the numbers captured and killed, in early June Eureka men petitioned General Wright and Governor Stanford for "independent volunteer companies" and arms. Continued clashes, such as a July 28 Redwood Creek episode in which three whites and two Indians died, motivated nearby Arcata men to organize a vigilante force. George W. Ousley became their captain, and they cooperated closely with regulars. On August 21, Captain Ousley led "thirty citizens and seventeen soldiers" to massacre six Wiyot people at a Light's Prairie village where one attacker died. Eighteen soldiers under Lieutenant Campbell and thirty-six vigilantes under Ousley then followed the survivors—many of whom were wounded—to Little River. There, on August 24, they massacred some twenty-two to forty people before burning the camp and retreating with a single wounded volunteer.[33]

Lippitt's men continued to take prisoners and by early September, held 874 people at Fort Humboldt. On September 14, authorities loaded 833 of them onto the steamer *Panama* and shipped them north to Crescent City, to be marched to Smith River Valley. As we shall see, institutionalized neglect led to additional deaths there on a federal reservation. The violent capture of California Indians as well as their containment under lethal conditions constituted important components of the killing machine. The traffic in unfree California Indians constituted another cog in the crushing machinery of genocide.[34]

1862 SLAVE RAIDING

The practice of murdering California Indian adults in order to kidnap and sell young women and children for a profit likely reached its zenith in 1862. That January, Lippitt reported that individuals and groups were constantly "kidnapping Indian children, frequently attacking the rancherias, and killing the parents for no other purpose." To the south, Captain Ketchum reported from Fort Baker, in April, that substantial numbers of men planned, once winter snows had melted "to make a business of killing the bucks wherever they can find them and selling the women and children into slavery." Two months later, another officer reported from Mattole Valley that "kidnapping is extensively practiced by a gang who live in the neighboring mountains" and that such crimes are "coupled with other barbarities, murder, rape, &c., which no pen can do justice to." Lethal kidnapping was widespread. In July, a correspondent reported that in "Mendocino, Humboldt, Del Norte and Klamath [there] flourishes a class of pestilent whites whose business it is, or has been until recently, to kill Indian 'bucks' and squaws for the purpose solely of getting and selling their children." The next month, the same correspondent described "Indian Baby Hunters" ranging from Sonoma to the Oregon border and concluded, "You may hear them talk of the operation of cutting to pieces an Indian squaw in their indiscriminate raids for babies as 'like slicing old cheese.'" Again, state and federal policies helped to facilitate both the genocidal crimes of "forcibly transferring children of the group to another group" and widespread and systematic killing.[35]

US soldiers may also have sometimes been complicit in genocidal crimes of "forcibly transferring children of the group to another group." Lassik/Wailaki woman Lucy Young recollected how, in 1862, a white man took her "Li'l sister . . . away. Never see her no more. . . . Mother lost her at Fort Seward." Here, soldiers failed to protect an Indian child. Young herself suffered kidnapping at the hands of a white man who "had cowhide rope. . . . Give woman good whipping with that." Young also recalled another instance in which soldiers captured a group of women and children in the Eel River region: "But this time, only the women were taken to Fort Seward. The children were all taken south and never heard of again." Thus, the army seems to have facilitated the permanent separation of these Indian children from their families and communities.[36]

California Indians resisted servitude by escaping, but whites frequently responded with deadly force, compounding the death toll associated with California's systems of Indian servitude. Young, who escaped captivity multiple times, recollected: "Young woman been stole by white people, come back. Shot through lights and liver. Front skin hang down like apron. She tie up with cotton dress. Never die, neither." Others were less fortunate. In some instances, whites massacred California Indian villages in retaliation for absenteeism or running away. It remains difficult to estimate how many California Indians died in slave raids and attempted escapes, but in 1862 the numbers may have reached into the hundreds. According to an October *Daily Alta California* article, "Rumor says that about one hundred children have been taken through Lake county this summer, for sale" and that raiders catch children in Humboldt and Mendocino counties "after killing their parents." The slavers also shot children who attempted to escape.[37]

The number of California Indians living in bondage under US rule may have peaked in 1862. At a local level, one writer later reported that in Ukiah "there were few families in town that did not have from one to three Indian children." At a regional level, a correspondent estimated a kidnapped Indian child in "every fourth white man's house" in northwestern California. Up and down the state, whites held California Indians as both de jure and de facto unfree laborers. As far south as San Diego County, rancher Cave Couts used state laws to ensnare Southern California Indians as de jure wards, apprentices, indentured servants, and leased convicts as well as de facto debt peons. Anti-Indian campaigns continued, in part, because the gears of the killing machine meshed with California's lucrative trade in unfree California Indian labor.[38]

ROUND VALLEY REGION VIGILANTE KILLINGS, 1862

Meanwhile, genocidal violence continued in the Round Valley region. On April 3, Captain Ketchum reported that whites had recently massacred seventeen Indian men near Eel River. Several weeks later, after some Achumawi or Atsugewi people fled Round Valley Reservation and killed an Indian boy and Hiram Watson of Grindstone, Stone Creek vigilantes massacred at least thirteen of them, taking two prisoners, while losing one man killed and another mortally wounded. Several months later, on August 4, the *Red Bluff Independent* reported another massacre near "Stony Creek" in which eleven Indians and a white man died. The paper concluded by stoking the fires of genocidal hatred: "Extermination of the red devils will have to be resorted to before the people in proximity to rancherias will be safe, or our mountain roads traveled with any degree of safety except by parties of well armed men."[39]

Vigilantes were already putting such sentiments into practice on Round Valley Reservation. In late July, Hanson reported that some men stabbed to death and hanged four or five reservation Indians. Several days later, twenty-seven vigilantes surrounded a group of sleeping Wailaki on the reservation near Upper Station because they feared that the hungry Wailaki might rustle stock. It would be another slaughter motivated by suspicion alone. At daylight the vigilantes massacred perhaps forty-five Wailaki people while just one of their own was wounded.[40]

During a December Army Court of Investigation, evidence of reservation supervisor James Short's involvement in this massacre emerged. James McHenry, who admitted participating in the atrocity, testified that—prior to the massacre— Supervisor Short had told him that "he did not see the use of men going into the mountains to hunt Indians when they were here on the Reservation" and that Short had loaned him a "pistol the evening before the attack." Thus, as in the Horse Canyon Massacre, Short played an indirect, but important supporting role. Another confessed Upper Station massacre perpetrator, Martin Corbett, added, "The Reservation employees knew that the Indians were to be attacked." As US Army major Edward Johnson concluded, Indians "had always been told by the white men, 'Come on the reservation; we do not want to kill you,' but that they had been invariably deceived and killed." High-ranking Washington officials, well aware of the Upper Station Massacre and Short's complicity, kept him on as reservation supervisor. The massacre of California Indians had become so routine that even those employed to protect them aided and abetted such atrocities without fear of repercussions.[41]

Indeed, policymakers in Washington understood that the reservations could be dangerous for California Indians. On November 26, 1862, Indian Affairs Commissioner William P. Dole reported that California Indians "are not even unmolested upon the scanty reservations we set apart for their use." Dole explained: "Upon one pretext or another, even these are invaded by the whites, and it is literally true that there is no place where the Indian can experience that feeling of security which is the effect of just and wholesome laws." Despite such reports, the Indian Affairs Office and army rarely acted to protect California Indians.[42]

RESERVATIONS AND STARVATION, 1862–1863

In fact, many California Indians continued to face institutionalized starvation conditions on federal reservations. In April 1862, the *Red Bluff Beacon* reported that at Nome Lackee Reservation, internees "draw no rations from the government—that they have neither 'beef, pork or flour' fed to them, except it be to two or three 'bucks and squaws,' kept in and around the buildings at the old headquarters." In August, the *Humboldt Times* reported Indians "who ran away from the Mendocino Reservation to keep from starving to death." Starvation conditions at Round Valley Reservation that year are particularly well documented. In October, the *Red Bluff Beacon* reported Round Valley Indians "in starving condition" fleeing "in the hope of escaping death by starvation." Possibly describing this exodus, Tome-ya-nem recollected meeting with the Round Valley Reservation supervisor, telling him that his "people were starving," declaring his intention to leave, and then leading some 500 Konkow people east in search of food. Meanwhile, Round Valley Reservation rations continued to diminish. By December, reservation employee J.M. Robinson testified: *"There is nothing for them to eat."* James McHenry also testified that Indians "said they had nothing to eat here." That same month, Captain Charles Douglas reported daily rations of just "two to three ears of corn to each Indian big or little," or 160 to 390 calories per person per day. The reservation possessed hundreds of cattle, but—as on other California reservations—federal decision makers refused to revise the policies that were causing starvation.[43]

Smith River Reservation, established in 1862, soon became another lethal federal detention center. In July 1863, California's Indian Affairs superintendent lamented: "The unsettled condition of three-fourths or more of the Indians, who have been compelled to lie on the cold, damp ground . . . has [in combination with venereal pathogens transmitted by soldiers] caused disease, and death in many instances." Neglect compounded these conditions. Inmates received no farming tools, and "only an occasional Indian wear[s] a whole garment, and not a whole blanket could be found among 100 Indians." Thus, "Their constant inquiry was: 'When *Captain* Lincoln, *big chief,* send Indian plenty blankets?'" Unsurprisingly, the population declined. By 1868, the superintendent explained: "The number of Indians at Smith river has decreased, not only by escapes but by severe sickness among them; measles, diarrhoea, and other epidemics." Inadequate clothing, substandard shelter, insufficient nutrition, and poor medical care all contributed. Indeed, confinement to federal reservations was a death sentence for many of the state's Indian people, whether they were starved to death, worked to death, shot, hanged, massacred, or died of sickness there. For those who escaped, life beyond the reservations remained perilous. The state laws that had stripped Indians of meaningful legal protection remained in force, vigilantes continued to kill with impunity, and the US Army persisted in launching lethal operations against California Indians.[44]

In late December 1862, the leader Lassik surrendered at or near Fort Seward, ending the resistance campaign that he and his followers began when they escaped from the institutionalized neglect and death at Smith River Reservation that September. Surrender would prove fatal. The *Mendocino Herald* reported that Lassik and his followers "took cold and died," adding, "We suspect the 'cold' they died with was mainly cold lead." A letter from Fort Seward soon specified, "Five of Lassux' band died with the same kind of 'cold' as himself." This was, however, a gross underestimate.[45]

Lucy Young, whose father was a Lassik, recollected the sights, sounds, and smells of that horrific day: "At last I come home [to Fort Seward]. . . . Before I get there, I see big fire. . . . Same time awfully funny smell. I think: Somebody got lotsa wood." Young then went to her house to find "everybody crying. Mother tell me: 'All our men killed now.' She say white men there, others come from Round Valley, Humboldt County too, kill our old uncle, Chief Lassik, and all our men." The vigilantes massacred the surrendered Lassik men execution style: "Stood up about forty Inyan in a row with rope around neck. 'What this for?' Chief Lassik askum. 'To hang you, dirty dogs,' white men tell it. 'Hanging, that's dog's death,' Chief Lassik say." Lassik remonstrated, "We done nothing, be hung for," and demanded: "'Must we die, shoot us.' So they shoot. All our men." The perpetrators of this carefully premeditated atrocity now destroyed the evidence: "Then build fire with wood and brush Inyan men been cut for days, never know their own funeral fire they fix. Build big fire, burn all them bodies. That's funny smell I smell before I get to house. Make hair raise on back of neck. Make stomach sick, too." As Young explained: "White people want our land, want destroy us." The mass killing continued.[46]

KILLING THE YANA, 1862–1863

To the southeast, over the Coast Range and east of the Sacramento River, Yana people in the foothills and mountains continued to hold out against deportation and death that summer. In June 1862, unidentified Indians—who may have been avenging the theft of their own children—killed three white children and a teamster near Rock Creek Canyon. Furious immigrants now advocated the annihilation of local Indians. On July 1, the *Red Bluff Independent* reported: "The general expression is, that the prowling savages must be effectually wiped

A photographer made this portrait of Lucy Young
(Lassik/Wailaki) at Zenia in Trinity County late in
her life. In 1862, she escaped repeated beatings in
a white man's house only to come home on the
very day that whites massacred the men of her
community. C. Hart Merriam(?), "Mrs. Lucy
Young; Zenia, Calif. July 1, 1922," photograph,
1922, in C. Hart Merriam Collection of Native
American Photographs. Courtesy of The Bancroft
Library, University of California, Berkeley.

out," before insisting that "every Indian" in the mountains to the east be "exterminated." That night, vigilantes attacked an Indian camp, presumably Yana,
killing "several." Three days later, the *Independent* reported the "breaking up
of an Indian camp [probably Yana] four miles from [Dye's] mill," before concluding, "that punishment should be extermination." In the local tradition of
fundraising for private Yana-hunting expeditions, on July 22, veteran Indian
killer Harmon Good began soliciting money to campaign until "the guilty are

extinct." The next month, the *Independent* called for "the extermination of the red devils."[47]

Good's posse was already heeding that call. "East of Red Bluff" they shot an Indian on August 3 before storming a "Big Antelope" Creek village, killing and scalping seventeen, mortally wounding at least six others, and capturing six children. The Marysville *Appeal* concluded: "They are determined to drive off or exterminate the Indians." Robert Anderson recollected that "a day or two later," when Good and Sandy Young passed by, Good displayed "eight fresh scalps that he had tied to his saddle," presumably to present as proof of his campaign's lethality or for his personal collection of scalps, forty of which he displayed in a poplar tree outside his house. Good then reported that on August 14, his posse attacked a Mill Creek camp, killing four men and capturing twenty-one women and children. At least one observer described Good's campaign as overtly genocidal. Yale scientist William H. Brewer visited the Rock Creek area in October, and in November he wrote that the "volunteers . . . had killed indiscriminately all the wild Indians they could find, male or female." Such killing also occurred to the north in the Pit River region. On November 17, thirty-five soldiers and volunteers—exemplifying cooperation between regulars and vigilantes—encircled an Achumawi village and massacred at least eleven people, including women and children.[48]

The following June, Yana-hunters—including Anderson and Good—returned to the field, where they murdered at least ten more people. Far to the southeast, a much larger Indian-hunting campaign—involving hundreds of vigilantes and California Volunteers—unfolded near the Nevada border in the region between Mono Lake and Owens Lake.[49]

THE FIRST "OWENS VALLEY WAR," FEBRUARY 1862–MAY 1863

Protected by 13,000-foot summits to the east, the soaring Sierras to the west, and the searing Mojave to the south, Owens Valley's indigenous peoples had little contact with non-Indians prior to 1861. Over thousands of years, Owens Valley Paiute-Shoshones (living north of Owens Lake) and Western Shoshones (living south of the lake) made the most of the region and its resources. In the Sierra, Inyo, and White Mountains they hunted deer and mountain sheep or harvested nutritious pine nuts. In the valley, they stalked rabbits and antelope, collected insects, and gathered berries, seeds, and tubers. To maximize yields, the peoples of the valley built dams and irrigation canals to channel water from Sierra creeks east to the plants that they harvested and to the forage eaten by the animals that they hunted. In the 1850s, before the white invasion, such systems

In this photograph, three Indian hunters pose with Ned(?), Harmon Good's
California Indian servant and ultimately Good's possible executioner (see page 334).
Unknown artist. Left to right: "Jay Salisbury, Sandy Young, Hi [Harmon]
Good, and Indian Lad [Ned?]" photograph, before May 7, 1870.
Courtesy of the Pioneer History Museum, Oroville, California.

helped to sustain perhaps 1,000–2,000 Owens Valley Paiute-Shoshones and an
unknown number of Western Shoshones.[50]

Back in 1859, US Army captain John "Blackjack" Davidson had visited and
had explained to Owens Valley Indian leaders his belief "that their Country
was set apart—exempt from settlement—for their use so long as they maintained
honest and peaceful habits." This never happened. In keeping with the policy of denying California Indians large reservations, federal officials did not set
aside the eighty-mile-long valley or surrounding areas for the Indian peoples
who owned and inhabited them. This was probably due in part to the discovery of gold north of Mono Lake in 1859 and at nearby Aurora, Nevada, in 1860.
During the summer and fall of 1861, ranchers unleashed hundreds of cattle to
fatten in Owens Valley for sale to miners, beginning a process of environmental transformation that dramatically diminished traditional Indian food
sources.[51]

Owens Valley Paiute-Shoshone people traditionally inhabited houses like this one. Andrew A. Forbes(?), "Untitled [Photograph of a family outside a Paiute wikiup, Owens Valley, California]" photograph, undated. Courtesy of the Braun Research Library Collection, Autry National Center, Los Angeles, P.2338.

In 1861, immigrant violence against Paiute-Shoshone people precipitated the first "Owens Valley War." That fall, whites reportedly killed a Paiute-Shoshone(?) Indian and raped three young females—including the daughter of Paiute-Shoshone chief Shoandow—sowing seeds that soon bore violent fruit. "No goodee cow man" became a Paiute-Shoshone refrain as the bitter winter of 1861–1862, following the decreased harvests caused by the pressures of white invasion, drove some Owens Valley Indians to hunt the invaders' stock. Immigrants retaliated by killing Paiute-Shoshones in January. Paiute-Shoshones resisted white aggression and even negotiated a local treaty with ranchers. However, whites soon broke the peace by murdering Chief Shoandow and others when they asked for the return of stolen horses. Amid this violence, a Mojave Indian refugee named Joaquin Jim now became "war chief" and began campaigning to drive the invaders and their destructive animal herds away. In the meantime, "a prospector named Taylor" reportedly killed ten Paiute-Shoshones at Benton, near the Nevada border, before they killed him.[52]

In keeping with well-established California patterns of genocide, forty vigilantes elected Charles S. Anderson captain in March and soon began killing. "A force of settlers" now drove "a small band of Jim's warriors," suspected of murdering two white men, north to the blue waters of Mono Lake. Anderson's vigilantes then killed or drowned all of them, at least fifteen men. On March 22, a correspondent reported that Indians had killed two whites on Owens River. The following morning, Anderson and twenty vigilantes carried out a genocidal massacre, slaying as many as thirty-seven Paiute-Shoshones near present-day Lone Pine and burning their village, but sustaining not more than three men wounded.[53]

Vigilantes from central California and Aurora, Nevada, now arrived to provide additional firepower. After finding two white men's corpses at what is now Big Pine, the combined force of fifty-two men killed and scalped an Indian before moving north. On April 6, they attacked "near Bishop's ranch." Although presumably not as well armed, Paiute-Shoshone warriors repulsed them, likely spurred to mount a desperate defense by the knowledge of what could happen to them and their families if they failed to hold the line. It was another California Indian triumph against superior firepower, but a costly victory. An eyewitness reported that two vigilantes and twelve or fifteen Indians died before the posse retreated south.[54]

Army lieutenant colonel George S. Evans's thirty-three Second California cavalrymen and fifty Nevada dragoons now arrived to reinforce the vigilantes. On April 9, some 120 vigilantes and soldiers collaborated to attack an estimated 500–700 Paiute-Shoshones who again mounted a successful but costly defense, killing two attackers but themselves losing "five to fifteen or more" killed. Two more whites and an unknown number of Paiute-Shoshones died in additional skirmishes.[55]

The goal of the US soldiers and vigilantes was total annihilation. Nevada Indian agent Warren Wasson arrived to make peace but reported that Colonel Evans and the vigilantes desired "only to exterminate them." Evans repeatedly attacked Owens Valley Indians, and lost two men, but eventually ran low on provisions. So with the other troops, civilians, and thousands of cattle and sheep, Evans evacuated the valley in mid-April. General Wright now ordered Evans to "chastise them severely." In the language of mid-nineteenth-century California military commanders, such orders were code for mass killing. Second California Cavalry saddler John C. Willet explained: "When the soldiers reached the foot of Owens Lake they were instructed to kill all the Indians they saw."[56]

On June 24, Colonel Evans reached the lake with some 250 soldiers, killing two Western Shoshone or Paiute-Shoshone men, taking eleven prisoners, and destroying a large quantity of food, presumably with the intention of starving the survivors. On July 4, he established Fort Independence and resolved to "keep the Indians out of the valley and in the hills, so that they can have no opportunity of gathering and preserving their necessary winter supplies, and . . . will be compelled to sue for peace." Accordingly, a leader named Chief George negotiated "a temporary peace" with Captain E.A. Rowe on July 5. As Evans reported, "Since I came into the valley and commenced killing and destroying whenever I could find an Indian to kill or his food to destroy [they] changed their tune and were anxious for peace." Several months later, in October, super-intending Indian agent for Southern California John P.H. Wentworth negotiated a treaty promising a 2,000-acre reservation as well as rations, blankets, and an-nuity goods. Yet, unlike its payments for California Indian-hunting militia opera-tions, Congress never granted Wentworth's request for $30,000 to pay for these items. The United States thus failed to fulfill the treaty promises made to the Owens Valley Paiute-Shoshone people.[57]

As a result, Paiute-Shoshone people, who had not been able to gather winter food stores, did not receive promised supplies. Presumably starving and driven to desperation as a result, in February 1863 they killed at least three immigrants and on March 3 wounded six soldiers. Nine days later, the *Visalia Delta* reported Captain George's escape as well as further clashes in which at least two soldiers, two immigrants, and an unknown number of Indians died. The army responded with a new killing campaign. A combined force of "120 soldiers and 35 citizen volunteers" first slew an unknown number of Paiute-Shoshone people near Big Pine before killing "some half dozen Indians" elsewhere. On March 19, twenty soldiers and auxiliaries massacred as many as thirty-three Paiute-Shoshone or Western Shoshone people at Owens Lake. No army reports of this attack seem to exist, perhaps because it was a one-sided genocidal massacre in which soldiers and their supporters slew dozens of Indians without suffering a single fatality.[58]

The army now poured men and arms into the valley to facilitate large-scale killing. On April 10, Captain Ropes led 120 soldiers and thirty-five auxiliaries against hundreds of Paiute-Shoshones north of Big Pine Creek, killing several, and sustaining several men wounded. The following day, the *Esmeralda Star* reported seventy-one more California cavalrymen entering the valley with a howitzer and fifty "muskets for the use of the citizens." Annihilationist killing ensued. On April 17, an Owens River correspondent reported that "two compa-nies of cavalry have been fighting the Indians four days and have killed 150. Two more companies have been ordered from Aurora and one from Visalia. They say they will kill all the Indians in the valley."[59]

Some Paiute-Shoshone now fled southwest over the Sierras, seeking refuge among Tubatulabal Indians. Yet, the thousands of California Volunteers patrolling the state made escape almost impossible. California Cavalry captain Moses A. McLaughlin of the US Army reported that at dawn on April 19 he and his men surrounded an Indian camp some ten miles from Keysville, on the Kern River. "I had the bucks collected together and informed José Chico and the citizens who had arrived that they might choose out those whom they knew to have been friendly . . . the others, to the number of thirty-five, for whom no one could vouch, were either shot or sabered . . . none escaped." An unrepentant McLaughlin considered such mass murder efficacious, arguing that "such examples will soon crush the Indians and finish the war in this and adjacent valleys." He concluded that this genocidal war would end in Indians' total physical annihilation: "They will soon either be killed off, or pushed so far in the surrounding deserts that they will perish by famine."[60]

Six days later, McLaughlin assumed command at Fort Independence and soon launched a brutal May offensive. His goal was to kill or capture all surviving Owens Valley Indians. On May 3, soldiers trapped a Paiute-Shoshone group in the Inyo Mountains, where they killed four. Soldiers killed four more near Owens Lake, and vigilantes then three more. The hunt was relentless. McLaughlin reported: "Scarcely a day passed without two or three of them being found and killed, and everything being destroyed that could be of use to the living." On May 16, he again threatened total annihilation. Sending prisoners as message bearers, he announced that if Indians failed to surrender within two weeks "no more prisoners would be taken, neither men, women, nor children . . . and that a price would be set upon their heads." On May 21, the Owens River expressman reported that soldiers had recently killed three more and taken six prisoners. Two days later, Captain George surrendered with his people, telling McLaughlin "that many of the women and children had died for want of water." By May 26, McLaughlin held some 300 prisoners. Ben Tibbitts, a Paiute-Shoshone survivor from Big Pine, remembered these events. In his unpublished 1935 autobiography, he explained that at a Big Pine diplomatic barbecue an army "Captain" had offered peace if Owens Valley Indians would all come to Fort Independence and "go to work for our white friends." However, after "we went down to Fort Independence . . . we were captured and kept." The betrayal now turned lethal.[61]

Tubatulabal chief Jose Pacheco—employed as McLaughlin's "guide and interpreter"—later described an all but forgotten massacre. In an 1864 letter to

General Wright, Pacheco explained that Indians in Owens Valley surrendered after being promised food, clothing, and protection. Yet, as soon as they surrendered, "I was required to point out the Kern river [Tubatulabal] Indians who had been engaged in the war, and they were all (thirty-four in number) immediately taken outside the camp and shot and sabered by the soldiers." McLaughlin had once again intentionally massacred disarmed prisoners en masse. One can only imagine Pacheco's pain at having been used to select his own tribesmen, and perhaps kin, for mass murder at the hands of his employers. This was yet another massacre committed by US Army soldiers, men paid with US taxpayer dollars.[62]

On June 4, 1863, the *Visalia Delta* proclaimed: "The Owens River War is over." McLaughlin's men had "not only destroyed the Indians' provisions, but discovered and guarded all the springs so closely that they actually died of thirst!" On July 11, some 100 soldiers deported at least 908 and perhaps as many as 1,000 or more Owens Valley Indians to the west. Some defied removal and fled. Others may have died en route. Eleven days after setting out and crossing the mountains, 850 of them arrived at Fort Tejon, south of the San Joaquin Valley. Meanwhile, the slaughter continued. In July, August, and September, vigilantes killed at least seventeen more Indian people in Owens Valley, losing three men of their own. In total, soldiers and vigilantes had killed at least 331 California Indian people in the Owens and Kern River valleys since the beginning of 1862.[63]

Government officials apparently preferred to kill California Indians rather than make peace or honor treaties. As superintending agent Wentworth concluded on September 1, had Congress appropriated the $30,000 to establish the promised reservation, "No Indian war would have been waged." Unsurprisingly, the victors failed to adequately feed or clothe their Tejon Reservation prisoners. The US Army stopped feeding them in October, and hungry Owens Valley Indians began fleeing. Most were gone by January 1864. By April of that year, Pacheco explained from Fort Tejon: "I do not think we get the provisions and clothing intended for us by our Great Father; the agents keep it from us, and sell it to make themselves rich, while we and our children are very poor, hungry and naked." The situation was grim: "The acorns are all gone . . . game is very scarce [and] there is little else to eat than tulle roots and a little clover." As a result, "Nearly every day some of them leave," despite the threat of being shot for doing so. Pacheco concluded, "There are only two hundred and fifty-seven here now, nearly all squaws and little children." These mothers must have faced an agonizing choice. They could keep their children at a place without adequate food and watch them slowly die of starvation, or they could take them on a long and dangerous journey back to a homeland filled with invaders who wanted to kill them. The decision of Congress to leave the treaty unratified and unfunded, compounded by the army's unwillingness to feed and clothe their Tejon prisoners and federal officials' disinterest in changing this situation, soon led to even larger-scale Owens Valley killings in 1864.[64]

NORTHWESTERN CALIFORNIA VIGILANTE AND ARMY OPERATIONS, JANUARY–MAY 1863

The thousands of soldiers now serving in California—fed, clothed, armed, and paid directly by the federal government—made it possible for the US Army to field multiple large-scale Indian-hunting campaigns simultaneously. Even as commanders deployed California Volunteers to hunt Indians in the Owens Valley near the Nevada border, they fielded additional units to kill and capture other Indians hundreds of miles to the northwest in the lush and densely wooded coastal region near Oregon.

These March, April, and May 1863 army operations followed local lobbying and multiple killings by vigilantes. At a January 3 Eureka meeting, immigrants called for Northern California Indian Affairs Superintendent Hanson's removal and recommended that 500 volunteers begin hunting Indians. That same month, a Klamath County Grand Jury called for militiamen to wage war. The legislative delegation of Del Norte, Humboldt, and Klamath counties now visited General Wright and asked him to suggest to Governor Stanford that militiamen be called out. Wright complied. Sensing voter frustration with his Indian policy, on January 7 Stanford proclaimed: "There should be absolute protection to our citizens from these repeated incursions of hostile Indians." But it would be the US Army's California Volunteers, rather than the state's militiamen, who were to secure such "absolute protection." Between January 21 and February 5, Wright asked Stanford to call out ten new companies of California Volunteers for Humboldt District service and by February 7 Stanford had done so. Stanford thus worked with Wright to field a major US Army operation. Meanwhile, between January 9 and February 17, vigilantes killed at least thirty-six Indians at Ball Creek, "Iaqua Ranch," Fort Seward, and nearby areas.[65]

Second California Infantry Captain Henry Flynn then launched a March campaign to the Eel River's north and middle forks. By April 1, he reported having killed at least forty-seven Indian males and females while capturing thirty-seven others in four engagements. He speculated that his men had killed sixty-four Indians, if not more. During the first eleven days of April, Flynn's thirty-five soldiers attacked a Nongatl rancheria near Big Bend, on the Eel River's north fork, killing thirty to thirty-eight Indians, taking "40 squaws and children prisoners" and losing one man "shot in the heart with an arrow." On April 9, following the murder of "George Bowers, of Williams' Valley," Second California Infantrymen "found a small camp" in the area and as "they would not surrender . . . six [Yuki?] bucks were here killed, not one of the whole party getting away." On May 9, Second California Infantrymen attacked Sinkyone people near Shelter Cove, killing four, wounding "3 . . . so badly that I found it useless to bring them along, [and capturing] 1 boy and 5 squaws." In fewer than three months, California Volunteers had killed at least 87 Indians, and perhaps as many as 123 or more.[66]

THE ARMY'S "TWO-YEARS' WAR" BEGINS

As the US Army prepared to muster the new California Volunteer companies called for by Governor Stanford, the *Humboldt Times* gloated that "an opportunity is now offered to rid our county forever from the curse of Indians at the expense of the Federal Government." The paper added: "The Indians once exterminated or removed, our county would soon take its place among the most flourishing in the State." Where bureaucracy had delayed and constrained federal funding for state militia operations, the creation of the US Army's California Volunteers made it possible for the federal government to directly fund California citizen Indian hunters. The US Army paid and supplied its California Volunteers directly. Thus, some whites continued to see federal money as the key to the violent elimination of California's original inhabitants and, ultimately, unfettered access to economic prosperity.[67]

Accustomed to underwriting state militia Indian hunting, Sacramento legislators also financially supported the army's new campaign. First, they authorized Humboldt County to levy a tax of $0.50 per $100 to provide additional pay to the county's volunteers. Most important, in the state's tradition of financing Indian hunting, legislators raised money to help recruit additional California Volunteers statewide. On April 27, Stanford approved "An Act for the Relief of the Enlisted Men of the California Volunteers in the service of the United States." The bill allowed the state to issue up to $600,000 in bonds with which to pay California Volunteers an extra $5 per month, above and beyond their regular army pay. Passed as the army was preparing to muster new California Volunteer companies into service, the bill helped lure California men to enlist, thus expanding the number of soldiers available to hunt California Indians.[68]

The six companies of California men who mustered into the army between May 1863 and March 1864 became known as the Mountaineer Battalion, the first two mustering in on May 30, 1863, at Fort Humboldt and on June 2 at Arcata. Nine days later, Mountaineer Battalion lieutenant colonel Stephen G. Whipple—the former owner of the *Humboldt Times*—took over the Humboldt District command from Colonel Lippitt, and a new campaign began. Northwestern California Indians resisted, but the Mountaineer Battalion repeatedly defeated and destroyed outnumbered and outgunned California Indians. By July 23, they had killed at least twenty unidentified Indians without losing any soldiers.[69]

Indian killing also flared to the south in and around Round Valley Reservation that month, reinforcing that institution's reputation as a place of death for California Indians. Fearing that hungry Round Valley Indians were planning an uprising, soldiers and colonists went into the mountains and killed at least four Yuki people. Others then murdered two more Indians on suspicion of involvement in an attempted murder before summarily hanging five to eight others at Round Valley.[70]

The number of Indians being indiscriminately killed by California Volunteers now exceeded even General Wright's tolerance. On August 7, he warned Whipple "that no indiscriminate murder of Indians is permitted." Still, Wright did not halt the campaign or remove Whipple from command. In the military language of the day, he merely ordered more targeted violence, instructing Whipple to "let the troops impress upon the Indians by their acts that the guilty ones will be severely punished and the peaceful be protected." Still, this letter may have been mere political insurance against future criticism. Wright soon gave Whipple additional manpower to carry out his killing campaign and deployed two more companies of Mountaineers to join the operation several weeks later.[71]

THE KONKOW MAIDU TRAIL OF TEARS, SEPTEMBER 1863

Even when California Volunteers were not shooting Indians, their enforcement of federal removal policies sometimes led to mass death. The most notorious such case is known as the Konkow Maidu Trail of Tears, which unfolded amid rising regional violence. In early June 1863, vigilantes hanged five presumably Konkow Maidu Indians at Helltown in Butte County. Possibly in response, unidentified Indians killed two white children, in what would be one of several attacks on immigrants in Konkow Maidu territory that July. No recorded Indian voices from this period explain the motives behind these assaults, but evidence suggests that multiple Indian peoples had retreated into the mountains of Yahi Yana territory to fight a defensive guerrilla war. Whether a multitribal group or solely Yanas, they would have been people backed into a corner with nowhere to run, little to lose, and few options. These attacks—and others like them—may have been their last desperate bid to drive the invaders away.[72]

Whatever motivated the killings, they inspired a wave of organized vigilante violence and calls for removal backed by the threat of genocide. On July 24, the Oroville Guards murdered two Maidu men and a boy peacefully working at a butcher shop. The following day, the *Oroville Union* enthused that whites had already "sent several to the 'big hunting ground'" before offering a murderous benediction, "May unbounded success attend them, and may they never take one male prisoner." On July 26, whites tied two Indians to a tree before shooting and scalping them at Chico. They also slew two Maidu people at Yankee Hill. Finally, on July 27, vigilantes massacred five Konkow farmhands at Missouri Bend, including three boys, a woman, and a ten-year-old girl. That same day, hundreds of "infuriated" whites gathered at Pence's Ranch and "passed a resolution that the superintending agent should be requested to remove every Indian in the county of Butte within thirty days . . . and [that] any left after that time should be killed." At a second, August 28 public meeting at Pence's Ranch, vigilantes reported having removed 435 Indians to Chico, voted to raise 150 men to complete this project, and resolved that Indians who refused removal from Butte County "shall be exterminated." Federal decision makers thus chose to remove the Konkow near Chico and called on California Volunteers to help.[73]

On September 4, 1863, California Cavalry captain Augustus W. Starr began marching 461 Konkow Maidu people from Chico to Round Valley Reservation, ninety miles and a mountain range away. Starr commanded twenty-three California cavalrymen, "14 citizen wagons," and a "Government wagon with 6 mules." Neither the army nor the Indian Office had adequately prepared to care for the hundreds of men, women, children, and elders that they now marched across Northern California. Prisoners—some of whom apparently had malaria—began suffering "very much for want of water" on the second day and found only "very brackish and disagreeable" water in Stony Creek. Conditions deteriorated as they ascended into the mountains and the fourteen civilian wagons returned to Chico. On September 14, Captain Starr abandoned "150 Indians not able to travel" at "Mountain House, [reportedly] leaving them four weeks' provisions." Starr now pushed on with 311 prisoners and reached Round Valley on September 18 "with 277 Indians, 32 dying en route and 2 escaping."[74]

The reservation proved inhospitable. That very day a correspondent reported ranchers' massacre of ten Wailaki people nearby. Konkows who were left behind on the road faced even worse conditions. Starr reported that there was no extra reservation food to take back to the 150 abandoned deportees and after dropping off the 277 prisoners, on September 21, Starr departed for Chico, presumably passing the abandoned Konkows, but failing to mention them in his report. On September 27, Second California Infantry captain Charles D. Douglas visited Round Valley and described the prisoners "in an almost dying condition through sickness and gross neglect of duty of the present supervisor." Douglas also learned "that nearly 200 sick Indians are scattered . . . for forty miles, and that they are dying by tens for want of care and medical treatment and from lack of food."[75]

Douglas sent Round Valley Reservation supervisor James Short to rescue them. After thirteen days Short, who had a record of aiding and abetting massacres on and near his reservation, had rescued only some of them. He later reported that "about 150 sick Indians were scattered along the trail for 50 miles . . . dying at the rate of 2 or 3 per day. They had nothing to eat . . . and the wild hogs were eating them up either before or after they were dead." Dismal planning created a disaster compounded by a callous, limited response that left dozens and perhaps hundreds of Konkow people dead. In the aftermath, the army and the Indian Office received reports describing the Konkow Maidu Trail of Tears, but decision makers left the federal government's California Indian policy unchanged. Lethal and institutionalized federal neglect thus continued to synchronize with the gears of the killing machine. And the federal government kept pouring money into the hunting and indiscriminate killing of California Indians.[76]

MORE FEDERAL MONEY FOR PAST MILITIA CAMPAIGNS

Even in the midst of a national civil war that stretched federal finances to their limits, US congressmen reaffirmed their commitment to California Indian hunting by fulfilling the promise of Congress to support past California volunteer militia expeditions. On September 5, 1863, the California treasury received $218,489.29 from the United States for the militia operations of 1854–1859. The amount was less than half of the $497,572.38 that California had claimed under the 1861 act because the federal government disallowed many of California's claims. Still, at over $218,000, the payment conveyed a financial expression of federal support for California Indian-hunting operations, particularly given that the United States was fighting an expensive war at the time. In combination with prior payments, this sum brought the total value of direct federal funding for past California militia operations to over $1 million, to say nothing of the weapons and other items that the federal government gave to California and its militias. This 1863 payment thus resoundingly underscored federal support for operations against California Indians, which the army's California Volunteers now continued.[77]

CONCLUDING THE "TWO-YEARS' WAR,"
SEPTEMBER 1863–DECEMBER 1864

In the final months of 1863, Whipple's Humboldt District campaign slowly continued killing and capturing northwestern California Indians, and on September 23, he defensively reported: "To hunt them out and kill or capture them is the slow work of months." Under his amateur leadership the Mountaineers made few sorties, perhaps deterred by fall rains and winter snows. But they did kill at least eight Whilkut people by November 17, before two additional California Volunteer companies arrived in the region. Their howitzer fire may then have killed a substantial number during their December 26 bombardment of a Whilkut village. Yet, after the Whilkut people retreated, the Mountaineers found only two Whilkut dead. Soon thereafter, yet another California Volunteer company arrived to reinforce Whipple's command.[78]

Some of Whipple's Mountaineers dehumanized all Indians in order to rationalize further annihilation. In an open New Year's Day letter, one wrote that he wanted northwestern California Indians "wiped out." He reviled them as "fiendish devils" and insisted that "to be tolerant with them—treat them anything like human beings—will no longer suffice. It won't answer to acknowledge them as belligerents; even the thinnest-skinned sympathizer with 'Lo! the poor Indian,' is down on him at last." After unknown forces killed six whites on Salmon River, the *Shasta Courier* reported that the commander of Fort Jones was organizing "to drive the Indians into the mountains or exterminate them" and predicted "that the cry will soon be 'extermination.'" Whipple's Mountaineers then killed or mortally injured at least nineteen Mattoles and other Indians, while capturing twenty-one Mattoles and others in late January and early February.[79]

Determined to end the campaign, on February 6, 1864, General Wright ordered West Point graduate, career officer, and Ninth U.S. Infantry Captain Henry M. Black to Fort Humboldt with 250 more California infantrymen to relieve Whipple and "push the war to a close" with "decisive measures." The fresh troops and new commander arrived on February 17, as Whipple reported having captured some 200 prisoners, people who would presumably soon be sent to the dire conditions of California reservations. Two new Mountaineer companies mustered in during February and March. Thus, sixteen companies of soldiers now operated

Photographer Mathew Brady made
this portrait of Henry Black in his US Army
colonel's uniform during the early 1860s. Mathew
Brady, "Col. Henry M. Black," photograph, ca.
1860–ca. 1865. Courtesy of National Archives and
Records Administration, Brady National
Photographic Art Gallery, 526913.

in the Humboldt Military District (covering Del Norte, Humboldt, Klamath, Mendocino, Napa, and Sonoma counties), and surviving Indians found it increasingly difficult to evade the 1,100 soldiers searching for them.[80]

Black's campaign to capture and kill northwest California Indians through surprise attacks on villages began at dawn on February 29, when Mountaineers killed three men and took five women and children prisoners between Mad River and Redwood Creek. On March 12, the Sixth California Infantry attacked Yuroks "at the mouth of the Klamath . . . almost exterminating the band under chiefs 'Jack' and 'Stone,'" before soldiers executed both leaders at Fort Gaston. A Second California Infantry detachment in the Eel River region then killed at least twenty-five men and captured ten women and children by March 28. Meanwhile, a correspondent reported that Captain Simpson's Company E was taking no male prisoners. Black had returned to old tactics, issuing "a special order that all Indian men taken in battle shall be hung at once; the women and children to be humanely treated." A correspondent from Orleans observed that Black "has introduced a new method of treating hostile Indian prisoners—hangs them all." Black's approach garnered substantial approbation. The correspondent concluded, "That style of dealing with a murdering Digger is very effective, and meets with universal approval by the citizen inhabitants of the hostile region. It seems to be a general sentiment here [Orleans] that a mean 'Digger' only becomes a 'good Indian' when he is dangling at the end of a rope, or has an ounce of lead in him."[81]

Black unleashed a surge of killing. Between early April and May 28, his men slew at least sixty-five Indian people, wounded others, and took at least thirty-five prisoners, almost all women and children. Overwhelming manpower and firepower, pitted against northwest California Indians' dwindling resources, shrinking population, and need to protect women, children, and elders, made for grossly asymmetric engagements. Only three of Black's soldiers were killed during this period.[82]

Having slain perhaps 100 people or more, from February to June, Black began to focus on capturing, rather than killing. By early June, he held 500 prisoners at Fort Humboldt. General Wright had changed tactics. On June 30, Austin Wiley, the former *Humboldt Times* editor-turned-California Indian Affairs superintendent, reported: "General Wright informs me that the hostilities in Humboldt, Klamath, and Trinity counties may now be considered virtually closed [and] that pretty much all the Indians, including the hostile ones, are ready to surrender." Still, soldiers sometimes resorted to ambush, entrapment, and murder of male captives, encouraged by local exhortations to "take no prisoners." Between July 11 and early September, Mountaineers and Sixth California Infantry men shot dead or hanged eight Sinkyone and Mattole people.[83]

That July, Superintendent Wiley demonstrated how peace could be forged without bloodshed. Rather than let soldiers attack the seventy-five armed Hupa men and their families in Hoopa Valley, on August 21, he concluded a treaty with the "Hoopa, South Fork, Redwood, and Grouse Creek Indians." The treaty disarmed hundreds in return for food, hunting rights, clothing, education, medical care, protection, and a new reservation. Many colonists were outraged, and a public meeting in Eureka blasted the treaty. Wiley had broken the unwritten rule against making federal government treaties with California Indians. Yet, in 1865 Congress appropriated $59,959.55 to buy out Hoopa Valley colonists, the government duly paid them, obtained legal title to the valley, and eventually established the Hoopa Valley Indian Reservation on the Trinity

River. The reservation stands today as a reminder of what might have been in California: an economical and peaceful diplomatic alternative to mass murder.[84]

Perhaps inspired by Wiley's peace offensive, in the summer and fall of 1864, some soldiers began capturing large numbers of prisoners, and reporting almost no killing. In August, California Volunteer Lieutenant Taylor brought thirty Mattole to Fort Humboldt. From July 19 to September 15, Captain John Simpson captured 161 Indians in the upper Eel River region. In one instance he surrounded a large group of Wailaki people and "told them through Indian interpreters to surrender and they would not be killed." Although some tried to escape, Simpson would not let his men fire and eventually captured eighty-eight people. In another comparatively peaceful operation, from October 5 to December 4, Lieutenant Thomas Middleton reported capturing fifty-nine people without killing anyone. And, in January 1865, Middleton brought in twenty-three Trinity River Indians.[85]

Still, some saw the ongoing campaign as one of annihilation. On September 1, 1864, Wiley warned US Indian Affairs commissioner William P. Dole that the "destructive Indian war" in "Humboldt, Klamath, and Trinity" counties "promised to end only in the extermination of the Indians." The systematic murder of captured Indian men now compelled the new Pacific Department commander to act. On November 23, Major General Irvin McDowell issued an order noting "that officers in this Department have assumed to act in a summary manner in reference to Indians charged with crimes; and there are cases where they have had Indians executed by the troops." McDowell emphasized: "This is against all law, is no way to be justified, and will not be sanctioned." Thus, he ordered, "Hereafter no officer or soldier will execute or aid in executing any Indian prisoners on any pretext whatever. If an Indian commits any crime, the military may hold him under guard until the civil authority can take charge of him." Parts of the killing machine could be stopped when federal policymakers chose to take action.[86]

VIGILANTES' NORTHEASTERN SACRAMENTO VALLEY CAMPAIGN, SEPTEMBER–OCTOBER 1864

To the east, in the Sacramento River Valley and its eastern tributaries, immigrants granted Indians no such legal rights. On September 8 and 9, Indians killed Catherine Allen at "Big Cow Creek, about thirty miles from Shasta" and a Mrs. John Jones "about four miles from Copper City," possibly to avenge the murder of two Indian plowmen employed by whites. Following California's well-established pattern, farmers, ranchers, and miners quickly formed two vigilante companies: forty Copper City men and "30 to 50" from Millville and Cow Creek. Yet, whereas prior Sacramento River Valley killing campaigns had primarily targeted Indians in the mountains or villages near white settlements, these operations set a new precedent by also targeting Indians working for and living with whites in the lowlands. Yana people were the primary targets in this new extermination campaign.[87]

Irvin Ayres later recalled that after a "mass meeting" vigilantes killed "two or three Indian lads who had been brought up in white families on Oak Run and who were living with these families at the time" as well as an Indian near the Cow Creek mill. These murders initiated the new pattern of killing so-called domesticated Indians. On September 10, the *Copper City Pioneer* summarized the report of a Mr. Worley, who described some sixty vigilantes from Cow Creek "killing the domesticated Diggers indiscriminately." These killers reportedly "confined their attacks to tame and friendly Indians." A week later, the *Shasta Courier* added: "The Millville company, it is reported, are bent on extermination and are killing indiscriminately all of Indian blood, wherever found." The *Courier* lamented: "Many of the domesticated Indians who had for years been living in peace on the ranches on the opposite side of the river, molesting nobody, have been exterminated, and at our present writing no one can tell where the bloody business will end." The paper continued: "The Indians about Shasta and other localities in the county, alarmed at the threats of extermination, are fleeing to the mountains for safety."[88]

In 1884, linguist and author Jeremiah Curtin visited the upper Sacramento Valley, where he interviewed both whites and Indians to assemble a detailed, if disjointed, narrative of the 1864 genocidal killing campaign against the Yanas. He wrote that the two vigilante parties "fell upon the Yanas immediately, sparing neither sex nor age [and] had resolved to exterminate the whole nation." His interviews yielded descriptions of ruthless slaughter: "At Millville . . . white men seized two Yana girls and a man. These they shot about fifty yards from the village hotel. At another place they came to the house of a white woman who had a Yana girl, seven or eight years of age. They seized this child, in spite of the woman, and shot her through the head." Their leader proclaimed: "We must kill them, big and little," as "nits will be lice." Elsewhere, "a few miles north of Millville lived a Yana girl named Eliza, industrious and much liked by those who knew her. She was working for a farmer at the time." When the posse arrived Eliza pleaded: "Don't kill me; when you were here I cooked for you, I washed for you, I was kind to you; I never asked pay of you; don't kill me now."

Unmoved, the killers "took Eliza, with her aunt and uncle . . . and shot the three." Curtin specified: "My informant counted eleven bullets in Eliza's breast [and] saw her . . . skull was broken."[89]

Murderous vigilantes searched systematically for Yana people on white farms, but not all employers complied. At a Little Cow Creek farm, vigilantes "found three Yana men threshing hayseed in a barn" and killed them. The murderers then entered the farmhouse and found "the three wives of the men killed in the barn." The women were screaming when the pregnant "farmer's wife hurried out with a quilt, threw it around the three women, and stood in front of them, holding the ends of the quilt. 'If you kill them you will kill me' she said, facing the party." According to Curtin, "To kill, or attempt to kill, under such conditions, would be a deed too ghastly for even such heroes; so they went away, swearing that they would kill the 'squaws' later." Real heroes intervened. "These three Indian women were saved [and] taken beyond the reach of danger by two white men." Two men from Redding also rescued about a dozen others. Regrettably, tales of such courage, decency, and rescue were rare.[90]

Killing squads punctuated small-scale slayings, such as a Bear Creek "killing," with large-scale massacres. "At one place they killed an Indian woman and her infant, at another three women. In the town of Cottonwood they killed twenty Yanas of both sexes." According to Curtin, "The most terrible slaughter in any place was near the head of Oak Run, where *three hundred* Yanas had met at a religious dance. These were attacked in force, and *not a soul escaped*." Still, "The slaughter went on day after day till the entire land of the Yanas was cleared." When the campaign ended, "the whole number of surviving Yanas of pure and mixed blood was not far from fifty."[91]

Why did the killers suddenly turn on Indian people peacefully working for other whites in the upper Sacramento River Valley? Curtin emphasized three motives: "An intense feeling of indignation at the murder" of the two white women, "unspeakable contempt for Indians," and "plundering." According to Curtin, "It was not uncommon for a single [Yana] person of them to have from $40 to $60. One informant told me that a man showed a friend of his $400 which he had taken from murdered Indians. Money and everything of value that the Yanas had was snatched up by these robbers." As in earlier phases of the California genocide, here too greed was an important motivator for mass murderers.[92]

Death-dealing vigilantes also moved east into the mountains near Mount Lassen. By September 24, "the Copper City and Millville Companies [had] united," raised over $100, and recently killed twelve or thirteen "Antelope [Yana] Indians." According to the *Red Bluff Independent*, "The Millville party are exterminating the whole race of Diggers in that section." On October 3, some

Achumawi women carried their children in
cradleboards like this one, which allowed them to
care for a small child while working or traveling.
Note this cradleboard's finely woven and
elegantly decorated shade. Edward S. Curtis,
"Achomawi Mother and Child," photograph, 1923.
Courtesy of Library of Congress, Prints &
Photographs Division, Edward S. Curtis
Collection, LC-USZ62-110225.

thirty men led by the widower Jones killed perhaps eight Indians who had
fled to the Sacramento's west side "for safety." Some aimed to expel or destroy
all regional Indians. On October 8, Millville men resolved that any Indians
found between the Pit River, Antelope Creek, the Sacramento, and the Cas-
cade crest would have ten days to leave, after which "it shall be the privilege
of our company . . . to exterminate or expel said Indians."[93]

Vigilantes thus targeted the Achumawi. Ayres recalled "in their thirst for
vengeance they threatened to visit the Pitt River Country and attack Shavehead

and his tribe." However, California Cavalry major Henry B. Mellen, commanding Fort Crook, warned "the citizens of the Sacramento Valley in the neighborhood of Millville, not to come up and attack the Pitt River Indians, for if they did they would find someone else to fight besides squaws and papooses." Mellen deterred the vigilantes, but not before they had taken their campaign deep into eastern Yana territory and perhaps beyond. "Matlock, who lived on a ranch about half way between Red Bluff and Fort Crook," told Ayres "that he had himself seen three squaws who had been shot by white people, lying dead in a yard with young papooses crawling over them and trying to suck their breasts." Extant written reports indicate that the northeastern Sacramento Valley campaign of 1864 left at least 361 Indians dead, but suggest that this genocidal frenzy of vigilante killing actually took far more lives.[94]

On October 15, 1864, Modoc leaders—whose people had bravely withstood five campaigns launched against them between 1851 and 1856—signed a treaty with the US government, ceding their ancestral homeland for payments, education, other benefits, and a shared reservation in the southern Oregon lands of the Klamath Indians. The demographic impact of successive genocidal campaigns had left the Modoc with little ability to reject the treaty. That year, Chief Schonchin summarized his nation's devastation at white hands, "Once my people were like the sand along yon shore. Now I call to them, and only the wind answers. Four hundred strong young men went with me to war with the Whites; only eighty are left." That fall, Indian agents counted just 339 Modocs at Fort Klamath, Oregon, down from a total Modoc population of some 1,000 to 2,000 or more in 1851. By 1864, other California Indian peoples were facing similarly catastrophic population declines, but continued to resist annihilationists against tremendous odds.[95]

THE SECOND "OWENS VALLEY WAR," NOVEMBER 1864–JANUARY 1865

Returning to their homes from the starvation conditions of Fort Tejon, hungry Owens Valley Paiute-Shoshone and Western Shoshone refugees struggled to survive in a land transformed by immigrants and their voracious stock. Cattle and other newly introduced animals ate important sources of traditional Indian food and competed with game for forage. The newcomers diverted water from indigenous aqueducts, shot the game animals, and felled the pine nut–bearing trees on which the region's indigenous people depended. To survive, and perhaps to resist the invaders, Owens Valley Indians began taking cattle. By September 1864, whites had started to fear new attacks and some fled the valley. In response, immigrants rode to Owens Valley Indian villages, warning that further "hostile acts" would be punished "without mercy." A minimum of two whites and five Indians then died in at least three separate incidents, two of which involved horse rustling.[96]

Perhaps in response to this violence, on December 30, Paiute-Shoshone or Western Shoshone Indians attacked the McGuire Ranch "between Little and Owen Lakes," burning the house, mortally wounding Mrs. McGuire, and killing her young son. Enraged immigrants now murdered "a friendly Indian" at Bend City, gunned down four Paiute-Shoshone prisoners at Lone Pine, and killed three others "near Black Rocks." They also "organized with the intention of killing, or in fact exterminating the whole Indian race in the neighborhood of the Owen River country at least." Thus began a new wave of genocidal killing in the valley and surrounding areas.[97]

On New Year's Day 1865, twenty to seventy Fort Independence men under a Captain Greenly started for the McGuire Ranch. At Lone Pine they saw the bodies of Mrs. McGuire and her son. "Infuriated," they immediately encircled a nearby Paiute-Shoshone village and "killed nearly every Indian in it; slaughtering men, women and children; those who escaped were overtaken and killed as they ran." A Lone Pine resident who described the atrocity estimated that fifty or more had been massacred that day, and explained that "the party had gone in pursuit of others—sworn to kill every Indian in the valley, or wherever they should find them."[98]

Three days later, at dawn on January 5, fourteen vigilantes surprised, "corralled and slaughtered" as many as "ONE HUNDRED MEN, WOMEN AND CHILDREN," or more, on the eastern shore of Owens Lake near the mouth of Owens River. On January 17, a correspondent wrote that "the whites are killing off the Indians on all sides." Meanwhile, reports record the killing of at least twenty-one additional Owens Valley Indian people in multiple incidents.[99]

Such reports, sometimes published under headings like "INDIANS DISAPPEARING," described the final stage of the process by which invaders purposely hunted the indigenous people of the Owens Valley to the brink of extinction. Camouflaged as a legitimate martial contest, and for years after seen as such by students reading texts by historians who reinforced this misconception, the "Second Owens Valley War" had killed between 62 and 184 or more Owens Valley Paiute-Shoshone and Western Shoshone people. Although a January 18, 1866, letter reported that whites "kill [Owens Valley Indians] on sight" and in August soldiers killed "several" on the east side of Owens Lake, the 1865 Owens Valley killing campaign marked an end of sorts. No vigilante operation would ever again kill such large numbers of California Indians. With the removal or destruction of most California Indians, the California genocide was ending. There remained few free California Indians left to hunt and kill.[100]

SCATTERED KILLINGS AND MASSACRES, 1865–1866

As the Civil War ground toward General Robert E. Lee's surrender at Appomattox on Palm Sunday 1865, the army's California Indian campaigns were winding down. The last of the Mountaineers Battalion mustered out on June 14, and other California Volunteer units had either already mustered out or soon followed. However, some did not demobilize until 1867. By 1865, California's Indian Affairs superintendent reported fewer than 34,000 surviving California Indians, down from perhaps 150,000 in 1845, which accounted in part for the decline in Indian hunting. The decline of the killing machine, however, was a more important factor. Deprived of the government-supported soldiers who had carried out most of California's Civil War–era killing campaigns, the state's fifteen-year-old killing machine slowed almost to a halt. Without overt rhetorical, monetary, and material support from Sacramento and Washington, DC, large, sustained Indian-hunting campaigns became difficult to organize and finance. Soldiers and vigilantes still occasionally massacred California Indians, but the killing machine entered what appeared to be a terminal decline: functioning in fits and starts, while slowly dying from 1865 to 1871.[101]

A single California massacre occurred in 1865 following Lee's surrender at Appomattox. Continuing to mark his career with blood, having led the slaying of eight Yahi Yana people in March, veteran Indian killer Harmon Good, along with Robert Anderson, directed the massacre of as many as sixteen or more other Yahi Yanas at the Three Knolls near Mill Creek at dawn on August 13 or 14.[102]

Annihilationist sentiment still ran high. On September 23, 1865, the *Weekly Trinity Journal* proclaimed it "a good time for the New River people to establish the precedent of killing every Indian who shows himself." Less than two weeks later, the *Humboldt Journal* insisted that "predatory bands should be speedily exterminated." In December, the *Chico Courant* advocated organizing armed men "to wipe out of existence the mischievous Indians inhabiting the Eastern counties of this State." The following year, the *Courant* thundered: "It is a mercy to the red devils to exterminate them, and a saving of many white lives . . . there is only one kind of treaty that is effective—cold lead." The *Shasta Courier* added: "Extermination is the only sure protection . . . and the sooner the remedy is applied the better." Massacres—unsurprisingly—continued and, when the US Army participated, the result was large-scale slaughter.[103]

Early in 1866 vigilantes from northeastern California's Surprise Valley, set out after Northern Paiute Indian "thieves" much as they had done in August 1864, when they had surrounded and massacred at least a dozen Indians, ten miles northwest of the valley. Now, however, Northern Paiute warriors successfully repulsed them. These men also made off with forty head of cattle, presumably to feed community members struggling to survive as immigrants, their stock, and their hunting reduced the supply of traditional Northern Paiute foods and access to them. When not outmanned and outgunned, California Indians could still hold their own. Thus, the vigilantes called upon Second California Cavalry units still serving in Surprise Valley at Fort Bidwell and across the border in Nevada at Smoke Creek. At least seventy-eight cavalrymen and auxiliaries now pursued the Northern Paiutes and "overhauled [them] at Guano valley, about fifty miles northeast of Fort Bidwell" in Oregon. On February 15, 1866, they charged the Northern Paiutes and then for six hours methodically hunted them in the rocks, killing about eighty Indians, according to most sources, and an additional thirty-five females, according to another. One white man was killed and six or seven wounded. In response the *Yreka Weekly Union* proclaimed, "GOOD WORK." It was another deadly collaboration between vigilantes and US soldiers, and it underscored the fact that the genocide waged against California Indians was often the product of partnerships between civilians and government employees.[104]

Without the lure of potential state support, vigilantes could no longer rally the men, supplies, financing, or firepower necessary for such large killings. Still, they continued to launch limited sorties and take California Indian lives in 1866. In April, following a robbery, Anderson and other veteran Indian killers slew two Yanas and wounded others at a Deer Creek village. In June, five men attacked a Papoose Valley camp near Eagle Lake—killing four Atsugewi men and wounding a fifth—simply because they did not like their look. In August, after Indians mortally wounded a Bavarian woman, vigilantes killed at least five Yanas at an Antelope Creek village. Yanas apparently tried to hide, but some sources suggest that vigilantes also massacred as many as thirty at a cave north of Dye Creek. Millville men then "killed four or five" more "at a cave on the head of Antelope Creek." That same year, Good and three others set out and "ten [Yana] victims bit the dust" on Deer Creek.[105]

When supported by soldiers, vigilantes were more lethal. In early November 1866, "soldiers and citizens from Surprise Valley" set out to avenge the killing of a vigilante. "West of Warner Basin and north of Surprise Valley," they surrounded a group of Northern Paiutes at night. "As the first gray streaks of morning became visible in the east, they commenced moving slowly and cautiously upon the foe, contracting the circle which they had formed in the night, until they were upon the enemy, when the work of slaughter commenced.—Fourteen Indians were left dead upon the ground, and many carried off by the survivors as they escaped."[106]

DISMANTLING CALIFORNIA INDIAN SERVITUDE

In 1865, slave raiding and related killings continued to take California Indian lives and to retard demographic recovery. Whites kidnapped and held some 20,000 California Indians in various forms of servitude between 1850 and 1863 alone. Many of them were children. Scholars estimate that perhaps 3,000 to 4,000 or more children were victims of such practices between 1852 and 1867. For decades, California Indians fought against and weakened California's un-free Indian labor regimes by hiding from kidnappers and slave raiders, resisting their attacks, and escaping when captured. The Civil War then unleashed sustained army campaigns against California Indians that increased slave raiding, but the war also catalyzed the dismantling of the laws that had made California Indian servitude both widespread and profitable.[107]

On January 1, 1863, President Abraham Lincoln put his Emancipation Proclamation into force, freeing slaves in the rebel states. On April 27 of the same year, Governor Stanford signed an act repealing those portions of the legislature's 1850 and 1860 acts that had allowed for the legal custodianship and indenture of Indians in California. Despite these repeals, Indian prisoner leasing remained legal, and murderous illegal slave raiding continued.[108]

Consequently, California's deadly systems of Indian servitude endured. In December 1863, William Brewer wrote from Crescent City, "It has for years been a regular business to steal Indian children . . . and sell them . . . and it is said that some of the kidnappers would often get the consent of the parents by shooting them." Murder continued to accompany kidnapping in 1865. For example, raiders stabbed a crippled Indian boy to death when he tried to stop them from taking his ten-year-old sister. At the same time, masters could be monstrous. That August, Bob Hildreth bound his Indian servant to a rope and dragged him behind his horse until "the Indian was terribly mangled, his arms being twisted off in his shoulders." Nearby, another "Indian slaveholder . . . shot one the other day, because he would not stand and be whipped." That same month, a journalist concluded: "Slavery exists in California in precisely the same condition that it did until lately in the Southern States. There the blacks; here in almost every county Indians are unlawfully held as chattels."[109]

In 1865 and 1867, Congress further weakened California Indian servitude. The Thirteenth Amendment outlawed "involuntary servitude, except as punishment for crime" and California's legislature ratified it less than two weeks later. Yet the amendment, like California's constitution, permitted convict labor and supposedly voluntary forms of bondage such as debt peonage. Illegal Indian servitude also continued. On January 1, 1867, an Indian Affairs investigator described Indian slavery as "not uncommon" in California. Later that year, Congress banned "peonage," further weakening California's systems of Indian servitude. Nevertheless, Indian convict leasing remained legal until 1937, kidnapping continued, and illicit California Indian slavery persisted. However, when new state civil and penal codes went into effect in 1873, judges and juries could no longer summarily reject Indian testimony without breaking the law. Those participating in the trafficking of California Indian people thus lost a major legal advantage, and unfree California Indian labor declined thereafter.[110]

POST–CIVIL WAR KILLING, 1867–1871

From 1867 to 1871, the number and lethality of violent incidents against Indians also steadily declined. In the first three months of 1867, vigilantes and US cavalrymen killed nineteen California Indians in three separate incidents. In some regions, genocidal sentiment remained intense. In April, the *Daily Alta California* reported that many whites in far Northern California "feel as if the sooner the savages are exterminated, the better." Egged on by supporters, genocidal killing continued. That year, vigilantes slew at least twenty-four people in Yana territory. In rare cases whites protected Indians. That September, a Mrs. V.V. Wilson of Oregon Gulch, in Trinity County, shot and killed a man who came to her house to whip or kill "her Indian boy." Had Wilson's determination to protect California Indians been more common, many lives might have been spared. Yet 1867 ended with another massacre. To the west, vigilantes struck an Achumawi encampment in Long Valley, where they murdered at least nine men.[111]

Better equipped, better trained, and better able to field sustained operations, US Army expeditions killed more Indians. On September 22, 1867, General George Crook—still carrying the arrow embedded in his thigh by an Achumawi archer in 1857—led several hundred US Army soldiers and Indian auxiliaries south from Oregon and into California on the west side of Goose Lake. In northeastern California, his men killed perhaps a dozen Indians in four days. Some 125 of Crook's men then surrounded approximately seventy-five Paiutes, thirty Achumawis, and a few Modocs in a lava field near what is today the town of Likely, California. Crook's objective was annihilation: "The General said the siege should be continued . . . until the red devils were all killed or starved to death." He recollected: "I never wanted dynamite so bad." How many Paiutes, Achumawis, and Modocs died in the three-day-long Battle of the Infernal Caverns may never be known. Soldiers counted at least eight Indian bodies, but contemporary sources estimated fifteen to twenty Indians killed before survivors escaped. Seven of Crook's men died in the attack.[112]

Killings continued in 1868, but declined in frequency. Early that year, US soldiers massacred twenty Owens Valley Indians, and vigilantes near Woodland, in Yolo County, tied five Indians to stakes before shooting them "in cold blood." In May, vigilantes and soldiers collaborated in the massacre of sixteen Northern Paiutes in upper Surprise Valley, losing just one of their own men killed. In November, vigilantes slew and scalped at least six Nongatl men near the Van Duzen River. Others killed Indian men in the Round Valley region that year. Still, California's murderous wave of genocidal killings had crested years before. Only sporadic killings continued.[113]

In 1869, the year that Ulysses S. Grant assumed the presidency, regulars and vigilantes killed four Nongatl men and four Nongatl women in two January attacks near Larabee Creek, and in March soldiers assaulted a Nongatl rancheria near the same creek, slaying an unknown number of Nongatl people and losing one soldier killed. That spring, the hardened Indian-murderer Harmon Good led a night ambush and "killed several" Yanas on or near Deer Creek.[114]

In May 1870, locals found Good, "Who devoted his time to hunting and killing Indians . . . pierced with twelve bullets and his head smashed with rocks." Yana survivors may thus have exacted some small measure of retribution for Good's many genocidal crimes against them.[115]

No reports of massacres exist for 1870, in part because it had become much harder for killers to find California Indians to kill. That year, census takers counted just 7,241 California Indians (almost certainly an undercount), but anthropologist C. Hart Merriam later estimated an 1870 California Indian population of 30,000 people. California Indian resistance and accommodation strategies played an important role in this large discrepancy. By 1870, many surviving California Indians seem to have been in hiding or successfully concealing their Indian identities as a survival strategy. Others resided with non-Indians, either willingly or unwillingly, and thus gained a measure of protection from Indian hunters. Some California Indian women lived with non-Indian men, and in 1870, California's Superintendent of Public Instruction reported 1,194 California Indian children, ages five to fifteen, residing in non-Indian households. Although no guarantee of safety, living with non-Indians provided some protection from killing squads, which were usually unwilling to murder California Indians living with non-Indians. This combination of factors made it increasingly difficult to find California Indians to kill in 1870.[116]

The last known large-scale massacre of California Indian people took place in 1871. After losing a steer near the headwaters of Mill Creek, four ranchers tracked Yanas to a cave and massacred "about thirty" people there. In 1915, Frank Norvell explained, "In the cave with the meat were some Indian children. Kingsley could not bear to kill these children with his 56-calibre Spencer rifle. 'It tore them up so bad.' *So he did it with his 38-calibre Smith and Wesson revolver.*" As the shots echoed across that rugged canyon, it seemed that the genocide of California Indians had finally come to a close. State and federal officials no longer poured men, money, arms, and supplies into killing campaigns that targeted California Indians. Yet, events in Modoc country would soon bring one final state-sponsored annihilation attempt.[117]

CONCLUSION

April 11, 1873, "broke fair and calm." It was Good Friday, but the four US peace commissioners and their translators sat uneasily in their saddles as they rode out into the lava beds of Modoc country—a "Hell with the fires gone out." Commanders had positioned hundreds of regular US soldiers and state militiamen to the east and west of the lava fields that morning, but could they protect the commissioners during this volatile truce in California's last Indian war?[1]

Modocs had lived peacefully and productively in their ancestral lands for more than two years after leaving Oregon's Klamath Reservation. Nevertheless, on July 6, 1872, the US Indian Affairs commissioner had ordered Oregon's Indian Affairs superintendent to return them to "Klamath Reservation—peaceably, if you possibly can; but forcibly, if you must." Four months later, US cavalrymen and local auxiliaries used deadly force in attempting to carry out this directive. It remains unclear who shot first, but Modoc leader John Schonchin insisted, "white men shoot first. I tell no lie." Captain James Jackson reported simply that at Lost River, "I poured in volley after volley among their worst men." As Modocs fled, Jackson's troops torched the village. The cavalrymen killed at least one Modoc man, and a sick Modoc woman burned to death in the flames. That same day, local white men opened fire in a second Modoc village across Lost River, slaying "an infant in its mother's arms." Defending themselves, Modocs killed one civilian attacker and another civilian they mistook for an assailant. US special commissioner to the Modocs Alfred Meacham wrote that in these two incidents, attackers killed two Modoc babies, a girl, and one or two women. John Schonchin explained, "I gave them all my land, water, grass, everything . . . yet they shoot me [as well as] squaws, children, little girl." Enraged by these assaults on peaceful villages, renegade Modocs then killed a dozen local white men, but spared white women. Thus began the infamous

1872–1873 Modoc War, during which a handful of Modocs held off the US Army, California volunteers, and Oregon militiamen for more than six months.[2]

Anticipating further violence, Kintpuash—usually remembered as Captain Jack—led Modoc people into the lava beds and to what became known as Captain Jack's Stronghold, a series of fortified volcanic caverns and trenches within that sea of jagged rock. Some 165 Modoc people—including men, women, children, and elders—now dug in. They subsisted on limited supplies and waited. Having lost hundreds of people and many villages during the six previous anti-Modoc campaigns, they likely anticipated the worst. Kintpuash himself had suffered because of this genocidal violence. He later explained, "When I was a little boy, [California militia Captain] Ben Wright murdered my father and forty-three others who went into his camp to make peace" at the 1852 Lost River Massacre. As a result of such experiences, the Modocs in the Stronghold likely expected the revival of the killing machine.[3]

By December 21, US Army soldiers, California volunteers, Oregon militiamen, and Indian scouts besieged Kintpuash's people in what is now Lava Beds National Monument. Having brought in howitzers, 400 men assaulted Captain Jack's Stronghold early on the morning of January 17, 1873. Given their overwhelming numbers and firepower, the regular soldiers and militiamen anticipated a swift victory. Yet, as Brevet Major General Frank Wheaton reported, the rugged terrain with its "miles of rocky fissures, caves, crevices, gorges, and ravines," obstructed his assault, as did an "unusually dense" fog. Modocs used the volcanic landscape and thick mist to their advantage. They moved, largely unseen, through the lava fields' rock formations to concealed positions from which they demonstrated their marksmanship and halted the attack. By the time the soldiers, volunteers, militiamen, and scouts retreated that evening, one Modoc and a dozen attackers lay dead. Kintpuash's people had accomplished the seemingly impossible. Having held off an enemy far larger and better armed than themselves, they remained defiant in their rock fortress. Chastened, the army and its auxiliaries settled into a siege that continued for months.[4]

Frustration mounted, and, on March 13, the head of the US Army, General William T. Sherman, suggested that he would tolerate genocide as a solution to the stalemate. That day, Sherman—a veteran of military service in California—told General E.R.S. Canby that if the Modocs failed to cooperate, "I trust you will make such use of the Military force that no other Indian tribe will imitate their example, and that no other reservation for them will be necessary except graves among their chosen lava-beds." Once again coiled, the killing machine was ready to strike. This was precisely what the Modocs—who had repeatedly suffered massacres and surprise attacks committed by whites—feared. Although

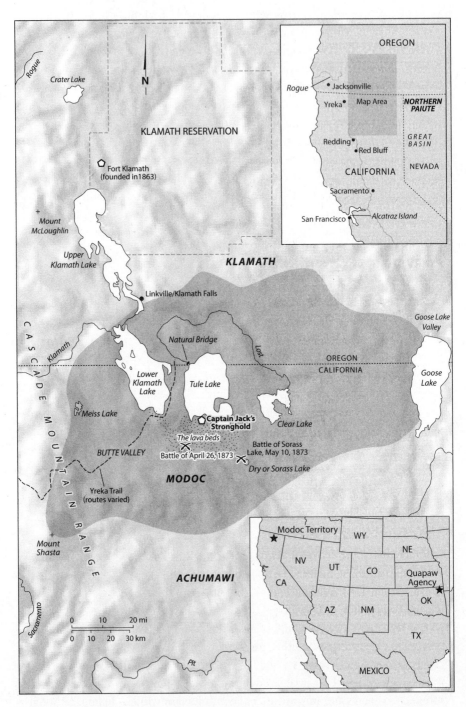

The Modoc War, 1872–1873

Kintpuash (Modoc) frequently visited the
Northern California town of Yreka in the
1860s. T.N. Wood made this portrait of Kintpuash
there in 1864. T.N. Wood, "Captain Jack
[Kintpuash]," gelatin silver print, 1864. Courtesy of
the Braun Research Library Collection, Autry
National Center, Los Angeles, P.482.

unaware of Sherman's command, the Modocs could see that Canby's "system
of gradual compression" was tightening the perimeter around them, increasing
his troop strength, and bringing his patrols closer to the Stronghold. The
Modocs were now wary to the point of planning their own preemptive attack.[5]

As the peace commissioners rode toward their Good Friday meeting with
Kintpuash and his lieutenants, they had reason to be uneasy. US forces did not
have the decisive upper hand and had been humiliated by Modoc warriors.
Worse, their Modoc interpreter—a woman named Winema, or Toby Riddle—
had repeatedly warned them that the besieged Modocs were finished with the

In 1872, Modoc people retreated to Captain Jack's Stronghold in the lava beds,
where they held out for months against hundreds of US soldiers, California
volunteers, and Oregon militiamen. Modocs used caverns like this one as
concealed sanctuaries in which they sought protection from small arms
fire and the army's artillery barrages. Unknown artist, "The Modoc War—
Captain Jack's Cave in the Lava Beds," engraving(?), 1873, in *Harper's
Weekly Journal of Civilization*, June 28, 1873, 545. Author's collection.

months of negotiating and were planning to assassinate them. Tensions were
indeed rising among the Modocs in the lava beds. They had little food or water.
They feared being killed. And, some were calling on Kintpuash to take drastic
action. The very night before, warriors advocating violence had rushed him at
a general public meeting, pulled a woman's shawl and bonnet over his head
and mocked him as a "Woman! Coward! [and] Whitefaced squaw!" Kintpuash
responded by struggling free to proclaim his willingness to kill and to die. It

was within this context that Alfred Meacham, the Reverend Eleasar Thomas, L.S. Dyar, their translators, and the chief negotiator, General Canby, rode into that "black ocean tumbled into a thousand fantastic shapes, a wild chaos of ruin, desolation and barrenness."[6]

The Modoc envoys warmly welcomed them to the meeting grounds, perhaps still hoping to negotiate a diplomatic solution, but this new round of talks soon ran into familiar obstacles. General Canby—who had served as an officer in California from 1849 to 1851—demanded that the Modocs surrender themselves as prisoners of war to the US Army. The Modocs remained adamant that Canby withdraw his troops, to demonstrate good faith, and promise them ownership of some small portion of their homeland instead of removing them from it. Neither side would back down. Eventually, the Modoc representative John Schonchin insisted: "Take away the soldiers, and give us Hot Creek, or stop talking." But before Schonchin's demands could be completely translated, Kintpuash rose and gave the signal, "Ot we kantux-e" or *"all ready"*![7]

Perhaps with the 1852 Lost River Massacre in mind, Kintpuash had organized a preemptive strike. He drew a revolver from his coat, aimed at General Canby's head, and pulled the trigger. The pistol failed to fire but Canby stood rooted to the spot. Kintpuash then revolved the pistol's cylinder and shot Canby in the face, just below his left eye. A moment later, the Modoc warrior Boston Charley shot the Reverend Thomas "in the left breast." Canby and Thomas stumbled away as the other whites scattered, but Modocs quickly killed both men. Meacham, meanwhile, pulled out a concealed derringer, stuck it against John Schonchin's chest and squeezed the trigger. Yet his gun also failed to fire, even when he pulled the trigger a second time. Meacham now ran, the Modocs shot him repeatedly, and he eventually fell motionless, but not before shooting Schonchin. Both men survived.[8]

At about the same time, on the eastern side of the jagged lava beds, Curley Headed Jack and several other Modoc men initiated what at first appeared to be a spontaneous conversation with the US infantry lieutenants William L. Sherwood and W.H. Boyle. It was another trap. As the lieutenants left the meeting ground, Modoc men began shooting and mortally wounded Sherwood.[9]

The killings of Sherwood, Thomas, and especially Canby—the first and only regularly commissioned US Army general ever killed by American Indians—inspired the head of the army to order a final, genocidal campaign. On April 12, Sherman telegraphed the new field commander, West Point graduate and Brevet Major General Alvan Gillem, via his commanding officer, "The President . . . authorizes me to instruct you to make the attack so strong and persistent that their fate may be commensurate with their crime. You will be fully justified in their utter extermination." Perhaps informed by the years he had spent in California as an officer and a civilian, off and on from 1848 to 1857, the US Army's highest-ranking general considered "utter extermination"—what we would today call total genocide—a valid military strategy that he could order while conveying the instructions of another man who had served as an army officer in California: President Ulysses S. Grant. On April 13, Gillem's commander, Major General J.M. Schofield, forwarded this order to him with an ominous endorsement of his own: "Let your work be done thoroughly." The following day, General Schofield made his command unmistakably clear, "Nothing short of their prompt and sure destruction will satisfy the ends of justice or meet the expectations of the Government." Once again, the killing machine had been ordered into genocidal action, this time by the highest-ranking general in the United States and one of his subordinate generals.[10]

Gillem now attempted to carry out these orders. His artillery pieces began pounding the Stronghold, and, on April 14, hundreds of troops started closing in for the coup de grâce. Fighting a disciplined rearguard action, Kintpuash's fifty-five to seventy warriors slowly retreated ever closer to the Stronghold. On the third morning of the assault, Gillem declared his intent: "We will endeavor to end the Modoc War today. . . . Let us exterminate the tribe." Yet Gillem, like General Wheaton before him, underestimated the Modocs. When his soldiers finally breached the Stronghold's fortifications and stormed its caverns, they found the sanctuary all but abandoned. The Modocs had quietly slipped away on the night of April 16, having inflicted twenty-three casualties. The Modocs lost perhaps sixteen people in Gillem's attack and its immediate aftermath.[11]

Still, the spirit of annihilation animated some soldiers in the Stronghold. They shot an elderly woman to death, murdered and scalped a wounded old man, and kicked a severed Modoc head. Such barbarities were unsurprising given the orders and attitudes of President Grant's generals. That same day, General Sherman wrote of Kintpuash's Modocs, "The order to attack is against the whole, and if all be swept from the face of the earth, they themselves have invited it." From the field, Gillem reported, "I have dislodged the Modocs from their stronghold in the lava beds. They are moving southward. No effort will be spared to exterminate them."[12]

Gillem would never achieve his genocidal goal. On April 26, Modoc warriors attacked US Army soldiers patrolling the lava beds. The regulars panicked, and Modoc marksmen killed twenty-three of Gillem's troops, wounding nineteen others, and losing perhaps one Modoc man in the process. Eventually, the Modoc warrior Scarfaced Charley stopped the attack, calling out to the soldiers,

During the 1872–1873 siege of Captain Jack's Stronghold, Modoc people defended themselves and their families using fortified volcanic lava trenches like this one. As they ran low on food, water, and supplies, their position became increasingly precarious, and US Army commanders eventually decided to exterminate them. William Simpson(?), "The Modoc Indians in the Lava Beds," engraving(?), 1873, in *Illustrated London News*, June 7, 1873, 536. Author's collection.

"All you fellows that aint dead had better go home. We don't want to kill you all in one day." Modocs thus let the rest of the patrol live, but Sherman replaced Gillem with Brevet Major General Jefferson C. Davis (not to be confused with the ex-Confederate leader).[13]

Over the next two weeks, Kintpuash's people kept moving through the barren lava beds but became desperate for supplies. On May 10, Kintpuash and a small group of warriors engaged regular soldiers at Dry or Sorass Lake, southeast of the lava beds, in an attempt to obtain supplies for their people. Just one Modoc died, but the soldiers and their Paiute auxiliaries routed Kintpuash.

More important, by capturing their horses and ammunition, the soldiers crippled Modoc resistance in what the *Army and Navy Journal* called "a decisive victory." Desperate for food and water, the fragmenting, exhausted, and poorly armed Modocs now became easier to kill. Although Modocs avoided troops, on May 18 cavalrymen killed two men and three women. Realizing their vulnerability and fearing death, survivors began surrendering. Soldiers and auxiliaries captured others. From this point on, most of the direct, state-sponsored killing ceased. Why?[14]

The US Army abandoned its attempt to exterminate the Modocs for a variety of reasons. The new officer commanding the operation, General Davis, was likely reluctant to kill civilians given that, as a Union officer during the Civil War, he had abandoned ex-slaves as Confederate cavalrymen advanced, which led to many civilian deaths and the temporary loss of his command. His men may have had their own concerns. In January 1873, California Indians had at last become eligible to serve as witnesses in California criminal trials. This removed an important element of the legal system that had long protected Indian killers from successful prosecution by denying Indians the right to testify against whites in criminal trials. Grant and his administration may also have been rethinking their approach. Thousands of miles to the east, Indian advocates like the Quaker Lucretia Mott and Philadelphia's Radical Club were pressuring President Grant, Interior Secretary Columbus Delano, and Indian Affairs Commissioner Edward Smith to prevent the army from exterminating the Modocs. Compounding these factors, the eyes of the world were on this last California Indian war. Correspondents writing for newspapers in Chicago, London, New York, Sacramento, San Francisco, and Yreka were onsite, thus ensuring that any violence against the surrendering Modocs would become national and even international news.[15]

Still, some men wanted to continue killing Modocs, even after they had surrendered or were captured. On June 8, two horsemen—probably Oregon militiamen—attacked a wagon bearing captured Modocs and at point-blank range shot four men dead and wounded a woman. Sherman also wanted some Modocs killed. He wrote to General Philip Sheridan: "I'm sorry that Jack & most of the Modocs were not killed in the taking." He also ordered General Schofield, Davis's commander, to have "some" Modocs "tried by court martial and shot." However, when Davis prepared in June to summarily hang "8 or 10 ringleaders," Schofield stopped him, so as to allow the US attorney general to decide whether to try the defendants in a civil or military court. An absurd kangaroo court-martial—in which the six Modoc defendants served as their own lawyers, their translators testified against them, and the men they had just fought helped to judge their case—soon found the defendants guilty and sentenced them to death. Still, as historian Boyd Cothran has explained, "Throughout July and August, President Grant and Secretary of the Interior Columbus Delano were inundated with requests for executive clemency." Finally, Lucretia Mott "burst in upon [an] elegant dinner party" and all but forced President Grant to commute the sentences of the two youngest Modoc defendants, Barncho and Slolux.[16]

Nevertheless, at 10:20 A.M. on October 3, 1873, soldiers hanged Kintpuash, John Schonchin, Boston Charley, and Black Jim before cutting off and shipping their heads to the Army Medical Museum in Washington, DC. Thus ended the final act of the last major military campaign against California Indians, which had killed up to thirty-nine or more Modocs. As in many prior California Indian-killing operations, the US government paid the bill, which was at least $477,015.12. And, as in many previous campaigns, Congress voted to reimburse nonfederal actors for their participation, giving California, Oregon, and "citizens thereof" $74,709.41 in 1883. However, the federal government's role in destroying Modoc lives did not end there.[17]

Modoc survivors, like many California Indians, now faced federal incarceration that was often fatal. Imprisoned on Alcatraz Island in October 1873, Barncho died of scrofula (a form of tuberculosis) less than two years later. Federal officials also deported 153 Modocs to Oklahoma's Quapaw Agency in 1873. Institutionalized neglect and disease, exacerbated by corruption, killed more than a third of these detainees by 1881. Many of them—including Kintpuash's young daughter Rosie—are buried in a quiet graveyard that their descendants still tend today. Despite such deaths at Quapaw, the California Indian genocide was coming to a close in 1873.[18]

Lethal violence against California Indians did continue, sometimes with authorities' acquiescence. For example, on the morning of January 26, 1879, a gang of armed vigilantes "mercilessly slaughtered" four presumably Miwok men at Humbug Gulch near Mariposa. Authorities quickly arrested five suspects. Yet the prosecution's case collapsed after the court ruled that because the Indian eyewitnesses "did not understand the nature of an oath" their testimony was "not admissible under the law." The court thus employed racism to work around the 1873 California penal code, which had barred judges and juries from summarily rejecting Indian testimony, so as to continue the tradition of granting legal impunity to those who murdered California Indians. Nevertheless, the systematic and direct, large-scale killing of California Indians ended in 1873.[19]

This photograph depicts sixteen of the Modoc prisoners deported to Oklahoma in 1873. Back row, left to right: Steamboat Frank, Shacknasty Jim, Scarfaced Charley, Captain Melville Wilkinson, Bogus Charley, William (Weium) Faithful, and Long Jim. Bottom row, left to right: Princess Mary's niece, unknown, Bogus Charley's wife and child, Long Jim's wife, Kintpuash's wife Lizzie, Kintpuash's daughter Rosie, Kintpuash's sister Princess Mary, and Samuel Clinton's wife and child. For names, see James, *Modoc*, 182–183. Unknown artist, "Modoc Prisoners of War," photograph, 1873. Courtesy of the Modoc Tribe of Oklahoma.

UNDERSTANDING GENOCIDE IN CALIFORNIA AND BEYOND

State and federal policies, in combination with vigilante violence, played major roles in the near-annihilation of California Indians during the first twenty-seven years of US rule. From 1846 to 1873, colonization policies, abductions, diseases, homicides, executions, battles, massacres, institutionalized neglect on federal reservations, and the willful destruction of indigenous villages and their food stores seem to have reduced California Indian numbers by at least 80 percent, from perhaps 150,000 to some 30,000. In less than three decades newcomers—with the support of both the state and federal governments—nearly exterminated California's Indians (see Table C.1).

Table C.1 California Indian Population Decline, 1845–1880

Year	Source	Estimated total California Indian population
1845	Cook (1976)	~150,000
1849	Merriam (1905)	100,000
1850	Cook (1976); Collier (1935)	100,000–110,000+
1851	Barbour and Wozencraft (1851)	200,000–300,000
1852	McKee (1852); Beale (1852); State Census (1852); Merriam (1905)	32,529–200,000
1853	Beale (1853)	100,000
1854	Schoolcraft (1854)	48,000
1856	Hittell (1897?); Merriam (1905); Henley (1856)	48,100–60,600+
1860	Federal Census (1860); Merriam (1905)	17,798–35,000
1865	Cook (1976); Maltby (1865)	~25,000–33,860
1870	Federal Census (1870); Merriam (1905)	7,241–30,000
1880	Federal Census (1880); Collier (1935); Merriam (1905)	16,277–20,500

Sources: For 1845: Cook, Population of California Indians, 44. For 1849: Merriam, "Indian Population of California," 600. For 1850: Cook, Population of California Indians, 44, and Collier in US Senate, Hearings before the Committee on Indian Affairs United States Senate Seventy-Fourth Congress First Session on S. 1793, 6. For 1851: Barbour and Wozencraft, March 1851, summarized in USOIA, Annual Report, 1855, note, 255. For 1852: R. McKee in SDU, January 27, 1852, 2; Beale to Lea, November 22, 1852, S. Exec. Doc. 4, 33rd Cong., Special Sess., 1853, serial 688, 379; 1852 census in Hurtado, Indian Survival on the California Frontier, 108, and Merriam, "Indian Population of California," 600. For 1853: E.F. Beale, Superintendent Indian Affairs to G.W. Manypenny, Esq., Commissioner of Indian Affairs, August 22, 1853, H. Exec. Doc. 1, Pt. 1, 33rd Cong., 1st Sess., 1853, serial 710, 467. For 1854: Henry R. Schoolcraft to Hon. Geo. W. Manypenny, Commissioner of Indian Affairs, November 18, 1854, S. Exec. Doc. 13, 33rd Cong., 2nd Sess., 1854, serial 751, 8. For 1856: Hittell, in Merriam, "Indian Population of California," 599; Merriam, "Indian Population of California," 600; and Thos J. Henley, Superintendent Indian Affairs to Hon. George W. Manypenny, Commissioner of Indian Affairs, September 4, 1856, in USOIA, Annual Report, 1856, 245–246 [Henley's figures total 60,600, not 61,600 as he wrote in his report]. For 1860: US Department of the Interior, Statistics of the Population of the United States, Embracing the Tables of Race, Nationality, Sex, Selected Ages, and Occupations, 16, and Merriam, "Indian Population of California," 600. For 1865: Cook, Population of California Indians, xv, and Charles Maltby, Superintendent Indian Affairs, California to Hon. D.W. Cooley, Com'r Indian Affairs, Washington, DC, September 15, 1865, in USOIA, Annual Report, 1865, 116. For 1870: US Department of the Interior, Statistics of the Population of the United States, 1872, 16, and Merriam, "Indian Population of California," 600. For 1880: US Department of the Interior, Statistics of the Population of the United States, 1882, 3; Collier, in US Senate, Hearings before the Committee on Indian Affairs United States Senate Seventy-Fourth Congress First Session on S. 1793, 6; and Merriam, "Indian Population of California," 600.

That California Indians survived is remarkable. As historian William Bauer Jr. has observed, while "the specter of genocide and the drastic population decline hangs over the narrative" of California Indian history, the epic of California Indian survival is "a story worthy of marvel." That thousands endured and maintained their traditions is a testament to their tenacious defiance and intelligent survival strategies against overwhelming odds. With a population estimated at 150,000 people in 2009, many California Indians are today enrolled members of the state's 109 federally recognized tribes. Many live on or near more than 100 federal Indian reservations in California as well as individual federal trust allotments. Other California Indians, such as the Shastas and Winnemem Wintus, belong to the scores of California tribes petitioning for federal recognition as sovereign nations and the important cultural, economic, territorial, and political rights associated with that status under state and federal law. Still other California Indian people reside on or near reservations in Oregon, Oklahoma, and beyond. No matter what their status under federal law, tens of thousands of California Indian people live and work among non-Indians in cities, suburbs, and towns across North America. Many are the descendants of genocide survivors. For many of them, the legacy of this catastrophe endures. Painful and persistent, the genocide is an event that some seek to understand and commemorate because it is so rarely acknowledged by non-Indians but so important to California Indian identities and current issues. Historical trauma, access to natural resources, control of land, and federal recognition are just some of the important present-day issues connected to the genocide that their ancestors endured.[20]

The legacy of the state's genocidal past remains hidden in plain sight and raises awkward questions when brought into focus. Californians can no longer elect the perpetrators of genocide to high office, as they did in 1882 by placing retired army officer George Stoneman—who participated in Lyon's genocidal 1850 campaign—in the governor's mansion. And few would now display "a blanket lined with Indian scalps" as one California man did in the early twentieth century. Still, the names of genocide perpetrators and their supporters are inscribed across the state. Many California place names—such as Alpine County's Carson Pass, Alameda County's City of Fremont, and Lake County's Kelseyville—commemorate men directly responsible for leading the killing of large numbers of California Indians, even as they obscure the presence of California Indians. Some supporters of killing campaigns are similarly honored. In 1878, Serranus Hastings donated $100,000 to found Hastings College of Law in San Francisco. California's oldest law school is thus named after a man who helped to lead the assembly, financing, and state-sponsorship drive for Walter Jarboe's genocidal

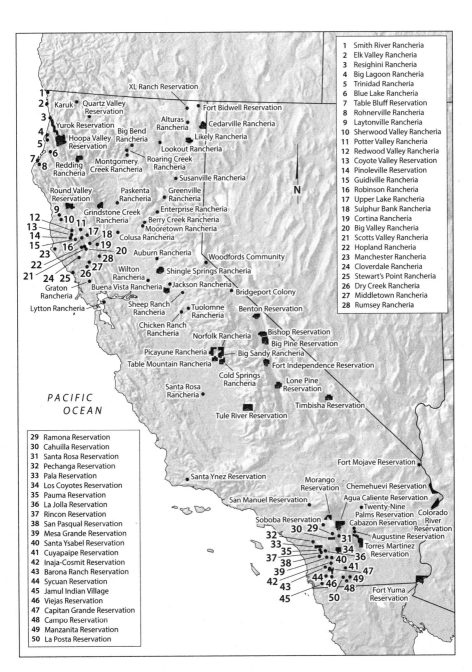

Some federally recognized California Indian lands, 2016

Map legend (1–28):

1 Smith River Rancheria
2 Elk Valley Rancheria
3 Resighini Rancheria
4 Big Lagoon Rancheria
5 Trinidad Rancheria
6 Blue Lake Rancheria
7 Table Bluff Reservation
8 Rohnerville Rancheria
9 Laytonville Rancheria
10 Sherwood Valley Rancheria
11 Potter Valley Rancheria
12 Redwood Valley Rancheria
13 Coyote Valley Reservation
14 Pinoleville Reservation
15 Guidiville Rancheria
16 Robinson Rancheria
17 Upper Lake Rancheria
18 Sulphur Bank Rancheria
19 Cortina Rancheria
20 Big Valley Rancheria
21 Scotts Valley Rancheria
22 Hopland Rancheria
23 Manchester Rancheria
24 Cloverdale Rancheria
25 Stewart's Point Rancheria
26 Dry Creek Rancheria
27 Middletown Rancheria
28 Rumsey Rancheria

Map legend (29–50):

29 Ramona Reservation
30 Cahuilla Reservation
31 Santa Rosa Reservation
32 Pechanga Reservation
33 Pala Reservation
34 Los Coyotes Reservation
35 Pauma Reservation
36 La Jolla Reservation
37 Rincon Reservation
38 San Pasqual Reservation
39 Mesa Grande Reservation
40 Santa Ysabel Reservation
41 Cuyapaipe Reservation
42 Inaja-Cosmit Reservation
43 Barona Ranch Reservation
44 Sycuan Reservation
45 Jamul Indian Village
46 Viejas Reservation
47 Capitan Grande Reservation
48 Campo Reservation
49 Manzanita Reservation
50 La Posta Reservation

Map labels:

XL Ranch Reservation
Karuk
Quartz Valley Reservation
Fort Bidwell Reservation
Alturas Rancheria
Cedarville Rancheria
Yurok Reservation
Big Bend Rancheria
Likely Rancheria
Hoopa Valley Reservation
Lookout Rancheria
Redding Rancheria
Montgomery Creek Rancheria
Roaring Creek Rancheria
Susanville Rancheria
Round Valley Reservation
Paskenta Rancheria
Greenville Rancheria
Enterprise Rancheria
Grindstone Creek Rancheria
Berry Creek Rancheria
Mooretown Rancheria
Colusa Rancheria
Auburn Rancheria
Woodfords Community
Wilton Rancheria
Shingle Springs Rancheria
Graton Rancheria
Buena Vista Rancheria
Jackson Rancheria
Bridgeport Colony
Lytton Rancheria
Sheep Ranch Rancheria
Tuolomne Rancheria
Benton Reservation
Chicken Ranch Rancheria
Norfolk Rancheria
Bishop Reservation
Big Pine Reservation
Picayune Rancheria
Big Sandy Rancheria
Table Mountain Rancheria
Fort Independence Reservation
Cold Springs Rancheria
Lone Pine Reservation
Santa Rosa Rancheria
Timbisha Reservation
Tule River Reservation
PACIFIC OCEAN
Fort Mojave Reservation
Santa Ynez Reservation
Morango Reservation
Chemehuevi Reservation
San Manuel Reservation
Agua Caliente Reservation
Twenty-Nine Palms Reservation
Colorado River Reservation
Soboba Reservation
Cabazon Reservation
Augustine Reservation
Torres Martinez Reservation
Fort Yuma Reservation
N

Eel River Rangers militia expedition in 1859. Leland Stanford and his wife later donated more than $20 million to found Stanford University. One of the state's premier academic institutions thus bears the family name of a governor who raised California Volunteers for lethal Civil War–era army campaigns against California Indians and signed legislation that helped to fund such operations. Both Hastings and Stanford built their colossal fortunes, in part, on California real estate. Both men thus profited from the theft of California Indian land. Having helped to facilitate genocide, they then used some of their wealth to create institutions that have benefited many people.[21]

Addressing such complex legacies is an ongoing process. In 2004, the City of Eureka deeded sixty acres of Duluwat Island—site of the 1860 Tuluwat massacre—to the Wiyot Tribe. In 2011, authorities renamed San Francisco's Burnett Child Development Center due to its namesake's profound racism, and in 2014 Long Beach changed the name of its Peter H. Burnett Elementary School for similar reasons. Still, the genocide suffered by California Indians is not a required topic in the state's public schools, and it is still possible to drive on Burnett Street in San Francisco, Weller Way in Sacramento, and Fremont Street in San Diego. More important, few people know that genocide helped to facilitate the conquest and colonization of the very land and natural resources on which contemporary California was built. The legacies of California's genocide remain widespread but largely unknown.[22]

Fortunately, a more revealing public history of the California genocide is slowly emerging. Revised official historical landmark plaques at sites like the location of the 1850 Bloody Island Massacre publicly memorialize some of the atrocities committed against California Indian people. Unfortunately, these historically accurate memorials related to genocide in California are few and far between. However, California Indians themselves are raising awareness with their own commemorations such as the annual Tolowa candlelight vigil at the site of the 1853 Yontocket Massacre, the yearly Wiyot candlelight vigil to commemorate the 1860 Tuluwat Massacre, and the annual Nome Cult Walk in which participants retrace the 1863 Konkow Maidu Trail of Tears. Even so, few have carefully considered why the events that took place in California constituted genocide.[23]

The California Indian catastrophe fits the two-part legal definition set forth in the UN Genocide Convention. First, various perpetrators demonstrated, in word and deed, their "intent to destroy, in whole or in part, a national, ethnical, racial or religious group as such." Second, at different times a variety of perpetrators committed examples of all five acts of genocide listed in the convention.

In 2013, members of the Round Valley Indian Tribe commemorated the one-hundredth anniversary of the Konkow Maidu Trail of Tears by walking the route. Unknown artist, "Members of the Round Valley Indian Tribe retrace the 1863 route of the Nome Cult Walk, a forced relocation of Indians from Chico, Calif., to Covelo, CA.," photograph, 2013. Courtesy of the United States Forest Service.

"Killing members of the group" occurred in more than 370 massacres, as well as in hundreds of smaller killings, individual homicides, and executions. Primary and secondary sources indicate that from 1846 to 1873 individuals, vigilantes, California state militiamen, and US soldiers killed at least 9,492 to 16,094 California Indians, and probably many more. Because primary sources for many incidents did not report a specific number killed on every occasion—instead using vague terms like "several," "many," "a multitude," or "the whole village"—and because some killings either produced several different death toll estimates or went unreported, we will never know the total number of California Indian people killed between 1846 and 1873. By way of contrast, sources indicate that California Indians killed fewer than 1,500 non-Indians during this period.[24]

Other acts of genocide proliferated too. Many rapes and beatings occurred, and these meet the Convention's definition of "causing serious bodily harm" to victims on the basis of their group identity and with the intent to destroy the group. The sustained military and civilian policy of demolishing California Indian villages and their food stores while driving Indians into inhospitable desert and mountain regions amounted to "deliberately inflicting on the group conditions of life calculated to bring about its physical destruction in whole or in part." Some Office of Indian Affairs employees administering federal Indian reservations in California—which Cook called "concentration camps"—committed the same genocidal crime. Further, because malnutrition and exposure predictably lowered fertility while increasing the number of miscarriages and stillbirths, some state and federal decision makers also appear guilty of "imposing measures intended to prevent births within the group." Finally, the state of California, slave raiders, and federal officials were all involved in "forcibly transferring children of the group to another group." Three thousand to 4,000 or more California Indian children suffered such forced transfers between 1852 and 1867 alone. By breaking up families and communities, forced removals also constituted "imposing measures intended to prevent births within the group." In effect, the state legalized abduction and enslavement of Indian minors; slavers exploited indenture laws; federal officials prevented US Army intervention to protect the victims; and in some cases slavers followed in the wake of army campaigns to capture Indian minors for enforced servitude. Sufficient evidence exists to designate the California Indian catastrophe a case of genocide, according to the UN definition. However, in order to understand this catastrophe as genocide, it is important to address the role of disease, genocidal intent in the absence of a written plan, and nonstate actors as agents of genocide.[25]

Disease played an important role in the California Indian population decline under US rule. Smallpox killed perhaps 150 Modocs in 1847 as well as substantial numbers of other California Indians during the 1854–1855 outbreak. The smallpox epidemic of 1862–1863 then ranged from Southern California to the Sacramento Valley. Malaria also likely took California Indian lives. Meanwhile, venereal diseases, which decreased reproduction through sterility and fetal death, were well documented. Observers reported sick Indians, particularly on federal Indian reservations plagued by institutionalized neglect, and many California Indians did die of disease. However, the massive population decline of 1846–1873 was also the product of direct killings that were perpetrated by human actors. These killings were, in turn, tolerated and often sponsored by both state and federal authorities.[26]

One intellectual legacy of the Nazi Holocaust—"for many, the paradigm case of genocide"—is an assumption that "intent to destroy" must be verbalized by a national leader like Adolf Hitler, or articulated in an official written plan like the 1942 Wannsee Conference Protocol. If so, designating the California Indian catastrophe as genocide is problematic. No US president spoke or wrote of their intent to kill all California Indians. State governors Burnett and Weller did verbally declare that the physical destruction of all California Indians was inevitable. On January 7, 1851, Governor Burnett publicly proclaimed that "a war of extermination will continue to be waged between the races, until the Indian race becomes extinct," adding that "the inevitable destiny of the race is beyond the power or wisdom of man to avert." On August 11, 1852, Senator Weller—who became California's governor in 1858—went further. He told his fellow US senators that California Indians "will be exterminated before the onward march of the white man" explaining, "humanity may forbid, but the *interest* of the white man demands their extinction." Still, only Burnett made such a pronouncement while he was governor. And apart from authorizing the planning of militia expeditions, extant primary sources document no state or federal leader articulating any *plan* to "destroy" the Indians of California. From this evidence, one might mistakenly conclude that state and federal officials were innocent of genocide in this case. However, international case law does not require prosecutors to produce a written plan for genocide in order to convict a party of that crime. In 1998, the International Criminal Tribunal for Rwanda ruled that Jean-Paul Akayesu was guilty of genocide based on his documented intent and action, stating that he was "culpable because he knew or should have known that the act committed would destroy, in whole or in part, a group." This certainly applied to some California and US leaders. Moreover, some of them further demonstrated genocidal intent as a conscious desire to destroy the group in whole or in part.[27]

Many state and federal government officials, as well as US Army and Office of Indian Affairs personnel, were well aware of what was happening to California Indians between 1846 and 1873. As we have seen, Indian Office officials, US Army officers, California militiamen, and other government officials frequently reported massacres and other genocidal acts. Even if officials did not read these government reports, California newspapers reported in detail on the mass murder of California Indians as it happened, frequently invoking terms like *extermination*, a nineteenth-century equivalent of the word *genocide*. Moreover, army officers, journalists, Indian Office employees, and concerned citizens frequently warned of the need either to change California Indian policy to protect California Indians or see the state's Indian population physically exterminated. Others simply urged the latter course. Still, the responsible state and federal officials took few actions to protect California Indians. Far more incriminating than this passivity were the active roles that state and federal officials played in physically destroying California Indians. Beyond the explicit statements of two men who served as state governor, state and federal policymakers tended to express genocidal intent more in deeds than in words.

Elected California officials were the primary architects of annihilation. Legislators created a legal environment in which California Indians had almost no rights, thus granting those who attacked them virtual impunity. Moreover, two governors threatened annihilation, and both governors and elected officials cooperated in building a killing machine. California governors called out or authorized no fewer than twenty-four state militia expeditions against Indians between 1850 and 1861, which killed 1,342 to 1,876 or more California Indian people. State legislators also passed three bills—in 1851, 1852, and 1857—that raised up to $1.51 million to fund these operations, usually ex post facto. By demonstrating that the state would not punish Indian killers, but instead reward them, state militia expeditions inspired an even greater number of vigilante killings. Finally, in 1863, after the US Army supplanted the state militia as the primary state-sponsored Indian-killing force, California legislators passed a bill allowing the state to raise an additional $600,000 to encourage more men to enlist as California Volunteers. Thus, some California officials seem to have been guilty of genocide, conspiracy to commit genocide, direct public incitement to commit genocide, attempt to commit genocide, and complicity in genocide. Yet, despite their leading role, Californians did not act alone.

The US Army played a crucial part in the California genocide, first creating the exclusionary legal system, then setting genocidal precedents, helping to build the killing machine, directly participating in killing, and finally taking control of it. Martial rule over California, between 1846 and 1850, created the legal foundations on which California state legislators built their anti-Indian laws. Martial law policies dehumanized California Indians, segregated them, limited their geographic movement, made it easier for non-Indians to distinguish which Indians they could kidnap or kill without offending authorities, and, finally, made Indians working for non-Indians captive laborers while potentially criminalizing those tens of thousands who were still free. Next, the army's 1850 Clear Lake campaign set important precedents for mass murder and its acceptance by the army, press, judiciary, United States Senate, and California public. The army's delivery of thousands of weapons and accoutrements, as well as untold quantities of ammunition, then helped to arm Indian-hunting state militia expeditions. Even more important, professionally trained, heavily armed soldiers had the power to stop vigilantes and militiamen from killing Indians—as demonstrated in multiple instances—but they rarely did so. Instead, they often participated. In the late 1850s, soldiers began to reassume the mantle of perpetrators, and during the Civil War the army supplanted militiamen as the primary state-sponsored Indian killers. US Army generals deployed California Volunteers, often commanded by regular, professional officers, to kill and massacre hundreds of California Indians in some of the largest and longest-lasting campaigns against them. In total, US Army soldiers killed at least 1,688 to 3,741 California Indians between 1846 and 1873, making the army more lethal than the state militias. Ultimately, some members of the US Army were guilty of genocide, conspiracy to commit genocide, attempt to commit genocide, and complicity in genocide.

If state legislators were the main architects of genocide, federal officials helped to lay the groundwork, became the final arbiters of the design, and ultimately paid for most of its official execution. US senators played a pivotal role in making victims of California Indians. In 1852, they repudiated the eighteen treaties signed between federal treaty commissioners and California Indians, thus dispossessing Indians of their remaining land and their negotiating role, while dramatically increasing their vulnerability by denying them land rights and full federal protection. Federal officials then repeatedly abdicated responsibility for California Indian affairs. They failed to adequately feed and care for California Indians on federal reservations. Moreover, rather than deploy substantial numbers of regular soldiers to protect Indians and serve as a buffer between colonists and Indians, they allowed state militiamen to hunt and kill California Indians. Congress could have reined in state militia activities or simply withheld funding for militias. Instead, it passed two major funding bills—in 1854 and 1860—allocating up to $1,324,259.65 to reimburse California for past militia expeditions, retrospectively endorsing them, financially supporting them, and thus fueling additional genocidal operations. By 1863, the federal government had given California more than $1 million for its militia campaigns. Congress never explicitly called for California Indians' extermination, but it emphatically approved genocide ex post facto by paying California for the killings carried out by its militia. Of course, by 1863, the US Army had taken over as the primary state-sponsored killer, and Congress controlled that institution's budget. Indeed, federal legislators paid for some or all of many lethal campaigns against California Indians. These ranged from Frémont's murderous 1846 operations to Lyon's genocidal 1850 rampage and from the state's deadly 1850–1861 militia expeditions to army killing campaigns before, during, and after the Civil War. Congress stopped paying for large-scale anti-California Indian operations only when, in 1883, it finished paying over $477,000 for the 1872–1873 war against the Modocs. Thus, some federal officials were guilty of genocidal crimes, as defined by the UN Genocide Convention.

Policy conflicts did exist. Members of the Office of Indian Affairs, army, California legislature, and US Senate disputed California Indian policy. Special Agent J. Ross Browne pleaded for changes. Soldiers sometimes protected Indians.

Many officials advocated for California Indian welfare, including a few state legislators. Kentucky senator John Crittenden even spoke out against the "slavery and oppression and murders" of California Indians. These critiques showed that alternative policies were conceivable, proposed, and possible. However, the fact remains that an anti-Indian US Congress and leaders like Jefferson Davis won the day. The result was genocide.[28]

Another intellectual legacy of the Holocaust is the erroneous assumption that genocide perpetrators must be national or state actors. Genocide is the work of individuals who kill, kidnap, and otherwise act to destroy a specific group. There is no requirement that perpetrators be government leaders or government employees. Indeed, the UN Genocide Convention designates "constitutionally responsible rulers, public officials or private individuals" as possible agents of genocide. In California, individuals and vigilante groups killed many more Indians than either militiamen or US Army soldiers. However, they could not have killed so many California Indians without Sacramento's support and Washington's acquiescence. State laws and policies, coupled with federal unwillingness to protect California Indians, made vigilantes' murderous freedom of action possible. Had there been no legal framework for kidnapping California Indian children, or had federal officials ordered the US Army either to protect California Indians or simply to stop massacring them, elements of the genocide could have been eliminated. In the end, whoever the direct agents, genocide rarely takes place without government complicity.[29]

Like California Indians, Native Americans across the country suffered a devastating population decline following the arrival of newcomers. Before contact, perhaps five million or more indigenous people inhabited what is now the continental United States. By 1900, the federal government counted fewer than 250,000 survivors. What caused this catastrophe? Diseases, colonialism, and war all played important roles, but was something more sinister also to blame?[30]

Academics and others have long debated whether or not Native Americans, or any groups of them, suffered genocide during the conquest and colonization of the Americas. The question of genocide in US history remains an important subject, given that the near obliteration of its indigenous peoples remains one of the formative events in the nation's history. As in many other Western Hemisphere countries, the Native American population cataclysm in the United States played a foundational role in facilitating the conquest and colonization of millions of square miles, the real estate and natural resources on which the country was built. Thus, how we explain the Native American population catastrophe informs how we understand the making of the United States and its colonial origins. Beyond interpretations of US history, the stakes include important issues such as public acknowledgment, apology, reparations, natural resources, land, American Indian sovereignty, and national character. Despite these high stakes, the question remains unresolved, in part because of the deadlocked American genocide debate.[31]

White violence against Native Americans had been a topic of discussion for centuries by 1880. In that year, however, the conversation took a dramatic turn. Former US Indian Affairs commissioner George Manypenny now released the first book addressing instances of extermination, genocide's nineteenth-century linguistic equivalent, across the history of the United States and its colonial precursors. The following year, author Helen Hunt Jackson chronicled atrocities and massacres in her now famous book, *A Century of Dishonor: A Sketch of the United States Government's Dealings with Some of the Indian Tribes*. In 1889, author and future president Theodore Roosevelt disparaged these books by Manypenny and Jackson, calling them "worse than valueless," and the debate was on.[32]

Fifty-four years later, jurist Raphaël Lemkin minted a new term for discussing crimes of "extermination." He called the phenomenon genocide. Soon he and others began using the concept to evaluate American Indian history. In 1987, anthropologist Russell Thornton released the first scholarly book addressing genocide in the continental United States as a whole. He asserted that genocide was one of multiple causes of Indian depopulation, but that only in certain cases did it cause total extermination. Three years later, historian Frank Chalk and sociologist Kurt Jonassohn argued that Indians suffered genocide in colonial New England and in the nineteenth-century United States. In 1992, American studies scholar David Stannard asserted that all Native Americans were victims of disease and genocide "from almost the instant of first human contact between Europe and the Americas." Other scholars also claimed that genocide had taken place against American Indians and controversial ethnic studies scholar Ward Churchill insisted that genocide began with invasion and continued into the post–Cold War era as "genocidal . . . Internal Colonialism." In his book *Blood and Soil*, historian Ben Kiernan then carefully documented examples of genocide in "Colonial North America, 1600–1776," as well as "Genocide in the United States."[33]

Critics of these views have asserted that Native Americans infrequently, or never, suffered genocide. In 1992, historian James Axtell proclaimed "'genocide' . . . inaccurate as a description of the vast majority of encounters between Europeans and Indians." Two years later, religious studies scholar Steven Katz called "the depopulation of the New World . . . largely an *unintended* tragedy." In 1997, historian Robert Utley insisted that using the word *genocide* to describe American

Indian experiences under US rule "grossly falsifies history." Historian William Rubinstein then went further. He claimed that "American policy towards the Indians . . . never actually encompassed genocide." The same year, historian Guenter Lewy agreed: "Genocide was never American policy, nor was it the result of policy." In 2014, historian Gary Anderson added that although "genocide did not occur in America," American Indians did suffer "ethnic cleansing" and "crimes against humanity."[34]

Two factors polarize the American genocide debate. First, only some participants use the UN Genocide Convention as their definition, even though 147 countries have signed or are parties to it, a growing body of case law supports it, and it remains the only authoritative international legal definition. Just as important, many participants emphasize rendering a verdict of genocide or not genocide for the entire history of the United States, before and after 1776, or even the entire Western Hemisphere from 1492 to the present. As Hurtado wrote of California Indians, "Generalization is difficult." Across the United States, Indian population declines took place at different rates, over millions of square miles, and across centuries. Colonial, state, and federal policymaking personnel changed over time, as did their governments' Indian policies. Moreover, hundreds of tribes were involved; their resistance and accommodation strategies varied, and changed over time. Thus, despite the fact that histories of violence against Native Americans abound, the details revealed by the California case suggest the need for more local and regional studies to provide the data that permit an assessment of genocide's occurrence, variability, and frequency, or absence, in other regions, in the United States as a whole, and elsewhere in the Americas, from Patagonia to the Arctic.[35]

Assessing the question of genocide in the United States and beyond without an agreed-upon definition or detailed case studies makes it difficult to reach comprehensive conclusions. Thornton showed the way forward by deploying brief tribal case studies to support his arguments. Stannard then touched on the role of both genocidal intent and genocidal actions. More recently, Kiernan demonstrated the importance of regional studies, emphasizing genocidal intent, command structures, and genocidal massacres. Nevertheless, as historian Dan Stone has observed, "It is remarkable that, given the enormous historiography on the colonial period and frontier conflict [in North America], there is not more that directly addresses the question of genocide."[36]

The direct and deliberate killing of Indians in California between 1846 and 1873 was more lethal and sustained that anywhere else in the United States or its colonial antecedents. Yet there remains a need for additional detailed studies addressing other regions and peoples within and beyond the United States.

The variables present in the California genocide did not recur in precisely the same combination, or at the same intensities, in the histories of other Native American peoples. In some other cases, disease was the overwhelming cause of mortalities. Both state and federal (or colonial and metropolitan) decision makers were not complicit in every case. Other Indian peoples employed different survival and resistance strategies, for example, fleeing contact zones or killing larger numbers of colonizers than California Indians did. Finally, in other cases, colonizers may have committed fewer or no genocidal crimes while the causes and rates of death differed. We need to build on our existing knowledge, with new research, in order to understand the full picture for the United States, North America, and the Western Hemisphere. However, this book has presented a workable methodology for examining potential cases of genocide in the Americas and beyond.[37]

The UN Genocide Convention provides historians with a standardized, internationally recognized rubric and a coherent legal definition that may be consistently applied. This book has suggested that scholars should rigorously consider every potential case in consistent terms. Just as important, we should consider each on a case-by-case or region-by-region basis, not just in California, but nationwide and internationally—to create a scholarly precision in our use of a politically explosive term—and to seriously consider the balance between variables like disease and the five categories of genocidal crimes described in the Genocide Convention. Thus, without claiming a universality of the California case, this book points the field toward clear and consistent definitional standards and application. Detailed case studies are an important element of genocide studies—a field often dominated by theoretical, and especially definitional, debates—because case studies provide a powerful tool with which to understand genocide and combat its denial around the world.

Native Americans experienced and reacted to conquest and colonization in varied ways. Rigorously examining this range of cases, using the Genocide Convention to evaluate both genocidal intent and genocidal acts, will help to move the discussion of genocide in the United States toward clarity. Unbraiding each region's story from the tapestry of American Indian history, and bringing each into sharper relief, will create a clearer, more vivid portrait of Native American experiences, and of US history as a whole. Such investigations may be painful, but they will help all Americans, both Indian and non-Indian, to make more accurate sense of our past and our selves.

NOTES

INTRODUCTION

1. Bancroft, *Works*, 22:224; Sloat, in *DAC*, July 10, 1852, 2; *DAC*, July 10, 1852, 2; Smith, *War with Mexico*, 1:334–335; Sloat, Fort Sacramento Papers. For the salute and roar, see *DAC*, July 10, 1852, 2; Bancroft, *Works*, 22:231; Smith, *War with Mexico*, 1:335. For "pine trees," see Sherman, *Recollections of California*, 9. Cook estimated some 150,000 California Indians alive in 1845. See Cook, *Population of California Indians*, 44. California's Indian population in 1846 is disputed.

2. For 1769: Cook, *Population of California Indians*, 43. Cook's precontact population estimate of 310,000 is disputed. In 1875, Stephen Powers estimated 705,000; in 1905, C. Hart Merriam estimated 260,000; in 1925, Alfred Kroeber estimated 133,000 alive in 1770; and in 1963 Martin Baumhoff estimated 350,000. See Powers, "California Indian Characteristics," 308; Merriam, "Indian Population of California," 598; Kroeber, *Handbook of the Indians of California*, 882–883; Baumhoff, "Ecological Determinants," 226. For 1845 population: Cook, *Population of California Indians*, 44. For mission deaths: Cook, "Conflict, I," 16. Robert F. Heizer and Albert B. Elsasser estimated 60,200 deaths in *Natural World of the California Indians*, 226. For quotation, see Mc-Williams, *Southern California Country*, 29. For spectrum: see Francis F. Guest, "Excerpts from A Special Article By Rev. Francis F. Guest, O.F.M.," in Costo and Costo, *Missions of California*, 223–232; Guest, *Hispanic California Revisited*; Geiger, *Life and Times of Fray Junípero Serra*; Costo and Costo, *Missions of California*.

3. Cook estimated 150,000 California Indians alive in 1845. See Cook, *Population of California Indians*, 44. For 1870 estimate, see Merriam, "Indian Population of California," 600. Census takers recorded just 7,241 California Indians that year, almost certainly an undercount. See US Department of the Interior, *Statistics of the Population*, 1872, 16. For 1880 population, again likely an undercount, see US Department of the Interior, *Statistics of the Population*, 1882, 3. In 1943, Sherburne Cook argued that "60 per cent of the population decline [under US rule was] due to disease," while dislocation, starvation, and homicide, roughly in that order, also contributed to

the decline. He republished this argument in 1976. In 1978, Cook posited, "the direct causes of death were disease, the bullet, exposure, and acute starvation," without specifying any causal hierarchy (Cook, "Conflict, III," 24; Sherburne F. Cook, "Historical Demography," in Heizer, *Handbook of North American Indians*, 8:93). According to historian Albert Hurtado, the population "decrease was a consequence of the gold rush: disease, starvation, homicide, and a declining birthrate for native people took a heavy toll" (Hurtado, *Indian Survival*, 1). Cook, "Historical Demography," 93. Historian Gary Clayton Anderson challenged Cook's 1845 population estimate of 150,000. Using selected US Army and Indian Office documents, while rejecting many other sources, Anderson claimed that "by summer 1851 . . . the total Native population then living outside the ranching community in California north of Los Angeles was at most 19,500." See Anderson, *Ethnic Cleansing and the Indian*, 192–205; for quotation, see 193.

4. Bancroft, *Works*, 24:474; John Collier, Commissioner of Indian Affairs, in US Senate, *Hearings before the Committee on Indian Affairs*, 6; Caughey, *California*, 379–391, 381; Cook, "Conflict, III," 106, 115, 5. Anderson rejected Cook's quantitative conclusions, instead claiming, "evidence suggests that approximately two thousand Indians were murdered in California during and after the gold rush." Anderson did not explain how he arrived at this figure. See Anderson, *Ethnic Cleansing and the Indian*, 194, 217.

5. Lemkin, *Axis Rule*, xi–xii, chap. 9. Lemkin's introduction was dated 1943. UN, *Convention*, 280.

6. UN, *Convention*, 280.

7. Lemkin, *Lemkin on Genocide*, 3; McDonnell and Moses, "Raphael Lemkin," 502. For more on Lemkin's unpublished writing about Native Americans and genocide, see John Docker, "Are Settler-Colonies Inherently Genocidal? Re-reading Lemkin," in Moses, *Empire, Colony, Genocide*, 81–101. For Lemkin's death, see "Deaths," *New York Times*, August 31, 1959, 21.

8. For twenty-two definitions proffered since 1959, see Jones, *Genocide*, 16–20.

9. LeBlanc, *United States and the Genocide Convention*, 1; Jones, *Genocide*, 16–20; UN, "Treaty Collection"; Caughey, *California*, 379; Cook, "Conflict, III," 5, 9.

10. Novick, *Holocaust in American Life*, 133; Arendt, *Eichmann in Jerusalem*; Baron, "First Wave," 90. See also Kramer, *Judgment at Nuremberg*; Hilberg, *Destruction of the European Jews*. For histories addressing violence against American Indians, see, for example, Brown, *Bury My Heart*, and Jennings, *Invasion of America*.

11. Kroeber and Heizer, *Almost Ancestors*, 19; Coffer, "Genocide of the California Indians"; Norton, *Genocide in Northwestern California*; Garner, *Broken Ring*, 107; Rawls, *Indians of California*, 171; Thornton, *American Indian Holocaust*, 201; Hurtado, *Indian Survival*, 135; William T. Hagen, "How the West Was Lost," in Hoxie, *Indians in American History*, 193.

12. For quotation, see Wilshire, *Get 'Em All! Kill 'Em!*, 18. Kohl, "Ethnocide and Ethnogenesis," 91–100; Chalk and Jonassohn, *History and Sociology of Genocide*, see 203 for assertion of genocide against American Indians and 197–199, 201–203 for references to the Yuki genocide; Fein, "Contextual and Comparative Studies," 80–82.

13. Stannard, *American Holocaust*, 142; Churchill, *Little Matter of Genocide*, 427n. According to Dan Frosch, Ward Churchill "was dismissed by the university [of Colo-

rado, Boulder] in July 2007 on grounds that he had plagerized and falsified parts of his research on the persecution of American Indians" (Frosch, "Fired Professor Defends 9/11 Remarks," *New York Times*, March 24, 2009, A15). For other scholars who mentioned genocide in California, see Del Castillo, *Treaty of Guadalupe Hidalgo*, 70; White, "Morality and Mortality," 35; Field, "Genocide and the Indians of California"; Lewis, *Neither Wolf nor Dog*, 84; Hauptman, *Tribes and Tribulations*, 5; Wilson, *Earth Shall Weep*, 228; Patricia Nelson Limerick, in James Brooke, "Less to Celebrate at This Gold Rush Anniversary," *New York Times*, March 22, 1998, 16; Trafzer and Hyer, *"Exterminate Them!*," 1; Hine and Faragher, *American West*, 249; Kevin Starr, "Introduction," in Starr and Orsi, *Rooted in Barbarous Soil*, 7; Sousa, "'They Will Be Hunted Down'," 193–209; Mann, *Dark Side of Democracy*, 76; Wilshire, *Get 'Em All! Kill 'Em!*, 29; Kiernan, *Blood and Soil*, 349–354; Bauer, *We Were All Like Migrant Workers Here*, 204. Historian Gary Clayton Anderson disagreed. He argued that, "A series of inhuman acts—murder, war crimes, and certainly ethnic cleansing—occurred, extending over a dozen years, but collectively they do not amount to state-sanctioned genocide." See Anderson, *Ethnic Cleansing and the Indian*, 217.

14. Heizer and Almquist, *Other Californians*, 23–137; Heizer, *Destruction of California Indians*; Heizer, *They Were Only Diggers*; Trafzer and Hyer, *"Exterminate Them!"* For case studies, see Norton, *Genocide in Northwestern California*; Carranco and Beard, *Genocide and Vendetta*; Thornton, *American Indian Holocaust*, 109–113, 200–210; Madley, "Patterns of Frontier Genocide," 176–181; Baumgardner, *Killing for Land* (Baumgardner mentioned genocide but ultimately framed the Round Valley catastrophe as conflict, see 18, 116, 122, 258); Madley, "California's Yuki Indians," 303–332; Benjamin Madley, "When 'The World Was Turned Upside Down': California and Oregon's Tolowa Indian Genocide, 1851–1856," in Jones, *New Directions*, 170–196; Benjamin Madley, "Genocide of California's Yana Indians," in Totten and Parsons, *Centuries of Genocide*, 16–53; Benjamin Madley, "California and Oregon's Modoc Indians: How Indigenous Resistance Camouflages Genocide in Colonial Histories," in Woolford, Benvenuto, and Hinton, *Colonial Genocide*, 95–130. Coffer devoted a few pages to Anglo-Americans' attempts to exterminate California Indians. In 1984, Rawls dedicated thirty pages to "extermination." In 1993, Field devoted thirty-eight pages to "The American Period: Isolation and Extermination." Kiernan then dedicated six pages to genocide in California. See Coffer, "Genocide of the California Indians," 8–15; Rawls, *Indians of California*, 171–201; Field, "Genocide and the Indians of California," 47–62, 76–99; Kiernan, *Blood and Soil*, 349–354. Secrest, *When the Great Spirit Died*; Lindsay, *Murder State*.

15. Some works addressing American exceptionalism include Lipset, *American Exceptionalism*; McEvoy-Levy, *American Exceptionalism*; and Glickstein, *American Exceptionalism*. For comparisons of genocide in California with genocides elsewhere, see Madley, "Patterns of Frontier Genocide," and Sousa, "'They Will Be Hunted Down.'" Sociologist Michael Mann posited a relationship between democracy and ethnic cleansing in *Dark Side of Democracy*.

16. For population figure, see Lightfoot and Parrish, *California Indians*, 3. For quotation, see Duran, Firehammer, and Gonzalez, "Liberation Psychology," 292. For more on

intergenerational trauma, see Danieli, *International Handbook*. In 2007, several hundred Indian and non-Indian participants at the Thirty-seventh United Indian Health Services Annual Board and Staff Meeting for northwestern California discussed this issue following a presentation by the author on genocide in California.

17. Eric Yamamoto and Liann Ebesuaga, "Report of Redress: The Japanese American Internment," in Greiff, *Handbook of Reparations*, 257–258, 269–270, 274. For gaming revenues, see Alan Meister summarized in Howard Stutz, "Indian Gaming Revenue Hits Record $28.3 Billion in 2013," *Las Vegas Review-Journal*, March 31, 2015, D1.

18. As early as 1875, ethnographer Stephen Powers remarked that California Indians "are forbidden by their religious ideas to speak of the dead" (Powers, "California Indian Characteristics," 304).

19. Heizer and Almquist, *Other Californians*, 27. It is difficult to know exactly how many California Indians non-Indians killed, given that, as historian Clare McKanna has pointed out, "In [nineteenth-century] California, homicides committed in isolated rural areas were commonly attributed to American Indians, particularly if there were no witnesses." See McKanna, *Race and Homicide*, 22. For reports of non-Indians killed by California Indians, see online Appendix 4.

20. For more on this debate, see Madley, "Reexamining the American Genocide Debate," 98–139. As historian Dan Stone observed, "It is remarkable that, given the enormous historiography on the colonial period and frontier conflict [in North America] there is not more that directly addresses the question of genocide." See Stone, *Historiography of Genocide*, 3.

CHAPTER 1. CALIFORNIA INDIANS BEFORE 1846

1. For Owens Lake, see Reheis, "Dust Deposition," 25999. For San Francisco Bay, see California State Coastal Conservancy et al., *San Francisco Bay*, 12. For Tulare Lake, see ECORP Consulting, "Tulare Lake Basin Hydrology," 4.

2. Loud, "Ethnogeography and Archaeology," 232–233; Frank R. LaPena, "Wintu," in Heizer, *Handbook of North American Indians*, 8:325; Catherine S. Fowler and Sven Lindblad, "Northern Paiute," in D'Azevedo, *Handbook of North American Indians*, 11:439; Warren L. D'Azevedo, "Washoe," in D'Azevedo, *Handbook of North American Indians*, 11:477; Maurice L. Zigmond, "Kawaiisu," in D'Azevedo, *Handbook of North American Indians*, 11:404; Campbell Grant, "Island Chumash," in Heizer, *Handbook of North American Indians*, 8:526; Lowell John Bean, "Cahuilla," in Heizer, *Handbook of North American Indians*, 8:579; Albert B. Elsasser, "Basketry," in Heizer, *Handbook of North American Indians*, 8:626–641.

3. Scholars dispute the date when humans first appeared in California. In 2003, archaeologist Brian Fagan asserted that "We do not know exactly when the first human settlers entered California, but it was certainly before 11,200 B.C., possibly as much as a thousand years earlier." In 2012, archaeologist John M. Erlandson asserted, "We must now consider the possibility that the California coast was first settled by humans at least 15,000 years ago." The creation stories and oral traditions of some

California Indian tribes describe how they originated in and have always inhabited lands now within California. See Fagan, *Before California*, 22; John M. Erlandson, "A Land by the Sea: An Ocean View of California Archaeology," in Jones and Perry, *Contemporary Issues*, 31. For Quechan farming, see Forde, "Ethnography of the Yuma Indians," 109; Anderson, *Tending the Wild*. See also Lewis, *Patterns of Indian Burning*, and Lowell John Bean and Harry Lawton, "Some Explanations for the Rise of Cultural Complexity in Native California with Comments on Proto-Agriculture and Agriculture," in Lewis, *Patterns of Indian Burning*, v–xlviii.

4. See, for example, Cronon, *Changes in the Land*.

5. Francis Drake, *World*, 79–80; Vizcaíno in Bolton, *Spanish Exploration*, 91–92.

6. Nettie Reuben, in Bright, "Karok Language," 287; T.R. Garth, "Atsugewi," in Heizer, *Handbook of North American Indians*, 8:243; D'Azevedo, "Washoe," 477; Kroeber, "Patwin and Their Neighbors," 279; Norman L. Wilson and Arlean H. Towne, "Nisenan," in Heizer, *Handbook of North American Indians*, 8:389; William J. Wallace, "Southern Valley Yokuts," in Heizer, *Handbook of North American Indians*, 8:450; DuBois, "Religion of the Luiseño Indians," 141.

7. For Konkow and Maidu, see Francis A. Riddell, "Maidu and Konkow," in Heizer, *Handbook of North American Indians*, 8:375; for Miwoks, see Richard Levy, "Eastern Miwok," in Heizer, *Handbook of North American Indians*, 8:405; for Lake Miwoks, see Catherine A. Callaghan, "Lake Miwok," in Heizer, *Handbook of North American Indians*, 8:266. For salting, drying, and smoking, see Callaghan, "Lake Miwok," 266, and Bright, "Karok Language," 182. For meat and bone meal, see Patti J. Johnson, "Patwin," in Heizer, *Handbook of North American Indians*, 8:355; Krober, "Handbook of the Indians of California," 294. For examples of buckskin and pelts for clothing, sinews for bows and bowstrings, feathers for regalia, and bones, horns, and hoofs for fashioning tools and making medicine, see Bright, "Karok Language," 184; LaPena, "Wintu," fig. 5, 330; Walter Goldschmidt, "Nomlaki," in Heizer, *Handbook of North American Indians*, 8:343, 344; Shirley Silver, "Shastan Peoples," in Heizer, *Handbook of North American Indians*, 8:217, Riddell, "Maidu and Konkow," 373–374.

8. For ovens and cooking, see Chester King, "Protohistoric and Historic Archaeology," in Heizer, *Handbook of North American Indians*, 8:66, and Anderson, *Tending the Wild*, 266–270. For more on acorns, pine nuts, and grass seeds, see Heizer and Elsasser, *Natural World of the California Indians*, 91–100, 82. For grasshoppers, see Young in Young and Murphey, "Out of the Past," 359. The Achumawi, for example, gathered "bear berries, buckthorn berries, chokecherries, currants, elderberries, gooseberries, Oregon grape, huckleberries, manzanita berries, plumb, skunk berries, salmonberries, and service berries" (D.L. Olmsted and Omer C. Stewart, "Achumawi," in Heizer, *Handbook of North American Indians*, 8:229). For Manzanita cider, see Heizer and Elsasser, *Natural World of the California Indians*, 105. For Sierra mint and other teas, see Riddell, "Maidu and Konkow," 374, and Anderson, *Tending the Wild*, 269. For granaries, see Anderson, *Tending the Wild*, 54.

9. William J. Wallace, "Hupa, Chilula, and Whilkut," in Heizer, *Handbook of North American Indians*, 8:165; Sam Bat'wī in Sapir, "Yana Texts," 72; Young and Murphey,

"Out of the Past," 359; Theodore Stern, "Klamath and Modoc," in Walker, *Handbook of North American Indians*, 12:448–449, 452; Charles R. Smith, "Tubatulabal," in Heizer, *Handbook of North American Indians*, 8:444.

10. Drucker, "Tolowa," 234, 236–237; Isabell Kelly, "Coast Miwok," in Heizer, *Handbook of North American Indians*, 8:416; Campbell Grant, "Eastern Coastal Chumash," in Heizer, *Handbook of North American Indians*, 8:515, 517. For mollusks, see Heizer and Elsasser, *Natural World of the California Indians*, 82. For examples of drying, smoking, and salting, see Bright, "Karok Language," 291, 374; Wallace, "Hupa, Chilula, and Whilkut," 165, and Roberta S. Greenwood, "Obispeño and Purisimeño Chumash," in Heizer, *Handbook of North American Indians*, 8:522. For examples of tribes that ground salmon bones, see Kroeber, "Handbook of the Indians of California," 294.

11. Margolin, *Way We Lived*, 6.

12. The number of precontact North American indigenous languages is disputed. In 1997, linguists Shirley Silver and Wick R. Miller estimated "about 250 in Canada and the United States." In 1999, linguist Marianne Mithun wrote that "nearly 300 distinct, mutually unintelligible languages are known to have been spoken north of the Rio Grande before the arrival of Europeans. Many more have disappeared with little trace. . . . While the languages of Europe are classified into just three families, Indo-European, Finno-Ugric, and Basque, those of North America constitute over 50." See Silver and Miller, *American Indian Languages*, 7; Mithun, *Languages of Native North America*, 1. The number of precontact California Indian languages and language families is also disputed. For example, in 1978 linguist William F. Shipley estimated sixty-four to eighty languages divided into six families, in 1994 linguist Leanne Hinton estimated over 100 languages from at least five families, and in 2011 anthropologist Victor Golla estimated seventy-eight languages and at least five families in an area that extended somewhat beyond California. See William F. Shipley, "Native Languages of California," in Heizer, *Handbook of North American Indians*, 8:80; Hinton, *Flutes of Fire*, 13; Golla, *California Indian Languages*, 1, 2. For quotation ("as mutually . . . "), see Margolin, *Way We Lived*, 2.

13. Sally McLendon and Robert L. Oswalt, "Pomo: Introduction," in Heizer, *Handbook of North American Indians*, 8:276; Jerald Jay Johnson, "Yana," in Heizer, *Handbook of North American Indians*, 8:361; Kroeber, "Nature of Land-Holding Groups," 39.

14. For an overview of trade, see Sample, "Trade and Trails in Aboriginal California." Trade is also covered extensively in Heizer, *Handbook of North American Indians*, 8.

15. Powers, "California Indian Characteristics," 302; Heizer and Elsasser, *Natural World of the California Indians*, 25.

16. For a history of California before contact with Europeans, see Fagan, *Before California*.

17. "The Voyage of Juan Cabrillo," in Wagner, *Spanish Voyages*, 93.

18. Weber, *Spanish Frontier*, 238–241; Fray Junípero Serra to General Don Teodoro de Croix, April 28, 1782, in Serra, *Writings*, 4:127; Monroy, *Thrown among Strangers*, 44–45.

19. Hackel, *Children of Coyote*, 65.

20. According to Hackel, "Children below age nine they baptized without hesitation, but Indians nine and older had to demonstrate a basic comprehension of Catholicism

beforehand. Typically, pre-baptismal instruction took months, if not years. In later decades, once Serra was gone [in 1784], it would last only weeks" (Hackel, *Junípero Serra*, 199, 236). For quotation, see Palóu, *Historical Memoirs*, 3:50.

21. Cook argued that "the entrance of the military into the active field of proselytizing ended the era of true voluntary conversion . . . during the decade 1790–1800," in "Conflict, I," 74. Scholar Richard Steven Street asserted that Franciscans employed coercion and consent to obtain California Indian workers (*Beasts of the Field*, 23–25). Historian James Sandos asserted: "There was . . . no forced recruitment of gentiles for missionization" (Sandos, *Converting California*, 103). Hackel observed that in Spanish California, "Indian labor took numerous forms and stages between freedom and unfreedom" (Hackel, *Children of Coyote*, 295). De Neve, in Beilharz, *Felipe De Neve*, 52; Asisara, in Mora-Torres, *Californio Voices*, 95; Rogers, Journal, December 2, 1826.

22. Cook, "Conflict, I," 95; Archibald, "Indian Labor," 181; Rupert Costo and Jeannette Costo, "Bigotry in Academia Malevolent and Benign," in Costo and Costo, *Missions of California*, 187; Sánchez, *Telling Identities*, 55; Sandos, *Converting California*, 110; Hackel, *Children of Coyote*, 281.

23. Sandos, *Converting California*, 49–50; Fray Junípero Serra to Fernando Rivera y Moncada, July 31, 1775, in Serra, *Writings*, 4:425, and Fray Junípero Serra to Colonel and Governor Don Felipe de Neve, January 7, 1780, in Serra, *Writings*, 3:413.

24. Fr. Antonio de la Concepcíon [Horra] to Viceroy, July 12, 1798, in Beebe and Senkewicz, *Lands of Promise*, 272; De Borica, in Beebe and Senkewicz, *Lands of Promise*, 270; Viceroy, in Beebe and Senkewicz, *Lands of Promise*, 271.

25. César, "Recollections of My Youth," 42; Asisara, in Harrison, *History of Santa Cruz*, 46, 47. Historian Lisbeth Haas has pointed out that "the humiliation of being whipped, the fear created by the whipping, its treatment as a public spectacle, and the viewers' responses to their leadership and loved ones being physically hurt to the point of potential death emphasize the violent and traumatic circumstances ever possible at the mission" (Haas, *Saints and Citizens*, 81).

26. Hackel, *Children of Coyote*, 363.

27. Jayme, *Letter of Luís Jayme*, 40, 44–48, 38; Junípero Serra to Antonio Maria de Bucareli y Ursua, May 21, 1773, in Serra, *Writings*, 1:363. Historian James Sandos concluded that, among Spanish soldiers in California, "sexual abuse of Indian women, including rape, became a serious problem" (Sandos, *Converting California*, 7).

28. Hackel, *Children of Coyote*, 226; Ortega, in Antonia I. Castañeda, "Sexual Violence in the Politics and Policies of Conquest: Amerindian Women and the Spanish Conquest of Alta California," in Heineman, *Sexual Violence*, 23; Serra to Bucareli, May 21, 1773, in Serra, *Writings*, 1:363; Woqoch, summarized by Fernando Librado, in Librado, Harrington, and Hudson, *Breath of the Sun*, 52–53.

29. Hackel, *Children of Coyote*, 226; Eulalia Callis, in Beebe and Senkewicz, *Lands of Promise*, 237; Hurtado, *Intimate Frontiers*, 27.

30. Hackel, *Children of Coyote*, 226.

31. Cook estimated 4,060 "based on 3,205 for 15 missions," in "Conflict, I," 61. For testimonies, see Bancroft, *Works*, 18:711n33. For nine additional testimonies and details on each of the twenty-three escapees, see Milliken, *Time of Little Choice*, 299–303. Historian

George Phillips observed that "fleeing from the missions became a collective expression of rebellion" (Phillips, *Indians and Intruders*, 82).

32. De Neve, in Milliken, *Ethnogeography and Ethnohistory*, 56; Piña, in Beebe and Senkewicz, *Lands of Promise*, 370–374.

33. Tápis, in Engelhardt, *Santa Barbara Mission*, 80–81; Pérouse, *Monterey in 1786*, 82; María Solares, summarized in Laird, *Encounter*, 18.

34. Tarakanoff, *Statement of My Captivity*, 14; Beechey, *Narrative of a Voyage*, 2:19. "The Black Legend," a British tradition of anti-Spanish propaganda also known as *La Leyenda Negra*, may have influenced Beechey's criticism.

35. For example, Pueblo Indians rose up against Franciscan missionaries and Hispanic colonists in 1680, driving them out of New Mexico. For San Diego, see Fray Vicente Fuster to Reverend Father President Fray Junípero Serra, November 28, 1775, in Serra, *Writings* 2:449–458. For San Luis Obispo, see Bancroft, *Works*, 18:298–299. For Purísima Concepción and San Pedro y San Pablo de Bicuner, see Bancroft, *Works*, 18:362–364, and Santiago, *Massacre at the Yuma Crossing*, 115.

36. Brown, "Pomponio's World"; Lieutenant Martinez, in Brown, "Pomponio's World," 14; Sandos, "Lavantamiento!" For Estanislao, see Juan Bojorges, in Cook, "Expeditions to the Interior," 166, Hurtado, *Indian Survival*, 43–44, and Sandos, *Converting California*, 170–172.

37. The 1821 Plan of Iguala, http://scholarship.rice.edu/jsp/xml/1911/20697/3/aa00005tr.tei .html; José María Echeandía, "Decreto de Emancipacion á favor de Neófitos, July 25, 1826," in Bancroft, *Works*, 20:102–103. For early petitions and "freedom" quotation, see Haas, *Saints and Citizens*, 141–147. For 1833 proclamation, see José Figueroa, "Prevenciones provisionales para la emancipacion de Indios reducidos," July 15, 1833, in Bancroft, *Works*, 20:328n50. For 1833 Mexican congressional secularization, see "Decreto del Congreso Mejicano secularizando los Misiones, 17 de Agosto de 1833," in Bancroft, *Works*, 20:336n61. For 1834, see, José Figueroa, "Reglamento Provisional para la secularizacion de las Misiones de la Alta California, 9 de Agosto, 1834," in Bancroft, *Works*, 20:342n4. Librado in Librado, Harrington, and Hudson, *Breath of the Sun*, 91; Portilla, in Engelhardt, *San Luis Rey Mission*, 96. For mission secularization in the 1830s and 1840s, see Jackson and Castillo, *Indians, Franciscans*, chap. 5, and Salomon, *Pío Pico*, chap. 4.

38. Hackel, *Junípero Serra*, 238.

39. Fray Junípero Serra to Reverend Father Guardian [Francisco Pangua] and Discretorium, August 31, 1774, in Serra, *Writings*, 2:167; Cook, "Conflict, I," 59, 16; Sherburne F. Cook, "Historical Demography," in Heizer, *Handbook of North American Indians*, 8:92.

40. Herman James, in Oswalt, "Kashaya Texts," 277.

41. Street, *Beasts of the Field*, 100; Forsyth, *History of the Peoples of Siberia*, 36–151; Slezkine, *Arctic Mirrors*, 11–45; Crowell, *Archaeology*, 12–53; Gibson, "Russia in California," 210, 211; Figueroa, in Street, *Beasts of the Field*, 100. For more on Fort Ross and surrounding Russian agriculture, see Gibson, *Imperial Russia*, 112–139, and Lightfoot, *Indians, Missionaries, and Merchants*.

42. Finkelman, "Law of Slavery," 438; Almaguer, *Racial Fault Lines*, 48; Hurtado, *Indian Survival*, 211; Edward Castillo, "The Impact of Euro-American Exploration and Set-

tlement," in Heizer, *Handbook of North American Indians*, 8:105; P.B. Reading to Philip P. Green, February 7, 1844, 3 in Reading Collection, CSL; Steger, "Chronology of the Life of Pierson Barton Reading," 365; Revere and Chief Hallowney, in Revere, *Tour of Duty*, 130, 134, 132. Historian George Phillips argued that "the secularization of the missions did not free the neophytes but placed them under different management" (Phillips, *Vineyards and Vaquero*, 165).

43. For a longer-term sense of how Mexican California's racial hierarchies built on Spanish legacies, see Weber, *Bárbaros*. Weber, *Mexican Frontier*, 211; Monroy, *Thrown among Strangers*, 100–103; Almaguer, *Racial Fault Lines*, 49–50.

44. Cook, "Epidemic of 1830–1833," 310. Cook cited primary-source evidence suggesting a substantial Central Valley Indian population. For more on this epidemic, see Ahrens, "John Work." Warner, in Gilbert, *History of San Joaquin*, 11–12. For additional primary-source accounts of the epidemic, see Cook, "Epidemic of 1830–1833," 316–319. Warner first reported the epidemic in *LAS*, August 29, 1874, 1. For death toll, see Cook, "Epidemic of 1830–1833," 322, and Cook, "Historical Demography," 92.

45. Historian Alfred W. Crosby coined the phrase "virgin soil epidemics," and defined them as "those in which the populations at risk have had no previous contact with the diseases that strike them and are therefore immunologically almost defenseless" (Crosby, "Virgin Soil Epidemics," 289). Tac, "Indian Life and Customs," 98. For more on Tac, see Haas and Luna, *Pablo Tac*.

46. For Miramontes Epidemic, see Cook, "Conflict, II," 17–18, and Cook, "Historical Demography," 92. For 1844 smallpox epidemic, see Cook, "Smallpox," 187–191; Hackel, *Children of Coyote*, 422; and Cook, "Conflict, II," 18. For death toll summary, see Cook, "Historical Demography," 92–93.

47. For 1826, which may have been massacres or battles, see Bancroft, *Works*, 20:109. For a report of forty-four killed in this expedition, see Bean and Mason, *Diaries and Accounts*, 84. For 1833, see Cook, "Conflict, II," 9, 54, 9. For 1837, see José Maria Amador, "Memorias sobre la Historia de California," in Cook, "Expeditions to the Interior," 197–198. For Clear Lake, see Davis, *Sixty Years in California*, 342; Sherman, "Sherman Was There [Part 3]," 49–51; Juan Bojorges, in Heizer, *Collected Documents*, 67–70. For Moth Island Massacre, see Salvador Vallejo to M.G. Vallejo, March 13, 1843, in Bancroft, *Works*, 21:362n28, and Bancroft, *Works*, 21:362–363; M.G. Vallejo to *comandante* of Sonoma, April 1, 1843, in Cook, "Conflict, II," 9. For Hallowney quotation, see Revere, *Tour of Duty*, 132.

48. Cook argued that, due to the epidemic, Indians "in the heart of California . . . could offer but the shadow of opposition to the gold-mining flood which swept over it in 1849" (Cook, "Epidemic of 1830–1833," 322). Ahrens later argued that the 1833 epidemic "contributed to the American colonial conquest of the region" ("John Work," 1).

49. For pigeons, see Mayfield, *Uncle Jeff's Story*, 41–42.

50. For pine nuts and Owens Valley Paiute-Shoshones, see Steward, "Basin-Plateau Aboriginal Groups," 50. For Yuroks and shellfish, see Arnold R. Pilling, "Yurok," in Heizer, *Handbook of North American Indians*, 8:137. For Southern Valley Yokuts' tule mat houses, see Wallace, "Southern Valley Yokuts," 450–451. For the wide distribution

of flutes among California Indians, see William J. Wallace, "Music and Musical Instruments," in Heizer, *Handbook of North American Indians*, 8:647.

CHAPTER 2. PRELUDE TO GENOCIDE

1. J.J. Abert, Col. Corps T.E. to Brevet Captain J.C. Frémont, February 12, 1845, in Jackson and Spence, *Expeditions of Frémont*, 1:396; John O'Sullivan, in *United States Magazine, and Democratic Review*, 17, no. 85 (July and August 1845), 5. On February 28, 1845, US congressmen voted to annex the Republic of Texas and on March 1, President John Tyler signed the bill, enraging Mexicans, most of whom considered Texas a rebellious province. See *Daily National Intelligencer*, March 1, 1845, 2–3. For Frémont's meeting with Polk, see Frémont, *Memoirs*, 418, 420.

2. For Frémont's 1843–1844 expedition, see Frémont, *Memoirs*, 169–410. Frémont recalled that "in arranging this expedition, the eventualities of war were taken into consideration" (Frémont, *Memoirs*, 422). Historian Joshua Paddison wrote: "Frémont's timing was not accidental; he knew that there was a growing resentment among newly emigrated Americans toward the Mexican government and hoped to encourage a revolt" (Paddison, *World Transformed*, 260). For Frémont's journey from the Arkansas River to California's Central Valley, see Frémont, *Memoirs*, 428–440. For Frémont's actions during this period, see Bancroft, *Works*, 22:chap. 1 and Harlow, *California Conquered*, 61–73. For final quotation, see Nevins, *Frémont*, 1:261.

3. Frémont, *Memoirs*, 473. Expedition member Thomas E. Breckenridge agreed with this date in Breckenridge, "Memoirs," Folder 3, 52. According to Harry L. Wells and W.L. Chambers, Frémont and his men stayed at Lassen's Ranch from March 30 to April 14, 1846 (Wells and Chambers, *History of Butte County*, 1:57). Carson, *Kit Carson's Own Story*, 69.

4. "Roster of the 1845–47 Expedition," in Jackson and Spence, *Expeditions of Frémont*, 2:487–488; Bancroft, *Works*, 22:7, 16; Martin, "Narrative," MSS C-D 122, 2–3; Breckenridge, "Memoirs," Folder 3, 24; Hanson, *Hawken Rifle*, 33. For volunteers, see Bancroft, *Works*, 22:7, 16; Wells and Chambers, *History of Butte County*, 1:57. For arrival timing, see Breckenridge, "Memoirs," Folder 4, 56. Giles, *Shasta County*, 200–201, 202n21. Giles's date contradicts Martin's recollection that after arriving at Lassen's he was gone "10 or 12 days" and then returned to join an expedition against local Indians. Martin's recollection placed the encounter perhaps four to seven days later (Martin, "Narrative," 13). Breckenridge wrote that the group "started north again on April 14th" ("Memoirs," Folder 3, 52).

5. Martin, "Narrative," 13. Martin's "tongue of land" probably existed during his 1846 visit. However, the Sacramento's channel moved to sever Bloody Island from the riverbank. See Steger and Jones, *Place Names*, 18. In 1949, Giles argued that the Indians were on an island (Giles, *Shasta County*, 200–201). In 1991, Dottie Smith agreed (*Dictionary of Early Shasta County*, 16). In 2000, David Roberts mistakenly located these events some fifty miles to the south, near present-day Vina (Roberts, *Newer World*, 152). Two twentieth-century local historians contend that these Indians were Yana people, but this location seems to have been west of Yana territory and well

inside Wintu territory (see Giles, *Shasta County*, 200–201, and Smith, *Dictionary of Early Shasta County*, 16). For foods, see Powers, "California Indians," 532–533, and Du Bois, "Wintu Ethnography," 9–21. In 1943, Cook estimated 2,950 Wintus but revised that number to 5,300 in 1976. In 1978, LaPena estimated 14,250, apparently misunderstanding Cook's combined estimate for Wintus, Wintuns, and Patwins as an estimate for Wintus alone. Cook, "Conflict, I," 180; Cook, *Population of California Indians*, 19; LaPena, "Wintu," in Heizer, *Handbook of North American Indians*, 8:325.

6. For political organization, see Du Bois, "Wintu Ethnography," 9–21, 24, 28–30. For trade, see Du Bois, "Wintu Ethnography," 24, and Powers, "California Indians," 533.

7. Carson, *Kit Carson's Own Story*, 69; Breckenridge, "Memoirs," Folder 4, 56; Martin, "Narrative," 13–14.

8. Tustin, "Recollections," MSS C-D 216, 4. Tustin located these events at Julien's Ranch. Other primary sources place them near Reading's Ranch.

9. Breckenridge, "Memoirs," Folder 4, 56; Tustin, "Recollections," 4; Sam Hawken, in Hanson, *Hawken Rifle*, 37. For harmless arrows, see Tustin, "Recollections," 4. Martin, "Narrative," 14; Breckenridge, "Memoirs," Folder 4, 56.

10. Tustin, "Recollections," 4; Wells and Chambers, *History of Butte County*, 1:57. Bancroft described the massacre as a "battle," in *Works*, 22:22.

11. Breckenridge, "Memoirs," Folder 4, 56; Martin, "Narrative," 14; Tustin, "Recollections," 4–5. Martin noted, "Some of the inds. escaped to the neighboring mts." (*With Frémont to California*, 7).

12. Frémont, *Memoirs*, 474; Tustin, "Recollections," 5.

13. Breckenridge, "Memoirs," Folder 4, 56, 57; Carson, *Kit Carson's Own Story*, 69–70.

14. Martin, *With Frémont to California*, 8. According to Breckenridge, expedition members received these orders after Indians attacked the expedition at Klamath Lake (Breckenridge, "Memoirs," Folder 4, 55).

15. For orders and retaliation, see Frémont, *Memoirs*, 488–491; Carson, *Kit Carson's Own Story*, 71; Breckenridge, "Memoirs," Folder 4, 54. The exact contents of the orders delivered to Frémont are unknown and remain a subject of speculation. For Frémont's determination to "square accounts" and subsequent attacks, see Frémont, *Memoirs*, 492–494, 495–497; Carson, *Kit Carson's Own Story*, 72–75. Because these killings took place well inside of Oregon and targeted Oregon Indians they do not appear in the online appendixes. On July 6, 1846, the United States annexed California. According to navy lieutenant Joseph Warren Revere, "On the seventh of July Commodore Sloat . . . hoisted the American flag at Monterey" (Revere, *Tour of Duty*, 77).

16. Kuper, *Genocide*, 10.

17. In 1846, California's non-Indian population was "about 10,000." See *Californian*, August 22, 1846, 1; Bryant, *What I Saw*, 286. The non-Indian population then increased to perhaps 13,000 or 14,000 prior to the gold rush.

18. Breckenridge, "Memoirs," Folder 4, 62.

19. Joseph, in Hurtado, *John Sutter*, 80; Bryant, *What I Saw*, 448; Murray, "Narrative," MSS C-D 132, 95; Buffum, *Six Months*, xv; Case, "Reminiscences of Wm. M. Case," 281.

20. Hastings, *Emigrants' Guide*, 132; Lienhard, *Pioneer at Sutter's Fort*, 68; Hurtado, *John Sutter*, 78; Chamberlain, "Memoirs," MSS C-D 57, 20; Sutter, "Reminiscences,"

MSS C-D 14, 45. Sutter recalled capturing Mission Indian slave raiders who had attacked American River Indians and when "fourteen confessed to the crime of murder . . . I ordered them shot" (Sutter, "Reminiscences," 45–46).

21. Frémont, *Geographical Memoir*, 38; Revere, *Tour of Duty*, 101; Farnham, *Life, Travels and Adventures*, 346; Bryant, *What I Saw*, 450, 446; Rufus B. Sage reported, "A single individual frequently owns from eight to ten thousand head of horses and mules; and, not rarely, even as high as fifteen or twenty thousand" (Sage, *Scenes in the Rocky Mountains*, 195). For California Indian *vaqueros*, or cowboys, see Bryant, *What I Saw*, 346, 424; Lienhard, *Pioneer at Sutter's Fort*, 59; Revere, *Tour of Duty*, 84, 144; Taylor, *Eldorado*, 1:129.

22. Frémont, *Geographical Memoir*, 22; Bryant, *What I Saw*, 241, 243, 244–245. For the number of Indians employed by Sutter, see M'Collum, *California As I Saw It*, 56; Colton, *Three Years in California*, 434; Wiggins, "Reminiscences," MSS C-D 175, 4; Hurtado, *Indian Survival*, 49. Buffum wrote that Sutter's "wheat-fields were very extensive, and his cattle soon numbered five thousand, the whole labour being performed by Indians" (Buffum, *Six Months*, 54).

23. *Californian*, July 10, 1847, 2; July 13, 1847, letter in *California Star*, July 24, 1847, 2.

24. Bryant, *What I Saw*, 321, 322, 338, 372, 371. Chester S. Lyman also reported on Thomas Larkin's "Indian cook" in Monterey in an August 1, 1847, journal entry (Lyman, *Around the Horn*, 223). For guides, see George M. Hayden, June 5, 1847, entry in Hayden Diaries, MSS C-F, 2:184, and Bryant, *What I Saw*, 242, 353. For loggers, see *California Star*, October 23, 1847, 3. For a ferryman in December 1847, see *California Star*, January 22, 1848, 3. For sailors, see Lienhard, *Pioneer at Sutter's Fort*, 38–39, 103.

25. Some of these men included Theodore Cordua, Henry Fitch, the Kelsey brothers, Thomas Larkin, Robert Livermore, Pierson Reading, Johann Sutter, Mariano and Salvador Vallejo, Charles Weber, and George C. Yount. For the size of Salvador Vallejo's estate, see Revere, *Tour of Duty*, 92. For the quotation, see Vallejo, "Notas históricas," MSS C-D 22, 46.

26. Hurtado, *Intimate Frontiers*, 40, 44; Cook, "Conflict, III," 77.

27. Hurtado, *Indian Survival*, 63–65; Lienhard, *Pioneer at Sutter's Fort*, 53–54, 61; Hurtado, *John Sutter*, 39; Yates, "Sketch of a Journey," MSS C-E 95, 6, 4–5; Lienhard, *Pioneer at Sutter's Fort*, 76, 75. On March 8, 1844, Frémont reported "a number of [Indian] girls at the fort, in training for a future woolen factory" (Frémont, *Report of the Exploring Expedition*, 246).

28. Case, "Notes By William M. Case," 169; Shaw, "Dictation," MSS C-D 334, 3; Bauer, "Statement," MSS C-D 40, 12; Lienhard, *Pioneer at Sutter's Fort*, 39, 53, 153; Ryan, *Personal Adventures*, 2:244, 240, 260.

29. Buffum, *Six Months*, 44, 45.

30. For rumors, see Bancroft, *Works*, 22:78–82. For the taking of Sonoma, see Revere, *Tour of Duty*, 63–64; Bancroft, *Works*, 22:145–146.

31. For prisoners, see Revere, *Tour of Duty*, 64; Bancroft, *Works*, 22:127, 121. For June 20, see Bancroft, *Works*, 22:170. For Sonoma and Sacramento, see J.C. Frémont to Hon. Thomas H. Benton, July 25, 1846, in Jackson and Jackson, *Expeditions of Frémont*, 2:183. For Bear Flaggers, see Harlow, *California Conquered*, 112–113; Bancroft, *Works*,

22:179, 184. For Fort Sutter, see Revere, *Tour of Duty*, 71; Schmölder, *Emigrant's Guide*, 45; Bancroft, *Works*, 22:244.

32. For Sutter Buttes, see Frémont, *Memoirs*, 517–518. For Indian recruits, see Jonathan Misroon to Edward Kern, August 8, 1846, in Kern, "Fort Sutter Collection," vol. 9, ms 27; Misroon to Kern, August 16, 1846, in Kern, "Fort Sutter Collection," vol. 9, ms 27; J.W. Revere, Lieut. U.S. Navy Commanding California Volunteers to Acting Capt. E.M. Kern Comdg garrison, September 16, 1846, in Kern, "Fort Sutter Collection," vol. 13, ms 42; Edward M. Kern Commanding Fort Sacramento, Requirements, October 14, 1846, in Kern, "Fort Sutter Collection," vol. 22, ms 84; Wiggins, "Reminiscences," 9; Lienhard, *Pioneer at Sutter's Fort*, 8; Sage, *Scenes in the Rocky Mountains*, 197; Sutter, "Reminiscences," 42; Hurtado, *John Sutter*, 76; Sutter, "Reminiscences," 75, 59; Wiggins, "Reminiscences of William Wiggins," 9; Hurtado in Lawrence and Lawrence, *Violent Encounters*, 110; Revere, *Tour of Duty*, 73; Hurtado, *John Sutter*, 198. For quotation, see Misroon to Kern, August 8, 1846.

33. For Joseph and Paul Revere, see Cavanaugh, *In Lights and Shadows*, 151. For quotation, see Revere, *Tour of Duty*, 70, 71. For enrollment and Frémont's appointment, see Bancroft, *Works*, 22:303; September 3, 1846, journal entry, in Bryant, *What I Saw*, 267. See also Pay Roll of Garrison at "Fort Sacramento" entered by Lieut. J.W. Revere U.S.N., in Kern, "Fort Sutter Collection," vol. 23, ms. 94.

34. Revere, *Tour of Duty*, 79, 81, 112, 137, 147, 152, 154; Colton, October 29, 1846, journal entry, in Colton, *Three Years in California*, 82.

35. Edw. M. Kern, Roll of the Men Composing Garrison at Fort Sacramento New Helvetia A[lta] C[alifornia] from Nov 9th 1846 to March 9th 1847, Mch 31, 1847, in Kern, "Fort Sutter Collection," vol. 23, ms 97; Bryant, *What I Saw*, 359, 365–366. Frémont also suggested that Delaware Indians were part of Company H in his *Memoirs*, 598.

36. Jacobs, "Muster Roll." For scouting, see Bryant, *What I Saw*, 388. For pickets and Natividad, see Frémont, *Memoirs*, 598, 594–595. For capitulation, see *Articles of Capitulation*, in Jackson and Spence, *Expeditions of Frémont*, 2:253. For discharge, see Pierson B. Reading, Paymaster, California Battalion to [illegible], January 27, 1847, Reading Collection, Box 286, Folder 14.

37. Bryant wrote, "Some of these are clothed in shirts and blankets, but a large portion of them are entirely naked" (*What I Saw*, 267).

38. James Clyman, "Diary," MSS C-E 116, 123; Bryant, September 3, 1846, journal entry, in Bryant, *What I Saw*, 268, 270. Both Wiggins, who visited Sutter in the 1840s, and Lienhard also remembered Sutter feeding his Indian employees from troughs. See Wiggins, "Reminiscences," 4 and Lienhard, *Pioneer at Sutter's Fort*, 68.

39. Bryant, *What I Saw*, 268.

40. *Californian*, September 15, 1847, 3. This cannibalism charge may have stemmed from the fact that a man named Fowler, one of the Vallejo's neighbors, had a ranch known as "Rancho Carne Humana," or "Human Flesh Ranch," in northern Napa Valley.

41. Colton, *Three Years in California*, 25; *Californian*, August 15, 1846, 1.

42. R.F. Stockton, Commander-in-Chief, and Governor of the Territory of California, "To the People of California," August 17, 1846, in Bryant, *What I Saw*, 299; *Californian*, August 22, 1846, 2; W.T. Sherman, A.A.A. Genl. to John Burton, Alcalde Pueblo de

San Jose, September 6, 1847, NARA, "Records of the 10th Military Department, 1846–51," Record Group 98, Microfilm Series M210, Reel 1:112 [hereafter RG98, M210]; *Californian*, September 26, 1846, 1.

43. Bancroft, *Works*, 22:432–433; Secretary of the Navy to Commodore Stockton, November 5, 1846, in Willey, *Transition Period*, 30; Bancroft, *Works*, 22:437; Johnson, *Fremont Court Martial*, 47, 51.

44. To the Commander of the U.S. Forces New Helvetia, February 28, 1847, in Kern, "Fort Sutter Collection," vol. 22, ms 82. For campaign, see *California Star*, March 20, 1847, 2; Midshipman Hoodworth, summarized in Jas A Hardee, 2 Lieut 3 Artillery, Maj. 7° Reg NY Vols. to General S.W. Kearney, Commanding, 10° Mil: Dep: Monterey, California, April 8, 1847, NARA, RG98, M210, Reel 2:n.p.; J.L. Fulsom, Capt. Asst. Qr. Mr. to Major Thos. [illegible], Div. Head, U.S.A., April 10, 1847, NARA, RG98, M210, Reel 2:n.p.; *California Star*, April 10, 1847, 2. Kern described launching three separate attacks, each at a different location, over two days, and convincing local Indians to stop stock raiding. Kern reported killing at least ten, but made no mention of a single, decisive engagement. See Edw. M. Kern Commg Sac. Dist. To Joseph B. Hull (Commanding Northern Department), March 30, 1847, in Kern, "Fort Sutter Collection," vol. 21, ms 83.

45. For Indian stock rustling in California, see Zappia, "Indigenous Borderlands." R.B. Mason Col. 1 Dragoons U.S.A. to alcaldes José Salazar and Henrique Ayala, April 10, 1847, in Archives of California, 63:330.

46. Bryant, *What I Saw*, 226. It is possible that the violence this chief referred to occurred in California under Mexican rule.

47. E.J. Babe, Magistrate of Nappa, Northern District of California to Lieut Harrison Comndg Military forces at Sonoma, March 17, 1847, NARA, RG98, M210, Reel 2:n.p. That same day, US marine lieutenant G.W. Harrison reported from Sonoma that whites had "stormed" an Indian "village and attempted to take some of them into servitude—were resisted and lost one of their number, not however without killing four of their opponents" (Geo Harrison to Capt. DuPont, March 17, 1847, NARA, RG98, M210, 2: Document 21); Jn. A. Sutter to Gen. S.W. Kearney, May 18, 1847, in Archives of California, 63:86; "gentleman residing at the fort," quoted in *California Star*, July 24, 1847, 2. J.A. Sutter, Sub-agent for the Indians on the Sacramento and San Joaquin rivers to R.B. Mason, Colonel 1st Dragoons, Governor, Commander-in-Chief of the land forces in California, July 12, 1847, S. Exec. Doc. 18, 31st Cong., 1st Sess., 1850, serial 557, 351.

48. Clark, summarized in Mansfield, *History of Butte County*, 189–190; Sutter to Mason, July 14, 1847, S. Exec. Doc. 18, 31st Cong., 1st Sess., 1850, serial 557, 351; Capt. Folsom, Assist. Qr.-Master to Gov. Mason, August 15, 1847, in Archives of California, 63:90; L.W. Boggs & M.G. Vallejo [acting as judges] to Gov Mason, October 30, 1847, in Archives of California, 63:124. Street argued that "military authorities never again made an effort to impede kidnapping" (*Beasts of the Field*, 110).

49. Lieut. William T. Sherman to Capt. Henry Naglee, September 9, 1847, NARA, RG98, 210, Reel 1:n.p. For burning and capturing, see Hayden, September 1847 journal entry in Hayden Diaries, vol. 2. For firing squad narrative and aftermath, see New York

volunteer, summarized in Ryan, *Personal Adventures*, 1:130–134; Wozencraft, "Indian Affairs," 1877, MSS C-D 204.

50. *California Star*, January 15, 1848, 3; Tinkham, *History of San Joaquin*, 51.

51. Pacific in *California Star*, February 26, 1848, 2; *Californian*, March 15, 1848, 2.

CHAPTER 3. GOLD, IMMIGRANTS, AND KILLERS FROM OREGON

1. *Californian*, March 15, 1848, 2; Bancroft, *Works*, 23:56.

2. Drawing on Hurtado's work, historian Jean O'Brien has asserted that the discovery was "the collective product of Indian and non-Indian labor" (O'Brien, "Indians and the California Gold Rush," in Sleeper-Smith, Barr, O'Brien, Shoemaker, and Stevens, eds., *Why You Can't Teach United States History without American Indians*, 106). For quotation, see *California Star*, June 10, 1848, 2. For geology, see Hill, *Geology*, 66.

3. Richard Levy, "Eastern Miwok," in Heizer, *Handbook of North American Indians*, 8:398–413; Norman L. Wilson and Arlean H. Towne, "Nisenan," in Heizer, *Handbook of North American Indians*, 8:387–397.

4. R.B. Mason, Colonel, 1st Dragoons, commanding to Brig. Gen. R. Jones, Adjutant General, U.S. Army, August 17, 1848, H. Exec. Doc. 1, 30th Cong., 2nd Sess., 1848, serial 514, 60; Colton, August 16, 1848, journal entry, in Colton, *Three Years in California*, 252; McIlhany, *Recollections of a '49er*, 39; Sutter, "Discovery of Gold," 197.

5. *Sacramento Transcript*, June 24, 1850, 2; Bidwell, "Dictation," 57.

6. *Californian*, August 14, 1848, 2; Grimshaw, "Narrative of life," MSS C-D 95, 45; Mason to Jones, August 17, 1848, 60.

7. Wilson and Towne, "Nisenan," 389–390; Levy, "Eastern Miwok," 402–403; Gerstäcker, *California Gold Mines*, 81.

8. Mason to Jones, August 17, 1848, 60; Buffum, *Six Months*, 92; James Clayman to *Friend Ross*, December 25, 1848, in *Daily Sentinel and Gazette*, July 4, 1849, 3; Johnson, *Experiences of a Forty-Niner*, 240. For more on California Indian gold miners see Rawls, "Gold Diggers," 28–45.

9. Findla, "Statement," MSS C-D 79, 5–6, 6; Thomas O. Larkin to Secretary of State James Buchanan, June 28, 1848, in Revere, *Tour of Duty*, 249; Colton, August 28, 1848, journal entry in Colton, *Three Years in California*, 253; W.T. Sherman, 1st Lieut. 3rd Art'y to Gen. Geo. Gibson, Com. Gen. Subs. Washington City, DC, August 5, 1848, in Sherman, *Letter*, 7.

10. For Sutter's employees, see June 30, 1848, letter in *Californian*, July 15, 1848, 3. The Reverend Samuel H. Willey encountered "Indian cooks" in Monterey, presumably in 1849 (Willey, "Personal Memoranda," MSS C-D 176, 92). In an April 1849 letter from San Francisco, J.D. Stephenson reported that "a woman servant, Indian or Chilean," earned "from $40 to $60; washing, $6 per dozen" (quoted in Wyman, *California Emigrant Letters*, 160). In 1849, Bayard Taylor encountered Indian "washerwomen" in San Francisco (*Eldorado*, 2:31). In 1849, E. Sandford Seymour declared, "In California such a thing as a white servant is unknown" (*Emigrant's Guide*, 44).

11. For non-Indian population estimates, see Bancroft, *Works*, 23:3, and Rohrbough, *Days of Gold*, 8.

12. *Californian*, September 16, 1848, 2. Bancroft, *Works*, 23:167. For November and December 1848 population estimates, see *DAC*, November 29, 1849, 2. William Gwin, John Frémont, George Wright, and Edward Gilbert, "Memorial. To the Honorable Senate and House of the Representatives of the United States of America in Congress assembled," March 12, 1850, in Browne, *Report of the Debates*, Appendix, 23.

13. Bancroft, *Works*, 30:43; W.T. Sherman to E.O.C. Ord, October 28, 1848, in Sherman, *California Gold Fields*, n.p.; Correspondent, in *California Star & Californian*, December 2, 1848, 3; *California Star & Californian*, December 2, 1848, 2; Burnett, "Recollections," MSS P-A 12, 325.

14. Addis, "Whitman Masssacre," 221–258. See also Jeffrey, *Converting the West*, 205–222. Yellow Bull, in Curtis, *North American Indian*, 8:81. For dissatisfaction with pay, see Hurtado, *Indian Survival*, 84.

15. Bancroft, *Works*, 29:686; Victor, *Early Indian Wars*, 169, 179, 222.

16. *DAC*, May 30, 1850, 2; Ross, "Narrative," MSS P-A 63, 10–11.

17. Juan Bernal, "Memoria," in Cook, "Expeditions to the Interior," 194–195; Grover, in Johnson, *Sights in the Gold Region*, 186; Green, "Life and Adventures," MSS C-D 94, 12, 17.

18. *California Star & Californian*, November 18, 1848, 2; Grimshaw, "Narrative of life," 46.

19. *DAC*, May 30, 1850, 2; Green, "Life and Adventures," 17.

20. *Daily National Intelligencer*, December 6, 1848, 2.

21. For early 1849 non-Indian population estimates, see *DAC*, November 29, 1849, 2, and Gwin, Fremont, Wright, and Gilbert, "Memorial," in Browne, *Report of the Debates*, Appendix, 23. For end of June estimates, see *DAC*, July 2, 1849, 2, and Gwin, Fremont, Wright, and Gilbert, "Memorial," in Browne, *Report of the Debates*, Appendix, 23. Bancroft estimated that "the number of white inhabitants at the close of 1849 [was] not over 100,000," concluding that it "approached 95,000" (*Works*, 23:159). Arthur H. Clark asserted that in 1849, 91,405 passengers disembarked in San Francisco (*Clipper Ship Era*, 101). M'Collum, *California As I Saw It*, 34. For quotation, see de Massey, "Frenchman in the Gold Rush [Part 1]," 7.

22. For the supposed Indian peril in books, see Stillson, *Spreading the Word*, 6. *New York Herald*, December 1, 1846, 2; St. Louis journalist, quoted in *DAC*, August 23, 1849, 6.

23. Unruh, *Plains Across*, 185, 408.

24. Ibid., 229; Pawnee, May 15, 1849, in *Missouri Republican*, June 4, 1849, 2; Potter in Geiger and Bryarly, *Trail to California*, 27. Stillson interpreted the groups' firearms as indicating "an unusually great fear of Indians" (*Spreading the Word*, 75). For $6 million, see Marks, *Precious Dust*, 250.

25. Woods, *Sixteen Months*, 21, 26; M'Collum, *California As I Saw It*, 6; Gerstäcker, *Gerstäcker's Travels*, 146, 155; Ananias Pond, December 5, 1849, entry, in Pond, Journal 1.

26. Cassin, "Cassin's Few Facts," MSS C-D 55, 1; Kane, "Statement," MSS C-D 208, 1; Sedgley, *Overland to California*, 4–5.

27. Report of the Secretary of the Interior, T. Ewing to The President of the United States, December 3, 1849, in CG, December 3, 1849, 23; Downie, *Hunting for Gold*, 21.

28. *Placer Times*, July 14, 1849, 2 (page 2 is also dated July 20, 1849); J.P. Taylor to brother, November 21, 1849, in *Statesman*, February 15, 1850, 3; M'Collum, *California As I Saw It*, 56, 58; McIlhany, *Recollections of a '49er*, 34–35.

29. Sayward, "Pioneer Reminiscences," MSS C-D 197, 5, 7–8; Letts, *California Illustrated*, 112 (Letts seems to have been working near Mormon Bar at the time); Tyson, *Diary of a Physician*, 63.

30. Perry, *Travels, Scenes and Sufferings*, 89.

31. Pond, September 8, 1849, entry, Pond Journal 1; Lienhard, *Pioneer at Sutter's Fort*, 182.

32. On November 8, 1849, Colton estimated "some fifty thousand persons . . . drifting up and down these slopes of the great Sierra . . . in quest of gold" (Colton, *Three Years in California*, 314). Gerstäcker estimated about "70,000 men working . . . at the diggings" by the "autumn of 1849" (*Gerstäcker's Travels*, 141).

33. *DAC*, January 18, 1849, 2.

34. *Sacramento Transcript*, June 24, 1850, 2.

35. Coronel, *Tales of Mexican California*, 62.

36. Sutter, summarized in Johnson, *Sights in the Gold Region*, 140; Lienhard, *Pioneer at Sutter's Fort*, 186.

37. Konnock, in Lienhard, *Pioneer at Sutter's Fort*, 186; Sutter, summarized in Johnson, *Sights in the Gold Region*, 140. For a brief survey of state-sponsored scalp bounties beginning in colonial times, see Madley, "Reexamining the American Genocide Debate," 114–117.

38. For April 12, see Johnson, *Sights in the Gold Region*, 152. For rapes and initial murders, see Bancroft, *Works*, 23:100–101, fn.24. For the Murderer's Bar killing, see Johnson, *Sights in the Gold Region*, 170; *Placer Times*, May 5, 1849, 1; E. Gould Buffet, June 20, 1849, in Wyman, *California Emigrant Letters*, 141–142. According to William M. Case, "Six Columbia River men were killed on the eleventh day of April, 1849, about thirteen miles from Coloma, on the North Fork of the American River" ("Notes by William M. Case," 169). Beals, "Ethnology of the Nisenan," 364. For the killing of two men upstream, see E.G.B., letter in *DAC*, May 10, 1849, 2. The *Placer Times* (May 5, 1849, 1) agreed that after five miners were killed, others were attacked "on the Middle Fork of the American." These two events are conflated as one killing of seven men in Ryan, *Personal Adventures*, 2:299–301.

39. Delavan, *Notes on California*, 46; Sutter, summarized in Johnson, *Sights in the Gold Region*, 140.

40. Johnson, *Sights in the Gold Region*, 157–158. The *Placer Times* (May 5, 1949, 1) reported this "party" killing only two Indians who had "attempted to escape."

41. Johnson, *Sights in the Gold Region*, 170–171; Case, "Reminiscences of Wm. M. Case," 285.

42. N.S. Bestor to W.T. Sherman, April 19, 1849, in Gay, *James W. Marshall*, 257; Johnson, *Sights in the Gold Region*, 171. The *Daily Alta California* (May 1, 1849, 2) reported that "twenty-five Oregonians went in pursuit of the Indians." E.G.B., letter in *DAC*, May 10, 1849, 2; Case, "Notes," 171. The *Daily Alta California* agreed that the killing occurred at "a large *rancheria* on Wever's [Weber's] creek" (*DAC*, May 1, 1849, 2). Case recollected that the killing happened "about twenty miles from Coloma" ("Notes,"

171). For death toll and prisoner numbers, see Ross, "Narrative," 15; *DAC*, May 1, 1849, 2; E.G.B. letter in *DAC*, May 10, 1849, 2; Johnson, *Sights in the Gold Region*, 180, 181; Case, "Notes," 171; Ryan, *Personal Adventures*, 2:300–301; Ross recollected only fifteen captives, all men ("Narrative," 15).

43. Johnson, *Sights in the Gold Region*, 179, 180.

44. Ibid., 181.

45. *DAC*, May 1, 1849, 2; E.G.B. letter, in *DAC*, May 10, 1849, 2; Johnson, *Sights in the Gold Region*, 181–182; Ross, "Narrative," 15–16. According to William M. Case and Fannie Clayton—both of whom were in Coloma at the time—Indian women survivors of the Weber's Creek Massacre identified the prisoners as the murderers of Oregonians. See Case, "Notes," 171, and Clayton, "Mrs. Fannie Clayton's Account," 183. For April 19 killing, see Grant, summarized in Johnson, *Sights in the Gold Region*, 182; *DAC*, May 1, 1849, 2; E.G.B. letter in *DAC*, May 10, 1849, 2; Henshaw, "Statement," MSS C-D 100, 1; Case, "Notes," 173; Clayton, paraphrased in Clayton, "Mrs. Fannie Clayton's Account," 183; Ross, "Narrative," 17; Johnson, *Sights in the Gold Region*, 182; Ryan, *Personal Adventures*, 2:301.

46. Case, "Notes," 173–174; Ross, "Narrative," 17; Case, "Reminiscences of Wm. M. Case," 287. For Ross quotation, see Ross, "Narrative," 17. For final Case quotation, see Case, "Reminiscences of Wm. M. Case," 287 (see also Case, "Notes," 174). Delavan, *Notes on California*, 46.

47. Case, "Notes," 175.

48. M'Collum, *California As I Saw It*, 51; Grimshaw, "Narrative of life," 46–47.

49. Case, "Reminiscences of Wm. M. Case," 288; Hurtado, *John Sutter*, 253; Case, "Notes," 178–179. For more on Free Labor ideology and its variations, see Foner, *Free Soil*.

50. *Placer Times*, May 5, 1849, 1, 2; Wm. Daylor letter in *Placer Times*, May 12, 1849, 1.

51. Daylor letter in *Placer Times*, May 12, 1849, 1; *Placer Times*, May 5, 1849, 1.

52. *Placer Times*, May 5, 1849, 1; *DAC*, May 1, 1849, 2; Chester S. Lyman, May 4, 1849, journal entry in Lyman, *Around the Horn*, 293.

53. *DAC*, May 1, 1849, 2; *Placer Times*, June 30, 1849, 2 (also dated July 9, 1849); *Placer Times*, July 21, 1849, 2 (also dated July 25, 1849); Pfaelzer, *Driven Out*.

54. M'Collum, *California As I Saw It*, 51–52. For first Shaw quotation, rainy season, attack, and second Shaw quotation, see Shaw, *Golden Dreams*, 102, 89, 108.

55. Shaw, *Golden Dreams*, 109–111. Some of the villagers were spared.

56. Angel, *History of Placer County*, 357–359.

57. Connor, "Connor's Early California," MSS C-D 60, 3–4.

58. Ibid.

59. Kelly, *Excursion to California*, 2:142–148.

60. Augustin W. Hale, December 27, 1849, journal entry, in Hale, Diary 1, January 5, 1849–December 5, 1849, Box 6 (1); Augustin W. Hale, January 2, January 31, February 10, February 22, and February 23, 1850, journal entries, in Hale, Diary 4, Dec. 25, 1849–Apr. 18, 1850, Box 6 (4).

61. Deloria, *Indians in Unexpected Places*, 15–21.

62. William Perkins, February 1, 1850, journal entry, in Perkins, *El Campo de Los Sonoraenses*, MSS C-D 5179, 39, 41–42.

63. La Motte, "Statement," MSS C-D 44, 7, 8.

64. "California Blood Stain," 129, 131, 129; *Marysville Appeal*, May 12, 1861, 2.

65. Israel S.P. Lord, March 10, 1850, journal entry, in Lord, "*At the Extremity*," 220; T. Butler King, H. Exec. Doc. 59, 31st Cong., 1st Sess., 1850, serial 577, 7.

66. De Massey, "Frenchman in the Gold Rush [Part 2]," 154; Gihon, "Incident of the Gold Bluff," 649. Scholar Tony Platt thinks that these events could have taken place at Big Lagoon (personal communication with Platt, August 14, 2008).

67. *Sacramento Transcript*, April 5, 1850, 2; *Sacramento Transcript*, April 12, 1850, 2; Angel, *History of Placer County*, 359; A Yuba Miner to Messrs. Editors, April 14, 1850, in *Sacramento Transcript*, April 25, 1850, 2.

68. Geo. Woodman, paraphrased in *Sacramento Transcript*, May 4, 1850, 2; *Placer Times*, May 8, 1850, 3; *Sacramento Transcript*, May 9, 1850, 2.

69. *Sacramento Transcript*, May 9, 1850, 2.

70. H. Day, Capt. 2nd Inf. to Col. Winn, May 13, 1850, in *Sacramento Transcript*, May 30, 1850, 2; To Messrs. Editors, May 14, 1850, in *Sacramento Transcript*, May 23, 1850, 1; Day to Winn, May 13, 1850, in *Sacramento Transcript*, May 30, 1850, 2.

71. To Messrs. Editors, May 14, 1850, in *Sacramento Transcript*, May 23, 1850, 1; Mr. Sargent, in William S. Byrne, "Historical Sketch of Grass Valley," in Bean, *Bean's History and Directory*, 186–187. For report of mourning, see To Messrs. Editors, May 14, 1850, in *Sacramento Transcript*, May 23, 1850. 1. For Nisenan widows' mourning rituals, see Wilson and Towne, "Nisenan," 392–393.

72. *DAC*, March 11, 1850, 2.

CHAPTER 4. TURNING POINT

1. Based on interviews with Pomo informants, conducted between 1903 and 1906, anthropologist S.A. Barrett referred to the ranch both as "the Lupillomi rancho" and "Big Valley" ("Material Aspects of Pomo Culture," 408). Max Radin, "Introduction," in Benson, "Stone and Kelsey 'Massacre,'" 266, 268, 266.

2. Benson, "Stone and Kelsey 'Massacre,'" 269. Barrett presented a similar series of events in "Material Aspects of Pomo Culture," 408. L.L. Palmer described Augustine as "chief of the Hoolanapos" (*History of Napa*, 2:50).

3. Sally McLendon and Michael J. Lowy, "Eastern Pomo and Southeastern Pomo," in Heizer, *Handbook of North American Indians*, 8:306–323.

4. Sally McLendon and Robert L. Oswalt, "Pomo: Introduction," in Heizer, *Handbook of North American Indians*, 8:274–276; Sally McLendon and Michael J. Lowy, "Eastern Pomo and Southeastern Pomo," in Heizer, *Handbook of North American Indians*, 8:283; Heizer and Elsasser, *Natural World*, 86; Jesse O. Sawyer, "Wappo," in Heizer, *Handbook of North American Indians*, 8:256–263.

5. Menefee, *Historical and Descriptive Sketch*, 229; Sherman, "Sherman Was There [Part 3]," 57–58; Bancroft, *Works*, 22:110n21; Hanrahan, *Historical Napa Valley*, 91–92; Palmer, *History of Napa*, 2:45.

6. Palmer, *History of Napa*, 2:50; Benson, "Stone and Kelsey 'Massacre,'" 269; Palmer, *History of Napa*, 2:34; Augustine, in Palmer, *History of Napa*, 2:58.

7. Fogel and Engerman, *Time on the Cross*, fig. 18, 76; Fogel, *Without Consent*, 69–71; Phillips, *Life and Labor*, 177. The internal US trade in African American slaves flourished during this period.

8. Davis, *Inhuman Bondage*, 194.

9. Thomas Knight, "Statement of Early Events," MSS C-D 110, 15; Palmer, *History of Napa*, 2:50; Benson, "Stone and Kelsey 'Massacre,'" 268, 269.

10. Augustine, in Palmer, *History of Napa*, 2:59; Knight, "Statement of Early Events," 15–16; Barrett, "Material Aspects of Pomo Culture," 408; Benson, "Stone and Kelsey 'Massacre,'" 268–269; Palmer, *History of Napa*, 2:56; Benson, "Stone and Kelsey 'Massacre,'" 268.

11. Yount, *Chronicles of the West*, 218; Benson, "Stone and Kelsey 'Massacre,'" 269; Palmer, *History of Napa*, 2:56.

12. Benson, "Stone and Kelsey 'Massacre,'" 268; Knight, "Statement of Early Events," 16; Yount, *Chronicles of the West*, 217.

13. For the numbers and identities of those taken by Kelsey and where he took them, see Augustine and Palmer, in Palmer, *History of Napa*, 2:54, 59; Cook, "Conflict, III," 57; Kaplan et al., *Sheemi Ke Janu*, 76; Justice of the Peace Peter Campbell, Sonoma, California to U.S. Commissioner of Indian Affairs, Orlando Brown, June 1, 1851, NARA, RG75, M234, Reel 32:C672, 3. For the selling off of supplies, see Palmer, *History of Napa*, 2:55. For Barrett quotation, see Barrett, "Material Aspects of Pomo Culture," 408. For Augustine quotations, see Augustine, in Palmer, *History of Napa*, 2:59. For malaria outbreak, see Palmer, *History of Napa*, 2:55. For death toll estimates, see Knight, "Statement of Early Events," 16; Palmer, *History of Napa*, 2:55; Cook, "Conflict, III," 57n74.

14. Augustine, in Palmer, *History of Napa*, 2:60; Palmer, *History of Napa*, 2:59–60.

15. Barrett, "Material Aspects of Pomo Culture," 409; Benson, "Stone and Kelsey 'Massacre,'" 269–270.

16. Three sources locate the ranch headquarters and killings near Kelseyville: Menefee, *Historical and Descriptive Sketch*, 229; Augustine, in Palmer, *History of Napa*, 2:59; Barrett, "Material Aspects of Pomo Culture," 408. Augustine, summarized in Palmer, *History of Napa*, 2:60. According to the *Daily Alta California*, Andrew Kelsey "was killed . . . by a party of Indians, for cruelty to one of their tribe." Campbell added that the killings were meant to avenge Benjamin Kelsey's murder of an Indian man in Sonoma "about January 1850" (this almost certainly took place in 1849). Yount claimed that Indians killed Stone and Kelsey because the two had "seize[d] & imprison[ed] the principal Chief of the nation & [kept] him in chains." John McKee, who visited the Clear Lake region in 1851, suggested that Indians killed Stone and Kelsey for "their own impudence and cruelty to the Indians working for them." Knight argued that "in revenge" for the mining expedition deaths, "they murdered Andy Kelsey," and according to Benson's discussion with participants, "The starvation of the indians was the cause of the massacre of stone and Kelsey." *DAC*, September 13, 1850, 2; Campbell to Brown, June 1, 1851, 4; Yount, *Chronicles of the West*, 217–218; John McKee, S. Exec. Doc. 4, 33rd Cong., Special Senate Sess., 1853, serial 688, 142; Knight, "Statement of Early Events," 16; Benson, "Stone and Kelsey 'Massacre,'" 269.

17. Anthropologist Robert F. Heizer's 1973 *Collected Documents on the Causes and Events in the Bloody Island Massacre of 1850* provided an important introduction to the Stone and Kelsey killings and their aftermath. Using a variety of new sources, this chapter builds on Heizer's pathbreaking work to better understand the Stone and Kelsey killings and their aftermath.

18. Barrett, "Material Aspects of Pomo Culture," 409; Benson, "Stone and Kelsey 'Massacre,'" 270; Augustine, in Palmer, *History of Napa*, 2:60; Yount, *Chronicles of the West*, 218.

19. Benson, "Stone and Kelsey 'Massacre,'" 270; Augustine, in Palmer, *History of Napa*, 2:50, 61; Benson, "Stone and Kelsey 'Massacre,'" 270. Benson's description of these events roughly parallels Barrett's, in "Material Aspects of Pomo Culture," 409.

20. Barrett, "Material Aspects of Pomo Culture," 409; Benson, "Stone and Kelsey 'Massacre,'" 270–271; Barrett, "Material Aspects of Pomo Culture," 409. See also Augustine, in Palmer, *History of Napa*, 2:61. Augustine recollected that once Kelsey crossed the creek "an old Indian caught him there and struck him on the head with a stone and killed him" (quoted in Palmer, *History of Napa*, 2:61). First Lieutenant J.W. Davidson recovered Kelsey's body and reported: "Mr. Kelsey . . . was killed with five wounds, two of arrow wounds" (J.W. Davidson, 1st Lieut. 1st Dragoons, Commanding to Major E.R.S. Canby, Asst. Adj. Gen. Monterey, Cal., January 6, 1850, S. Exec. Doc. 52, 31st Cong., 1st Sess., 1850, serial 561, 65).

21. Augustine, in Palmer, *History of Napa*, 2:60; Benson, "Stone and Kelsey 'Massacre,'" 271; Augustine, in Palmer, *History of Napa*, 2:61.

22. Altschule, "Exploring the Coast Range," 321; Herr, *Story of the U.S. Cavalry*, 24, 28, 41, 24, 25; Butterworth, *Soldiers on Horseback*, 58.

23. Cullum, *Biographical Register*, 2:231; Davidson to Canby, January 6, 1850, S. Exec. Doc. 52, 31st Cong., 1st Sess., 1850, serial 561, 64. See also Barrett, "Material Aspects of Pomo Culture," 409; Davidson to Canby, January 6, 1850, 66.

24. Suscol Intertribal Council website, http://www.suscolcouncil.org/NativeHistory .html; Heizer, "Archaeology of the Napa Region," 324; Sawyer, "Wappo," 261.

25. Nash, in Barrett, "Material Aspects of Pomo Culture," 409; Barrett, "Ethno-Geography," 269–270; Sawyer, "Wappo," 257; Nash, interviewed December 5, 1902, and in Barrett, "Material Aspects of Pomo Culture," 409–410; Sawyer, "Wappo," 259–260.

26. Wright, *Early Upper Napa Valley*, 14, 21.

27. Ibid., 21; Sawyer, "Wappo," 260. Wright's confusion over Davidson's point of departure was likely due to Benicia's being the US Army's main Northern California base in 1849 and 1850.

28. Davidson to Canby, January 6, 1850, 64–65.

29. Ibid., 65; McClendon and Oswalt, "Pomo," in Heizer, *Handbook of North American Indians*, 8:276.

30. Davidson to Canby, January 6, 1850, 65.

31. Smith, *War with Mexico*, 2:377; Persifer F. Smith, Bvt. Maj. Gen., Commanding the Dep. to Lieut. Col. W.G. Freeman, Asst. Adjt. General, January 12, 1850, S. Exec. Doc. 52, 31st Cong., 1st Sess., 1850, serial 561, 89; J. Hooker, Assistant Adjutant-General

[writing for General Persifor F. Smith] to Brev. Brig. Gen. Bennet Riley, Comdg. 10th Mil. Department, February 26, 1850, S. Exec. Doc. 52, 31st Cong., 1st Sess., 1850, serial 561, 84.

32. Hooker [writing for General Smith] to Riley, 83; *San Francisco Herald*, May 31, 1850, in *DAC*, June 1, 1850, 2.

33. Isabell Kelly, "Coast Miwok," in Heizer, *Handbook of North American Indians*, 8:415.

34. Sonoma correspondent, March 2, 1850, in *DAC*, March 11, 1850, 2; Sawyer, "Wappo," 257; Yount, *Chronicles of the West*, 221.

35. William H. Brewer to Edgar Brewer, November 17, 1861, in Brewer, *Up and Down California*, 225; J. Bennett in Cal. 1850, *People v. Smith, et al.*, 1 Cal. 9, 1850 WL; Sonoma correspondent, March 2, 1850, in *DAC*, March 11, 1850, 2; Yount, *Chronicles of the West*, 221.

36. Yount, *Chronicles of the West*, 221; Sonoma correspondent, March 2, 1850, in *DAC*, March 11, 1850, 2. For tribal territories, see McLendon and Oswalt, "Pomo," 278, and Kelly, "Coast Miwok," 415.

37. J.W.B, March 4, 1850, in *DAC*, March 16, 1850, 2; Menefee, *Historical and Descriptive Sketch*, 23; J.W.B, March 4, 1850, in *DAC*, March 16, 1850, 2.

38. Campbell to Brown, June 1, 1851, 4; Knight, "Statement of Early Events," 16; *DAC*, September 13, 1850, 2.

39. Woodward, *Life of Lyon*, 153; J.W.B, March 4, 1850, in *DAC*, March 16, 1850, 2.

40. Rockwell D. Hunt, "The Birth of the Commonwealth," in Shuck, *History of the Bench*, 42–44.

41. Yount, *Chronicles of the West*, 221.

42. J.W.B, March 4, 1850, in *DAC*, March 16, 1850, 2.

43. Yount, *Chronicles of the West*, 221; *DAC*, March 19, 1850, 2; Knight, "Statement of Early Events," 16; Major General Persifor F. Smith to the Editors, May 31, 1850, *San Francisco Herald*, June 1, 1850, in *DAC*, June 3, 1850, 2; Thos J Henley, Supt Indn. Affrs to Hon. J.W. Denver, Comr. Indn. Affairs, November 30, 1857, NARA, RG75, M234, Reel 35:1445–1447. See also Campbell to Brown, June 1, 1851, 4; Yount, *Chronicles of the West*, 221; Menefee, *Historical and Descriptive Sketch*, 23; Knight, "Statement of Early Events," 16.

44. J. Bennett in Cal. 1850, *People v. Smith, et al.*, 1 Cal. 9; Mooney, *Dictionary*, 6:365; Henley to Denver, November 30, 1857, 1445–1447.

45. Henley to Denver, November 30, 1857, 1445–1447; Veritas, September 10, 1850, in *DAC*, September 28, 1850, 2. Samuel Kelsey later returned to Sonoma and lived there openly (*DAC*, April 2, 1854, 2).

46. Kelly, "Coast Miwok," 421; Loeb, "Pomo Folkways," 289; Sawyer, "Wappo," 260; *DAC*, March 19, 1850, 2.

47. *DAC*, March 11, 1850, 2; *DAC*, March 13, 1850, 2.

48. Heitman, *Historical Register*, 2:400; *DAC*, May 28, 1850, 2. The *DAC* identified their informant as "Capt. J.B. Frisbie" (*DAC*, June 1, 1850, 2).

49. N. Lyon, Brevet Captain 2d Infantry, Commanding Expedition to Major E.R.S. Canby, Assistant Adjutant General, Monterey, California, Headquarters Tenth Military Department, May 22, 1850, S. Exec. Doc.1, Part 2, 31st Cong., 2nd Sess., 1850, serial 587,

81; George Gibbs, in Schoolcraft, *Archives of Aboriginal Knowledge*, 3:100; Woodward, *Life of Lyon*, 168, 170; Menefee, *Historical and Descriptive Sketch*, 229; Hanrahan, *Historical Napa Valley*, 96. McLendon and Lowy wrote, "The Southeastern Pomo and the Eastern Pomo of Big Valley seem to have largely been able to avoid the troops" ("Eastern Pomo and Southeastern Pomo," 319). Benson, "Stone and Kelsey 'Massacre,'" 271.

50. Cullum, *Biographical Register*, 2:75; Lyon to Canby, May 22, 1850, 81; Cullum, *Biographical Register*, 2:280; Lyon to Canby, May 22, 1850, 81; Gibbs, August 19, 1851, journal entry, in Schoolcraft, *Archives of Aboriginal Knowledge*, 3:109; Lyon to Canby, May 22, 1850, 82.

51. Persifer F. Smith, Brevet Major General, Commanding Division to Captain Irwin McDowell, Assistant Adjutant General, Headquarters of the Army, May 25, 1850, S. Exec. Doc.1, Part 2, 31st Cong., 2nd Sess., 1850, serial 587, 78.

52. Hooker [for Smith] to Riley, February 26, 1850, 83.

53. Augustine, in Palmer, *History of Napa*, 2:62; Lyon to Canby, May 22, 1850, 82.

54. Benson, "Stone and Kelsey 'Massacre,'" 271–272.

55. Lyon to Canby, May 22, 1850, 82; Smith to McDowell, May 25, 1850, 78; Augustine, in Palmer, *History of Napa*, 2:62; Benson, "Stone and Kelsey 'Massacre,'" 272. Artillery may have played a decisive role. Though Augustine emphasized that *"the cannon were not fired at all,"* Menefee wrote: "The cannon was brought into use, loaded with grape and canister, and at the first discharge produced the utmost dismay among the Indians . . . resistance was forgotten." Bancroft added that Lyon's "troops . . . first drove them from their concealment with a howitzer." Palmer asserted that "canister shots . . . went plowing madly through their numbers, strewing the ground with dead and dying." According to Hanrahan, "Captain [Lyon] ordered the artillery turned loose on the Indians." Menefee, Bancroft, Palmer, and Hanrahan may all have confused the use of artillery at an earlier engagement with this amphibious assault, but after bringing howitzers and an artillery officer all the way to Clear Lake would Lyon not have used them? Moreover, from the lakeshore the island would have been within a mountain howitzer's range. Augustine, in Palmer, *History of Napa*, 2:62; Menefee, *Historical and Descriptive Sketch*, 230; Bancroft, *Works*, 24:458; Palmer, *History of Napa*, 2:57; Hanrahan, *Historical Napa Valley*, 97.

56. Lyon to Canby, May 22, 1850, 82; Smith to McDowell, May 25, 1850, 78.

57. Frisbie, summarized and quoted in *DAC*, May 28, 1850, 2.

58. J.W. Davidson to the Editors, May 30, 1850, in *DAC*, June 8, 1850, 2; Smith to the Editors of the *San Francisco Herald*, May 31, 1850, in *San Francisco Herald*, June 1, 1850, in *DAC*, June 3, 1850, 2. For Frisbie's May 31 statement, see *DAC*, June 1, 1850, 2.

59. Benson, "Stone and Kelsey 'Massacre,'" 272.

60. *DAC*, June 27, 1850, 2; Lyon to Canby, May 22, 1850, 82; Palmer, *History of Napa*, 2:58.

61. Gibbs, August 11, 1851, journal entry, in Schoolcraft, *Archives of Aboriginal Knowledge*, 3:100.

62. McLendon and Lowy, "Eastern Pomo and Southeastern Pomo," 315; Benson, "Stone and Kelsey 'Massacre,'" 272.

63. McLendon and Lowy, "Eastern Pomo and Southeastern Pomo," 315; Lyon to Canby, May 22, 1850, 82; July 19, 1853, letter from Sonoma, in *DAC*, July 28, 1853, 1; Woodward, *Life of Lyon*, 171; Menefee, *Historical and Descriptive Sketch*, 230; Augustine, in Palmer, *History of Napa*, 2:62; Merriam, in Heizer, *Collected Documents*, 46; Hanrahan, *Historical Napa Valley*, 97.

64. Sherman, "Sherman Was There [Part 3]," 54; Allen B. Sherman, introduction, in Sherman, "Sherman Was There [Part 1]," 259; Sherman, "Sherman Was There [Part 3]," 54; Jensen, "Big Foot's Followers," 198; Ostler, *Plains Sioux*, 345; Underhill, *Nevves from America*, 39; Mason, *Brief History*, 10; Cave, *Pequot War*, 151; Captain Velasco to the Viceroy, March 22, 1601, and Alonso Sanchez to Rodrigo del Rio, February 28, 1599, in Hammond and Rey, *Don Juan de Oñate*, 2:614–615, 1:427.

65. Lyon to Canby, May 22, 1850, 82 (see also Menefee, *Historical and Descriptive Sketch*, 230); Carpenter and Millberry, *History of Mendocino*, 129. The 1942 marker describes a "battle," and the 2005 marker notes that "dragoons . . . massacred nearly the entire Native population of the island."

66. Lyon to Canby, May 11, 1850, 82; Barrett, "Material Aspects of Pomo Culture," 410; Barrett, "Ethno-Geography," 189; McLendon and Lowy, "Eastern Pomo and Southeastern Pomo," 319; Sydney J. Jones, "Pomo," in Malinowski and Sheets, *Gale Encyclopedia*, 152.

67. Gibbs, August 23, 1851, journal entry, in Schoolcraft, *Archives of Aboriginal Knowledge*, 3:113–114; Benson, "Stone and Kelsey 'Massacre,'" 272.

68. Lyon to Canby, May 22, 1850, 82.

69. Ibid.; McLendon and Oswalt, "Pomo," 282; Barrett, "Ethno-Geography," 176; Lyon to Canby, May 22, 1850, 82. According to Barrett, Cokadjal was located on a pond ("Ethno-Geography," 176).

70. Smith to McDowell, May 25, 1850, 79; Woodward, *Life of Lyon*, 172; Benson, "Stone and Kelsey 'Massacre,'" 272. Barrett wrote that "Captain Lyons told the interpreter to tell the Indians to come out and meet for a parley," but that "none came [and] thereupon the soldiers fired into the houses" ("Material Aspects of Pomo Culture," 411). This is inconsistent with Smith's, Woodward's, and Benson's narratives. Had Lyon offered parley, he would have been directly disobeying Smith's orders.

71. Lyon to Canby, May 22, 1850, 82; Smith to McDowell, May 25, 1850, 79; Augustine, in Palmer, *History of Napa*, 2:62. There appears to be no conclusive evidence as to whether or not the soldiers used artillery in this attack.

72. Barrett, "Material Aspects of Pomo Culture," 411; Lyon to Canby, May 22, 1850, 82; Benson, "Stone and Kelsey 'Massacre,'" 272–273.

73. Benson, "Stone and Kelsey 'Massacre,'" 272; Alcantara, summarized in Kaplan et al., *Sheemi Ke Janu*, 79.

74. Lyon to Canby, May 22, 1850, 82; Augustine, in Palmer, *History of Napa*, 2:62; "Indians who escaped" in Barrett, "Ethno-Geography," 176; Barrett, "Material Aspects of Pomo Culture," 412; Lyon to Canby, May 22, 1850, 82. See also Woodward, *Life of Lyon*, 173.

75. Lyon to Canby, May 22, 1850, 82; Elliot, in Kaplan et al., *Sheemi Ke Janu*, 80.

76. Revere, *Tour of Duty*, 140; Altschule, "Exploring the Coast Range," 312, 322. It is possible that this was a description of the Cokadjal Massacre.

77. Altschule, "Exploring the Coast Range," 322, 323. For cremation, see Loeb, "Pomo Folkways," 286.
78. Altschule, "Exploring the Coast Range," 322.
79. Ibid., 323.
80. Benson, "Stone and Kelsey 'Massacre,'" 273.
81. Barrett, "Material Aspects of Pomo Culture," 412; Lyon to Canby, May 22, 1850, 83; Bancroft, *Works*, 24:458n; *DAC*, August 26, 1850, 2; Lyon to Canby, May 22, 1850, 83; Barrett, "Material Aspects of Pomo Culture," 412.
82. Lyon's report arrived on July 9 and Smith's on July 17. The government published and distributed both reports as Senate Executive Documents in December 1850. See Lyon to Canby, May 22, 1850, 83, and Smith to McDowell, May 25, 1850, 81.
83. Bancroft, *Works*, 24:211.
84. *DAC*, May 27, 1850, 2; *DAC*, June 8, 1850, 2; *San Francisco Herald*, May 31, 1850, in *Stockton Times*, June 8, 1850, 4.
85. San Francisco *Watchman*, June 1850, in *DAC*, June 3, 1850, 2.
86. *San Francisco Herald*, May 31, 1850, in *DAC*, June 1, 1850, 2; *Daily Picayune*, July 3, 1850, 1; *New York Herald*, July 8, 1850, 1; *Daily National Intelligencer*, July 10, 1850, 4; *DAC*, December 10, 1850, 2; *New York Herald*, July 8, 1850, 1.
87. John Winthrop, June 15, 1637, journal entry, in Winthrop, *Winthrop's Journal*, 1:222; Bradford and Deane, *History of Plymouth Plantation*, 357; Green, "Medals of Wounded Knee," 203.
88. Phillips, *Damned Yankee*, 70.
89. Smith to McDowell, May 25, 1850, 79.
90. Anderson, *Conquest of Texas*, 246; Smith, in Rodenbough, ed., *From Everglade to Cañon*, 166; Bash, "Notes," MSS C-D 5129, 8; Heitman, *Historical Register*, 21; Bash, "Notes," 8.
91. Cullum, *Biographical Register*, 2:231–232.
92. Ibid., 2:281; Stoneman, "Autobiographical Statement," MSS C-D 757, 10; Cullum, *Biographical Register*, 2:282; Fordney, *George Stoneman*, 142–144. Stoneman retired as a full major general, but President Ulysses S. Grant revoked that promotion (Fordney, *George Stoneman*, 156–157). Stoneman, "Autobiographical Statement," 10, 11.
93. Lyon to Canby, May 22, 1850, 83; Lyon, *Last Political Writings*, 21; "Captain's Commission of Nathaniel Lyon"; Phillips, *Damned Yankee*, 72; Secretary of War Simon Cameron to Brigadier-General Nathaniel Lyon, May 17, 1861, in Woodward, *Life of Lyon*, 257; Cullum, *Biographical Register*, 2:74.
94. West, *Contested Plains*, 305. Eyewitness Sand Creek death toll estimates vary dramatically. The commander of the operation, Colonel John Chivington, as well as his subordinate, Major Jacob Downing, estimated 500 to 600 killed. See Hoig, *Sand Creek Massacre*, 183, 186–187, Appendix.
95. When Frémont's troops massacred California Indians on the Sacramento River in 1846, they were not acting on orders from a staff officer.
96. *DAC*, May 29, 1850, 2.

CHAPTER 5. LEGISLATING EXCLUSION AND VULNERABILITY

1. Almaguer, *Racial Fault Lines*, 48; Hurtado, *Indian Survival*, 211.
2. *Californian*, November 7, 1846, 2.
3. Ibid.
4. Colton and the council published their ordinance in eleven issues of the Monterey *Californian*, in both English and Spanish, over four months. *Californian*, January 16, 1847, 3; January 23, 1847, 4; January 28, 1847, 2; February 6, 1847, 4; February 13, 1847, 4; February 20, 1847, 4; February 27, 1847, 4; March 6, 1847, 4; March 13, 1847, 4; March 27, 1847, 4; April 3, 1847, 4. In 1836, California's Mexican governor Mariano Chico "made a sweeping order that every Indian, found away from his residence without license from the alcalde, administrator or missionary, should be arrested and sentenced to labor on the public works" (Hittell, *History of California*, 2:221. See also Haas, *Saints and Citizens*, 164).
5. *California Star*, February 20, 1847, 4; March 6, 1847, 4. These versions of Montgomery's proclamation varied slightly from the original. *California Star*, August 28, 1847, 1–2.
6. US Bureau of the Census, "California," in *State and County QuickFacts*; *Californian*, June 19, 1847, 2; W.L. Marcy, Secretary of War to the President, December 2, 1847, in CG, December 7, 1847, 17; H.W. Halleck, Lieutenant of Engineers and Secretary of State for California, "Circular to Indian Agents and Others," in *California Star*, September 18, 1847, 3. For California stock rustling, see Zappia, "Indigenous Borderlands," 193–220.
7. Halleck, "Circular," in *California Star*, September 18, 1847, 3. William H. Ellison observed: "These measures . . . bear close resemblance to the black codes of the south" ("Federal Indian Policy," 43).
8. Governor Brevet Brigadier General R. Riley, "PROCLAMATION OF THE GOVERNOR, *Recommending the formation of a State Constitution, or a plan of a Territorial Government*," June 3, 1849, in Browne, *Report of the Debates*, 3–4.
9. Browne, *Report of the Debates*, 7; Taylor, *Eldorado*, 1:99, 90; Sherman, *Recollections of California*, 49; Conway, *Monterey*, 62; Colton, in Conway, *Monterey*, 62.
10. Taylor, *Eldorado*, 1:99, 100. For Semple's height, see Bancroft, *California Pioneer Register*, 323. Taylor described the hall, in *Eldorado*, 1:100. For delegates' ages, see Bancroft, *Works*, 23:288, and Browne, *Report of the Debates*, 478–479. For birthplaces, see Browne, *Report of the Debates*, 478–479. Numerous delegates, including Johann (John) Sutter and Mariano Vallejo, employed California Indians on their ranches. Hugo Reid, representing San Gabriel, had an Indian wife. See Hansen, *Search for Authority*, 150. Taylor wrote that Manuel Dominguez was the convention's "Indian member" (*Eldorado*, 1:107). Semple, in Browne, *Report of the Debates*, 37.
11. Bancroft, *Works*, 23:288; Botts, in Browne, *Report of the Debates*, 63; *The Treaty of Guadalupe Hidalgo, as Ratified by the United States and Mexican Governments, 1848*, in del Castillo, *Treaty of Guadalupe Hidalgo*, 187–190. The 1824 Mexican Constitution had granted Indians full citizenship.

12. For Foster's biographical information, see Colton, *Three Years in California*, 11, and Bancroft, *California Pioneer Register*, 148. Foster, in Browne, *Report of the Debates*, 63; Priestley, *Mexican Nation*, 272, 295.

13. Hastings, in Browne, *Report of the Debates*, 63–64; Dimmick, in Browne, *Report of the Debates*, 64; Gwin, in Browne, *Report of the Debates*, 65. For biographical information on Hastings, Dimmick, and Gwin, see Colton, *Three Years in California*, 11.

14. Botts and Gwin, in Browne, *Report of the Debates*, 66; Dimmick, in Browne, *Report of the Debates*, 67.

15. Taylor, *Eldorado*, 1:90–91. The sun set that evening in Monterey at 6:19 P.M. The moon rose at 2:33 A.M. the next day. US Naval Observatory, "Complete Sun and Moon Data"; Browne, *Report of the Debates*, 68.

16. For biographical information, see Colton, *Three Years in California*, 11. Hoppe, Wozencraft, and McCarver, in Browne, *Report of the Debates*, 69–70.

17. Dent, paraphrased in Browne, *Report of the Debates*, 70; Tefft, in Browne, *Report of the Debates*, 70–71. For biographical information on Dent and Tefft, see Colton, *Three Years in California*, 11.

18. Browne, *Report of the Debates*, 73.

19. Ibid., 304; Halleck, in Browne, *Report of the Debates*, 305; Taylor, *Eldorado*, 1:107; de la Guerra, in Browne, *Report of the Debates*, 305.

20. Browne, *Report of the Debates*, 478, 305–306; McCarver and Hoppe, in Browne, *Report of the Debates*, 306. For biographical information, see Colton, *Three Years in California*, 11. Sherwood, in Browne, *Report of the Debates*, 306; Hurtado, *John Sutter*, 261–262; de la Guerra, in Browne, *Report of the Debates*, 306–307.

21. Browne, *Report of the Debates*, 304. "Yeas.—Messrs. Carillo, Covarrubias, De la Guerra, Dimmick, Dominguez, Foster, Gilbert, Hill, Halleck, Hollingsworth, Larkin, Lippitt, Ord, Pedrorena, Rodriguez, Reid, Shannon, Stearns, Sansevaine, Tefft, Vallejo—21. Nays.—Messrs. Aram, Botts, Brown, Crosby, Gwin, Hanks, Hoppe, Hobson, Hastings, Jones, Lippincott, Moore, McCarver, McDougal, Norton, Price, Sutter, Sherwood, Steuart, Vermeule, Walker, Wozencraft.—22" (Browne, *Report of the Debates*, 307).

22. J. Ross Browne to Lucy Browne, October 1, 1849, in Browne, *Muleback to the Convention*, 40–41; Taylor, *Eldorado*, 1:101, 107. For Dominguez's biographical information, see Browne, *Report of the Debates*, 478.

23. De la Guerra, in Browne, *Report of the Debates*, 323; Vermeule, in Browne, *Report of the Debates*, 341; Browne, *Report of the Debates*, 341.

24. Browne, *Report of the Debates*, 108; 1849 California Constitution, in Browne, *Report of the Debates*, appendix, IV; DAC, September 5, 1853, 1.

25. Joseph Aram, Elam Brown, Henry A. Tefft, W.M. Stewart, and J.M. Covarrubias served as assemblymen. E.O. Crosby, Benjamin Lippincott, Mariano G. Vallejo, Thomas L. Vermeule, and Pablo de la Guerra served as state senators (Browne, *Report of the Debates*, 478–479, and Bancroft, *Works*, 23:309–310).

26. Rockwell D. Hunt, "Birth of the Commonwealth," in Shuck, *History of the Bench*, 42, 44.

27. Governor Peter H. Burnett, "Governor's Message," in California, *Senate Journal*, 1849, 41; Bancroft, *Works*, 23:308.

28. California, *Senate Journal*, 1849, 224; Bancroft, *Works*, 23:308–309; Taylor, *Eldorado*, 1:133; Bidwell's bill, summarized in Hurtado, *Indian Survival*, 129–130. For more on Bidwell's bill, including substantial portions of the text, see Gillis and Magliari, *John Bidwell and California*, 251–253 and 291–293.

29. California, *Statutes*, 1850, 102; California, *Senate Journal*, 1849, 23–24. California legislators enfranchised nonwhites in the 1879 California Constitution. See California, *Statutes*, 1880, xxiv.

30. California, *Journal of the Proceedings*, 1849, 576, 1205; California, *Senate Journal*, 1849, 384; California, *Journal of the Proceedings*, 1849, 1284.

31. Langum, *Law and Community*, 79. On this same page Langum noted: "Indians were regarded as inferior beings and were treated somewhat more harshly than ordinary defendants. . . . Similarly, there was a tendency to treat the defendants for the crimes committed upon even those Indians living within the settled areas with somewhat more leniency."

32. California, *Statutes*, 1850, 408–410; Caughey, *California*, 380; Street, *Beasts of the Field*, 122. On April 30, 1855, California legislators passed "An Act To punish Vagrants, Vagabonds, and Dangerous and Suspicious Persons." It applied to "All persons except Digger Indians," but its penalties were less draconian than those imposed on Indians under the 1850 act and made no provisions for convict leasing. California, *Statutes*, 1855, 217–218.

33. California, *Statutes*, 1850, 409.

34. Ibid.

35. Ibid., 230. Only qualified electors could serve as jurors in California courts, so Indians—who had just been denied the franchise—could not serve as jurors (ibid., 288). California, *Statutes*, 1851, 48, 114.

36. California, *Statutes*, 1854, 67; California, *Statutes*, 1855, 179. Because only qualified electors could serve as jurors in California courts, Indians—denied the franchise in 1850—were also prevented from becoming jurors. California, *Statutes*, 1850, 288, 441. As late as 1861 the fourth edition of a California law and court procedures compendium presented the general 1854 civil procedure law excluding Indians from being witnesses as valid law. California, *California Practice Act*, 220. California, *Penal Code*, 455; *People v. McGuire*; Fernandez, "Except a California Indian," 165.

37. McKanna, *Race and Homicide*, 90. In his study, McKanna documented only one conviction of a white man for the homicide of an Indian (*Race and Homicide*, 95). In at least one instance a non-Indian California mob lynched a white man for murdering an Indian (*DAC*, March 1, 1854, 2). Crook, *General George Crook*, 16.

38. Gerber, "Origin of California's Export Surplus," 41–43; Bancroft, *Works*, 24:478; quoted by Arkansas senator William King Sebastian, in *CG*, March 3, 1853, 1085.

39. Bell, *Reminiscences*, 48–49; Phillips, "Indians in Los Angeles," 448.

40. California Superintendent of Indian Affairs Beale to Commissioner of Indian Affairs Lea, September 30, 1852, S. Exec. Doc. 57, 32nd Cong., 2nd Sess., 1853, serial 665, 9; E.F. Beale, Superintendent Indian Affairs to Luke Lea, Commissioner of Indian

Affairs, Washington, DC, November 22, 1852, S. Exec. Doc. 4, 33rd Cong., Spec. Sess., 1853, serial 688, 378.

41. R.N. Woods, in J.H. Jenkins to Superintendent Beale, January 13, 1853, S. Exec. Doc. 57, 32nd Cong., 2nd Sess., 1853, serial 665, 10.

42. Thos J Henley, Sup Ind Affairs, Cal to Hon Geo W Manypenny, Comr of Indian Affairs, April 14, 1856, NARA, RG75, M234, Reel 35:312; Stevenson to Henley, July 31, 1856, in USOIA, *Report of the Commissioner of Indian Affairs*, 1856, 251.

43. CG, September 13, 1850, 1791; Frémont, in CG, September 13, 1850, 1793.

44. Frémont in CG, September 14, 1850, 1816; CG, September 14, 1850, 1816 and September 16, 1850, 1828.

45. Gwin in CG, September 14, 1850, 1816; CG, September 28, 1850, 2023; US Congress, *Statutes at Large and Treaties*, 9:519.

46. Ibid., 9:558; A.S. Loughery, Acting Commissioner to Messrs. Redick McKee, Geo. W. Barbour, O.M. Wozencraft (Commissioners), in S. Exec. Doc. 4, 33rd Cong., Spec. Sess., 1853, serial 688, 8–9; George E. Anderson and Robert F. Heizer, "Treaty-making by the Federal Government in California 1851–1852," in Anderson, Ellison, and Heizer, *Treaty Making*, 26; DAC, December 18, 1850, 2; DAC, January 12, 1851, 2.

47. Redick, McKee, Geo. W. Barbour, and O. M. Wozencraft, *"To the People of California, residing in the vicinity of the Indian Troubles,"* January 13, 1851, in DAC, January 14, 1851, 2; DAC, May 31, 1851, 2; Shasta to *Daily Alta California*, n.d., in DAC, February 9, 1852, 2.

48. L. Lea, Commissioner to Messrs. Redick McKee, Geo. W. Barbour, O.M. Wozencraft, May 22, 1851, in S. Exec. Doc. 4, 33rd Cong., Spec. Sess., 1853, serial 688, 15.

49. Redick McKee to Hon. Luke Lea, Commissioner of Indian Affairs, March 24, 1851, in S. Exec. Doc. 4, 33rd Cong., Spec. Sess., 1853, serial 688, 67; Ellison, "Federal Indian Policy in California, 1846–1860," 54–55; Heizer, *Eighteen Unratified Treaties*, 1, 12–15; Goodrich, "Legal Status," 95; Heizer, *Eighteen Unratified Treaties*, Map 1; DAC, February 8, 1851, 2; O.M. Wozencraft, United States Indian Agent to Hon. Luke Lea, Commissioner of Indian Affairs, October 14, 1851, in S. Exec. Doc. 4, 33rd Cong., Spec. Sess., 1853, serial 688, 207; Anderson and Heizer, "Treaty-making by the Federal Government in California 1851–1852," 26; *Los Angeles Star*, in Almaguer, *Racial Fault Lines*, 145. Attacks on the treaties also appeared in the *San Francisco Herald* on August 2, 1851, 2, and *Sacramento Placer Times and Transcript*, September 24, 1851, 2.

50. Bigler, in California, *Senate Journal*, 1852, 79; *Weekly Alta California*, February 14, 1852, 2.

51. "Majority and Minority Reports of the Special Committee to Inquire into the Treaties made by the United States Commissioners with the Indians of California," in California, *Senate Journal*, 1852, 600, 601. According to Goodrich, "The resolutions do not appear to have been finally acted upon by the [state] Assembly." See Goodrich, "Legal Status," 96.

52. "Majority and Minority Reports," in California, *Senate Journal*, 1852, 603.

53. "Report of the California Assembly Committee to Inquire into the Treaties Made by the United States Indian Commissioners with the Indians of California," in California, *Senate Journal*, 1852, 202; California, *Journal of the Third Session*, 1852, 396–397.

54. "Majority and Minority Reports," in California, *Senate Journal*, 1852, 597; "Report of the California Assembly Committee," in California, *Journal of the Third Session*, 1852, 203; McCorkle, in *CG*, March 26, 1852, 890; "Report of the Secretary . . . communicating a copy of the correspondence between the Department of the Interior and the Indian agents in California," S. Exec. Doc. 4, 33rd Cong., Spec. Sess., 1853, serial 688, 319–320; Goodrich, "Legal Status," 96.

55. Ellison, "Rejection of California Indian Treaties [Part 2]," 4; United States, *Journal of the Executive Proceedings of the Senate of the United States of America*, 8:417–420; US Congress, *Congressional Record*, January 18, 1905, 1021; Kelsey, "California Indian Treaty Myth," 233. For an analysis of why the Senate rejected the treaties see Banner, *Possessing the Pacific*, 183–189.

56. Heizer, *Eighteen Unratified Treaties*.

57. George Falconer Emmons, "Replies to Inquiries Respecting the Indian Tribes of Oregon and California," in Schoolcraft, *Archives of Aboriginal Knowledge*, 3:210, 221.

58. Beale to Lea, November 22, 1852, in S. Exec. Doc. 4, 33rd Cong., Spec. Sess., 1853, serial 688, 378–379.

59. Report of the Secretary of the Interior, Secretary of the Interior Alex H.H. Stuart to the President, December 4, 1852, in *CG*, December 4, 1852, 18.

60. Message of the President of the United States, President Millard Fillmore to Fellow-Citizens of the Senate, and of the House of Representatives, December 6, 1852, in *CG*, December 6, 1852, 3.

61. Major General John Wool to U.S. Senators D.C. Broderick and Wm. Gwin, January 28, 1857, 2, Interior Department Appointment Papers. Held-Poage Library, Ukiah, California; Ellison, "Federal Indian Policy," 61; Wool to Broderick and Gwin, January 28, 1857, 4.

62. *The Cherokee Nation v. The State of Georgia*, 30 U.S. 1 (1831).

63. Historians Howard R. Lamar and Samuel Truett have observed that "California Indians rarely, if ever, became part of Anglo-American society." Lamar and Truett, "The Greater Southwest and California from the Beginning of European Settlement to the 1880s," in Trigger and Washburn, *Cambridge History*, 1:2:99.

64. Collier, in US Senate, *Hearings before the Committee on Indian Affairs*, 6.

CHAPTER 6. RISE OF THE KILLING MACHINE

1. Shea, "To Defend Virginia."

2. For Paspahas: Percy, "'Trewe Relacyon,'" 271–272. For Mystic: Mason, *Brief History*, 10. For Rhode Island: Jennings, *Invasion of America*, 312. For Gnadenhütten: Heckewelder, *Narrative of the Mission*, 320–321, and David Zeisberger, April 7, 1782, entry, in Zeisberger, *Diary*, 1:85. For Hillabee: James White, Brig. Gen. to John Cocke, Major-general, November 24, 1813, in *Weekly Register*, December 25, 1813, 282–283, and Major General John Cocke to General [Andrew Jackson], November 27, 1813, in Andrew Jackson Papers. For Bad Axe: Jung, *Black Hawk War*, 172.

3. California, *Senate Journal*, 1849, 308; California, *Statutes*, 1850, 190, 192–193 (exceptions included California state militia veterans, US military veterans, and those who

paid $2 to avoid service for a year); Hurtado, *John Sutter*, 299. See also *DAC*, June 28, 1853, 2. The most comprehensive study of this militia system remains Dayton, "California Militia, 1850–1866."

4. California's State Archives contain documents related to 303 volunteer California state militia units but do not contain muster rolls for Colusa, Fresno, Glenn, Imperial, Inyo, Kern, Kings, Lake, Madera, Mendocino, Merced, Modoc, Riverside, San Benito, or Ventura counties for the 1851–1866 period. Thus, many more militia units exited during this time. For the 35,000 estimate see Root Cellar, *California State Militia*, ii, 1396–1465. For procedures, see California, *Statutes*, 1850, 145–148, 190–196.

5. *DAC*, February 4, 1850, 2. The First California Guards, founded in 1849, succeeded the San Francisco Guards, founded in 1848. See *Californian*, September 2, 1848, 3, and September 9, 1848, 3, and Soulé, Gihon, and Nisbet, *Annals of San Francisco*, 702. For more on social militias, see Dayton, "'Polished Boot,'" 359–368.

6. Root Cellar, *California State Militia*, 1432–1446.

7. Sociologist Martin Shaw has argued that "instances of genocide—not only the Holocaust, but also Armenia and Rwanda—have been clearly connected with war contexts, and this is an overwhelmingly empirical trend" (Shaw, *What Is Genocide?* 43).

8. Thos. J. Green, Major-General, 1st Division, California Militia to Peter H. Burnett, Governor of California, May 16, 1850, in California, *California Legislature*, 1851, 763; Gudde, *California Place Names*, 230.

9. Thos. J. Green, Major-General, 1st Division, California Militia to Peter H. Burnett, Governor of California, May 25, 1850, in California, *California Legislature*, 1851, 764–765. The *Placer Times* (May 20, 1850, 2) reported what may have been the first attack: on May 17, "a party of 30 went out from Nicolaus and killed four" Indians "near Johnson's Ranch" after "A teamster from Nicolaus was found dead." For treaty text, see *Placer Times*, May 29, 1850, 2.

10. *Placer Times*, May 20, 1850, 2; *DAC*, May 23, 1850, 2; *DAC*, May 29, 1850, 2.

11. Peter H. Burnett, Com. in Chief to Maj. Gen. Thomas J. Green, June 3, 1850, in California, *California Legislature*, 1851, 768. An 1857 act appropriated up to $20,000 for 1850 and 1851 Nevada County expeditions. See California, *Statutes*, 1857, 262–263.

12. J.C.W., in *Placer Times*, June 3, 1850, 3; Samuel Kip to *Daily Alta California*, June 9, 1850, in *DAC*, June 18, 1850, 2; R.W. to the editor, June 29, 1850, in *DAC*, July 3, 1850, 2; Extract of letter, dated Trinidad City, July 2, in *DAC*, July 10, 1850, 3; Gihon, "Incident of the Gold Bluff," 655–660; Extract of letter, dated Trinidad City, July 2, in *DAC*, July 10, 1850, 3; Gihon, "Incident of the Gold Bluff," 660. In January 1851, James Bruff passed through what was probably the remnants of this village, north of Gold Bluff. Bruff wrote, "I am informed, that last summer, some Indians of this village . . . wounded two [miners]. They had previously murdered several white men. The miners attacked the village, killed 7 or 8 of the savages" (Bruff, *Gold Rush*, 1120, 946); Eidsness, "Initial Cultural Resources Study," 16. Tony Platt kindly provided this quotation and source.

13. Pancoast, *Quaker Forty-Niner*, 298–299; Daniel B. Woods reported what were probably the same events (*Sixteen Months*, 138).

14. Phillips, *Chiefs and Challengers*, 71–72; Chamberlain, *My Confession*; Theodoro, December 10, 1850, in *DAC*, January 8, 1851, 2. According to historian Clifford Trafzer, "11 or 12 ferrymen lost their lives that day" (Trafzer, *Yuma*, 76).

15. Peter H. Burnett, Gov.+Commander in Chief to J.H. Bean, Major General of the 4th Division, California Militia, June 1, 1850, *IWP*, F3753:2; Peter H. Burnett, Gov. +Com: in Chief to Maj. Genl. J.H. Bean, June 4, 1850, *IWP*, F3753:3; J.H. Bean, Major General, Commanding 4th Division Cal. Militia, "Gen. Orders No. 1," July 9, 1850, *IWP*, F3753:4; J.H. Bean, Major Genl., Commanding 4th Division Cal. Militia, "Gen. Orders No. 2," n.d., *IWP*, F3753:5; Jos. C. Morehead, Quarter-Master General, State of California to the Governor of the State of California, January 21, 1851, in California, *California Legislature*, 1851, 608; Guinn, *History of the State*, 226–227; Peter H. Burnett, Gov:+Com: in Chief to Maj. Genl. J.H. Bean, 4th Div. Cal:Mila, September 4, 1850, *IWP*, F3753:7; Comptroller, "Expenditures," 115; Morehead to Governor, January 21, 1851, in California, *California Legislature*, 1851, 608.

16. Comptroller, "Expenditures," 115; Morehead to Governor, January 21, 1851, in California, *California Legislature*, 1851, 607. Civil authorities also provided arms and ammunition (ibid., 609).

17. Mr. Freaner, in *Weekly Placer Times*, June 29, 1850, 2; Wells, *History of Siskiyou*, 121–122; Ross, "Narrative," 19; Gold Hunter to Gentlemen, July 15, 1850, in *DAC*, September 12, 1850, 2; Massey, "Frenchman in the Gold Rush [Part 3]," 229, 231; Revere, Album, MSS HM56913, 29–46 (in 1831, French foreign minister Horace Sébastiani probably coined the phrase "Order reigns in Warsaw" to reference Russia's suppression of the 1830–1831 Polish Uprising); Sytax to Editors, in *DAC*, August 20, 1850, 2.

18. Augustin W. Hale, August 10, 1850, journal entry, in Hale, Diaries, Diary 7, August 1–28, 1850, Box 6(7); *Sacramento Transcript*, October 11, 1850, 2.

19. *Stockton Journal*, in *DAC*, July 19, 1850, 2. Sometime before September 8, vigilantes killed two Shasta Indians and wounded others near Beaver River (probably Scott River). John E. Ross shot three Indians between Scott Bar and the Sacramento. In October, Mormons in Eastern California "killed and scalped six Digger Indians, in revenge for thirty [stolen] mules," even though their victims did not have the mules. A week later, following the killing of a white man, vigilantes murdered seven or eight Konkow or Maidu people on the Feather River's west branch. For Bear River, see Augustin W. Hale, September 8, 1850, journal entry, in Hale, Diaries, Diary 8, Aug. 28–Sep. 30, 1850, Box 6(8). For Ross, see Ross, "Narrative," 22. For Eastern California, see Franklin Langworthy, October 10, 1850, journal entry made near Mormon Station in Carson Valley, in Langworthy, *Scenery of the Plains*, 155. For Feather River, see Mr. Ford, paraphrased in *Marysville Herald*, October 22, 1850, 2.

20. Rogers, in California, *California Legislature*, 1851, 795; Peter H. Burnett, Gov. & Com. in Chief to William Rogers, Sheriff of Eldorado, October 25, 1850, *IWP*, F3753:9; Wm. Rogers, Col. Commanding to Brig. Genl. Winn, October 29, 1850, and L.H. McKinney, Lieut. Col. Com. Horses to Col. Rogers, October 28, 1850, *IWP*, F3753:10; Wm. Rogers, Col. Comdg. to Brig Genl. A.M. Winn, November 4, 1850, *IWP*, F3753:16; C.W. Boone, Major Comdg. to Col. Wm. Rogers, November 4, 1850, *IWP*, F3753:14; Comptroller, "Expenditures," 36.

21. Haskins, *Argonauts of California*, 148; A.M. Winn, Brig. Gen., 2° Brig. 10th Div. Cm. to Peter H. Burnett, November 11, 1850, *IWP*, F3753:24; Peter H. Burnett, Gov. + Comd. in Chief to Wm. Rogers, Commander of the Expedition in Eldorado County November 15, 1850, *IWP*, F3753:27; Wm. Rogers, Major Commanding to Brig. Gen. Winn, December 10, 1850, *IWP*, F3753:37.

22. *Placer Times* summarized in and commented on, in *DAC*, December 15, 1850, 2; Alfred Barstow, "Statement," MSS C-D 37, 5–6.

23. La Motte, "Statement," 11; *DAC*, November 11, 1850, 2; Menefee, *Historical and Descriptive Sketch Book*, 23; Bruff, December 14, 1850, journal entry, in *Gold Rush*, 465; *DAC*, December 15, 1850, 2. In January the *Daily Alta California* reiterated that "the Indians are peaceably disposed" (*DAC*, January 12, 1851, 2).

24. *New York Tribune*, May 17, 1850, 8; Galbraith, *Money*, 42; *DAC*, December 15, 1850, 2; *DAC*, January 12, 1851, 2. See also *DAC*, January 21, 1851, 2.

25. Phillips, *Indians and Intruders*, 105; Wm. Graham, letter in *Sacramento Transcript*, January 20, 1851, 2; W Graham to Messrs Editors, January 25, 1851, in *Sacramento Transcript*, January 29, 1851, 2; Redick McKee to Hon. Luke Lea Commr. Indn. Affairs, Washington, February 11, 1851, NARA, RG75, M234, Reel 32:328.

26. Jackson, in Richardson, *Compilation*, 2:521; Horace Greeley, *New-Yorker*, March 24, 1838, 9.

27. Farnham, *Travels in the Californias*, 413; *California Star*, February 26, 1848, 2; *DAC*, December 15, 1850, 2; *DAC*, December 30, 1850, 2.

28. Peter H. Burnett, "Governor's Message," in California, *California Legislature*, 1851, 15.

29. McKee, Barbour, and Wozencraft, *"To the People of California, residing in the vicinity of the Indian Troubles,"* January 13, 1851, in *DAC*, January 14, 1851, 2.

30. Correspondents reported four whites killed that month but no Indian deaths. See Johnston to Burnett, January 2, 1851, *IWP*, F3753:46; C.D. Gibbes to the Editors, December 29, 1850, in *Stockton Times*, January 11, 1851, 1. For quotations see Gibbes to Editors, December 23, 1850, in *Stockton Times*, January 4, 1851, 3; *DAC*, January 1, 1851, 2; Johnston to Burnett, January 2, 1851, *IWP*, F3753:46. For Pleasant Valley see *Sacramento Transcript*, January 8, 1851, 2.

31. Several Eye-Witnesses to *Sonora Herald*, January 7, 1851, in *Stockton Times*, February 12, 1851, 1; James Burney to Governor Peter H. Burnett, January 13, 1851, *IWP* F3753:48. T.G. Palmer participated in the operation and reported that seventy-seven vigilantes took part. T.G. Palmer to My Dear Father, January 16, 1851, in Bunnell, *Discovery of the Yosemite*, 30; *Stockton Times*, January 8, 1851, 2. See also Mr. Southern of "Moquelumne Hill," in *Stockton Times*, January 25, 1851, 1. For massacre see *DAC*, January 21, 1851, 2; *Sacramento Transcript*, January 23, 1851, 2.

32. Palmer to Father, January 16, 1851, in Bunnell, *Discovery of the Yosemite*, 31–33; Burney to Burnett, January 13, 1851, *IWP*, F3753:48; Express Rider, January 19, 1851, in *Marysville Herald*, January 24, 1851, 3.

33. Samuel Merritt, H.V. Richardson, and James Miller to Governor Peter H. Burnett, January 2, 1851, *IWP*, F3753:47; J.M. Bondurant, County Judge, Richard Daly, County Attorney, David Easton and "seventy others" to Governor P.H. Burnett, January 13, 1851, *IWP*, F3753:49; James Burney to Sir, January 13, 1851, in *IWP*, F:3753:48; John

McDougal, Govr + Commander in Chief to James Birney, Shff, Agua Frio, Mariposa Co., January 13, 1851, *IWP*, F:3753:50.

34. Executive Office to Hon. D. Broderick, Prest. Senate, January 18, 1851, *IWP*, F3753:51; Jno. McDougal to The Legislature of California, January 18, 1851, *IWP*, F3753:52.

35. Bunnell, *Discovery of the Yosemite*, 13–16 (Bunnell did not mention Indian casualty numbers); Jno. McDougal to Col. J. Neely Johnson, January 25, 1851, in California, *California Legislature*, 1851, 674; R.W. to Messrs. Editors, February 4, 1851, in *DAC*, February 7, 1851, 2; Comptroller, "Expenditures," 23.

36. California, *Statutes*, 1851, 520–521; California, *California Legislature*, 1851, 1077–1078; "An Act prescribing the Amount of Compensation and Mode of Payment to Persons who have Performed Military Services for the State of California, and Expenses incurred therein," in California, *Statutes*, 1851, 489–490; California, *California Legislature*, 1851, 1368, 853–854; *Sacramento Transcript*, March 3, 1851, 2; *SDU*, March 31, 1851, 2; *SDU*, summarized in *DAC*, July 30, 1851, 2; R.W., September 24, 1851, in *DAC*, October 5, 1851, 2.

37. California, *Statutes*, 1851, 490; Comptroller, "Expenditures," 24–36, 37, 115.

38. *Sacramento Transcript*, January 30, 1851, 2.

39. Perkins, January 12, 1851, journal entry, in Perkins, *El Campo de Los Sonoraenses*, 104; Mountaineer, January 26, 1851, in *Stockton Times*, February 8, 1851, 2; *Stockton Times*, February 8, 1851, 2; *Stockton Times*, February 12, 1851, 3; Agua Fria correspondent, in *Stockton Times*, February 19, 1851, 3; *Stockton Times*, February 26, 1851, 1; Yankee Hill correspondent, in *DAC*, February 15, 1851, 2.

40. C.D. Gibbes to the Editors, in *Stockton Times*, February 19, 1851, 3.

41. J. Neeley Johnson, paraphrased in G.W. Barbour, R. McKee and O.M. Wozencraft to Hon. Luke Lea Esq., February 17, 1851, NARA, M234, Reel 32:106 (emphasis added).

42. Adam Johnston to Hon. L. Lea, Commissioner of Indn Affairs, March 7, 1851, NARA, RG75, M234, Reel 32:214; N.B. Lewis, Agent by order of James D. Savage, Maj. Com'd Battalion to Gov. John McDougal, March 9, 1851, in *DAC*, March 20, 1851, 2.

43. Persifer F. Smith, Brevet Major-General Commanding Pacific Division to Brevet-Major General R. Jones, Adjutant-General of the Army, March 13, 1851, H. Exec. Doc. 2, part 1, 32nd Cong., 1st Sess., 1851, serial 634, 137–138.

44. Jno. McDougal to the Senate and House of Assembly, March 15, 1851, *IWP*, F3753:60; Special Correspondence to *Daily Alta California*, March 16, 1851, in *DAC*, March 19, 1851, 2; California, *Statutes*, 1851, 402.

45. *DAC*, March 17, 1851, 2; *Stockton Times*, March 26, 1851, 2; March 16, 1851, journal entry in Eccleston, *Mariposa Indian War*, 33.

46. Kuykendall, in Bunnell, *Discovery of the Yosemite*, 143; Cameron, in Bunnell, *Discovery of the Yosemite*, 162; *DAC*, April 4, 1851, 2; April 27 and April 28, 1851, journal entries in Eccleston, *Mariposa Indian War*, 70, 71; John Bowling to Major Savage, May 15, 1851, in *DAC*, June 12, 1851, 2; May 17, 1851, journal entry, in Eccleston, *Mariposa Indian War*, 87; Bunnell, *Discovery of the Yosemite*, 170. For burnings, see March 29, April 24, April 26, April 27, May 7, and May 15, 1851, journal entries, in Eccleston, *Mariposa Indian War*, 48–49, 67–70, 82, 86; John Bowling, Captain, Co. B to Major Savage, April 29, 1851, in *DAC*, June 11, 1851, 2; R.E. Russell, Serg't Major California

Battalion to M.B. Lewis, Adjutant, May 17, 1851, in *DAC*, June 12, 1851, 2; *Stockton Journal*, May 31, 1851, paraphrased in *DAC*, June 3, 1851, 2. There were 560 enrolled in the Mariposa Battalion and Monterey Expedition, in combination, but at least 518 in the Mariposa Battalion (Comptroller, "Expenditures," 23).

47. James McMany, in Hayes, "Hayes Scrapbooks," vol. 39, item 1; Lewis Granger, February 4, 1851, in *DAC*, February 14, 1851, 2; J.H. Bean, Major General of the Fourth Division California Militia to His Excellency John McDougal, Governor and Command in Chief, February 9, 1851, *IWP*, F3753:117; Petition of Citizens of Los Angeles to Genl. Joshua Bean in reference to Indian difficulties, n.d., *IWP*, F3753:118; Jno. McDougal to Maj. Gen. Joshua Bean, March 1, 1851, *IWP*, F3753:119; Comptroller, "Expenditures," 77; *LAS*, May 24, 1851, 2; *LAS*, June 7, 1851, in Hayes, "Hayes Scrapbooks," vol. 39.

48. William Rogers, Major to General A.M. Winn, February 22, 1851, *IWP*, F3753:41; Comptroller, "Expenditures," 63; *DAC*, May 15, 1851, 2.

49. Wm. Rogers, Major Commanding to His Excellency John McDougal, Governor, December 10, 1851, in California, *Journal of the Third Session*, 1852, 430–431; *Placer Times*, summarized in *DAC*, May 28, 1851, 2; Rogers to McDougal, December 10, 1851, in California, *Journal of the Third Session*, 1852, 431; E.S. Lovell to Messrs. Editors, July 2, 1851, in *DAC*, July 6, 1851, 2; Rogers, to McDougal, December 10, 1851, in California, *Journal of the Third Session*, 1852, 431; A.M. Winn, Brig. Gen. to Gov. McDougal, July 21, 1851, in *DAC*, July 25, 1851, 2.

50. *DAC*, June 3, 1851, 2; Comptroller, "Expenditures," 23. In combination, 560 men enrolled in the Mariposa Battalion and Monterey Expedition, but at least twenty-two enrolled in the Monterey Expedition (Comptroller, "Expenditures," 23).

51. Meyer, *Bound for Sacramento*, 146.

52. Mr. Ashby, paraphrased in *SDU*, March 24, 1851, 2; *Memorial and Biographical History*, 131; E.D. Walker to Gen. D.F. Douglas, March 25, 1851, in *Stockton Times*, March 26, 1851, 3; Mr. Curtis, paraphrased in *SDU*, April 18, 1851, 2; *Sacramento Transcript*, April 28, 1851, 3; A.T., Trinity Diggings, near the Mouth of Weaver Creek, May 2, 1851, in *Marysville Herald*, May 10, 1851, 2.

53. John Marshall, April 22, 1851, in *DAC*, April 27, 1851, 2; T.J.R., May 30, 1851, in *DAC*, July 2, 1851, 2; Wells, *History of Siskiyou*, 104; P.B. Reading to O.M. Wozencraft, June 28, 1851, in *DAC*, July 14, 1851, 2; G.R.S., July 1, 1851, in *Marysville Herald*, July 17, 1851, 2.

54. Meyer, *Bound for Sacramento*, 279n4.

55. *DAC*, July 7, 1851, 2.

56. A. French to *Marysville Herald*, July 6, 1851, in *DAC*, July 23, 1851, 2 (Harvey described the Indians in the first massacre as "Pitt river Indians," often considered dangerous by whites, but it is unlikely that Achumawi people would be so far from home. More likely, Harvey sought to justify his massacre of unoffending Wintu people); A. French to *Marysville Herald*, July 15, 1851, in *DAC*, July 23, 1851, 2.

57. *DAC*, March 21, 1851, 2; John McDougal to the Senate and House of Assembly, April 25, 1851, in California, *California Legislature*, 1851, 1716. About this time, however, Morehead, California's quartermaster general, illegally "sold . . . a large portion

of said arms" and fled with the proceeds. See McDougal to the Senate and House of Assembly, April 25, 1851, in California, *Journals of the Legislature*, 1851, 1716–1717. Still, the larceny proved only a temporary setback.

58. Governor John McDougal to His Excellency, Millard Fillmore, President of the United States, March 1, 1851, H. Exec. Doc. 2, part 1, 32nd Cong., 1st Sess., 1851, serial 634, 139. For gold production see, Rohrbough, *Days of Gold*, 35.

59. C.N. Conrad, Secretary of War to His Excellency John McDougal, Governor of California, April 30, 1851, H. Exec. Doc. 2, 32nd Cong., 1st Sess., 1851, serial 634, 140–142.

60. Peters, *Public Statutes*, 2:490–491; Conrad to McDougal, April 30, 1851, 142; Quarter M. General W.H. Richardson, "Report of the Quarter M. General," December 15, 1851, in California, *Senate Journal*, 1852, 517–518.

61. Richardson, "Report of the Quarter M. General," 517; Comptroller, "Expenditures," 87; *DAC*, July 26, 1851, 2.

62. *DAC*, September 20, 1851, 2.

63. According to the 1873 recollection of a person who had been in the area at the time, in 1851 "Oregonians had ruthlessly killed two Indians, and provoked by this means the massacre of unoffending travelers" migrating through Modoc country to Oregon and California (May 7, 1873, Special Correspondent's letter in *New York Times*, May 24, 1873, 2); Johansen and Pritzker, *Encyclopedia*, 4:1142; James, *Modoc*, 19; Theodore Stern, "Klamath and Modoc," in Walker, *Handbook of North American Indians*, 12:448–449, 452; Turner, "Scraps of Modoc History," 21; Stern, "Klamath and Modoc," 446; Allison, *Cultural Landscape*, 39; Stern, "Klamath and Modoc," 446–466.

64. Ross, "Narrative," 22–23; Statement of W.T. Kershaw, November 21, 1857, in H. Mis. Doc. 47, 35th Cong., 2nd Sess., 1859, serial 1016, 41 (hereafter, Kershaw statement); Murray, *Modocs and Their War*, 19–21; William R. Fanning, in Wells, *History of Siskiyou*, 123–125; Kershaw statement, 42; Benjamin Madley, "California and Oregon's Modoc Indians: How Indigenous Resistance Camouflages Genocide in Colonial Histories," in Woolford, Benvenuto, and Hinton, *Colonial Genocide*, 119, 95.

65. *LAS*, in *DAC*, November 13, 1851, 2; Phillips, *Chiefs and Challengers*, 75.

66. Antonio Garra to Juan Antonio, December 2, 1851, in *LAS*, December 20, 1851, 2; Phillips, *Chiefs and Challengers*, 78–79; Comptroller, "Expenditures," 95; Geo. H. Davis, Secy. to His Excellency John McDougall, Governor of the State of California, November 24, 1851, *IWP*, F3753:140.

67. Phillips, *Chiefs and Challengers*, 88; Comptroller, "Expenditures," 77; Whaley to Eloise, December 17, 1851, in Phillips, *Chiefs and Challengers*, 89, 82; *San Diego Herald*, December 18, 1851, 2; Phillips, *Chiefs and Challengers*, 92–93; J.H. Bean Maj. Genl comdg 4th Div. Cal. State Militia to His Excellency John McDougal, January 1, 1852, *IWP*, F3753:144. For trial details, see Phillips, *Chiefs and Challengers*, 95–110.

68. *LAS*, January 3, 1852, 2; Bean to McDougal, January 1, 1852, *IWP*, F3753:144; *San Diego Herald*, January 17, 1852, 2; W. McKinstry, Adjt. General to Gen. Joshua Bean, Major General 4th Division, Cal. Militia, January 12, 1852, *IWP*, F3752:146; Comptroller, "Expenditures," 95. The Comptroller reported the cost and total number of men enrolled in the Los Angeles and Utah Expeditions together. Thus it is impossible

to know precisely how many men served in each or how much each cost (Comptroller, "Expenditures," 77).

69. Wozencraft, in *SDU*, February 2, 1852, 2; *SDU*, February 17, 1852, 2; *Marysville Herald*, in *SDU*, February 20, 1852, 2; Mr. Taylor, in *SDU*, February 28, 1852, 2; Josiah Roop, March 1, 1852, in *SDU*, March 9, 1852, 2; *SDU*, March 5, 1852, 2.

70. Redick McKee, United States Indian Agent for Northern California to His Excellency John Bigler, Governor of California, April 5, 1852, in California, *Senate Journal*, 1852, 712.

71. John Bigler to Hon. Redick McKee, April 9, 1852, in California, *Senate Journal*, 1852, 714–716; Redick McKee, U.S. Indian Agent, Northern California to Governor John Bigler, April 12, 1852, in California, *Senate Journal*, 1852, 720.

72. U.S. Indian Commissioner Redick McKee to *Daily Alta California*, March 21, 1852, in *DAC*, April 5, 1852, 2. "T.J.R." later wrote from Trinidad to report the same killings, "in which some 40 Indians were killed, and two white men wounded" (T.J.R. to Editors, May 12, 1852, in *DAC*, May 16, 1852, 2); R. McKee to Messrs Editors in *DAC*, May 21, 1852, 2; McKee to *Daily Alta California*, March 21, 1852, in *DAC*, April 5, 1852, 2.

73. McKee to Bigler, April 5, 1852, in California, *Senate Journal*, 1852, 712–713; *Weekly Alta California*, March 27, 1852, 1.

74. J.W. Denver, R.T. Sprague, Thomas H. Coats, Samuel Fleming, E.D. Pearce, [and] Geo. O. McMullin to his Excellency John Bigler, April 5, 1852, in California, *Senate Journal*, 1852, 703–704; *Shasta Courier*, paraphrased in Redick McKee to Governor John Bigler, April 12, 1852, in California, *Senate Journal*, 1852, 720; Redick McKee, U.S. Indian Agent for Northern California to Br. General E.A. Hitchcock, April 7, 1852, in California, *Senate Journal*, 1852, 716–717; John Bigler to Brevet Brig. General E.A. Hitchcock, Commanding Pacific Division, April 8, 1852, in California, *Senate Journal*, 1852, 705–706.

75. *SDU*, April 13, 1852, 2; General Hitchcock to Governor Bigler, April 16, 1850, in California, *Senate Journal*, 1852, 711.

76. J.A. Luckett to Editors, *Shasta Courier*, April 18, 1852, in *SDU*, April 27, 1852, 2; Petitioners to the Governor of the State of California, April 18, 1852, *IWP*, F3753:195.

77. Letter dated Weaverville, April 25, 1852, in *Shasta Courier*, in *SDU*, May 3, 1852, 3; Carr, *Pioneer Days*, 195, 198; Knapp, "Old Californian's Pioneer Story," 508; Franklin August Buck to Marcy Sewall Bradley, June 9, 1852, HM60481, Franklin Augustus Buck Papers, 1846–1853, Box 1, L15 C6; *DAC*, May 4, 1852, 2; Cox, *Annals of Trinity County*, 115, 116; Fred Stacer, in *Golden Era*, November 15, 1879, 3; Grace McKibbin, summarized in Shriner, *Thunder up the Creek*, 237; McKibbin, *In My Own Words*, 15; Carr, *Pioneer Days*, 198; Cox, *Annals of Trinity County*, 116; Knapp, "Old Californian's Pioneer Story," 508.

78. California, *Statutes*, 1852, 59.

79. "Fort Reading Military reservation," H. Doc. 35, 44th Cong., 2nd Sess., 1876, serial 1769, 1.

80. Barry, *Up and Down*, 126–128; *DAC*, May 10, 1852, 2; *Shasta Courier*, May 15, 1852, paraphrased in *DAC*, May 18, 1852, 2; Crow Creek informant, in *SDU*, June 28,

1852, 3; *SDU*, July 5, 1852, 2; Gillis and Magliari, *John Bidwell and California*, 258–259 and 300–301; *Stockton Journal*, July 13, 1852, 2; O.M. Wozencraft, U.S.A. to Hon Gov Bigler, July 13, 1852, in Bigler, "John Bigler Papers," MSS, C-B 639, 3; *Shasta Courier*, July 17, 1852, in *SDU*, July 19, 1852, 3; [*Shasta?*] *Courier*, in *SDU*, July 29, 1852, 2.

81. Tushingham, "Development of Intensive Foraging," ii, table 21, 234; Richard Gould, "Tolowa," in Heizer, *Handbook of North American Indians*, 8:135; Drucker, "Tolowa," 241–244; Gould, "Tolowa," 130; Chase, *They Pushed Back*, 11–12; Reed, "*Neeyu Nn'ee min' Nngheeyilh Naach'aaghitlhni*," xiii; Drucker, "Tolowa," 231–235; Gould, *Archaeology*, 80–85. For late twentieth-century precontact Tolowa population estimates, see Cook, "Aboriginal Population," 101; Baumhoff, "Ecological Determinants," 231; Thornton, *American Indian Holocaust*, 207; Bommelyn and Bommelyn, *Now You're Speaking Tolowa*, x; Reed, "Research Notes"; Drucker, "Tolowa," 226–227; Gould, "Tolowa," 128–133.

82. Manypenny, *Our Indian Wards*, 154–155. This probably occurred in 1852 or 1853.

83. Sally Bell, in Nomland, "Sinkyone Notes," 166–167.

84. *Echo*, July 21, 1852, in *DAC*, July 28, 1852, 2.

85. Ellison, "Rejection of California Indian Treaties," 4; Kenny, *History and Proposed Settlement*, 18.

86. John B. Weller, August 11, 1852, in *CG*, August 12, 1852, 21:2175.

87. "An Act making Appropriation for the current and contingent Expenses of the Indian Department, and for fulfilling Treaty Stipulations with various Indian Tribes, for the Year ending June [30, 1853]," in US Congress, *Statutes at Large and Treaties*, 10:56; Gwin, in *CG*, August 28, 1852, 2438; E.A. Hitchcock, Col. 2d Infantry, B.B. General, commanding, Headquarters, Pacific Division, October 31, 1852, S. Exec. Doc. 4, 33rd Cong., Spec. Sess., 1853, serial 688, 374–375. Several scholars have misunderstood this cut as a reduction "to $20,000," because they have cited a misquotation of Gwin, in *LAS*, October 30, 1852, 1.

88. Wells, "Ben Wright Massacre," 317; Chas. McDermitt to John Bigler, Governor of the State of California, December 19, 1852, in California, *California Legislature*, 1853, Appendix, Doc. no. 21, 2, 3. Wells wrote that one escaped ("Ben Wright Massacre," 317); Benj Wright to Gentlemen, September 2, 1852, *IWP*, F3753:203.

89. Special Correspondent's letter, May 7, 1873, in *New York Times*, May 24, 1873, 2; Report of the Committee on Indian Affairs in California, *California Legislature*, 1853, Doc. no. 33, 4; Walling and Munro-Fraser, *Illustrated History*, 205; R.A. Clark, April 23, 187[3?], in *San Francisco Chronicle*, May 7, 1873, 3; Wright to Gentlemen, September 2, 1852, *IWP*, F3753:203. For death toll estimates, see H.S. Lewis to Bigler, September 7, 1852, *IWP*, F3753:211; McDermitt to Bigler, December 19, 1852, in California, *California Legislature*, 1853, Appendix, Doc. 21, 3; Kershaw statement, 42; J.C. Burgess, summarized in Klamath Agency Correspondent, July 1, 1873, in *New York Times*, July 17, 1873, 2; Wells, *History*, 131; Walling and Munro-Fraser, *Illustrated History*, 205; Wells, "Ben Wright Massacre," 318; Kershaw statement, 42. For scalping, see Bradford, *Biographical Sketches*, 39.

90. John E. Ross, Colonel 9th Regiment O.M. to Geo. L. Curry, Acting Governor and Commander-in-chief, November 10, 1854, in H. Mis. Doc. 47, 35th Cong., 2nd Sess.,

1859, serial 1016, 15, and Ross, "Narrative," 25. Kershaw reported twenty-two bodies (Kershaw statement, 42); Nathaniel Todd later reported thirty-six "murdered by the Modoc Indians on the southern Oregon emigrant road" in August 1852 (Todd, in H. Mis. Doc. 47, 35th Cong., 2nd Sess., 1859, serial 1016, 57). In 1857, former Oregon superintendent of Indian Affairs Joel Palmer reported that Wright found eighteen to twenty bodies and that Ross's party found about a dozen (Joel Palmer to B.F. Dowell, Esq., December 17, 1857, in H. Mis. Doc. 47, 35th Cong., 2nd Sess., 1859, serial 1016, 54–56). Wells also wrote of thirty-six bodies ("Ben Wright Massacre," 318). For the estimate of seventy-five, see Meacham, "Report of A.B. Meacham, Special Commissioner to the Modocs, Upon the Late Modoc War," October 5, 1872, in USOIA, *Annual Report*, 1873, 79. Old Schonchin in Special Correspondent's letter, May 7, 1873, in *New York Times*, May 24, 1873, 2.

91. Wright to Gentlemen, September 2, 1852, *IWP*, F3753:203; To His Excellency John Bigler, Governor of the State of California, September 7, 1852, *IWP*, F3753:204; H.S. Lewis to Gov. Bigler, September 7, 1852, *IWP*, F3753:211.

92. E.A. Hitchcock to Bigler, September 15, 1852, NARA, RG393, M2114, Reel 1:392; Jas. Strawbridge to Rains, September 28, 1852, in *SDU*, October 4, 1852, 2; Wells, *History of Siskiyou*, 131; Wells, "Ben Wright Massacre," 318; Walling and Munro-Fraser, *Illustrated History*, 206; Strobridge, *Regulars in the Redwoods*, 45; [Shasta] *Courier*, in *DAC*, November 8, 1852, 2; Report of the Committee on Indian Affairs in California, *California Legislature*, 1853, Doc. no. 33, 4. The "hunting Indians" quotation is from *Courier*, in *DAC*, November 8, 1852, 2. Englishman William Barry participated in an 1852 action that may have been an additional massacre by Wright's men. Barry, who subsequently moved to Australia, wrote in 1878 that, after receiving news of immigrants killed by Modocs, some 800 whites "set out to exact a severe retaliation." Probably exaggerating, given that no other sources report an 1852 anti-Modoc operation of this scale, Barry recalled that after locating some 600 Modocs at "a small lake," Wright's men charged as "darkness set in" but could not locate their quarry. However, at "daylight, when the Indians showed in a body . . . we immediately charged them, shooting down men, women, squaws, and papooses indiscriminately." Barry continued, "The slaughter—for it could hardly be called a fight—was over in half an hour, and we reckoned that scarcely fifty out of the mob escaped; the rest were despatched to the 'happy hunting-grounds' without the slightest show of mercy." Barry, shot in the leg during the attack, recollected, "The loss on our side was trifling, ten killed and twenty wounded, the onslaught being so sudden that the foe could not make any stand at all." Because this massacre is not mentioned in any other source, it is possible that Barry was simply exaggerating another known massacre carried out by Wright. See Barry, *Up and Down California*, 123, 124.

93. E.A. Hitchcock, Colonel 2d Infantry, Brevet Brigadier General, Com'g to Colonel S. Cooper, Adjutant General U.S. Army, March 31, 1853, H. Exec. Doc. 76, 34th Cong., 3rd Sess., 1857, serial 906, 78; Turner, "Scraps of Modoc History," 23; Correspondent to *Shasta Courier*, November 21, 1852, in *DAC*, December 2, 1852, 2; McDermitt to Bigler, December 19, 1852, 3; Hitchcock to Cooper, March 31, 1853, 78; Kershaw statement, 42; Turner, "Scraps of Modoc History," 23; Wells, *History of Siskiyou*, 133; Wells,

"Ben Wright Massacre," 320; Modoc leader Captain Jack in Special Correspondent's letter, May 7, 1873, in *New York Times*, May 24, 1873, 2; Brady, *Northwestern Fights and Fighters*, 231; Frank Riddle, who was married to the Modoc woman Wi-me-ma and was one of Wright's men, paraphrased in Thompson, *Reminiscences of a Pioneer*, 83; Riddle, *Indian History*, 31.

94. Kershaw statement, 42–43; Wells, *History of Siskiyou*, 133. Hitchcock, Barry, and Jeff Riddle all reported similar details. See Hitchcock to Cooper, March 31, 1853, 78; Barry, *Up and Down California*, 124, 125; Riddle, *Indian History*, 32. For final quotation, see Correspondent to *Shasta Courier*, November 21, 1852, in *DAC*, December 2, 1852, 2.

95. Report of the Committee on Indian Affairs, on the Claims of Wright and McDermitt's Command in California, *California Legislature*, 1853, Appendix, Doc. 33, 4; Chief Schonchin, summarized in *New York Times*, July 17, 1873, 2; McDermitt to Bigler, December 19, 1852, 3; Report of the Committee on Indian Affairs, on the Claims of Wright and McDermitt's Command in California, *California Legislature*, 1853, Appendix, Doc. 33, 4; Thompson, *Modoc War*, xvii.

96. California, *Statutes*, 1853, 95–96, 134; Douthit, "Between Indian and White Worlds," 410.

97. Comptroller, "Expenditures," 101.

98. *SDU*, October 4, 1852, 2.

99. Census estimates, summarized in *DAC*, December 23, 1853, 2. For an analysis of the 1852 California census, see Harris, "California Census of 1852," 59–64.

100. William Sebastian, in *CG*, March 3, 1853, 1085.

101. Annual Report of the State Comptroller, 1853, 46, in California, *California Legislature*, 1853, Appendix, Doc. no. 1; *Shasta Courier*, April 2, 1853, 2.

102. *Marysville Herald* correspondent, summarized and quoted in *DAC*, January 22, 1853, 2; J.A. Benson to *Sacramento Daily Union*, *SDU*, February 3, 1853, 2; *SDU*, February 9, 1853, 2.

103. Correspondent to *Stockton Journal*, in *SDU*, February 5, 1853, 2. According to the *Shasta Courier*, "Impelled by hunger," Indians north of Shasta were "fighting for food with a fury unparalleled in the history of our intercourse with them." Moreover, "Hunger is the great cause of their recent attacks" (*Shasta Courier*, March 26, 1853, 2). On February 25, John Breckenridge killed an Indian and took a prisoner whom whites later lynched at Moon's Ranch. At dawn on March 1, a "Mr. Carter of Butte county" led vigilantes in the massacre of thirteen Indians, including "three women," to avenge stolen stock (*SDU*, March 5, 1853, 2).

104. Wells, *History of Siskiyou*, 134; Cox, *Annals of Trinity County*, 121–122; G.C. Lusk, Trinity, March 5, 1853, in *SDU*, March 29, 1853, 3; J.R. to Eds. Union, March 13, 1853, in *SDU*, March 29, 1853, 3.

105. "Miner" to *Sacramento Daily Union*, March 7, 1853, in *SDU*, March 15, 1853, 2; *DAC*, March 30, 1853, 2; *Shasta Courier*, March 26, 1853, 2.

106. General E.A. Hitchcock to Governor John Bigler, November 18, 1853, in California, *Journal of the Legislature*, 1854, 32–33; *Shasta Courier*, March 26, 1853, 2; *Shasta Courier*, April 16, 1853, 2; *Shasta Courier*, April 23, 1853, 2.

107. *Del Norte Record*, June 26, 1880, 2; Collins, *Understanding Tolowa Histories*, 35; SDU, April 30, 1853, 2; G.C. Lusk, in *SDU*, May 7, 1853, 2; Weston, May 6 journal entry, in Weston, *Life in the Mountains*, 9–13; *Columbia Gazette*, in DAC, May 24, 1853, 2.

108. *Yreka Mountain Herald*, July 30, 1853, in *Shasta Courier*, August 6, 1853, 2 (see also Hutchings, January 20, 1855, journal entry, in Hutchings, "Diary," MSS 2003/176 cz, 17–18); *Yreka Mountain Herald* "Extra!," August 7, 1853, scrap in Beinecke Library kindly provided by George Miles; Mr. Thornbury, *Mountain Echo* editor, in *SDU*, August 18, 1853, 2; Riddle, *Indian History*, 15–17. For an example of a soldier who killed an Indian in 1853, see *Shasta Courier*, March 26, 1853, in DAC, March 30, 1853, 2.

109. Riddle, *Indian History*, 19.

110. *Yreka Mountain Herald* "Extra!," August 7, 1853; *Yreka Mountain Herald*, in DAC, August 15, 1853, 2; *Daily Evening Herald*, August 11, 1853, 2; *Yreka Mountain Herald*, in *Shasta Courier*, August 27, 1853, 2.

111. J.S.W. to Editors, August 14, 1853, in DAC, August 19, 1853, 2; Dowell, Correspondence and Papers, MS P-A 133, 5–6.

112. DAC, August 21, 1853, 2; DAC, August 27, 1853, 2; DAC, August 15, 1853, 2.

113. Abo. to Eds. Courier, September 3, 1853, in *Shasta Courier*, September 10, 1853, 1; Curtis, *North American Indian*, 13:91. According to Tolowa dance maker Loren Bommelyn, whites razed Xaa-wan'-k'wvt in 1853 (personal communication, August 9, 2011). October 28, 1853, letter from Fort Lane, in *Oregon Statesman*, November 22, 1853, 4; DAC, December 1, 1853, 1; Lucius Fairchild to J.C. Fairchild and Family, October 16, 1853, in Fairchild, *California Letters*, 157. On October 24, soldiers killed eight to fifteen Indians, potentially Tolowa refugees, on Illinois Creek. See letter, October 28, in *Oregon Statesman*, November 22, 1853, 4; DAC, December 1, 1853, 1.

114. Drucker, "Tolowa," 226, 244; Bommelyn and Bommelyn, *Now You're Speaking Tolowa*, x; Reed, "*Neeyu Nn'ee min' Nngheeyilh Naach'aaghitlhni*," xiii.

115. Peters(?), in *Del Norte Record*, June 26, 1880, 2; Peters, in Coan, "Del Norte Indian," 20–22.

116. Lopez and family, in C. Hart Merriam notes, in Baumhoff, "California Athabascan Groups," 226; Richards, in Gould, "Indian and White Versions," 32–33; Brown, in Gould, "Indian and White Versions," 35–36; Sam Lopez, in Clausen and Spitzner, *Del Norte Bites*, 11 (Jerry Rohde kindly provided this source); Bommelyn, in Norton, *Genocide in Northwestern California*, 54–56; Collins, *Understanding Tolowa Histories*, 35.

117. In Ernie Coan's unpublished 1933 manuscript, Peters recollected at least twenty killed, but an unsigned 1880 *Del Norte Record* article—almost certainly an earlier Peters recollection given nearly identical wording—stated that "an eye witness says that he stood in one place and counted seventy bodies," presumably after the killing had concluded, and thus after many victims had already been immolated or thrown into Lake Earl. These conditions help explain why this 1880 estimate concluded that "perhaps the souls of as many more were sent to . . . the Great Spirit"—for a total of as many as 140 killed, why Bledsoe later estimated "a large number" killed, and why in 1916 Smith River resident Asa Crook reported: "The number killed, including men, women and children is estimated at one hundred fifty." See Peters, in Coan,

"Del Norte Indian," 21; Peters(?), in *Del Norte Record*, June 26, 1880, 2; Bledsoe, *History of Del Norte County*, 20; Asa Crook, in Baldwin, "History of Smith River." Lopez, in Clausen and Spitzner, *Del Norte Bites*, 11; Thornton, "Social Organization," 192; Reed, "*Neeyu Nn'ee min' Nngheeyilh Naach'aaghitlhni,*" 61.

118. *Memorial and Biographical History*, 113–114; Wells and Chambers, *History of Butte County*, 217; *Memorial and Biographical History*, 114; *San Francisco Herald*, January 1, 1854, in *Shasta Courier*, January 7, 1854, 2.

119. *Yreka Mountain Herald*, in DAC, December 26, 1853, 2.

120. *Pictorial Union*, January 1, 1854, 2. During January, newspapers reported five killed "at Burnt Ranch, on Trinity River," seven Tolowas slain "about ten miles up" Smith River, and eight Tolowas killed near "the mouth of Smith's River." See *Shasta Courier*, January 14, 1854, 2; *Crescent City* purser, summarized in DAC, January 19, 1854, 2; DAC, January 19, 1854, 2.

121. S.G. Whipple, W.D. Aylett and A.J. Butler to his Excellency John Bigler Governor of the State of California, *IWP*, F3753:228; Wm. C. Kibbe, Quartermaster General to the County Judge of Klamath Co., January 31, 1854, *IWP*, F3753:229. Klamath County no longer exists.

122. DAC, February 1, 1854, 1; *Shasta Courier*, February 11, 1854, 2; Strobridge, *Regulars in the Redwoods*, 72; *Mountain Herald*, January 21, 1854, in SDU, February 2, 1854, 1; *Shasta Courier*, February 11, 1854, 2.

123. *Shasta Courier*, January 21, 1854, 2. See also SDU, February 13, 1854, 2. John A. Dreibelbis to His Excellency John Bigler, April 13, 1854, *IWP*, F3753:233; Gardiner Brooks, summarized in *Shasta Courier*, February 25, 1854, 2.

124. List of names of Officers and Privates of Company of Volunteers Organized at Pittsburgh Shasta County California on Monday the 20th of Feby 1854, *IWP*, F3753:230; Comptroller, "Expenditures," 122; Dreibelbis to Bigler, April 13, 1854, *IWP*, F3753:233; *Shasta Courier*, March 4, 1854, 2. The *Courier* dated the attack February 24 with twenty-two killed. Dreiblebis thought it occurred on February 15 with twenty-one killed. Dreibelbis to Bigler, April 13, 1853, F3753:233; G.W., to Editors Courier, April 2, 1854, in *Shasta Courier*, April 8, 1854, 2.

125. G.W. to Editors, April 2, 1854, in *Shasta Courier*, April 8, 1854, 2; Dreibelbis to Bigler, April 13, 1853, F3753:233; Comptroller, "Expenditures," A1.

126. Karl to Messrs. Editors, March 18, 1854, in *Shasta Courier*, March 25, 1854, 2; *Daily Democratic State Journal*, March 14, 1854, 2. On March 11, 1854, the *Butte Record* reported that after a cattle theft near Tehama, vigilantes massacred twenty-three Yahi Yana Indians in Dry Creek Canyon (*Butte Record*, March 11, 1854, 2). The *Daily Democratic State Journal* reported a similar atrocity in Colusa County, which may in fact have been this same massacre (*Daily Democratic State Journal*, March 14, 1854, 2).

127. Colonel W. Willer, summarized in DAC, March 29, 1854, 2.

128. Hittell, *General Laws*, 532; California, *Statutes*, 1913, 57; Goodrich, "Legal Status," 94n47.

129. Fernandez, "Except a California Indian," 163. In early April, the *Shasta Courier* had reported that "during the last five months 63 McCloud Indians and 40 Pitt River

Indians have been killed by the miners" (*Shasta Courier*, summarized in *DAC*, April 12, 1854, 2). On April 15, the *Daily Alta California* estimated that "since the beginning of winter 65 McCloud Indians [Wintu] and 49 Pitt Indians [Achumawi] have been shot down" (*DAC*, April 15, 1854, 1). Also in April, the *Yreka Mountain Herald* reported "the camp of some Indians in Shasta Valley . . . pitched into and cleaned out" as well as "four Indians . . . killed by some whites on Trinity River" (*Yreka Mountain Herald*, in *DAC*, May 1, 1854, 2).

130. Thornton, *American Indian Holocaust*, 201, 203; Lynn, *Story of the Stolen Valley*, 4; Tassin, "Chronicles, I," 25; Foster, "Summary of Yuki Culture," 176; Powers, *Tribes of California*, 128; Malinowski and Sheets, *Gale Encyclopedia*, 4:239. For demographers' precontact population estimates, see Cook, "Aboriginal Population," 108, 127; Thornton, *American Indian Holocaust*, 203. For some primary source population estimates, see Tassin, "Chronicles, I," 25; Potter, "Reminiscences," MSS C-D 5136:2, 1; Simmon Storms to Tho. Henley, 20 June 1856, NARA, RG75, M234, Reel 35:475. For ethnographic information, see Virginia Miller, "Yuki, Huchnom, and Coast Yuki," in Heizer, *Handbook of North Ameican Indians*, 8:249–255.

131. Asbill and Shawley, *Last of the West*, 18, 19; Palmer, *History of Mendocino*, 459, 595, 596. According to anthropologist Virginia Miller, "One aged Yuki man living in Round Valley" later "denie[d] this account of the discovery of Round Valley. He says instead that [while] the Asbill-Kelsey party did kill one Yuki boy. . . . The Yuki pursued the white men at the time" (Miller, "Yuki," 46–47).

132. John Bigler to Hon. Winslow S. Pierce, June 30, 1853, in California, *California Legislature*, 1855, 63–64; Gwin in *CG*, December 7, 1853, 14; *CG*, December 14, 1853, 33.

133. *California Legislature*, 1855, 63–69; US Congress, *Statutes at Large and Treaties*, 10:582–583. Killings multiplied during the second half of 1854. Between August and early November, Oregon militiamen patrolling northeastern California's Oregon Trail killed at least thirty Modocs and Paiutes in one-sided engagements. In November, Churn Town residents "killed several . . . savages." And "in the latter part of 1854," twenty vigilantes killed seven Wintu people, destroyed a village, and murdered four prisoners at the mouth of Hayfork Creek. Whites then killed perhaps "eleven or twelve" Indians between the south and main forks of the Trinity that winter. For Oregon militia expedition, see Delazon Smith and A.P. Dennison, January 31, 1856, in H. Mis. Doc. 47, 35th Cong., 2nd Sess., 1859, serial 1016, 29; L.F. Grover and James Kelly, January 13, 1857, in H. Mis. Doc. 47, 35th Cong., 2nd Sess., 1859, serial 1016, 31; Jesse Walker to John Ross, November 6, 1854, in H. Mis. Doc. 47, 35th Cong., 2nd Sess., 1859, serial 1016, 12–13. For Churn Town, see *Shasta Courier*, November 25, 1854, 2. One J.J.T. refuted this report, in *Shasta Courier*, December 2, 1854, 2. For Hayfork and Trinity, see Cox, *Annals of Trinity County*, 84–87.

CHAPTER 7. PERFECTING THE KILLING MACHINE

1. Loren Bommelyn, "Purpose of Nee-dash."

2. On the night of December 30–31, 1854, the moon was 94 percent illuminated and waxing. United States Naval Observatory, "Complete Sun and Moon Data."

3. In 1854, all of what is now Del Norte County was part of Klamath County. For arma-
ments, see Military Records, Bins 3415-1 and 3493-1; Wm. L Kibbe, Quartermaster
General to the County Judge of Klamath Co., January 31, 1854, *IWP*, F3753:229; John
Bigler, Governor State of California, September 11, 1854, in Military Records, Bin
3409-3; "Invoice of Ordnance + Armament Stores turned over to Capt. D.W. Thorpe
for use of the Coast Rangers," in Military Records, Bin 3409-3.

4. *Crescent City Herald*, January 10, 1855, 2; Bledsoe, *History of Del Norte County*, 32;
Muster Roll of the Coast Rangers of Klamath County, California, U.S.A., in Military
Records, Bin 3409-3; D.W. Thorpe, in "Requisition, Coast Rangers," Military Records,
Bin 3409-3; 1940 WPA study, http://www.militarymuseum.org/KlamathMounted%20
Rangers.html; White informants, interviewed in the 1960s, in Warburton and Endert,
Indian Lore, 167–168; *Crescent City Herald*, January 3, 1855, 2. For Indian death toll
estimates, see *Crescent City Herald*, January 3, 1855, 2; Anderson Myers, First Lieu-
tenant Coast Rangers to Adjutant General of Calia, March 10, 1855, in Military Records, Bin 3413-5, Coast Rangers; Bledsoe, *History of Del Norte County*, 32; White
informants, in Warburton and Endert, *Indian Lore*, 168; Tolowa informants, in
Thornton, "Social Organization," 192; Tolowa informants, in Collins, *Understanding
Tolowa Histories*, 36; Anderson Myers to Adjutant General, March 10, 1855. As in some
other California massacres, attackers killed many people in the water or threw their
victims' bodies into it, thus making an accurate body count difficult for them to
obtain.

5. *Crescent City Herald*, January 3, 1855, 2.

6. *Crescent City Herald*, January 17, 1855, 2 (the treaty text is in this article); Chase, *They
Pushed Back*, 44. Chase's narrative may be an inaccurate retelling of the Etchulet
massacre.

7. *SDU*, January 19, 1855, 2; January 22, 1855, letter in *SDU*, February 3, 1855, 2; *Yreka
Herald*, summarized in *SDU*, January 19, 1855, 2.

8. *HT*, January 27, 1855, 2; E to *Yreka Herald*, January 18, 1855, in *DAC*, January 27, 1855,
2; *HT*, January 27, 1855, 2; Judge Fletcher of Klamath County, paraphrased in *DAC*,
February 20, 1855, 2.

9. Stephen Smith to Mssr's McDonald & Young, January 5, 1855, in Rosborough,
"Special Indian Agent," 203; Bledsoe, *Indian Wars*, 164; *HT*, January 20, 1855, 2;
Mr. Strawbridge, in *HT*, January 13, 1855, 2; F. Buzelle to Capt. H.W. Judah, 4th US
Infantry, January 16, 1855, in *HT*, February 3, 1855, 2.

10. *HT*, January 20, 1855, 2; *HT*, January 27, 1855, 2; Fletcher, paraphrased in *DAC*, February
20, 1855, 2.

11. *HT*, January 27, 1855, 2; Comptroller, "Expenditures," 38–43; *HT*, January 20, 1855, 2;
January 22, 1855, letter in *Crescent City Herald*, January 31, 1855, 2; *HT*, January 20,
1855, 2.

12. F. Buzelle to Capt. Best, January 25, 1855, in *HT*, February 3, 1855, 2; *HT*, February 3,
1855, 2; *SDU*, February 3, 1855, 2; *HT*, February 10, 1855, 2; *HT*, February 17, 1855, 2.

13. Fletcher, paraphrased in *DAC*, February 20, 1855, 2; *HT* February 17, 1855, 2; Comptroller, "Expenditures," 38; *HT*, February 24, 1855, 2; *Crescent City Herald*, March 19,
1855, 2. By February 24, the *Humboldt Times* reported an absolute minimum of

twenty-five or thirty Indians killed, but this was an underestimate (*HT*, February 24, 1855, 2). For Judah report, see Judah, summarized in John E. Wool, Major General to Lieut. Col. L. Thomas, Assistant Adjutant General, April 11, 1855, S. Exec. Doc. 1, Part 2, 34th Cong., 1st Sess., 1855, serial 811, 75.

14. Comptroller, "Expenditures," 39, 41; Bledsoe, *Indian Wars*, 174–175 (the *Humboldt Times* reported that Judah's forces "killed one of Chiponish's party." *HT*, April 21, 1855, 2); *HT*, May 26, 1855, 2; Comptroller, "Expenditures," 39, 41; Bledsoe, *Indian Wars*, 176. Two other militia companies remained active, but their operations during this time are obscured by a lack of extant sources.

15. February 10, 1855, letter to *Daily California Statesman*, February 15, 1855, 2.

16. Oberly, *Sixty Million Acres*, 37. For the 1855 Bounty Land Law text, see *Crescent City Herald*, May 2, 1855, 1.

17. *Crescent City Herald*, April 25, 1855, 4.

18. California, *Statutes*, 1855, 136–143; California, "Report of the Controller of State. January, 1857," A, in California, *Appendix to Assembly Journals*, 1857, 87; Office of Quartermaster and Adj't General, "Annual Report of the Quarter-Master and Adjutant-General," 5, 4, in California, *Appendix to Assembly Journals*, 1856.

19. Kibbe, *Volunteer*, iii; John Bigler, General and Commander in Chief, General Order, September 10, 1855, in California Adjutant General's Office, *Military Department, Adjutant General, General Orders, 1855–1924* B3473-4; Sec of War Jefferson Davis to John Bigler, Governor of California, December 24, 1855 in California Adjutant General's Office, *Military Department, Adjutant General, Adjutant General's Office Records, 1848–1861* VB358. For an advertisement for Kibbe's manual, see *DAC*, December 1, 1855, 1.

20. *Grass Valley Telegraph*, in *DAC*, April 7, 1855, 2; *DAC*, April 7, 1855, 2.

21. Jeffn. Davis, Secretary of War to Hon. R.M. McClellan, Secretary of the Interior, May 23, 1855, NARA, RG75, M234, Reel 34:1000; Robt White to Col. T.J. Henley, August 9, 1855, NARA, RG75, M234, Reel 34:667; Robt. White to Col. T.J. Henley, August 20, 1855, NARA, RG75, M234, Reel 34:685.

22. *Yreka Mountain Herald*, in *SDU*, June 14, 1855, 3; *HT*, June 16, 1855, 2. In 1854, whites reportedly massacred eleven Indian people in Yreka (Bailey Diary, in Smith, *History of Del Norte County*, 39).

23. P.A. Chalfant, in *Morning Call*, January 4, 1885, 1. Chalfant stipulated, "I won't be positive as to the exact month, or even certain as to the year, though every incident herein stated is given as a literal occurrence."

24. *HT*, July 14, 1855, 2.

25. *Yreka Union*, in *DAC*, August 4, 1855, 2; Wells, *History of Siskiyou*, 138; Walling and Munro-Fraser, *Illustrated History*, 238; Comptroller, "Expenditures," 27–32; Walling and Munro-Fraser, *Illustrated History*, 238. Whites killed "five Indians . . . at Hamburgh Bar," on the Klamath, another Indian on the Scott River, and on July 30 or 31 lynched two Indians and shot one at Yreka and "six . . . on Humbug." See *Yreka Union*, in *SDU*, August 9, 1855, 2; *HT*, August 11, 1855, 2; Wells, *History of Siskiyou*, 139; *Yreka Union*, in *SDU*, August 9, 1855, 2. Horsley & Barrow's Express report, July 31, 1855, in *DAC*, August 6, 1855, 2; Walling and Munro-Fraser, *Illustrated History*, 238.

26. Comptroller, "Expenditures," 27; Walling and Munro-Fraser, *Illustrated History*, 238–240; Comptroller, "Expenditures," 30, 101; Wells, *History of Siskiyou*, 141. A seventh company mustered in on October 10, but its operations are obscured by a lack of extant evidence.

27. Chief Weimah in Hutchings, October 1, 1855, journal entry in Hutchings, Diary, 138; Bumpis summarized by Correspondent, October 21, 1855, in *SDU*, October 24, 1855, 2.

28. *DAC*, October 20, 1855, 2; *DAC*, October 22, 1855, 2; *Marysville Herald*, October 23, 1855, 2; *Sonora Herald*, in *SDU*, October 23, 1855, 3; *SDU*, November 2, 1855, 2; *Nevada Journal*, November 16, 1855, 2.

29. "Chief of the Fall River Band," in Curtis, *North American Indian*, 13:133; Major General John Wool, Commander of the Department of the Pacific, to Lt. Col. Lorenzo Thomas, Assistant Adjutant General, Headquarters of the Army, New York City, November 3, 1855, S. Exec. Doc. 26, 34th Cong., 1st Sess., 1856, serial 819, 50; *Nevada Journal*, in *DAC*, November 18, 1855, 2; Anonymous correspondent, in *SDU*, December 29, 1855, 3.

30. *Shasta Courier*, January 12, 1856, 2; *Shasta Republican*, March 8, 1856, 2; *San Francisco Herald*, April 4, 1856, 2; *HT*, April 5, 1856, 2; *Shasta Republican*, April 19, 1856, 2; Mr. Skillman, in *SDU*, April 19, 1856, 2; T.J. Moorman, in *SDU*, April 22, 1856, 2.

31. *Shasta Republican*, April 19, 1856, 2; Mr. Skillman, in *SDU*, April 19, 1856, 2; T.J. Moorman, in *SDU*, April 22, 1856, 2; *Shasta Republican*, April 19, 1856, 2; letter to *Marysville Express*, in *HT*, May 10, 1856, 2; *San Francisco Herald*, April 4, 1856, 2.

32. California, *Statutes*, 1856, 87–89. The increased "Military Tax" yielded higher revenues of $5,812.82 between July 1, 1856, and June 30, 1857. However, after legislators lowered the per man tax to twenty-five cents, in 1857, annual revenues fell to $3,682.06. See G.H. Whitman, "Annual Report of the Comtroller of State, for 1857," A, in California, *Appendix to Assembly Journals*, 1858; A.R. Melony, "Annual Report of the Controller of State, for the Year 1858," A, in California, *Appendix to Journals of Assembly*, 1859.

33. David N Gilmore to His Excellency J Neely Johnson, May 5, 1856, *IWP*, F3753:284; William C. Kibbe, "Annual Report of the Quarter-Master and Adjutant General," December 15, 1856, 8, in California, *Appendix to Assembly Journals*, 1857; May 6, 1856, postscript in Gilmore to Johnson, May 5, 1856, *IWP*, F3753:284; E.Y. Naylor, Quartermaster and Commissary to Gen. Wm. C. Kibbe, August 26, 1856, in William C. Kibbe, "Annual Report of the Quarter-Master and Adjutant General," 10–11, in California, *Appendix to Assembly Journals*, 1857. The Comptroller ultimately reported thirty-one militiamen enrolled in this expedition (Comptroller, "Expenditures," 124).

34. Telegram, May 5, in *DEB*, May 5, 1856, 2; *Daily San Joaquin Republican*, May 6, 1856, 2; Foster De Master Captain of the Tulare Mounted Riflemen to the Governor of the State of California, April 30, 1856, *IWP*, F3753:244; Kibbe, "Annual Report of the Quarter-Master and Adjutant General," December 15, 1856, 14; W.H.J. to Editors, in *Volcano Weekly Ledger*, May 17, 1856, 2.

35. Mr. Nicols, in *Mariposa Gazette*, May 13, 1856, in *SDU*, May 20, 1856, 2; *LAS*, May 8, 1856, 3.

36. J. Neeley Johnson, paraphrased in G.W. Barbour, R. McKee and O.M. Wozencraft to Hon. Luke Lea Esq., February 17, 1851, NARA, RG75, M234, Reel 32:106; *Evening Journal*, paraphrased in *SDU*, May 10, 1856, 2; J. Neeley Johnson to Dr. George, May 8, 1856, *IWP*, F3753:246; Comptroller, "Expenditures," 125; *Evening Journal*, paraphrased in *SDU*, May 10, 1856, 2; Careless, May 15, 1856, in *Daily San Joaquin Republican*, May 21, 1856, 2; *SDU*, May 15, 1856, 2; *Stockton Argus*, summarized in *SDU*, June 12, 1856, 2; Careless, May 15, 1856, in *San Joaquin Republican*, May 21, 1856, 2; E.F. Beale Brig Genl 1st Brig 1st Division to J. Neely Johnson Governor State of Cal, July 12, 1856, *IWP*, F3753:263.

37. Beale to Johnson, July 12, 1856, *IWP*, F3753:263; E[.]F. Beale Brigadier General to His Excellency, J. Neely Johnson, Governor of the State of California, June 10, 1856, *IWP*, F3753:249; Menefee and Dodge, *History of Tulare*, 24. Beale to Johnson, July 12, 1856, *IWP*, F3753:263; Beale to Johnson, June 10, 1856, *IWP*, F3753:249; Beale to Johnson, July 12, 1856, *IWP*, F3753:263; *SDU*, July 1, 1856, 3; *SDU*, August 27, 1856, 3; W.W. Allen, in *San Joaquin Republican*, August 23, 1856, 2.

38. Bradford, *Biographical Sketches*, 48–51; Geo. to Editor Republican, August 18, 1856, in *Shasta Republican*, August 23, 1856, 2; Bledsoe, *Indian Wars*, 207.

39. Yreka correspondent, in *Marysville Daily Herald*, November 18, 1855, 2; J.D. Cosby, Maj. Gen. Com. Per C.W. Lizer Adjt. to His Excellency J. Neely Johnson, June 12, 1856, *IWP*, F3753:293. Cosby was probably referring to the murders of Charles W. Greene and Thomas Stewart "on McKinney's creek, in Siskiyou county" and the June 9 "murder of a Mr. Gibson and Mr. Coe, about eight miles west of Willow Springs, in Shasta county" (*Yreka Union*, in *SDU*, June 21, 1856, 3). R.C. Wood's "spy company" went into service on June 12, 1856 (Comptroller, "Expenditures," Modoc Expedition, 14).

40. J. Neely Johnson to John E. Wool, Maj Genl Comdg Pacific Division, June 17, 1856, *IWP*, F3753:294; J. Neely Johnson to Hon. John Cosby, Major Gen'l Commanding 6th Division Cal. Mil., August 4, 1856, *IWP*, F3753:296; *Yreka Union*, in *SDU*, August 5, 1856, 1; Comptroller, "Expenditures," Modoc Expedition, 8–13; *Yreka Chronicle*, August 7, 1856, in *SDU*, August 11, 1856, 1; *Yreka Union*, August 7, 1856, in Wells, *History of Siskiyou*, 142. Captain H.M. Judah, stationed at Fort Jones, denied the accuracy of these reports (Judah, in Wells, *History of Siskiyou*, 143).

41. Johnson to Cosby, August 4, 1856, *IWP*, F3753:296.

42. D.L. Olmsted and Omer C. Stewart, "Achumawi," in Heizer, *Handbook of North American Indians*, 8:225–235; Malinowski and Sheets, *Gale Encyclopedia*, 4:14–18.

43. August 19, 1856, letter in *Siskiyou Chronicle*, August 28, 1856, in *SDU*, September 2, 1856, 1; *Shasta Republican*, August 30, 1856, 2; August 19, 1856, letter in *Siskiyou Chronicle*, August 28, 1856, in *SDU*, September 2, 1856, 1; *Shasta Republican*, August 30, 1856, 2; August 19, 1856, letter in *Siskiyou Chronicle*, August 28, 1856, in *SDU*, September 2, 1856, 1; *Shasta Republican*, August 30, 1856, 2; August 19, 1856, letter to *Yreka Union*, summarized in *Shasta Republican*, August 30, 1856, 2.

44. Jargon to Editors Yreka Union, September 4, in *Yreka Union*, September 11, 1856, in *SDU*, September 17, 1856, 1; *SDU*, October 8, 1856, 2.

45. Correspondent, September 29, 1856, in *SDU*, October 17, 1856, 2; Major R.C. Wood, in *Yreka Union*, October 9, 1856, in *SDU*, October 17, 1856, 2; Strobridge, *Regulars in the Redwoods*, 133; *Shasta Republican*, September 13, 1856, 2. On September 8, Judah came into Yreka and reported "killing five and wounding another" at Hat Creek (*Yreka Union*, September 11, 1856, in *SDU*, September 17, 1856, 1).

46. Correspondent, September 29, 1856, in *Yreka Union*, October 9, 1856, in *SDU*, October 17, 1856, 2; Correspondent, October 3, 1856, in *Yreka Union*, October 9, 1856, in *SDU*, October 17, 1856, 2; Correspondent in *Yreka Union*, October 16, 1856, in *SDU*, October 21, 1856, 2; Comptroller, "Expenditures," Modoc Expedition, 9–12, 22.

47. Comptroller, "Expenditures," Modoc Expedition, A6; Cosby, paraphrased in Wells, *History of Siskiyou*, 143.

48. On July 8, Weller introduced a bill to force Davis to pay. However, senators' reluctance to pay the private investors who held California's "War Debt" bonds overwhelmed Weller's power as Senate Military Affairs Committee chairman and the bill died in committee (*CG*, July 8, 1856, 1567). For Judah P. Benjamin and the Confederacy, see Meade, *Judah P. Benjamin*, 159–207, 244–256.

49. *CG*, July 22, 1856, 1669; *CG*, July 29, 1856, 1777–1778; *CG*, August 1, 1856, 1846; *CG*, August 15, 1856, 2122–2125; Smith and Denver, "Report of Commissioners of California War Debt," January 5, 1857, in California, *Senate Journal*, 1858, 48–49.

50. *SDU*, January 17, 1860, 2.

51. H.Y.L., October 2, 1856, in *HT*, October 4, 1856, 2; *HT*, October 4, 1856, 2; Bledsoe, *Indian Wars*, 208; *HT*, November 15, 1856, 2; Hittell, *History of California*, 3:915.

52. *DEB*, September 1, 1856, 1; Metlar, *Northern California*, 7.

53. *MMR*, 3; Benjamin Arthur deposition, February 28, 1860, *MMR*, 51; John Burgess deposition, February 28, 1860, *MMR*, 24; John Lawson deposition, February 27, 1860, *MMR*, 68; Arthur deposition, *MMR*, 51; Dryden Lacock deposition, February 25, 1860, *MMR*, 49; Dryden Lacock deposition, February 25, 1860, *IWP*, F3753:441.

54. J. Neely Johnson, January 7, 1857, in California, *Senate Journal*, 1857, 29, 36. For small militia-related funding bills, see California, *Senate Journal*, 1857, 147, 286, 381, 395.

55. *DAC*, March 23, 1857, 2 (emphasis added); *Shasta Republican*, April 4, 1857, 2. The *Republican* later published a *Trinity Journal* denial that claimed, "Nothing of the kind ever happened" (*Shasta Republican*, April 25, 1857, 4).

56. California, *Appendix to Assembly Journals*, 1857, 722; California, *Senate Journal*, 1857, 793; California, *Statutes*, 1857, 262–263.

57. "Chief of the Fall River Band," in Curtis, *North American Indian*, 13:133; G. Whitney, summarized in *Yreka Union Extra*, in *Butte Record*, February 21, 1857, 2; *Shasta Republican*, February 14, 1857, 2; *Yreka Union*, paraphrased in *Butte Record*, May 2, 1857, 3; *Shasta Republican*, February 14, 1857, 2; *Shasta Republican*, March 14, 1857, 2; *Yreka Union*, in *DAC*, March 5, 1857, 2; *Shasta Republican*, March 14, 1857, 2. Lockhart later claimed to have poisoned only one Indian during the summer of 1856 but did not deny having left poison-laced flour in 1857 (*Shasta Republican*, March 28, 1857, 2).

58. Lockhart, in *Shasta Republican*, March 28, 1857, 2; Woodbridge, "Tragedy of Pit River," 641–642. The *Sacramento Daily Union* does not seem to contain the report

mentioned by the anonymous informant. However, the informant may have been referring to the *Yreka Union*, located much closer to Shasta than the *Sacramento Daily Union*. There are very few extant copies of the *Yreka Union* so it is difficult to verify this supposition. Robert Bennett to Edward Bennett, June 9, 1623, in Kingsbury, *Records of the Virginia Company*, 4:220–222. William Scott deposition, March 2, 1860, *MMR*, 22.

59. Comptroller, "Expenditures," 74. On or about April 1, they killed one person and severely wounded another. On April 7, they surprised and massacred sixteen people. Then they killed three more. Lockhart and five others mustered out on April 18 and reported a total of nineteen killed and "many wounded." See *Shasta Republican*, April 11, 1857, 2; Wiley J. Fox, in *Yreka Union*, in *Butte Record*, May 2, 1857, 3; Samuel R. Lockhart to *Shasta Courier*, April 21, 1857, in *SDU*, April 28, 1857, 2; Comptroller, "Expenditures," 74; Lockhart to *Shasta Courier*, April 21, 1857, in *SDU*, April 28, 1857, 2. "Chief of the Fall River Band," in Curtis, *North American Indian*, 13:133–134; *Yreka Union*, May 7, 1857, in *SDU*, May 12, 1857, 1; *Yreka Union*, paraphrased in *SDU*, May 20, 1857, 2; Comptroller, "Expenditures," 74.

60. "Chief of the Fall River Band," in Curtis, *North American Indian*, 13:134.

61. *State Register and Year Book of Facts*, 122.

62. Mr. Jenner, summarized in *Yreka Union*, in *DAC*, July 6, 1857, 2; Crook, *General George Crook*, xix, 39. On June 7, they killed three to five Achumawis. On June 26, they killed another, and on June 27, they killed two more. See Simeon Oldom, paraphrased in *Shasta Republican*, June 20, 1857, 3; *Siskiyou Chronicle*, in *SDU*, June 27, 1857, 3; Crook, *General George Crook*, 42; *Yreka Union*, July 2, 1857, in *SDU*, July 8, 1857, 2; Crook, *General George Crook*, 42–43.

63. Lieut. Saunders, summarized in *Yreka Union*, July 16, 1857, in *SDU*, July 20, 1857, 2; Crook, *General George Crook*, 45; "A private letter from Lt.C., to a gentleman in [Shasta]," in *Shasta Republican*, July 18, 1857, 2 (Crook did not mention the July 7 massacre in his autobiography); Lieut. Dryer, paraphrased in *Butte Record*, July 11, 1857, 4; *Yreka Union*, in *SDU*, August 5, 1857, 2; *Yreka Union*, in *Shasta Republican*, August 8, 1857, 2 (Crook recollected that the July 25 massacre took place on July 27, in *General George Crook*, 47; Lieut. Sanders reported thirty killed in this massacre, in *SDU*, August 4, 1857, 2); Crook, *General George Crook*, 53; *Shasta Republican*, August 1, 1857, 3; Lieutenant McCall, paraphrased in *Yreka Chronicle*, August 27, 1857, in *SDU*, September 1, 1857, 3; Crook, *General George Crook*, 52.

64. *Red Bluff Beacon* and Mr. Chaffee, paraphrased in *Shasta Republican*, June 20, 1857, 2; J. Williams, paraphrased in *SDU*, October 24, 1857, 2; Fairfield, *Fairfield's Pioneer History*, 83, 85; J. Williams, paraphrased in *SDU*, October 24, 1857, 2.

65. *SDU*, April 8, 1857, 3.

66. *DAC*, May 12, 1857, 1; *Tehama Advocate*, paraphrased in *DAC*, October 6, 1857, 1; *DAC*, May 13, 1857, 2; *Mariposa Gazette*, in *DAC*, February 7, 1858, 1; Wallace, *Long Bitter Trail*, 81, 87; Foreman, *Traveler in Indian Territory*, 120; Thornton, *American Indian Holocaust*, 118.

67. Mr. Peilsticker, paraphrased in *Butte Record*, October 18, 1856, 2; Yoi'-mut, in F.F. Latta, "Little Journeys in the San Joaquin," in *Livingston Chronicle*, September 2,

1937, 4; Andrew Freeman, in Goldschmidt, "Nomlaki Ethnography," 313; Kroeber, *Ishi in Two Worlds*, 47.

68. Yoi'-mut, in Latta, "Little Journeys in the San Joaquin," *Livingston Chronicle*, September 2, 1937, 4; Baumgardner, *Yanks in the Redwoods*, 101; J.L. Clapp, in J. Ross Browne, Special Agt Treas'y Dept. to Hon. Chas. E. Mix, Commissioner of Indian Affairs, November 1, 1858, in Heizer, *Destruction of California Indians*, 122; Matteo, in Deposition of John P. Simpson, August 12, 1858, NARA, RG75, M234, Reel 36:333; Deposition of H.L. Ford, August 16, 1858, NARA, RG75, M234, Reel 36:342. According to reservation employee William H. Ray, Matteo said that "his people ~~were starving~~ would starve," in Deposition of William H. Ray, August 16, 1858, NARA, RG75, M234, Reel 36:363; Simpson deposition, August 12, 1858, 331. Baumgardner, *Yanks in the Redwoods*, 205; G.J. Rains, Major 4th Infy. Comdg., Actg. Ind. Agent to Hon. Thos. J. Hendricks, Commissioner of Indian Affairs, April 30, 1860, NARA, RG75, M234, Reel 37:1161; Tome-ya-nem, in Tassin, "Con-Cow Indians," 10.

69. G. Bailey, Special Agent Interior Department, to Charles E. Mix, Commissioner of Indian Affairs, November 4, 1858, in USOIA, *Annual Report*, 1858, 298; Edward Johnson, Br'vt Maj. and Capt. to W.W. Mackall, Ass't Adg't-Gen, August 21, 1859, in California, *Correspondence Relative to Indian Affairs in Mendocino County*, 9; Browne, "Coast Rangers," 311; Edward D. Castillo, "Impact of Euro-American Exploration and Settlement," in Heizer, *Handbook of North American Indians*, 8:111.

70. Major General John Wool to U.S. Senators D.C. Broderick and Wm. Gwin, January 28, 1857, 2, 4, Interior Department Appointment Papers; Arthur deposition, *MMR*, 51. Indian Agent Simon Storms, who became very wealthy using Indian labor, "testified that only three Indians died while provisioning" the reservation. See Bauer, *We Were All Like Migrant Workers Here*, 40, 38.

71. Reed, *"Neeyu Nn'ee min' Nngheeyilh Naach'aaghitlhni,"* 81; C.H..Rundell, 2d Lieutenant 4th Infantry, Commanding Detachment to Lieutenant F.H. Bates, 4th Infantry, Commanding Fort Humboldt, California, June, 1856, H. Exec. Doc. 1, Pt. 2, 34th Cong., 3rd Sess., 1856, serial 894, 151; Jasper Janes, in *Northern Californian*, in *HT*, June 23, 1860, 2; H.P. Heintzelman to T.J. Henley, July 13, 1857 in USOIA, *Annual Report*, 1857, 391–392; *Crescent City Herald*, August 5, 1857, 2; *Crescent City Herald*, August 12, 1857, 2; John G. Hyatt, Acting Clerk, Klamath Reservation, November 23, 1857, in *Crescent City Herald*, December 2, 1857, 2; Crook, *General George Crook*, 57; James Mathews, R.H. Parris, and Stephens, in *HT*, November 28, 1857, 2; Bledsoe, *Indian Wars*, 224–225.

72. *HT*, July 17, 1858, 2; *HT*, October 2, 1858, 2.

73. In January, a posse led by Rudolph Klotz killed "ten or twelve [Yana] Indians" and, on February 4, "Adolf," of Todd's Valley, reported five Indians killed in various engagements. After Yuki Indians reportedly ambushed William Mantle, Round Valley farmer Isaac Shannon recollected that he and others "went out and killed 14 Indians." See *Red Bluff Beacon*, February 2, 1858, 2; Adolf, Todd's Valley, February 4, 1858, in *SDU*, February 6, 1858, 3; Charles Eberle deposition, February 22, 1860, *MMR*, 35; Isaac Shannon deposition, February 28, 1860, *MMR*, 72. Isaac Roop to Editor Republican, April 22, 1858, in *Shasta Republican*, May 8, 1858, 1; Correspondent to *SDU*,

May 4, 1858, 2; Dow and Hines, in Fairfield, *Fairfield's Pioneer History*, 114–115; *SDU*, May 12, 1858, 2; Dow and Hines, in Fairfield, *Fairfield's Pioneer History*, 116–118; *Oroville Advertiser*, in *DAC*, May 9, 1858, 1; Mr. Garlow, in *Butte Record*, May 10, 1858, in *SDU*, May 12, 1858, 2; J.L. Adams, summarized in *Red Bluff Beacon*, May 26, 1858, 2; E.W. Inskeep to Editors, April 28, 1858, and editor in *Red Bluff Beacon*, May 5, 1858, 2; Correspondent to *Sacramento Daily Union*, May 3, 1858, in *SDU*, May 6, 1858, 1; Delaney, "Adventures of Captain Hi Good," 1.

74. *HT*, June 19, 1858, 2; *HT*, June 26, 1858, 2; *HT*, July 17, 1858, 2; G.J. Rains, Major, 4th Infy. Comdg. Act. Indn. agent to Honorable Thos. J. Hendricks, April 30, 1860, NARA, RG75, M234, 37:1160; *HT*, July 17, 1858, 2; *Yreka Union*, July 29, 1858, in *DEB*, August 4, 1858, 3; *DAC*, August 5, 1858, 1; Brown, "Indian Wars in Trinity," 37; F.E.W., Reservation, Klamath River, July 20, 1858, in *Crescent City Herald*, July 28, 1858, 2; *HT*, August 7, 1858, 2; *Trinity Journal*, in *HT*, July 10, 1858, 2 (in this same issue, the *Humboldt Times* denied "an attack had been made upon the Indians on Mad river when the [*Trinity Journal*] item was written"); *Shasta Courier*, July 31, 1858, in *SDU*, August 3, 1858, 1.

75. *HT*, September 18, 1858, 2; J. Ross Browne, "Report of J. Ross Browns in relation to a probably Indian War in California resulting from difficulties In the Vicinity of Humboldt Bay," September 29, 1858, NARA, RG75, M234, Reel 36:436.

76. A. Wiley, Editor and Proprietor "Humboldt Times" to His Excellency John B. Weller, August 14, 1858, in California, *Senate Journal*, 1859, 671–674; Burch to Weller, n.d., paraphrased in *Sacramento Mercury*, in *DAC*, August 15, 1858, 2; John B. Weller, Gov. + Com in Chief to Genl. S.H. Dosh, Brig. Genl. 2nd Brigade 6th Division, September 5, 1858, *IWP*, F3753:335; W.W. Markoll, A.A. General to his Excellency, John B. Weller, Gov. State of Cal., September 6, 1858, in *HT*, September 25, 1858, 2; Kibbe, paraphrased in *Marysville Express*, in *DAC*, September 21, 1858, 2; *HT*, September 25, 1858, 2.

77. Anonymous to *Daily Alta California*, September 30, 1858, in *DAC*, October 1, 1858, 2.

78. Bledsoe, *Indian Wars*, 241–242; Cox, *Annals of Trinity County*, 130; *SDU*, October 18, 1858, 2; *HT*, October 2, 1858, 2.

79. Governor Weller to General S. H. Dosh, September 5, 1858, *IWP*, F3753:336; S.H. Dosh, Brig. Gen. commanding 2nd Brigade, 6th Division to the citizens of Shasta, Trinity and Humboldt Counties, October 6, 1858, in *Shasta Courier*, October 9, 1858, 2; *HT*, October 9, 1858, 2; *Yreka Union*, October 14, 1858, in *SDU*, October 18, 1858, 2; Comptroller, "Expenditures," 60.

80. *HT*, October 30, 1858, 2; *Trinity Journal*, November 6, 1858, 1; Wm. C. Kibbe, Quartermaster and Adjutant-General to His Excellency, John B. Weller, Governor State of California, April 7, 1859, in California, *Senate Journal*, 1859, 667; *HT*, November 20, 1858, 2; *HT*, December 4, 1858, 2; Settler to A. Wiley, December 4, 1858, in *HT*, December 11, 1858, 2; Mr. Jones, in *Northern Californian*, December 22, 1858, 2; *Shasta Courier*, January 1, 1859, 3.

81. Kibbe, paraphrased in *Northern Californian*, extra, January 22, 1859, 2, in *Northern Californian*, January 26, 1859, 2; A messenger to Gen. Kibbe, in *Northern Californian*, January 26, 1859, 2; *HT*, January 29, 1859, 2; *HT*, February 5, 1859, 2; Kibbe to Weller, April 7, 1859, 667–668.

82. _HT_, March 26, 1859, 2; Kibbe to Weller, April 7, 1859, 668, 670, 667; California, _Statutes_, 1859, 295; Bledsoe, _Indian Wars_, 262–278.

83. Isaac W. Shannon deposition, February 28, 1860, _IWP_, F3753:462; _Tehama Gazette_, December 11, 1858, in _SDU_, December 7, 1858, 3; Cloverdale correspondent, January 5, 1859, in _DAC_, January 9, 1859, 1; S.C. Hastings, paraphrased in _DAC_, January 11, 1859, 1. In what was probably a description of the same incident, H.L. Hall testified that "in December 1858," after four or six horses had been killed, "I went up to the Rancheria with JW Smith, Charles McLean, and William Vaughn. We found some 18 or 20 Indians who ran as soon as they saw us. I think 8 or 10 were killed and the balance escaped." Hall's posse then murdered the one person they found in the village (H.L. Hall deposition, February 26, 1860, _IWP_, F3758:449). For killing of forty see E. Smith to Editors Alta, January 18, 1859, in _DAC_, January 20, 1859, 1. For final killings see Lawson deposition, February 27, 1860, _MMR_, 69.

84. S.C. Hastings, paraphrased in _SDU_, January 13, 1859, 2; Browne, "Coast Rangers," 312; _DAC_, January 20, 1859, 2.

85. Baumgardner, _Killing for Land_, 90; Strobridge, _Regulars in the Redwoods_, 184–185; Dillon deposition, _MMR_, 59.

86. Edward Dillon, 2nd Lieut. 6th Inft. to Bvt. Major E. Johnson, 6th Infy Comdg, Fort Miller, March 23, 1859, April 2, addendum, _IWP_, F3753:356; informant, paraphrased in _Petaluma Journal_, in _DAC_, April 16, 1859, 1. Heizer mistakenly attributed this quotation to 1857 (_They Were Only Diggers_, 47–48).

87. Female Indian prisoner, in _Shasta Courier_, January 29, 1859, 2; "Monthly Record of Current Events," 382.

88. Hydesville informant to Friend Wiley, May 11, 1859, in _HT_, May 14, 1859, 2; A.B. Hardcastle, May 15(?), 1859 entry, in A.B. Hardcastle, "[Journal of a] March," _CT_ 2511; Hardcastle, May 17, 1859, journal entry; _DEB_, September 1, 1856, 1; Hardcastle, May 20, 1859, journal entry; _Trinity Journal_, May 21, 1859, 2.

89. Hydesville correspondent, May 31, 1859, in _HT_, June 4, 1859, 2; _HT_, May 28, 1859, 2; Hydesville correspondent and Ed. Turk, summarized in _HT_, June 11, 1859, 2.

90. Hardcastle, May 31, June 3, and June 5, 1859 journal entries; _HT_, August 20, 1859, 2; _HT_, September 17, 1859, 2.

91. US Department of the Interior, _Statistics of the Population of the United States, Embracing the Tables of Race, Nationality, Sex, Selected Ages, and Occupations_, 16; Merriam, "Indian Population of California," 600 (California's Indian population in 1849 is contested); _DAC_, June 26, 1859, 2.

92. Correspondent to _Martinez Gazette_, February 4, 1859, in _SDU_, February 9, 1859, 3; Chooksa Homar, in Zappia, _Traders and Raiders_, 130; anonymous correspondent from "Bishop's party," n.d., in _DAC_, April 19, 1859, 1; Samuel A. Bishop to Col. Hoffman, n.d., in _DAC_, April 17, 1859, 1; Yesar, April 24, 1859, in _DAC_, May 7, 1859, 1.

93. K., August 6, 1859, in _LAS_, August 20, 1859, 1; Anonymous to Capt. Hancock, U.S.A., n.d., in _LAS_, August 27, 1859, 2.

94. Amos Figel and others to Gov. John B. Weller, May 9, 1859, James W. Smith and others to Gov. John B. Weller, May 14, 1859, Hon. Newell Hall and others to Gov. John B.

Weller, May 15, 1859, Thomas James and others to Gov. John B. Weller, May 15, 1859, and Messrs. Harrison and Bradley to Gov. J.B. Weller, May 16, 1859, in Kibbe, *Report*, 13–19; Sauber, "True Tales of the Old West," 127; *Red Bluff Beacon*, April 6, 1859, 2; *Red Bluff Beacon*, April 27, 1859, 2; *Shasta Republican*, May 28, 1859, 2; Telegram dated Red Bluff, May 22, 1859, in *DAC*, May 24, 1859, 1.

95. Order of Gen. Clark to Capt. F.F. Flint, May 19, 1859, in Kibbe, *Report*, 21; F.F. Flint to Gen. Kibbe, July 12, 1859, in Kibbe, *Report*, 26; Mr. Davis, paraphrased in *Shasta Republican*, May 28, 1859, 2; *Tehama Gazette*, paraphrased in *DAC*, June 20, 1859, 2; Anderson, *Fighting the Mill Creeks*, 10; Mr. Davis, paraphrased in *Shasta Republican*, May 28, 1859, 2; *Red Bluff Beacon*, May 25, 1859, 2; *Shasta Herald*, June 11, 1859, 2; *Red Bluff Beacon*, June 15, 1859, 2; Anderson, *Fighting the Mill Creeks*, 10.

96. Anderson, *Fighting the Mill Creeks*, 11; Waterman, "Yana Indians," 44; Kroeber, *Ishi in Two Worlds*, 67; Anderson, *Fighting the Mill Creeks*, 21, 27, 23, 24; *Red Bluff Beacon*, August 3, 1859, 2.

97. *Red Bluff Beacon*, August 24, 1859, 2; Anderson, *Fighting the Mill Creeks*, 38–42; Schoonover, "Kibbe's Campaign," 11. On August 3, the *Red Bluff Beacon* reported that "last week" the posse killed five Indians and a white man "between the headwaters of Butte and Deer Creek." The next day they apparently massacred "ten Indians, including one squaw." Correspondents also reported a massacre "about two miles from [Forks of Butte] on the ridge in the direction of Chico creek" in which whites killed two children, two women, and five men while wounding four others "perhaps fatally." See *Red Bluff Beacon*, August 3, 1859, 2; Correspondence to *Union*, July 28, 1859, in *SDU*, August 6, 1859, 2; *Butte Herald* correspondent, July 29, 1859, in *DAC*, August 9, 1859, 1. For quotations, see "citizens of the 'Forks of Butte,'" in *SDU*, August 20, 1859, 1, and *Red Bluff Beacon*, August 31, 1859, 2.

98. Gov. John B. Weller to Gen. W.C. Kibbe, July 4, 1859, in Kibbe, *Report*, 24; Kibbe to Weller, n.d., in Kibbe, *Report*, 26; Weller to Kibbe, August 2, 1859, in Kibbe, *Report*, 28; Kibbe, *Report*, 5; Comptroller, "Expenditures," 66; Potter, "Reminiscences," 10; "Pit River Expedition," www.militarymuseum.org/KibbeRangers.html.

99. Kibbe, *Report*, 5–7; Indian Agent Vincent E. Geiger to Sup't Indian Affairs J.Y. McDuffie, August 31, 1859, in USOIA, *Annual Report*, 1859, 440.

100. George Lount, in *DAC*, January 26, 1860, 1; Charles Hazlett, in *Shasta Herald*, September 10, 1859, 2; *Shasta Courier*, September 17, 1859, 2; Kibbe to *Bulletin*, in *SDU*, December 31, 1859, 3; *Shasta Herald*, August 27, 1859, 2; *Shasta Courier*, in *DAC*, August 30, 1859, 2.

101. Kibbe to *Bulletin*, in *DEB*, December 29, 1859, 1; Potter, "Reminiscences," 10; Lount, in *DAC*, January 26, 1860, 1.

102. Lount, in *DAC*, January 26, 1860, 1.

103. Ibid. For some death toll estimates, see Captain J.T. Langley, summarized by George H. Dobbins in a telegram dated September 6, 1859, from Yreka, in *SDU*, September 7, 1859, 2; *Shasta Courier*, September 17, 1859, 2; Henry Landt, in *Plumas Argus*, October 1, 1859, in *DAC*, October 6, 1859, 1; Kibbe volunteer to editor, October 8, 1859, in *Weekly Trinity Journal*, October 15, 1859, 2.

104. "Chief of the Fall River Band," in Curtis, *North American Indian*, 13:134.

105. Lount, summarized in *DAC*, January 26, 1860, 1; Telegram dated Marysville, Sept. 11—9 P.M., in *DAC*, September 11, 1859, 1; *Yreka Union*, in *DEB*, September 28, 1859, 3; "Belden, the Honey Lake Expressman," in *Plumas Standard*, in *SDU*, October 26, 1859, 3.

106. Landt, paraphrased in *Plumas Argus*, October 1, 1859, in *DAC*, October 6, 1859, 1.

107. S., October 10, 1859, in *Red Bluff Beacon*, October 26, 1859, 1; *Red Bluff Beacon*, October 12, 1859, 2; *Shasta Herald*, October 15, 1859, 2; Kibbe, paraphrased in *Sacramento Daily Bee*, October 14, 1859, 2.

108. *SDU*, October 18, 1859, 2; *SDU*, October 25, 1859, 2; *Plumas Argus*, in *SDU*, November 12, 1859, 2.

109. H.W.S. to Editors Union, November 1, 1859, in *SDU*, November 8, 1859, 3; *Red Bluff Beacon*, December 7, 1859, 2; Southern, *Our Storied Landmarks*, 81.

110. Kibbe, *Report*, 6–7; Comptroller, "Expenditures," 66–68. Most of Kibbe's rangers mustered out in mid-December.

111. Kibbe, *Report*, 7; *Shasta Herald*, January 21, 1860, 2; Glacus, December 16, 1859, in *New York Times*, January 12, 1860, 2; Kibbe, *Report*, 7, 9. Expedition member Potter recalled, "We brought away more than 1500 Indian; about half of whom were Konkows, and Kimshews" (Potter, "Reminiscences," 9).

112. Johnson, quoted in Tassin, "Chronicles, I," 27–28.

113. S.C. Hastings deposition, March 13, 1860, *MMR*, 30; Johnson, in Secrest, *When the Great Spirit Died*, 298; Garrett, "Destruction of the Indian," 65.

114. Garrett, "Destruction of the Indian," 65; Shuck, *History of the Bench*, 456; *SDU*, January 16, 1860, 2; *Shasta Herald*, August 27, 1859, 3; Edward Johnson to W. Mackall, August 21, 1859, *IWP*, F3753:378; letter summarized in Garrett, "Destruction of the Indian," 66; Weller to Jarboe, September 6, 1859, paraphrased in *SDU*, January 16, 1860, 2.

115. For late September, see A Stock Raiser, October 1, 1859, in *Sonoma County Journal*, October 7, 1859, 2; *Petaluma Journal*, October 1, 1859, in *DAC*, October 9, 1859, 1. For October 12, see W.S. Jarboe, October 16, in *Santa Rosa Democrat*, in *DEB*, November 7, 1859, 2. For November 18, see Capt. Jarboe to Capt. S.D. Goodrich, November 28, 1859, in *DEB*, January 4, 1860, supplement, 2. For December 9, see *Santa Rosa Democrat*, December 20, 1859, in *DAC*, January 1, 1860, 1; Observer to Editors Union, January 23, 1860, in *SDU*, February 1, 1860, 4. For massacre of seventeen, see S.P. Storms, in *Tehama Gazette*, in *DAC*, December 12, 1859, 1. For December 13, see "A member of Jarboe's company," summarized in *Santa Rosa Democrat*, December 20, 1859, in *DAC*, January 1, 1860, 1. For December 19, see Mr. White, in *Sonoma County Journal*, January 20, 1860, 2. For late December and December 31, see "A writer to the Santa Rosa *Democrat*," summarized in *Weekly Humboldt Times*, January 21, 1860, 2. The newspaper did not report all of the massacres in the region. Frazier reported the December killings of thirty-eight Indians between Round Valley and Long Valley (Frazier deposition, February 22, 1860, California, *Appendix to Journals of Assembly*, 1860, 14). Hildreth reported the killing of seventeen Indians in Round Valley and environs before February, 1860 (Hildreth deposition, February 24, 1860, *IWP*, F3753:443).

116. California Superintendent of Indian Affairs J.Y. McDuffie to Commissioner of Indian Affairs A.B. Greenwood, September 4, 1859, S. Exec. Doc. 46, 36th Cong., 1st Sess., 1860, serial 1033, 10; J. Ross Browne to A. Greenwood, October 18, 1859, NARA, RG75, M234, Reel 37:69; Johnson, in Tassin, "Chronicles, I," 30; Johnson, in Strobridge, *Regulars in the Redwoods*, 189.

117. W. Jarboe to John Downey, February 18, 1860, *IWP*, F3753:432; *DEB*, February 24, 1860, 2; H.H. Buckles deposition, February 23, 1860, *MMR*, 29; *DAC*, January 22, 1860, 1. Historian Gary Clayton Anderson called Jarboe's death toll "very likely an exaggeration" (*Ethnic Cleansing and the Indian*, 215). However, a variety of sources described Jarboe's killing campaign, reporting that in just six massacres between late September and December 31, 1859, Jarboe's men killed at least 182 people. Thus, it seems entirely possible that he killed many more. Indeed, the *Daily Alta California* suggested that Jarboe's company killed more than 400 people.

118. John Weller to W. Jarboe, September 8 and October 23, 1859, *IWP*, F3753:382, 399; Garrett, "Destruction of the Indian," 69; W. Jarboe to John Weller, December 3, 1859, *IWP*, F3753:401; *SDU*, January 16, 1860, 2.

119. *DAC*, January 22, 1860, 1; *SDU*, January 20, 1860, 2; Correspondent, January 20, 1860, in *DEB*, January 21, 1860, 2; *Northern Journal*, February 2, 1860, 2; *LAS*, March 24, 1860, 2.

120. Correspondent, January 18, 1860, in *DAC*, January 19, 1860, 1; Observer to Editors Union, January 23, 1860, in *SDU*, February 1, 1860, 4.

121. A Taxpayer of California, January 15, 1860, in *DEB*, January 21, 1860, 2; *Petaluma Argus*, in *SDU*, February 3, 1860, 2; *SDU*, February 2, 1860, 2; *SDU*, February 23, 1860, 2; *DEB*, February 24, 1860, 2.

122. *SDU*, February 24, 1860, 2; Correspondent, February 13, 1860, in *DAC*, February 14, 1860, 1.

123. Correspondent, February 25, 1860, in *DAC*, February 25, 1860, 1; *HT*, December 17, 1859, 2; Mat. to Friend Wiley, December 20, 1859, in *HT*, December 24, 1859, 2.

124. Rains to Hendricks, April 30, 1860, 1162; Comptroller, "Expenditures," 75; Rains to Hendricks, April 30, 1860, 1162. The *Humboldt Times* reported that the company formed on February 4 and consisted of a dozen officers and fifty-five privates (*HT*, February 11, 1860, 2). Rains to Hendricks, April 30, 1860, 1163. On February 25, the *Humboldt Times* hinted at supporting such aims: "The Indians are killing the stock . . . in the backcountry and will continue to do so until they are driven from that section, or exterminated" (*HT*, February 25, 1860, 2).

125. *Northern Californian*, February 29, 1860, 2; Scharnhorst, *Bret Hart*, 13; An Eye-Witness to the Editor, in *DEB*, March 13, 1860, 3. For death toll estimates, see Charles Rossiter, February 26, 1860, in *DEB*, March 2, 1860, 3; J.A. Lord, in *DEB*, February 28, 1860, 2; Glaucus, March 16, 1860, in *New York Times*, April 12, 1860, 8; Rains to Hendricks, April 30, 1860, 1163–1164; Female survivor, summarized by Robert Gunther, in Genzoli and Martin, *Redwood Cavalcade*, 12. Duluwat Island is also known as Bloody Island, Gunther Island, and Indian Island.

126. Dandy Bill, in Loud, "Ethnogeography and Archaeology," 333; Rains to Hendricks, April 30, 1860, 1163; Lord, in *DEB*, February 28, 1860, 2; Gunther, in Genzoli and

Martin, *Redwood Cavalcade*, 12; *HT*, March 3, 1860, 2. Humboldt County Sheriff B. Van Ness added that "about 80 are *known* to have been killed" but this was almost certainly an underestimate (B. Van Ness, February 29, 1860, in *DEB*, March 2, 1860, 3).

127. *HT*, March 3, 1860, 2; Eye-Witness, in *DEB*, March 13, 1860, 3; Rains to Hendricks, April 30, 1860, 1164; Glaucus, March 16, 1860, in *New York Times*, April 12, 1860, 8; *HT*, March 3, 1860, 2; *HT*, March 17, 1860, 2; Scharnhorst, *Bret Hart*, 14. On August 31, 1862, a Humboldt Bay correspondent reported that "vigorous efforts have been made by the Grand Jury of Humboldt county to bring to justice . . . those engaged in the Indian Island massacres, but without success for want of evidence. The names of some half dozen different parties to the latter enterprise are whispered with suspicion among the better informed, and four of them, it is said, have already been killed by the Indians in retaliation" (Correspondence to Union, August 31, 1862, in *Bancroft Scraps*, 36:100–101).

128. Correspondent, in *Bulletin*, in *SDU*, March 15, 1860, 2; *DAC*, February 29, 1860, 1; *San Francisco Herald*, March 3, 1860, 2; Swift, *Modest Proposal*.

129. The Assembly passed the bill by a vote of forty-nine to nineteen whereas the Senate passed it by twenty-five to five. For these votes and Phelps/Wheeler quotation, see Correspondent, March 9, 1860, in *DAC*, March 10, 1860, 1, and Correspondent, March 17, 1860, in *DAC*, March 18, 1860, 1.

130. *MMR*, 6; *SDU*, April 9, 1860, 2; California, *Statutes*, 1860, 173.

131. Latham, Wilson, and Crittenden, in *CG*, May 26, 1860, 2366–2368.

132. Gwin, in *CG*, May 26, 1860, 2368.

133. Correspondent to *Bulletin*, June 1, 1860, in *DEB*, June 1, 1860, 2; C.F. Kauffman, "The Nosea Indians: A Reminiscence of Sierra Township, Tehama County," newspaper clipping ca. 1882, in Gans, "Scrapbook," 26–28; Anti-Thug to *Bulletin*, March 31, 1860, in *DEB*, April 11, 1860, 3; G.J. Rains, Major 4th Infantry, Comdg Post. to Lieutenant J.W. Cleary, U.S.A., n.d., in *SDU*, May 26, 1860, 2.

134. Carlin to Ford, April 14, 1860, Carlin to Mackall, April 25, 1860, and Carlin to Hamilton and Oliver, April 25, 1860, in Strobridge, *Regulars in the Redwoods*, 199–200; *Northern Californian*, June 13, 1860, 3; *Tuolumne Courier*, July 28, 1860, in *SDU*, August 1, 1860, 3; E. Swift, paraphrased in *DAC*, December 9, 1860, 1; Mr. Tracey, paraphrased in *HT*, December 8, 1860, 3.

135. Casebier, *Carleton's Pah-Ute Campaign*, 1; *LAS*, May 12, 1860, 2; E.K. Fuller, in *Deseret News*, June 13, 1860, 5.

136. California, *Statutes*, 1860, 196–197. Michael Magliari kindly provided insights into the workings of this amendment.

137. *CG*, May 26, 1860, 2366–2368.

138. John G. Downey, Governor, January 7, 1861, in California, *Senate Journal*, 1861, 39.

139. Deputy Sheriff Witt, in *Mendocino Herald*, January 18, 1861, in *DEB*, January 26, 1861, 1; February 4, 1861, telegram, in *SDU*, February 5, 1861, 2; *HT*, February 2, 1861, 3; *HT*, February 9, 1861, 3; *HT*, February 23, 1861, 2, 3; Stephen Goff, in *HT*, March 9, 1861, 3; Correspondent, February 22, 1861, in *DAC*, February 27, 1861, 1.

CHAPTER 8. THE CIVIL WAR IN CALIFORNIA
AND ITS AFTERMATH

1. South Carolina Constitutional Convention, "Ordinance of Secession," December 20, 1860, Document Number S 131053, South Carolina Department of Archives and History, Columbia, South Carolina; *CG*, December 22, 1860, 172; *CG*, January 10, 1861, 283; "An Act for the Payment of Expenses incurred in the Suppression of Indian Hostilities in the State of California," in US Congress, *Statutes at Large, Treaties, and Proclamations*, 12:199–200.

2. These included the 1854 Shasta, 1855 Siskiyou, 1855 Klamath and Humboldt, 1855 San Bernardino, 1856 Klamath, 1856 Modoc, 1856 Tulare, 1858–1859 Klamath and Humboldt, and 1859 Pit River expeditions. Congress excluded Jarboe's controversial 1859–1860 Mendocino Expedition. See *CG*, February 22, 1861, 1112.

3. Bledsoe, *Indian Wars*, 324; G.J. Rains, Major 4th Infantry Comdg. Post to Lieutenant J.W. Cleary, n.d., in *SDU*, May 26, 1860, 2; Rains to McLearry, in Bledsoe, *Indian Wars*, 323–324.

4. A.S. Johnson, Bv't. Br'g Gen'l to His Excellency, John G. Downey, Governor of the State of California, March 25, 1861, in *HT*, April 6, 1861, 2; *HT*, April 13, 1861, 3; John Rher, in *HT*, April 20, 1861, 2; Jos. B. Collins, First Lieut., Fourth Infty., Co. B. Sixth U.S. Infty. to Capt. Charles Lovell, April 15, 1861, WOR 1:50:1, 18.

5. *Evening Alta*, February 25, 1861, in *DAC*, February 26, 1861, 1; Johnston to Thomas, April 9, 1861, WOR 1:50:1, 463–464; Jefferson Davis, April 8, 1862, WOR 1:52:2, 298; Bledsoe, *Indian Wars*, 343.

6. *HT*, May 18, 1861, 3; Strobridge, *Regulars in the Redwoods*, 241; *HT*, June 1, 1861, 2; Strobridge, *Regulars in the Redwoods*, 241; Green Wilkinson, June 22, 1861, in *HT*, June 29, 1861, 2.

7. Jos. B. Collins, First Lieutenant, Fourth Infantry to Capt. Charles S. Lovell, May 9, 1861, WOR 1:50:1, 12; *HT*, May 18, 1861, 3; Jos. B. Collins, First Lieutenant, Fourth Infantry to Capt. Charles S. Lovell, Sixth Infantry, June 18, 1861, WOR 1:50:1, 18–19; Correspondent, in *HT*, June 15, 1861, 3.

8. *San Francisco Herald*, June 20, 1861, 2; *HT*, June 22, 1861, 2.

9. Jas. P. Martin, Second Lieutenant, Seventh Infantry to Capt. C.S. Lovell, Sixth Infantry, June 27, 1861, WOR 1:50:1, 19–21; "Letter to Mr. B. Adams, from South Fork Eel river," summarized in *HT*, May 25, 1861, 2; Martin to Lovell, June 27, 1861, WOR 1:50:1, 19–21; Strobridge, *Regulars in the Redwoods*, 241.

10. *HT*, July 20, 1861, 2; Bledsoe, *Indian Wars*, 347; Jas. P. Martin, Second Lieutenant, Seventh Infantry to Capt. C.S. Lovell, Sixth Infantry, July 25, 1861, WOR 1:50:1, 21; Wm. P. Dole, Commissioner of Indian Affairs, November 27, 1861, in USOIA, *Annual Report*, 1861, 23–24; Geo. M. Hanson, Superintending Agent Indian Affairs, Northern District of California, to Hon. William P. Dole, Commissioner of Indian Affairs, July 14, 1861, in USOIA, *Annual Report*, 1861, 149.

11. *Red Bluff Independent* correspondent, in *Marysville Appeal*, January 4, 1861, 2; *HT*, February 23, 1861, 3; Magliari, "Free State Slavery," table 1, 170–171; Heizer and Almquist, *Other Californians*, 54–56.

12. *Boston Transcript* correspondent, in *Farmer's Cabinet*, September 20, 1861, 2; *Marysville Appeal*, October 17, 1861, 3.

13. Geo. M. Hanson, Superintending Agent Indian Affairs, Northern District of California, to Hon. Wm. P. Dole, Commissioner of Indian Affairs, December 31, 1861, in USOIA, *Annual Report*, 1862, 315.

14. *Shasta Herald*, May 9, 1861, in *Marysville Appeal*, May 12, 1861, 2.

15. T.M. Ames to Editor, June 20, 1861, in *San Francisco Herald*, June 20, 1861, 2; June 27, 1861, letter to *Petaluma Journal*, in *Marysville Appeal*, July 9, 1861, 1; Biaggi, "Shelter Cove Scalping," 7; *HT*, July 27, 1861, 2; *HT*, August 10, 1861, 3; Deputy Sheriff Ham to *Douglas City Gazette*, in *SDU*, August 13, 1861, 3; *SDU*, August 20, 1861, 1.

16. Hanson to Dole, July 14, 1861, in USOIA, *Annual Report*, 1861, 150; *Mendocino Herald*, February 5, 1861, 1.

17. S.P. Storms, October 15, 1861, in *DEB*, October 23, 1861, 3; *Red Bluff Beacon*, October 24, 1861, 2; Tome-ya-nem, in Tassin, "Con-Cow Indians," 11.

18. Tome-ya-nem, in Tassin, "Con-Cow Indians," 11; Storms, October 15, 1861, in *DEB*, October 23, 1861, 3; *Red Bluff Beacon*, October 24, 1861, 2. For some death toll estimates, see Storms, October 15, 1861, in *DEB*, October 23, 1861, 3; Short, summarized in a telegram printed in *SDU*, October 23, 1861, 1; *Red Bluff Beacon*, October 24, 1861, 2; Perpetrators, summarized in Potter, "Reminiscences," 13; Tassin, "Chronicles. II," 180.

19. *Red Bluff Beacon*, October 24, 1861, 2.

20. Geo. M. Hanson, Supt Ind Affs N. Dist. Cal. to Ho. Chas. E. Mix, July 23, 1861, NARA, RG75, M234, Reel 38:144; Browne, "Coast Rangers," 314, 313, 310–312.

21. Geo. M. Hanson, Superintending Agent Indian Affairs, Northern District of California, to Hon. William P. Dole, Commissioner of Indian Affairs, July 15, 1861, in USOIA, *Annual Report*, 1861, 147; Hanson to Dole, December 31, 1861, in USOIA, *Annual Report*, 1862, 314.

22. *HT*, July 27, 1861, 2; *HT*, August 24, 1861, 2; *DAC*, September 14, 1861, 1; Jas. Ryan, Brig. Genl. Cala. Mila. to His Excellency John G. Downey, September 9, 1861, in Military Records, Bin 3409-3; *HT*, October 19, 1861, 3. On October 10, they killed two men and took eleven women and children prisoners at Larabee Creek (*HT*, October 19, 1861, 2, 3). On October 20, Indian hunters charged a rancheria "between Bear River ridge and Eel River," killing two Indians and losing one man mortally wounded (*HT*, October 26, 1861, 2).

23. *DAC*, October 26, 1861, 2; *DEB*, October 25, 1861, 2.

24. *HT*, November 9, 1861, 2; *Humboldt Times Extra*, November 18, 1861, in *SDU*, November 30, 1861, 2; *HT*, November 23, 1861, 3; *HT*, November 30, 1861, 2; G.W. Werk to Maj. Wm. C. Martin, December 18, 1861, in *HT*, December 21, 1861, 2; Francis J. Lippitt, Col. Second California Vol. Infantry to Maj. R.C. Drum, Assistant Adjutant-General, Department of the Pacific, March 5, 1862, WOR 1:50:1, 907. Bledsoe wrote that Werk's men engaged Indians fifteen times, killed seventy-five, and wounded seventy-five while suffering one killed and eight wounded (Bledsoe, *Indian Wars*, 357).

25. *New York Herald,* April 13, 1861, 1; Simon Cameron, Secretary of War to Governor of California, July 24, 1861, WOR 1:50:1, 543; John G. Downey, in California, *California Men,* 12–13; Simon Cameron, Secretary of War to Hon. John G. Downey, Governor of California, August 14, 1861, WOR 1:50:1, 569.

26. McPherson, *Battle Cry of Freedom,* 274–275; California, *California Men,* 11–13; Kennedy, *Population of the United States,* 28; 1852 census estimates, summarized in *DAC,* December 23, 1853, 2.

27. G. Wright, Brigadier-General to Brig. Gen. Lorenzo Thomas, Adjutant-General U.S. Army, December 10, 1861, WOR 1:50:1, 757.

28. Francis J. Lippitt, Col. Second California Vol. Infantry to Maj. R.C. Drum, Assistant Adjutant-General, Department of the Pacific, January 12, 1862, WOR 1:50:1, 803; California, *California Men,* 418; John Hanna, Jr., Acting Assistant Adjutant-General, Humboldt Military District to Capt. Charles Heffernan, Company K, Second Infantry California Volunteers, March 8, 1862, WOR 1:50:1, 916; Lippitt to Drum, January 12, 1862, WOR 1:50:1, 803.

29. James Beith to James McHary, January 21, 1862, in Beith, Letterbook, 116, 118; *HT,* February 15, 1862, 3; *HT,* April 5, 1862, 2; *HT,* April 12, 1862, 3; D.B. Akey, Captain Company E, Second Cavalry California Volunteers to Col. F.J. Lippitt, April 12, 1862, WOR 1:50:1, 86.

30. On April 7, Lippitt reported only one Indian killed during recent engagements. That day, Akey's men killed two, and on April 10, one of Lippitt's officers brought forty-two Indian prisoners to Fort Humboldt (WOR 1:50:1, 53–54; WOR 1:50:1, 86; *HT,* April 12, 1862, 3); G. Wright, Brigadier-General, U.S. Army, Commanding to Col. Francis J. Lippitt, Second Infantry California Volunteers, Commanding District Humboldt, April 7, 1862, WOR 1:50:1, 992 (emphasis added); Colonel Francis J. Lippitt, "General Orders No. 4," WOR 1:50:1, 994; John Hanna, Jr., Acting Assistant Adjutant-General to Capt. C.D. Douglas, March 26, 1862, WOR 1:50:1, 956. Lieutenant Flynn's force first captured three Yurok prisoners and killed one "upon their attempting to escape." On April 26, Captain Thomas Ketchum's men attacked Indians "near Eel River" killing five men and women before taking two dozen women, children, and teenagers prisoners. That same day, Lieutenant Staples's troops killed at least fifteen, but took perhaps thirty-seven prisoners, "mostly squaws and children." Between May 14 and June 7, California infantrymen killed or mortally wounded at least fifteen Indians in the Mad River and Mattole Valley region, while capturing perhaps ninety-six people. See *HT,* April 19, 1862, 2; Thos. E. Ketchum, Captain, Third Infantry California Vols. to Lieut. John Hanna, Jr., Actg. Asst. Adjt-Gen., Humboldt Military District, April 28, 1862, WOR 1:50:1, 79 (the *Humboldt Times* [May 3, 1862, 2] reported only four killed); Lippitt to Drum, May 20, 1862, WOR 1:50:1, 55; *SDU,* May 10, 1862, 2; Lippitt to Drum, May 20, 1862, in California, *California Men,* 420; Lippitt to Drum, May 20, 1862, WOR 1:50:1, 56; Francis J. Lippitt, Col. Second California Vol. Infantry to Maj. R.C. Drum, Assistant Adjutant-General, Department of the Pacific, June 25, 1862, WOR 1:50:1, 59.

31. H. Mannheim to Lieutenant-Colonel Olney, June 6, 1862, WOR, 1:50:1, 1120; *HT,* June 14, 1862, 1; John Hanna, Jr., First Lieut. and Adjt. Second Infty., California Vols.,

Actg. Asst. Adjt. Gen., Special Orders No. 68, WOR 1:50:1, 1126; Charles G. Hubbard, First Lieut., Second Infantry California Vols. to Col. Francis J. Lippitt, June 20, 1862, WOR 1:50:1, 74.

32. *HT,* June 21, 1862, 2; Volunteer to Editor, June 30, 1862, in *DEB,* July 12, 1862, 3; Francis J. Lippitt, Col. Second Infantry California Vols. to Maj. R.C. Drum, Assistant Adjutant-General, Department of the Pacific, July 12, 1862, WOR 1:50:1, 60.

33. For June 9 and 10 meetings in Eureka, see *HT,* June 14, 1862, 1. Wright replied that Lippitt's eleven companies of soldiers were doing an adequate job, having captured over 250 Indians, and promised that "the volunteer soldiers of California [would] go on battling with the savage foes until a permanent peace shall be obtained." Still, Wright did promise Stanford that he would send three more companies to the area. See G. Wright, Brigadier-General to Hon. W. Van Dyke, June 12, 1862, WOR 1:50:1, 1134–1135; G. Wright, Brigadier-General to His Excellency Leland Stanford, Governor of the State of California, June 17, 1862, WOR 1:50:1, 1143–1144. For two Indians killed by soldiers in June, see WOR 1:50:1, 60, 80. G. Wright, Brigadier-General to Brig.-Gen. L. Thomas, Adjutant-General, U.S. Army, July 25, 1862, in California, *California Men,* 507; *HT,* August 2, 1862, 2; *HT,* August 23, 1862, 2; P.B. Johnson, Lieutenant, Second Infantry, California Volunteers to Capt. C.D. Douglas, Second Infantry, California Vols., August 23, 1862, WOR 1:50:1, 76–77; *HT,* August 30, 1862, 2; Correspondent, August 31, 1862, in *SDU,* September 18, 1862, 1; Francis J. Lippitt, Col. Second California Vol. Infantry to Lieut. Col. R.C. Drum, Assistant Adjutant-General, Department of the Pacific, WOR 1:50:1, 66; Bledsoe, *Indian Wars,* 396–398.

34. On October 21, Flynn killed one Indian near Hydesville (H. Flynn, Captain, Second Infantry California Volunteers to First Lieut. John Hanna, Jr., Acting Assistant Adjutant-General, October 21, 1862, WOR 1:50:1, 179). *HT,* September 6, 1862, 2; *HT,* September 20, 1862, 3.

35. Lippitt to Drum, February 12, 1862, WOR 1:50:1, 803; Thomas E. Ketchum, Captain, Third Infantry California Volunteers to Lieut. John Hanna, Jr., Acting Assistant Adjutant-General, April 3, 1862, WOR 1:50:1, 982; Hubbard to Lippitt, June 20, 1862, WOR 1:50:1, 74; Correspondent, July 15, 1862, in *SDU,* July 19, 1862, 3; Correspondent, August 31, 1862, in *SDU,* September 18, 1862, 1.

36. Young, in Young and Murphey, "Out of the Past," 358, 355; Young, summarized in Essene, "Culture Element Distributions," 89.

37. Young, in Young and Murphey, "Out of the Past," 358. For examples of massacres perpetrated in response to absenteeism and flight, see E.W. Inskeep to Editors, April 28, 1858, and editor, in *Red Bluff Beacon,* May 5, 1858, 2, and *DEB,* June 1, 1860, 2. *DAC,* October 5, 1862, 2.

38. Carpenter, "Among the Diggers," 391; Correspondent, July 15, 1862, in *SDU,* July 19, 1862, 3; Magliari, "Free Soil, Unfree Labor," 371–373.

39. Thomas E. Ketchum, Captain, Third Infantry California Volunteers to Lieut. John Hanna, Jr., Acting Assistant Adjutant-General, WOR 1:50:1, 982; May 4 dispatch in *Nevada Democrat,* May 6, 1862, 2; May 6 telegram, in *DEB,* May 6, 1862, 1; *Red Bluff Beacon,* May 8, 1862, 2; Tom Gelrick, May 4, 1862, in *SDU,* May 5, 1862, 4; *Red Bluff Independent,* August 4, 1862, in Heizer, *They Were Only Diggers,* 56.

40. George M. Hanson, Superintendent, Agent Indian Affairs, Northern District California to Hon. William P. Dole, Commissioner Indian Affairs, August 18, 1862, in USOIA, *Annual Report*, 1862, 320; James Short testimony, December 18, 1862, in *MLRV*, 8; Hanson to Dole, August 18, 1862, NARA, RG75, M234, 38:590–591; Potter, "Reminiscences," 15–16; James McHenry testimony, December 19, 1862, in *MLRV*, 23; Potter, "Reminiscences," 15–16; *Mendocino Herald*, August 8, 1862, 2; Hanson to Dole, August 18, 1862, in USOIA, *Annual Report*, 1862, 320. For the wounded attacker, see Potter, "Reminiscences," 16; James Short testimony, in *MLRV*, 8. Round Valley resident Elijah Potter later recalled, "Twenty-two I think was buried in a trench" and "half as many more were found among the willows" so that in December 1862, three Round Valley whites reported only twenty-two or twenty-three "Indians, of all sexes and ages" massacred. James Short testimony, in *MLRV*, 8, 14; D.M. Dohrman testimony, December 19, 1862, in *MLRV*, 16; Green Short testimony, December 19, 1862, in *MLRV*, 21.
41. McHenry testimony, December 19, 1862, in *MLRV*, 23; Martin Corbett testimony, December 19, 1862, in *MLRV*, 24; Johnson, quoted in Tassin, "Chronicles, I," 29.
42. "Report of the Commissioner of Indian Affairs, November 26, 1862," in USOIA, *Annual Report*, 1862, 39.
43. X to editor, in *Red Bluff Beacon*, April 17, 1862, 2; *HT*, August 23, 1862, 2; *Red Bluff Beacon*, October 9, 1862, 2; Tome-ya-nem, in Tassin, "Con-Cow Indians," 11; J.M. Robinson testimony, December 18, 1862, in *MLRV*, 12; McHenry testimony, December 19, 1862, in *MLRV*, 24; Capt. C.D. Douglas, in Baumgardner, *Killing for Land*, 242. A medium ear of cooked corn contains eighty to 130 calories. See Ensminger et al., *Foods and Nutrition Encyclopedia*, 1:489, 972, 980.
44. George Hanson to William Dole, July 18, 1863, in USOIA, *Annual Report*, 1863, 94; B.C. Whiting to N.G. Taylor, October 10, 1868, in USOIA, *Annual Report*, 1868, 127.
45. Mr. Gilkey, summarized in *HT*, January 3, 1863, 3; Young, in Young and Murphey, "Out of the Past," 353; Francis J. Lippitt, Colonel Second Infantry California Volunteers, Commanding Humboldt Military District to Lieut. Col. R.C. Drum, Assistant Adjutant-General, Department of the Pacific, October 13, 1862, WOR 1:50:2, 170; *Mendocino Herald*, in *HT*, January 24, 1863, 2; letter, summarized in *HT*, January 24, 1863, 2.
46. Young, in Young and Murphey, "Out of the Past," 354, 358.
47. *SDU*, June 26, 1862, 2; *Red Bluff Semi-Weekly Independent*, July 1, 1862, 2. Anderson recollected that, "the feeling against the Indians was so bitter that it was proposed to make a general cleanup, even of the friendly Indians" (Anderson, *Fighting the Mill Creeks*, 55). *Butte Record*, July 5, 1862, 2; *Red Bluff Semi-Weekly Independent*, July 4, 1862, 2; Harmon Good, July 22, 1862, in *Red Bluff Beacon*, July 23, 1862, 2; *Red Bluff Semi-Weekly Independent*, August 4, 1862, in Heizer, *They Were Only Diggers*, 56.
48. *Red Bluff Semi-Weekly Independent*, August 8, 1862, 2; *Marysville Appeal*, August 9, 1862, 2; Delaney, "Adventures of Hi Good," 1; Anderson, *Fighting the Mill Creeks*, 55; Member of Good's posse to the Union, in *SDU*, August 21, 1862, 2; Volunteer, August 11, 1862, in *SDU*, August 15, 1862, 2; *Marysville Appeal*, August 9, 1862, 2; Anderson, *Fighting the Mill Creeks*, 55; Moak, *Last of the Mill Creeks*, 31; Harmon A. Good, August 18, 1862, in *Red Bluff Beacon*, August 21, 1862, 3; Brewer, *Up and Down California*, 338; A.L. Tunison diary, in Fairfield, *Fairfield's Pioneer History*, 293–294.

49. Anderson remembered that he and two others attacked a Yana camp near "the breaks of Mill Creek," killing seven and leaving two "badly wounded." Delaney recalled that after "Indians stole" stock from a Deer Creek ranch, Anderson and Good killed three more. See Anderson, *Fighting the Mill Creeks*, 66, 70, and Delaney, "Adventures of Captain Hi Good," 1.

50. Jedediah S. Smith crossed the Owens Valley in 1826, with a group of trappers in the first recorded visit by non-Indians (Chalfant, *Story of Inyo*, 95). Jelmer W. Eerkens, "The Evolution of Social Organization, Settlement Patterns and Population Densities in Prehistoric Owens Valley," in Pauketat, *Oxford Handbook*, 201; Steward, "Basin-Plateau Aboriginal Groups," 50–54, 34; Sven Liljeblad and Catherine Fowler, "Owens Valley Paiute," in D'Azevedo, *Handbook of North American Indians*, 11:417. For more on indigenous Owens Valley irrigation, see Steward, "Ethnography," 247; A.W. Von Schmidt and J.R. Vineyard, in Chalfant, *Story of Inyo*, 74, 15; H.T. Chichester, summarized in *LAS*, August 21, 1858, 2.

51. J.W. Davidson, Capt. 1 Dragoons to 1 Lt. C.H. Ogle, Adjutant, 1st Dragoons, n.d., in Wilke and Lawton, *Expedition of Capt. Davidson*, 21. For the discovery of gold north of Mono Lake in 1859, see Chalfant, *Story of Inyo*, 127. For the Aurora gold discovery in 1860, see Carlson, *Nevada Place Names*, 43. J.W.A. Wright, in *Daily Evening Post*, November 22, 1879, 2; *Inyo Register*, February 11, 1904, 1.

52. Wright, in *Daily Evening Post*, November 22, 1879, 2; Geo. S. Evans, Lieutenant-Colonel Second Cavalry California to Maj. R.C. Drum, April 29, 1862, *WOR* 1:50:1, 46; Chalfant, *Story of Inyo*, 148; Diomed, May 10, 1862, in *SDU*, May 19, 1862, 1; Wright, in *Daily Evening Post*, November 22, 1879, 2; Chalfant, *Story of Inyo*, 150; *Inyo Register*, February 18, 1904, 1; Wright, in *Daily Evening Post*, November 22, 1879, 2; G. Wright, Brigadier-General to Brig. Gen. L. Thomas, Adjutant-General, U.S. Army, March 31, 1862, *WOR* 1:50:1, 966–967; Wright, in *Daily Evening Post*, November 22, 1879, 2; Wright, to Thomas, March 31, 1862, *WOR* 1:50:1, 966–967; Evans to Drum, April 29, 1862, *WOR* 1:50:1, 46; *Inyo Register*, February 18, 1904, 1.

53. Diomed, May 10, 1862, in *SDU*, May 19, 1862, 1; Chalfant, *Story of Inyo*, 152; *Chico Weekly Courant*, December 18, 1868, 2; Wright, in *Daily Evening Post*, November 22, 1879, 2; March 22, 1862, letter in *SDU*, March 26, 1862, 2; Diomed, May 10, 1862, 1; Evans to Drum, April 29, 1862, *WOR* 1:50:1, 46; Wright, in *Daily Evening Post*, November 22, 1879, 2.

54. Diomed, May 10, 1862, in *SDU*, May 19, 1862, 1; Chalfant, *Story of Inyo*, 156–157; *Inyo Register*, January 22, 1914, 1; Diomed, May 10, 1862, 1; Chalfant, *Story of Inyo*, 156–157.

55. Wright, in *Daily Evening Post*, November 22, 1879, 2; Diomed, May 10, 1862, in *SDU*, May 19, 1862, 1; Evans to Drum, April 29, 1862, *WOR* 1:50:1, 47–48; Diomed, May 10, 1862, 1; *Silver Age*, in *HT*, May 31, 1862, 2; *Inyo Register*, January 22, 1914, 1; *Silver Age*, in *HT*, May 31, 1862, 2.

56. Warren Wasson to His Excellency James W. Nye, Governor and ex officio Superintendent Indian Affairs, Carson City, Nevada Territory, in USOIA, *Annual Report*, 1862, 225; *Silver Age*, in *HT*, May 31, 1862, 2. Geo. S. Evans, Lieutenant-Colonel, Second Cavalry California Volunteers to Maj. R.C. Drum, Assistant Adjutant-General, U.S. Army, July 9, 1862, *WOR* 1:50:1, 148; John C. Willet, in Chalfant, *Story of Inyo*, 168–169.

57. Wright, in *Daily Evening Post*, November 22, 1879, 2; Go. S. Evans, Lieutenant-Colonel, Second Cavalry California Volunteers to Lieut. William Forrey, July 1, 1862, *WOR* 1:50:1, 146; Chalfant, *Story of Inyo*, 169; Evans to Drum, July 9, 1862, *WOR* 1:50:1, 149; Wright, in *Daily Evening Post*, November 22, 1879, 2; John P.H. Wentworth, Superintending Agent to William P. Dole, Commissioner of Indian Affairs, December 3, 1862, in USOIA, *Annual Report*, 1863, 105–106.

58. Correspondent, March 4, 1863, in *SDU*, March 12, 1863, 2; Mr. White, in *Visalia Delta*, March 12, 1863, 2; Wright, in *Daily Evening Post*, November 22, 1879, 2; Correspondent, in *Visalia Delta*, April 2, 1863, 2; Correspondent, March 25, 1863, in *DAC*, April 8, 1863, 1; Chalfant, *Story of Inyo*, 187; Milo Page, in Wright, in *Daily Evening Post*, November 22, 1879, 2; Chalfant, *Story of Inyo*, 185; Correspondent, in *Visalia Delta*, April 2, 1863, 2. In a series of reports of questionable veracity and specificity, Chalfant suggested more civilian casualties (*Story of Inyo*, 175–179).

59. California, *California Men*, 181; Chalfant, *Story of Inyo*, 185–186; *Esmeralda Star*, April 11, 1863, in *SDU*, April 16, 1863, 2; Benedict to H.G. Hanks, April 17, 1863, summarized in *Sacramento Daily Bee*, April 27, 1863, 3.

60. M.A. McLaughlin, Capt., Second Cav. California Vols. to Col. R.C. Drum, Assistant Adjutant-General, April 24, 1863, *WOR* 1:50:1, 208–209. Two other sources reported between thirty-two and forty Owens Valley and Kern River Indian men massacred that morning (Correspondent, April 19, 1863, to *Visalia Delta*, and Correspondent, n.d., in *Visalia Delta*, April 23, 1863, 2).

61. McLaughlin to Drum, April 24, 1863, *WOR* 1:50:1, 209; M.A. McLaughlin, Captain, Second Cavalry California Volunteers to Col. R.C. Drum, Assistant Adjutant-General, May 26, 1863, *WOR* 1:50:1, 211; California, *California Men*, 181, 182; *Inyo Register*, February 26, 1914, 1; McLaughlin to Drum, May 26, 1863, *WOR* 1:50:1, 211–212; White, in *Visalia Delta*, May 21, 1863, in *DEB*, May 26, 1863, 2; McLaughlin to Drum, May 26, 1863, *WOR* 1:50:1, 211–212; Ben Tibbitts, "Autobiography of Ben Tibbitts," 6–8, in Essene, "Fort Independence Paiute," Film 2216. The Big Pine Paiute Tribe of the Owens Valley kindly shared this source.

62. Jose Pacheco to General Wright, April 16, 1864, in *SDU*, April 28, 1864, 1. William Rawlinson kindly provided this source.

63. *Visalia Delta*, June 4, 1863, 3; Correspondent, in *DAC*, July 31, 1863, 1; Captain Ropes 2d California Cavalry to *Esmeralda Star*, July 30, 1863, in USOIA, *Annual Report*, 1863, 100; Tibbitts, "Autobiography," 8; Robert Daley deposition in US Congress, *Condition of the Indian Tribes*, 496; USOIA, Southern District of California, September 1, 1863, in USOIA, *Annual Report*, 1863, 99; Ropes, in *Esmeralda Star*, July 30, 1863, in USOIA, *Annual Report*, 1863, 100; Page, in *Inyo Register*, February 26, 1914, 1; Chalfant, *Story of Inyo*, 196; Ezra D. Merriam, in Chalfant, *Story of Inyo*, 196–198.

64. Wentworth, December 3, 1862, in USOIA, *Annual Report*, 1863, 99; E. Sparrow Purdy, Assistant Adjutant-General to Capt. M.A. McLaughlin, Commanding Fort Tejon, October 13, 1863, *WOR* 1:50:2, 645; Phillips, *Bringing Them under Subjection*, 248; Pacheco to Wright, April 16, 1864, in *SDU*, April 28, 1864, 1.

65. *HT*, January 10, 1863, 1; Bledsoe, *Indian Wars*, 401–403; California, *Senate Journal*, 1863, 33; G. Wright, Brigadier-General to His Excellency Leland Stanford, Governor

of the State of California, January 21, 1863, WOR 1:50:2, 291; Leland Stanford, Governor to Brig. Gen. George Wright, January 22, 1863, WOR 1:50:2, 292; G. Wright, Brigadier-General to His Excellency Leland Stanford, Governor of the State of California, February 5, 1863, and Leland Stanford, Governor, Proclamation, February 7, 1863, WOR 1:50:2, 303–304, 305–306. For January 9 to February 17 killings, see *HT*, January 17, 1863, 2, and K.N. Gear, summarized in *HT*, March 7, 1863, 2.

66. In March, Flynn's men first murdered an Indian guide. They then massacred eleven people on the Eel River's North Fork, losing one soldier killed before taking women and children prisoners. Next, they massacred nine people and then killed eight more on the Middle Fork of Eel River. Finally, Flynn's men massacred between eighteen and forty-three or more others on the Middle Fork of Eel River (H. Flynn, Captain, Second Infantry California Volunteers to Lieut. Charls H. Barth, Adjutant Second Infantry California Volunteers, April 1, 1863, WOR 1:50:1, 194–195). *HT*, April 11, 1863, 2; C.D. Douglas, Captain, Second Infantry California Volunteers to Lieut. Col. R.C. Drum, April 11, 1863, WOR 1:50:1, 203–204; Wm. E. Hull, Captain Second California Volunteer Infantry to First Lieut. Charles H. Barth, Actg. Asst. Gen., Humboldt Mil. Dist., May 21, 1863, WOR 1:50:1, 196. A Yuki Indian named Hope-no-clan later confessed to killing Bowers, and US Army soldiers executed him on December 7, 1864 (Tassin, "Chronicles, II," 174).

67. *HT*, March 7, 1863, 2.

68. California, *Statutes*, 1863, 662–666; *HT*, March 21, 1863, 2.

69. California, *California Men*, 827–831. For change of command see Chas. H. Barth., First Lieut. and Adjt. Second Infantry California Volunteers, General Orders No. 4, July 13, 1863, WOR 1:50:2, 522. On July 3, Captain Long reported "that his company" had "killed four." On July 8, Indians engaged soldiers escorting a pack train on Redwood Creek, leaving ten soldiers wounded and "six Indians . . . killed on the ground." On July 11, the *Humboldt Times* reported that Lieutenant Geer's men had given one Indian "passage to the 'happy hunting ground'" and that Sergeant Bradford's men had killed "three bucks" and taken a woman prisoner. Finally, on July 23, Ousley's company killed six Indians on Grouse Creek. See *HT*, July 4, 1863, 3; *HT*, July 11, 1863, 2; *HT*, July 18, 1863, 2; July 25, 1863, letter in Beith, Letterbook, 201; *HT*, July 11, 1863, 3; *HT*, August 1, 1863, 3.

70. C.D. Douglas, Captain, Second Infantry California Volunteers to Lieut. Col. R.C. Drum, Asst. Adjt. Gen., July 26, 1863, WOR 1:50:1, 231; Americus, August 8, 1863, in *DEB*, August 14, 1863, 3; G.M. Hanson, Superintending Agent Northern District California to William P. Dole, Commissioner of Indian Affairs, August 22, 1863, in USOIA, *Annual Report*, 1863, 98.

71. R.C. Drum, Assistant Adjutant-General to Lieut. Col. S.G. Whipple, Mountaineer Batt., Comdg., Dist. of Humboldt, August 7, 1863, WOR 1:50:2, 558. On August 29, Mountaineer Company C mustered in at Arcata to be joined two days later by Company E at Fort Humboldt. Company D mustered in during 1864. See California, *California Men*, 828, 830.

72. Correspondent to the Union, June 8, 1863, in *SDU*, June 11, 1863, 2; G.M. Hanson, Superintending Agent to William P. Dole, Commissioner of Indian Affairs, August 4,

1863, in USOIA, *Annual Report*, 1863, 95–96; Wells and Chandler, *History of Butte County*, 2:219; Carson, *Captured*, 2, 6.

73. *Oroville Union*, August 1, 1863, in Bancroft Scraps, 36:116; *San Francisco Bulletin*, August 6, 1863, 2; *Oroville Union*, July 25, 1863, 3; *Marysville Appeal*, July 28, 1863, 3; Gillis and Magliari, *John Bidwell and California*, 272; G.M. Hanson, Superintending Agent to William P. Dole, Commissioner of Indian Affairs, August 4, 1863, and attached J.F. Eddy to G.M. Hanson, in USOIA, *Annual Report*, 1863, 96; Hanson n.d., to Dole, August 4, 1863, in USOIA, *Annual Report*, 1863, 96; *Marysville Appeal*, July 29, 1863, 3; Mansfield, *History of Butte County*, 211, 212.

74. Augustus W. Starr, Captain, Second Cavalry California Volunteers to Lieutenant-Colonel Hooker, Sixth Infantry California Volunteers, September 25, 1863, WOR 1:50:2, 635. See also Charles D. Douglas, Captain, Second Infantry California Volunteers to Lieut. Col. R.C. Drum, Assistant Adjutant-General, September 27, 1863, WOR 1:50:2, 629. Of the "about 800 Indians" gathered on his ranch before the removal, John Bidwell wrote that, "It being the sickly season many were dying daily" (Bidwell in Gillis and Magliari, *John Bidwell and California*, 304). For malaria, see Shover, "John Bidwell's Role in the 1863 Indian Removal from Chico, Part 2, and Through 1866."

75. C.H. Eberle, September 12, 1863, in *Mendocino Herald*, September 18, 1863, 3; Starr to Hooker, September 25, 1863, WOR 1:50:2, 636; Douglas to Drum, September 27, 1863, WOR 1:50:2, 629.

76. Short, in Baumgardner, *Killing for Land*, 212.

77. *SDU*, September 12, 1863, 2. For prior federal payments totaling $814,456.84, see Smith and Denver, "Report of Commissioners of California War Debt," January 5, 1857, in California, *Senate Journal*, 1858, 48–49.

78. S.G. Whipple, Lieut. Col. First Battalion Mountaineers to Lieut. Col. R.C. Drum, Asst. Adjt. Gen., Dept. of the Pacific, September 23, 1863, WOR 1:50:1, 235. In September, soldiers killed an Indian in a boat and took two prisoners. On November 13, Captain Miller attacked Indians dressing beef near "Thomas Ranch" and "Big Bar and South Fork of Trinity," killing two as they swam away. Four days later, near Willow Creek, Ousley's Mountaineers killed five to seven Indians and wounded ten others. Five of the Mountaineers suffered wounds. See Wm. S.R. Taylor, Maj. 1st Batt. Mountaineers to Col. R.C. Drum, Assistant Adjutant-General, September 19, 1863, WOR 1:50:1, 238; A. Miller, Capt. Company C, First Battalion Mountaineers to Maj. W.S.R. Taylor, November 15, 1863, and Wm. S.R. Taylor, Maj. 1st Batt. Mountaineers to Lieut. Col. R.C. Drum, Assistant Adjutant-General, November 18, 1863, WOR 1:50:1, 240; *HT*, November 28, 1863, 2; George W. Ousley, Captain, First Battalion Mountaineers to Maj. W.S.R. Taylor, Commanding Fort Gaston, November 18, 1863, WOR 1:50:1, 421; *HT*, December 19, 1863, 2; *HT*, January 23, 1864, 3. For bombardment, see *HT*, January 2, 1864, 3; George W. Ousley, Capt. Com'nd'g, Co. B, 1st B.M., C.V. to J.E. Wyman, January 11, 1864, in *HT*, January 16, 1864, 3; and *HT*, February 13, 1864, 2.

79. Traveler to the Union, January 1, 1864, in *SDU*, January 15, 1864, 2; Dispatch, January 19, 1864, in *SDU*, January 22, 1864, 2; Neely, January 22, 1864, in *HT*, January 30, 1864, 2; Dispatch, January 18, 1864, in *Yreka Semi-Weekly Union*, January 23, 1864, 2; *Shasta Courier*, January 23, 1864, 2. On January 26, Lieutenants Hempfield and Middleton

killed one Indian and mortally wounded two others "near Jonathon Lyon's farm." On February 2, Lieutenant William Frazier and twelve Mountaineers surprised two Upper Mattole villages, killing thirteen or fourteen men and a woman while capturing twenty-one. Soon thereafter, soldiers killed three more Indians on the Salmon River. See Nelly to Editors Times, January 28, 1864, in *HT*, February 6, 1864, 2; *HT*, February 20, 1864, 3; California, *California Men*, 830; Bledsoe, *Indian Wars*, 254; telegram, February 18, 1864, in *DEB*, February 19, 1864, 3.

80. R.C. Drum, Assistant Adjutant-General to Col. H.M. Black, Sixth Infantry California Vols., February 6, 1864, WOR 1:50:2, 742 (note: Black became a colonel in the California Volunteers); California, *California Men*, 720; H.M. Black, Colonel Sixth Infantry California Volunteers to Lieut. Col. S.G. Whipple, First Battalion Mountaineers, February 18, 1864, WOR 1:50:2, 759; S.G. Whipple, Lieut. Col., First Battalion Mountaineers to Lieut. Col. R.C. Drum, February 16, 1864, WOR 1:50:2, 753; California, *California Men*, 830, 831; G. Wright, Brigadier-General to Col. E.D. Townsend, Asst. Adjt. Gen., Hdqrs. of the Army, February 29, 1864, WOR 1:50:2, 772. For the geographic scope of the Humboldt Military District, see Eicher and Eicher, *Civil War High Commands*, 828–829. For troop strength, see Correspondent, March 20, 1864, in *SDU*, March 28, 1864, 2.

81. K. Geer, Lieut., Co. A, First Batt. Mountaineers to First Lieut. A.W. Hanna, Adjutant First Battalion Mountaineers, March 8, 1864, WOR 1:50:1, 287; *HT*, March 12, 1864, 2; Guidon to Editors, March 29, 1864, in *DAC*, April 19, 1864, 1; William E. Hull, Captain, Second Infantry California Vols. To Acting Assistant Adjutant-General, Humboldt Military District, March 31, 1864, WOR 1:50:1, 257; Correspondent, March 20, 1864, in *SDU*, March 28, 1864, 2; Correspondent, in *HT*, April 2, 1864, 3; Klamath, March 18, 1864, to Editors Union, in *Yreka Semi-Weekly Union*, March 30, 1864, 2.

82. In early April, Hull's Second California Infantry men massacred twenty-five or twenty-six Indian men and took fifteen women and children prisoner "near the North Fork of Eel River." On April 28, Sergeant Wheeler's Second California Infantry men killed eight men and took a dozen women and children prisoner at "Big Bend, on Eel River." At dawn on May 2, Mountaineer lieutenants Geer and Taylor surrounded a village and killed three or six men and three women while capturing four women and children. Lieutenant Middleton's Mountaineers then engaged Trinity Indians, losing three men but killing eleven Indians. On May 23, Lieutenant Geer led more than forty Mountaineers, Sixth California Infantry men, and auxiliaries in massacring at least eleven people before taking four women and children prisoners "on the Trinity border." On May 28, Lieutenant Frazier's Mountaineers attacked Mattole people near the South Fork of Mattole River, leaving two men "lying on the beach, food for bears." That afternoon, Sergeant Wilson and nine other Mountaineers attacked a rancheria near the Trinity River, killing three men and a woman and wounding one or two others. See *HT*, April 16, 1864, 2; Bledsoe, *Indian Wars*, 444; William E. Hull, Captain Second Infantry, California Volunteers to First Lieut. James Ulio, Acting Assistant Adjutant-General, Humboldt Military District, April 30, 1864, WOR 1:50:1, 260; *HT*, May 7, 1864, 2; K. Geer, First Lieutenant Company A, First Battalion Mountaineers to Maj. T.F. Wright, Sixth Infantry California Volunteers, May 2, 1864, WOR 1:50:1, 291; *HT*, May 21, 1864, 3; K. Geer, First Lieutenant

Company A, First Battalion Mountaineers to Maj. Thomas F. Wright, Sixth Infantry California Volunteers, May 25, 1864, WOR 1:50:1, 294; Henry Powell, summarized by D.E. Gordon, May 27, 1864, in *Weekly Trinity Journal*, June 4, 1864, 2; W.W. Frazier, Second Lieutenant Company E, First Battalion Mountaineers, n.d., WOR 1:50:1, 299; Abraham Miller, Captain, First Battalion Mountaineers to Lieut. James Ulio, Adjutant Sixth Volunteer Infantry, June 1, 1864, WOR 1:50:1, 284.

83. Austin Wiley, Superintendent Indian Affairs to Hon. W.P. Dole, Commissioner Indian Affairs, June 4, 1864, in USOIA, *Annual Report*, 1864, 128; Austin Wiley, Superintendent Indian Affairs to W.P. Dole, Commissioner Indian Affairs, June 30, 1864, in USOIA, *Annual Report*, 1864, 130; *Weekly Trinity Journal*, July 16, 1864, 2. On July 11, Frazier's Mountaineers ambushed Indians "between Bull creek and Rainbow ridge," killing one and severely wounding another. On August 16, Sergeant Hines's Sixth California Infantry men hanged two captured Indians and shot two others dead. Geer's Mountaineers, meanwhile, hunted down the last known free Mattole band, killing two men and a woman, and capturing eight women in multiple incidents. See *HT*, July 23, 1864, 3; *HT*, September 3, 1864, 3; *HT*, September 17, 1864, 2.

84. USOIA, *Annual Report*, 1864, 135–136; *HT*, October 1, 1864, 3; *HT*, May 6, 1865, 3; *HT*, September 2, 1865, 3.

85. *HT*, August 6, 1864, 3; J.P. Simpson, Captain, First Battalion Mountaineers to First Lieut. A.W. Hanna, Jr. Adjutant First Battalion Mountaineers, October 1, 1864, WOR 1:50:1, 391; Thomas Middleton, Second Lieut. Co. C., First Batt. of Mountaineers to Lieut. A.W. Hanna, Adjutant First Battalion of Mountaineers, November 5, 1864, and December 4, 1864, WOR 1:50:1, 394–395; *HT*, January 14, 1865, 2.

86. Austin Wiley, Superintendent Indian Affairs to W.P. Dole, Commissioner Indian Affairs, September 1, 1864, in USOIA, *Annual Report*, 1864, 116; Cullum, *Biographical Register*, 1:712; Irvin McDowell, in *SDU*, December 10, 1864, 2.

87. *Shasta Courier*, September 10, 1864, 2; *Shasta Courier*, September 17, 1864, 2; Curtin, *Creation Myths*, 517, 2–3; David Matlock, summarized in Irvin Ayres, "Notes," MSS C-D 301, 1886, 2–3; *Shasta Courier*, September 17, 1864, 2.

88. Ayres, "Notes," 3; *Copper City Pioneer*, September 10, 1864, in *Shasta Courier*, September 17, 1864, 2; *Shasta Courier*, September 17, 1864, 2.

89. Curtin, *Creation Myths*, 517–518.

90. Ibid., 518–519.

91. "A Private Informant," in Waterman, "Yana Indians," 51; Curtin, *Creation Myths*, 519 (emphasis added).

92. Curtin, *Creation Myths*, 519, 520.

93. *Shasta Courier*, September 24, 1864, 2; *Red Bluff Independent*, September 26, 1864, in *Marysville Appeal*, September 30, 1864, 3; *Shasta Courier*, October 8, 1864, 2; *Shasta Courier*, October 15, 1864, 2.

94. Ayres, "Notes," 3–4.

95. USOIA, *Annual Report*, 1865, 104–105; Sc[h]onchin, in Turner, "Scraps of Modoc History," 23; J.W. Huntington to Wm. Dole, December 10, 1864, in USOIA, *Annual Report*, 1865, 101–102. The total Modoc population probably exceeded 339 people in October 1864. For the 1851 Modoc population, see Benjamin Madley, "California and

Oregon's Modoc Indians: How Indigenous Resistance Camouflages Genocide in Colonial Histories," in Woolford, Benvenuto, and Hinton, *Colonial Genocide*, 117.

96. Dean et al., *Weaving a Legacy*, 19–20; Thos. Mahony, John B. Hughes, P.B. Tripp, [and 21 Others] to Major-General MD Dowell, Commander of the Forces of California, n.d., WOR 1:50:2, 989; Wright, in *Daily Evening Post*, November 22, 1879, 2. On November 14, a correspondent reported two miners killed in the White Mountains on the valley's eastern rim. Whites then killed an Indian reportedly trying to steal horses. On December 22, R.A. Washington reported that Indians east of Owens River had killed two white men and taken their horses before other whites killed the horse thieves and others. See J.S. Broder Ed. Union, November 14, 1864, in *Esmeralda Union*, November 21, 1864, 3; Correspondent, November 14, 1864, in *SDU*, November 26, 1864, 2; *Aurora Union*, November 18, 1864, in *SDU*, November 24, 1864, 3; *Esmeralda Union*, November 18, 1864, 3; R.A. Washington, Pi-Ute Interpreter to Maj. C. McDermitt, Second California Volunteer Cavalry, December 22, 1864, WOR 1:50:2, 1114.

97. G. to Messrs. Editors, n.d., in *Esmeralda Union*, January 7, 1865, 3; Unattributed recollection, quoted in Chalfant, *Story of Inyo*, 222; G. to Editors, n.d., in *Esmeralda Union*, January 7, 1865, 3; Chalfant, *Story of Inyo*, 224.

98. Correspondent, January 2, 1865, in *Visalia Delta*, January 11, 1865, 2; George Lechler, paraphrased in *Los Angeles Tri-Weekly News*, January 21, 1865, 2. For death toll estimates see Correspondent, January 2, 1865, in *Visalia Delta*, January 11, 1865, 2; Lechler, paraphrased in *Los Angeles Tri-Weekly News*, January 21, 1865, 2; Chalfant, *Story of Inyo*, 222. Greenly agreed that his posse "killed nearly all the Indians who were there," in Cadmium, January 8, 1865, in *DAC*, January 22, 1865, 1.

99. Captain Greenly, summarized by Cadmium, January 8, 1865, in *DAC*, January 22, 1865, 1; Montgomery district gentleman summarized in *Esmeralda Union*, January 18, 1865, 2; Montgomery correspondent, January 17, 1865, in *Esmeralda Union*, January 21, 1865, 2; Wright, in *Daily Evening Post*, November 22, 1879, 2; Works Progress Administration, *California*, 38; Caughey, *California*, 384; Correspondent, January 17, 1865, in *Esmeralda Union*, January 21, 1865, 2. Whites killed two "eight miles below Bishop creek," two more near Big Pine, and seventeen others near Taboose Ranch. See Correspondent, January 17, 1865, in *Esmeralda Union*, January 21, 1865, 2; *Esmeralda Union*, January 18, 1865, 2; Wright, in *Daily Evening Post*, November 22, 1879, 2.

100. *SDU*, January 26, 1865, 2; January 18, 1866, letter in Chalfant, *Story of Inyo*, 226; Chalfant, *Story of Inyo*, 226.

101. HT, June 17, 1865, 2; California, *California Men*; Charles Maltby, Superintendent Indian Affairs, California to Hon. D.W. Cooley, Com'r Indian Affairs, Washington, DC, September 15, 1865, in USOIA, *Annual Report*, 1865, 116; Cook, *Population of California Indians*, 44.

102. *SDU*, March 27, 1865, 3; Delaney, "Adventures of Captain Hi Good," 1; Dispatch, August 15, 1865, in *SDU*, August 16, 1865, 2; *Union Record*, August 19, 1865, 3; Daniel Klauberg, in *Union Record*, August 26, 1865, 3.

103. *Weekly Trinity Journal*, September 23, 1865, 2; *Humboldt Journal*, October 5, 1865, in *Bancroft Scraps*, 36:28; *Red Bluff Independent*, December 27, 1865, 3; *Chico Weekly Courant*, July 28, 1866, 2; *Shasta Courier*, September 29, 1866, 2.

104. Snow Shoe to Editors Appeal, August 13, 1864, in *Marysville Appeal*, August 23, 1864, 2; B.A. Farmer to J.K. Luttrell, March 2, 1866, in *SDU*, March 12, 1866, 2; Correspondent to the Union, March 4, 1866, in *SDU*, March 14, 1866, 2; Correspondent, in *Red Bluff Independent*, March 14, 1866, 3; *Humboldt Register*, March 17, 1866, 2; *Yreka Weekly Union*, March 24, 1866, 2.

105. Moak, *Last of the Mill Creeks*, 24–26; *Chico Weekly Courant*, April 14, 1866, 3; William Dow, in Fairfield, *Fairfield's Pioneer History*, 397–398; Mr. Dodge, summarized in *Shasta Courier*, August 25, 1866, 2; *Shasta Courier*, September 1, 1866, 2; *Red Bluff Independent*, September 5, 1866, 2; Waterman, "Yana Indians," 51; Fred Dersch, paraphrased in Southern, *Our Storied Landmarks*, 94–95; *Shasta Courier*, September 22, 1866, 2; *Shasta Courier*, October 6, 1866, 2; Delaney, "Adventures of Captain Hi Good," 1.

106. *Shasta Courier*, October 13, 1866, 2; *Susanville Sagebrush*, November 10, 1866, in *Shasta Courier*, November 17, 1866, 2.

107. Robert F. Heizer, "Indian Servitude in California," in Washburn, *Handbook of North American Indians*, 4:415; Cook, "Conflict, III," 315; Edward D. Castillo, "The Impact of Euro-American Exploration and Settlement," in Heizer, *Handbook of North American Indians*, 8:109.

108. The Emancipation Proclamation, January 1, 1863, http://www.archives.gov/exhibits/featured_documents/emancipation_proclamation/transcript.html; California, *Statutes*, 1863, 743.

109. Brewer, *Up and Down California*, 493; *Shasta Courier*, November 18, 1865, 2; Correspondent to Union, August 13, 1865, in *SDU*, August 19, 1865, 2; *California Police Gazette*, August 26, 1865, 2.

110. Robert Brady and US House of Representatives, *The Constitution of the United States of America as Amended: Unratified Amendments, Analytical Index*, 16; Rob't J. Stephens, Special Commissioner, & c. to Hon. Lewis V. Bogy, Commissioner of Indian Affairs, January 1, 1867, in USOIA, *Annual Report*, 1867, 117; 18 United States Code, Chapter 77 § 1581–1588; California, *Statutes*, 1936, 1005, 1180; California, *Penal Code*, 455, 536; California, *Code of Civil Procedure*, 605.

111. In January, vigilantes killed seven Northern Paiutes near Surprise Valley. In March, vigilantes massacred seven Indians east of San Bernardino and US cavalrymen killed five Paiute-Shoshone men east of Owens Valley. See H., March 30, 1867, in *Plumas National*, April 27, 1867, 3; *San Bernardino Guardian*, April 6, 1867, in Hayes, "Hayes Scrapbooks," vol. 39; Thomas Franklin to Editors Alta, March 13, 1867, in *DAC*, March 23, 1867, 1. For *Daily Alta California* quotation, see *DAC*, April 24, 1867, 2. Vigilantes killed seven Yana people on Antelope Creek in May, two on Antelope Creek in mid-June, seven or more at Ink's Creek on June 27, and eight or nine others in the Antelope Creek region that fall. See *Red Bluff Independent*, May 22, 1867, 3; *Shasta Courier*, June 22, 1867, 2; *Red Bluff Independent*, July 3, 1867, 3; *Shasta Courier*, May 23, 1868, 2. For Wilson, see *Shasta Courier*, summarized in *Red Bluff Independent*, September 18, 1867, 2. Fairfield, *Fairfield's Pioneer History*, 415–416.

112. Robinson, *General Crook*, 96; Bourke, "General Crook," 645; Joe, in *Owyhee Avalanche*, November 2, 1867, 1; Crook, *General George Crook*, 155n3; Crook, quoted by Joe, in *Owyhee Avalanche*, November 2, 1867, 2; Crook, *General George Crook*, 154;

J.M. Bassett, October 28, 1867, in *Yreka Weekly Union*, November 2, 1867, 3; Military Express, October 28, 1867, in *DAC*, October 29, 1867, 1, and *SDU*, October 29, 1867, 2; Joe, in *Owyhee Avalanche*, November 2, 1867, 2; Correspondent, November 14, 1867, in *SDU*, December 5, 1867, 5; Indian survivor, paraphrased in Minchno, *Deadliest Indian War*, 264; Minchno, *Deadliest Indian War*, 265; Crook, *General George Crook*, 155n3.

113. A. to Editors, in *DAC*, March 2, 1868, 1; Correspondent, in *DAC*, February 22, 1868, 1; *Susanville Sagebrush*, May 16, 1868, 3; [Illegible] to Editor Times, November 29, 1868, in *HT*, December 5, 1868, 3; *Shasta Courier*, December 5, 1868, 2; *Red Bluff Independent*, December 10, 1868, 2; *Trinity Journal*, December 5, 1868, 2; "Hayfork," 26–27; Potter, "Reminiscences," 2.

114. *HT*, January 9, 1869, 3; *HT*, April 10, 1869, 3; Delaney, "Adventures of Captain Hi Good," 1.

115. *SDU*, May 7, 1870, 4.

116. US Department of the Interior, *Statistics of the Population of the United States, Embracing the Tables of Race, Nationality, Sex, Selected Ages, and Occupations*, 16; Merriam, "Indian Population of California," 600; O.T. Fitzgerald, "Fourth Biennial Report of the Superintendent of Public Instruction for the school years 1870 and 1871," in California, *Appendix to Journals of Senate and Assembly*, 1:106.

117. Mr. Novall [Norvell] and D.B. Lyon, in Waterman, "Yana Indians," 59. Theodora Kroeber thought that this massacre took place in "1870, 1871, or 1872" (Kroeber, *Ishi in Two Worlds*, 239).

CONCLUSION

1. Wells, *History of Siskiyou*, 153; Jesse Applegate, in Dillon, *Burnt-Out Fires*, 160.

2. F.A. Walker to T.B. Odeneal, July 6, 1872, H. Exec. Doc. 122, 43rd Cong., 1st Sess., 1874, serial 1607, 263; Schonchin in *New York Herald*, February 28, 1873, 3 (Kintpuash also "directly denied that the Indians shot first" [*New York Herald*, February 28, 1873, 4]); James Jackson to John Green, December 2, 1872, H. Exec. Doc. 122, 43rd Cong., 1st Sess., 1874, serial 1607, 42–43; Murray, *Modocs and Their War*, 89; Meacham, *Wi-ne-ma*, 81; Murray, *Modocs and Their War*, 88–89; Meacham, *Wi-ne-ma*, 80–81; Jackson to Green, December 2, 1872, 44. The Modoc War began on November 29, 1872, when the US Army attacked the Modocs on Lost River, and it effectively ended on June 1, 1873, with Kintpuash's surrender. See Cothran, *Remembering the Modoc War*, 1, 64.

3. Murray, *Modocs and Their War*, 243; Quinn, *Hell with the Fire Out*, 157; Captain Jack, in Special Correspondent's letter, May 7, 1873, in *New York Times*, May 24, 1873, 2.

4. Thompson, *Modoc War*, 28, 29; Frank Wheaton, Bvt. Maj. Gen. to Gen. E.R.S. Canby, Commanding Department of the Columbia, January 19, 1873, H. Exec. Doc. 122, 43rd Cong., 1st Sess., 1874, serial 1607, 50–51; Frank Wheaton, Lieut. Col. Twenty-first Infantry, Bvt. Maj. Gen. to Brig. Gen. E.R.S. Canby, Commanding Dep. of the Columbia and Military Division of the Pacific, n.d., H. Exec. Doc. 122, 43rd Cong., 1st Sess., 1874, serial 1607, 54; Wheaton, in Thompson, *Modoc War*, 43, 169.

5. W.T. Sherman, General to Gen. E.R.S. Canby, March 13, 1873, H. Exec. Doc. 122, 43rd Cong., 1st Sess., 1874, serial 1607, 70–71; Ed. R.S. Canby, Brigadier-General Commanding to General W.T. Sherman, March 16, 1873, H. Exec. Doc. 122, 43rd Cong., 1st Sess., 1874, serial 1607, 276; Thompson, *Modoc War*, 54–59.

6. "Trial of the Modoc Prisoners," H. Exec. Doc. 122, 43rd Cong., 1st Sess., 1874, serial 1607, 161; Murray, *Modocs and Their War*, 177–178; a soldier quoting Mark Twain, in Quinn, *Hell with the Fire Out*, 72.

7. Schonchin and Kintpuash, in Meacham, October 5, 1872, in USOIA, *Annual Report*, 1873, 78.

8. Meacham, *Wigwam and War-Path*, 492, 495–497; Murray, *Modocs and Their War*, 189.

9. Murray, *Modocs and Their War*, 192–193; Boyle, "Personal Observations," MSS PA96, n.d., 55–57.

10. W.T. Sherman, General to Gen. Schofield, April 12, 1873, in *DAC*, April 14, 1873, 1; J.M. Schofield, Major General to Gen. Gillem, April 13, 1873, in *DAC*, April 14, 1873, 2; John M. Schofield to Gillem, April 14, 1873, in *Army and Navy Journal*, April 26, 1873, 585. Historian Boyd Cothran called the Modoc War a "five-month-long peace negotiation turned campaign of extermination" (*Remembering the Modoc War*, 1).

11. Meacham, *Wigwam and War-Path*, 522–523; Thompson, *Modoc War*, 168; Gillem to Mason, April 16, 1873, in Hagen, *Modoc War*, 2:1061. A summary of multiple death toll estimates appeared in Thompson, *Modoc War*, 74–76, 168, 170.

12. Quinn, *Hell with the Fire Out*, 143; Sherman to Dear Sir, April 17, 1873, in *Army and Navy Journal*, April 26, 1873, 586–587; A.C. Gillem, Colonel Commanding to Major-General Schofield, April 17, in *DAC*, April 19, 1873, 1.

13. Thompson, *Modoc War*, 82, 92; Scarfaced Charlie, in Glassley, *Pacific Northwest Indian Wars*, 196; Murray, *Modocs and Their War*, 236.

14. Murray, *Modocs and Their War*, 243, 246–251; *Army and Navy Journal*, May 17, 1873, 630; H.C. Hasbrouck, in Brady, *Northwestern Fights and Fighters*, 324.

15. Glatthaar, *March to the Sea*, 64; Murray, *Modocs and Their War*, 204; California, *Penal Code*, 455; *People v. McGuire*, 1872; Lucretia Mott, Elizabeth S. Bladen and E.M. Davis of the Radical Club and others to Ulysses S. Grant, President of the United States, Columbus Delano Secy of the Interior and E.P. Smith Commissioner of Indian Affairs and others, April 19, 1873, in Hagen, *Modoc War*, 1:885–886; Knight, *Following the Indian Wars*, 104–158.

16. *DAC*, June 10, 1873, 1 (for additional details on this killing, see newspaper clippings in Hagen, *Modoc War*, 2:1071–1072); Sherman to Sheridan, June 3, 1873, in Athern, *William Tecumseh Sherman*, 303; W.T. Sherman to J.M. Schofield, June 3, 1873, H. Exec. Doc. 122, 43rd Cong., 1st Sess., 1874, serial 1607, 86; Jeff C. Davis to Assist. Adjut. General, June 5, 1873, in Hagen, *Modoc War*, 2:1028; Thompson, *Modoc War*, 120–122; Cothran, *Remembering the Modoc War*, 71; Murray, *Modocs and Their War*, 285–286, 297; Quinn, *Hell with the Fire Out*, 180. Cothran has asserted that army Major H.P. Curtis, the judge advocate who prosecuted the Modoc men, successfully petitioned on behalf of Barncho and Slolux (*Remembering the Modoc War*, 72).

17. Thompson, *Modoc War*, 124–125, 126; "Cost of Modoc War," H. Exec. Doc. 185, 43rd Cong., 1st Sess., 1874, serial 1610, 2, 3; "An act to reimburse the State of Oregon and State of California and the citizens thereof for moneys paid by said States in the suppression of Indian hostilities during the Modoc war in the years eighteen hundred and seventy-two and eighteen hundred and seventy-three," in US Congress, *Statutes at Large of the United States of America, From December, 1881, to March, 1883*, 22:399–400.

18. *Rock*, August, 1915, 3; H.C. Hasbrouck to Samuel Breck, November 5, 1873, in H. Exec. Doc. 122, 43rd Cong., 1st Sess., 1874, serial 1607, 102; Albert L. Hurtado, "The Modocs and the Jones Family: Quaker Administration of the Quapaw Agency, 1873–1879," in Smith, *Oklahoma's Forgotten Indians*, 86–107; USOIA, *Annual Report*, 1881, 278. The army sent two of the original 155 prisoners—Barncho and Slolux—to Alcatraz (Murray, *Modocs and Their War*, 297).

19. *Mariposa Gazette*, February 1, 1879, 3; *Mariposa Gazette*, April 26, 1879, 3.

20. Bauer, *We Were All Like Migrant Workers Here*, 204. For population, see Lightfoot and Parrish, *California Indians*, 3. For the number of federally recognized tribes, reservations, and tribes petitioning for federal recognition, see http://www.courts.ca .gov/3066.htm. In 2007, legal scholar Angela Riley explained, "As presently constituted under federal law, tribal sovereignty ensures that Indian tribes enjoy the same inherent rights of self-government over their members and retained territories as any other nation, except as limited by the doctrine of discovery, treaty-based cessions of authority, or explicit congressional abrogation under the plenary power doctrine. Tribal sovereignty is embodied in hundreds of treaties between Indian nations and the colonial powers, referenced in the U.S. Constitution, recognized by a vast body of Supreme Court jurisprudence, and affirmed by numerous congressional acts." See Riley, "(Tribal) Sovereignty and Illiberalism," 807.

21. Waterman, "Ishi, the Last Yahi Indian," 530; Gudde, *California Place Names*, 55, 114–115, 162. For Hastings, see Shuck, *Bench and Bar*, 243–244; Buckles deposition, February 23, 1860, *MMR*, 28; H.L. Hall deposition, February 26, 1860, *MMR*, 42; Lacock deposition, February 28, 1860, *MMR*, 49–50; Hastings deposition, March 13, 1860, *MMR*, 30. For Stanford, see *New York Times*, August 10, 1891, 11; Tutorow, *Governor*.

22. Jessica Cejnar, "Indian Island Cleanup Nearly Finished; Wiyot Tribe Searching for Additional Project Funding," *Times Standard*, June 13, 2012, http://www.times-standard .com/20120613/indian-island-cleanup-nearly-finished-wiyot-tribe-searching-for-additio nal-project-funding; Robin Hindery, "San Francisco School Swaps out Name of Racist Governor," *San Jose Mercury News*, May 20, 2011, http://www.mercurynews.com/ci _18104528; Lauren Williams, "L.B. School Dropping Racist Governor's Name," *Orange County Register*, December 28, 2014, central B.

23. In 2005, the State Department of Parks and Recreation, the Lucy Moore Foundation, the California Department of Transportation, and the US Forest Service dedicated a new monument near the site of the massacre titled "Bloody Island Bo-no-po-ti." It reads, "One-fourth mile west is the island called Bo-no-po-ti (Old Island), now Bloody Island. It was a place for Native gatherings until May 15, 1850. On that date, a regiment of the 1st Dragoons of the US Cavalry, commanded by Capt. Nathaniel Lyon

and Lt. J.W. Davidson, massacred nearly the entire Native population of the island. Most were women and children. This act was in reprisal for the killing of Andrew Kelsey and Charles Stone who had long enslaved, brutalized, and starved indigenous people in the area. The island, now a hill surrounded by reclaimed land, remains a sacred testament to this sacrifice of innocents." For commemorations, see *Del Norte Triplicate*, December 18, 2013, http://www.triplicate.com/Northcoast-Life /Northcoast-Life/Annual-vigil-open-to-public; *Times Standard*, February 25, 2011, http://www.times-standard.com/20110225/wiyot-tribe-holding-annual-candlelight-vigil -for-indian-island;   http://blogs.usda.gov/2013/11/21/tribes-remember-the-nome-cult -trail/.

24. For Indians killed between 1846 and 1873, see online appendixes 1, 2, and 3. For non-Indians killed between 1846 and 1873 by Indians in California, see online Appendix 4.

25. Cook, *Population of California Indians*, 45. For forcible transfers of children, see Cook, "Conflict, III," 61, and Castillo, "The Impact of Euro-American Exploration and Settlement," in Heizer, *Handbook of North American Indians*, 8:109. Other countries have addressed systematic child kidnapping as genocide. For example, see National Inquiry into the Separation of Aboriginal and Torres Strait Islander Children from Their Families, *Bringing Them Home*.

26. Powers, "California Indians. No. VIII.—The Modocs," 536; *Nevada Journal*, May 27, 1855, 2; Magliari, "Free State Slavery," 191; Phillips, "Indians in Los Angeles, 1781–1875," 448–449; *LAS*, January 31, 1863, 2; Thompson, "Insalubrious California," 57–63.

27. Wilshire, *Get 'Em All! Kill 'Em!*, 18; Burnett, "Governor's Message," in California, *California Legislature*, 1851, 15; Weller, August 11, 1852, in *CG*, August 12, 1852, 2175. For International Criminal Tribunal for Rwanda quotation, see Schabas, *Genocide in International Law*, 212.

28. Crittenden, in *CG*, May 26, 1860, 2336.

29. UN, *Convention on Genocide*, 280.

30. Estimates of the precontact American Indian population in what would become the continental United States remain contested. In 1987, demographer Russell Thornton estimated "5+million" in "the coterminous United States" (Thornton, *American Indian Holocaust*, 32, 60). The US Indian Office reported 243,299 American Indians in 1887, and the federal Census Bureau reported 237,196 in 1900 (US Department of the Interior, *Annual Reports of the Department of the Interior for the Fiscal Year Ended June 30, 1900*, 48, and US Bureau of the Census, *Indian Population in the United States and Alaska, 1910*, 10). According to Thornton, "the single most important factor in American Indian population decline was an increased death rate due to diseases introduced from the Eastern Hemisphere" (Thornton, *American Indian Holocaust*, 44).

31. For more on this debate, see Madley, "Reexamining the American Genocide Debate," 98–139.

32. In *Our Indian Wards*—which ranged from colonial times through the 1870s—Manypenny described and quoted instances of Indians exterminated, threats and plans to exterminate Indians, concerns regarding Indians' extermination, and the

process of extermination (Manypenny, *Our Indian Wards*, 14, 99, 122, 142, 175, 176, 180, 187, 195, 198, 204, 209, 287, 432). Jackson, *A Century of Dishonor*, 339; Roosevelt, *Winning of the West*, 1:334. Roosevelt did concede that "the English had exterminated or assimilated the Celts of Britain, and they substantially repeated the process with the Indians of America" (Roosevelt, *Winning of the West*, 1:11).

33. Lemkin, *Lemkin on Genocide*, 3; McDonnell and Moses, "Raphael Lemkin," 502. For some of those who began using the concept of genocide to evaluate American Indian history, see Buffy Sainte-Marie, "My Country 'Tis of Thy People You're Dying," on the album *Little Wheel Spin and Spin* (1966) (political scientist Adam Jones kindly provided this citation); Sturtevant and Stanley, "Indian Communities," 17; Native American activists in Matthiessen, *In the Spirit of Crazy Horse*, 415, 429, 478; Norton, *Genocide in Northwestern California*; Todorov, *Conquest of America*, 5. Thornton, *American Indian Holocaust*, xvi, 44; Frank Chalk and Kurt Jonassohn, "Indians of the Americas, 1492–1789," in Chalk and Jonassohn, *History and Sociology of Genocide*, 173–180; Chalk and Jonassohn, "Indians of the United States in the Nineteenth Century," in Chalk and Jonassohn, *History and Sociology of Genocide*, 195–203; Stannard, *American Holocaust*, xii. For some other scholars who claimed that American Indians suffered genocide, see M. Annette Jaimes, "Introduction: Sand Creek: The Morning After," in Jaimes, *State of Native America*, 3; Lenore A. Stiffarm and Phil Lane Jr., "The Demography of Native North America: A Question of American Indian Survival," in Jaimes, *State of Native America*, 37. Churchill, *Little Matter of Genocide*, 97, 159, 289–290; Kiernan, *Blood and Soil*, 213–248, 310–363. Many other scholars have asserted that American Indians suffered genocide.

34. Axtell, *Beyond 1492*, 261; Katz, *Holocaust in Historical Context*, 20; Robert M. Utley, "Total War on the American Indian Frontier," in Boemeke, Chickering, and Förster, *Anticipating Total War*, 401, 399 (Utley did acknowledge that "in one sense the concept of genocide is relevant: cultural genocide," 400); Rubinstein, *Genocide*, 53; Lewy, "Were American Indians Victims?," 63; Anderson, *Ethnic Cleansing and the Indian*, 7, 13, 50, 51, 64, 177, 209, 241, 272, 286, 309, 328, 337.

35. Hurtado, *Indian Survival*, 7. Some twenty-first-century histories addressing violence against Native Americans include Richter, *Facing East from Indian Country*; Anderson, *Conquest of Texas*; Blackhawk, *Violence over the Land*; Jacoby, *Shadows at Dawn*; Silver, *Our Savage Neighbors*; DeLay, *War of a Thousand Deserts*; Cave, *Lethal Encounters*; Lindsay, *Murder State*; Cothran, *Remembering the Modoc War*.

36. Stone, "Introduction," in Stone, *Historiography of Genocide*, 3.

37. In 1987, anthropologist Russell Thornton argued that "the largest, most blatant, deliberate killings of North American Indians by non-Indians surely occurred in California" and in the year 2000 historians Robert Hine and John Faragher concluded that California was the site of "the clearest case of genocide in the history of the American frontier." See Thornton, *American Indian Holocaust*, 201, and Hine and Faragher, *American West*, 249.

BIBLIOGRAPHY

ARCHIVAL SOURCES

Akerman, J.L. "J.L. Akerman Journal, 1849 September 23–1854 February 1." Bancroft Library, 1854.

Andrew Jackson Papers, Library of Congress, Washington, DC, n.d.

Archives of California. Vol. 63. Bancroft Library, n.d.

Ayres, Irvin. "Notes furnished by and concerning Irvin Ayres, Esq're, to be digested and used by Mr. Hubert Howe Bancroft in preparing his history of the Pacific slope." Bancroft Library, 1886.

Baldwin, Marian. "History of Smith River, California." Humboldt State University Library, 1916.

Bancroft Scraps. 23 vols. Bancroft Library, n.d.

Barstow, Alfred. "Statement of Alfred Barstow, a Pioneer of 1849." Bancroft Library, 1877.

Bash, L.H. "Notes on the Life of Brevet Major General Persifor Frazer Smith, U.S.A. Compiled from Official Reports, Contemporary Newspapers, Memoirs, etc." Bancroft Library, 1927.

Bauer, John A. "Statement of John A. Bauer, a Pioneer of 1849." Bancroft Library, 1877.

Beith, James. Letterbook, 1854–1867. Bancroft Library, n.d.

Bidwell, John. "Dictation from John Bidwell." Bancroft Library, 1891(?).

Bigler, John. "John Bigler Papers, 1850–1869." Bancroft Library, n.d.

Boyle, W.H. "Personal Observations on the Conduct of the Modoc War." Bancroft Library, n.d.

Breckenridge, Thomas E. "Thomas E. Breckenridge Memoirs, 1894." Folders 1–5. Western Historical Manuscripts Collection, University of Missouri at Columbia.

Buck, Franklin Augustus. Franklin Augustus Buck Papers. 1846–1966, Box 1. Huntington Library, n.d.

Burnett, Peter H. "Recollections of the Past." Bancroft Library, 1878.

"Captain's Commission of Nathaniel Lyon, June 11, 1851." Nathaniel Lyon Papers, History and Genealogy Unit, Connecticut State Library, Hartford.

Cassin, Francis. "Cassin's Few Facts: Statement of a few facts on California By Francis Cassin (pioneer of 1849)." Bancroft Library, 1878.

Chamberlain, John. "Memoirs of California since 1840." Bancroft Library, 1877.

Clyman, James. "Diary of Col. James Clyman of Napa Co., 1844–1846." Bancroft Library, 1871.

Coan, Ernie. "The Del Norte Indian." Humboldt State University Library, 1933.

Connor, John W. "Connor's Early California: Statement of a few recollections on Early California." Bancroft Library, 1878.

Doble, John. "Doble's Diary, 1851–1854." Bancroft Library, n.d.

Dowell, Benjamin Franklin. Correspondence and Papers, 1855–1886. Bancroft Library, n.d.

Dustin, Daniel. "Letters of Daniel Dustin, 1850–1857." Rauner Library, n.d.

Essene, Frank J. complier. "Fort Independence Paiute Ethnographic Notes, 1935 in Ethnological Documents of the Department and Museum of Anthropology, University of California, Berkeley, 1875–1958." Bancroft Library, n.d.

Findla, James. "Statement of a few events in early days of Cal. as given by James Findla, for Bancroft Library." Bancroft Library, 1878.

Gans, Judge Herbert South. "Judge Herbert South Gans Scrapbook." Tehama County Library, n.d.

Geer, Knyphausen. "Captain Knyphausen Geer: His Life and Memoirs." Bancroft Library, n.d.

Green, Alfred A. "Life and Adventures of a 47-er of California." Bancroft Library, 1878.

Grimshaw, William Robinson. "William Robinson Grimshaw, His narrative of life and events in California during flush times, particularly the years 1848–50, including a biographical sketch of himself." Bancroft Library, 1872.

Hagen, Olaf T., ed. *Modoc War: Official Correspondence and Documents, 1865–1878.* 2 vols. San Francisco: Government publication, 1942. Bancroft Library.

Hale, Augustin W. Diaries 1 and 3–14. Augustin W. Hale Papers, 1775–1909. Huntington Library, n.d.

Hardcastle, A.B. "[Journal of a] March from Ft. Bridger, W.T., to Benicia, Calif., [and of an expedition against the Indians from] Ft. Humboldt to Yager Creek [and back with maps of the route]." In Cave Johnson Couts Papers, 1832–1951. Huntington Library, n.d.

Hayden, George M. George M. Hayden Diaries, vols. 1 and 2, 1846–1848. Bancroft Library, n.d.

Hayes, Benjamin, comp. "Hayes Scrapbooks, 1847–1875." 138 vols. Bancroft Library, n.d.

Henshaw, Joshua S. "Statement of Historical Events in California in early times after Am.-occupn." Bancroft Library, 1878.

Hutchings, James Mason. James Mason Hutchings Diary, 1848–1855. Bancroft Library, n.d.

Iturbide, Augustin de. "Plan of Iguala." February 24, 1821. http://scholarship.rice.edu/jsp/xml/1911/20697/3/aa00005tr.tei.html.

Jacobs, R. "Muster Roll of Capt. R. Jacobs Company (H) California Battalion [illegible] Commanded by Lieut. Col. J.C. Fremont from October 1846." Fresno Genealogical Society. http://www.rootsweb.ancestry.com/~cafcgs/Fremont/rosterh.htm.

Kane, Michael. "Statement of Michael Kane." Bancroft Library, 1878.

Kern, Edward Meyer, comp. "Fort Sutter Collection: A Transcript of the Fort Sutter Papers together with the Historical Commentaries Accompanying Them." Huntington Library, 1921.

Knight, Thomas. "Statement of Early Events in California By Thomas Knight (a pioneer of 1845) for Bancroft Library." Bancroft Library, 1879.

La Motte, H.D. "Statement of H.D. La Motte." In La Motte Family Papers, 1802–1970. Bancroft Library, n.d.

Martin, Thomas S. "Narrative of John C. Fremont's Exped. to California in 1845–6 and subsequent events in Cal. down to 1853, including Fremont's Exploring Exploration of 1848." Bancroft Library, 1878.

Murray, Walter. "Narrative of a California Volunteer." Bancroft Library, 1878.

Nahl, C. del [Charles Nahl]. *Hutchings' California Scenes.* Placerville, CA: James M. Hutchings, 1854. Huntington Library.

Perkins, William. "El Campo de Los Sonoraenses or Three Years Residence in California, 1849–1852." Bancroft Library, n.d.

Pond, Ananias. Ananias Pond Journal 1. Huntington Library, n.d.

Potter, Elijah Renshaw. "Reminiscences of the early history of northern California and of the Indian troubles." Bancroft Library, n.d.

Reading, Pierson B. Reading Collection, 1843–1868. California State Library, n.d.

Revere, Joseph Warren. Album (1848–1870). Huntington Library, 1870.

Rogers, Harrison G. Journal, November 1826–January 1827. William Henry Ashley Collection, 1811–1975. Missouri History Museum Archives, n.d.

Ross, John E. "Narrative of an Indian Fighter." Bancroft Library, 1878.

Sayward, W.T. "Pioneer Reminiscences." Bancroft Library, 1882.

Shaw, William J. "Dictation." Bancroft Library, 1886.

Sloat, John D. Commander in Chief of the United States Naval Forces in the Pacific Ocean to the Inhabitants of California, July 7, 1846. Fort Sacramento Papers with Historical Commentaries, vol. 3. Huntington Library.

Stoneman, George. "Autobiographical Statement." Bancroft Library, 1888(?).

Sutter, John A. "Reminiscences." Bancroft Library, 1876.

Tustin, William Isaac. "Recollections of Early Days in California." Bancroft Library, 1880.

Vallejo, José Manuel Salvador. "Notas históricas sobre California." Bancroft Library, 1874.

Wiggins, William. "Reminiscences of William Wiggins who came to California in 1840 on the 'Lusanne.'" Bancroft Library, 1877.

Willey, Samuel H. "Personal Memoranda on California." Bancroft Library, 1878.

Wozencraft, O.M. "Indian Affairs, 1849–1850." Bancroft Library, 1877.

Yates, John. "Sketch of a Journey in the Year 1842 from Sacramento California through the Valley by John Yates of Yatestown." Bancroft Library, 1872.

GOVERNMENT DOCUMENTS

Brady, Robert, and US House of Representatives. *The Constitution of the United States of America as Amended: Unratified Amendments, Analytical Index.* Washington, DC: Government Printing Office, 2007.

California. *Appendix to Journal of the Seventh Session of the Assembly of the State of California, Begun on the Seventh Day of January, One Thousand Eight Hundred and Fifty-Six, and Ended on the Twenty-First Day of April, One Thousand Eight Hundred and Fifty-Six, at the City of Sacramento.* Sacramento: James Allen, 1856.

California. *Appendix to Assembly Journals for the Eighth Session of the Legislature of the State of California.* Sacramento: James Allen, 1857.

California. *Appendix to Assembly Journals of the Ninth Session of the Legislature of the State of California.* Sacramento: John O'Meara, 1858.

California. *Appendix to Journals of Assembly, of the Tenth Session of the Legislature of the State of California.* Sacramento: John O'Meara, 1859.

California. *Appendix to Journals of Assembly, of the Eleventh Session of the Legislature of the State of California.* Sacramento: C.T. Botts, 1860.

California. *Appendix to Journals of Senate and Assembly, of the Nineteenth Session of the Legislature of the State of California.* 4 vols. Vol. 1. Sacramento: T.A. Springer, 1872.

California. *The California Practice Act: Being an act entitled "An act to regulate proceedings in civil cases in the courts of justice in this state," passed April 29, 1851; also, "An Act concerning the Courts of Justice of this State, and Judicial Officers," passed May 19, 1853; and also, "An Act concerning Forcible Entries and Unlawful Detainers," passed April 22, 1850.* Edited by Henry J. Labatt. 4th ed. San Francisco: H.H. Bancroft, 1861.

California. *The Code of Civil Procedure of the State of California,* compiled by Warren Olney. San Francisco: Sumner Whitney, 1872.

California. *Correspondence Relative to Indian Affairs in Mendocino County.* Sacramento: Chas. T. Botts, 1859.

California. *The General Laws of the State of California, from 1850 to 1864, Inclusive: Being a Compilation of all Acts of a General Nature Now in Force, with Full References to Repealed Acts, Special and Local Legislation, and Statutory Constructions of the Supreme Court.* Compiled by Theodore H. Hittell. San Francisco: H.H. Bancroft, 1865.

California. *Journal of the Proceedings of the House of Assembly of the State of California; at its First Session begun and held at Puebla de San José, on the Fifteenth Day of December, 1849.* San José: J. Winchester, 1850.

California. *Journal of the Senate of the State of California; At their First Session Begun and Held at Puebla de San José, on the Fifteenth Day of December, 1849.* San José: J. Winchester, 1850.

California. *Journals of the Legislature of the State of California; At its Second Session: Held at the City of San Jose, Commencing on the Sixth Day of January, and Ending on the First Day of May, 1851.* N.p.: Eugene Casserly, 1851.

California. *Journal of the Third Session of the Legislature of the State of California, Begun on the 5th Day of January, 1852, and Ended on the 4th Day of May, 1852, at the Cities of Vallejo and Sacramento.* San Francisco: G.K. Fitch and V.E. Geiger, 1852.

California. *Journal of the Fourth Session of the Legislature of the State of California, Begun on the Third Day of January, 1853, and Ended on the Nineteenth Day of May, 1853, at the Cities of Vallejo and Benicia.* San Francisco: George Kerr, 1853.

California. *Journal of the Fifth Session of the Legislature of the State of California, Begun on the Second Day of January, 1854, and Ended on the Fifteenth Day of May, 1854, at the Cities of Benicia and Sacramento.* Sacramento: B.B. Redding, 1854.

California. *Journal of the Sixth Session of the Legislature of the State of California, Begun on the First Day of January, 1855, and Ended on the Seventh Day of May 1855, at the City of Sacramento.* Sacramento: B.B. Redding, 1855.

California. *Journal of the Eighth Session of the Senate of the State of California, Begun on the Fifth Day of January, One Thousand Eight Hundred and Fifty-Seven, and Ended on the Twenty-Ninth Day of April, One Thousand Eight Hundred and Fifty-Seven, at the City of Sacramento.* Sacramento: James Allen, 1857.

California. *Journal of the Ninth Session of the Senate of the State of California, Begun on the Fourth Day of January, One Thousand Eight Hundred and Fifty-Eight, and Ended on the Twenty-Sixth Day of April, One Thousand Eight Hundred and Fifty-Eight, at the City of Sacramento.* Sacramento: John O'Meara, 1858.

California. *Journal of the Senate of the State of California, at the Tenth Session of the Legislature, Begun on the Third Day of January, 1859, and Ended on the Nineteenth Day of April, 1859, at the City of Sacramento.* Sacramento: John O'Meara, 1859.

California. *Journal of the Senate of the State of California, at the Twelfth Session of the Legislature, Begun on the Seventh Day of January, 1861, and Ended on the Twentieth Day of May, 1861, at the City of Sacramento.* Sacramento: C.T. Botts, 1861.

California. *The Journal of the Senate, During the Fourteenth Session of the Legislature of the State of California: 1863.* Sacramento: Benj. P. Avery, 1863.

California. *Majority and Minority Reports of the Special Joint Committee on the Mendocino War.* Sacramento: Charles T. Botts, State Printer, 1860.

California. *The Penal Code of the State of California.* Annotated by Creed Haymond and John C. Burch. San Francisco: A.L. Bancroft, 1874.

California. *Records of California Men in the War of the Rebellion, 1861 to 1867.* Compiled by Richard H. Orton. Sacramento: State Office, J.D. Young, Supt. State Printing, 1890.

California. *The Statutes of California, Passed at the First Session of the Legislature. Begun the 15th Day of Dec. 1849, and Ended the 22d Day of April, 1850, at the City of Pueblo de San José.* San José: J. Winchester, 1850.

California. *The Statutes of California, Passed at the Second Session of the Legislature: Begun the Sixth Day of January, 1851, and Ended on the First Day of May, 1851, at the City of San Jose.* N.p.: Eugene Casserly, 1851.

California. *The Statutes of California, Passed at the Third Session of the Legislature, Begun on the Fifth of January, 1852 and Ended on the Fourth Day of May, 1852, at the Cities of Vallejo and Sacramento.* San Francisco: G.K. Fitch and V.E. Geiger, 1852.

California. *The Statutes of California, Passed at the Fourth Session of the Legislature, Begun on the Third of January, 1853, and Ended on the Nineteenth Day of May, 1853, at the Cities of Vallejo and Benicia.* San Francisco: George Kerr, 1853.

California. *The Statutes of California passed at the Fifth Session of the Legislature, Begun on the Fourth of January, 1854, and Ended on the Fifteenth Day of May, 1854, at the Cities of Benicia and Sacramento.* Sacramento: B.B. Redding, 1854.

California. *The Statutes of California, Passed at the Sixth Session of the Legislature, Begun on the First Day of January, One Thousand Eight Hundred and Fifty-five, and Ended on the Seventh Day of May, One Thousand and Eight Hundred and Fifty-five, at the City of Sacramento*. Sacramento: B.B. Redding, 1855.

California. *Statutes of California, Passed at the Seventh Session of the Legislature, Begun on the Seventh Day of January, One Thousand Eight Hundred and Fifty-Six, and Ended on the Twenty-First Day of April, One Thousand Eight Hundred and Fifty-Six, at the City of Sacramento*. Sacramento: James Allen, 1856.

California. *The Statutes of California, Passed at the Eighth Session of the Legislature, 1857*. Sacramento: James Allen, 1857.

California. *The Statutes of California, Passed at the Tenth Session of the Legislature, 1859*. Sacramento: John O'Meara, 1859.

California. *The Statutes of California, Passed at the Eleventh Session of the Legislature, 1860: Begun Monday, the Second Day of January, and Ended on Monday, the Thirtieth Day of April*. Sacramento: Charles T. Botts, 1860.

California. *The Statutes of California, Passed at the Fourteenth Session of the Legislature, 1863: Begun on Monday, the Fifth Day of January, and Ended on Monday, the Twenty-Seventh Day of April*. Sacramento: Benj. P. Avery, 1863.

California. *Statutes of California Passed at the Twenty-Third Session of the Legislature, 1880*. Sacramento: J.D. Young, 1880.

California. *The Statutes of California and Amendments to the Codes Passed at the Fortieth Session of the Legislature 1913 Began on Monday, January Sixth, and Adjourned on Tuesday, May Twelfth, Nineteen Hundred and Thirteen*. Sacramento: Bancroft-Whitney Company, 1913.

California. *Statutes of California, Extra Session of the Fifty-First Legislature 1936 Began Monday, May Twenty-Fifth, and Adjourned Tuesday, May Twenty-Sixth, Nineteen Hundred and Thirty-Six*. Sacramento: J. Winchester, 1937.

California Adjutant General's Office. *Military Department, Adjutant General, Adjutant General's Office Records, 1848–1861 VB358*. California State Archives, Sacramento, n.d.

California Adjutant General's Office. *Military Department, Adjutant General, General Orders, 1855–1924 B3473-4*. California State Archives, Sacramento, n.d.

California Adjutant General's Office. *Military Department, Adjutant General, Indian War Papers F3753*. California State Archives, Sacramento, n.d.

California and Randall Milliken. *Ethnogeography and Ethnohistory of the Big Sur District, California State Park System, during the 1770–1810 Time Period*. Sacramento: State of California Department of Parks and Recreation, 1990.

The Cherokee Nation v. The State of Georgia, 30 U.S. 1 1831.

Comptroller of the State of California. "Expenditures for Military Expeditions Against the Indians During the Years 1850–1859." California State Archives, Sacramento, n.d.

Interior Department. Appointment Papers. Held-Poage Library, Ukiah, CA, n.d.

Judicial Branch of California. "California Tribal Communities." http://www.courts.ca.gov /3066.htm.

Kennedy, Joseph C.G. *Population of the United States in 1860: Compiled from the Original Returns of the Eighth Census, Under the Direction of the Secretary of the Interior.* Washington, DC: Government Printing Office, 1864.

Kenny, Robert W. *History and Proposed Settlement Claims of California Indians.* Sacramento: State Printing Office, 1944.

Kibbe, William C. *Report of the Expedition Against the Indians in the Northern Part of this State.* Sacramento: C.T. Botts, 1860.

Lincoln, Abraham. "The Emancipation Proclamation, January 1, 1863." http://www.archives .gov/exhibits/featured_documents/emancipation_proclamation/transcript.html.

Martial Law in Round Valley, Mendocino Co., California, The Causes which led to that Measure, the Evidence, As Brought out by a Court of Investigation ordered by Brig. Gen. G. Wright, Commanding U.S. Forces on the Pacific. Ukiah City, CA: Herald Office, 1863.

Military Records. California State Archives, Sacramento, n.d.

National Inquiry into the Separation of Aboriginal and Torres Strait Islander Children from Their Families. *Bringing them home: Report of the National Inquiry into the Separation of Aboriginal and Torres Strait Islander Children from Their Families.* Sydney: Human Rights and Equal Opportunity Commission, 1997.

Naval Historical Center. *Dictionary of American Naval Fighting Ships.* Series edited by James L. Mooney. 9 vols. Vol. 6. Washington, DC: Government Printing Office, 1976.

Oregon. *The Early Indian Wars of Oregon: Compiled from the Oregon Archives and Other Original Sources with Muster Rolls.* Compiled by Francis Fuller Victor. Salem, OR: Frank C. Baker, 1894.

The People v. McGuire. 45 Cal. 56, 1872.

The People v. Smith et. al. 1 Cal. 9, 1850.

Richardson, James D., ed. *A Compilation of the Messages and Papers of the Presidents, 1789–1897.* 10 vols. Vol. 2. Washington, DC: Bureau of National Literature, 1896.

South Carolina Constitutional Convention. "Ordinance of Secession," December 20, 1860. Document no. S 131053, South Carolina Department of Archives and History, Columbia.

United Nations. "Convention on the Prevention and Punishment of the Crime of Genocide, Adopted by the General Assembly of the United Nations on 9 December 1948." *Treaty Series,* vol. 78, no. 1021.

United Nations. "Treaty Collection." http://treaties.un.org/Pages/ViewDetails.aspx?src =TREATY&mtdsg_no=IV-1&chapter=4&lang=e.

US Bureau of the Census. "American Indian and Alaska Native Alone and Alone or in Combination by Population of Tribe for California." Table 19. http://www.census.gov /census2000/states/ca.html.

US Bureau of the Census. "California." In *State and County QuickFacts.* http://quickfacts .census.gov/qfd/states/06000.html.

US Bureau of the Census. *Indian Population in the United States and Alaska, 1910.* Washington, DC: Government Printing Office, 1915.

US Congress. *Condition of the Indian Tribes.* Washington, DC: Government Printing Office, 1867.

US Congress. *The Congressional Globe.* http://memory.loc.gov/ammem/amlaw/.

US Congress. *Congressional Record: Containing the Proceedings and Debates of the Fifty-Eighth Congress, Third Session.* 157 vols. Vol. 39. Washington, DC: Government Printing Office, 1905.

US Congress. H. Exec. Doc. 1. 30th Cong., 2nd Sess., 1848, serial 514.

US Congress. H. Exec. Doc. 59. 31st Cong., 1st Sess., 1850, serial 577.

US Congress. H. Exec. Doc. 2. 32nd Cong., 1st Sess., 1851, serial 634.

US Congress. H. Exec. Doc. 1, Pt. 1. 33rd Cong., 1st Sess., 1853, serial 710.

US Congress. H. Exec. Doc. 1, Pt. 2. 34th Cong., 3rd Sess., 1856, serial 894.

US Congress. H. Exec. Doc. 76. 34th Cong., 3rd Sess., 1857, serial 906.

US Congress. H. Mis. Doc. 47. 35th Cong., 2nd Sess., 1859, serial 1016.

US Congress. H. Exec. Doc. 122. 43rd Cong., 1st Sess., 1874, serial 1607.

US Congress. H. Exec. Doc. 185. 43rd Cong., 1st Sess., 1874, serial 1610.

US Congress. H. Exec. Doc. 35. 44th Cong., 2nd Sess., 1876, serial 1769.

US Congress. S. Exec. Doc. 18. 31st Cong., 1st Sess., 1850, serial 557.

US Congress. S. Exec. Doc. 52. 31st Cong., 1st Sess., 1850, serial 561.

US Congress. S. Exec. Doc. 1, Pt. 2. 31st Cong., 2nd Sess., 1850, serial 587.

US Congress. S. Exec. Doc. 57. 32nd Cong., 2nd Sess., 1853, serial 665.

US Congress. S. Exec. Doc. 4. 33rd Cong., Special Sess., 1853, serial 688.

US Congress. S. Exec. Doc. 13. 33rd Cong., 2nd Sess., 1854, serial 751.

US Congress. S. Exec. Doc. 1, Pt. 2. 34th Cong., 1st Sess., 1855, serial 811.

US Congress. S. Exec. Doc. 26. 34th Cong., 1st Sess., 1856, serial 819.

US Congress. S. Exec. Doc. 46. 36th Cong., 1st Sess., 1860, serial 1033.

US Congress. *The Public Statutes at Large of the United States of America, from the Organization of the Government in 1789, to March 3, 1845.* Edited by Richard Peters. 8 vols. Vol. 2. Boston: C.C. Little and J. Brown, 1845.

US Congress. *The Statutes at Large and Treaties of the United States of America from December 1, 1851, to March 3, 1855.* Edited by George Minot. 125 vols. Vol. 10. Boston: Little, Brown, 1855.

US Congress. *The Statutes at Large, Treaties, and Proclamations, of the United States of America.* Edited by George P. Sanger. 18 vols. Vol. 12. Boston: Little, Brown, 1863.

US Congress. *The Statutes at Large of the United States of America, from December, 1881, to March, 1883, and Recent Treaties, Postal Conventions, and Executive Proclamations.* 125 vols. Vol. 22. Washington, DC: Government Printing Office, 1883.

US Department of Agriculture. "Tribes Remember the Nome Cult Trail." http://blogs.usda.gov/2013/11/21/tribes-remember-the-nome-cult-trail/.

US Department of the Interior. *Annual Reports of the Department of the Interior for the Fiscal Year Ended June 30, 1900: Indian Affairs—Report of the Commissioner and Appendixes.* Washington, DC: Government Printing Office, 1900.

US Department of the Interior. *The Statistics of the Population of the United States, at the Tenth Census, Embracing . . . Occupations.* Washington, DC: Government Printing Office, 1882.

US Department of the Interior. *The Statistics of the Population of the United States, Embracing the Tables of Race, Nationality, Sex, Selected Ages, and Occupations.* Washington, DC: Government Printing Office, 1872.

US National Archives and Records Administration. "Letters Received by the Office of Indian Affairs, 1824–80." Record Group 75, Microfilm Series M234. Washington, DC: National Archives, n.d.

US National Archives and Records Administration. "Records of the 10th Military Department, 1846–51." Record Group 98, Microfilm Series M210. Washington, DC: National Archives, n.d.

US National Archives and Records Administration. "Selected Records of the General Accounting Office Relating to Fremont Expeditions and the California Battalion, 1842–1890." Record Group 217, Microfilm Series T135. Washington, DC: National Archives, n.d.

US National Archives and Records Administration. "War Department Records of the Division and Department of the Pacific, 1847–1873." Record Group 393, Microfilm Series M2114. Washington, DC: National Archives, n.d.

US Naval Observatory. "Complete Sun and Moon Data for One Day." http://aa.usno.navy.mil/data/docs/RS_OneDay.php.

US Office of Indian Affairs. *Annual Report of the Commissioner of Indian Affairs, Transmitted with the Message of the President at the Opening of the First Session of the Thirty-Fourth Congress, 1855.* Washington, DC: A.O.P. Nicholson, 1856.

US Office of Indian Affairs. *Report of the Commissioner of Indian Affairs, Accompanying the Annual Report of the Secretary of the Interior, for the Year 1856.* Washington, DC: A.O.P. Nicholson, 1857.

US Office of Indian Affairs. *Report of the Commissioner of Indian Affairs, Accompanying the Annual Report of the Secretary of the Interior for the Year 1857.* Washington, DC: William A. Harris, 1858.

US Office of Indian Affairs. *Report of the Commissioner of Indian Affairs, Accompanying the Annual Report of the Secretary of the Interior, for the Year 1858.* Washington, DC: William A. Harris, 1858.

US Office of Indian Affairs. *Report of the Commissioner of Indian Affairs, Accompanying the Annual Report of the Secretary of the Interior, for the Year 1859.* Washington, DC: George W. Bowman, 1860.

US Office of Indian Affairs. *Report of the Commissioner of Indian Affairs, Accompanying the Annual Report of the Secretary of the Interior, for the Year 1861.* Washington, DC: Government Printing Office, 1861.

US Office of Indian Affairs. *Report of the Commissioner of Indian Affairs for the Year 1862.* Washington, DC: Government Printing Office, 1863.

US Office of Indian Affairs. *Report of the Commissioner of Indian Affairs, for the Year 1863.* Washington, DC: Government Printing Office, 1864.

US Office of Indian Affairs. *Report of the Commissioner of Indians Affairs, for the Year 1864.* Washington, DC: Government Printing Office, 1865.

US Office of Indian Affairs. *Report of the Commissioner of Indian Affairs for the Year 1865.* Washington, DC: Government Printing Office, 1865.

US Office of Indian Affairs. *Report on Indian Affairs, by the Acting Commissioner, for the Year 1867.* Washington, DC: Government Printing Office, 1868.

US Office of Indian Affairs. *Annual Report of the Commissioner of Indian Affairs, for the Year 1868.* Washington, DC: Government Printing Office, 1868.

US Office of Indian Affairs. *Report of the Commissioner of Indian Affairs, Made to the Secretary of the Interior, for the Year 1869*. Washington, DC: Government Printing Office, 1870.

US Office of Indian Affairs. *Annual Report of the Commissioner of Indian Affairs to the Secretary of the Interior for the Year 1873*. Washington, DC: Government Printing Office, 1874.

US Office of Indian Affairs. *Annual Report of the Commissioner of Indian Affairs to the Secretary of the Interior for the Year 1881*. Washington, DC: Government Printing Office, 1881.

US Senate. *Hearings before the Committee on Indian Affairs United States Senate Seventy-Fourth Congress First Session on S. 1793*. Washington, DC: Government Printing Office, 1935.

US Senate. *Journal of the Executive Proceedings of the Senate of the United States of America*. 146 vols. Vol. 8. Washington, DC: Government Printing Office, 1887.

US War Department. *The War of the Rebellion: A Compilation of the Official Records of the Union and Confederate Armies*. 4 series, 130 vols. Series 1, vol. 50, pt 1. Washington, DC: Government Printing Office, 1897.

US War Department. *The War of the Rebellion: A Compilation of the Official Records of the Union and Confederate Armies*. 4 series, 130 vols. Series 1, vol. 50, pt. 2. Washington, DC: Government Printing Office, 1897.

US War Department. *The War of the Rebellion: A Compilation of the Official Records of the Union and Confederate Armies*. 4 series, 130 vols. Series 1, vol. 52, pt. 2. Washington, DC: Government Printing Office, 1898.

PERIODICALS

Army and Navy Journal (New York)

Butte Record (Oroville, CA)

California Farmer and Journal of Useful Sciences (San Francisco)

Californian (Monterey, CA / San Francisco)

California Police Gazette (San Francisco)

California Star (San Francisco)

California Star & Californian (San Francisco)

Chico Weekly Courant (Chico, CA)

Covered Wagon (Redding, CA)

Crescent City Herald (Crescent City, CA)

Daily Alta California / Weekly Alta California (San Francisco)

Daily California Statesman (Sacramento)

Daily Democratic State Journal (Sacramento)

Daily Evening Bulletin (San Francisco)

Daily Evening Herald (Marysville, CA)

Daily Evening Post (San Francisco)

Daily National Intelligencer (Washington, DC)

Daily Picayune (New Orleans)

Daily San Joaquin Republican (Stockton, CA)
Daily Sentinel and Gazette (Milwaukee)
Del Norte Record (Crescent City, CA)
Del Norte Triplicate (Crescent City, CA)
Deseret News (Salt Lake City)
Esmeralda Star (Aurora, CA)
Esmeralda Union (Aurora, NV)
Farmer's Cabinet (Amherst, NH)
Golden Era (San Francisco)
Grass Valley Telegraph (Grass Valley, CA)
Harper's Weekly Journal of Civilization (New York)
Humboldt Register (Unionville, NV)
Humboldt Times / Weekly Humboldt Times (Eureka, CA)
Hutchings' California Magazine (San Francisco)
Illustrated London News
Inyo Register (Bishop, CA)
Las Vegas Review-Journal
Livingston Chronicle (Livingston, CA)
Los Angeles Star
Los Angeles Tri-Weekly News
Mariposa Gazette (Mariposa, CA)
Marysville Appeal (Marysville, CA)
Marysville Herald (Marysville, CA)
Mendocino Herald (Ukiah, CA)
Missouri Republican (Saint Louis, MO)
Morning Call (San Francisco)
Napa Register (Napa, CA)
Nevada Democrat (Nevada, CA)
Nevada Journal (Nevada, CA)
New-Yorker
New York Herald
New York Times
New York Tribune
Northern Californian (Arcata, CA)
Northern Journal (Yreka, CA)
Orange County Register (Santa Ana, CA)
Oregon Statesman (Salem, OR)
Oroville Union (Oroville, CA)
Owyhee Avalanche (Silver City, ID)
Pictorial Union (Sacramento)
Pioneer (San Francisco)
Placer Times / Weekly Placer Times (Sacramento)
Plumas National (Quincy, CA)
Quincy Union (Quincy, CA)

Red Bluff Beacon (Red Bluff, CA)

Red Bluff Independent / *Red Bluff Semi-Weekly Independent* / *Weekly People's Cause* (Red Bluff, CA)

Reno Crescent (Reno, NV)

Rock (Alcatraz, CA)

Sacramento Daily Bee

Sacramento Daily Union

Sacramento Placer Times and Transcript

Sacramento Transcript

San Bernardino Guardian (San Bernardino, CA)

San Diego Herald

San Francisco Chronicle

San Francisco Herald

San Jose Mercury News

Sentinel (Red Bluff, CA)

Shasta Courier (Shasta, CA)

Shasta Republican (Shasta, CA)

Sonoma County Journal (Petaluma, CA)

Southern News (Los Angeles)

Statesman (Columbia, MO)

Stockton Times / *Stockton Times and Tualumne City Intelligencer* (Stockton, CA)

Susanville Sagebrush (Susanville, CA)

Times Standard (Eureka, CA)

Trinity Journal / *Weekly Trinity Journal* (Weaverville, CA)

Union Record / *Weekly Union Record* (Oroville, CA)

United States Magazine, and Democratic Review (New York, NY)

Visalia Delta (Visalia, CA)

Volcano Weekly Ledger (Volcano, CA)

Weekly Register (Baltimore, MD)

Yreka Mountain Herald (Yreka, CA)

Yreka Union / *Yreka Semi-Weekly Union* / *Yreka Weekly Union* (Yreka, CA)

PRIMARY AND SECONDARY SOURCES

Addis, Cameron. "The Whitman Massacre: Religion and Manifest Destiny on the Columbia Plateau, 1809–1858." *Journal of the Early Republic* 25, no. 2 (Summer 2005): 221–258.

Ahrens, Peter. "John Work, J.J. Warner, and the Native American Catastrophe of 1833." *Southern California Quarterly* 93, no. 1 (Spring 2011): 1–32.

Allison, John. *The Cultural Landscape of the Klamath, Modoc, and Yahooskin Peoples: Spirit, Nature, History.* Chiloquin, OR: Klamath Tribes, 1994.

Almaguer, Tomás. *Racial Fault Lines: The Historical Origins of White Supremacy in California.* Berkeley: University of California Press, 1994.

Altschule, Herman. "Exploring the Coast Range in 1850." *Overland Monthly and Out West Magazine* 11, no. 63 (March 1888): 320–326.

Anderson, Gary Clayton. *The Conquest of Texas: Ethnic Cleansing in the Promised Land, 1820–1875*. Norman: University of Oklahoma Press, 2005.

Anderson, Gary Clayton. *Ethnic Cleansing and the Indian: The Crime That Should Haunt America*. Norman: University of Oklahoma Press, 2014.

Anderson, George E., W.H. Ellison, and Robert F. Heizer. *Treaty Making and Treaty Rejection by the Federal Government in California, 1850–1852*. Socorro, NM: Ballena Press, 1978.

Anderson, M. Kat. *Tending the Wild: Native American Knowledge and the Management of California's Natural Resources*. Berkeley: University of California Press, 2005.

Anderson, Robert A. *Fighting the Mill Creeks: Being a Personal Account of Campaigns against Indians of the Northern Sierras*. Chico, CA: Chico Record Press, 1909.

Angel, Myron, ed. *History of Placer County, California, with Illustrations and Biographical Sketches of Its Prominent Men and Pioneers*. Oakland, CA: Thompson and West, 1882.

Archibald, Robert. "Indian Labor at the California Missions: Slavery or Salvation?" *Journal of San Diego History* 24, no. 2 (Spring 1978): 172–182.

Arendt, Hannah. *Eichmann in Jerusalem: A Report on the Banality of Evil*. New York: Viking Press, 1963.

Asbill, Frank, and Argle Shawley. *The Last of the West*. New York: Carlton Press, 1975.

Athern, Robert G. *William Tecumseh Sherman and the Settlement of the West*. Norman: University of Oklahoma Press, [1956] 1995.

Axtell, James. *Beyond 1492: Encounters in Colonial North America*. New York: Oxford University Press, 1992.

Bancroft, Hubert H. *The Works of Hubert Howe Bancroft*. 39 vols. Vol. 18. San Francisco: A.L. Bancroft, 1884.

Bancroft, Hubert H. *The Works of Hubert Howe Bancroft*. 39 vols. Vol. 20. San Francisco: A.L. Bancroft, 1885.

Bancroft, Hubert H. *The Works of Hubert Howe Bancroft*. 39 vols. Vol. 21. San Francisco: A.L. Bancroft, 1886.

Bancroft, Hubert H. *The Works of Hubert Howe Bancroft*. 39 vols. Vol. 22. San Francisco: History Company, 1886.

Bancroft, Hubert H. *The Works of Hubert Howe Bancroft*. 39 vols. Vol. 23. San Francisco: History Company, 1888.

Bancroft, Hubert H. *The Works of Hubert Howe Bancroft*. 39 vols. Vol. 24. San Francisco: History Company, 1890.

Bancroft, Hubert H. *The Works of Hubert Howe Bancroft*. 39 vols. Vol. 29. San Francisco: History Company, 1886.

Bancroft, Hubert H. *The Works of Hubert Howe Bancroft*. 39 vols. Vol. 30. San Francisco: History Company, 1888.

Bancroft, Hubert Howe. *California Pioneer Register and Index, 1542–1848: Including Inhabitants of California, 1769–1800 and List of Pioneers*. Baltimore: Regional, 1964.

Banner, Stuart. *Possessing the Pacific: Land, Settlers, and Indigenous People from Australia to Alaska*. Cambridge, MA: Harvard University Press, 2007.

Baron, Lawrence. "The First Wave of American 'Holocaust' Films, 1945–1959." *American Historical Review* 115, no. 1 (February 2010): 90–114.

Barrett, S.A. "The Ethno-Geography of the Pomo and Neighboring Indians." *University of California Publications in American Archaeology and Ethnology* 6, no. 1 (February 1908): 1–332.

Barrett, S.A. "Material Aspects of Pomo Culture." *Bulletin of the Public Museum of the City of Milwaukee* 20, pt. 2 (August 1952): 265–507.

Barry, William Jackson. *Up and Down: Or, Fifty Years' Colonial Experiences in Australia, California, New Zealand, India, China, and the South Pacific; Being the Life History of Capt. W.J. Barry.* London: Sampson Low, Marston, Searle, and Rivington, 1878.

Bartlett, John Russell. *Personal Narrative of Explorations and Incidents in Texas, New Mexico, California, Sonora, and Chihuahua connected with the United States and Mexican Boundary Commission, during the Years 1850, '51, '52, and '53.* 2 vols. Vol. 2. New York: D. Appleton, 1854.

Bates, D.B. *Incidents on Land and Water, or Four years on the Pacific coast, Being a narrative of the burning of the ships Nonantum, Humayoon and Fanchon, together with many startling adventures on sea and land.* Boston: J. French, 1857.

Bauer, William J., Jr. *We Were All Like Migrant Workers Here: Work, Community, and Memory on California's Round Valley Reservation, 1850–1941.* Chapel Hill: University of North Carolina Press, 2009.

Baumgardner, Frank H. *Killing for Land in Early California: Indian Blood at Round Valley.* New York: Algora, 2005.

Baumgardner, Frank H. *Yanks in the Redwoods: Carving Out a Life in Northern California.* New York: Algora, 2010.

Baumhoff, Martin. "California Athabascan Groups." *University of California Anthropological Records* 16, no. 5 (August 1, 1958): 157–237.

Baumhoff, Martin. "Ecological Determinants of Aboriginal California Populations." *University of California Publications in American Archaeology and Ethnology* 49, no. 2 (May 28, 1963): 155–235.

Beals, Ralph L. "Ethnology of the Nisenan." *University of California Publications in American Archaeology and Ethnology* 31, no. 6 (March 29, 1933): 335–414.

Bean, Edwin F. *Bean's History and Directory of Nevada County, California.* Nevada, CA: Daily Gazette Book and Job Office, 1867.

Bean, Lowell John, and William Marvin Mason. *Diaries and Accounts of the Romero Expeditions in Arizona and California, 1823–1826.* Los Angeles: W. Ritchie Press, 1962.

Beebe, Rose Marie, and Robert M. Senkewicz. *Lands of Promise and Despair: Chronicles of Early California, 1535–1846.* Berkeley, CA: Heyday Books, 2001.

Beechey, Frederick. *Narrative of a Voyage to the Pacific and Beering's Strait, to Co-operate with the Polar Expeditions: Performed in His Majesty's Ship Blossom, Under the Command of Captain F.W. Beechey, R.N. in the Years 1825, 26, 27, 28.* 2 vols. Vol. 2. London: Henry Colburn and Richard Bentley, 1831.

Beilharz, Edwin A. *Felipe De Neve: First Governor of California.* San Francisco: California Historical Society, 1971.

Bell, Horace. *Reminiscences of a Ranger or, Early Times in Southern California.* Los Angeles: Yarnell, Caystile and Mathes, 1881.

Benson, William Ralganal. "The Stone and Kelsey 'Massacre' on the Shores of Clear Lake in 1849: The Indian Viewpoint." *California Historical Society Quarterly* 11, no. 3 (September 1932): 266–273.

Biaggi, John, Jr. "Shelter Cove Scalping." *Mendocino County Historical Society Newsletter* 3, no. 1 (August 1964): 7–8.

Blackhawk, Ned. *Violence over the Land: Indians and Empires in the Early American West.* Cambridge, MA: Harvard University Press, 2006.

Bledsoe, A.J. *Indian Wars of the Northwest: A California Sketch.* San Francisco: Bacon, 1885.

Bledsoe, Anthony Jennings. *History of Del Norte County, California, with a Business Directory and Traveler's Guide.* Eureka, CA: Wyman, 1881.

Boemeke, Manfred F., Roger Chickering, and Stig Förster, eds. *Anticipating Total War: The German and American Experiences, 1871–1914.* Cambridge: Cambridge University Press, 1999.

Bolton, Herbert Eugene. *Spanish Exploration in the Southwest, 1542–1706.* New York: Charles Scribner's, 1916.

Bommelyn, Loren. "Purpose of Nee-dash (interview)." https://vimeo.com/30036441.

Bommelyn, Loren, and Lena Bommelyn. *Now You're Speaking Tolowa.* Arcata, CA: Center for Indian Community Development, Humboldt State University, 1995.

Bourke, John G. "General Crook in the Indian Country." *Century Magazine* 41, no. 5 (March 1891): 643–660.

Bradford, Ward. *Biographical Sketches of the Life of Major Ward Bradford, Old Pioneer: As Related by the Author, Who is Eighty-three Years of Age and Nearly Blind.* N.p.: Self-published, 1893(?).

Bradford, William. *History of Plymouth Plantation.* Edited by Charles Deane. Boston: Privately Printed, 1856.

Brady, Cyrus. *Northwestern Fights and Fighters.* New York: McClure, 1907.

Brewer, William H. *Up and Down California in 1860–1864.* Edited by Francis P. Farquhar. Berkeley: University of California Press, [1966] 1974.

Bright, William. "The Karok Language." *University of California Publications in Linguistics* 13 (July 19, 1957): 1–458.

Brown, Alan K. "Pomponio's World." *Argonaut* 6 (May 1975): 1–20.

Brown, Dee. *Bury My Heart at Wounded Knee: An Indian History of the American West.* New York: Holt, Reinhart and Winston, 1970.

Brown, Millard. "Indians Wars in Trinity, 1858–1865." *Yearbook of the Trinity County Historical Society* (1969): 36–42.

Browne, J. Ross. "The Coast Rangers: A Chronicle of Adventures in California." *Harper's New Monthly Magazine* 23, no. 135 (August 1861): 306–16.

Browne, J. Ross. *Muleback to the Convention: Letters of J. Ross Browne, Reported to the Constitutional Convention.* San Francisco: Book Club of California, 1950.

Browne, J. Ross. *Report of the Debates in the Convention of California, on the Formation of the State Constitution, in September and October, 1849.* Washington, DC: John T. Towers, 1850.

Bruff, J. Goldsborough. *Gold Rush: The Journals, Drawings and Other Papers of J. Goldsborough Bruff.* Edited by Georgia Willis Read and Ruth Gaines. New York: Columbia University Press, 1949.

Bryant, Edwin. *What I Saw in California: Being the Journal of a Tour, by the Emigrant Route and South Pass of the Rocky Mountains, Across the Continent of North America, the Great Desert Basin, and through California, in the years 1846, 1847.* New York: D. Appleton, 1848.

Buffum, E. Gould. *Six Months in the Gold Mines: From a Journal of Three Years' Residence in Upper and Lower California, 1847–1849.* Philadelphia: Lee and Blanchard, 1850.

Bunnell, Lafayette Houghton. *Discovery of the Yosemite and the Indian War of 1851 Which Led to That Event.* Los Angeles: G.W. Gerlicher, 1911.

Butterworth, W.E. *Soldiers on Horseback: The Story of the United States Cavalry.* New York: Norton, 1967.

"A California Blood Stain." *Hutchings' California Magazine* 3, no. 3 (September 1858): 129–131.

California State Coastal Conservancy and Ocean Protection Council et al. *San Francisco Bay Subtidal Habitat Goals Reports: Conservation Planning for the Submerged Areas of the Bay.* Oakland, CA: J.T. Litho, 2010.

Carlson, Helen S. *Nevada Place Names: A Geographical Dictionary.* Reno: University of Nevada Press, 1974.

Carpenter, Aurelius O., and Percy H. Millberry. *History of Mendocino and Lake Counties, California with Biographical Sketches of The Leading Men and Women of the Counties Who Have Been Identified with Their Growth and Development from the Early Days to the Present.* Los Angeles: Historic Record Company, 1914.

Carpenter, Helen. "Among the Diggers of Thirty Years Ago, Part II." *Overland Monthly and Out West Magazine* 21, no. 124 (April 1893): 389–399.

Carr, John. *Pioneer Days in California: By John Carr.* Eureka, CA: Times Publishing, 1891.

Carranco, Lynwood, and Estle Beard. *Genocide and Vendetta: The Round Valley Wars of Northern California.* Norman: University of Oklahoma Press, 1981.

Carson, A. Thankful. *Captured by the Mill Creek Indians: A True Story of the Capture of the Sam Lewis Children in the year 1863; Incidents in the Early History of Butte County by the Sole Survivor.* Chico, CA: N.p., 1915.

Carson, Kit. *Kit Carson's Own Story of His Life, As dictated to Col. And Mrs. D.C. Peters about 1856–1857, and never before published.* Edited by Blanche C. Grant. Taos, NM: Santa Fe New Mexican Publishing, 1926.

Case, William M. "Notes By William M. Case. Supplementary to his 'Reminiscences,' published in the September Quarterly, Volume I, Number 3." Edited by H.S. Lyman. *Quarterly of the Oregon Historical Society* 2, no. 2 (June 1901): 168–179.

Case, William M. "Reminiscences of Wm. M. Case." Edited by H.S. Lyman. *Quarterly of the Oregon Historical Society* 1, no. 3 (September 1900): 269–295.

Casebier, Dennis G. *Carleton's Pah-Ute Campaign.* Norco, CA: King's Press, 1972.

Caughey, John Walton. *California.* New York: Prentice-Hall, 1940.

Cavanaugh, Cam. *In Lights and Shadows: Morristown in Three Centuries.* Morristown, NJ: The Joint Free Public Library of Morristown and Morris Township, 1986.

Cave, Alfred A. *Lethal Encounters: Englishmen and Indians in Colonial Virginia.* Santa Barbara, CA: ABC-CLIO, 2011.

Cave, Alfred A. *The Pequot War.* Amherst: University of Massachusetts Press, 1996.

César, Julio. "Recollections of My Youth at San Luis Rey Mission: The Memories of a Full-Blooded Indian, of Affairs and Events Witnessed at One of California's Most Famous 'Cathedrals of the Sun.'" Translated by Nellie Van de Grift Sanchez. *Touring Topics* 22 (November 1930): 42–43.

Chalfant, W.A. *The Story of Inyo.* Bishop, CA: Chalfant Press, 1933.

Chalk, Frank, and Kurt Jonassohn. *The History and Sociology of Genocide: Analyses and Case Studies.* New Haven, CT: Yale University Press, 1990.

Chamberlain, Samuel. *My Confession: Recollections of a Rogue.* Austin: Texas State Historical Association, 1996.

Chase, Doris. *They Pushed Back the Forest.* Colfax, CA: Self-published, 1959.

Church, Andrew S. "Memoirs of Andrew S. Church." *Quarterly of the Society of California Pioneers* 3, no. 4 (December 1926): 153–201.

Churchill, Ward. *A Little Matter of Genocide: Holocaust and Denial in the Americas, 1492 to the Present.* San Francisco: City Lights Books, 1997.

Clark, Arthur H. *The Clipper Ship Era: An Epitome of Famous American and British Clipper Ships, Their Owners, Builders, Commanders, and Crews, 1843–1869.* New York: G.P. Putnam's Sons, 1912.

Clausen, Barbara, and Beverly Spitzner. *Del Norte Bites: History and Recipes.* N.p.: Babe Publications, 1996.

Clayton, Fannie. "Mrs. Fannie Clayton's Account of the Indian Troubles in California in 1849." Edited by H.S. Lyman. *Quarterly of the Oregon Historical Society* 2, no. 2 (June 1901): 180–184.

Coffer, William E. "Genocide of the California Indians, with a Comparative Study of Other Minorities." *Indian Historian* 10, no. 2 (Spring 1977): 8–15.

Collins, John. *Understanding Tolowa Histories: Western Hegemonies and Native American Responses.* New York: Routledge, 1998.

Colton, Walter. *Three Years in California.* New York: A.S. Barnes, 1851.

Conway, J.D. *Monterey: Presidio, Pueblo, and Port.* Monterey, CA: Arcadia, 2003.

Cook, S.F. "The Aboriginal Population of the North Coast of California." *University of California Anthropological Records* 16, no. 3 (October 11, 1956): 81–130.

Cook, S.F. "The Conflict between the California Indian and White Civilization, I. The Indian versus the Spanish Mission." *Ibero-Americana* 21 (January 23, 1943): 1–194.

Cook, S.F. "The Conflict between the California Indian and White Civilization, II. The Physical and Demographic Reaction of the Nonmission Indians in Colonial and Provincial California." *Ibero-Americana* 22 (February 10, 1943): 1–55.

Cook, S.F. "The Conflict between the California Indian and White Civilization, III. The American Invasion, 1848–1870." *Ibero-Americana* 23 (April 20, 1943): 1–115.

Cook, S.F. "The Epidemic of 1830–1833 in California and Oregon." *University of California Publications in American Archaeology and Ethnology* 43, no. 3 (May 10, 1955): 303–326.

Cook, S.F. "Expeditions to the Interior of California Central Valley, 1820–1840." *University of California Anthropological Records* 20, no. 5 (February 1, 1962): 151–213.

Cook, Sherburne F. *The Conflict between the California Indian and White Civilization.* Berkeley: University of California Press, 1976.

Cook, Sherburne F. *The Population of the California Indians, 1769–1970.* Berkeley: University of California Press, 1976.

Cook, Sherburne F. "Smallpox in Spanish and Mexican California, 1770–1845." *Bulletin of the History of Medicine* 7, no. 2 (February 1939): 153–191.

Coronel, Antonio Franco. *Tales of Mexican California: Cosas de California.* Translated by Diane de Avalle-Arce and edited by Doyce B. Nunis Jr. Santa Barbara, CA: Bellerophon Books, 1994.

Costo, Rupert, and Jeanette Henry Costo. *The Missions of California: A Legacy of Genocide.* San Francisco: Indian Historian Press, 1987.

Cothran, Boyd. *Remembering the Modoc War: Redemptive Violence and the Making of American Innocence.* Chapel Hill: University of North Carolina Press, 2014.

Cox, Isaac. *The Annals of Trinity County; Containing a history of the discovery, settlement and progress, together with a description of the resources and present condition of Trinity County. As also sketches of important events that have transpired therein from its settlement to the present time.* San Francisco: Commercial Book and Job Steam Printing Establishment, 1858.

Cronon, William. *Changes in the Land: Indians, Colonists, and the Ecology of New England.* New York: Hill and Wang, 1983.

Crook, George. *General George Crook: His Autobiography.* Edited by Martin F. Schmitt. Norman: University of Oklahoma Press, 1946.

Crosby, Alfred W. "Virgin Soil Epidemics as a Factor in the Aboriginal Depopulation in America." *William and Mary Quarterly* 33, no. 2 (April 1976): 289–299.

Crowell, Aron L. *Archaeology and the Capitalist World System: A Study from Russian America.* New York: Plenum Press, 1997.

Cullum, George W. *Biographical Register of the Officers and Graduates of the U.S. Military Academy at West Point, N.Y. from its Establishment, in 1802, to 1890 with the Early History of the United States Military Academy.* 5 vols. Boston: Houghton, Mifflin, 1891.

Curtin, Jeremiah. *Creation Myths of Primitive America in Relation to the Religious History and Mental Development of Mankind.* London: Williams and Norgate, 1899.

Curtis, Edward S. *The North American Indian: Being A Series of Volumes Picturing and Describing the Indians of the United States and Alaska.* Edited by Frederick Webb Hodge. 20 vols. Vol. 8. Norwood, MA: Plimpton Press, 1911.

Curtis, Edward S. *The North American Indian: Being A Series of Volumes Picturing and Describing the Indians of the United States, the Dominion of Canada, and Alaska.* Edited by Frederick Webb Hodge. 20 vols. Vol. 13. Norwood, MA: Plimpton Press, 1924.

Curtis, Edward S. *The North American Indian: Being A Series of Volumes Picturing and Describing the Indians of the United States, the Dominion of Canada, and Alaska.* Edited by Frederick Webb Hodge. 20 vols. Vol. 14. Norwood, MA: Plimpton Press, 1924.

Danieli, Yael, ed. *International Handbook of Multigenerational Legacies of Trauma.* New York: Plenum Press, 1998.

Davis, David Brion. *Inhuman Bondage: The Rise and Fall of Slavery in the New World.* New York: Oxford University Press, 2006.

Davis, William H. *Seventy-Five Years in California; A History of Events and Life in California: Personal, Political, and Military.* San Francisco: John Howell, 1929.

Davis, William Heath. *Sixty Years in California: A History of Events and Life in California; Personal, Political and Military.* San Francisco: A.J. Leary, 1889.

Dayton, Dello G. "The California Militia, 1850–1866." Ph.D. diss., University of California at Berkeley, 1951.

Dayton, Dello G. "'Polished Boot and Bran New Suit': The California Militia in Community Affairs." *California Historical Society Quarterly* 37, no. 4 (December 1958): 359–368.

D'Azevedo, Warren L., vol. ed. *Handbook of North American Indians.* Series edited by William Sturtevant. 20 vols. Vol. 11. Washington, DC: Smithsonian Institution, 1986.

Dean, Sharon E., Peggy S. Ratcheson, Judith W. Finger, Ellen F. Daus, and Craig D. Bates. *Weaving a Legacy: Indian Baskets and the People of Owens Valley, California.* Salt Lake City: University of Utah Press, 2004.

Delaney, Dan. "The Adventures of Captain Hi Good." *Northern Enterprise* (Chico, CA), June 7, 1872, 1–3.

Delavan, James. *Notes on California and the Placers: How to Get There and What to Do Afterwards.* New York: H. Long, 1850.

DeLay, Brian. *War of a Thousand Deserts: Indian Raids and the U.S.-Mexican War.* New Haven, CT: Yale University Press, 2008.

del Castillo, Richard Griswold. *The Treaty of Guadalupe Hidalgo: A Legacy of Conflict.* Norman: University of Oklahoma Press, 1990.

Deloria, Philip J. *Indians in Unexpected Places.* Lawrence: University Press of Kansas, 2004.

Dillon, Richard H. *Burnt-Out Fires.* Englewood Cliffs, NJ: Prentice-Hall, 1973.

Dillon, Richard H. *Texas Argonauts: Isaac H. Duval and the California Gold Rush.* San Francisco: Book Club of California, 1987.

Douthit, Nathan. "Between Indian and White Worlds on the Oregon-California Border, 1851–1857: Benjamin Wright and Enos." *Oregon Historical Quarterly* 100, no. 4 (Winter 1999): 402–433.

Downie, William. *Hunting for Gold: Reminiscences of Personal Experience and Research in the Early Days of the Pacific Coast From Alaska to Panama.* San Francisco: California Publishing, 1893.

Drake, Francis. *The World Encompaffed by Sir Francis Drake, Being his next voyage to that to Nombre de Dios formerly imprinted; Carefully collected out of the notes of Mafter Francis Fletcher Preacher in this imployment, and divers others . . .* London: Nicholas Bovrne, 1628.

Drucker, Philip. "The Tolowa and their Southwest Oregon Kin." *University of California Publications in American Archaeology and Ethnology* 36, no. 4 (October 22, 1937): 221–300.

DuBois, Constance Goddard. "The Religion of the Luiseño Indians of Southern California." *University of California Publications in American Archaeology and Ethnology* 8, no. 3 (June 27, 1908): 69–186.

Du Bois, Cora. "Wintu Ethnography." *University of California Publications in American Archaeology and Ethnology* 36, no. 1 (October 15, 1935): 1–147.

Duran, Eduardo, Judith Firehammer, and John Gonzalez. "Liberation Psychology as the Path Toward Healing Cultural Soul Wounds." *Journal of Counseling and Development* 86, no. 3 (Summer 2008): 288–295.

Eccleston, Robert. *The Mariposa Indian War, 1850–1851. Diaries of Robert Eccleston: The California Gold Rush, Yosemite, and the High Sierra.* Edited by C. Gregory Crampton. Salt Lake City: University of Utah Press, 1957.

ECORP Consulting. "Tulare Lake Basin Hydrology and Hydrography: A Summary of the Movement of Water and Aquatic Species." Prepared for the United States Environmental Protection Agency, April 12, 2007.

Eicher, John H., and David H. Eicher. *Civil War High Commands.* Stanford, CA: Stanford University Press, 2001.

Eidsness, Janet. "Initial Cultural Resources Study for Proposed Hazard Tree Removal and Water Tank Replacement Project, Big Lagoon Park Company Community in Humboldt County, California." November 5, 2007. In possession of Tony Platt.

Ellison, W.H. "The Federal Indian Policy in California, 1846–1860." *Mississippi Valley Historical Review* 9, no. 1 (June 1922): 37–67.

Ellison, W.H. "Rejection of California Indian Treaties: A Study in Local Influence on National Policy." *Grizzly Bear* 37, no. 217 (May 1925): 4–5, 86.

Ellison, W.H. "Rejection of California Indian Treaties: A Study in Local Influence on National Policy." *Grizzly Bear* 37, no. 218 (June 1925): 4–5, supplement 7.

Engelhardt, Zephyrin. *San Luis Rey Mission.* San Francisco: James H. Barry, 1921.

Engelhardt, Zephyrin. *Santa Barbara Mission.* San Francisco: James H. Barry, 1923.

Ensminger, Audrey H. et al. *Foods and Nutrition Encyclopedia.* 2 vols. Vol. 1. Boca Raton, FL: CRC Press, 1994.

Essene, Frank. "Culture Element Distributions: XXI Round Valley." *University of California Anthropological Records* 8, no. 1 (August 7, 1942): 1–97.

Fagan, Brian. *Before California: An Archaeologist Looks at Our Earliest Inhabitants.* Walnut Creek, CA: Alta Mira Press, 2003.

Fairchild, Lucius. *California Letters of Lucius Fairchild.* Edited by Joseph Schafer. Madison: State Historical Society of Wisconsin, 1931.

Fairfield, Asa Merrill. *Fairfield's Pioneer History of Lassen County, California . . . and Many Stories of Indian Warfare Never before Published.* San Francisco: H.S. Crocker, 1916.

Farnham, Thomas J. *Life, Travels and Adventures in California, and Scenes in the Pacific Ocean.* New York: William H. Graham, 1846.

Farnham, Thomas J. *Travels in the Californias, and Scenes in the Pacific Ocean.* New York: Saxton and Miles, 1844.

Fein, Helen, "Contextual and Comparative Studies II: Other Genocides." *Current Sociology* 38, no. 1 (March 1990): 79–91.

Fernandez, Ferdinand F. "Except a California Indian: A Study in Legal Discrimination." *Southern California Quarterly* 50, no. 2 (June 1968): 161–175.

Field, Margaret A. "Genocide and the Indians of California, 1769–1873." Master's thesis, University of Massachusetts, Boston, 1993.

Finkelman, Paul. "The Law of Slavery and Freedom in California, 1848–1860." *California Western Law Review* 17, no. 3 (Spring 1981): 437–464.

Fogel, Robert William. *Without Consent or Contract: The Rise and Fall of American Slavery.* New York: Norton, 1989.

Fogel, Robert William, and Stanley L. Engerman. *Time on the Cross: The Economics of American Negro Slavery.* Boston: Little, Brown, 1974.

Foner, Eric. *Free Soil, Free Labor, Free Men: The Ideology of the Republican Party before the Civil War.* New York: Oxford University Press, 1970.

Forde, C. Daryll. "Ethnography of the Yuma Indians." *University of California Publications in Archaeology and Ethnology* 28, no. 4 (December 12, 1931): 83–278.

Fordney, Ben Fuller. *George Stoneman: A Biography of the Union General.* London: McFarland, 2008.

Forsyth, James. *A History of the Peoples of Siberia: Russia's North Asian Colony, 1581–1990.* New York: Cambridge University Press, 1992.

Foster, George M. "A Summary of Yuki Culture." *University of California Anthropological Records* 5, no. 3 (December 30, 1944): 155–244.

Frémont, J.C. *Report of the Exploring Expedition to the Rocky Mountains in the Year 1842, and to Oregon and North California in the Years 1843–'44.* Washington, DC: Gales and Seaton, 1845.

Frémont, John Charles. *Geographical Memoir upon Upper California, in Illustration of his Map of Oregon and California by John Charles Frémont: Addressed to the Senate of the United States.* Washington, DC: Wendell and Van Benthuysen, 1848.

Frémont, John Charles. *Memoirs of My Life, By John Charles Frémont.* Chicago: Belford, Clark, 1887.

Galbraith, John Kenneth. *Money: Whence It Came, Where It Went.* Boston: Houghton Mifflin, 1975.

Garner, Van H. *The Broken Ring: The Destruction of the California Indians.* Tucson, AZ: Westernlore Press, 1982.

Garrett, Gary E. "The Destruction of the Indian in Mendocino County, 1856–1860." Master's thesis, Sacramento State College, 1969.

Gay, Theressa. *James W. Marshall, the Discoverer of California Gold: A Biography.* Georgetown, CA: Talisman Press, 1967.

Geiger, Maynard J. *The Life and Times of Fray Junípero Serra, O.F.M.: Or The Man Who Never Turned Back (1713–1784), A Biography.* 2 vols. Washington, DC: Academy of American Franciscan History, 1959.

Geiger, Vincent, and Wakeman Bryarly. *Trail to California: The Overland Journal of Vincent Geiger and Wakeman Bryarly.* Edited by David Morris Potter. New Haven, CT: Yale University Press, 1945.

Genzoli, Andrew M., and Wallace E. Martin. *Redwood Cavalcade: Pioneer Life, Times.* Eureka, CA: Schooner Features, 1968.

Gerber, Jim. "The Origin of California's Export Surplus in Cereals." *Agricultural History* 67, no. 4 (Fall 1993): 40–57.

Gerstäcker, F. *Scènes de la Vie Californienne par F. Gerstäcker.* Translated by Gustave Revilliod. Genève: Imprimerie de Jules-Gme Fick, 1859.

Gerstäcker, Friedrich. *California Gold Mines*. Oakland, CA: Biobooks, [1854] 1946.

Gerstäcker, Friedrich. *Gerstäcker's Travels: Rio de Janeiro—Buenos Ayres—Ride Through the Pampas—Winter Journey Across the Cordilleras—Chile-Valparaiso—California and the Gold Fields*. London: T. Nelson, 1854.

Gibson, James R. *Imperial Russia in Frontier America: The Changing Geography of Supply of Russian America, 1784–1867*. New York: Oxford University Press, 1976.

Gibson, James R. "Russia in California, 1833: Report of Governor Wrangel." *Pacific Northwest Quarterly* 60, no. 4 (October 1969): 205–215.

Gihon, Thomas. "An Incident of the Gold Bluff Excitement." *Overland Monthly and Out West Magazine* 18, no. 108 (December 1891): 646–660.

Gilbert, Frank T. *History of San Joaquin County, California*. Oakland, CA: Thompson and West, 1879.

Giles, Rosena A. *Shasta County, California: A History*. Oakland, CA: Biobooks, 1949.

Gillis, Michael J., and Michael F. Magliari. *John Bidwell and California: The Life and Writings of a Pioneer, 1841–1900*. Spokane, WA: Arthur H. Clark, 2004.

Glassley, Ray Hoard. *Pacific Northwest Indian Wars: the Cayuse War of 1848, the Rogue River Wars of the '50s, the Yakima War, 1853–56, the Coeur d'Alene War, 1857, the Modoc War, 1873, the Nez Perce War, 1877, the Bannock War, 1878, the Sheepeater's War of 1879*. Portland, OR: Binfords and Mort, 1953.

Glatthaar, Joseph T. *The March to the Sea and Beyond: Sherman's Troops in the Savannah and Carolinas Campaigns*. New York: New York University Press, 1985.

Glickstein, Jonathan A. *American Exceptionalism, American Anxiety: Wages, Competition, and Degraded Labor in the Antebellum United States*. Charlottesville: University of Virginia Press, 2002.

Goldschmidt, Walter. "Nomlaki Ethnography." *University of California Publications in American Archaeology and Ethnology* 42, no. 4 (May 22, 1951): 303–443.

Golla, Victor. *California Indian Languages*. Berkeley: University of California Press, 2011.

Gonzales-Day, Ken. *Lynching in the West, 1850–1935*. Durham, NC: Duke University Press, 2006.

Goodrich, Chauncey Shafter. "The Legal Status of the California Indian." *California Law Review* 14, no. 2 (January 1926): 83–100.

Gould, Richard A. *Archaeology of the Point St. George Site, and Tolowa Prehistory*. Berkeley: University of California Press, 1966.

Gould, Richard A. "Indian and White Versions of 'The Burnt Ranch Massacre': A Study in Comparative Ethnohistory." *Journal of the Folklore Institute* 3, no. 1 (June 1966): 30–42.

Grabhorn, Jane Bissell, ed. *A California Gold Rush Miscellany, Comprising: The Original Journal of Alexander Barrington, Nine Unpublished Letters from the Gold Mines, Reproductions of Early Maps and Towns from California Lithographs; Broadsides, & c., & c*. San Francisco: Grabhorn Press, 1934.

Green, Jerry. "The Medals of Wounded Knee." *Nebraska History* 75 (Summer 1994): 200–208.

Greiff, Pablo de. *The Handbook of Reparations*. New York: Oxford University Press, 2006.

Gudde, Erwin, G. *California Place Names: The Origin and Etymology of Current Geographical Names*. 3rd rev. ed. Berkeley: University of California Press, 1969.

Guest, Francis F. *Hispanic California Revisited: Essays by Francis F. Guest, O.F.M.* Edited by Doyce B. Nunis Jr. Santa Barbara, CA: Santa Barbara Mission Archive Library, 1996.

Guinn, J.M. *History of the State of California and Biographical Record of Coast Counties, California.* Chicago: Chapman, 1904.

H., M.R., "A Rare Maidu Portrait." *Masterkey* 28, no. 5 (September–October 1954): 195.

Haas, Lisbeth. *Saints and Citizens: Indigenous Histories of Colonial Missions and Mexican California.* Berkeley: University of California Press, 2014.

Haas, Lisbeth, and James Luna. *Pablo Tac, Indigenous Scholar: Writing on Luiseño Language and Colonial History, c. 1840.* Berkeley: University of California Press, 2011.

Hackel, Steven W. *Children of Coyote, Missionaries of Saint Francis: Indian–Spanish Relations in Colonial California, 1769–1850.* Chapel Hill: University of North Carolina Press, 2005.

Hackel, Steven W. *Junípero Serra: California's Founding Father.* New York: Hill and Wang, 2013.

Hammond, George P., and Agapito Rey, eds. *Don Juan de Oñate: Colonizer of New Mexico, 1595–1628.* 2 vols. Albuquerque: University of New Mexico Press, 1953.

Hanrahan, Virginia. *Historical Napa Valley.* Napa, CA: Napa County Historical Society, 1949(?).

Hansen, Woodrow James. *The Search for Authority in California.* Oakland, CA: Biobooks, 1960.

Hanson, Charles E., Jr. *The Hawken Rifle: Its Place in History.* Chadron, NE: Fur Press, 1979.

Harlow, Neal. *California Conquered: War and Peace on the Pacific, 1846–1850.* Berkeley: University of California Press, 1982.

Harris, Dennis E. "The California Census of 1852: A Note of Caution and Encouragement." *Pacific Historian* 28, no. 2 (Summer 1984): 59–64.

Harrison, E.S. *History of Santa Cruz County, California.* San Francisco: Pacific Press, 1892.

Haskins, C.W. *The Argonauts of California: Being the Reminiscences of Scenes and Incidents That Occurred in California in Early Mining Days.* New York: Fords, Howard and Hulbert, 1890.

Hastings, Lansford Warren. *The Emigrants' Guide, to Oregon and California . . . and all Necessary Information Relative to the Equipment, Supplies, and the Method of Traveling.* Cincinnati: George Conclin, 1845.

Hauptman, Laurence M. *Tribes and Tribulations: Misconceptions about American Indians and Their Histories.* Albuquerque: University of New Mexico Press, 1995.

"Hayfork: Valley of Abundance." *Yearbook of the Trinity County Historical Society* (1955): 25–27.

Heckewelder, John. *A Narrative of the Mission of the United Brethren Among the Delaware and Mohegan Indians, from its Commencement, in the Year 1740, to the Close of the Year 1808.* Philadelphia: M'Carty and Davis, 1820.

Heineman, Elizabeth D., ed. *Sexual Violence in Conflict Zones: From the Ancient World to the Era of Human Rights.* Philadelphia: University of Pennsylvania Press, 2011.

Heitman, Francis B. *Historical Register and Dictionary of the United States Army from Its Organization, September 29, 1789, to March 2, 1903.* 5 vols. Vol. 2. Washington, DC: Government Printing Office, 1903.

Heizer, Robert F., ed. "The Archaeology of the Napa Region." *University of California Anthropological Records* 12, no. 6 (December 15, 1953): 225–358.

Heizer, Robert F., ed. *Collected Documents on the Causes and Events in the Bloody Island Massacre of 1850.* Berkeley: University of California Press, 1973.

Heizer, Robert F., ed. *The Destruction of California Indians: A Collection of Documents from the Period 1847 to 1865 in Which Are Described Some of the Things That Happened to Some of the Indians of California.* Santa Barbara, CA: Peregrine Smith, 1974.

Heizer, Robert F. *The Eighteen Unratified Treaties of 1851–1852 between the California Indians and the United States Government.* Berkeley: University of California Press, 1972.

Heizer, Robert F., vol. ed. *Handbook of North American Indians.* Series edited by William Sturtevant. 20 vols. Vol. 8. Washington, DC: Smithsonian Institution, 1978.

Heizer, Robert F., ed. *They Were Only Diggers: A Collection of Articles from California Newspapers, 1851–1866, on Indian and White Relations.* Ramona, CA: Ballena Press, 1974.

Heizer, Robert F., and Alan Almquist. *The Other Californians: Prejudice and Discrimination under Spain, Mexico, and the United States to 1920.* Berkeley: University of California Press, 1971.

Heizer, Robert F., and Albert B. Elsasser. *The Natural World of the California Indians.* Berkeley: University of California Press, 1980.

Helper, Hinton R. *The Land of Gold. Reality Versus Fiction.* Baltimore: H. Taylor, 1855.

Herr, John K. *The Story of the U.S. Cavalry, 1775–1942.* Boston: Little, Brown, 1953.

Hilberg, Raul. *The Destruction of the European Jews.* Chicago: Quadrangle Books, 1961.

Hill, Mary. *Geology of the Sierra Nevada.* Rev. ed. Berkeley: University of California Press, 2006.

Hine, Robert V., and John Mack Faragher. *The American West: A New Interpretive History.* New Haven, CT: Yale University Press, 2000.

Hinton, Leanne. *Flutes of Fire: Essays on California Indian Languages.* Berkeley, CA: Heyday Books, 1994.

Hitchcock, Ethan Allan. *A Traveler in Indian Territory: The Journal of Ethan Allan Hitchcock, Late Major-General in the United States Army.* Edited by Grant Foreman. Cedar Rapids, IA: Torch Press, 1930.

Hittell, Theodore H. *History of California.* 4 vols. Vol. 2. San Francisco: N.J. Stone, 1898.

Hoig, Stan. *The Sand Creek Massacre.* Norman: University of Oklahoma Press, 1961.

Hoxie, Frederick, ed. *Indians in American History: An Introduction.* Arlington Heights, IL: Harlan Davidson, 1988.

Hurtado, Albert L. *Indian Survival on the California Frontier.* New Haven, CT: Yale University Press, 1988.

Hurtado, Albert L. *Intimate Frontiers: Sex, Gender, and Culture in Old California.* Albuquerque: University of New Mexico Press, 1999.

Hurtado, Albert L. *John Sutter: A Life on the North American Frontier.* Norman: University of Oklahoma Press, 2007.

Hurtado, Albert L. "The Modocs and the Jones Family Indian Ring: Quaker Administration of the Quapaw Agency, 1873–1879." In *Oklahoma's Forgotten Indians*, edited by Robert E. Smith, 86–107. Oklahoma City: Oklahoma Historical Society, 1981.

Jackson, Donald, and Mary Lee Spence, eds. *The Expeditions of John Charles Frémont*. Vol. 1: *Travels from 1838 to 1844*. Urbana: University of Illinois Press, 1970.

Jackson, Donald, and Mary Lee Spence, eds. *The Expeditions of John Charles Frémont*. Vol. 2: *The Bear Flag Revolt and the Court-Martial*. Urbana: University of Illinois Press, 1973.

Jackson, Helen Hunt. *A Century of Dishonor: A Sketch of the United States Government's Dealings with Some of the Indian Tribes*. New York: Harper, 1881.

Jackson, Robert H., and Edward Castillo. *Indians, Franciscans, and Spanish Colonization: The Impact of the Mission System on California Indians*. Albuquerque: University of New Mexico Press, 1995.

Jacoby, Karl. *Shadows at Dawn: A Borderlands Massacre and the Violence of History*. New York: Penguin Press, 2008.

Jaimes, M. Annette, ed. *The State of Native America: Genocide, Colonization, and Resistance*. Boston: South End Press, 1992.

James, Cheewa. *Modoc: The Tribe That Wouldn't Die*. Happy Camp, CA: Naturegraph, 2008.

"A Jaunt to Honey Lake Valley and Noble's Pass." *Hutchings' California Magazine* 1, no. 12 (June 1857): 529–541.

Jayme, Luís. *Letter of Luís Jayme, O.F.M., San Diego, October 17, 1772*. Translated and edited by Maynard J. Geiger. Los Angeles: Dawson's Book Shop, 1970.

Jeffrey, Julie Roy. *Converting the West: A Biography of Narcissa Whitman*. Norman: University of Oklahoma Press, 1991.

Jennings, Francis. *The Invasion of America: Indians, Colonialism, and the Cant of Conquest*. Chapel Hill: University of North Carolina Press, 1975.

Jensen, Richard E. "Big Foot's Followers at Wounded Knee." *Nebraska History* 71, no. 4 (Winter 1990): 194–212.

Johansen, Bruce Elliott, and Barry M. Pritzker, eds. *Encyclopedia of American Indian History*. 4 vols. Vol. 4. Santa Barbara, CA: ABC-CLIO, 2008.

Johnson, Kenneth M. *The Fremont Court Martial*. Los Angeles: Dawson's Book Shop, 1968.

Johnson, Theodore T. *Sights in the Gold Region, and Scenes by the Way*. 2nd ed. New York: Baker and Scribner, 1850.

Johnson, William Graham. *Experiences of a Forty-Niner*. N.P.: Printer illegible, 1892.

Jones, Adam. *Genocide: A Comprehensive Introduction*. 2nd ed. New York: Routledge, 2010.

Jones, Adam, ed. *New Directions in Genocide Research*. New York: Routledge, 2012.

Jones, Terry L., and Jennifer E. Perry, eds. *Contemporary Issues in California Archaeology*. Walnut Creek, CA: Left Coast Press, 2012.

Jung, Patrick J. *The Black Hawk War of 1832*. Norman: University of Oklahoma Press, 2007.

Kaplan, Victoria Dickler, Florence Anderson, Carmen Christy, Priscilla Hunter, Frances Jack, Iris Martinez, and David Rapport. *Sheemi Ke Janu: Talk from the Past: A History of the Russian River Pomo of Mendocino County.* Ukiah, CA: Ukiah Title VII Project, Ukiah Unified School District, 1984.

Katz, Steven T. *The Holocaust in Historical Context: The Holocaust and Mass Death before the Modern Age.* New York: Oxford University Press, 1994.

Kelly, William. *An Excursion to California over the Prairie, Rocky Mountains, and Great Sierra Nevada.* 2 vols. Vol. 2. London: Chapman and Hall, 1851.

Kelsey, Harry. "The California Indian Treaty Myth." *Southern California Quarterly* 55, no. 3 (Fall 1973): 225–238.

Kibbe, William C. *The Volunteer: Containing Exercises and Movements of Infantry, Light Infantry, Riflemen and Cavalry, Compiled from the Most Approved Works, and Dedicated to the Volunteers of California.* Sacramento: B.B. Redding, 1855.

Kiernan, Ben. *Blood and Soil: A World History of Genocide and Extermination from Sparta to Darfur.* New Haven, CT: Yale University Press, 2007.

Kingsbury, Susan Myra, ed. *The Records of the Virginia Company of London.* 4 vols. Vol. 4. Washington, DC: Government Printing Office, 1935.

Knapp, W. Augustus. "An Old Californian's Pioneer Story.—II." *Overland Monthly and Out West Magazine* 10, no. 59 (November 1887): 499–518.

Knight, Oliver. *Following the Indian Wars: The Story of the Newspaper Correspondents among the Indian Campaigners.* Norman: University of Oklahoma Press, 1960.

Kohl, Seena B. "Ethnocide and Ethnogenesis: A Case Study of the Mississippi Band of Choctaw, A Genocide Avoided." *Holocaust and Genocide Studies* 1, no. 1 (January 1986): 91–100.

Kramer, Stanley, dir. *Judgment at Nuremberg.* Roxlom Films, 1961.

Kroeber, A.L. *Handbook of the Indians of California.* Washington, DC: Government Printing Office, 1925.

Kroeber, A.L. "The Nature of Land-Holding Groups in Aboriginal California." *University of California Archaeological Survey* 56 (1962): 19–58.

Kroeber, A.L. "The Patwin and Their Neighbors." *University of California Publications in Archaeology and Ethnology* 29, no. 4 (February 27, 1932): 253–423.

Kroeber, Theodora. *Ishi in Two Worlds: A Biography of the Last Wild Indian in North America.* Berkeley: University of California Press, [1961] 2002.

Kroeber, Theodora, and Robert F. Heizer. *Almost Ancestors: The First Californians.* Edited by David F. Hales. San Francisco: Sierra Club, 1968.

Kuper, Leo. *Genocide: Its Political Use in the Twentieth Century.* New Haven, CT: Yale University Press, 1981.

Laird, Carobeth. *Encounter with an Angry God: Recollections of My Life with John Peabody Harrington.* Banning, CA: Malki Museum Press, 1975.

Langum, David J. *Law and Community on the Mexican California Frontier: Anglo-American Expatriates and the Clash of Legal Traditions, 1821–1846.* Norman: University of Oklahoma Press, 1987.

Langworthy, Franklin. *Scenery of the Plains, Mountains and Mines: Or A Diary Kept Upon the Overland Route to California, by way of the Great Salt Lake: Travels in the Cities, Mines, and Agricultural Districts—Embracing the return by the Pacific Ocean and Central America, In the Years 1850, '51, '52 and '53.* Ogdensburgh, NY: J.C. Sprague, 1855.

Lawrence, Deborah, and Jon Lawrence. *Violent Encounters: Interviews on Western Massacres*. Norman: University of Oklahoma Press, 2011.

LeBlanc, Lawrence J. *The United States and the Genocide Convention*. Durham, NC: Duke University Press, 1991.

Lemkin, Raphaël. *Axis Rule in Occupied Europe: Laws of Occupation, Analysis of Government, Proposals for Redress*. Washington, DC: Carnegie Endowment for International Peace, Division of International Law, 1944.

Lemkin, Raphaël. *Lemkin on Genocide*. Edited by Steven Leonard Jacobs. Lanham, MD: Lexington Books, 2012.

Letts, J.M. *California Illustrated: Including a Description of the Panama and Nicaragua Routes*. New York: William Holdredge, 1852.

Lewis, David Rich. *Neither Wolf nor Dog: American Indians, Environment, and Agrarian Change*. New York: Oxford University Press, 1994.

Lewis, Henry T. *Patterns of Indian Burning in California: Ecology and Ethnohistory*. Ramona, CA: Ballena Press, 1973.

Lewy, Guenter. "Were American Indians the Victims of Genocide?" *Commentary* 118, no. 2 (September 2004): 55–63.

Librado, Fernando, John Harrington, and Travis Hudson. *Breath of the Sun: Life in Early California as Told by a Chumash Indian, Fernando Librado to John P. Harrington*. Banning, CA: Malki Museum Press, 1979.

Lienhard, Heinrich. *A Pioneer at Sutter's Fort, 1846–1850: The Adventures of Heinrich Lienhard*. Translated and edited by Marguerite Eyer Wilbur. Los Angeles: Calafía Society, 1941.

Lightfoot, Kent G. *Indians, Missionaries, and Merchants: The Legacy of Colonial Encounters on the California Frontiers*. Berkeley: University of California Press, 2005.

Lightfoot, Kent G., and Otis Parrish. *California Indians and Their Environment: An Introduction*. Berkeley: University of California Press, 2009.

Lindsay, Brendan C. *Murder State: California's Native American Genocide, 1846–1873*. Lincoln: University of Nebraska Press, 2012.

Lipset, Seymour Martin. *American Exceptionalism: A Double-Edged Sword*. New York: Norton, 1996.

Loeb, Edwin M. "Pomo Folkways." *University of California Publications in American Archaeology and Ethnology* 19, no. 2 (September 29, 1926): 149–404.

Lord, Israel Shipman Pelton. *"At the Extremity of Civilization": A Meticulously Descriptive Diary of an Illinois Physician's Journey in 1849 along the Oregon Trail to the Goldmines and Cholera of California, Thence in Two Years to Return by Boat Via Panama*. Edited by Necia Dixon Liles. Jefferson, NC: McFarland, 1995.

Loud, Llewellyn L. "Ethnogeography and Archaeology of the Wiyot Territory." *University of California Publications in American Archaeology and Ethnology* 14, no. 3 (December 1918): 221–436.

Lyman, Chester S. *Around the Horn to the Sandwich Islands and California, 1845–1850*. Edited by Frederick J. Teggart. New Haven, CT: Yale University Press, 1924.

Lynn, Rena. *The Story of the Stolen Valley*. Willits, CA: L and S, 1977.

Lyon, Nathaniel. *The Last Political Writings of Gen. Nathaniel Lyon, U.S.A. with a Sketch of his Life and Military Services.* Edited by Richard Henry Stoddard. New York: Rudd and Carlton, 1861.

Madley, Benjamin. "California's Yuki Indians: Defining Genocide in Native American History." *Western Historical Quarterly* 39, no. 3 (Autumn 2008): 303–332.

Madley, Benjamin. "Patterns of Frontier Genocide, 1803–1910: The Aboriginal Tasmanians, the Yuki of California, and the Herero of Namibia." *Journal of Genocide Research* 6, no. 2 (June 2004): 167–192.

Madley, Benjamin. "Reexamining the American Genocide Debate: Meaning, Historiography, and New Methods." *American Historical Review* 120, no. 1 (February 2015): 98–139.

Magliari, Michael. "Free Soil, Unfree Labor: Cave Johnson Couts and the Binding of Indian Workers in California, 1850–1867." *Pacific Historical Review* 73, no. 3 (August 2004): 349–390.

Magliari, Michael F. "Free State Slavery: Bound Indian Labor and Slave Trafficking in California's Sacramento Valley, 1850–1864." *Pacific Historical Review* 81, no. 2 (May 2012): 155–192.

Malinowski, Sharon, and Ann Sheets, eds. *The Gale Encyclopedia of Native American Tribes.* 4 vols. Vol. 4. Detroit: Gale, 1998.

Mann, Michael. *The Dark Side of Democracy: Explaining Ethnic Cleansing.* New York: Cambridge University Press, 2005.

Mansfield, George C. *History of Butte County California with Biographical Sketches of The Leading Men and Women of the County Who Have Been Identified with Its Growth and Development from the Early Days to the Present.* Los Angeles: Historic Record Company, 1918.

Manypenny, George W. *Our Indian Wards.* Cincinnati: Robert Clarke, 1880.

Margolin, Malcolm, ed. *The Way We Lived: California Indian Stories, Songs and Reminiscences.* Berkeley: Heyday Books and the California Historical Society, 1981.

Marks, Paula Mitchell. *Precious Dust: The American Gold Rush Era, 1848–1900.* New York: William Morrow, 1994.

Martin, Oscar F. "Pioneer Sketches.—I. The Old Lassen Trail." *Overland Monthly and Out West Magazine* 2, no. 7 (July 1883): 74–82.

Martin, Thomas S. *With Frémont to California and the Southwest 1845–1849.* Edited by Ferol Egan. Ashland, OR: Lewis Osborne, 1975.

Mason, Jesse D. *The History of Amador County, California, With Illustrations and Biographical Sketches of its Prominent Men and Pioneers.* Oakland, CA: Thompson and West, 1881.

Mason, John. *A Brief History of the Pequot War: Especially of the Memorable Taking of their Fort at Mistick in Connecticut in 1637.* Boston: S. Kneeland and T. Green, 1736.

Massey, Ernest de. "A Frenchman in the Gold Rush [Part I]." Translated by Marguerite Eyer Wilbur. *California Historical Society Quarterly* 5, no. 1 (March 1926): 2–43.

Massey, Ernest de. "A Frenchman in the Gold Rush [Part II]." Translated by Marguerite Eyer Wilbur. *California Historical Society Quarterly* 5, no. 2 (June 1926): 139–177.

Massey, Ernest de. "A Frenchman in the Gold Rush [Part III]." Translated by Marguerite Eyer Wilbur. *California Historical Society Quarterly* 5, no. 3 (September 1926): 218–254.

Matthiessen, Peter. *In the Spirit of Crazy Horse.* New York: Viking Press, 1983.

Mayfield, T.J. *Uncle Jeff's Story: A Tale of a San Joaquin Valley Pioneer and His Life with the Yokuts Indians*. Edited by F.F. Latta. Tulare, CA: Tulare Times, 1929.

M'Collum, William S. *California As I Saw It: Pencillings by the Way of Its Gold and Gold Diggers! And Incidents of Travel by Land and Water*. Buffalo, NY: George H. Derby, 1850.

McComish, Charles Davis, and Rebecca T. Lambert. *History of Colusa and Glenn Counties California with Biographical Sketches of the Leading Men and Women of the Counties Who Have Been Identified with Their Growth and Development from the Early Days to the Present*. Los Angeles: Historic Record Company, 1918.

McDonnell, Michael A., and A. Dirk Moses. "Raphael Lemkin as Historian of Genocide in the Americas." *Journal of Genocide Research* 7, no. 4 (December 2005): 501–529.

McEvoy-Levy, Siobhán. *American Exceptionalism and US Foreign Policy: Public Diplomacy at the End of the Cold War*. New York: Palgrave, 2001.

McGrath, Roger D. *Gunfighters, Highwaymen, and Vigilantes: Violence on the Frontier*. Berkeley: University of California Press, 1984.

McIlhany, Edward Washington. *Recollections of a '49er*. Kansas City, MO: Hailman Printing, 1908.

McKanna, Clare V., Jr. *Race and Homicide in Nineteenth-Century California*. Reno: University of Nevada Press, 2002.

McKibbin, Grace. *In My Own Words: Stories, Songs, and Memories of Grace McKibbin, Wintu*. Edited by Alice Shepherd. Berkeley, CA: Heyday Books, 1997.

McPherson, James M. *Battle Cry of Freedom: The Civil War Era*. New York: Oxford University Press, 1988.

McWilliams, Carey. *Southern California Country: An Island on the Land*. New York: Duell, Sloan, and Pearce, 1946.

Meacham, A.B. *Wigwam and War-Path; or the Royal Chief in Chains*. Boston: John P. Dale, 1875.

Meacham, A.B. *Wi-ne-ma (The Woman-Chief) and Her People*. Hartford, CT: American Publishing, 1876.

Meade, Robert Douthat. *Judah P. Benjamin: Confederate Statesman*. New York: Oxford University Press, 1943.

A Memorial and Biographical History of Northern California, Illustrated. Chicago: Lewis Publishing, 1891.

Menefee, C.A. *Historical and Descriptive Sketch Book of Napa, Sonoma, Lake and Mendocino, Comprising Sketches of Their Topography, Productions, History, Scenery, and Peculiar Attractions*. Napa, CA: Reporter Publishing, 1873.

Menefee, Eugene L., and Fred A. Dodge. *History of Tulare and Kings Counties California with Biographical Sketches of the Leading Men and Women of the Counties Who Have Been Identified with Their Growth and Development From the Early Days to the Present*. Los Angeles: Historic Record Company, 1913.

Merriam, C. Hart. "The Indian Population of California." *American Anthropologist* 7, no. 4 (October–December 1905): 594–606.

Metlar, George W. *Northern California, Scott and Klamath Rivers, their Inhabitants and Characteristics—its Historical Features—Arrival of Scott and his Friends—Mining Interests*. Yreka, CA: Union Printing Office, 1856.

Meyer, Carl. *Bound for Sacramento: Travel-Pictures of a Returned Wanderer Translated from the German by Ruth Frey Axe.* Translated by Ruth Frey Axe. Claremont, CA: Sauders Studio Press, 1938.

Miller, Virginia Peek. "The Yuki: Culture Contact to Allotment." Ph.D. diss., University of California at Davis, 1973.

Milliken, Randall. *Time of Little Choice: The Disintegration of Tribal Culture in the San Francisco Bay Area, 1769–1810.* Menlo Park, CA: Ballena Press, 1995.

Michno, Gregory. *The Deadliest Indian War in the West: The Snake Conflict, 1864–1868.* Caldwell, ID: Caxton Press, 2007.

Mithun, Marianne. *The Languages of Native North America.* Cambridge: Cambridge University Press, 1999.

Moak, Sim. *The Last of the Mill Creeks and Early Life in Northern California.* Chico, CA: N.p., 1923.

Monroy, Douglas. *Thrown among Strangers: The Making of Mexican Culture in Frontier California.* Berkeley: University of California Press, 1990.

"Monthly Record of Current Events." *Hutchings' California Magazine* 3, no. 8 (February 1859): 381–383.

Mora-Torres, Gregorio, ed. and trans. *Californio Voices: The Oral Memoirs of José María Amador and Lorenzo Asisara.* Denton: University of North Texas Press, 2005.

Morse, Edwin Franklin. "The Story of a Gold Miner: Reminiscences of Edwin Franklin Morse." *California Historical Society Quarterly* 6, no. 3 (September 1927): 205–237.

Moses, A. Dirk, ed. *Empire, Colony, Genocide: Conquest, Occupation, and Subaltern Resistance in World History.* New York: Berghahn Books, 2008.

Murray, Keith A. *The Modocs and Their War.* Norman: University of Oklahoma Press, 1959.

Navarro, Ramón Gil. *The Gold Rush Diary of Ramón Gil Navarro.* Translated and edited by María del Carmen Ferreyra and David S. Reher. Lincoln: University of Nebraska Press, 2000.

Nevins, Allan. *Frémont, The West's Greatest Adventurer, Being a Biography from certain hitherto unpublished sources of General John C. Frémont, Together with his Wife, Jesse Benton Frémont, and Some Account of the Period of Expansion which Found a Brilliant Leader in the Pathfinder.* 2 vols. New York: Harper, 1928.

Nomland, Gladys Ayer. "Bear River Ethnography." *University of California Anthropological Records* 2, no. 2 (March 17, 1938): 91–126.

Nomland, Gladys Ayer. "Sinkyone Notes." *University of California Publications in American Archaeology and Ethnology* 36, no. 2 (December 31, 1935): 149–178.

Norton, Jack. *Genocide in Northwestern California: When Our Worlds Cried.* San Francisco: Indian Historian Press, 1979.

Novick, Peter. *The Holocaust in American Life.* Boston: Houghton Mifflin, 1999.

Oberly, James W. *Sixty Million Acres: American Veterans and the Public Lands before the Civil War.* Kent, OH: Kent State University Press, 1990.

Ostler, Jeffrey. *The Plains Sioux and U.S. Colonialism from Lewis and Clark to Wounded Knee.* Cambridge: Cambridge University Press, 2004.

Oswalt, Robert L. "Kashaya Texts." *University of California Publications in Linguistics* 36 (September 1, 1964): 1–337.

Paddison, Joshua, ed. *A World Transformed: Firsthand Accounts of California before the Gold Rush*. Berkeley, CA: Heyday Books, 1999.

Palmer, L.L. *History of Napa and Lake Counties, California . . . and Biographical Sketches of Early Settlers and Representative Men*. 2 vols. San Francisco: Slocum, Bowen, 1881.

Palmer, Lyman. *History of Mendocino County, California . . . in which is embodied the raising of the Bear Flag*. San Francisco: Alley, Bowen, 1880.

Palóu, Francisco. *Historical Memoirs of New California by Francisco Palóu, O.F.M.* Edited and Translated by Herbert Bolton. 4 vols. Berkeley: University of California Press, 1926.

Pancoast, Charles Edward. *A Quaker Forty-Niner: The Adventures of Charles Edward Pancoast on the American Frontier*. Edited by Anna Paschall Hannum. Philadelphia: University of Pennsylvania Press, 1930.

Pauketat, Timothy R., ed. *The Oxford Handbook of North American Archaeology*. New York: Oxford University Press, 2012.

Percy, George. "'A Trewe Relacyon'—Virginia from 1609 to 1612." Reprinted in *Tyler's Quarterly Historical and Genealogical Magazine* 3, no. 4 (April 1922): 259–282.

Pérouse, Jean François de la. *Monterey in 1786: The Journals of Jean François de La Pérouse*. Edited by Malcolm Margolin. Berkeley, CA: Heyday Books, 1989.

Perry, Elder J.A. *Travels, Scenes and Sufferings in Cuba, Mexico, and California*. Boston: Redding, 1853.

Pfaelzer, Jean. *Driven Out: The Forgotten War Against Chinese Americans*. Berkeley: University of California Press, 2007.

Phillips, Christopher. *Damned Yankee: The Life of General Nathaniel Lyon*. Columbia: University of Missouri Press, 1990.

Phillips, George Harwood. *"Bringing Them under Subjection": California's Tejón Indian Reservation and Beyond, 1852–1864*. Lincoln: University of Nebraska Press, 2004.

Phillips, George Harwood. *Chiefs and Challengers: Indian Resistance and Cooperation in Southern California*. Berkeley: University of California Press, 1975.

Phillips, George Harwood. *Indians and Intruders in Central California, 1769–1849*. Norman: University of Oklahoma Press, 1993.

Phillips, George Harwood. "Indians in Los Angeles, 1781–1875: Economic Integration, Social Disintegration." *Pacific Historical Review* 49, no. 3 (August 1980): 427–451.

Phillips, George Harwood. *Vineyards and Vaqueros: Indian Labor and the Economic Expansion of Southern California, 1771–1877*. Norman, OK: Arthur H. Clark, 2010.

Phillips, Ulrich Bonnell. *Life and Labor in the Old South*. Columbia: University of South Carolina Press, [1929] 2007.

Pigman, Walter Griffith. *The Journal of Walter Griffith Pigman*. Edited by Ulla Stanley Fawks. Mexico, MO: Walter G. Stanley, 1942.

Powers, Stephen. "California Indian Characteristics." *Overland Monthly and Out West Magazine* 14, no. 4 (April 1875): 297–309.

Powers, Stephen. "The California Indians. No. VIII.—The Modocs." *Overland Monthly and Out West Magazine* 10, no. 6 (June 1873): 535–545.

Powers, Stephen. "The California Indians. No. XII.—The Wintoons." *Overland Monthly and Out West Magazine* 12, no. 6 (June 1874): 530–540.

Powers, Stephen. "Tribes of California." In *Contributions to North American Ethnology,* vol. 3. Edited by John Wesley Powell. Washington, DC: Government Printing Office, 1877. Reprinted as Robert F. Heizer, ed., *Tribes of California.* Berkeley: University of California Press, 1976.

Priestly, Herbert Ingram. *The Mexican Nation: A History.* London: Macmillan, 1923.

Quinn, Arthur. *Hell with the Fire Out: A History of the Modoc War.* Boston: Faber and Faber, 1997.

Rawls, James J. "Gold Diggers: Indian Miners in the California Gold Rush." *California Historical Quarterly* 55, no. 1 (Spring 1976): 28–45.

Rawls, James J. *Indians of California: The Changing Image.* Norman: University of Oklahoma Press, 1984.

Reed, Annette. "*Neeyu Nn'ee min' Nngheeyilh Naach'aaghitlhni: Lha't'i Deeni Tr'vmdan' Natlhsri*—Rooted in the Land of Our Ancestors, We Are Strong: A Tolowa History." PhD diss., University of California at Berkeley, 1999.

Reed, Annette. "Research Notes." http://www.csus.edu/pubaf/journal/spring2005/12research.htm.

Reheis, Marith C. "Dust Deposition Downwind of Owens (Dry) Lake, 1991–1994: Preliminary Findings." *Journal of Geophysical Research* 102, no. D22 (November 1997): 25999–26008.

Revere, Joseph Warren. *A Tour of Duty in California; Including a Description of the Gold Region: And an Account of the Voyage Around Cape Horn; with Notices of Lower California, the Gulf and Pacific Coasts, and the Principal Events Attending the Conquest of the Californias.* Edited by Joseph N. Balestier. New York: C.S. Francis, 1849.

Richter, Daniel K. *Facing East from Indian Country: A Native History of Early America.* Cambridge, MA: Harvard University Press, 2001.

Riddle, Jeff C. *The Indian History of the Modoc War and the Causes that Led to It.* San Francisco: Marnell, 1914.

Riley, Angela R. "(Tribal) Sovereignty and Illiberalism." *California Law Review* 95, no. 3 (June 2005): 799–848.

Roberts, David. *A Newer World: Kit Carson, John C. Frémont, and the Claiming of the American West.* New York: Simon and Schuster, 2000.

Robinson, Charles M. *General Crook and the Western Frontier.* Norman: University of Oklahoma Press, 2001.

Rodenbough, Theo. F., comp. *From Everglade to Cañon with the Second Dragoons, (Second United States Cavalry): An Authentic Account of Service in Florida, Mexico, Virginia, and the Indian Country, including the Personal Recollections of Prominent Officers, with . . .* New York: D. Van Nostrand, 1875.

Rohrbough, Malcolm J. *Days of Gold: The California Gold Rush and the American Nation.* Berkeley: University of California Press, 1997.

Roosevelt, Theodore. *The Winning of the West.* 4 vols. Vol. 1. New York: G.P. Putnam's, 1889.

Root Cellar, Sacramento Genealogical Society. *California State Militia: Index to the Muster Rolls of 1851–1866.* Sacramento: The Society, 1999.

Rosborough, Alex J. "A.M. Rosborough, Special Indian Agent." *California Historical Society Quarterly* 26, no. 3 (September 1947): 201–207.

Rubinstein, William D. *Genocide: A History.* Harlow, UK: Pearson Longman, 2004.

Ryan, William Redmond. *Personal Adventures in Upper and Lower California, in 1848–9; With the Author's Experience at the Mines.* 2 vols. London: William Shoberl, 1850.

Sage, Rufus B. *Scenes in the Rocky Mountains, and in Oregon, California, New Mexico, Texas, and The Grand Prairies; or Notes by the Way, During an Excursion of Three Years, with a Description of the Countries Passed Through, Including their Geography, Geology, Resources, Present Condition, and the Different Nations Inhabiting Them.* Philadelphia: Carey and Hart, 1846.

Sainte-Marie, Buffy. *Little Wheel Spin and Spin.* LP recording, Vanguard, 1966.

Salomon, Carlos Manuel. *Pío Pico: The Last Governor of Mexican California.* Norman: University of Oklahoma Press, 2010.

Sample, L.L. "Trade and Trails in Aboriginal California." *Reports of the University of California Archaeological Survey* 8 (September 15, 1950): 1–30.

Sánchez, Rosaura. *Telling Identities: The California Testimonios.* Minneapolis: University of Minnesota Press, 1995.

Sandos, James A. *Converting California: Indians and Franciscans in the Missions.* New Haven, CT: Yale University Press, 2004.

Sandos, James A. "Lavantamiento! The 1824 Chumash Uprising Reconsidered." *Southern California Quarterly* 67, no. 2 (Summer 1985): 109–133.

Santiago, Mark. *Massacre at the Yuma Crossing: Spanish Relations with the Quechans, 1779–1782.* Tucson: University of Arizona Press, 1998.

Sapir, Edward. "Yana Texts." *University of California Publications in American Archaeology and Ethnology* 9, no. 1 (February 19, 1910): 1–235.

Sauber, H.H. "True Tales of the Old West, XV.—Hi Good and the 'Mill Creeks'." *Overland Monthly and Out West Magazine* 30, no. 176 (August 1897): 122–127.

Schabas, William A., *Genocide in International Law: The Crime of Crimes.* New York: Cambridge University Press, 2000.

Schaeffer, L.M. *Sketches of Travels in South America, Mexico and California.* New York: James Egbert, 1860.

Scharnhorst, Gary. *Bret Hart: Opening the American Literary West.* Norman: University of Oklahoma Press, 2000.

Schmölder, B. *The Emigrant's Guide to California, Describing its Geography, Agricultural and Commercial Resources.* London: Pellham Richardson, 1848.

Schoolcraft, Henry R. ed. *Archives of Aboriginal Knowledge.* 6 vols. Vol. 3. Philadelphia: J.B. Lippincott, 1860.

Schoonover, Steve. "Kibbe's Campaign." *Dogtown Territorial Quarterly* 20 (Winter 1994): 10–11, 44–49.

Secrest, William B. *When the Great Spirit Died: The Destruction of the California Indians, 1850–1860.* Sanger, CA: Word Dancer Press, 2003.

Sedgley, Joseph. *Overland to California in 1849.* Oakland, CA: Butler and Bowman, 1877.

Serra, Junípero. *Writings of Junípero Serra*. Edited by Antonine Tibesar. 4 vols. Washington, DC: Academy of American Franciscan History, 1955–1966.

Seymour, E. Sandford. *Emigrant's Guide to the Gold Mines, with a Map of California, and a Sketch of the Country, Containing Instructions Relative to Nine Different Routes, Especially the Route by the South Pass*. Chicago: R.L. Wilson, 1849.

Shaw, Martin. *What Is Genocide?* Cambridge, UK: Polity, 2007.

Shaw, William. *Golden Dreams and Waking Realities: Being the Adventures of a Gold-Seeker in California and the Pacific Islands*. London: Smith, Elder, 1851.

Shea, William Lee. "To Defend Virginia: The Evolution of the First Colonial Militia, 1607–1677." PhD diss., Rice University, 1975.

Sherman, Edwin A. "Sherman Was There: The Recollections of Major Edwin A. Sherman [Part I]." *California Historical Society Quarterly* 23, no. 3 (September 1944): 259–281.

Sherman, Edwin A. "Sherman Was There: The Recollections of Major Edwin A. Sherman (Continued) [Part III]." *California Historical Society Quarterly* 24, no. 1 (March 1945): 47–72.

Sherman, William T. *A Letter of Lieut. W.T. Sherman Reporting on Conditions in California in 1848*. Carmel, CA: Thos. W. Norris, 1947.

Sherman, William T. *Recollections of California, 1846–1861*. Oakland, CA: Biobooks, 1945.

Sherman, William T. *W.T. Sherman, The California Gold Fields in 1848: Two letters from Lt. W. T. Sherman, U.S.A.* Berkeley, CA: Bancroft Library, 1964.

Shover, Michele. "John Bidwell's Role in the 1863 Indian Removal from Chico, Part 2, and through 1866." *Dogtown Territorial Quarterly* 50 (Summer 2002): 34–59.

Shriner, Herk. *Thunder up the Creek To-Mo-Kus Waket-Awl-Wa-Mem: The Story of the Bridge Gulch Massacre*. Weaverville, CA: Ruin River, 2005.

Shuck, Oscar T. *Bench and Bar in California*. San Francisco: Occident Printing House, 1889.

Shuck, Oscar T., ed. *History of the Bench and Bar of California: being biographies of many remarkable men, a store of humorous and pathetic recollections, accounts of important legislation and extraordinary cases, comprehending the judicial history of the state*. Los Angeles: Commercial Printing House, 1901.

Silver, Peter Rhoads. *Our Savage Neighbors: How Indian War Transformed Early America*. New York: W.W. Norton, 2008.

Silver, Shirley, and Wick R. Miller. *American Indian Languages: Cultural and Social Contexts*. Tucson: University of Arizona Press, 1997.

Simpson, Henry I. *The Emigrant's Guide to the Gold Mines: Three Weeks in the Gold Mines, or Adventures with the Gold Diggers of California in August, 1848*. New York: Joyce, 1848.

Sleeper-Smith, Susan, Juliana Barr, Jean M. O'Brien, Nancy Shoemaker, and Scott Manning Stevens, eds. *Why You Can't Teach United States History without American Indians*. Chapel Hill: University of North Carolina Press, 2015.

Slezkine, Yuri. *Arctic Mirrors: Russia and the Small Peoples of the North*. Ithaca, NY: Cornell University Press, 1994.

Smith, Dottie. *The Dictionary of Early Shasta County History.* Cottonwood, CA: D. Smith, 1991.

Smith, Esther Ruth. *The History of Del Norte County, California: Including the Story of Its Pioneers with Many of Their Personal Narratives.* Oakland, CA: Holmes Book, 1953.

Smith, Justin H. *The War with Mexico.* 2 vols. Vol. 1. New York: Macmillan, 1919.

Soulé, Frank, John H. Gihon, and James Nisbet. *The Annals of San Francisco; Containing a Summary of the History of the First Discovery, Settlement, Progress, and Present Condition of California, and a Complete History of All the Important Events Connected with its Great City: To Which Are Added, Biographical Memoirs of Some Prominent Citizens.* New York: D. Appleton, 1854.

Sousa, Ashley Riley. "'They Will Be Hunted Down Like Wild Beasts and Destroyed!' A Comparative Study of Genocide in California and Tasmania." *Journal of Genocide Research* 6, no. 2 (June 2004): 193–209.

Southern, May Hazel. *Our Storied Landmarks, Shasta County, California.* San Francisco: P. Balakshin Printing, ca. 1942.

Stannard, David E. *American Holocaust: The Conquest of the New World.* New York: Oxford University Press, 1992.

Starr, Kevin, and Richard J. Orsi, eds. *Rooted in Barbarous Soil: People, Culture, and Community in Gold Rush California.* Berkeley: University of California Press, 2000.

The State Register and Year Book of Facts: For the Year 1859. San Francisco: Henry G. Langley and Samuel A. Morison, 1859.

Steger, Gertrude A. "A Chronology of the Life of Pierson Barton Reading." *California Historical Quarterly* 22, no. 4 (December 1943): 365–371.

Steger, Gertrude A., and Helen Hinckley Jones. *Place Names of Shasta County.* Glendale, CA: La Siesta Press, 1966.

Steward, Julian H. "Basin-Plateau Aboriginal Sociopolitical Groups." *Smithsonian Institution Bureau of American Ethnology Bulletin* 120 (1938): 1–346.

Steward, Julian H. "Ethnography of the Owens Valley Paiute." *University of California Publications in American Archaeology and Ethnology* 33, no. 3 (September 6, 1933): 233–350.

Stillson, Richard T. *Spreading the Word: A History of Information in the California Gold Rush.* Lincoln: University of Nebraska Press, 2006.

Stone, Dan, ed. *The Historiography of Genocide.* New York: Palgrave Macmillan, 2008.

Street, Richard Steven. *Beasts of the Field: A Narrative History of California Farmworkers, 1769–1913.* Stanford, CA: Stanford University Press, 2004.

Strobridge, William F. *Regulars in the Redwoods: The U.S. Army in Northern California, 1852–1861.* Spokane, WA: Arthur H. Clark, 1994.

Sturtevant, William C., and Samuel Stanley. "Indian Communities in the Eastern States." *Indian Historian* 1, no. 3 (Summer 1968): 15–19.

Sutter, John. "The Discovery of Gold in California." *Hutchings' California Magazine* 2, no. 5 (November 1857): 193–202.

Swift, Dr. [Jonathan]. *A Modest Proposal For preventing the Children of Poor People From being a Burthen to Their Parents or Country, and For making them Beneficial to the Publick.* Reprint. London: J. Roberts, 1729.

Tac, Pablo. "Indian Life and Customs at Mission San Luis Rey: A Record of California Mission Life Written by Pablo Tac, an Indian Neophyte (Rome, ca. 1835)." Translated and edited by Minna Hewes and Gordon Hewes. *Americas* 9, no. 1 (July 1952): 87–106.

Tarakanoff, Vassili. *Statement of My Captivity among the Californians.* Translated by Ivan Petroff and edited by Arthur Woodward. Los Angeles: Glen Dawson, 1953.

Tassin, A.G. "Chronicles of Camp Wright. I." *Overland Monthly and Out West Magazine* 10, no. 55 (July 1887): 24–32.

Tassin, A.G. "Chronicles of Camp Wright.—II." *Overland Monthly and Out West Magazine* 10, no. 56 (August 1887): 169–186.

Tassin, A.G. "The Con-Cow Indians." *Overland Monthly and Out West Magazine* 4, no. 19 (July 1884): 7–14.

Taylor, Bayard. *Eldorado, or, Adventures in the Path of Empire; Comprising a Voyage to California, via Panama; Life in San Francisco and Monterey; Pictures of the Gold Region; and Experiences of Mexican Travel.* 2 vols. London: George Routledge, 1850.

Thompson, Erwin N. *Modoc War: Its Military History and Topography.* Sacramento, CA: Argus Books, 1971.

Thompson, Kenneth. "Insalubrious California: Perception and Reality." *Annals of the Association of American Geographers* 59, no. 1 (March 1969): 50–64.

Thompson, William. *Reminiscences of a Pioneer.* San Francisco: Self-published, 1912.

Thornton, Russell. *American Indian Holocaust and Survival: A Population History since 1492.* Norman: University of Oklahoma Press, 1987.

Thornton, Russell. "Social Organization and the Demographic Survival of the Tolowa." *Ethnohistory* 31, no. 3 (Summer 1984): 187–196.

Tinkham, George H. *History of San Joaquin County California with Biographical Sketches of the Leading Men and Women of the County Who Have Been Identified with Its Growth and Development from the Early Days to the Present.* Los Angeles: Historic Record Company, 1923.

Todorov, Tzvetan. *The Conquest of America: The Question of the Other.* Translated by Richard Howard. New York: Harper and Row, 1984.

Totten, Samuel, and William S. Parsons, eds. *Centuries of Genocide: Essays and Eyewitness Accounts.* New York: Routledge, 2013.

Trafzer, Clifford E. *Yuma: Frontier Crossing of the Far Southwest.* Wichita, KS: Western Heritage Books, 1980.

Trafzer, Clifford E., and Joel R. Hyer, eds. *"Exterminate Them!" Written Accounts of the Murder, Rape, and Slavery of Native Americans during the California Gold Rush, 1848–1868.* East Lansing: Michigan State University Press, 1999.

Trigger, Bruce R., and Wilcomb E. Washburn, eds. *The Cambridge History of the Native Peoples of the Americas.* Vol. 1: *North America.* Part 2. 2 vols. Cambridge, UK: Cambridge University Press, 1996.

Turner, William M. "Scraps of Modoc History." *Overland Monthly and Out West Magazine* 11, no. 1 (July 1873): 21–25.

Tushingham, Shannon. "The Development of Intensive Foraging Systems in Northwestern California." PhD diss., University of California at Davis, 2009.

Tutorow, Norman E. *The Governor: The Life and Legacy of Leland Stanford, A California Colossus.* 2 vols. Spokane, WA: Arthur H. Clark, 2004.

Tyson, James L. *Diary of a Physician in California; Being the Result of Actual Experience, Including Notes of the Journey by Land and Water, and Observations on the Climate, Soil, Resources of the Country, Etc.* New York: D. Appleton, 1850.

Uldall, Hans Jørgen, and William Shipley. "Nisenan Texts and Dictionary." *University of California Publications in Linguistics* 46 (1966): 1–282.

Underhill, John. *Newes from America; or, A New and Experimentall Discoverie of New England . . .* London: I.D. for Peter Cole, 1638.

Unruh, John D., Jr. *The Plains Across: The Overland Emigrants and the Trans-Mississippi West, 1840–60.* Urbana: University of Illinois Press, 1979.

Wagner, Henry R. *Spanish Voyages to the Northwest Coast of America in the Sixteenth Century.* San Francisco: California Historical Society, 1929.

Walker, Deward, Jr., vol. ed. *Handbook of North American Indians.* Series edited by William Sturtevant. 20 vols. Vol. 12. Washington, DC: Government Printing Office, 1998.

Wallace, Anthony F.C. *The Long Bitter Trail: Andrew Jackson and the American Indians.* New York: Hill and Wang, 1993.

Walling, A.G. *Illustrated History of Lane County, Oregon.* Portland, OR: A.G. Walling, 1884.

Warburton, Austen D., and Joseph F. Endert. *Indian Lore of the North California Coast.* Santa Clara, CA: Pacific Pueblo Press, 1966.

Washburn, Wilcomb, vol. ed. *Handbook of North American Indians.* Series edited by William Sturtevant. 20 vols. Vol. 4. Washington, DC: Smithsonian Institution, 1988.

Waterman, T.T. "Ishi, the Last Yahi Indian." *Southern Workman* 46, no. 10 (October 1917): 528–537.

Waterman, T.T. "The Yana Indians." *University of California Publications in American Archaeology and Ethnology* 13, no. 2 (February 27, 1918): 35–102.

Weber, David J. *Bárbaros: Spaniards and Their Savages in the Age of Enlightenment.* New Haven, CT: Yale University Press, 2005.

Weber, David J. *The Mexican Frontier, 1821–1846: The American Southwest under Mexico.* Albuquerque: University of New Mexico Press, 1982.

Weber, David J. *The Spanish Frontier in North America.* New Haven, CT: Yale University Press, 1992.

Wells, Harry L. "The Ben Wright Massacre." *West Shore* 10, no. 10 (October 1884): 314–320.

Wells, Harry L. *History of Siskiyou County, California, Illustrated with Views of Residences, Business Buildings and Natural Scenery, and Containing Portraits and Biographies of its Leading Citizens and Pioneers.* Oakland, CA: D.J. Stewart, 1881.

Wells, Harry L. "The Modocs in 1851." *West Shore* 10, no. 5 (May 1884): 132–134.

Wells, Harry L., and W.L. Chambers. *The History of Butte County, California, in Two Volumes.* 2 vols. San Francisco: Harry L. Wells, 1882.

West, Elliot. *The Contested Plains: Indians, Goldseekers, and the Rush to Colorado.* Lawrence: University of Kansas Press, 1998.

Weston, S. *Life in the Mountains, or, Four months in the Mines of California.* Providence, RI: E.P. Weston, 1854.

White, Richard. "Morality and Mortality." *New Republic* 208, no. 3 (January 18, 1993): 33–36.

Wilke, Philip J., and Harry W. Lawton, eds. *The Expedition of Capt. J.W. Davidson from Fort Tejon to the Owens Valley in 1859.* Socorro, NM: Ballena Press, 1976.

Willey, Samuel H. *The Transition Period of California, From a Province of Mexico in 1846 to a State of the American Union in 1850.* San Francisco: Whitaker and Ray, 1901.

Wilshire, Bruce. *Get 'Em All! Kill 'Em! Genocide, Terrorism, Righteous Communities.* Lanham, MD: Lexington Books, [2004] 2005.

Wilson, James. *The Earth Shall Weep: A History of Native America.* New York: Grove Press, 1998.

Winthrop, John. *Winthrop's Journal, "History of New England," 1630–1649.* Edited by James Kendall Hosmer. 2 vols. Vol. 1. New York: Charles Scribner's, 1908.

Woodbridge, Bradford. "True Tales of the Old West: XIV—A Tragedy of Pit River." *Overland Monthly and Out West Magazine* 29, no. 174 (June 1897): 640–642.

Woods, Daniel B. *Sixteen Months at the Gold Diggings.* New York: Harper, 1851.

Woodward, Ashbel. *Life of General Nathaniel Lyon.* Hartford, CT: Case, Lockwood, 1862.

Woolford, Andrew, Jeff Benvenuto, and Alexander Laban Hinton, eds. *Colonial Genocide in Indigenous North America.* Durham, NC: Duke University Press, 2014.

Works Progress Administration. *California: A Guide to the Golden State.* New York: Hastings House, 1939.

Wright, Elizabeth Cyrus. *The Early Upper Napa Valley.* Calistoga, CA: Napa County Historical Society, January 1928, reprint 1991.

Wyman, Walker D., ed. *California Emigrant Letters.* New York: Bookman Associates, 1952.

Young, Lucy, and Edith V.A. Murphey. "Out of the Past: A True Indian Story Told by Lucy Young, of Round Valley Indian Reservation to Edith V.A. Murphey." *California Historical Society Quarterly* 20, no. 4 (December 1941): 349–364.

Yount, George C. *George C. Yount and His Chronicles of the West, Comprising Extracts from His "Memoirs" and from the Orange Clark "Narrative."* Edited by Charles L. Camp. Denver, CO: Old West Publishing, 1966.

Zappia, Natale A. "Indigenous Borderlands: Livestock, Captivity, and Power in the Far West." *Pacific Historical Review* 81, no. 2 (May 2012): 193–220.

Zappia, Natale A. *Traders and Raiders: The Indigenous World of the Colorado Basin, 1540–1859.* Chapel Hill: University of North Carolina Press, 2014.

Zeisberger, David. *Diary of David Zeisberger, A Moravian Missionary Among the Indians of Ohio.* Translated and edited by Eugene Bliss. 2 vols. Vol. 1. Cincinnati: Robert Clark, 1885.

INDEX

Page numbers in *italics* indicate maps and illustrations.

Achumawi people, 43, 204, 208, 219, 222, 225, 233, 241, 243–244, 247–250, 254–257, 261, 271–274, 276, 296, 304, 309, 327, 333, 334; basket-maker, 248, precontact, 247–248
Acoma Massacre, 132
Act for the Government and Protection of Indians (1850), 158–159
Agency, in annihilation of Indians, 185
Ahwahanee people, 194
Akayesu, Jean-Paul, 353
Akey, D.B., 301
Alcantara, Salome, 134
Alcatraz Island, 345
Allgeier, Nicholaus, 55
Almquist, Allan, 7, 12
Altschule, Herman, 136–137
Amador, José Maria, 40
American Indian activism, 6
American Indian Religious Freedom Act (1978), 10
American Indians, debate over genocide of, 356–359
Anderson, Charles S., 312
Anderson, Gary, 358
Anderson, M. Kat, 18
Anderson, Robert, 270, 271, 272, 309, 330, 331

Anderson, W., 124
Angel, Myron, 98
Annihilation. *See* Extermination
Antonio, Juan (leader), 203
Apologies, 9
Apprentice system, 65, 286–287, 293, 304
Arapaho people, massacre of, 142
Archibald, Robert, 27
Armistead, Lewis, 269
Arms and ammunition, Indians denied access to, 227–228
Armstrong, L., 180
Army, US: ability to stop mass murder, 204, 242, 245, 266; attempt to stop "Red Cap War," 235, 237; Bloody Island Massacre, 127–133, 139–140; California Indians in, 56, 57–59; California Volunteers, 222, 299–303, 309, 314, 316–320, 321, 350, 354–355; Cayuse men in, 75; collaboration with militiamen, 215; collaboration with vigilantes, 302, 309, 312, 313, 331, 334; compared to vigilantes, 224, 267, 331–332; condoning of massacres by, 142; departure of most regulars from California, 299; facilitation of separation of children from communities, 303–304; 1st Dragoons,

Army, US (cont.)
115–120, 127, 128, 131, 136 (*see also*
Davidson, John W.); and forced
removal, 257; Fort Reading, 207; Indian
killing by, 45–50, 57, 61–62, 116–118,
129–133, 203, 227, 139, 237, 245–246, 249,
256–257, 268, 269–270, 286, 290,
292–293, 302, 307, 312–318, 321–324, 330,
331–332, 333, 334, 336, 342, 343, 345;
Indian policies, 260, 266, 290, 300–301;
lack of action on Indian killing, 219;
Lovell's campaign, 290–293; massacres
by, 40–50, 116, 129–139, 249, 268,
269–270, 290, 292, 313, 314, 315, 316,
317, 322, 323, 331–332; Modoc War,
336–345; and Mojave War, 268–270;
numbers of California Indians killed
by, 175, 355; in Owens Valley, 310,
312–313; prevented from protecting
Indians, 352; and protection of Indians,
242, 245, 266; and protection of
reservations, 171, 260; refusal to
intervene in kidnapping/slave raiding,
240; in retaliation for killing of Stone
and Kelsey, 115 (*see also* Davidson,
John W.; Smith, Persifor F.); role in
California Indian catastrophe, 14,
354–355; in Siskiyou Volunteer Rangers
Expedition, 215; support for militias, 181,
237, 246, 272; torture of children by, 137;
transformation of Indian killing by,
299–300 (*see also* California Volunteers);
"Two-Years' War," 317–318, 321–324. *See
also* Indian killing; Massacres, Indian;
Villages, destruction of
Arthur, Benjamin, 252, 253
Asbill, Frank, 228–229
Asbill, Pierce, 229
Asisara, Lorenzo, 27, 30
Assimilation, *vs.* exclusion, 149
Atsugewi people, 19, 222, 247, 256, 271, 272,
275, 276, 296, 304, 331
Attorneys, 160

Augustine (Shuk), 103, 105, 109, 110, 111,
112, 113, 114, 115, 129, 132, 134
Axtell, James, 357
Aylett, W.D., 225
Ayres, Irvin, 325, 327, 328

Babe, E.J., 64
Bailey, Goddard, 260
Bancroft, Hubert Howe, 3, 138, 168
Baptism, 27, 33, 36
Barbour, George W., 164, 165, 186, 193.
See also Treaty commissioners
Barncho, 345
Barrett, S.A., 110, 112, 113, 115, 116, 132, 133,
134
Barry, William Jackson, 207
Barstow, Alfred, 184
Bartlett, Washington A., 147
Battery Point Massacre, 220, 223
Battle of the Infernal Caverns, 334
Battle of Yreka Pass, 227
Battles: defined, 11; massacres disguised
as, 12, 255, 329; under Mexican rule,
39–40
Ba-Tus, 103, 114
Bauer, John A., 56
Bauer, William, Jr., 348
Baume, Charles, 296
Baumgardner, Frank, 258
Beale, Edward F., 161–162, 168, 170, 246
Bean, Joshua, 180, 181, 203
Bear Flaggers, 57, 58, 107, 175
Beechy, Frederick, 34
Bell, Horace, 161
Bell, Sally, 210, 211
Benjamin, Judah P., 250, 251
Benson, William Ralganal (leader), 103,
105, 107, 108, 109, 110, 111, 112, 115, 128,
129, 130, 131, 133, 134, 137
Berreyesa, Sisto, 85–86
Berries, 21–22, 23, 43, 45, 71, 106, 201, 209,
210, 248, 309
Bestor, Norman, 88

Biaggi, John, Jr., 295

Bidwell, John, 70, 157–158, 208

Bigler, John, 165, 168, 204, 205, 206, 207, 208, 215, 225, 226, 229–230, 232, 238, 240

Big Valley Ranch, 103, 106, 107, 109, 110–114. *See also* Kelsey, Andrew; Retaliation, for killing of Stone and Kelsey; Stone, Charles

Bill, Dandy, 283

Births, prevention of, 4, 63, 172, 182, 260, 261, 287, 293, 297, 352

Bishop, Samuel A., 269

Black, Henry M., 321–323

Black Jim, 345

Blood and Soil (Kiernan), 357

Bloody Island Massacre, 127–133, 139–140, 350; *Daily Alta California* on, 139. *See also* Clear Lake Indians; Lyon, Nathaniel

Bloody Point Massacre, 213–214

Bommelyn, Loren, 224

Boston Charley, 341, 345

Boston Transcript, 293

Botts, Charles T., 150, 152

Bounties, for Indian heads/scalps, 86, 197, 198, 205, 270, 295

Bounty Land Laws, 237–238

Bowling, John, 190

Boyle, W.H., 341

Bradford, Ward, 246

Bradford, William, 140

Breckenridge, John, 220, 270–271

Breckenridge, Thomas E., 45, 46, 47, 48, 51

Brewer, William H., 309, 332

Bridge Gulch Massacre, 206–207

Brown, Amelia, 223

Brown, Bob (*tawin t^{h}ewis*), 207

Brown, Elam, 158

Browne, J. Ross, 154–155, 260, 262, 265, 279, 280, 297, 355

Bruff, J. Goldsborough, 184

Bryant, Edwin, 52, 53, 58, 59, 60–61, 63

Buckles, H.H., 280

Buffum, E. Gould, 56

Bunnell, Lafayette, 189

Burgess, John, 252

Burnett, Peter H., 74, 124, 157, 158, 174, 178, 179, 180, 181, 182, 183, 186, 187, 188, 189, 192, 193, 198, 350, 352, 353

Burney, James, 188, 189, 190

Burton, John, 62

Bush, George H.W., 9

Butte County, 318–319

Buzelle, Frank, 235, 236

Cahuilla people, 17. *See also* Antonio, Juan (leader); Chapuli (leader)

California: in 1846, 40–41; admitted to Union, 157; constitution, 123, 156; criminal justice system, 138; establishment of civilian government, 148–149, 157; Indian population, 3, 217, 268, 328, 334, 347, 348; map of, nineteenth century, 2; missions, forts, and towns, 28; non-Indian population, 74, 77–78, 217, 256, 300; political status, 123–124; Polk's desire to acquire, 42; precontact, 16–26; Russo-Hispanic Period, 1, 3, 26–41; self-government of, 123–124; US conquest of, 1, 56–59; US rule in, 50; War Debt, 218, 225, 229, 230, 238, 250, 253; War Fund, 253

California Blades, 94, 98

California Cavalry, 299, 301, 312, 313, 314, 319, 328, 330, 331

California Constitutional Convention, 149–156, 163–164

California Indians: control of movement of, 148; cremation, wood engraving of, 176; cultural and political units of, 23; death rate of, 3; depopulation of, 3, 38–39, 171, 328, 346, 347, 356 (*see also* Catastrophe, California Indian); diets, 18–23; diversity of, 23, 26; federal recognition of, 348; languages, 23, 24; legal status, 27, 29–30, 32, 34, 170, 171,

California Indians (cont.)
348; perceived as indistinguishable, 119;
population, 3, 23, 217, 268, 328, 330, 334,
347, 348; relationships with each other,
25; relationship with colonists, 50–66,
142–144; situation of in 1852, 168, 170;
survival of, 348; trade between, 18, 22,
23, 25, 43, 45, 106, 201, 209, 228; tribal
identity of, 15; tribes, 17, 24 (*see also
individual tribes*); use of term, 15;
violence against non-Indians, 12 (*see
also* Indian depredations). *See also*
Extermination, war of; Massacres,
Indian; Miners, California Indians
Californian (San Francisco), 53, 61, 62, 66,
67, 70, 74
California Star (San Francisco), 53, 65,
147, 186
California Star & Californian (San
Francisco), 74, 77
California Supreme Court, 14, 124–125,
138, 142, 182, 277. *See also* Hastings,
Serranus C.
California Volunteers, 299–303, 309, 314,
316–320, 321, 337, 350, 354–355. *See also*
"Owens Valley War"
Californios, 40, 50, 51, 54, 56, 59, 66, 72,
73, 101, 109, 145, 149, 153–154, 155, 156.
See also Spanish speakers
Cameron, Simon, 299
Campbell, Peter, 123
Canby, E.R.S., 337, 340, 341
Captain George, 313, 314
Captain Jack (leader). *See* Kintpuash
(Captain Jack)
Captain Jack's Stronghold, 337, 339, 340,
342
Carson, Kit, 42, 43, 45, 47, 48, 49–50, 116
Case, William M., 52, 56, 88–89, 90, 91
Cassin, Francis, 81
Castillo, Edward, 38
Castro, José, 57
Casus belli, 57, 236, 269

Catastrophe, California Indian: architects
of, 354; Army's role in, 14, 354–355 (*see
also* Army); bureaucracy's role in, 14;
causes of death in, 11; effects of analysis
of, 8–9; evidence of, 10–13; genocidal
characteristics of, 350–352; as genocide,
352; government complicity in, 356;
government's awareness of, 353;
government's role in, 354, 355–356;
lawmakers' role in, 14; legacies of, 348,
350; numbers killed in, 12–13, 14, 351;
precedents to, 40; public history of, 350;
scholarship on, 6–8; support for, 13, 14.
See also Extermination; Extermination,
war of; Indian killing; Massacres,
Indian
Caughey, John Walton, 3, 6, 159
Cayuse Indians, 74–75
Cayuse War, 74–75, 76
Central Mines, 13, 67, 68, 69, 71, 74, 77,
82, 92, 98, 101, 178; campaign to expel
all nonwhites from, 92–93 (*see also*
Catastrophe, California Indian).
See also Gold Rush
Century of Dishonor, A (Jackson), 357
Certificate system, 147
César, Julio, 30
Chalfant, P.A., 241
Chalk, Frank, 7, 357
Chamberlain, John, 52, 55
Chapo (leader), 133
Chapuli (leader), 203
Chase, Doris, 234
Chechee, 65
Cheyenne people, massacre of, 142
Chico Courant, 330
Chief of the Fall River Band, 243, 254,
255, 274
Children, California Indian; difficulty in
finding evidence of genocide, 175–176;
killing of, 11, 15, 40, 48, 50, 64, 86, 119,
122, 128, 130, 131, 132, 134, 180, 197, 207,
213, 219, 221, 232, 243, 244, 255, 258, 262,

265, 266, 270, 271, 273, 274, 277, 279, 280, 281, 282, 283, 284, 286, 287, 295, 296, 297, 301, 302, 309, 329, 335, 336; laws regarding 158, 286–287, 293–295, 303–304, 309, 332, 335; numbers kidnapped, 332; policies regarding, 176; and protection of by whites, 180, 209, 301, 323; removal of, 38, 52, 63, 64, 92, 161, 162, 171, 172, 175–176, 182, 240, 255, 260, 269, 285; residing in non-Indian households, 175, 209, 304, 334–335; separation of from community, 240, 255, 287, 303–304; torture of, 137. *See also* Kidnapping; Sexual assaults; Slave raiding; Slavery, Indian, Slaves, Indian; Slave trade, Indian

Chilula people, 252

Chimariko people, 295

Chinese (people), 93, 224, 225, 226

Choctaw people, 257

Chumash people, 17, 22, 35. *See also* Kitsepawit (Fernando Librado); Solares, María

Churchill, Ward, 7, 357

Citizenship, of Indians, 151, 152, 156, 162–163, 171

Civil rights, of California Indians, 145, 156. *See also* Exclusion, legal

Civil rights activism, 6

Civil War, 14, 173, 289, 330, 332; California soldiers in, 299; and transformation of killing machine, 299–300

Clapp, J.L., 258

Clark, John A., 64

Clayman, James, 71

Clayton, John, 97

Clean sweep policy, 301, 302

Clear Lake Indians: languages of, 118; plans to exterminate, 127–128. *See also* Clear Lake Wappo people; Eastern Pomo people; Lake Miwok people; Pomo people; Retaliation, for killing of Stone and Kelsey; Wappo people

Clear Lake massacres, 40, 128–133, 144, 173, 249. *See also* Bloody Island Massacre; Davidson, John W.; Lyon, Nathaniel; Retaliation, for killing of Stone and Kelsey; Smith, Persifor F.

Clear Lake Wappo people, 103, 106, 107, 112, 116, 132. *See also* Wappo

Cleary, J.W., 290

Clyman, James, 60

Coast Miwok people, 22, 120, 122, 125. *See also* Pomponio (leader)

Coast Rangers, 232, 234, 250

Coffer, William, 6

Cokadjal Massacre, 133–135, 138–139, 142, 173

Collier, John, 3, 171

Collins, Joseph B., 290, 292

Coloma, 87, 88, 89–90, 91

Colton, David D., 255

Colton, Walter, 59, 70, 71–72, 147

Columbia Gazette, 220

Commissioners of Indian Affairs, 3, 123, 161, 162, 164, 165, 168, 171, 185, 193, 209, 279, 293, 305, 324, 336, 344, 357

Congressional Medal of Honor, 140

Connor, John W., 94, 95

Conquest, defensive, 96

Conrad, Charles Magill, 142, 199

Convict leasing, 158–159, 332, 333

Cook, Sherburne, 3, 4, 6, 12, 27, 39, 54, 352

Copper City Pioneer, 325

Corbett, Martin, 305

Cordua, Theodore, 53

Coronel, Antonio, 85–86

Corporal punishment, 29–30, 32–34, 158, 159, 294

Cosby, John D., 247–250

Cosby (Crosby), Jim, 221

Costanoan people, 33. *See also* Asisara, Lorenzo

Costo, Jeannette, 3

Costo, Rupert, 3

Cothran, Boyd, 345

Courts, 6, 10, 124–125, 138, 159–160, 162, 172, 344, 345

Covelo, 258. *See also* Round Valley Reservation

Cow Creek Massacre, 241

Cox, Isaac, 263

Creek people, 174, 257

Crescent City Herald, 232, 234, 237

Crimes, against Indians: Bidwell's proposals on, 157; and exclusion from courts, 158, 159–160; lack of punishment for, 31, 64, 65, 91, 159, 160–161, 172, 182–183, 294–295; by ranchers, 107, 109–114; Supreme Court's view of, 138

Crimes, by Indians: extralegal process for, 128; punishment for, 64–65, 160

Criminal law, 5

Crittenden, John, 285, 356

Crook, George, 160–161, 256–257, 290, 333–334

Crosby (Cosby), Jim, 221

Culture, policies designed to strip Indian children of, 10, 176

Curley Headed Jack, 341

Currency, seashell, 23, 43, 45, 87, 106, 111

Cupeño people, 203. *See also* Garra, Antonio; Garra's Uprising

Curtin, Jeremiah, 325–326

Cyrus, Enoch, 117

Cyrus family ranch, 117

Daily Alta California (San Francisco), 76, 77, 225; calls for extermination, 144, 222, 298; description of Bloody Island Massacre, 129–130; on effects of Gold Rush on food supplies, 184; on extermination, 139, 201, 222; on federal funding of Indian killing, 253; on First El Dorado Expedition, 184; on "foreigners," 93; on formation of Confederacy, 290; genocidal sentiment in, 92, 333; on Indian attacks, 219; on Indian-related panic in Southern

Mines, 188; on Indian voting rights, 156; on Jarboe's rangers, 280, 298; justification of genocide by, 179; on kidnapping, 240, 304; on killing campaigns, 198; on Lyon's campaign, 127, 130, 139; on Mariposa Battalion, 194; on massacres, 284, 298; McKee's letter to, 205; on militias, 184, 195; on numbers of California Indians killed, 184, 268, 280–281; on Oregonians, 76; on plans for extermination, 127; predictions of extermination, 243, 268; propagation of myth of inevitable extinction, 186; on Round Valley killings, 266; on Second El Dorado Expedition, 195, on slave raiding, 304; on treaties, 164, 165, 201, 225; on vigilantes, 125, 127; on violence toward Indians, 84, 100, 123, 125; on war of extermination, 222

Daily Appeal (Marysville), 309

Daily Evening Bulletin (San Francisco), 252, 267, 281, 284, 298–299

Daily Evening Herald (Marysville), 221

Davidson, John W., 115, 116–120, 127, 128, 129, 130, 131, 136, 137, 138, 139, 141, 310

Davis, Jefferson (Secretary of War), 116, 230, 237–238, 240, 243, 250, 290, 356

Davis, Jefferson C. (Brevet Major General), 343, 344

Day, Hannibal, 99

Daylor, William, 71, 91, 92

De Borica, Diego, 30

Debt peonage, 29, 37, 38, 147, 159, 161, 333. *See also* Labor, unfree; Servitude, Indian

Deer Creek, 99, 178, 179, 270, 271, 331

Dehumanization, 34, 37, 40, 50, 59–66, 84, 89, 93, 148, 321. *See also* Labor, unfree

De la Guerra, Pablo, 153–154, 156

Delano, Columbus, 344, 345

Delavan, James, 88, 90

Delaware people, 43, 47, 49, 173

Deloria, Philip J., 96
De Master, Foster, 245, 246
Demonization, 61, 224
De Neve, Felipe, 27, 29, 32
Dent, Louis, 152–153
Dentalia, 23, 43, 45, 87, 106, *111*
Dillon, Edward, 266, 277
Dimmick, Kimball, 151, 152, 153, 154
Disease, 3, 8, 11, 13, 26, 38–39, 40, 75, 78,
    90, 112, 168, 212, 259, 297, 320, 345, 346,
    352, 356, 357, 359; and European
    contact, 27; at missions, 35; on reserva-
    tions, 260, 306
Dixon, Sheriff, 206, 207
Dole, William P., 293, 305, 324
Dominguez, Manuel, 155
Dosh, S.H., 264
Douglas, Charles D., 302, 306, 320
Douglas, D.F., 197
Dowling, Robert, 188
Downey, John, 279, 282, 286, 287, 288, 290,
    298, 299
Downie, William, 81
Drake, Francis, 18
Duluwat Island, 282–283, 350
Dyar, L.S., 341

Eastern Pomo people, 103, 106, 107, 109,
    112, 132. *See also* Pomo people
Eccleston, Robert, 194
Echeandía, José María de, 35
Economies, California Indian, 18, 23, 25,
    40, 50, 71, 100–101, 238, 268, 348
Economy, California, 13, 50, 51, 52, 53, 54,
    66, 68, 71, 72, 73, 117, 145, 146, 165, 192
Eden Valley region, 265, 266, 277
Eel River Rangers, 277, 279–282, 350
Eichmann, Adolf, 6
El Dorado Expedition, First, 183–184,
    189, 191
El Dorado Expedition, Second, 195, 207
Elliot, Alice, 136
Ellison, James C., 267

Elsasser, Albert, 25
Emigrants, 184; arming of, 78, 80–81; fear
    of Indians, 78; killed by Indians, 78;
    numbers of during Gold Rush, 84, 100.
    See also Forty-eighters; Forty-niners;
    Gold Rush; Newcomers; Whites
Emmons, George Falconer, 168
Enfranchisement, for Indians, 150–156,
    157, 158, 164
Environment, management of, 18, 20, 23,
    309
Esmeralda Star, 313
Esselen people, 32
Estanislao, 35
Estill, James, 200–201
Etchulet Massacre, 232, 234, 250
Ethnohistory, 175
Evans, George S., 312, 313
Ewing, Thomas, 81
Exclusion, legal, 146, 156, 159–160, 172,
    344; *vs.* assimilation, 149; and debate
    over voting rights, 149–156. *See also*
    Courts
Execution, 203; as genocidal, 11–12; of
    prisoners, 90, 133, 160, 203, 204, 209,
    210, 224, 252, 270, 301, 305, 307, 314–315,
    318, 323, 324, 345, 346
Execution, extrajudicial, 84, 89, 90,
    96–97, 99, 242
Extermination: advocation of, 247;
    architects of, 354; calls for, 221, 222, 236,
    238, 240, 263, 264, 270, 275, 280, 305,
    307–308, 309, 330; as Crook's objective,
    334; *Daily Alta California* on, 100, 139,
    144, 179; as description of First El
    Dorado Expedition, 183; expectations
    of, 285; as goal in Owens Valley War,
    312, 314; justification of, 91, 185, 243;
    orders for, 127, 130, 139, 296, 337,
    341–342; perceived inevitability of, 144,
    212, 186, 243, 353; politicians on, 212,
    353; politicians' support for, 212;
    predictions of, 212, 242–243, 262, 321,

Extermination (cont.)
324; and Sherman, 337, 341–342; support for, 3, 13, 65–66, 144, 216, 221–222, 224, 243, 280, 281, 288, 298; threats of, 192–193; as topic of public discussion, 139, 243; treaties framed as alternative to, 164, 186, 201, 213; warnings of, 92, 167, 179, 192, 204, 218, 220, 222, 232–235, 244, 246, 252, 262–263, 267, 268, 277, 281, 295–298, 325. *See also* Catastrophe, California Indian; Indian killing

Extermination, war of, 40, 86, 88, 144, 164, 179, 183, 186, 187, 204, 205, 218, 219, 221, 222, 232, 234, 235, 238, 243, 244, 247, 252, 262, 263, 267, 275, 277, 280, 281, 288, 353

Extinction, inevitable, 144, 185–186, 212, 219, 243

Extraordinary Chambers in the Courts of Cambodia, 6

Fages, Pedro, 31
Fanning, William, 202
Faragher, John, 7
Farms, Indian labor on, 37, 51, 50, 52–53, 54
Farnham, Thomas J., 52, 185
Feather Dance, 222, 231
Fein, Helen, 7
Ferrymen, 54, 180
Figueroa, José, 35, 36
Fillmore, Millard, 142, 168, 170, 199, 200
1st Dragoons, 115–120, 127, 128, 129, 131, 136
First California Guards, 174
Fish, 22–23
Fitzgerald, Edward H., 181, 203, 215
Fitzgerald, George B., 203
Fitzgerald's Volunteers, 203
Flint, Franklin F., 270, 277
Floggings, at missions, 30, 32, 33
Flynn, Henry, 316
Food supplies/sources: destruction of, 95, 96, 188, 194, 218–219, 243, 310, 311, 313, 328; effects of Gold Rush on, 70–71, 95, 100, 184; effects of immigration on, 217;

and Indian policies, 227–228. *See also* Starvation

Ford, Henry L., 258
"Foreigners," 93
Fort Humboldt, 264, 267, 290, 300, 302, 318, 321, 323, 324
Fort Independence, 313, 314, 329
Fort Reading, 207, 225
Fort Ross Colony, 36–37, 39
Forts, 3, 13, 27, 29, 31, 57, 78, 142, 233, 242, 246, 269, 270, 272, 288, 291, 299, 303, 321, 322, 328, 331, 337, 342. *See also* Captain Jack's Stronghold; Fort Humboldt; Fort Independence; Fort Reading; Fort Ross Colony; Fort Seward; Fort Tejon
Fort Seward, 303, 304, 307, 316
Fort Tejon, 315–316, 328–329
Forty-eighters, 67–68, 70–72, 74. *See also* Gold Rush
Forty-niners, 77–78, 80–82. *See also* Gold Rush
Foster, Stephen, 151
Fowler, Henry, 121–122
Freedom, of California Indians, 148. *See also* Movement, freedom of
Free Labor ideology, 91
Freeman, Andrew, 258
Frémont, John C., 42, 43, 45, 46, 47, 48, 49, 51, 52, 53, 56, 57, 58, 59, 62, 158, 163, 355; charged with mutiny, 62; in conquest of California, 59; expedition of, 45–50; march to California, 42–43; movements of, 44; plan to conquer California, 57; Sacramento River Massacre, 45–48; use of California Indians in Army, 57–59
Freshwater ecosystems, 22
Fresno Reservation, 194, 245, 258, 297
Frisbie, John B., 127, 129–130, 131, 139

Galbraith, John Kenneth, 184
Game animals, 18, 19–20

Garner, Van H., 6

Garra, Antonio, 202, 203

Garra's Uprising, 202–204

Garrett, Gary, 280

Gathering, 20–22

Geiger, Maynard, 3

Geiger, V.E., 272, 293

Genocide: acts of, 13, 182, 240, 255, 260, 261, 287, 293, 297, 303, 350–352; American awareness of concept, 6; California Indian catastrophe as, 350–352 (*see also* Catastrophe, California Indian); and collective mindset, 61; concept of, 4–7; as concept to evaluate past with, 5; debate over definition of, 356–358; definitions of, 4–6, 8; difficulty in finding evidence of, 10, 175–176; intensification of, 245; intent in, 5; introduction of term, 357; justification of, 179, 330; legacy of, 348, 350; motive in, 5, 178, 183; perpetrators of, 356; written plan for, 352–353. *See also* Extermination; Extermination, war of; Intent, genocidal

Genocide, cultural, 11

Genocide, legally sanctioned, 173

Genocide, local, 68, 74, 86, 92

Genocide, of American Indians: debate over, 356–359

Genocide, of California Indians. *See* Catastrophe, California Indian; Extermination; Extermination, war of; Indian killing; Massacres, Indian; War of extermination

Genocide Convention. *See* United Nations Convention on the Prevention and Punishment of the Crime of Genocide

Genocide studies, 7

George (leader), 313, 314

George, S.G., 245

Gerstäcker, Friedrich, 71, 80

Gibbes, C.D., 187, 192

Gibbs, George, 131, 133

Gihon, Thomas, 97–98

Gila Expedition, 180–181, 191

Gillem, Alvan, 341, 342, 343

Gillespie, Archibald H., 48

Gold Rush, 13, 66, 69; announcement of, 67; arming of emigrants, 78, 80–81; beginning of, 67; and campaign to expel all nonwhites from the Central Mines, 92–93; and changes in relationships between Indians and whites, 101; and desire to eliminate Indian miners, 192; effects of on food supplies, 70–71, 95, 100, 101, 184; labor demand during, 70; labor done by California Indians during, 68, 70, 71, 73; and labor vacuum, 71–73; local genocide during, 68, 74, 86, 87, 92; number of immigrants during, 100; numbers of California Indians killed during, 100; organized attacks on Indians during, 93–96; and population of non-Indians, 77–78; revenues from, 184, 212–213; spread of exterminatory violence during, 96; systematic Indian killing during, 82–100; war of extermination during, 88. *See also* Central Mines; Miners, California Indian; Miners, Chinese; Miners, South American; Northern Mines; Oregonians; Southern Mines

Good, Harmon, 270, 308, 309, 310, 330, 331, 334

Goodrich, Chauncey Shafter, 168, 227

Government, US: acquiescence in extermination, 299; arming of militias, 200, 225; awareness of catastrophe, 353; failure to intervene in forced servitude, 240, 352; failure to provide supplies, 313; funding of army against Indians, 317, 345, 355; funding of militias, 175, 230, 250–252, 253, 284, 285, 289, 290, 299, 320–321, 345, 355; land bounties,

Government, US (cont.)
237–238; policies against California
Indians, 211–213, 260; refusal to grant
reservations, 211–212, 310; rejection of
treaties, 170, 172, 194, 201, 211, 315, 316,
355; role in California Indian catastro-
phe, 355–356; support for extermination,
295, 300; support for Indian killing, 293.
See also Senate, US
Graham, Julian, 124, 138
Graham, William, 184–185
Grain, 50, 53, 54, 145
Grant, Ulysses S., 334, 342, 344, 345
Grass Valley Telegraph, 240
Greeley, Horace, 185
Green, Alfred A., 76
Green, Thomas J., 178, 179, 181, 254
Greenwood, Alfred B., 279
Grimshaw, William Robinson, 70, 77, 91
Grouse Creek Massacre, 262
Guano Valley Massacre, 331
Guest, Francis, 3
Guides, 54, 58: execution of, 129, 235; for
Lovell's campaign, 290, 292, 293
Guilt, assumption of, 128; collective-guilt
argument, 119; "guilty tribe," 119, 120;
for killing of Stone and Kelsey, 133
Guns, Indians denied access to, 227–228
Gunther, Robert, 283
Gwin, William, 152, 158, 163, 200, 212–213,
230, 285

Hackel, Steven, 26, 30, 35
Hagen, William T., 7
Hale, Augustin, 96, 182
Hall, H.L., 255
Halleck, Henry W., 147–148, 153, 154
Hallowney (leader), 38, 40
Hanrahan, Virginia, 132
Hanson, George, 294–295, 296, 297, 298,
305, 316
Haraszthy, Agoston, 203
Hardcastle, A.B., 267–268

Hargrave, William, 122
Harper's, 297
Harte, Bret, 282, 284
Harvey, B.F., 198
Hastings, Lansford W., 151, 152
Hastings, Serranus C., 277, 348, 350
Hastings College of Law, 348
Hat Creek region, 272, 276
Heads, Indian, 86, 197, 198, 204, 223, 274,
286, 345
Heintzelman, Samuel P., 203
Heizer, Robert F., 6, 7, 12, 25
Henley, Thomas J., 125, 162, 240, 258, 260,
266, 285
Herman, James, 36
Hilberg, Raul, 6
Hildreth, Bob, 332
Hine, Robert, 7
History and Sociology of Genocide, The
(Chalk and Jonassohn), 7
Hitchcock, Ethan A., 206, 213, 215
Hittell, Theodore, 252
Holocaust, 6, 7, 10, 352, 356
Holocaust and Genocide Studies
(journal), 7
Homar, Chooksa, 268–269
Homicides, 11, 13
Hoopa Valley Reservation, 323–324
Hoppe, Jacob D., 152, 154
Horse Canyon Massacre, 296–297, 305
Horsley & Barrow's Express, 242
Hubbard, Charles, 302
Human agency, in annihilation of
Indians, 185
Human Flesh Ranch, 121–122
Humboldt Bay massacres, 282–284
Humboldt Cavalry, 282, 286
Humboldt Home Guards Expedition,
298–299
Humboldt Journal, 330
Humboldt Times, 235, 240, 241, 283, 318;
call for forced removal, 263; calls for
extermination or removal, 263, 264,

283–284, 317; on Collins's campaign, 292; encouragement of vigilantes, 240, 262; on killing by California Volunteers, 302; reports on Indian killing, 241, 262, 264, 283; on reservation conditions, 261, 306; on unfree labor regime, 293

"Humbug War," 241–242

Hunger, 27, 31, 32, 96, 205, 212, 218, 237, 244, 252, 258, 260, 297. *See also* Malnutrition; Starvation

Hunkpapa people, massacre of, 132

Hunting, 19, 23, 43, 51, 71, 95, 100, 110, 116, 227, 265, 331

Hupa people, 22, 181, 234, 323. *See also* Norton, Jack

Hurtado, Albert, 7, 38, 54, 91, 154, 358

Hyer, Joel, 7

Immigrants. *See* Emigrants; Newcomers; Whites

Incarceration, federal, 11, 257, 345

Incarceration, lethal, 8, 12, 13, 257, 345. *See also* Reservations

Indenture, 146, 286, 287, 293, 304, 332, 352. *See also* Servitude, Indian

Indian Affairs Office, 164, 213, 260, 305

Indian Affairs superintendents, 161, 216, 217, 306, 330, 336. *See also* Beale, Edward F.; Hanson, George; Henley, Thomas J.; McDuffie, James Y.; Wiley, Austin

Indian Baby Hunters, 303

Indian Civil Rights Acts (1968), 10

Indian depredations: collective reprisals for, 12, 181; encouragement of retaliation for, 188; motivations of Indians in, 96, 218–219, 243, 244, 252, 298, 328; retaliation for, 12, 61–62, 64–65, 84, 96, 98, 105, 184–185, 217, 218–219, 243, 244, 245, 252, 253, 262 (*see also* Vigilantes). *See also* Theft

Indian killing: by Army, 45–50, 57, 61–62, 116–118, 129–139, 203, 227, 237, 245–246,

249, 256–257, 268, 269–270, 286, 290, 292–293, 302, 307, 312–318, 321–324, 330, 331–334, 342, 343, 345; decline in, 334–335; decreased support for, 330; as defensive conquest, 96; for entertainment, 97, 244; federal support for, 230, 250–252, 253, 293, 317, 320–321, 345, 355; financial advantages of, 183–184, 195, 197–198; genocidal intent in, 100, 178, 179, 183, 197, 207; government culpability in, 266; Indian participation in, 296–297; institutionalization of, 195, 197, 207; killing of "domesticated" Indians, 325; lack of consequences for, 138–139, 182–183, 198, 226; local fundraising for, 270, 295, 308; militias' focus on, 216–217; motivations in, 127, 219; pretexts for, 96, 98, 116, 235, 241, 257, 263, 296; rationales for, 119; on reservations, 209, 296, 305, 318; state endorsement of, 175, 179, 181, 182, 186, 189, 317, 354 (*see also* Militias); state sponsorship of, end of, 344. *See also* Catastrophe, California Indian; Extermination, war of; Killing, pedagogic; Massacres, Indian; Militias; Vigilantes; *individual tribes; specific locations*

Indian policies, 149; Act for the Government and Protection of Indians, 158–159; of Army, 290, 300–301; Bidwell's bill on, 157–158; denial of access to arms, 227–228; federal, 211–213, 260; federal protest of, 161–162; institutionalization of, 192; Mexican, 1, 26, 37, 147, 151; regarding children, 176. *See also* Courts; Exclusion, legal; Voting rights, for Indians

Indians: Anglo-American attitudes toward, 119; debate over genocide of, 356–359; fear of, 77–81, 221; myth of inevitable extinction of, 185–186; perceptions of, 78, 90

Institutions, names of, 350
Intent, genocidal, 4, 5, 11, 12, 13, 63, 96, 100, 178, 179, 183, 197, 207, 235, 236, 302, 350–353, 358, 359; articulation of, 352–353
International Criminal Court, 6
International Criminal Tribunal for the Former Yugoslavia, 6
International Criminal Tribunal for Rwanda, 6, 253
Ipai people, 26, 31, 34

Jackson, Andrew, 185
Jackson, Helen Hunt, 357
Jackson, James, 336
Japanese Americans, 9
Jarboe, Walter S., 277, 279–282, 284, 285, 348
Joaquin Jim, 311, 312
Johnson, D.C., 226
Johnson, Edward, 260, 276–277, 279, 280, 305
Johnson, J. Neely, 190, 192, 193, 245, 247, 253
Johnson, Theodore T., 86–87, 88, 89, 90
Johnston, Adam, 193
Johnston, Albert Sidney, 290
Jonassohn, Kurt, 7, 357
Joseph, William, 51–52
Judah, Henry M., 225, 235, 236, 237, 249
Justice, vigilante, 176
Justice of the Peace for Indians, 157
J.W.B., 122, 123, 124

Kane, Michael, 81
Karuk people, 19, 181, 182, 197, 205, 234–235, 237, 244
Katz, Steven, 357
Kawaiisu people, 17
Kearney, Stephen, 62
Kelly, John, 124, 138
Kelsey, Andrew, 103, 106, 107, 109, 110, 111, 112, 113, 114, 115, 116, 117. *See also* Big

Valley Ranch; Retaliation, for killing of Stone and Kelsey
Kelsey, Benjamin, 107, 112, 123, 124, 125, 126, 138
Kelsey, Samuel, 123, 124, 125, 138
Kenny, Robert W., 212
Kern, Edward M., 57, 62
Kershaw, W.T., 202, 214
Ketchum, Thomas, 302, 303, 304
Kibbe, William C., 225, 232, 238, 239, 240, 264, 265, 270, 271–272, 274–276, 280, 281
Kidnapping, 26, 64, 96, 109, 161, 162, 171, 172, 182, 240, 287, 293–295, 303, 332. *See also* Slave raiding
Kiernan, Ben, 357, 358
Killing, categories of, 11–12. *See also* Battles; Execution; Homicides; Massacres, Indian
Killing, exterminatory. *See* Violence, exterminatory
Killing, of Indians. *See* Indian killing
Killing, pedagogic, 48, 95, 128, 137, 180, 181, 216
Killing campaigns. *See* Indian killing
King, T. Butler, 97
Kintpuash (Captain Jack), 337, 339, 340, 341, 342, 343, 345
Kitsepawit (Fernando Librado), 31, 35
Klamath and Humboldt Expedition, 234–237, 254
Klamath and Humboldt Expedition, Second, 263–265
Klamath Expedition, 245, 253
Klamath Mounted Rangers, 232, 234, 250
Klamath people, 49–50, 221, 222, 247, 328
Klamath Reservation (California), 237, 261, 298
Klamath Reservation (Oregon), 336
Klamath Rifles, 237
"Klamath War," 234–237
Knapp, Augustus W., 207
Knight, Thomas, 110, 112, 123

Konkow Maidu Trail of Tears, 318, 319–320, 350, 351

Konkow people, 20, 70, 204, 257, 259, 270, 271, 296, 306, 319; Chino village, 63. *See also* Bauer, William, Jr.; Clark, John A.

Konnock, 86

Kra-nas, 105, 114, 115

Kroeber, Theodora, 6, 258

Kuper, Leo, 50

Kuykendall, John, 190, 194

Labor, Indian: Bidwell's proposals on, 157–158; in Californian economy, 51–54, 73, 146; certificate system, 147; control of, 146–148; crimes against, 107, 109–114, 260–261, 332; as de facto slavery, 107, 109, 110, 147; demand for in Gold Rush, 70; dependence on, 13, 72, 73, 117, 145, 165; as disposable, 109, 110, 112, 260; Free Labor ideology, 91; at missions, 27; pass system, 65, 147–148; on ranches/farms, 51–52, 53–54. *See also* Labor, unfree; Servitude; Slavery, Indian; Slaves, Indian

Labor, unfree: before 1846, 52; acquisition of, 107; in Act for the Government and Protection of Indians, 158–159; California laws enabling, 158–161, 286–287, 304; decline in, 332–333; demand for, 217, 240; expansion of, 161, 286–287, 293; extermination considered means of eliminating, 91; federal protest of policies of, 161–162; under Mexican rule, 37–38, 40, 51–52; Montgomery's proclamation on, 146–147; resistance to, 32, 33, 107, 304, 332; under Russians, 36–37, 40; under Spanish, 27, 29. *See also* Convict leasing; Debt peonage; Dehumanization; Servitude, Indian; Slavery, Indian; Slaves, Indian; Slave trade, Indian

Lacock, Dryden, 253

Lake Miwok people, 20

La Motte, H.D., 96–97

Land: control of, 348; Indian land, 349; and opposition to treaties, 165–168; in reservations, 170; transfer of to non-Indians, 163 (*see also* Reservations; Treaties); in treaties, 164–165 (*see also* Reservations; Treaties)

Land bounties, 237–238

Land rights, of California Indians, 157, 162, 163–164, 166, 170, 171, 323, 355. *See also* Reservations; Treaties

Landt, Henry, 274

Language: of California Indians, 18, 23, 24; of Clear Lake Indians, 118; government suppression of, 10; policies designed to strip Indian children of, 176; of Pomo, 106; of Wappo, 106

Larkin, Thomas O., 71

Lassen, Peter, 43

Lassik (leader), 307

Lassik people, 307. *See also* Young, Lucy

Latham, Milton, 285, 289

Lawson, John, 252

Lea, Luke, 165, 168

Legal system, 344; under Spanish, Russian, and Mexican rule, 26. *See also* Courts; Exclusion, legal

Legislators, California: acquiescence in extermination, 204, 205–206; as architects of annihilation, 354; denial of Indian access to arms, 227–228; endorsement of Wright's campaign, 216; opposition to funding of militia expeditions, 284–285; role in California Indian catastrophe, 14; support for militias, 190, 207, 238, 244, 253, 285 (*see also* Militias, funding of). *See also* California Supreme Court

Leidesdorff, William A., 53

Lemkin, Raphaël, 4, 5, 357

Letts, John, 83

Lewis, H.S., 215

Lewis, James, 124, 138

Lewis, Jane, 87
Lewis, Tom, 85
Lewy, Guenter, 358
Librado, Fernando (Kitsepawit), 31, 35
Lienhard, Heinrich, 52, 54, 55, 56,
    83–84, 86
Lippitt, Francis J., 299, 300–301, 302,
    303, 318
Liquor, 159, 161
Lockhart, Harry, 254
Lockhart, Samuel, 254, 255
Longley, John, 272
Lopez, Sam, 223
Lord, Israel, 97
Lord, J.A., 283
Los Angeles Expedition, 203, 204
Los Angeles Star, 165, 202, 281
Lost River Massacre (1852), 215–216, 337,
    341
Loughery, Ardavan S., 164
Lount, George, 272–273
Lovell, Charles S., 290, 292–293, 298
Luckett, J.A., 206
Luiseño people, 19; eagle dancers, 17.
    See also César, Julio; Tac, Pablo
Lusk, G.C., 219
Lutario (leader), 179
Lutman, Henry, 220
Lyman, Chester, 92
Lyon, Nathaniel, 128, 129–142, 143,
    355

Macklay, James, 198
Mad River Basin, 262, 264, 267–268, 301,
    322
Maidu people, 60, 63, 73, 95, 166, 204,
    208, 257, 271, 272, 276, 319; man with
    arrows, 196
Maklaks. *See* Modoc people
Malaria, 38, 112, 319, 352
Ma-Laxa-Que-Tu, 105, 114
Malnutrition, 258, 259, 260, 352. *See also*
    Hunger

Manifest destiny, 42
Manypenny, George, 209, 357
Mariposa Battalion, 189, 190, 191, 192, 193,
    194
Marshall, James, 67, 89
Marshall, John (rancher), 197
Marshall, John (Supreme Court Justice),
    171
Martial law, 1, 61, 146–149, 354
Martin, James P., 292–293
Martin, Thomas S., 43, 45, 46, 47, 48
Marysville Appeal, 294
Marysville Herald, 204, 243
Mason, R.B., 62, 68, 70, 71, 116
Massacre, defined, 11
Massacre, genocidal, 50
Massacres, Indian, 140; acceptability of,
    140; by Army, 129, 315 (*see also* Army,
    US); Battery Point Massacre, 220, 223;
    Bloody Island Massacre, 127–133,
    139–140, 350; Bloody Point Massacre,
    213–214; Bridge Gulch Massacre,
    206–207; celebration of, 140; at Clear
    Lake, 40, 144, 173, 249; Cokadjal
    Massacre, 133–135, 138–139, 173; condon-
    ing of, 142; Cow Creek Massacre, 241;
    descriptions of, 325–326; difficulty in
    finding evidence of, 175–176, 209–210;
    disguised as battles, 12, 255, 329; by Eel
    River Rangers, 277; Etchulet Massacre,
    232; expansion of state sponsorship of,
    180; eyewitnesses to, 47, 129, 137,
    175–176, 210, 215–216, 223, 274, 282–283,
    312, 315; by forty-niners, 86; framing of,
    176; Grouse Creek Massacre, 262;
    Guano Valley Massacre, 331; Horse
    Canyon Massacre, 296–297, 305;
    Humboldt Bay massacres, 282–284;
    Indian oral histories of, 134, 207,
    209–210, 223–224, 243, 274, 307, 337;
    inspired by militias, 179; justification of,
    140; lack of punishment for, 138–139;
    Lost River Massacre (1852), 215–216, 337,

341; McKee's reports on, 204–205; under Mexican rule, 39–40; by militias, 173–174 (*see also* Militias); Mystic Massacre, 132, 140, 173; Needle Rock Massacre, 210; Oak Run Massacre, 326; by Oregonians, 76–77, 88–90, 93; Owens Lake Massacre (1865), 329; pedagogic aims of, 95 (*see also* Killing, pedagogic); pretexts for, 96, 116, 241, 244, 257, 296; Rolf's Ranch, 272–274, 285; Sacramento River Massacre, 45–48, 51; in Southern California, 202; survivors of, 209–210, 255; tactics of, 46–47, 50, 93, 95, 140; Tuluwat Massacre, 282–283, 284, 350; Upper Station Massacre, 305; by vigilantes (*see* Vigilantes); Whitman Massacre, 74–76; Yontocket Massacre, 222–224, 350. *See also* Catastrophe, California Indian; Extermination; Indian killing; Retaliation, for killing of Stone and Kelsey; Vigilantes; *individual tribes*

Massey, Ernest de, 78, 97, 181
Mass violence, preemptive, 46, 50, 222
Matteo (leader), 258
Mattole people, 181, 282, 287, 288, 302, 321, 323, 324
Mattole Valley killings, 240, 262–263, 302, 303
Mayacama, 116
McCarver, M.M., 152, 154
McCoon, Perry, 56
McCorkle, Joseph, 168
McDermitt, Charles, 213, 215, 216
McDougal, John, 186, 189, 190, 193, 194, 195, 199, 200, 203, 217
McDowell, Irvin, 324
McDuffie, James Y., 279
McGuire Ranch, 329
McHenry, James, 305, 306
McIlhany, Edward, 70, 82
McKanna, Clare, 160

McKee, Redick, 164, 165, 168, 185, 186, 193, 204, 205, 206. *See also* Treaty commissioners
McKibbin, Grace, 207
McLaughlin, Moses A., 314–315
McLearry, R.W., 290
M'Collum, William, 78, 80, 81, 90, 93
McWilliams, Carey, 3
Meacham, Alfred, 336, 341
Measles, 75, 306
Mellen, Henry B., 328
Mendocino Expedition, 276–280, 281, 284, 285
Mendocino Herald, 296, 307
Mendocino Reservation, 257, 258, 259, 265, 276, 297
Menefee, C.A., 122–123, 131
Mercado, Jesús, 40
Merriam, C. Hart, 132, 268, 334
Mervine, William, 1
Messic, I.G., 264
Metlar, George, 252
Mexican-American War, 51, 59; Indian soldiers in, 59, 75; Treaty of Guadalupe Hidalgo, 151, 152, 153, 154
Mexican Constitution, 151
Mexico: battles/massacres under rule of, 39–40; emancipation of mission Indians by, 35; independence from Spain, 35; policies/practices toward California Indians, 1, 26, 156, 158; unfree labor under rule of, 37–38
Meyer, Carl, 197
Middleton, Thomas, 324
Militias, 14; arming of, 175, 199, 200, 225, 232, 245; Army support for, 181, 237, 246, 272; Coast Rangers, 232, 234, 250; cost of campaigns, 354; decreased support for, 285–286, 287; Eel River Rangers, 277, 279–281, 350; El Dorado Expedition, First, 183–184, 189, 191; El Dorado Expedition, Second, 195; expectations of federal funding for, 189,

Militias (cont.)
199, 207, 253; federal funding of, 250–252, 253, 284, 289, 320–321; federal incentives for, 238; federal support for, 285; financial advantages of, 183–184, 191, 195; Fitzgerald's Volunteers, 203; focus on Indian killing, 216–217; funding of, 189, 190, 191–192, 207, 218, 230, 238, 244, 253–254, 281–282, 284; Gila Expedition, 180–181, 191; Green's campaign, 178–180, 254; Humboldt Home Guards Expedition, 298–299; justification of expeditions by, 189; Klamath and Humboldt Expedition, 234–237, 254; Klamath and Humboldt Expedition, Second, 263–265; Klamath Expedition, 245, 253; Klamath Mounted Rangers, 232, 234, 250; Klamath Rifles, 237; lack of consequences for, 279; lack of restraints on, 279; and land bounties, 237–238; Los Angeles Expedition, 203, 204; manuals for, 238, 244; Mariposa Battalion, 189–190, 191, 192, 193, 194; Mendocino Expedition, 276–280, 281, 284, 285; militia acts, 174, 238, 244, 253; Modoc Expedition, 247–250; Monterey Expedition, 195–196; Mounted Volunteers of Siskiyou County Expedition, 255; numbers of California Indians killed by, 175, 354; opposition to funding of, 284–285; pay for, 189, 190–191, 193–194; from Oregon, 75–76, 337, 344; Pit River Expedition, 271–276, 280, 281, 284; professionalization of, 238, 240, 244; rangers, 175; response to Garra Uprising, 203–204; San Bernardino Expedition, 254; Senate's support for, 289; Shasta Expedition, 226; Siskiyou Expedition (1855), 241–242, 253; Siskiyou Volunteer Rangers Expedition, 213–217; social militias, 174–175; suppliers of, 181, 183, 184, 191, 192; Trinity, Klamath, and

Clear Lake Expedition, 200–201; Tulare Expedition, 245–246, 254; Tulare Mounted Riflemen, 245; US dependence on, 173; Utah Expedition, 194; voluntary *vs.* compulsory, 174; Yosemite campaign, 194. *See also* Indian killing; Massacres, Indian; Villages, destruction of

Militia tax, 238, 244

Miners, California Indian, 68, 70–71, 72, 90–91, 92, 112, 192

Miners, Chinese, 93

Miners, South American, 93

Miners, white, 82. *See also* Forty-eighters; Forty-niners; Gold Rush; Newcomers

Miniconjou people, massacre of, 132

Minors, Indian, 158, 286–287. *See also* Children, California Indian

Missionaries, 3, 26, 27, 29, 33

Missions, 3, 26–36, 28; La Purisima, 35; San Buenaventura, 31; San Carlos, 32; San Diego, 34; San Fernando, 34; San Francisco, 32; San Gabriel, 27, 31; San Jose, 25, 35; San Juan Bautista, 35; San Luis Obispo, 34; San Luis Rey, 30, 35, 39; San Miguel, 54; Santa Barbara, 35; Santa Cruz, 27, 30, 35; Santa Ines, 35

Missroon, J.S., 58

Miwok people, 20, 22, 36, 39, 40, 57, 60, 64–65, 68, 70–71, 76, 82, 93, 95, 120, 123, 125, 180, 185, 190, 192, 218, 286, 345; Head-man, portrait of, 94

Modoc Expedition, 247–250

Modoc people, 22, 137–138, 201–202, 213–217, 220–221; 247, 249–250, 262, 333, 334; attacks on whites, 213, 215; final attempt at extermination of, 336–345; massacres of, 213–214, 215–216, 249–250; pattern of attacks on, 221; population decline, 328; prisoners, 346; resistance by, 216, 247; Riddle, 221; treaty signed by, 328

Modoc War, 336–345, 338, 340, 343, 346
Mojave people, 34, 268–270, 286.
    See also Jim, Joaquin
Mojave War, 268–270
Monterey, labor regime in, 147
Monterey Expedition, 195–196
Montgomery, John B., 146, 147
Morehead, J.C., 180–181
Motive, in genocide, 5, 178, 183
Mott, Lucretia, 344, 345
Mountaineer Battalion, 317–318, 321, 322, 323, 330
Mounted Volunteers of Siskiyou County Expedition, 255
Movement, freedom of, 148, 157, 354
Movement, of California Indians, 148
Munro-Fraser, J.P., 242
Murders, 13; inspired by militias, 179; lack of punishment for, 138–139, 160–161.
    See also Indian killing
Mystic Massacre, 132, 140, 173
Myth of inevitable extinction, 185–186, 243

Naglee, Henry, 64
Napa Valley, 110, 116, 117, 120, 121, 122, 124, 125
Narragansett people, 173
Nash (witness), 116–117
Nazis, 3, 4, 352, 356
Needle Rock Massacre, 210
Neglect, 7, 112, 260, 297, 303, 306, 307, 320, 345, 346, 352
Negotiation: Achumawi attempts at, 274; Lyon's rejection of, 128–129; Mattole attempts at, 262; Modoc attempts at, 215; in Modoc War, 341; Nisenan attempts at, 179, 195; orders against, 120; Owens Valley Paiute-Shoshone attempts at, 314; Pomo attempts at, 129; Tolowa attempts at, 234
Nevada (state), 151, 300
Nevada Journal, 243

Newcomers, 8; perceptions of Indians, 56, 78; population of, 54, 74, 77–78, 102, 217, 256, 300; relations with Indians, 10, 12, 15, 26, 73, 74, 83, 100, 102, 107, 198–199, 212, 328, 346, 356. *See also* Emigrants; Forty-eighters; Forty-niners; Whites
Newspapers: on California Indian catastrophe, 3; calls for extermination, 221, 222, 224, 240, 264, 270, 275, 296, 305, 307–308, 309, 330; condoning of massacres, 142; coverage of vigilante violence, 92, 138; criticism of massacres, 284; downplaying of massacres, 139–140; encouragement of vigilantes, 224; on humanity of Indians, 61; portrayals of Indians, 78; predictions of extermination, 144, 219, 242–243, 262–263, 267, 268; propagation of myth of inevitable extinction, 185, 186, 243; reports of extermination, 100, 130, 232, 234, 235, 252, 267, 275, 281, 295, 325; reports on massacres, 277, 297 (*see also* Massacres, Indian); support for extermination, 65–66, 221, 222, 224, 243; on treaties, 164–165, 194, 201, 225; warnings of extermination, 164, 179, 186, 204, 218, 220, 242–243, 244, 252, 281, 321. *See also individual newspapers*
New York Herald, 78, 140
New York Times, 213, 276
Nisenan people, 19, 57, 178, 179, 183; attacks on during Gold Rush, 98–99; in early Gold Rush, 67, 73; effects of Gold Rush on food supplies, 70–71; expeditions against, 85–86, 195; exterminatory violence against, 89; food sent by whites to, 90; genocidal campaigns against, 97; Green's campaign against, 178–179; killing of by forty-niners, 84–86; man with arrows, 196; massacres of, 85–86, 92, 98–99, 179, 183, 185, 195, 220; survivors, white attempts to help, 90;

Nisenan people (cont.)
  territory, 68; violence against, 77, 82,
  84, 86, 87–90, 91, 93–94, 98–99, 181,
  183, 195. *See also* Joseph, William;
  Lewis, Jane; Lewis, Tom; Weimah
  (leader)
Nome Cult Walk, 350, 351. *See also*
  Konkow Maidu Trail of Tears
Nome Lackee Reservation, 257, 271, 293,
  298, 306
Nomlaki people, 39, 95, 197. *See also*
  Freeman, Andrew
Nongatl people, 244, 252, 262, 263,
  264, 267, 268, 286, 287, 290, 292, 316,
  334
Non-Indians. *See* Californios; Whites
Nor-rel-muk Wintu people, 206–207
Northern Mines, 68, 69, 81, 97, 181,
  196–198, 206
Northern Paiute people, 17, 138, 262,
  331–332, 334
Norton, Jack, 6
Norvell, Frank, 335
Numtarimon (leader), 220
Nye, Michael C., 54

Oak Run Massacre, 326
Office of Indian Affairs, 164, 213, 305
Ohlone people, 22
Oklahoma, 257, 345, 348
Olney, James M., 302
Oral histories, 10, 11, 36, 133, 176, 179,
  209–210, 224
Oregon, 48, 170, 201, 209, 216, 345; attack
  on Whitmans, 74–75; Cayuse War, 76;
  Rogue River War, 221–224
Oregonians, 13, 74, 100, 101; attacks on
  California Indians, 76–77, 82–83, 84,
  86, 87–90, 91, 92, 93, 97; desire for
  revenge, 76; during Gold Rush, 74;
  hostility toward Indians, 74–76; rape by,
  87; retaliation for Whitman Massacre,
  75–76

Oroville Guards, 319
Ortega, José Francisco, 31
Ousley, George W., 302
Owens Lake Massacre (1865), 329
Owens Valley, 310, 316
Owens Valley Paiute-Shoshone people, 41,
  309, 311, 312, 313, 314, 328–329. *See also*
  "Owens Valley War"
"Owens Valley War": First, 309–316;
  Second, 328–329

Pacheco, Jose (leader), 314–315
Paiute people, 333, 334, 343
Palmer, L.L., 107, 109, 110, 131, 132
Pass system, 65, 147–148
Paternalism, 38
Patwin people, 19, 57
Pence, Manoah, 224
Pence's Ranch, 319
Pequot people, massacre of, 132, 140, 173
Perkins, William, 96
Pérouse, Jean François de la, 33
Perry, J.A., 83
Petaluma Argus, 281
Peters, J.M., 223
Pico, Andrés, 59
Pictorial Union (Sacramento), 224–225
Pierce, Winslow S., 230
Pit River Expedition, 271–276, 280, 281,
  284
Pit River Rangers, 272–274, 281
Pit River region, 204, 208, 248, 249, 250,
  254–255, 256, 272, 276, 281, 309, 327
Place names, 348, 350
Placer Times (Sacramento), 81, 92, 93, 179,
  183–184
Plumas Argus, 275
Poindexter, Captain, 245
Poison, 75, 254–255, 440
Polk, James K., 42, 77
Pomo people, 23, 36, 38, 39, 40, 41,
  128–133; photographs of, 105, 108, 111,
  113; territory of, 106; vigilante violence

against, 120–127. *See also* Alcantara, Salome; Benson, William Ralganal (leader); Big Valley Ranch; Cokadjal Massacre; Elliot, Alice; Kelsey, Andrew; Retaliation, for killing of Stone and Kelsey; Shuk (Chief Augustine); Stone, Charles; Yokaya people

Pomponio (leader), 34–35

Pond, Ananias, 81, 83

Portilla, Pablo de la, 35

Powers, Stephen, 25

Powhatan people, 255

Prigmore, James, 124, 138

Prisoners: deaths of, 302; execution of, 90, 133, 160, 203, 204, 209, 210, 224, 252, 270, 301, 305, 307, 314–315, 318, 323, 345, 346; execution of, prohibition of, 324; from Modoc War, 344–345; neglect of, 258–261, 297–298, 306–307, 315–316, 319–320; treatment of, 302–303

Protection, of Indians: and Army, 242, 245, 266, 277, 305; lack of, 170–172, 212, 240, 352; lack of for reservations, 170–171, 260–261, 277, 279; McKee's request for, 206; on reservations, 213; by residing in non-Indian households, 334–335; by whites, 246, 326, 328, 333, 344

Puebloan people, massacre of, 132

Quapaw Agency, 345

Quechan people, 18, 31, 34, 39, 180–181

Racial hierarchy, 159; under Mexican rule, 38, 60; under Spanish, 30

Racism, 7, 8, 15, 38, 60, 110, 150, 167, 345, 350

Radical Club, 344

Rains, Gabriel J., 258, 282, 286, 290

Ranches, Indian labor on, 37, 51, 52–53, 54, 73, 145

Rancho Carne Humana, 121–122

Rape of California Indian women, 56, 160, 162, 172, 198–199, 234, 261, 263, 303, 311,

351; at Big Valley Ranch, 110–111; by Oregonians, 87; by Spaniards, 31–32

Reading, Pierson B., 38, 204

Reading's Ranch, 43, 204

Reagan, Ronald, 9

Recognition, of tribes, 9, 348

Red Bluff Beacon, 270, 271, 275, 297, 306

Red Bluff Independent, 304–305, 307–308, 309, 326

"Red Cap War," 234–237

Removal, forced, 10, 15, 257–258, 271, 329, 352; and Army, 267; calls for, 164, 166, 263, 319; deaths during, 257–258; Konkow Maidu Trail of Tears, 318, 319–320, 350; lethality of, 257; Pit River Expedition, 264, 276; resistance to, 257, 258, 315. *See also* Reservations

Reparations, 9, 357

Repetition, in genocide, 13

Reproduction, prevention of, 63, 172, 182, 260

Reservations, 15, 348; as alternative to mass murder, 164, 263, 324; attempts to escape from, 261; authorization of, 170; complicity of employees of in massacres, 265, 305, 320; conditions on, 194, 237, 260–261, 276, 306–307, 352; escape from, 306, 307; executions on, 252, 318; federal troops on, 213; at Fort Lane, 242; Fresno Reservation, 194, 245, 258, 297; government's refusal to grant, 211–212, 310; Hoopa Valley Reservation, 323–324; Indian killing on, 209, 296, 305, 318; jurisdiction of, 170–171; Klamath Reservation (California), 237, 261; Klamath Reservation (Oregon), 336; lack of protection for, 170–171, 260–261; lethality of, 257, 260; malnutrition on, 258, 259, 260, 352; Mendocino Reservation, 257, 258, 259, 265, 276, 297; neglect on, 260, 297, 303, 306, 307, 320, 352; Nome Lackee Reservation, 257, 271, 293, 298, 306; proposed, 169; protection

Reservations (cont.)
of, 213; Round Valley Reservation,
258, 259, 260, 265–266, 296–297,
305–306, 318, 319; Smith River
Reservation, 306, 307; starvation on,
194, 258–259, 260, 265, 297–298, 306,
315; Tule River Reservation, 258;
uprisings on, 261; white opposition to,
165–168. *See also* Incarceration,
lethal; Removal, forced
Resistance, by California Indians, 12, 26,
40, 107, 178, 182, 199, 243, 244, 256, 304,
328; Garra's Uprising, 202–204; to
Missions, 32–35; by Modocs, 215, 216,
247, 336–345; by Mojaves, 268; by
Owens Valley Paiute-Shoshones, 311; to
removal, 257, 258, 315; retaliation for, 97,
244, 267, 304; by Yuroks, 97
Resources, natural, 328, 348. *See also*
Food supplies/sources
Retaliation, 90, 105, 167, 180, 234, 241, 304.
See also under Indian depredations;
Resistance; Vigilantes
Retaliation, for killing of Stone and
Kelsey, 114; 1st Dragoons campaign,
115–120, 127 (*see also* Davidson,
John W.). *See also* Bloody Island
Massacre; Clear Lake Indians; Clear
Lake massacres; Cokadjal Massacre;
Frisbie, John B.; Lyon, Nathaniel; Riley,
Bennett; Smith, Persifor F.
Revere, Joseph Warren, 38, 40, 58, 181
Richards, Eddie, 223
Riddle, Jeff, 221
Riddle, Toby (Winema), 339
Riley, Bennett, 119, 120, 124, 128, 149
Rogers, Harrison, 27
Rogers, William, 183, 195
Rogue River War, 221–224, 227
Rolf's Ranch, 272–274, 285
Roosevelt, Theodore, 357
Ross, John E., 76, 89, 90, 201–202, 214
Ross, William E., 262

Round Valley: killings in, 265–266;
Mendocino Expedition, 276–280;
numbers of California Indians killed in,
252–253; vigilante killings in, 229,
252–253, 255, 296, 304–305, 318
Round Valley Reservation, 258, 259, 260,
265–266, 296–297, 305–306, 318, 319
Rowe, E.A., 313
Rubinstein, William, 358
Russians, 26, 36–37
Russian American Company, 34
Ryan, William Redmond, 56, 64

Sacramento Daily Union, 206; on
extermination, 243; on federal funding
of militias, 251–252; on Indian hunting,
217; on Indian killing, 265; on Kibbe
expedition, 275; on Mendocino
Expedition, 281, 285; on payment for
militia campaigns, 281; on skeletons,
257; warnings of extermination, 281; on
war of extermination, 204, 218, 235, 243
Sacramento River Massacre, 45–48, 51
Sacramento Transcript, 70, 84, 98, 192
Sand Creek Massacre, 142
San Bernardino Expedition, 254
San Francisco, 61, 79, 256, 350; First
California Guards, 174; Hastings
College of Law, 348; labor regime in,
73, 147, 267
San Francisco harbor, 74, 79
San Francisco Herald, 130, 139, 140, 284,
292
Santa Rosa region, 120, 122, 123, 125, 143
Santiago (leader), 195
Sauk and Fox people, 174
Savage, James, 188, 190, 193
Savannah, USS, 1, 124, 125
Sayward, W.T., 82
Scalping, 49, 50, 78, 86, 88, 89, 97, 98, 99,
180, 182, 192, 197, 201, 204, 205, 207, 214,
216, 219, 220, 221, 224, 241, 252, 269, 270,
281, 286, 295, 309, 312, 319, 334, 342, 348

Scarfaced Charley, 342, 346
Schofield, J.M., 342, 344
Schonchin, John, 336, 341, 345
Schonchin, Old (leader), 215, 216, 328
Scott, William, 255
Seafood, 22–23, 32, 106
Sebastian, William, 217
Secession, 287, 289
Secrest, William, 7–8
Segregation, 148
Seigneurialism, 38
Semple, Charles D., 125
Semple, Robert, 149, 150
Senate, US: 138; approval of Clear Lake campaign, 142, 144, 354; and California Indian servitude, 287; condoning of massacres by, 142; debate of California Indian killings, 285; Fillmore's address to, 170; Frémont in, 163; policy toward California Indians, 213; reduction of appropriation for California Indians, 212–213, 260; rejection of treaties by, 165, 168, 170, 171, 194, 201, 211, 212, 218, 315, 316, 355; role in California Indian catastrophe, 355; support for Lyon, 141; support for militias, 250, 289 (*see also* Militias)
Serra, Junípero, 26, 27, 29, 31, 36
Servants, Indian, 53–54, 73, 122, 147, 287, 304, 332. *See also* Labor, Indian; Labor, unfree; Servitude; Slavery, Indian; Slaves, Indian
Servitude, Indian, 12, 38, 158–159; debated in Senate, 287; illegal, 333; legalization of system of, 147–148, 161; maintenance of existing systems of, 145, 146; numbers of Indians in, 304, 332; weakening of, 332, 333. *See also* Labor, Indian; Labor, unfree; Servants; Slave raiding; Slavery, Indian; Slaves, Indian
Settlers: use of term, 15. *See also* Newcomers
Sexual assaults, 31–32, 56, 160, 162, 172, 198–199, 234, 261, 263, 303, 311, 351; at

Big Valley Ranch, 107, 110–111, 114; by Oregonians, 87; by Spaniards, 31–32
Sexual slavery, 56
Shasta City, 197, 198, 208, 255
Shasta Courier, 206, 209, 219–220, 222, 225, 262, 264, 272, 321, 330, 325
Shasta Expedition, 226
Shasta Herald, 272, 275, 295
Shasta people, 43, 181, 182, 197, 205, 209, 220, 221, 222, 227, 241–242, 348
Shasta Republican, 254, 256
Shaw, William J., 56, 93
Sheridan, Philip, 344
Sherman, Edwin Allen, 132
Sherman, William T., 62, 64, 70, 72, 337, 341, 342, 343, 344
Sherwood, William L., 341
Sherwood, Winfield, 154
Shoandow (leader), 311
Short, James, 296, 305, 320
Shuk (Chief Augustine), 103, 105, 107, 109, 110, 111, 112, 113, 114, 115, 129, 132, 133, 134
Simpson, John P., 258, 324
Sinclair, John, 53, 70
Sinkyone people, 210, 252, 262, 286, 288, 292, 293, 295, 317, 323. *See also* Bell, Sally
Siskiyou Expedition (1855), 241–242, 253
Siskiyou Volunteer Rangers Expedition, 213–217
Slave pass system, 148
Slave raiding, 59, 62–64, 70, 73, 109, 162, 240, 269, 293–295, 303–304, 332, 352. *See also* Kidnapping
Slavery, Indian, 27, 29, 37, 60, 73, 91, 107, 109, 147, 148, 161, 162, 171, 198, 303, 332, 333, 356. *See also* Labor, unfree
Slaves, African American, 52, 109, 147, 162
Slaves, Indian, 27, 33, 38, 52, 68, 70, 91, 109–110, 146, 161, 260, 332. *See also* Big Valley Ranch
Slave trade, Indian, 109, 159, 161, 162, 198, 285, 303, 304

Sloat, John, 1
Slolux, 345
Smallpox, 39, 219, 352
Smith, Captain, 124, 138
Smith, Edward, 344
Smith, Persifor F., 119–120, 123, 124, 127, 128, 129, 130, 134, 138, 139, 141, 193
Smith, Stephen, 235
Smith River Reservation, 306, 307
Society, exclusion of California Indians from, 171, 172
Solares, María, 33
Soldiers, Indian: California Indians as, 56, 57–59; Cayuse men as, 75
Sonoma Valley, 120, 125, 127, 143
Sonora Herald, 243
Soule, Frank, 205–206
South Carolina, 289
Southern, May Hazel, 275
Southern Mines, 68, 69, 90, 93, 97, 187–188, 189–191, 192, 207
Southern Paiute people, 286
Spain/Spaniards, 26–36
Spanish speakers, 93. *See also* Californios
Specific intent, 5
Stanford, Leland, 301, 316, 317, 332, 350
Stanford University, 350
Stannard, David, 7, 357, 358
Starr, Augustus W., 319–320
Starvation, 3, 11, 12, 32, 111, 161, 168, 171, 184, 185, 217–218, 275; on Big Valley Ranch, 107, 110, 111, 114; on reservations, 194, 258–259, 260, 265, 297–298, 306, 315. *See also* Food supplies/sources
Starvation, institutionalized, 110, 258, 260, 297, 306
States' rights, 124
Stevenson, E.A., 162, 270
Stockton, Robert, 61, 62
Stockton Journal, 183
Stockton Times, 139, 194
Stone, Charles, 103, 106, 107, 109, 110, 111, 112, 113, 114, 115, 116, 117. *See also* Big

Valley Ranch; Retaliation, for killing of Stone and Kelsey
Stone, Dan, 358
Stoneman, George, 128, 129, 131, 136, 141–142, 348
Street, Richard Steven, 36, 159
Strobridge, William F., 293
Stuart, Alexander H.H., 170
Suffrage, for Indians, 150–156, 158, 164
Suspicion, as pretext for massacres, 241, 244, 305
Sutter, Johann, 52, 53, 55, 62, 64, 67, 70, 73, 154; on exterminatory violence, 86, 88; feeding of Indian laborers, 60–61; ranch, 60; on slave raiders, 64; use of Indian miners, 70
Sutter's Fort, 54, 57, 58, 59, 60
Systems of exchange, between Indians, 23, 25. *See also* Economies, California Indian; Trade, between Indians

Tac, Pablo, 39
Tamáhŭs, 75
Tápis, Estevan, 32
Taylor, Bayard, 155
Tefft, Henry A., 153, 154
Tenaya, 194
Tending the wild, 18
Terminology, 15
Testimony, Indian, 10, 157, 159, 160, 333, 344, 345
Theft: massacres triggered by, 76, 176, 184–185, 197, 202, 204, 206–207, 207–208, 219, 220, 221, 224, 226, 227, 243, 244, 246, 252, 262, 265, 266, 279, 286, 301, 331; motivations of Indians in, 12, 99, 185, 217, 218–219, 243, 252, 311; retaliation for, 105. *See also* Indian depredations
Thirteenth Amendment, 333
Thomas, Eleasar, 341
Thompson, Erwin, 216
Thornton, Russell, 6–7, 358

Tibbitts, Ben, 314

Tipai people, 31, 34

Tolowa people, 209, 220, 225, 245, 261; candlelight vigil, 350; massacres of, 209, 220, 222–224, 231–232, 234, 246

Tome-ya-nem (leader), 259, 296–297, 306

Tongva people, 31

Torture: in Act for the Government and Protection of Indians, 159; of Indian children, by Army, 137; of Indian laborers at Big Valley Ranch, 107, 110; at missions, 30, 32–34

Trade, between Indians, 18, 22, 23, 25, 43 45, 106, 201, 209, 228

Trafzer, Clifford, 7

Trail of Tears (Cherokee), 257

Trauma, historical, 9, 348

Treaties, Indian, 164, 169; as alternative to extermination, 164, 186, 201, 213; breaking of promises in, 168; Burnett's dismissal of, 186; government's failure to honor, 313, 315, 316; between Green and Nisenan, 179; and Indian killing, 195; Indians compelled to sign, 195, 201, 246; with Mattole Indians, 262; negotiating, 164; opposition to, 165–168, 323; promises in, 165; rejection of, 165, 168, 170, 171, 172, 194, 201, 211, 212, 218, 315, 316, 355; signed without killing, 195–196; support for, 194; and threats of annihilation, 192–193. *See also* Barbour, George W.; McKee, Redick; Treaty commissioners; Wozencraft, Oliver

Treaty commissioners, 164, 189, 192, 194, 355. *See also* Barbour, George W.; McKee, Redick; Treaties; Wozencraft, Oliver

Treaty of Cahuenga, 59

Treaty of Guadalupe Hidalgo, 151, 152, 153, 154

Trinity, Klamath, and Clear Lake Expedition, 200–201

Trinity Journal, 262, 267, 330

Tubatulabal people, 22, 314–315

Tulare Expedition, 245–246, 254

Tulare Mounted Riflemen, 245

Tule Lake, 46, 213, 214, 215, 249

Tule River Reservation, 258

Tuluwat Massacre, 282–283, 284, 350

Tustin, William Isaac, 46, 47–48

"Two Years' War," 317–318, 321–324

Tyson, James L., 83

Underwood, Edmund, 290, 292

United Nations Convention on the Prevention and Punishment of the Crime of Genocide (Genocide Convention), 4–6, 8, 11, 14, 172, 178, 179, 183, 259–260, 261, 287, 350–352, 355, 356, 358, 359

Upper Station Massacre, 305

Utah Expedition, 194, 207

Utley, Robert, 357–358

Vagrancy, 146, 159, 287. *See also* Labor, unfree

Vallejo, Mariano, 40, 57, 61

Vallejo, Salvador, 40, 54, 57, 107

Van Dyke, Walter, 301

Venereal diseases, 306, 352; syphilis, 260

Vermeule, Thomas, 156

Veterans, land bounties for, 237–238; pay for, 189

Vigilantes, 8, 13–14, 117, 143; 1858 campaigns by, 261–263; 1861 killings by, 295–297; arrested, 124–125; Breckenridge Expedition, 270–271; and California Supreme Court, 124–125, 138, 143–144; collaboration with Army, 215, 302, 309, 331, 331–332, 334; compared to Army, 224, 267, 331; decline in killings by, 286, 329; decreased support for, 331; destruction of Indian houses and food by, 210, 217, 218; encouragement of, 184, 191, 224, 262; February-March, 1850 campaigns by, 120–123; genocidal

Vigilantes (cont.)
nature of killings by, 176; Humboldt
Cavalry, 286; killings by, 88, 99, 206,
218, 222, 235, 242, 246, 252, 257, 267, 270,
308, 312, 314, 315, 316, 319, 325, 326, 333,
334; lack of consequences for, 143–144,
172, 183, 218, 224, 226, 307, 345; lack of
prosecution of, 125, 138, 143–144, 307;
lack of restraints on, 218, 241, 354, 356;
Lippitt on, 301; massacres by, 89, 98,
122, 179, 180, 188, 189, 190, 198, 202, 204,
206–207, 220–221, 223–224, 227, 232, 241,
242, 243–244, 253, 257, 266, 270,
272–274, 282–284, 286, 287, 301, 302,
307, 312, 318, 319, 326, 328, 329, 330,
331–332, 333, 334, 345 (*see also* Massacres,
Indian); motivations of, 127, 253, 326;
in Northeastern Sacramento Valley
Campaign, 324–328; numbers killed by,
123, 175, 356; precedents for violence by,
179; Oroville Guards, 319; in Owens
Valley, 312, 314, 315, 329; rejection of
legal system by, 128; role in near-
annihilation of California Indians, 346;
Round Valley region killings by, 229,
252–253, 255, 265–266, 287, 296,
304–305, 318; Smith's reluctance to
intervene in, 123, 124; in Southern
Mines, 187–190; survivors of, 125;
transformation into militiamen, 187,
190; violence in retaliation for killing of
Stone and Kelsey, 114, 120–127; white
opposition to, 122, 124, 301. *See also*
Indian killing; Massacres, Indian;
Villages, destruction of
Villages, destruction of, 64, 84, 88, 89, 95,
94, 96, 97, 98, 122, 123, 124, 132, 136, 137,
172, 179, 181, 184, 188, 190, 192, 194, 195,
197, 203, 204, 205, 210, 215, 218, 220, 223,
224, 227, 235, 241, 246, 247, 270, 273, 302,
312, 336, 337, 346, 351
Violence: categories of, 11–12; erosion of
cultural barriers to, 60, 100, 140–141,
171, 172; preemptive mass violence, 46,
50, 178–179, 222
Violence, exterminatory, 86–88, 95–96,
100, 139, 221. *See also* Extermination;
Extermination, war of; Massacres,
Indian
Violence, pedagogic. *See* Killing,
pedagogic
Visalia Delta, 313, 315
Vizcaíno, Juan Sebastián, 18
Voting rights, for Indians, 150–156, 157,
158, 164
Vulnerability, of California Indians, 158,
163, 171. *See also* Reservations; Treaties

Wailaki people, 22, 277, 296–297, 305, 319,
324. *See also* Bauer, William, Jr.;
Young, Lucy
Walling, Albert G., 242
Wannsee Conference Protocol, 352
Wappo people, 39, 103, 106, 107, 109, 112,
116–117, 132, 161; house interior, 118;
man, portrait of, 121; vigilante violence
against, 120–127. *See also* Big Valley
Ranch; Kelsey, Andrew; Kra-nas;
Retaliation, for killing of Stone and
Kelsey; Stone, Charles
War, just, 235
War bonds, 207, 208, 250, 252
War Debt, 218, 225, 229, 230, 238, 250, 253
War Fund, 253, 285
Warman, H.H., 247
Warner, J.J., 38, 167
War of extermination, 40, 86, 88, 144, 164,
179, 183, 186, 187, 204, 205, 218, 219, 221,
222, 232, 234, 235, 238, 243, 244, 247, 262,
263, 267, 275, 277, 280, 281, 353
Washoe people, 17, 19, 257, 261
Watchman (San Francisco), 139
Watmough, James H., 62
Weber, Charles, 65
Weber, Charles M., 71
Weimah (leader), 242

Weller, John B., 125, 212, 230, 250, 263, 270, 271–272, 275, 277, 279, 280, 281, 282, 352, 353

Wentworth, John P.H., 313, 315

Werk, G.W., 298, 299

Western Shoshone people, 309, 310, 313, 328–329. *See also* "Owens Valley War"

Whaley, Thomas, 203

Wheaton, Frank, 337, 342

Whilkut people, 22, 244, 246, 252, 262, 264, 267, 286, 290, 299, 301, 321

Whippings of Indians, 110, 294, 303; legally sanctioned, 159, 203; at missions, 29, 30, 32, 33

Whipple, Stephen D., 225, 298, 318, 321

White, Robert, 240

Whites: attacks on, 114–115, 194, 199, 203, 213–215, 269, 298, 307, 318, 324, 329, 336, 341; Bigler's defense of, 205; desire for Indian land, 307; blamed for violence, 199; numbers killed by Indians, 351; opposition to Indian killing, 127; opposition to reservations, 165–168; opposition to vigilante violence, 124; protection of Indians by, 90, 92, 117, 180, 246, 326, 328, 333, 344. *See also* Emigrants; Forty-eighters; Forty-niners; Newcomers; Settlers

Whitman Massacre, 74–76

Wiley, Austin, 323, 324

Wilkinson, Green, 290, 292

Willer, W., 227

Willet, John C., 312

Williams, W., 227

Wilson, Henry, 285

Wilson, Lieutenant, 116, 119

Wilson, V.V., 333

Winema (Toby Riddle), 339

Winn, A.M., 195

Winnemem Wintu people, 348. *See also* Wintu people

Winthrop, John, 140

"Wintoon War," 263–265

Wintu people, 17, 43, 45–48, 96, 97, 182, 197, 198, 204, 206–207, 208, 217, 219, 220, 225, 226, 244, 253, 262, 295–296, 348; village, 45, 46. *See also* Nor-rel-muk Wintu people; Winnemem Wintu people

Witnesses, 160, 344

Wiyot people, 17, 97, 181, 204, 252, 264, 282, 283, 302, 350

Women, California Indian: at Big Valley Ranch, 110–111; during Gold Rush, 73; food sent by whites to, 90; killing of, 11, 15, 40, 47, 48, 50, 86, 97, 98, 119, 122, 128, 130, 131, 132, 134, 180, 197, 205, 207, 213, 219, 221, 223, 227, 232, 236, 243, 244, 249, 255, 262, 265, 266, 267, 268, 270, 271, 273–274, 275, 277, 279, 280, 281, 282, 283, 284, 286, 287, 292, 293, 296, 297, 299, 301, 302, 303, 309, 326, 328, 329, 334, 336, 344; protection of by whites, 180, 301, 302, 323, 326, 333; rape of, 31–32, 56, 87, 107, 110–111, 160, 162, 172, 198–199, 234, 261, 263, 303, 311, 351; relationships with white men, 54–56, 273, 334; unfree laborers, 52, 303; whipping of, 30, 33, 303

Women, non-Indian, 54, 174, 270, 324, 326, 336; protection of California Indians by, 326, 333, 344

Woods, R.N., 162

Woodward, Ashbel, 131

Woodward, C., 237

Woodward, F.M., 235

Woodward, M., 237

Wool, John, 171, 243, 246, 247, 260

World Renewal ceremonies, 222, 231, 282

Wounded Knee, 132, 140

Wozencraft, Oliver, 152, 164, 165, 166, 186, 189, 193, 195, 204, 208. *See also* Treaties, Indian; Treaty commissioners

Wrangel, Ferdinand, 36

Wright, Ben, 202, 213–217, 337

Wright, Elizabeth Cyrus, 117
Wright, George, 300, 301, 302, 312, 315, 316, 318, 321, 323
Wright, Seaman, 282, 286

Xasis, 103, 105, 113, 114, 115

Yahi Yana people, 95, 184, 208, 224, 227, 257, 271, 286, 318–319, 330
Yana people, 22, 23, 43, 95, 96, 184, 197, 208, 224, 227, 241, 242, 244, 246, 257, 258, 262, 266, 270, 271, 276, 286, 307–309, 318–319, 325–326, 328, 330, 331, 333, 334, 335
Yates, John, 55
Yellow Bull, 75
Yoi'-mut, 258
Yokaya Pomo people, 133–135; warrior, 135

Yokuts people, 19, 41, 93, 190, 194, 195, 218, 245, 246, 258. *See also* Estanislao; Yoi'-mut
Yontocket Massacre, 222–224, 350
Yosemite campaign, 194. *See also* Mariposa Battalion
Young, Lucy, 21, 303–304, 307, 308
Young, Sandy, 309, 310
Yount, George C., 110, 112, 121, 122, 124
Yreka Mountain Herald, 220, 221, 222, 224, 225, 240
Yreka Northern Journal, 281
Yreka Weekly Union, 331
Yuki people, 7, 228–229, 244, 252, 265, 266, 277, 279, 280, 287, 296, 317, 318
Yuma people. *See* Quechan people
Yurok people, 41, 97–98, 179–180, 222, 234, 235, 302, 322; canoe on Trinity River, 236. *See also* "Red Cap War"